www.wadsworth.com

wadsworth.com is the World Wide Web site for Wadsworth and is your direct source to dozens of online resources.

At *wadsworth.com* you can find out about supplements, demonstration software, and student resources. You can also send email to many of our authors and preview new publications and exciting new technologies.

wadsworth.com
Changing the way the world learns®

Introduction to Physical Anthropology

Ninth Edition

Robert Jurmain
San Jose State University

Lynn Kilgore
Colorado State University

Wenda Trevathan
New Mexico State University

Harry Nelson

THOMSON
✳
WADSWORTH

Australia • Canada • Mexico • Singapore • Spain
United Kingdom • United States

Anthropology Editor: Lin Marshall
Developmental Editor: Robert Jucha
Assistant Editor: Analie Barnett
Editorial Assistant: Amanda Santana
Technology Project Manager: Dee Dee Zobian
Marketing Manager: Diane McOscar
Marketing Assistant: Michael Silverstein
Advertising Project Manager: Linda Yip
Project Manager, Editorial Production: Lisa Weber
Print/Media Buyer: Karen Hunt
Permissions Editor: Robert Kauser
Production Service: Hespenheide Design
Text and Cover Designer: Hespenheide Design

Photo Researcher: Hespenheide Design
Copy Editor: Janet Greenblatt
Illustrators: Alexander Productions, Randy Miyake,
    Paragon 3, Sue Sellars, Leslie Weller, Cyndie Wooley
Cover Images (clockwise): painted hands on cave wall:
    © Fulvio Roiter/CORBIS; x-ray of hands: © Stone/
    Getty Images; Indian woman painting hands: © Ric
    Ergenbright/CORBIS; chimpanzee: © E. A. Janes/Photo
    Researchers, Inc.; Da Vinci hands: © Sheila Terry/Science
    Photo Library
Cover Printer: Transcontinental/Interglobe
Compositor: Hespenheide Design
Printer: Transcontinental/Interglobe

Printed in Canada
1 2 3 4 5 6 7 06 05 04 03 02

For more information about our products, contact us at:
Thomson Learning Academic Resource Center
1-800-423-0563
For permission to use material from this text, contact us by:
Phone: 1-800-730-2214   Fax: 1-800-730-2215
Web: http://www.thomsonrights.com

Library of Congress Control Number: 2002100398

Student Edition ISBN 0-534-58788-7
Instructor's Edition ISBN 0-534-58789-5

Wadsworth/Thomson Learning
10 Davis Drive
Belmont, CA 94002-3098
USA

Asia
Thomson Learning
5 Shenton Way #01-01
UIC Building
Singapore 068808

Australia
Nelson Thomson Learning
102 Dodds Street
South Melbourne, Victoria 3205
Australia

Canada
Nelson Thomson Learning
1120 Birchmount Road
Toronto, Ontario M1K 5G4
Canada

Europe/Middle East/Africa
Thomson Learning
High Holborn House
50/51 Bedford Row
London WC1R 4LR
United Kingdom

Dedication

In December 2000, Harry Nelson, our colleague, friend, and co-author, passed away after an extended illness. Harry's rich and varied life was distinguished by accomplishment and service. Yet, owing to his quiet humility, many of his achievements were unknown to his colleagues or even to his family.

Harry was born in Pennsylvania and received his bachelor's degree from Bloomburg State College in Philadelphia. From there he went on to Columbia where he received his M.A. and then to Berkeley, where following World War II, he received his Ph.D. During the war, Harry served from 1943 to 1946 as an Army captain and was awarded decorations for combat duty, including a bronze star.

For the remainder of his life, Harry dedicated himself to being a teacher, mentor, and successful textbook author. Guided by more than 35 years of teaching experience at community colleges in California, including Foothill College from 1965–1986, and covering all areas of anthropology, Harry brought wisdom and balance to his writing. His awareness of student needs and his unflagging desire to enhance learning were the foundation of his teaching and writing—and these two facets of his approach remain the basis of our textbook. It is thus completely in character that Harry concluded the preface of our very first textbook (published in 1979) with an acknowledgment to his students:

"Finally, we thank our many students who, over the years,
helped us to see physical anthropology from their point of view."

1915–2000

Brief Contents

Contents

Lynn Kilgore

Courtesy, Fred Jacobs

CHAPTER 4
Heredity and Evolution

PART 2   Primates

CHAPTER 5
An Overview of the Primates

Lynn Kilgore

Courtesy, David Haring, Duke University Primate Center

Lynn Kilgore

PART 3   Hominid Evolution

Robert Jurmain

Reproduced with permission of the National Museums of Kenya, copyright reserved, courtesy of Alan Walker

Harry Nelson

Harry Nelson

Renee Lynn/Photo Researchers

Preface

Students occasionally ask us why textbooks require such frequent revisions. Perhaps in no period during the last 25 years since we began writing our first book, *Introduction to Physical Anthropology,* First Edition, has it been so clear why a revision was necessary. The Eighth Edition of *Introduction to Physical Anthropology* was published in the summer of 1999 and carried a 2000 copyright; however, in the last three years, new technologies have been developed and dramatic new discoveries made that challenge our interpretations of human evolution and affect virtually every aspect of physical anthropology.

For example, in the area of paleoanthropology, that is the study of ancient human or human-like species, exciting new fossil finds have come to light. Since 1999 the greatest number of new fossils has come from East Africa, but other exciting discoveries have been made in South Africa, the Republic of Georgia, and Portugal. These finds are more than simply numerous. They significantly challenge earlier interpretations concerning a variety of crucial issues relating to human evolution: the origins of the first members of the human family; when and how our ancestors first dispersed from Africa; the beginnings of modern humans; and, linked to this last topic, the fate of the Neandertals. So it is not an exaggeration when, in a new section of Chapter 10, we observe regarding paleoanthropological research that "we are certainly living in interesting times!"

This textbook is primarily about human evolution, and, as such, its main focus is a *biological* one. Without question, then, the revolution in molecular biology, culminating in 2000 with the publication of the first largely complete mapping of human DNA, has significantly influenced human evolutionary research. To comprehend and thus appreciate how evolution operates in any organism, *including* the human organism, an understanding of the nature and function of genes and of how genetic information is organized, transmitted, and altered is absolutely necessary. Moreover recent applications of these powerful new genetic technologies has allowed more accurate assessment of human diversity and more precise calibrations of ongoing evolutionary change within our species.

In addition to new discoveries and new technologies, another equally revolutionary transformation that has affected all intellectual pursuits concerns the manner in which information is disseminated. College students might perhaps take much of this for granted. But consider: When this text was first published in 1979 there was *no* Internet, nor were affordable personal computers available. The latter came on the scene very soon thereafter—and think of the changes which have come since!

One way to appreciate how basic and interrelated all these trends have become in scientific research is to reflect on the two major areas of advances just discussed—precise knowledge about DNA and use of new genetic technologies and information technology. Internationally based research into DNA, deriving from both publicly funded and private laboratories, has in the last decade accumulated a vast quantity of new data. New computer hardware and software had to be designed to allow researchers to store and analyze all this current information. Moreover, as each new piece of evidence is added to the detailed mapping of human genes, this information is instantly disseminated via the Internet to researchers all over the world.

This textbook is, naturally, much influenced by these contemporary trends. Much of the latest data we include here was researched using the Internet. We, however, also continue to rely on more formal printed forms of publication, and you will find a comprehensive bibliography at the back of the book. In this regard, it is noteworthy that, compared to the prior edition of this book, the Ninth Edition contains more than 120 new bibliographical citations relating to the most recent and most exciting groundbreaking research.

We, of course, recognize that students also use the Internet as a primary means for acquiring information. Thus, as topics are presented in each chapter, we provide orientation and direction for further research of relevant topics through updated end-of-chapter Internet and InfoTrac® College Edition exercises.

It is often said that the amount of scientific knowledge accumulates exponentially. That is, every year the pace of new discovery continues to accelerate. It may be difficult to imagine that in three years from now the fields of human biology and human evolution will be as much transformed as they have been in the last three years. Yet, if history is any teacher, we can anticipate there will be even *greater* changes, accumulating ever more rapidly.

From this recognition come both challenges and lessons. For you, as introductory students in a course about human evolution, the most advantageous way to learn is to acquire basic principles—rather than memorizing mountains of individual facts, many of which in the near future will most likely be revised or reinterpreted. By learning to apply all-purpose tools and mastering fundamental principles and key concepts of evolutionary theory basic to all life, you can arrive at an understanding of the place of the human species in the biological world. Perhaps the most valuable tool of all, however, is learning to apply critical thinking skills to all intellectual aspects of your life.

In its basic approach this text is designed to assist you in refining your critical thinking abilities. Indeed, a college education in general is largely oriented to serve the same goal, especially those courses in scientific disciplines. Accordingly, this book is more than simply an introduction to physical anthropology, it is also an introduction to science itself: How scientific data are gathered, how generalizations are deduced, and how these conclusions are tested. We weave this scientific approach throughout our presentation, but you will find it most explicitly stated in the Issues. In these boxed features you will read about several contemporary and potentially controversial topics, and you will also find critical thinking questions, challenging you to think about what you have read in a more rigorous, that is, *scientific,* way.

As our perspectives widen, we come to know and appreciate more completely the human condition. You will see that these widening perspectives have recently been extended ever farther back in time to the dawn of the most remote ancestors of the human family. At the same time, new genetic technologies have extended our knowledge to include the very chemical basis of what makes us alive, what makes us an animal, and indeed, what makes us human. Beyond our intellectual perspectives are personal and emotional viewpoints, which can also be transformed, sometimes unexpectedly so. In this textbook we discuss aspects of DNA individual identification, as well as forensic anthropological techniques of identifying other kinds of human physical remains. In the aftermath of September 11, 2001, can any of us ever think about these topics in quite the same way?

Where and how fast scientific investigation will take us in the next few years is difficult to imagine, and almost impossible to predict. Where do you think scientific research in human biology will lead us in the next five years? In the next ten years? Such prognostications are stimulating and good fun, but must remain largely conjectural. There is however a more pertinent question: Whatever comes, will you be ready?

What's New in the Ninth Edition?

As mentioned, we have considerably altered and updated this textbook from its last edition. We have expanded our coverage of stem cell research and cloning (Chapter 3), topics that in the last few years have become highly controversial. In addition, the new and increasingly precise evidence relating to human DNA sequencing impacts a variety of topics in this text. Since these developments are so crucial to all of human biology, we have discussed aspects of DNA technology and new genetically based methods that affect the treatment of disease (Chapter 3), our understanding of the genetic relationships among primates (Chapter 5), the sequencing of ancient DNA found in Neandertal fossil remains (Chapter 12), the use of contemporary genetic patterning to reconstruct the origins of modern humans (Chapter 13), advances in identifying and measuring genetic variation in human populations (Chapter 14), and the utility of this evidence for understanding larger patterns of human diversity (Chapter 15).

The chapters on nonhuman primates (Chapters 5, 6, and 7) have been refocused to emphasize and clarify the contemporary approach of behavioral ecology. Moreover, we continue with our emphasis on primate conservation and present new and disturbing data relating to a dramatic increase in the bushmeat trade (new Issue box, Chapter 5).

Chapter 8, which concentrates on macroevolution, includes a new section on the "definition of species," providing students with a more complete and more theoretical perspective. The chapters concerning hominid evolution (Chapters 9–13) have been extensively updated. New materials are included throughout these five chapters, including discoveries from East Africa (*Orrorin, Ardipithecus, Australopithecus,* and *Kenyanthropus*) as well as from South Africa, Western Asia, and Europe. All these discoveries have potentially great significance, in many cases requiring serious reevaluation of the course of human evolution. Thus, not only are the "nuts and bolts" presented (what, where, how old), but also the significance of each discovery is discussed—insofar as current analysis and publication permit.

Perhaps the most fundamental change to this text, however, is found in Chapter 16, our concluding chapter. This chapter has been retitled "Legacies of Human Evolutionary History," and the whole chapter has been refocused to reflect this title and to function more effectively as a capstone chapter for the book. In addition to coverage of human growth and development, new materials have been added on human behavioral ecology, the impact of humans on the planet, and the potential course of future human evolution.

Features

Issues are major boxed features, which are found at the end of every other chapter. Issues boxes focus on current controversial topics discussed and debated within the field of physical anthropology. Three Issues new to this edition are:

- Genetic Methods for Treating Trauma and Disease: Advances and Controversies (following Chapter 3)
- The Bushmeat Trade: Just When We Thought Things Couldn't Get Any Worse . . . (following Chapter 5)
- The Piltdown Caper: Who Dunnit? (following Chapter 9)

A Closer Look boxes are high-interest boxed features found throughout the book. They expand on the topic under discussion in the chapter by providing a more in-depth overview.

In-Chapter Learning Aids

- **Chapter outlines**, at the beginning of each chapter, list all major topics covered.
- A **running glossary** in the margins provides definitions of terms immediately adjacent to the text when the term is first introduced. A **full glossary** is provided in the back of the book.
- **Figures**, including numerous photographs, line drawings, and maps—most in full color—are carefully selected to clarify text materials, and they are placed to directly support discussion in the text.
- **Questions for Review** at the end of each chapter reinforce key points and encourage students to think critically about what they have read.
- **Suggested Further Reading**, also found at the end of each chapter, is carefully selected to direct interested students toward accessible and authoritative sources for further reading.
- **Full bibliographic citations** throughout the entire book provide sources from which the materials are drawn. This type of documentation guides students to published source materials and illustrates for students the proper use of referencing; all cited sources are listed in the comprehensive bibliography at the back of the book.
- **Resources on the Internet** is a learning aid found at the end of each chapter. Resources include Internet Exercises incorporating specific sites on the Internet. These exercises are designed to help students become more competent in using the Internet. **InfoTrac College Edition exercises** follow the Internet exercises and also direct students in effective use of this free online library.
- Icons are strategically placed throughout the text to integrate text materials with those found in the

Virtual Laboratories for Physical Anthropology CD-ROM, Third Edition, prepared by John Kappelman of the University of Texas at Austin. The icons are found in the margins, adjacent to related materials in the text, as follows:

 See the following section of the CD-ROM for topics covered in this chapter: Virtual Lab 2, sections II and III.

Acknowledgments

Over the years many friends and colleagues have assisted us with our books. For this edition we are especially grateful to the reviewers who so carefully commented on the manuscript and made such helpful suggestions: Cheryl A. Johnston, Ohio State University; Geoffrey Pope, William Patterson University; Andrew Kramer, University of Tennessee; Christopher Stonjanowski, Florida State University; Pat Lambert, Utah State University; Janel Tortorice, Rutgers University; Lorena Madrigal, University of South Florida; and Richard G. Wilkinson, University of Albany.

We also wish to thank at Wadsworth Publishing Lin Marshall, Senior Anthropology Editor; Reilly O'Neal, Editorial Assistant; Analie Barnett, Assistant Editor; Robert Jucha, Senior Development Editor; Diane McOscar, Executive Marketing Manager; Lisa Weber, Production Project Editor; Eve Howard, Editor in Chief; and Susan Badger, President and CEO. Moreover, for their unflagging expertise and patience we are grateful to our copy editor, Janet Greenblatt, our production coordinator, Gary Hespenheide and his skilled staff at Hespenheide Design, including Patti Zeman, production coordinator; Bridget Neumayr, proofreader/editor; and Stephanie Davila, designer.

To the many friends and colleagues who have generously provided photographs we are greatly appreciative: C.K. Brain, Günter Bräuer, Desmond Clark, Raymond Dart, Jean deRousseau, Denis Etler, Diane France, David Frayer, Kathleen Galvin, David Haring, Ellen Ingmanson, Fred Jacobs, Peter Jones, Arlene Kruse, Richard Leakey, Carol Lofton, Lorna Moore, John Oates, Bonnie Pedersen, Lorna Pierce, David Pilbeam, William Pratt, Judith Regensteiner, Sastrohamijoyo Sartono, Wayne Savage, Eugenie Scott, Rose Sevick, Elwyn Simons, Meredith Small, Fred Smith, H. Dieter Steklis, Judy Suchey, Li Tianyuan, Philip Tobias, Alan Walker, Milford Wolpoff, and Xinzhi Wu.

Robert Jurmain
Lynn Kilgore
Wenda Trevathan

Supplements

Supplements for Instructors

Technology Demo CD-ROM for Anthropology The Technology Demo CD-ROM introduces and demonstrates all of the key technology supplements that Wadsworth offers. The demos provide instructors with an overview of each supplement and a more detailed demonstration of exactly how to use each product. The Technology Demo CD comes in each Instructor's Edition of the text.

Instructor's Manual with Test Bank This comprehensive manual offers chapter outlines, learning objectives, key terms and concepts, lecture suggestions and enrichment topics as well as 40–60 test questions per chapter. Concise user guides for InfoTrac College Edition and WebTutor are included as appendices.

***ExamView*® Computerized and Online Testing** Create, deliver, and customize tests and study guides (both print and online) in minutes with this easy-to-use assessment and tutorial system. *ExamView* offers both a *Quick Test Wizard* and an Online Test Wizard that guide you step-by-step through the process of creating tests, while its unique "WYSIWYG" capability allows you to see the test you are creating onscreen exactly as it will print or display online. Using *ExamView*'s complete word processing capabilities, you can enter an unlimited number of new questions or edit existing questions.

Classroom Presentation Tools for Instructors

Wadsworth's Physical Anthropology Transparency Acetates 2003 A set of full-color acetates from Wadsworth's Physical Anthropology texts is available to help prepare lecture presentations.

Multimedia Manager for Anthropology: A Microsoft PowerPoint® Link Tool 2003 CD-ROM This 2003 CD-ROM contains digital media and PowerPoint presentations for all of Wadsworth's 2003 introductory Anthropology texts, placing images, lectures, and video clips at instructors' fingertips. Start with our preassembled PowerPoint Presentations, which include chapter outlines and key terms. Then easily add video and images from Wadsworth's Anthropology texts all included on the CD-ROM. Instructors can also add their own lecture notes and images to create a custom-made lecture presentation. The new Wadsworth Multimedia Manager also includes an exciting Earthwatch Institute Research Feature.

Wadsworth Anthropology Video Library Qualified adopters may select full-length videos from an extensive library of offerings drawn from excellent educational video sources such as *Films for the Humanities and Sciences*.

***CNN* Today Physical Anthropology Video Series, Volumes I–IV** The *CNN Today Physical Anthropology* Video Series is an exclusive series jointly created by Wadsworth and CNN for the physical anthropology course. Each video in the series consists of approximately 45 minutes of footage originally broadcast on CNN within the last several years. The videos are broken into short two- to seven-minute segments, which are perfect for classroom use as lecture launchers, or to illustrate key anthropological concepts. An annotated table of contents accompanies each video with descriptions of the segments and suggestions for their possible use within the course.

Supplements for Students

Study Guide This useful guide enables students to fully comprehend and appreciate what the text has to offer. Each chapter of the study guide features learning objectives, chapter outlines, key terms, extended applications, and practice tests consisting of 30–40 multiple-choice questions and 5–10 true/false questions with answers and page references, in addition to several short-answer and essay questions.

***Virtual Laboratories for Physical Anthropology* CD-ROM, Third Edition** By John Kappelman, University of Texas at Austin. The new edition of this interactive CD-ROM provides students with a hands-on computer component for doing lab assignments at school or at home. It encourages students to actively participate in their physical anthropology lab or course through the taking of measurements and the plotting of data, as well as giving them a format for testing their knowledge of important concepts. It contains full color images, video clips, 3-D animations, sound, and more. New to this edition is a special quizzing section where students can take online tutorial quizzes based on the 12 laboratories and have their answers scored and emailed to their instructor.

Supplementary Modules   There are free-standing full chapters on topics in physical anthropology not treated comprehensively in the textbook. Chapter content, format, and level are designed to exactly mirror that used in the book. Modules now available cover primate evolution and forensic anthropology. Others planned will cover human osteology/paleopathology and human ecology.

Lab Manual and Workbook for Physical Anthropology, **Fourth Edition**   Written by Diane France, this lab manual emphasizes human osteology, forensic anthropology, anthropometry, primates, human evolution, and genetics, and provides students with hands-on lab assignments to help make the concepts of physical anthropology much more clear. It contains short-answer questions, identification problems, and observation exercises.

Researching Anthropology on the Internet, **Second Edition**   Written by David Carlson, this useful guide is designed to assist anthropology students in all of their needs when doing research on the Internet. Part One contains general information necessary to get started and answers questions about security, the type of material available on the Internet, the information that is reliable and the sites that are not, the best ways to find research, and the best links to take students where they want to go. Part Two looks at each main discipline in anthropology and refers students to sites where the most enlightening research can be obtained.

Web Resources and Supplements for Instructors and Students

Anthropology Online: Wadsworth's Anthropology Resource Center

The Wadsworth Anthropology Resource Center contains a wealth of information and useful tools for both instructors and students. After logging on to the Wadsworth Anthropology home page at **http://anthropology .wadsworth.com,** click on Course Materials, Physical Anthropology, and the Jurmain book cover. Proceed to the Student Resources section by clicking "For Students." There, students will find many exciting chapter specific resources such as CNN video clips, crossword puzzles, Internet Exercises, InfoTrac College Edition Exercises, practice quizzes that calculate results which can then be emailed to instructors, and much more. Instructors too will find a wealth of materials such as an online Instructor's Manual and PowerPoint Lecture slides.

A Virtual Tour of Applying Anthropology   This special section of the Anthropology Web site serves as an online resource center for the anthropology student. Students will find Applied Anthropologists at Work, Graduate Studies information, Job Boards, Internships and Field Work, and an Essay on Careers with Video.

InfoTrac College Edition   Ignite discussions or augment lectures with the latest developments in anthropology and societal change. InfoTrac College Edition (available as a free option with newly purchased texts) gives instructors and students 4-months' free access to an easy-to-use online database of reliable, full-length articles (not abstracts) from hundreds of top academic journals and popular sources. Among the journals available 24 hours a day, seven days a week, are *American Anthropologist, Current Anthropology, Canadian Review of Sociology and Anthropology.* Contact your Wadsworth/Thomson learning representative for more information.

WebTutor Advantage™ on WebCT and Blackboard   For students, **WebTutor Advantage** offers real-time access to a full array of study tools, including chapter summaries, flashcards (with audio), practice quizzes, interactive maps and timelines, online tutorials, and Web links. Professors can use **WebTutor Advantage** to provide virtual office hours, post syllabuses, set up threaded discussions, track student progress on quizzes, and more. **WebTutor Advantage** provides rich communication tools, including a course calendar, asynchronous discussion, "real-time" chat, a whiteboard, and an integrated email system.

CHAPTER

1

Introduction

CONTENTS

DNA escaping from a bacterium (*Escherichia coli*)

Introduction

One day, perhaps at the beginning of the rainy season some 3.7 million years ago, two or three individuals walked across a grassland savanna in what is now northern Tanzania in East Africa. These individuals were early members of the taxonomic family **Hominidae**, the family that also includes ourselves, modern *Homo sapiens*. Fortunately for us (the living descendants of those distant travelers), a record of their passage on that long-forgotten day remains in the form of fossilized footprints, preserved in hardened volcanic deposits.

As chance would have it, shortly after heels and toes were pressed into the dampened soil and volcanic ash of the area, a volcano, some 12 miles distant, erupted. The ensuing ashfall blanketed everything on the ground surface, including the footprints of the **hominids** and those of numerous other species as well. In time, the ash layer hardened into a deposit, which preserved a quite remarkable assortment of tracks and other materials that lay beneath it (Fig. 1–1).

These now-famous Laetoli prints indicate that two hominids, one smaller than the other, perhaps walked side by side, leaving parallel sets of tracks. But because the prints of the larger individual are obscured, possibly by those of a third, it is unclear how many actually made that journey so long ago. What is clear from the prints is that they were left by an animal that habitually walked **bipedally** (on two feet). It is this critical feature that has led scientists to consider these ancient passersby as hominids.

Hominidae
The taxonomic family to which humans belong; also includes other, now extinct, bipedal relatives.

Hominids
Members of the family Hominidae.

Bipedally
On two feet. Walking habitually on two legs is the single most distinctive feature of the Hominidae.

FIGURE 1–1
Early hominid footprints at Laetoli. The tracks to the left were made by one individual, while those to the right appear to have been formed by two individuals, the second stepping in the tracks of the first.

See the following sections of the CD-ROM for topics covered in this chapter: Virtual Lab 1, sections I and II; Virtual Lab 2; Virtual Lab 3; and Virtual Lab 11.*

*This CD-ROM icon indicates additional material that can be found on the *Virtual Laboratories for Physical Anthropology* CD-ROM, which is further described in the preface to this book.

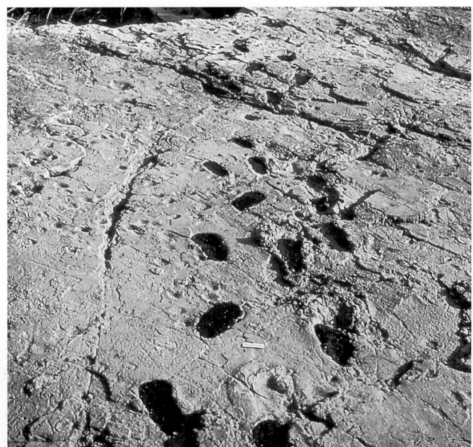

Courtesy, Peter Jones

In addition to the preserved footprints, scientists at Laetoli and elsewhere have discovered numerous fossilized skeletal remains of what we now call *Australopithecus afarensis.* These fossils and prints have volumes to say about the beings they represent, provided we can learn to interpret them.

What, then, have we actually gleaned from the meager evidence we possess of those creatures who beckon to us from an incomprehensibly distant past? Where did their journey take them that far-gone day, and why were they walking in that particular place? Were they foraging for food within the boundaries of their territory, or were they going to a nearby water source? Did the two (or three) indeed travel together at all, or did they simply use the same route within a short period of time?

We could ask myriad questions about these individuals, but we will never be able to answer them all. They walked down a path into what became their future, and their immediate journey has long since ended. It remains for us to sort out what little we can know about them and the **species** they represent. In this sense, their greater journey continues.

From the footprints and fossilized fragmentary skeletons, we know that these hominids walked upright. Thus, they were, in a great many respects, anatomically similar to ourselves, but their brains were only about one-third the size of ours. Although they may have used stones and sticks as tools, much as modern chimpanzees do, there is no current evidence to suggest they manufactured stone tools. In short, these early hominids were very much at the mercy of nature's whims. They certainly could not outrun most predators, and their lack of large canine teeth rendered them relatively defenseless.

Chimpanzees often serve as living models for our early ancestors, but in fact, the earliest hominids occupied a different habitat, exploited different resources, and probably had more to fear from predators than do chimpanzees. However much we may be tempted to compare early hominids to living species, we must remind ourselves that there is no living form that adequately represents them. Just like every other living thing, they were unique.

On July 20, 1969, a television audience numbering in the hundreds of millions watched as two human beings stepped out of a spacecraft and onto the surface of the moon. To anyone born after that date, this event is taken more or less for granted, even though it has not been repeated often. But the significance of that first moonwalk cannot be overstated, for it represents humankind's presumed mastery over the natural forces that govern our presence on earth. For the first time ever, people actually walked upon the surface of a celestial body that (as far as we know) has never given birth to biological life.

As the astronauts gathered geological specimens and frolicked in near weightlessness, they left traces of their fleeting presence in the form of footprints in the lunar dust (Fig. 1–2). On the atmosphereless surface of the moon, where no rain falls and no wind blows, the footprints remain undisturbed to this day. They survive as mute testimony to a brief visit by a medium-sized, big-brained creature who presumed to challenge the very forces that had created it.

We humans uncovered the Laetoli footprints, and we question the nature of the animal who made them. Perhaps one day, creatures as yet unimagined will ponder the essence of the being that made the lunar footprints. What do you suppose they will think?

We humans, who can barely comprehend a century, can only grasp at the enormity of 3.7 million years. We want to understand those creatures who traveled that day across the savanna. By what route did an insignificant but clever bipedal **primate** give rise to a species that would, in time, walk on the surface of a moon

Species
A group of organisms that can interbreed to produce fertile offspring. Members of one species are reproductively isolated from members of all other species (i.e., they cannot mate with them to produce fertile offspring).

© Bettmann/CORBIS

FIGURE 1–2
Human footprints left on the lunar surface during the *Apollo* mission.

Primate
A member of the order of mammals Primates (pronounced "pry-may´-tees"), which includes prosimians, monkeys, apes, and humans.

Introduction

some 230,000 miles from earth? How did it come to be that in the relatively short (geologically speaking) span of fewer than 4 million years, a fairly inconsequential animal evolved into the species that has developed the ability to dominate and destroy much (if not all) of life on the planet?

How did it happen that *Homo sapiens,* a result of the same evolutionary forces that produced all other life on this planet, gained the power to control the flow of rivers and alter the very climate in which we live? As tropical animals, how were we able to leave the tropics and disperse over most of the earth's land surfaces, and how did we adjust to local environmental conditions as we so expanded? How could our species, which numbered fewer than 1 billion individuals until the mid-nineteenth century, come to number more than 6 billion worldwide today and, as we now do, add another billion every 11 years?

These are some of the many questions that physical or biological anthropologists attempt to answer, and these questions are largely the focus of the study of human **evolution**, variation, and adaptation. These issues, and many more, are the topics covered directly or indirectly in this textbook, because physical anthropology is, in part, human biology seen from an evolutionary perspective.

As biological organisms, humans are subject to the same evolutionary forces as all other species. On hearing the term *evolution,* most people think of the appearance of new species. Certainly, new species formation is one consequence of evolution; however, biologists see evolution as an ongoing biological process with a precise genetic meaning. Quite simply, evolution is a change in the genetic makeup of a population from one generation to the next. It is the accumulation of such changes, over considerable periods of time, that can result in the appearance of a new species. Thus, evolution can be defined and studied at two different levels. At one level there are genetic alterations *within* populations. Although this type of change may not lead to the development of new species, it frequently results in variation between populations with regard to the frequency of certain traits. Evolution at this level is referred to as *microevolution.* At the other level is genetic change sufficient to result in the appearance of a new species, a process termed *macroevolution* or speciation. Evolution as it occurs at both these levels will be addressed in this text.

But physical anthropologists are not involved solely in the study of physiological systems and biological phenomena. When such topics are placed within the broader context of human evolution, another factor must also be considered: the role of **culture**. Culture is an extremely important concept, not only as it pertains to modern human beings, but also in terms of its critical role in human evolution. It has been said that there are as many definitions of culture as there are people who attempt to define it. Quite simply, and in a very broad sense, culture can be said to be the strategy by which humans adapt to the natural environment. In this sense, culture includes technologies that range from stone tools to computers; subsistence patterns ranging from hunting and gathering to agribusiness on a global scale; housing types, from thatched huts to skyscrapers; and clothing, from animal skins to high-tech synthetic fibers (Fig. 1–3). Because religion, values, social organization, language, kinship, marriage rules, gender roles, inheritance of property, and so on, are all aspects of culture, each culture shapes people's perceptions of the external environment, or **world view**, in particular ways that distinguish that culture from all others.

One fundamental point to remember is that culture is passed from one generation to the next independently of biological factors (i.e., genes). In other words, culture is *learned,* and the process of learning one's culture begins, quite literally, at birth. All humans are products of the culture in which they are raised, and since

Evolution
A change in the genetic structure of a population. The term is also frequently used to refer to the appearance of a new species.

Culture
All aspects of human adaptation, including technology, traditions, language, religion, marriage patterns, and social roles. Culture is a set of learned behaviors that is transmitted from one generation to the next by nonbiological means.

World view
General cultural orientation or perspective shared by members of a society.

(a)

(b)

(c)

(d)

most of human behavior is learned, it follows that most behaviors, perceptions, and reactions are shaped by culture.

It is important to emphasize, however, that even though culture is not genetically determined, the human *predisposition to assimilate culture and function within it is influenced by biological factors*. As you will see, many nonhuman animals especially primates, rely heavily on learned behavior, and chimpanzees, in particular, exhibit numerous aspects of culture. The predisposition for culture is perhaps the most critical component of human evolutionary history, and it was inherited from early hominid or prehominid ancestors. It may well have even existed in the common ancestor we share with chimpanzees. But in the course of human evolution, as you will see, the role of culture increasingly assumed an added importance. Over time, culture and biology interacted in such a way that humans are said to be the

FIGURE 1–3
(a) An early stone tool from East Africa. This artifact represents the oldest type of stone tools found anywhere. (b) Assortment of implements available today in a modern hardware store. (c) A Samburu woman building a simple, traditional dwelling of stems, plant fibers, and mud. (d) A modern high-rise apartment complex, typical of industrialized cities.

Biocultural evolution
The mutual, interactive evolution of human biology and culture; the concept that biology makes culture possible and that developing culture further influences the direction of biological evolution; a basic concept in understanding the unique components of human evolution.

Adaptation
Functional response of organisms or populations to the environment. Adaptation results from evolutionary change (specifically, as a result of natural selection).

Anthropology
The field of inquiry that studies human culture and evolutionary aspects of human biology; includes cultural anthropology, archaeology, linguistics, and physical anthropology.

result of **biocultural evolution.** In this respect, humans are unique among biological organisms.

Biocultural interactions have resulted in such anatomical, biological, and behavioral changes as increased brain size, reorganization of neurological structures, decreased tooth size, and development of language in humans, to list a few, and they even continue to be critical in changing disease patterns as well. As a contemporary example, rapid culture change (particularly in Africa) and changing social and sexual mores may have influenced evolutionary rates of HIV, the virus that causes AIDS. Certainly, these cultural factors influenced the spread of HIV throughout populations in both the developed and developing worlds.

The study of many of the biological aspects of humankind, including **adaptation** and evolution, could certainly be the purview of human biologists, and it frequently is. However, particularly in the United States, when such research also considers the role of cultural factors, it is placed within the discipline of **anthropology.**

What Is Anthropology?

Stated ambitiously but simply, anthropology is the study of humankind. (The term *anthropology* is derived from the Greek words *anthropos,* meaning "human," and *logos,* meaning "word" or "study of.") Anthropologists are not the only scientists who study humans, and the goals of anthropology are shared by other disciplines within the social, behavioral, and biological sciences. For example, psychologists and psychiatrists investigate various aspects of human motivation and behavior while developing theories that have clinical significance. Historians focus on recorded events in the past, but since their research concerns documented occurrences, it is limited to, at most, a few thousand years. The main difference between anthropology and such related fields is that anthropology integrates the findings of many disciplines, including sociology, economics, history, psychology, and biology.

The focus of anthropology is very broad indeed. Like other disciplines, anthropology is divided into numerous specialized subfields, but fundamentally its concentration is on human biological and cultural evolution. In short, anthropologists explore all aspects of what it means to be human.

In the United States, anthropology comprises three main subfields: cultural, or social, anthropology; archaeology; and physical, or biological, anthropology. Additionally, some universities include linguistic anthropology as a fourth area. Each of these subdisciplines, in turn, is divided into several specialized areas of interest. Following is a brief discussion of the main subdisciplines of anthropology.

Cultural Anthropology

Cultural anthropology is the study of all aspects of human behavior. It could reasonably be argued that cultural anthropology began in the fourth century B.C. with the Greek philosopher Aristotle, or even earlier. But for practical purposes, the beginnings of cultural anthropology are found in the nineteenth century, when Europeans became increasingly aware of what they termed "primitive" societies in Africa and Asia. Likewise, in the New World, there was much interest in the vanishing cultures of Native Americans.

Ethnographies
Detailed descriptive studies of human societies. In cultural anthropology, an ethnography is traditionally the study of a non-Western society.

The interest in traditional societies led numerous early anthropologists to study and record lifeways that unfortunately are now mostly extinct. These studies produced many descriptive **ethnographies** that became the basis for subsequent comparisons between groups. Early ethnographies emphasized various phenomena, such as religion, ritual, myth, use of symbols, subsistence strategies, technology, gender roles, child-rearing practices, dietary preferences, taboos, medical practices, and how kinship was reckoned.

Ethnographic accounts, in turn, formed the basis for comparative studies of numerous cultures. Such *cross-cultural* studies, termed *ethnologies,* broadened the context within which cultural anthropologists studied human behavior. By examining the similarities and differences between diverse cultures, anthropologists have been able to formulate many theories about the fundamental aspects of human behavior.

The focus of cultural anthropology shifted over the course of the twentieth century. But traditional ethnographic techniques, wherein anthropologists spend months or years living in and studying various societies, are still employed, although the nature of the study groups may have changed. For example, in recent decades, ethnographic techniques have been applied to the study of diverse subcultures and their interactions with one another in contemporary metropolitan areas. The subfield of cultural anthropology that deals with issues of inner cities is appropriately called *urban anthropology.* Among the many issues addressed by urban anthropologists are the relationships between ethnic groups, those aspects of traditional cultures maintained by immigrant populations, poverty, labor relations, homelessness, access to health care, and problems facing the elderly.

Medical anthropology is the subfield of cultural anthropology that explores the relationship between various cultural attributes and health and disease. One area of interest is how different groups view disease processes and how these views affect treatment or the willingness to accept treatment. When a medical anthropologist focuses on the social dimensions of disease, physicians and physical anthropologists may also collaborate. Indeed, many medical anthropologists have received much of their training in physical anthropology.

Economic anthropologists are concerned with factors that influence the distribution of goods and resources within and between cultures. Areas of interest include such topics as division of labor (by gender and age), factors that influence who controls resources and wealth, and trade practices and regulations.

Many cultural anthropologists are involved in gender studies. Such studies may focus on gender norms, how such norms are learned, and the specific cultural factors that lead to individual development of gender identity. It is also valuable to explore the social consequences if gender norms are violated.

There is also increasing interest in the social aspects of development and aging. This field is particularly relevant in industrialized nations, where the proportion of elderly individuals is higher than ever before. As populations age, the needs of the elderly, particularly in the area of health care, become social issues that require more and more attention.

Another relevant area for cultural anthropologists today is in the resettlement of refugees in many parts of the world. To develop plans that properly accommodate the needs of displaced peoples, governments may find the special talents of cultural anthropologists of considerable benefit.

Many of the subfields of cultural anthropology (e.g., medical anthropology) have practical applications and are pursued by anthropologists working outside the university setting. This approach is aptly termed *applied anthropology.* While most applied anthropologists regard themselves as cultural anthropologists, the designation is also sometimes used to describe the activities of archaeologists and physical anthropologists (see p. 14). Indeed, the various fields of anthropology, as they are practiced in the United States, overlap to a considerable degree, which, after all, was the rationale for combining them under the umbrella of anthropology in the first place.

Archaeology

Archaeology is discussed in Virtual Lab 11.

Artifacts
Objects or materials made or modified for use by hominids. The earliest artifacts tend to be tools made of stone or, occasionally, bone.

Material culture
The physical manifestations of human activities; includes tools, art, and structures. As the most durable aspects of culture, material remains make up the majority of archaeological evidence of past societies.

Archaeology is the study of earlier cultures and lifeways by anthropologists who specialize in the scientific recovery, analysis, and interpretation of the material remains of past societies. Although archaeology often deals with cultures that existed before the invention of writing (the period commonly known as *prehistory*), *historic archaeologists* examine the evidence of later, complex civilizations that produced written records.

Archaeologists are concerned with culture, but they differ from cultural anthropologists in that their sources of information are not living people but rather the **artifacts** and other **material culture** left behind by earlier societies. Obviously, no one has ever excavated such aspects of culture as religious belief, spoken language, or a political system. However, archaeologists assume that the surviving evidence of human occupation reflects some of those important but less tangible features of the culture that created them. Therefore, the material remains of a given ancient society may serve to inform us about the nature of that society.

The roots of modern archaeology are found in the fascination of nineteenth-century Europeans with the classical world (particularly Greece and Egypt). This interest was primarily manifested in the excavation (sometimes controlled, sometimes not) and removal of thousands of treasures and artifacts destined for the museums and private collections of wealthy Europeans.

New World archaeology has long focused on the pre-Columbian civilizations of Mexico and Central and South America (the Aztecs, Maya, and Inka). In the United States, archaeological interest was sparked particularly by the large earthen burial mounds found throughout much of the southeast. In fact, Thomas Jefferson conducted one of the first controlled excavations of a burial mound on his Virginia plantation in 1784. Importantly, his goal was not simply the recovery of artifacts; he specifically wished to address the question of how the mound was constructed.

Today, the main goal of archaeology is to answer specific questions pertaining to human behavior. Sites are not excavated simply because they exist or for the artifacts they may yield; excavation is conducted for the explicit purpose of gaining information about human behavior. Patterns of behavior are reflected in the dispersal of human settlements across a landscape and in the distribution of cultural remains within them. Through the identification of these patterns, archaeologists can elucidate the commonalities shared by many or all populations as well as those features that differ between groups. Research questions may focus on specific localities or peoples and attempt to identify, for example, various aspects of social organization, subsistence techniques, or the factors that led to the collapse of a civilization. Alternatively, inquiry may reflect an interest in broader issues relating to human culture in general, such as the development of agriculture or the rise of cities. But the design of most archaeological projects centers around a number of questions that address a wide range of interests, some specific and others broad.

Archaeology is a discipline that requires precise measurement, description, and excavation techniques, for it must be remembered that when a site is dug, it is also destroyed. Errors in excavation or recording result in the permanent loss or misinterpretation of valuable information. Therefore, contrary to what many people think, the science of archaeology is much more than simply digging up artifacts. Rather, archaeology is a multidisciplinary approach to the study of human behavior as evidenced by cultural remains.

For many projects, the specialized expertise of many disciplines is needed. Chemists, geologists, physicists, paleontologists, and physical anthropologists may all be required. Even the sophisticated satellite technologies of NASA have been called upon to locate archaeological sites.

In the United States, the greatest expansion in archaeology in recent years has been in the important area of _cultural resource management (CRM)_. This applied approach arose from environmental legislation requiring the archaeological evaluation and even excavation of sites that may be threatened by construction and other forms of development. Many contract archaeologists (so called because their services are contracted out to developers, government agencies, and municipalities) are affiliated with private archaeological consulting firms, state or federal agencies, or educational institutions. In fact, an estimated 40 percent of all archaeologists in the United States now fill such positions.

Archaeological techniques are used to identify and excavate not only remains of human cities and settlements, but also paleontological sites containing remains of extinct species, including everything from dinosaurs to early hominids. Together, prehistoric archaeology and physical anthropology form the core of a joint science called _paleoanthropology,_ described below.

Linguistic Anthropology

Linguistic anthropology is the study of human speech and language, including the origins of language in general as well as specific languages. By examining similarities between contemporary languages, linguists have been able to trace historical ties between languages and groups of languages, thus facilitating the identification of language families and perhaps past relationships between human populations.

There is also much interest in the relationship between language and culture: how language reflects the way members of a society perceive phenomena and how the use of language shapes perceptions in different cultures. For instance, vocabulary provides important clues as to the importance of certain items and concepts in particular cultures. The most famous example is the use of some 50 terms for snow among the Inuit (Eskimos), reflecting their need to convey specific information about the properties of this form of frozen precipitation. (For that matter, skiers also employ many more increasingly precise terms for snow than do nonskiers.)

Because the spontaneous acquisition and use of language is a uniquely human characteristic, it is a topic that holds considerable interest for linguistic anthropologists, who, along with specialists in other fields, study the process of language acquisition in infants. Since insights into the process may well have implications for the development of language skills in human evolution, as well as in growing children, it is also an important subject to physical anthropologists.

Physical Anthropology

Physical anthropology, as has already been stated, is the study of human biology within the framework of evolution, with an emphasis on the interaction between biology and culture. This subdiscipline is also referred to as _biological anthropology,_ and you will find the terms used interchangeably. _Physical anthropology_ is the original and traditional term, and it reflects the initial interests anthropologists had in describing human physical variation. The American Association of Physical Anthropologists, its journal, many college courses, and numerous publications retain this term. But the designation _biological anthropology_ reflects the shift in emphasis to more biologically oriented topics, such as genetics, evolutionary biology, nutrition, physiological adaptation, and growth and development. This shift occurred largely as a result of advances in the field of genetics, especially since the late 1950s and early 1960s. Although we have continued to use the traditional term in the title of this textbook, you will find that all the major topics pertain to biological matters.

The place of physical anthropology within the discipline of anthropology is discussed in Virtual Lab 1, section I.

Introduction

Physical anthropology is composed of several subdisciplines, or areas of specialization, the most significant of which are briefly described in the following paragraphs. The origins of physical anthropology are to be found in two principal areas of interest among nineteenth-century scholars. First, there was increasing concern among many scientists (at the time called *natural historians*) regarding the mechanisms by which modern species had come to be. In other words, increasing numbers of intellectuals were beginning to doubt the literal, biblical interpretation of creation. This does not mean that all natural historians had abandoned all religious explanations of natural occurrences. But scientific explanations emphasizing natural, rather than supernatural, phenomena were becoming increasingly popular in scientific and intellectual circles. Although few scientists were actually prepared to believe that humans had evolved from earlier forms, discoveries of several Neandertal fossils in the 1800s began to raise questions regarding the origins and antiquity of the human species.

The sparks of interest in biological change over time were fueled into flames by the publication of Charles Darwin's *Origin of Species* in 1859. Today, **paleoanthropology**, or the study of human evolution, particularly as evidenced in the fossil record, is one of the major subfields of physical anthropology (Fig. 1–4). There are now thousands of specimens of human ancestors housed in museum and research collections. Taken together, these fossils cover a span of at least 4 million years of human prehistory, and although incomplete, they provide us with significantly more knowledge than was available even 15 years ago. It is the ultimate goal of paleoanthropological research to identify the various early hominid species, establish a chronological sequence of relationships among them, and gain insights into their adaptation and behavior. Only then will there emerge a clear picture of how and when humankind came into being.

A second nineteenth-century interest that had direct relevance to anthropology was observable physical variation, particularly as seen in skin color. Enormous effort was aimed at describing and explaining the biological differences among various

origins

Paleoanthropology
The interdisciplinary approach to the study of earlier hominids—their chronology, physical structure, archaeological remains, habitats, etc.

FIGURE 1–4
Paleoanthropological research at Hadar, Ethiopia, during a field season in 1993.

Institute of Human Origins

comparing bodies across cultures

human populations. Although some endeavors were misguided, they gave birth to literally thousands of body measurements that could be used to compare people. Physical anthropologists use many of the techniques of **anthropometry** today, not only to study living groups, but also to study skeletal remains from archaeological sites (Fig. 1–5). Moreover, anthropometric techniques have considerable application in the design of everything from airplane cockpits to office furniture.

Anthropologists today are concerned with human variation because of its *adaptive significance* and also because they want to elucidate the genetic and other related evolutionary factors that act to produce variation. In other words, many traits that typify certain populations are seen as having evolved as biological adaptations, or adjustments, to local environmental conditions including infectious disease. Other traits may be the results of geographic isolation or the descent of populations from small founding groups. Examining biological variation between populations of any species provides valuable information as to the mechanisms of genetic change in groups over time, which is precisely what the evolutionary process is all about.

Modern population studies also examine other important aspects of human variation, including how various groups respond physiologically to different kinds of environmentally induced stress (Fig. 1–6). Such stresses may include high altitude, cold, or heat.

Other physical anthropologists conduct nutritional studies, investigating the relationships between various dietary components, cultural practices, physiology, and certain aspects of health and disease. Closely related to the topic of nutrition are investigations of human fertility, growth, and development. These fields of inquiry are fundamental to studies of adaptation in modern human populations, and they can provide insights into hominid evolution as well.

It would be impossible to study evolutionary processes, and therefore adaptation, without a knowledge of genetic principles. For this reason and others, **genetics** is a crucial field for physical anthropologists. Modern physical anthropology would not exist as an evolutionary science were it not for advances in the understanding of genetic principles.

Not only does genetics allow us to explain how evolutionary processes work, but today's anthropologists use recently developed genetic technologies to investigate evolutionary distances between living primate species (including humans). Moreover, genetic theories have been used (with much debate) to explain, among other things, the origins of modern *Homo sapiens*.

Primatology, the study of nonhuman primates, has become increasingly important since the late 1950s for several reasons (Fig. 1–7). Behavioral studies, especially those conducted on groups in natural environments, have implications for numerous scientific disciplines. Moreover, studies of nonhuman animal behavior have assumed a greater urgency in recent decades owing to concern over declining numbers of many species.

The behavioral study of any species provides a wealth of data pertaining to

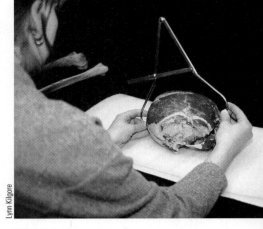
Lynn Kilgore

FIGURE 1–5
Anthropology student using spreading calipers to measure cranial length.

Anthropometry
Measurement of human body parts. When osteologists measure skeletal elements, the term *osteometry* is often used.

Genetics
The study of gene structure and action and the patterns of inheritance of traits from parent to offspring. Genetic mechanisms are the underlying foundation for evolutionary change.

Courtesy, Judith Regensteiner

FIGURE 1–6
Researcher using a treadmill test to assess a subject's heart rate, blood pressure, and oxygen consumption.

Primatology
The study of the biology and behavior of nonhuman primates (prosimians, monkeys, and apes).

(a)

(b)

FIGURE 1-7
(a) Yahaya Alamasi, a member of the senior field staff at Gombe National Park, Tanzania. Alamasi is recording behaviors in free-ranging chimpanzees. (b) Oakland Zoo docent uses a laptop computer to record behaviors of a captive chimpanzee.

Osteology
The study of skeletal material. Human osteology focuses on the interpretation of the skeletal remains of past groups. Some of the same techniques are used in paleoanthropology to study early hominids.

Paleopathology
The branch of osteology that studies the evidence of disease and injury in human skeletal (or, occasionally, mummified) remains.

adaptation. Because nonhuman primates are our closest living relatives, the identification of underlying factors related to social behavior, communication, infant care, reproductive behavior, and so on, aids in developing a better understanding of the natural forces that have shaped so many aspects of modern human behavior.

Moreover, nonhuman primates are important to study in their own right, and this is particularly true today because the majority of species are threatened or seriously endangered. Only through study will scientists be able to recommend policies that can better ensure the survival of many nonhuman primates and thousands of other species as well.

Primate paleontology, the study of the primate fossil record, has implications not only for nonhuman primates but also for hominids. Virtually every year, fossil-bearing beds in North America, Africa, Asia, and Europe yield important new discoveries. Through the study of fossil primates, we are able to learn much about factors such as diet or locomotion in earlier forms. By comparisons with anatomically similar living species, primate paleontologists can make reasoned inferences regarding behavior in earlier groups as well. Moreover, we hope to be able to clarify what we know about evolutionary relationships between extinct and modern species, including ourselves.

Osteology, the study of the skeleton, is central to physical anthropology. Indeed, it is so important that when many people think of physical anthropology, the first thing that comes to mind is bones. The emphasis on osteology exists in part because of the concern with the analysis of fossil material. Certainly, a thorough knowledge of the structure and function of the skeleton is critical to the interpretation of fossil material.

Bone biology and physiology are of major importance to many other aspects of physical anthropology, in addition to paleontology. Many osteologists specialize in studies that emphasize various measurements of skeletal elements. This type of research is essential, for example, to the identification of stature and growth patterns in archaeological populations.

One subdiscipline of osteology is the study of disease and trauma in archaeologically derived skeletal populations. **Paleopathology** is a prominent subfield that

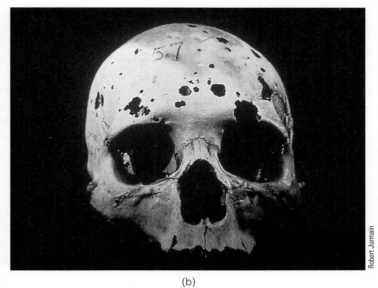

(b)

(a)

Lynn Kilgore

Robert Jurmain

FIGURE 1–8
(a) Healing fracture of a humerus (upper arm bone) in a skeleton from Nubia (Republic of the Sudan). (b) Cranial lesions, probably resulting from metastasized cancer.

investigates the incidence of trauma, certain infectious diseases (including syphilis and tuberculosis), nutritional deficiencies, and numerous other conditions that may leave evidence in bone (Fig. 1–8). In this area of research, a precise knowledge of bone physiology and response to insult is required.

A field directly related to osteology and paleopathology is **forensic anthropology.** Technically, this approach is the application of anthropological (usually osteological and sometimes archaeological) techniques to the law (Fig. 1–9). Forensic

Forensic anthropology
An applied anthropological approach dealing with legal matters. Physical anthropologists work with coroners and others in the analysis and identification of human remains.

FIGURE 1–9
Physical anthropologists Lorna Pierce (left) and Judy Suchey (center) working as forensic consultants. The dog has just located a concealed human cranium during a training session.

Courtesy, Lorna Pierce/Judy Suchey

anthropologists are commonly called on to help identify skeletal remains in cases of disaster or other situations where a human body has been found.

Forensic anthropologists have been involved in numerous cases having important legal, historical, and human consequences. They were prominent in the identification of the skeletons of most of the Russian imperial family, executed in 1918. They also participated in the identification of missing American soldiers in Southeast Asia. And most recently, many forensic anthropologists were mobilized to participate in the tragically overwhelming task of identifying the remains of victims of the September 11, 2001, terrorist attacks at the Pentagon and in New York City and Pennsylvania.

Anatomical studies constitute another important area of interest for physical anthropologists. In the living organism, bone and dental structures are intimately linked to the soft tissues that surround and act on them. Thus, a thorough knowledge of soft tissue anatomy is essential to the understanding of biomechanical relationships involved in movement. Such relationships are important to the accurate assessment of the structure and function of limbs and other components in fossilized remains. For these reasons and others, many physical anthropologists specialize in anatomical studies. In fact, several physical anthropologists hold professorships in anatomy departments at universities and medical schools.

Applied approaches in physical anthropology are numerous. And while *applied anthropology* is aimed at the practical application of anthropological theories and methods outside the academic setting, applied and academic anthropology are not mutually exclusive approaches. In fact, applied anthropology relies on the research and theories of academic anthropologists and at the same time has much to contribute to theory and techniques. Probably the majority of applied anthropologists are trained as cultural anthropologists, but perhaps the best-known example is provided by archaeologists working in cultural resource management (see p. 9). Within biological anthropology, forensic anthropologists provide a good example of the applied approach. But the practical application of the techniques of physical anthropology is not new. During World War II, for example, physical anthropologists, because of their expertise in measuring humans, were extensively involved in the design of gun turrets and airplane cockpits. Since that time, many physical anthropologists have pursued careers in genetic and biomedical research, public health, evolutionary medicine, medical anthropology, and conservation of nonhuman primates, and many hold positions in museums and zoos. In fact, a background in physical anthropology is excellent preparation for almost any career in the medical and biological fields.

From this brief overview, it can be seen that physical anthropology is the subdiscipline of anthropology that focuses on many varied aspects of the biological and behavioral nature of *Homo sapiens*. Humans are a product of the same forces that produced all life on earth. As such, we represent one contemporary component of a vast biological **continuum** at one point in time, and in this regard, we are not particularly unique. Stating that humans are part of a continuum does not imply that we are at the peak of development on that continuum. Depending on which criteria one uses, humans can be seen to exist at one end of the continuum or the other or somewhere in between. But humans do not necessarily occupy a position of inherent superiority over other species.

There is, however, one dimension in which human beings are truly unique, and that is intellect. After all, humans are the only species, born of earth, to stir the lunar dust. Humans are the only species to develop language and complex culture as a means of buffering the challenges posed by nature and by so doing eventually gain the power to shape the very destiny of the planet.

Continuum
A set of relationships in which all components fall along a single integrated spectrum. All life reflects a single *biological* continuum.

Physical Anthropology and the Scientific Method

Science is a process of understanding phenomena through observation, generalization, and verification. By this we mean that there is an **empirical** approach to gaining information through the use of systematic and explicit techniques. Because physical anthropologists are engaged in scientific pursuits, they adhere to the principles of the **scientific method,** whereby a research problem is identified and information subsequently gathered to solve it.

The gathering of information is referred to as **data** collection, and when researchers use a rigorously controlled approach, they are able to describe precisely their techniques and results in a manner that facilitates comparisons with the work of others. For example, when scientists collect data on tooth size in hominid fossils, they must specify precisely which teeth are being measured, how they are being measured, and what the results of the measurements are (expressed numerically, or **quantitatively**). Subsequently, it is up to the investigators to draw conclusions as to the meaning and significance of their measurements. This body of information then becomes the basis of future studies, perhaps by other researchers, who can compare their own results with those already obtained. The eventual outcome of this type of inquiry may be the acceptance or rejection of certain proposed facts and explanations.

Once facts have been established, scientists attempt to explain them. First, a **hypothesis,** or provisional explanation of phenomena, is developed. But before a hypothesis can be accepted, it must be tested by means of data collection and analysis. Indeed, the testing of hypotheses with the possibility of proving them false is the very basis of the scientific method.

Scientific testing of hypotheses may take several years (or longer) and may involve researchers who were not involved with the original work. In subsequent studies, other investigators may attempt to obtain the original results, but such repetition may not occur. For example, repeated failures to duplicate the results of highly publicized cold fusion experiments led most scientists to question and ultimately reject the claims made in the original research. While it is easier to duplicate original studies conducted in laboratory settings, it is equally important to verify data collected outside tightly controlled situations. In the latter circumstance, results are tested relative to other, often larger, samples. The predicted patterns will either be confirmed through such further research or be viewed as limited or even incorrect.

If a hypothesis cannot be falsified, it is accepted as a **theory.** A theory, then, is a statement of relationships that has a firm basis as demonstrated through testing and the accumulation of evidence. As such, it not only helps organize current knowledge, but should also predict how new facts may fit into the established pattern.

Use of the scientific method not only allows for the development and testing of hypotheses, but also permits various types of *bias* to be addressed and controlled. It is important to realize that bias occurs in all studies. Sources of bias include how the investigator was trained and by whom; what particular questions interest the researcher; what specific skills and talents he or she possesses; what earlier results (if any) have been established in this realm of study and by whom (e.g., the researcher, close colleagues, or those with rival approaches or even rival personalities); and what sources of data are available (e.g., accessible countries or museums) and thus what samples can be collected (at all or at least conveniently).

Application of the scientific method thus requires constant vigilance by all those who practice it. The goal is not to establish "truth" in any absolute sense, but rather to generate ever more accurate and consistent depictions and explanations of phenomena in our universe. At its very heart, scientific methodology is an exercise in rational thought and critical thinking (see Issue, pp. 19–20).

Science
A body of knowledge gained through observation and experimentation; from the Latin *scientia,* meaning "knowledge."

Empirical
Relying on experiment or observation; from the Latin *empiricus,* meaning "experienced."

Scientific method
A research method whereby a problem is identified, a hypothesis (or hypothetical explanation) is stated, and that hypothesis is tested through the collection and analysis of data. If the hypothesis is verified, it becomes a theory.

Data
(*sing.,* datum)
Facts from which conclusions can be drawn; scientific information.

Quantitatively
In a manner involving measurements of quantity and including such properties as size, number, and capacity. When data are quantified, they are expressed numerically and are capable of being tested statistically.

Hypothesis
(*pl.,* hypotheses)
A provisional explanation of a phenomenon. Hypotheses require verification.

Scientific testing
The precise repetition of an experiment or expansion of observed data to provide verification; the procedure by which hypotheses and theories are verified, modified, or discarded.

Theory
A broad statement of scientific relationships or underlying principles that has been at least partially verified.

A discussion of the scientific method can be found in Virtual Lab 3, section III.

The Anthropological Perspective

Perhaps the most important benefit you will receive from this textbook—and this course—is a wider appreciation of the human experience. To understand human beings and how our species came to be, it is necessary to broaden our viewpoint, both through time and over space. All branches of anthropology fundamentally seek to do this in what we call the *anthropological perspective.*

Physical anthropologists, for example, are keenly interested in how humans differ from and are similar to other animals, especially nonhuman primates. For example, we have defined *hominids* as bipedal primates, but what are the major components of bipedal locomotion, and how do they differ from, say, those in a quadrupedal ape? To answer these questions, we would need to study human locomotion and compare it with the locomotion seen in various nonhuman primates. Moreover, in addition to observing how humans walk while wearing shoes, we also would be interested in their pattern of locomotion while walking barefoot. Indeed, it would probably be useful to look at the locomotion of people who have never worn shoes, and to obtain these data, we would probably have to leave our own culture and study other quite geographically distant groups.

Through such a wider perspective, we can begin to grasp the contemporary diversity of the human experience and, in so doing, more fully understand both human potentialities and human constraints. And by extending our breadth of knowledge, it is easier to avoid the **ethnocentric** pitfalls inherent in a more limited view of humanity.

Ethnocentric
Viewing other cultures from the inherently biased perspective of one's own culture. Ethnocentrism often results in cultures being seen as inferior to one's own.

In addition to broadening perspectives over space (i.e., encompassing many cultures and ecological circumstances as well as nonhuman species), an anthropological perspective also extends our horizons *through time.* For example, in Chapter 16 we will discuss human nutrition. However, the vast majority of the kinds of foods currently eaten (coming from domesticated plants and animals) were unavailable prior to 10,000 years ago. Human physiological mechanisms for chewing and digesting foods nevertheless were already well established long before that date. These adaptive complexes go back many hundreds of thousands—perhaps even millions—of years. In addition to the obviously different diets prior to the development of agriculture (approximately 10,000 years ago), earlier hominids might well have differed from humans today in average body size, metabolism, and activity patterns. How, then, does the basic evolutionary "equipment" (i.e., physiology) inherited from our hominid forebears accommodate our modern diets? Clearly, the way to understand such processes is not just by looking at contemporary human responses, but also by placing them in the perspective of evolutionary development through time.

Indeed, most of the topics covered in this book—as most topics considered by all types of anthropologists—are addressed by using a broad application of the anthropological perspective. For physical anthropologists, such an approach usually means extending the perspective over space as well as through considerable periods of time.

We hope that the ensuing pages will help you develop an increased understanding of the similarities we share with other biological organisms and also of the processes that have shaped the traits that make us unique. We live in what may well be the most crucial period for our planet in the last 65 million years. We are members of the one species that, through the very agency of culture, has wrought such devastating changes in ecological systems that we must now alter our technologies or face potentially unspeakable consequences. In such a time, it is vital that we attempt to gain the best possible understanding of what it means to be human. We believe that the study of physical anthropology is one endeavor that aids in this attempt, and that is indeed the goal of this text.

SUMMARY

In this chapter, we have introduced the field of physical anthropology and have placed it within the overall context of anthropological studies. As a major academic area within the social sciences, anthropology also includes archaeology, cultural anthropology, and linguistic anthropology as its major subfields.

Physical anthropology itself includes aspects of human biology (emphasizing evolutionary perspectives), the study of nonhuman primates, and the hominid fossil record. Especially as applied to the study of early hominids (as incorporated within the interdisciplinary field of paleoanthropology), physical anthropologists work in close collaboration with many other scientists from the fields of archaeology, geology, chemistry, and many other disciplines.

In the next chapter, we present a brief overview of changes in scientific thought that led to the discovery of the basic principles of biological evolution. Evolution is the core of physical anthropology, and basic evolutionary processes explain the appearance of humans and our ancestors as well as human (and nonhuman) adaptation and variation.

QUESTIONS FOR REVIEW

1. What is anthropology? What are the major subfields of anthropology?
2. How does physical anthropology differ from other disciplines interested in human biology?
3. What is meant by biocultural evolution, and why is it important in understanding human evolution?
4. What are some of the primary areas of research within physical anthropology? Give two or three examples of the types of research pursued by physical anthropologists.
5. What is meant by the term *hominid?* Be specific.
6. What fields, in addition to physical anthropology, contribute to paleoanthropology?

SUGGESTED FURTHER READING

Ferraro, Gary, Wenda Trevathan, and Janet Levy. 1994. *Anthropology, an Applied Perspective.* St. Paul: West.
Spencer, Frank (ed.). 1982. *A History of Physical Anthropology.* New York: Academic Press.
Stiebing, William H., Jr. 1993. *Uncovering the Past: A History of Archaeology.* New York: Oxford University Press.

RESOURCES ON THE INTERNET

Wadsworth Anthropology Resource Center
http://anthropology.wadsworth.com

The companion website for this text includes a range of enrichment material focused on the chapter's topic. While online, you can enhance your understanding of the chapter by exploring one of the several additional Internet exercises, by researching topics, and by accessing full articles on InfoTrac College Edition. You can also reinforce the concepts by taking online practice exams.

Internet Exercises

Visit the major association of anthropologists in the United States, the American Anthropological Association. (If your search did not provide the link, try **www.aaanet.org**.) The American Anthropological Association represents anthropologists in all subdisciplines, and this site serves as a good indicator of the breadth of anthropology. Take time to explore the site thoroughly. Visit "About AAA" to learn more about the field and the association. Read "Careers in Anthropology." What could you do with a major in anthropology without going to graduate school?

InfoTrac College Edition
http://www.infotrac-college.com/wadsworth

Anthropology is a very broad discipline. Search InfoTrac College Edition for the subject *anthropology*. How many different topics are there? How many are related to biological or physical anthropology? How many are there for archaeology? Choose one subject not introduced in the text and read some of the articles about it. What makes this topic anthropological?

Evaluation in Science: Lessons in Critical Thinking

At the end of various chapters throughout this book, you will find a brief discussion of a contemporary topic. Some of these subjects are not usually covered in anthropology textbooks. However, we feel it is important to address such issues because scientists should not simply dismiss those views or ideas of which they are skeptical. Similarly, you should be reluctant to *accept* a view based solely on its personal appeal. Accepting or rejecting an idea based on personal feelings is as good a definition of "bias" as one could devise. Science is an approach—indeed, a *tool*—used to eliminate (or at least minimize) bias.

Scientific approaches of evaluation are, in fact, a part of a broader framework of intellectual rigor that is termed *critical thinking*. The development of critical thinking skills is an important and lasting benefit of a college education. Such skills enable people to evaluate, compare, analyze, critique, and synthesize information so that they will not accept all they hear and read at face value but will be able to reach their own conclusions. Critical thinkers are able to assess the evidence supporting their own beliefs (in a sense, to step outside themselves) and to identify the weaknesses in their own positions. They recognize that knowledge is not merely a collection of facts but an ongoing process of examining information to expand our understanding of the world.

In scientific inquiry, individual "facts" (or better put, *observations*) must be presented clearly, with appropriate documentation. That is the purpose of bibliographical citation, as exemplified throughout this textbook. Once "facts" are established, scientists attempt to develop explanations concerning their relationships. In this way, initial hypotheses can be broadened into more general and better-supported theories.

A crucial aspect of scientific statements is that they are *falsifiable;* that is, there must be a means of evaluating the validity of hypotheses and theories to demonstrate that the statements may be incorrect. In this way, scientific conclusions are constantly *tested*. Statements such as "Heaven exists" may well be "true" (i.e., describe some actual state), but there is no rational, *empirical* means (based on experience or experiment) by which to test it. Acceptance of such a view is thus based on faith rather than on scientific verification.

We should emphasize that perceived phenomena understood through faith do not necessarily conflict with empirical demonstration. In fact, precisely because there may be areas of knowledge beyond the reach of scientific inquiry, faith-based beliefs provide a powerful influence for many people. Furthermore, these beliefs need not (and for many individuals, scientist and nonscientist alike, do not) conflict with the demonstrable values of scientific thought.

One of the most appealing aspects of perspectives based in faith is that such beliefs are widely and comfortably accepted as true. In science, statements can be tested and falsified (indeed, this is a central component of the scientific method), but they can never completely be proved "true." Theories can simply be better substantiated and are thus more fully established. However, new evidence can also require modification of hypotheses and theories; and some theories might prove so inadequate as to be rejected altogether. Thus, Newton's theory of gravitation was substantially altered by Einstein's theory of relativity. The old theory of a "missing link" (a kind of halfway compromise between modern humans and modern apes) preceded modern evolutionary thinking and is now seen as simplistic, misleading, and, at a practical level, of no value.

This inherent aspect of scientific inquiry in which theories are always subject to ongoing evaluation is widely misunderstood, frequently with disturbing consequences. For example, as we will note in Chapter 2, claims are often made that evolution is "just a theory." Pronouncements like these, as related to the teaching of evolution in public schools, have found their way into court decisions in California and policy statements by the Alabama State Board of Education. In science, knowledge is always proposed, organized, and tested in the form of hypotheses and, more generally, as theories. Our understanding of the action of gravity is just a theory, and so is the sun-centered depiction of the solar system. These two theories have, of course, been supported by an overwhelming amount of highly consistent evidence—but *so has evolutionary theory.* The constraint that science can never establish absolute "truth" should not be confused with an inability to understand the world around us. The human brain is one product of 4 billion years of evolution on this planet, and by using this neurological structure, *Homo sapiens* has the ability to apply rational thought. In the last few hundred years, the scientific method has developed into the most powerful tool invented by our species to utilize these rational capabilities and, in so doing, to come to grips with the universe and how we fit into it.

Throughout this book, you will be presented with the results of numerous studies that utilize numerical data. For example, it might be stated that female chimpanzees eat more insects than male chimpanzees or that Neandertal males were bigger than females or that the gene for cystic fibrosis is more common in European populations than in other groups. First of all, you should always be cautious of generalizations. What is the specific nature of the argument? What data support it? Can these data be quantified? If so, how is this information presented? (*Note:* Always read the tables in textbooks or articles.)

Regardless of the discipline you ultimately study, at some point in your academic career you should take a course in statistics. Many universities now make statistics a general education requirement (sometimes under the category "quantitative reasoning"). Whether you are required

to take such an offering or elect to do so, we strongly encourage it. Statistics often seems a very dry subject, and many students are intimidated by the math it requires. Nevertheless, perhaps more than any other skill you will acquire in your college years, quantitative critical reasoning is a tool you will be able to use every day of your life.

The topics chosen for the chapter-closing issues are those that intrigue the authors, and we hope that you also will find them stimulating. Some subjects are of historical interest. In addition, we address several topics that relate to recent advances in science, as exemplified by newly developed genetic technologies (see Chapter 3). Here, in addition to challenging you to grasp the basic scientific principles involved, we also ask you to consider the *social implications* of scientific/technological advances.

A responsibility of an educated society is to be both informed and vigilant. The knowledge we possess and attempt to build on is neither "good" nor "bad"; however, the uses to which knowledge may be put have highly charged moral and ethical implications. Thus, a goal of the chapter-closing issues is to stimulate your interest and provide you with a basis to reach your own conclusions. Here are some useful questions to ask in making critical evaluations about these issues or any other controversial scientific topic:

1. What data are presented?
2. What conclusions are presented, and how are they organized (as tentative hypotheses or as more dogmatic assertions)?
3. Are these views the individual opinions of the authors, or are they supported by a larger body of research?
4. What are the research findings? Are they adequately documented?
5. Is the information consistent with information that you already possess? If not, can the inconsistencies be explained?
6. Are the conclusions (hypotheses) testable? How might one go about testing the various hypotheses that are presented?
7. If presentation of new research findings is at odds with previous hypotheses (or theories), must these hypotheses now be modified (or completely rejected)?
8. How do your own personal views bias you in interpreting the results?
9. Once you have identified your own biases, are you able to set them aside so as to evaluate the information objectively?
10. Are you able to discuss both the pros and cons of a scientific topic in an evenhanded manner?

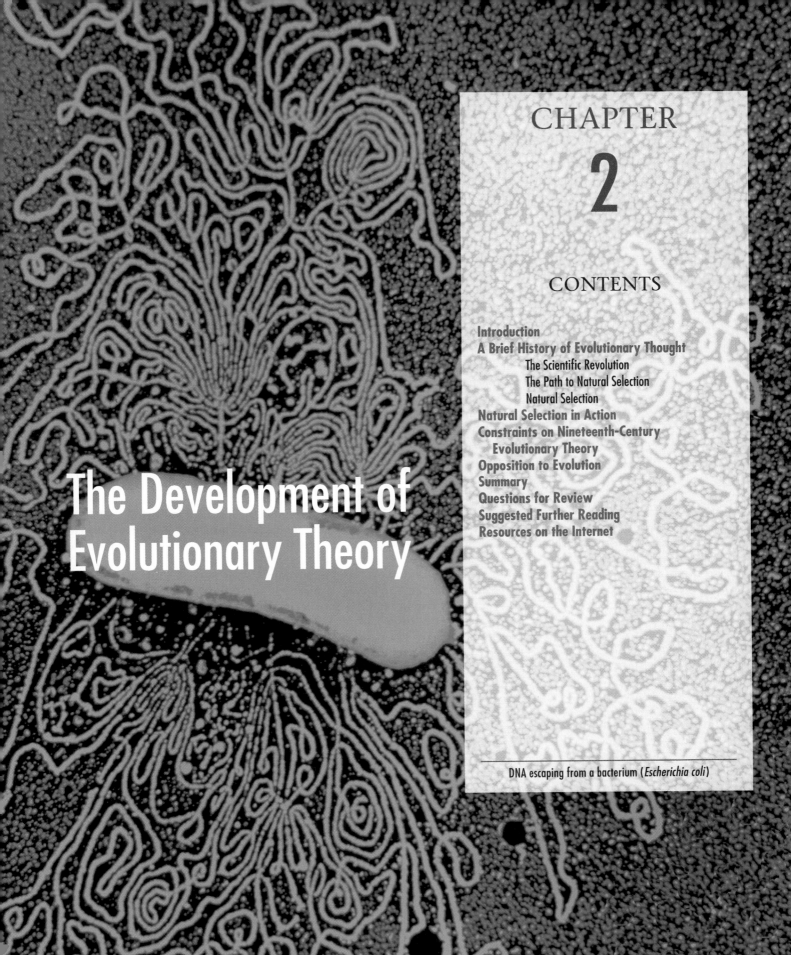

The Development of Evolutionary Theory

CHAPTER

2

CONTENTS

DNA escaping from a bacterium (*Escherichia coli*)

Evolution
A change in the genetic structure of a population. The term is also frequently used to refer to the appearance of a new species.

See the following sections of the CD-ROM for topics covered in this chapter: Virtual Lab 1, section II and Virtual Lab 2, section I.

Natural selection
The mechanism of evolutionary change first articulated by Charles Darwin; refers to genetic change or changes in the frequencies of certain traits in populations due to differential reproductive success between individuals.

Introduction

The term **evolution** is sometimes charged with emotion. The topic is often controversial, particularly in the United States, because some religious views hold that evolutionary statements run counter to biblical teachings. Indeed, as you are probably aware, there continues to be much opposition to the teaching of evolution in public schools.

Those who wish to denigrate evolution frequently insist that it is "only a theory"—in an attempt to reduce its status to supposition. Actually, to refer to a concept as "theory" is to lend it support. As we noted in Chapter 1, theories are general hypotheses that have been tested and subjected to verification through accumulated evidence. Evolution *is* a theory, one that has increasingly been supported by a mounting body of genetic evidence. It is a theory that has stood the test of time, and today it stands as the most fundamental unifying force in biological science.

Because physical anthropology is concerned with all aspects of how humans came to be and how we adapt physiologically to the external environment, the details of the evolutionary process are crucial to the field. Moreover, given the central importance of evolution to physical anthropology, it is valuable to know how the mechanics of the process came to be discovered. Additionally, to appreciate the nature of the controversy that continues to surround the issue today, it is important to examine the basic evolutionary principles within the social and political context in which the theory emerged.

A Brief History of Evolutionary Thought

The individual most responsible for the elucidation of the evolutionary process was Charles Darwin. But while Darwin was formulating his theory of **natural selection**, his ideas were being duplicated by another English naturalist, Alfred Russel Wallace.

That natural selection, the single most important mechanism of evolutionary change, should be proposed at more or less the same time by two British men in the mid-nineteenth century may seen highly improbable. But actually, it is not all that surprising. Indeed, if Darwin and Wallace had not made their simultaneous discoveries, someone else would have done so in short order. That is to say, the groundwork had already been laid, and many within the scientific community were prepared to accept explanations of biological change that would have been unacceptable even 25 years before.

Like other human endeavors, scientific knowledge is usually gained through a series of small steps rather than giant leaps. Just as technological innovation is based on past achievements, scientific knowledge builds on previously developed theories. (One does not build a space shuttle without first having invented the airplane.) Given this stepwise aspect of scientific discovery, it is informative to examine the development of ideas that led Darwin and Wallace independently to develop the theory of evolution by natural selection.

Throughout the Middle Ages, one predominant component of the European world view was *stasis*. That is, all aspects of nature, including all forms of life and their relationships to one another, were seen as fixed and unchanging. This view of natural phenomena was shaped in part by a feudal society that was very much a hierarchical arrangement supporting a rigid class system that had changed little for several centuries.

The world view of Europeans during the Middle Ages was also shaped by a powerful religious system. The teachings of Christianity were taken quite literally, and it was generally accepted that all life on earth had been created by God exactly as it existed in the present. Indeed, alterations in plants and animals were seen to be impossible because they would have run counter to God's plan. This belief that life forms could not change eventually came to be known in European intellectual circles as fixity of species.

Accompanying the notion of fixity of species was the belief that all God's creations were arranged in a hierarchy that progressed from the simplest organisms to the most complex. At the top of this linear sequence were humans. This concept of a ranked order of living things is termed the *Great Chain of Being* and was first proposed in the fourth century B.C. by the Greek philosopher Aristotle. Although position within the chain was based on physical similarities between species, no evolutionary or biological relationships were implied. Nor did "lower" forms move up the scale to become "superior" ones.

In addition, there was the common notion that the earth was "full" and that nothing new (such as species) could be added. Thus, it was believed that since the creation, no new species had appeared and none had disappeared, or become extinct. And since all of nature and the Great Chain of Being were created by God in a fixed state, change was inconceivable. Questioning the assumptions of fixity was ultimately seen as a challenge to God's perfection and could be considered heresy.

The plan of the entire universe was seen as the Grand Design—that is, God's design. In what is called the "argument from design," anatomical structures were viewed as planned to meet the purpose for which they were required. Wings, arms, eyes—all these structures were interpreted as neatly fitting the functions they performed, and nature was considered to be a deliberate plan of the Grand Designer.

The date the Grand Designer had completed his works was relatively recent—4004 B.C., according to Archbishop James Ussher (1581–1656), an Irish scholar who worked out the date of creation by analyzing the "begat" chapter of Genesis. Archbishop Ussher was not the first person to propose a recent origin of the earth, but he was responsible for providing a precise date for it.

The prevailing notion of the earth's brief existence, together with fixity of species, provided a formidable obstacle to the development of evolutionary theory because evolution requires time. Thus, in addition to overcoming the notion of fixity of species, scientists needed a theory of immense geological time in order to formulate evolutionary principles. In fact, until these prior concepts of fixity and time were fundamentally altered, it would have been unlikely that the idea of natural selection could even have been conceived.

The Scientific Revolution

What, then, upset the medieval belief in a rigid universe of planets, stars, plants, and animals? How did the scientific method as we know it today develop and, with the help of Newton and Galileo in the seventeenth century, demonstrate a moving, not static, universe?

The discovery of the New World and circumnavigation of the globe in the fifteenth century overturned some very fundamental ideas about the planet. For one thing, the earth could no longer be perceived as flat. Also, as Europeans began to explore the New World, their awareness of biological diversity was greatly expanded through exposure to plants and animals previously unknown to them.

There were other attacks on the complacency of traditional beliefs. In 1514, a Polish mathematician named Copernicus challenged Aristotle's long-believed assertion that the earth, circled by the sun, moon, and stars, was the center of the universe. Copernicus removed the earth as the center of all things by proposing a *heliocentric* (sun-centered) solar system.

Copernicus' theory did not attract widespread attention at the time, but in the early 1600s, it was restated and further substantiated by an Italian mathematics

Fixity of species
The notion that species, once created, can never change; an idea diametrically opposed to theories of biological evolution.

23

professor, Galileo Galilei. Galileo came into direct confrontation with the Catholic Church over his publications, to the extent that he spent the last nine years of his life under house arrest. Even so, in intellectual circles, the universe had changed from one of fixity to one of motion, although most scholars still believed that change was impossible for living forms.

Scholars of the sixteenth and seventeenth centuries developed methods and theories that revolutionized scientific thought. The seventeenth century, in particular, was a beehive of scientific activity. The works of such individuals as Keppler, Descartes, and Newton established the laws of physics, motion, and gravity. Other achievements included the discovery of the circulation of blood and the development of numerous scientific instruments, including the telescope, barometer, and microscope. These technological advances permitted investigations of natural phenomena and opened up entire worlds for discoveries such as had never before been imagined.

Scientific achievement increasingly came to direct as well as reflect the changing views of Europeans. Investigations of stars, planets, animals, and plants came to be conducted without significant reference to the supernatural. In other words, nature was seen as a mechanism, functioning according to certain universal physical laws, and it was these laws that scientists were seeking. Yet, most scientists still insisted that a First Cause initiated the entire system. The argument from design was still defended, and support for it continued well into the nineteenth century and, indeed, strongly persists even today.

The Path to Natural Selection

 The species concept and the Linnaean system of classification are found in Virtual Lab 1, section II.

Before early naturalists could begin to understand the forms of organic life, it was necessary to list and describe those forms. As attempts in this direction were made, scholars became increasingly impressed with the amount of biological diversity that confronted them.

John Ray   By the sixteenth century, a keen interest in nature's variation had developed, and by the mid-1500s, there were a few descriptive works on plants, birds, fish, and mammals. But it was not until the seventeenth century that the concept of species was clearly defined by Englishman John Ray (1627–1705), an ordained minister trained at Cambridge University.

Ray was the first to recognize that groups of plants and animals could be distinguished from other groups by their ability to reproduce with one another and produce offspring. Such groups of reproductively isolated organisms were placed into a single category he called *species* (*pl.,* species). Thus, by the late 1600s, the biological criterion of reproduction was used to define species much as it is today (Young, 1992), and upon its publication, the concept was enthusiastically received by the scientific community.

Ray also recognized that species frequently shared similarities with other species, and these he grouped together in a second level of classification he called the *genus* (*pl.,* genera). Ray was the first to use the labels *genus* and *species* in this manner, and they are the terms still in use today. But Ray was very much an adherent of fixity of species. His 1691 publication, *The Wisdom of God Manifested in the Works of Creation*, was intended to demonstrate God's plan in nature, and in this work Ray stressed that nature was a deliberate outcome of a Grand Design.

Carolus Linnaeus   One of the leading naturalists of the eighteenth century was Carolus Linnaeus (1707–1778), of Sweden (Fig. 2–1). He is best known for developing a classification of plants and animals, the *Systema Naturae* (Systems of Nature), first published in 1735.

Courtesy, Dept. of Library Services, American Museum of Natural History

FIGURE 2–1
Linnaeus developed a classification system for plants and animals.

Linnaeus standardized Ray's more sporadic use of two names (genus and species) for organisms, thus firmly establishing the use of **binomial nomenclature**. Moreover, he added two more categories: class and order. Linnaeus' four-level system of classification became the basis for **taxonomy**, the system of classification still used today.

Another of Linnaeus' innovations was to include humans in his classification of animals, placing them in the genus *Homo* and species *sapiens*. The inclusion of humans in this scheme was controversial because it defied contemporary thought that humans, made in God's image, should be considered separately and outside the animal kingdom.

Linnaeus was also a believer in fixity of species, although in later years, faced with mounting evidence to the contrary, he came to question this long-held assumption. Indeed, fixity of species was being challenged on many fronts, especially in France, where voices were being raised in favor of a universe based on change and, more to the point, in favor of the relationship between similar forms based on descent from a common ancestor.

Comte de Buffon Georges-Louis Leclerc (1707–1788), who was raised to the rank of count under the name Buffon, was Keeper of the King's Gardens in Paris (Fig. 2–2). He believed neither in the perfection of nature nor in the idea that nature had a purpose, as declared by the argument from design, but he did recognize the dynamic relationship between the external environment and living forms. In his *Natural History,* first published in 1749, he repeatedly stressed the importance of change in the universe, and he underlined the changing nature of species.

Buffon believed that when groups of organisms migrated to new areas of the world, each group would subsequently be influenced by local climatic conditions and would gradually change as a result of adaptation to the environment. Buffon's recognition of the external environment as an agent of change in species was an important innovation. However, he rejected the idea that one species could give rise to another.

Erasmus Darwin Erasmus Darwin (1731–1802) is today best known as Charles Darwin's grandfather (Fig. 2–3). However, during his life, this freethinking, high-living physician was well known in literary circles for his poetry and other writings. Chief among the latter was his *Zoonomia,* in which evolutionary concepts were expressed in verse.

More than 50 years before his grandson was to startle the world with his views on natural selection, Erasmus Darwin had expressed similar ideas and had even commented on *human* evolution. From letters and other sources, it is known that Charles Darwin had read and was fond of his grandfather's writings. But the degree to which the grandson's theories were influenced by the grandfather is not known.

Jean-Baptiste Lamarck Neither Buffon nor Erasmus Darwin codified his beliefs into a comprehensive system that attempted to *explain* the evolutionary process. The first European scientist to do so was the French scholar Jean-Baptiste Pierre Antoine de Monet Chevalier de Lamarck (1744–1829). (Thankfully, most references to Lamarck use only his surname.)

Expanding beyond the views of Buffon, Lamarck (Fig. 2–4) attempted to *explain* evolution. He postulated a dynamic interaction between organic forms and the environment, such that organic forms could become altered in the face of changing environmental circumstances. Thus, as the environment changed, an animal's activity patterns would also change, resulting in increased or decreased use of certain body parts. As a result of this use or disuse, body parts became altered.

Binomial nomenclature
(*binomial,* meaning "two names") In taxonomy, the convention established by Carolus Linnaeus whereby genus and species names are used to refer to species. For example, *Homo sapiens* refers to human beings.

Taxonomy
The branch of science concerned with the rules of classifying organisms on the basis of evolutionary relationships.

Courtesy, Dept. of Library Services, American Museum of Natural History

FIGURE 2–2
Buffon recognized the influence of the environment on life forms.

Corbis

FIGURE 2–3
Erasmus Darwin, grandfather of Charles Darwin, believed in species change.

FIGURE 2–4

Lamarck believed that species change was influenced by environmental change. He is best known for his theory of the inheritance of acquired characteristics.

Physical alteration occurred as a function of perceived bodily "needs." If a particular part of the body felt a certain need, "fluids and forces" would be directed toward that point and the structure would be modified to satisfy the need. Because the modification would render the animal better suited to its habitat, the new trait would be passed on to offspring. This theory is known as the *inheritance of acquired characteristics,* or the *use-disuse* theory.

One of the most frequently given examples of Lamarck's theory is the giraffe, who, having stripped all the leaves from the lower branches of a tree (environmental change), strives to reach those leaves on upper branches. As vital forces progress to tissues of the neck, the neck increases slightly in length, thus enabling the giraffe to obtain more food. The longer neck is subsequently transmitted to offspring, with the eventual result that all giraffes have longer necks than did their predecessors (Fig. 2–5a). Thus, according to the theory of acquired characteristics, *a trait acquired by an animal during its lifetime can be passed on to offspring.* Today we know this explanation to be inaccurate, for only those traits coded for by genetic information contained within sex cells (eggs and sperm) can be inherited (see Chapters 3 and 4).

Because Lamarck's explanation of species change was not genetically correct, his theories are frequently derided. Actually, Lamarck deserves much credit. He was the first to stress the importance of interactions between organisms and the environment in the evolutionary process. Moreover, Lamarck was one of the first

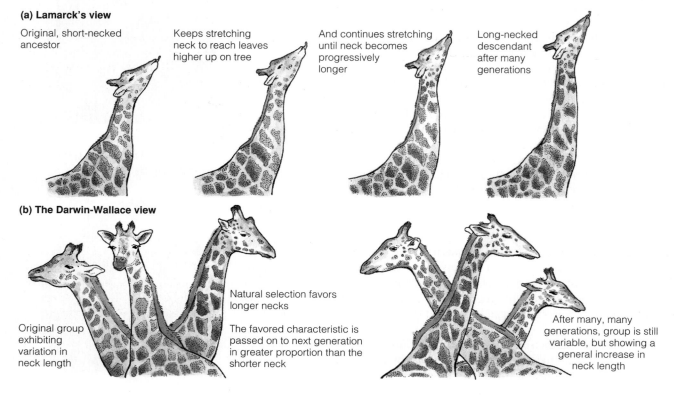

(a) Lamarck's view

Original, short-necked ancestor

Keeps stretching neck to reach leaves higher up on tree

And continues stretching until neck becomes progressively longer

Long-necked descendant after many generations

(b) The Darwin-Wallace view

Original group exhibiting variation in neck length

Natural selection favors longer necks

The favored characteristic is passed on to next generation in greater proportion than the shorter neck

After many, many generations, group is still variable, but showing a general increase in neck length

FIGURE 2–5

Contrasting ideas about the mechanism of evolution. (a) According to Lamarck's theory, acquired characteristics can be passed to subsequent generations. Thus, short-necked giraffes stretched their necks to reach higher into trees for food, and, according to Lamarck, this acquired trait was passed on to offspring, who were born with longer necks. (b) According to the Darwin-Wallace theory of natural selection, among giraffes there is variation in neck length. If having a longer neck provides an advantage for feeding, this trait will be passed on to a greater number of offspring, leading to an increase in the length of giraffe necks over many generations.

to acknowledge the need for a distinct branch of science that dealt solely with living things (i.e., separate from geology). For this new science, Lamarck coined the term *biology,* and a central feature of this new science was the notion of evolutionary change.

Georges Cuvier   The most vehement opponent of Lamarck was a young colleague, Georges Cuvier (1769–1832). Cuvier (Fig. 2–6) specialized in vertebrate paleontology, and it was he who introduced the concept of extinction to explain the disappearance of animals represented by fossils. Although a brilliant anatomist, Cuvier never grasped the dynamic concept of nature, and he adamantly insisted on the fixity of species. Just as the abundance of fossils in geological strata was becoming increasingly apparent, it also became more important to explain what they were. But rather than assume that similarities between certain fossil forms and living species indicated evolutionary relationships, Cuvier proposed a variation of a theory known as **catastrophism.**

Catastrophism held that the earth's geological features were the results of sudden, worldwide cataclysmic events, such as the Noah flood. Cuvier's version of catastrophism also postulated a series of regional disasters that destroyed most or all of the local plant and animal life. These areas of destruction were subsequently restocked with new forms that migrated in from neighboring, unaffected regions.

To be consistent with the fossil evidence, Cuvier also proposed that destroyed regions were repopulated by new organisms of a more modern appearance and that these forms were the results of more recent creation events. (The last of these creations is the one depicted in Genesis.) Thus, Cuvier's explanation of increased complexity over time avoided any notion of evolution while still being able to account for the evidence of change as preserved in the fossil record. (multiple creations)

Charles Lyell   Charles Lyell (1797–1875), the son of Scottish landowners, is considered the founder of modern geology (Fig. 2–7). He was a barrister by training, a geologist by avocation, and for many years Charles Darwin's friend and mentor. Before he met Darwin in 1836, Lyell had earned wide popular acclaim as well as acceptance in Europe's most prestigious scientific circles, thanks to his highly praised *Principles of Geology,* first published in three volumes in 1830–1833.

In this immensely important work, Lyell argued that the geological processes observed in the present are the same as those that occurred in the past. This theory, which has come to be known as **uniformitarianism,** did not originate entirely with Lyell, but had been proposed by James Hutton in the late 1700s. Nevertheless, it was Lyell who demonstrated that such forces as wind, water erosion, local flooding, frost, the decomposition of vegetable matter, volcanoes, earthquakes, and glacial movements all had contributed in the past to produce the geological landscape that exists in the present. Moreover, the fact that these processes could still be observed in operation indicated that geological change continued to occur and that the forces that drove such change were consistent, or *uniform,* over time. In other words, although various aspects of the earth's surface (e.g., climate, flora, fauna, and land surfaces) are variable through time, the *underlying processes* that influence them are constant.

The theory of uniformitarianism flew in the face of Cuvier's catastrophism and did not go unopposed. Additionally, and every bit as controversially, Lyell emphasized the obvious: namely, that for such slow-acting forces to produce momentous change, the earth must indeed be far older than anyone had previously suspected.

By providing an immense time scale and thereby altering perceptions of earth's history from a few thousand to many millions of years, Lyell changed the framework within which scientists viewed the geological past. Thus, the concept of "deep

FIGURE 2–6
Cuvier explained the fossil record as the result of a succession of catastrophes followed by new creation events.

Catastrophism
The view that the earth's geological landscape is the result of violent cataclysmic events. This view was promoted by Cuvier, especially in opposition to Lamarck.

Uniformitarianism
The theory that the earth's features are the result of long-term processes that continue to operate in the present as they did in the past. Elaborated on by Lyell, this theory opposed catastrophism and provided for immense geological time.

FIGURE 2–7
Lyell, the father of geology, stated the theory of uniformitarianism in his *Principles of Geology.*

FIGURE 2–8
Thomas Malthus' *Essay on the Principle of Population* led both Darwin and Wallace to the principle of natural selection.

Transmutation

The change of one species to another. The term *evolution* did not assume its current meaning until the late nineteenth century.

time" (Gould, 1987) remains one of Lyell's most significant contributions to the discovery of evolutionary principles. The immensity of geological time permitted the necessary time depth for the inherently slow process of evolutionary change.

Thomas Malthus　In 1798, Thomas Robert Malthus (1766–1834), an English clergyman and economist, wrote *An Essay on the Principle of Population,* which inspired both Charles Darwin and Alfred Wallace in their separate discoveries of the principle of natural selection (Fig. 2–8). In his essay, Malthus pointed out that if not kept in check by limited food supplies, human populations could double in size every 25 years. That is, population size increases exponentially while food supplies remain relatively stable.

Malthus focused on humans because the ability to increase food supplies artificially reduces constraints on population growth, and he was arguing for population control. However, the same logic could be applied to nonhuman organisms. In nature, the tendency for populations to increase is continuously checked by resource availability. Thus, there is constant competition for food and other resources. In time, the extension of Malthus' principles to all organisms would be made by both Darwin and Wallace.

Charles Darwin　Charles Darwin (1809–1882) was one of six children of Dr. Robert and Susanna Darwin (Fig. 2–9). Being the grandson of wealthy Josiah Wedgwood (of Wedgwood pottery fame) as well as of Erasmus Darwin, he grew up enjoying the lifestyle of the landed gentry in rural England.

As a boy, Darwin displayed a keen interest in nature and spent his days fishing and collecting shells, birds' eggs, and rocks. However, this developing interest in natural history did not dispel the generally held view of family and friends that he was not in any way remarkable. In fact, his performance at school was no more than ordinary.

After the death of his mother when he was eight, Darwin's upbringing was guided by his rather stern father and his older sisters. Because he showed little interest in, or aptitude for, anything except hunting, shooting, and perhaps science, his father, fearing Charles would sink into dissipation, sent him to Edinburgh University to study medicine. It was in Edinburgh that Darwin first became acquainted with the evolutionary theories of Lamarck and others.

During this time (the 1820s), notions of evolution were becoming much feared in England and elsewhere. Certainly, anything identifiable with postrevolutionary France was viewed with grave suspicion by the established order in England. Lamarck, especially, was vilified by most English academicians, the majority of whom were also members of the Anglican clergy.

This was also a time of growing political unrest in Britain. The Reform Movement, which sought to undo many of the wrongs of the class system, was under way, and as with most social movements, this one contained a radical faction. Because many of the radicals were atheists and socialists who also supported Lamarck's evolutionary theory, evolution came to be associated, in the minds of many, with atheism and political subversion. Such was the growing fear of evolutionary ideas that many believed that if it were generally accepted that nature evolved unaided by God, "the Church would crash, the moral fabric of society would be torn apart, and civilized man would return to savagery" (Desmond and Moore, 1991, p. 34). It is unfortunate that some of the most outspoken early proponents of **transmutation** were so vehemently anti-Christian, because their rhetoric helped establish the entrenched suspicion and misunderstanding of evolutionary theory that persists even today.

While at Edinburgh, the young Darwin spent endless hours studying with professors who were outspoken supporters of Lamarck. Darwin's second year in Edinburgh saw him examining museum collections and attending natural history lectures. Therefore, although he hated medicine and left Edinburgh after two years, his experience there was a formative period in his intellectual development.

Subsequently, Darwin took up residence at Christ's College, Cambridge, to study theology. (Although he was rather indifferent to religion, theology was often seen as a last resort by parents who viewed their sons as having no discernible academic leanings.) It was during his Cambridge years that Darwin seriously cultivated his interests in natural science, and he often joined the field excursions of botany classes. He also was immersed in geology and was a frequent and serious participant in geological expeditions.

It was no wonder that following his graduation in 1831 at age 22, he was recommended to accompany a scientific expedition that would circle the globe. Thus it was, after overcoming his father's objections, that Darwin set sail aboard the HMS *Beagle* on December 17, 1831 (Fig. 2–10). The famous voyage of the *Beagle* was to last for almost five years and would forever change not only the course of Darwin's life, but also the history of biological science.

Darwin went aboard the *Beagle* believing in fixity of species. But during the voyage, he privately began to have doubts. As early as 1832, for example, he noted in his diary that a snake with rudimentary hind limbs marked "the passage by which Nature joins the lizards to the snakes." He came across fossils of ancient giant animals that looked, except for size, very much like living forms in the same vicinity, and he wondered whether the fossils were the ancestors of those living forms.

Courtesy, Dept. of Library Services, American Museum of Natural History

FIGURE 2–9
Charles Darwin as a young man.

FIGURE 2–10
The route of the HMS *Beagle*.

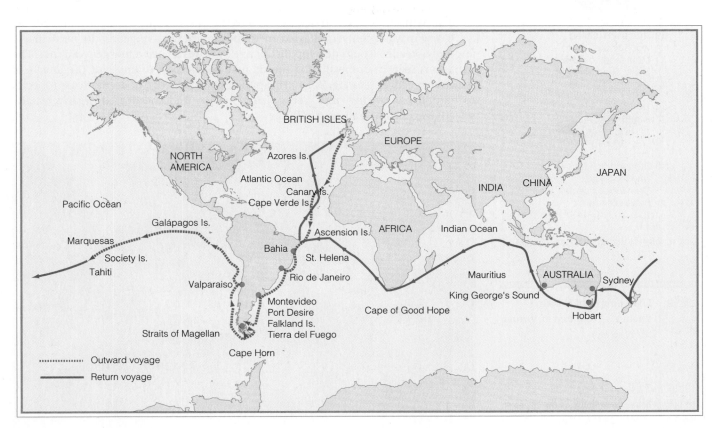

The Development of Evolutionary Theory

(a) Ground finch
Main food: seeds
Beak: heavy

(b) Tree finch
Main food: leaves, buds,
blossoms, fruits
Beak: thick, short

(c) Tree finch (called
woodpecker finch)
Main food: insects
Beak: stout, straight

(d) Ground finch (known as
warbler finch)
Main food: insects
Beak: slender

FIGURE 2–11
Beak variation in Darwin's Galápagos finches.

The example of Darwin's finches is presented in Virtual Lab 2, section I.

FIGURE 2–12
The Darwin home, Down House, in the village of Down, as seen from the rear garden. *On the Origin of Species* was written here.

During the famous stopover at the Galápagos Islands (see Fig. 2–10), Darwin noted that the flora and fauna of South America showed striking similarities to those of the Galápagos, as well as intriguing differences. Even more surprising, the inhabitants of the various islands differed slightly from one another.

For example, Darwin collected 13 different varieties of Galápagos finches. These varieties shared many structural similarities, and clearly they represented a closely affiliated group. But at the same time, they differed with regard to certain physical traits, particularly in the shape and size of their beaks (Fig. 2–11). Darwin also collected finches from the South American mainland, and these appeared to represent only one group, or species.

The insight that Darwin gained from the finches is legendary. He recognized that the various Galápagos finches had all descended from a common, mainland ancestor and had become modified in response to the varying island habitats and to altered dietary preferences. But actually, it was not until *after* he had returned to England that Darwin recognized the significance of the variation in beak structure. In fact, during the voyage, Darwin had paid little attention to the finches. It was only in retrospect that he considered the factors that could lead to the modification of 1 species into 13 (Gould, 1985; Desmond and Moore, 1991).

Darwin returned to England in October 1836 and almost immediately was accepted into the most eminent of scientific circles. He married his cousin Emma Wedgwood and moved to the village of Down, near London, where he spent the rest of his life writing on topics ranging from fossils to orchids (Fig. 2–12). But his overriding concern was the question of species change.

At Down, Darwin began developing his views on what he termed *natural selection*. This concept was borrowed from animal breeders, who "select" as breeding stock those animals that exhibit specific traits they hope to emphasize in offspring. Animals with undesirable traits are "selected against," or prevented from breeding.

Darwin was keenly interested in domestic animals—pigeons, in particular—and how breeders could develop distinctive varieties in just a few generations. (The variations seen in domestic dog breeds may be the best example of the effects of selective breeding. See Fig. 2–13.) He applied his knowledge of domesticated species to naturally occurring ones, recognizing that in undomesticated organisms, the selective agent was nature, not humans.

By the late 1830s, Darwin recognized that biological variation within a species was critically important. Furthermore, he acknowledged the importance of sexual reproduction in increasing variation. Then, in 1838, Darwin read Malthus' essay, and in it he found the answer to his question of how new species came to be. He accepted from Malthus that populations increase at a faster rate than do resources, and he inferred that in nonhuman animals, increase in population size is continuously checked by limited food supplies. He also accepted Lyell's observation that in nature there is a constant "struggle for existence." The idea that in each generation more offspring are born than survive to adulthood coupled with the notions of competition for resources and biological diversity were all Darwin needed to develop his theory of natural selection. He wrote: "It at once struck me that under these circumstances favourable variations would tend to be preserved, and unfavourable ones to be destroyed. The result of this would be the formation of a new species" (F. Darwin, 1950, pp. 53–54). Basically, this quotation summarizes the whole of natural selection theory.

Darwin wrote a short summary of his views on natural selection in 1842 and revised it in 1844. The 1844 sketch is similar to the argument he presented 15 years later in *On the Origin of Species,* but in 1844 he did not feel he had sufficient data to support his views, so he continued his research without publishing.

Darwin had another reason for not publishing what he knew would be, to say the least, a highly controversial work. As a member of the established order, he knew that many of his friends and associates were concerned with threats to the status quo, and evolutionary theory was viewed as a serious threat indeed. In addition, Darwin was a man to whom reputation was of paramount importance, and he was tormented by fears of bringing dishonor and public criticism to those he loved. Thus, he hesitated.

FIGURE 2–13
All domestic dog breeds share a common ancestor, the wolf. The extreme variation that dog breeds exhibit today has been achieved in a relatively short period of time through artificial selection. In this situation, humans allow only certain dogs to breed because they possess specific characteristics that humans want to emphasize. (We should note that not all traits deemed desirable by human breeders are advantageous to the dogs themselves.)

The Development of Evolutionary Theory

FIGURE 2–14
Alfred Russel Wallace independently uncovered the key to the evolutionary process.

Courtesy, Dept. of Library Services, American Museum of Natural History

Alfred Russel Wallace Unlike Darwin, Alfred Russel Wallace (1823–1913) was born into a family of modest means (Fig. 2–14). He went to work at the age of 14, and without any special talent and little formal education, he moved from one job to the next. He became interested in collecting plants and animals, and in 1848 he joined an expedition to the Amazon, where he acquired firsthand knowledge of natural phenomena. Then, in 1854, he sailed for Southeast Asia and the Malay Peninsula to continue his study and to collect bird and insect specimens.

In 1855, Wallace published a paper suggesting that species were descended from other species and that the appearance of new species was influenced by environmental factors (Trinkaus and Shipman, 1992). The Wallace paper spurred Lyell and others to urge Darwin to publish, but still he hesitated. Wallace and Darwin even corresponded briefly.

Then, in 1858, Wallace sent Darwin another paper titled "On the Tendency of Varieties to Depart Indefinitely from the Original Type." In this paper, Wallace described evolution as a process driven by competition and natural selection. Upon receipt of Wallace's paper, Darwin despaired. He feared that Wallace might be credited for a theory (natural selection) that he himself had formulated. He quickly wrote a paper presenting his ideas, and both the paper by Darwin and the one by Wallace were read before the Linnean Society of London in 1858. Neither author was present. Wallace was not in the country, and Darwin was mourning the very recent death of his young son.

The papers received little notice at the time, but at the urging of Lyell and others, Darwin completed and published his greatest work, *On the Origin of Species,** in December 1859. Upon publication, the storm broke, and it has not abated even to this day. While there was much praise for the book, the gist of opinion was negative. Scientific opinion gradually came to Darwin's support, assisted by Darwin's able friend, Thomas Huxley, who for years wrote and spoke in favor of natural selection. The riddle of species was now explained: Species were mutable, not fixed; and they evolved from other species through the mechanism of natural selection.

Natural Selection

Early in his research, Darwin had realized that selection was the key to evolution. With the help of Malthus' ideas, he saw *how* selection in nature could be explained. In the struggle for existence, those *individuals* with favorable variations would survive and reproduce; those with unfavorable variations would not.

For Darwin, the explanation of evolution was simple. The basic processes, as he understood them, are as follows:

1. All species are capable of producing offspring at a faster rate than food supplies increase.
2. There is biological variation within all species; except for identical twins, no two individuals are exactly alike.
3. Because in each generation more individuals are produced than can survive, owing to limited resources, there is competition between individuals. (*Note:* This statement does not imply that there is constant fierce fighting.)
4. Those individuals who possess favorable variations or traits (e.g., speed, disease resistance, protective coloration) have an advantage over individuals that do not possess them. By virtue of the favorable trait, these individuals are more likely to survive to produce offspring than are others.

---

*The full title is *On the Origin of Species by Means of Natural Selection, or the Preservation of Favoured Races in the Struggle for Life.*

5. The environmental context determines whether or not a trait is beneficial. That is, what is favorable in one setting may be a liability in another. In this way, which traits become most advantageous is the result of a natural process.

6. Traits are inherited and are passed on to the next generation. Because individuals who possess favorable traits contribute more offspring to the next generation than do others, over time, such traits become more common in the population; less favorable traits are not passed on as frequently and become less common. Those individuals who produce more offspring, compared to others, are said to have greater **reproductive success.**

7. Over long periods of geological time, successful variations accumulate in a population, so that later generations may be distinct from ancestral ones. Thus, in time, a new species may appear.

8. Geographical isolation may also lead to the formation of new species. As populations of a species become geographically isolated from one another, for whatever reasons, they begin to adapt to different environments. Over time, as populations continue to respond to different **selective pressures** (i.e., different ecological circumstances), they may become distinct species, descended from a common ancestor. The 13 species of Galápagos finches, presumably all descended from a common ancestor on the South American mainland, provide an example of the role of geographical isolation.

Before Darwin, scientists thought of species as entities that could not change. Because individuals within the species did not appear to be significant, they were not the object of study; therefore, it was difficult for many scientists to imagine how change could occur. Darwin, as we have pointed out, saw that variation among individuals could explain how selection occurred. Favorable variations were selected for survival by nature; unfavorable ones were eliminated.

This emphasis on the uniqueness of the individual led Darwin to natural selection as the mechanism that made evolution work. *Natural selection operates on individuals,* favorably or unfavorably, but *it is the population that evolves*. The unit of natural selection is the individual; the unit of evolution is the population.

Natural Selection in Action

A well-documented case of natural selection acting in modern populations concerns changes in pigmentation among peppered moths near Manchester, England (Fig. 2–15). Before the nineteenth century, the common variety of moth was a mottled gray color. This light, mottled coloration provided extremely effective camouflage against lichen-covered tree trunks. Also present, though less common, was a dark variety of the same species. While resting on light, lichen-covered trees, the

Reproductive success
The number of offspring an individual produces and rears to reproductive age; an individual's genetic contribution to the next generation, as compared to the contributions of other individuals.

Selective pressures
Forces in the environment that influence reproductive success in individuals. In the example of the peppered moth, birds applied the selective pressure.

FIGURE 2–15
Variation in the peppered moth. (a) The dark form is more visible on the light, lichen-covered tree. (b) On trees darkened by pollution, the lighter form is more visible.

33

dark, uncamouflaged moths were more visible to birds and were therefore eaten more often. (In this example, birds are the *selective agent,* and they apply *selective pressures* on moth populations.) Thus, in the end, the dark moths produced fewer offspring than the light, camouflaged moths. Yet, by the end of the nineteenth century, the common gray form had been almost completely replaced by the black variety.

What had brought about this rapid change? The answer lies in the rapidly changing environment of industrialized nineteenth-century England. Coal dust in the area settled on trees, killing the lichen and turning the bark a dark gray. Moths continued to rest on trees, but the gray (light) variety was increasingly conspicuous as the trees became darker. Consequently, they began to be preyed on more frequently by birds and contributed fewer genes to the next generation. In the late twentieth century, increasing control of pollutants allowed trees to return to their lighter, lichen-covered, preindustrial condition. As would be expected, the black variety of moth is now being supplanted by the gray.

The substance that produces coloration is a pigment called *melanin,* and the evolutionary shift in the peppered moth, as well as in many other moth species, is termed *industrial melanism*. Such an evolutionary shift in response to environmental change is called *adaptation*.

Although industrial melanism in peppered moths is still the most frequently cited example of natural selection, it is by no means the only one. Nineteenth-century naturalists described numerous examples of anatomical variations between populations of the same species, and they fully appreciated the fact that such populations occupied different localities and were isolated from one another. In fact, as early as 1833, C. L. Gloger published a book entitled *The Variation of Birds Under the Influence of Climate,* in which he pointed out that members of species living in humid climates tend to have darker plumage than those living in drier climates, a statement termed "Gloger's rule" (Young, 1992). Naturalists recognized that Golger's rule pertained to camouflage provided by darker plumage in regions with denser vegetation. But, they interpreted the relationship between the environment and protective coloration in Lamarckian terms. Today we know that such color variation is due to natural selection acting on variation that was already present, as in the moth example.

An example of Gloger's rule is provided by the house sparrow, also called the English sparrow because it was deliberately introduced into the New World from England in the 1850s when several of the birds were released in New York City. These birds rapidly spread across the United States, reaching California in only 20 years. Today they are found throughout the United States and in much of Canada and South America, and those that live in cooler, rainy areas, such as Vancouver, British Columbia, are typically dark, while those found in hotter, drier areas are lighter, sandy colored (Udvardy, 1977).

Another example of natural selection is provided by the medium ground finch of the Galápagos Islands. In 1977, drought conditions eliminated many of the plants that produced smaller, softer seeds, compelling a study population on the island of Daphne Major to feed on larger, harder seeds. The population already exhibited some variation in beak size, and during the drought, mortality rates were higher in birds with smaller beaks because they were less able to efficiently process the larger seeds. Consequently, although population size was dramatically reduced, average beak thickness in the survivors and their offspring was seen to increase, simply because thicker-beaked individuals were contributing more offspring to the next generation (i.e., they had greater reproductive success). But during the rains of the 1982–1983 El Niño event, smaller seeds became more plentiful and the pattern in beak size reversed itself, thus providing a beautiful illustration of how reproductive success is related to environmental conditions (Grant, 1975, 1986; Ridley, 1993).

The best illustration of natural selection, however, and certainly the one with potentially grave consequences for humans, in the increase in resistant strains of disease-causing microorganisms. When antibiotic therapy was introduced in the 1940s, it was hailed as the end of bacterial disease, but this notion did not take into account the fact that bacteria, like other organisms, possess genetic variability. Consequently, while exposure to an antibiotic will kill most bacteria in an infected individual, those pathogens with an inherited resistance to that particular therapy will survive and pass on their resistance to the next generation. Moreover, because bacteria produce new generations every few hours, antibiotic-resistant strains are continuously being produced. As a result, many types of infection no longer respond to treatment. For example, tuberculosis was once thought to be well controlled, but it has seen a resurgence in recent years because the bacterium that causes it no longer responds to antibiotic therapy. Similarly, the organism that is transmitted by mosquitoes and causes malaria has become resistant to the traditional preventive medication, chloraquin. And if that were not enough, many populations of mosquitoes have become resistant to the insecticide DDT, which is still used in many parts of the world to control the spread of malaria.

These examples provide numerous insights into the mechanisms of evolutionary change produced by natural selection:

1. *A trait must be inherited to have importance in natural selection.* A characteristic that is not hereditary (such as a temporary change in hair pigmentation brought about by dye) will not be passed on to succeeding generations. In moths, pigmentation is a demonstrated hereditary trait.

2. *Natural selection cannot occur without variation in inherited characteristics.* If, for example, all the peppered moths had initially been gray (you will recall that some dark forms were always present) and the trees had become darker, the survival and reproduction of all moths could have been so low that the population might have become extinct. Such an event is not unusual and without variation would nearly always occur. *Selection can work only with variation that already exists.*

3. **Fitness** *is a relative measure that will change as the environment changes.* Fitness is simply differential reproductive success. In the initial stage, the lighter moth was the more fit variety because they produced more offspring. But as the environment changed, the dark gray moths became more fit, and a further change reversed the adaptive pattern. It should be obvious that statements regarding the "most fit" life form mean nothing without reference to specific environments.

Fitness
Pertaining to natural selection, a measure of *relative* reproductive success of individuals. Fitness can be measured by an individual's genetic contribution to the next generation compared to that of other individuals.

The examples discussed so far show how different death rates influence natural selection (e.g., moths that die early tend to leave fewer offspring). But mortality is not the entire picture. Another important aspect of natural selection is fertility, for an animal that gives birth to more young would pass its genes on at a faster rate than one that bears fewer offspring. However, fertility is not the entire picture either, for the crucial element is the number of young raised successfully to the point at which they themselves reproduce. We may state this simply as *differential net reproductive success*. The way this mechanism works can be demonstrated through another example.

In a common variety of small birds called swifts, data show that giving birth to more offspring does not necessarily guarantee that more young will be successfully raised. The number of eggs hatched in a breeding season is a measure of fertility. The number of birds that mature and are eventually able to leave the nest is a measure of net reproductive success, or offspring successfully raised. The following tabulation shows the correlation between the number of eggs hatched (fertility) and the number of young that leave the nest (reproductive success) averaged over four breeding seasons (Lack, 1966):

Number of eggs hatched (fertility)	2 eggs	3 eggs	4 eggs
Average number of young raised (reproductive success)	1.92	2.54	1.76
Sample size (number of nests)	72	20	16

As the tabulation shows, the most efficient fertility number is three eggs, since that number yields the highest reproductive success. Raising two is less beneficial to the parents, since the end result is not as successful as with three eggs. Trying to raise more than three young is actually detrimental, since the parents may not be able to provide adequate nourishment for any of the offspring. An offspring that dies before reaching reproductive age is, in evolutionary terms, equivalent to never having been born in the first place. Actually, such a result may be an evolutionary minus to the parents, for this offspring will drain their resources and may inhibit their ability to raise other offspring, thereby lowering their reproductive success even further. Selection will favor those genetic traits that yield the maximum net reproductive success. If the number of eggs laid* is a genetic trait in birds (and it seems to be), natural selection in swifts should act to favor the laying of three eggs as opposed to two or four.

Constraints on Nineteenth-Century Evolutionary Theory

Darwin argued eloquently for the notion of evolution in general and the role of natural selection in particular, but he did not entirely comprehend the exact mechanisms of evolutionary change.

As we have seen, natural selection acts on *variation* within species. Neither Darwin nor anyone else in the nineteenth century understood the source of all this variation. Consequently, Darwin speculated about variation arising from "use"—an idea similar to Lamarck's. Darwin, however, was not as dogmatic in his views as Lamarck and most emphatically argued against inner "needs" or "effort." Darwin had to confess that when it came to explaining variation, he simply did not know: "Our ignorance of the laws of variation is profound. Not in one case out of a hundred can we pretend to assign any reason why this or that part differs, more or less, from the same part in the parents" (Darwin, 1859, pp. 167–168).

In addition to his inability to explain the origins of variation, Darwin also did not completely understand the mechanism by which parents transmitted traits to offspring. Almost without exception, nineteenth-century scholars were confused about the laws of heredity, and the popular consensus was that inheritance was *blending* by nature. In other words, offspring were expected to express intermediate traits as a result of a blending of their parents' contributions. Given this view, we can see why the actual nature of genes was unimaginable. Without any viable alternatives, Darwin accepted this popular misconception. As it turned out, a contemporary of Darwin's had systematically worked out the rules of heredity. However, the work of this Augustinian monk, Gregor Mendel (whom you will meet in Chapter 4), was not recognized until the beginning of the twentieth century.

---

*The number of eggs hatched is directly related to the number of eggs laid.

Opposition to Evolution

The publication of *On the Origin of Species* fanned the flames of controversy over evolution into an inferno, but the question had already been debated in intellectual circles for some years, with most people vehemently opposed to evolutionary theory. The very idea that species could give rise to other species was particularly offensive to many Christians because it appeared to be in direct conflict to the special creation event depicted in Genesis. People were horrified at the notion that humans might be biologically related to other animals and especially that they might share a common ancestor with the great apes. Even to make such a claim was degrading, for it denied humanity its unique and exalted place in the universe; in the minds of many, it denied the very existence of God.

The debate has not ended even now, almost 150 years later. For the majority of scientists today, evolution is fact. Indeed, the genetic evidence for it is indisputable, and anyone who appreciates and understands genetic mechanisms cannot avoid the conclusion that populations and species evolve. Moreover, the majority of Christians do not believe that biblical depictions are to be taken literally. But at the same time, surveys show that almost half of all Americans believe that evolution does not occur. There are a number of reasons for this.

The mechanisms of evolution are complex and do not lend themselves to simple explanations. To understand these mechanisms requires some familiarity with genetics and biology, a familiarity that most people do not possess. Moreover, people who have not been exposed to scientific training want definitive answers to complicated questions. But as you learned in Chapter 1, science does not prove truths, and it frequently does not provide definitive answers.

Another fact to consider is that while all religions offer explanations for natural phenomena, and some even feature the transformation of individuals from one form to another, none really proposes biological change over time. Most people, regardless of their culture, are raised in belief systems that do not emphasize biological continuity between species or offer scientific explanations for natural phenomena.

The relationship between science and religion has never been easy. While both serve, in their own ways, to explain phenomena, scientific explanations are based in data analysis and interpretation. Religion, meanwhile, is a system of beliefs not amenable to scientific testing and falsification; it is based in faith. Religion and science concern different aspects of the human experience, and although they use different approaches in areas where they overlap, they are not inherently mutually exclusive. In fact, many people see them as two sides of the same coin. Moreover, evolutionary theories are not considered anathema by all religions (or even by all forms of Christianity). Some years ago, the Vatican hosted an international conference on human evolution, and in 1996, Pope John Paul II issued a statement to the Pontifical Academy of Sciences acknowledging that "fresh knowledge leads to recognition of the theory of evolution as more than just a hypothesis." Today, the official position of the Catholic Church is that evolutionary processes do occur but that the human soul is of divine creation and not subject to evolutionary processes. Likewise, mainstream Protestants do not generally see a conflict. Unfortunately, those who believe in a literal interpretation of the Bible (termed fundamentalists) do not accept any form of compromise.

Reacting to rapid cultural changes after World War I, conservative Christians in the United States sought a revival of what they considered traditional values. In their view, one way to do this was to prevent any mention of Darwinism in public schools. The Butler Act, passed in Tennessee in 1925, was one result of this effort, and it banned the teaching of evolution in public schools in that state. To test the validity of the law, the American Civil Liberties Union persuaded John Scopes, a high school teacher, to be arrested and ultimately tried for teaching evolution.

The subsequent trial was the famous Scopes Monkey Trial, in which the well-known orator William Jennings Bryan was the prosecuting attorney. The lawyer for the defense was Clarence Darrow, a nationally known labor and criminal lawyer. The trial ended with the conviction of Scopes, who was fined $100. The case was appealed to the Tennessee Supreme Court, which upheld the law, and the teaching of evolution remained illegal in Tennessee. Eventually, several other states, mostly in the South, passed similar laws, and it was not until 1967 that the last two states (Tennessee and Arkansas) ceased to prohibit the teaching of evolution.

But the story does not end there. In the more than 75 years since the Scopes trial, religious fundamentalists have persisted in their attempts to remove evolution from public school curricula. Known as creationists because they explain the existence of the universe as a result of a sudden creation, they are determined either to eliminate the teaching of evolution or to introduce antievolutionary material into public school classes. In the past 20 years, creationists have insisted that "creation science" is just as valid a scientific endeavor as is the study of evolution. They argue that in the interest of fairness, a balanced view should be offered: If evolution is taught as science, then creationism should also be taught as science. But "creation science" is, by definition, not science at all. Creationists assert that their view is absolute and infallible. Consequently, creationism is not a hypothesis that can be tested, nor is it amenable to falsification. Because such testing is the basis of all science, creationism, by its very nature, cannot be considered science. It is religion.

Still, creationists have been active in state legislatures, promoting the passage of laws mandating the inclusion of creationism in school curricula. To this effect, the Arkansas state legislature passed Act 590 in 1981. But this law was challenged and overturned in 1982. Judge William Ray Overton, in his ruling against the state, found that "a theory that is by its own terms dogmatic, absolutist and never subject to revision is not a scientific theory." And he added: "Since creation is not science, the conclusion is inescapable that the only real effect of Act 590 is the advancement of religion." In 1987, the United States Supreme Court struck down a similar law in Louisiana.

So far, these and related laws have been overturned because they violate the principle of separation of church and state provided in the First Amendment to the Constitution. But this has not stopped the creationists, who have encouraged teachers to claim "academic freedom" to teach creationism. Also, they have dropped the term *creationism* in favor of less religious sounding terms, such as *intelligent design theory*. And as recently as August 1999, the Kansas state legislature adopted a policy that, had it not been overturned, could have eliminated evolution from standardized public school curricula. Moreover, antievolution feeling remains strong among politicians. In 1999, one very prominent U.S. congressman went so far as to say that the teaching of evolution is one of the factors behind violence in America today!

Although the courts have consistently ruled against the creationists, these religious fundamentalists have nevertheless had an impact on the teaching of evolution. Many public school teachers, seeking to avoid controversy, simply do not cover evolution, or they refer to it as "just a theory" (see p. 22). Thus, students may not be exposed to theories of evolution until they go to college—and only then if they take related courses. This consequence is ultimately to the detriment of the biological sciences (and education in general) in the United States.

SUMMARY

Our current understanding of evolutionary processes is directly traceable to developments in intellectual thought in western Europe over the last 300 years. In particular, the contributions of Linnaeus, Lamarck, Buffon, Lyell, and Malthus all had a significant impact on Darwin. The year 1859 marks a watershed in evolutionary theory, for in that year, the publication of Darwin's *On the Origin of Species* crystallized the understanding of the evolutionary process (particularly the crucial role of natural selection) and for the first time thrust evolutionary theory into the consciousness of the general public. Debates both inside and outside the sciences continued for several decades (and in some quarters persist today), but the theory of evolution irrevocably changed the tide of intellectual thought. Gradually, Darwin's formulation of the evolutionary process became accepted almost universally by scientists as the very foundation of all the biological sciences, physical anthropology included. As we begin the twenty-first century, contributions from genetics allow us to demonstrate the mechanics of evolution in a way unknown to Darwin and his contemporaries.

Natural selection is the central determining factor influencing the long-term direction of evolutionary change. How natural selection works can best be explained as differential reproductive success—in other words, how successful individuals are in leaving offspring to succeeding generations.

QUESTIONS FOR REVIEW

1. Trace the history of intellectual thought immediately leading to Darwin's theory.
2. What is fixity of species? Why did it pose a problem for the development of evolutionary thinking?
3. What was John Ray's major contribution to biology and the development of evolutionary theories?
4. In what ways did Linnaeus and Buffon differ in their approach to the concept of evolution?
5. What are the bases of Lamarck's theory of acquired characteristics? Why is this theory incorrect?
6. What was Lamarck's positive contribution to nineteenth-century evolutionary ideas?
7. Explain Cuvier's notion of catastrophism.
8. What did Malthus and Lyell contribute to Darwin's thinking on evolution?
9. Darwin approached the subject of species change by emphasizing individuals within populations. Why was this significant to the development of the concept of natural selection?
10. What evidence did Darwin use to strengthen his argument concerning evolution?
11. How did Darwin's explanation of evolution differ from Lamarck's?
12. What is meant by adaptation? Illustrate through the example of industrial melanism.
13. Define natural selection. What is a selective agent? Give an example.
14. Explain why the changes in coloration in populations of peppered moths and in some bird species serve as a good example of natural selection.
15. Explain why some people are opposed to the teaching of evolutionary principles.

SUGGESTED FURTHER READING

Burke, James. 1985. *The Day the Universe Changed*. Boston: Little, Brown.

Desmond, Adrian, and James Moore. 1991. *Darwin*. New York: Warner Books.

Gould, Stephen Jay. 1987. *Time's Arrow, Time's Cycle*. Cambridge, MA: Harvard University Press.

Grant, P. R. 1991. "Natural Selection in Darwin's finches." *Scientific American* 265(4): 82–87.

Mayr, Ernst. 2000. "Darwin's Influence on Modern Thought." *Scientific American* 283(1): 78–83.

Ridley, Mark. 1993. *Evolution*. Boston: Blackwell Scientific Publications.

Scott, Eugenie C. 1997. "Antievolutionism and Creationism in the United States." *Annual Review of Anthropology* 2: 263–289.

Trinkaus, Eric, and Pat Shipman. 1993. *The Neandertals*. New York: Knopf.

Young, David. 1992. *The Discovery of Evolution*. London: Natural History Museum Publications, Cambridge University Press.

RESOURCES ON THE INTERNET

 Wadsworth Anthropology Resource Center
http://anthropology.wadsworth.com

The companion website for this text includes a range of enrichment material focused on the chapter's topic. While online, you can enhance your understanding of the chapter by exploring one of the several additional Internet exercises, by researching topics, and by accessing full articles on InfoTrac College Edition. You can also reinforce the concepts by taking online practice exams.

Internet Exercises

As you learned in this chapter, Charles Darwin's theory of natural selection was influenced by the writings of numerous other naturalists. You can either use your search engine or go to **www.ucmp.berkeley.edu/history/evolution.html** to read more about these influential people and the development of evolutionary thought. Scroll down to "Preludes to Evolution" and click on the name of someone discussed in this chapter (perhaps Lamarck). What additional facts did you learn? Then choose someone not discussed in the textbook and write one or two paragraphs describing that person's contributions.

 InfoTrac College Edition
http://www.infotrac-college.com/wadsworth

A subject search in InfoTrac College Edition for *natural selection* will yield at least 100 current periodical references. Explore these references, and select and read at least one article (not just the abstract) pertaining to a topic you find especially interesting. How does this article illustrate and elaborate on the basic principles of natural selection as presented in Chapter 2?

CHAPTER

3

The Biological
Basis of Life

CONTENTS

DNA escaping from a bacterium (*Escherichia coli*)

See the following section of the CD-ROM for topics covered in this chapter: Virtual Lab 2, section II.

Introduction

This text is about human evolution and adaptation, both of which are intimately linked to life processes that involve cells, the replication and decoding of genetic information, and the transmission of this information between generations. Thus, to present human evolution and adaptation in the broad sense, we must first examine how life is organized at the cellular and molecular levels, and this, in turn, necessitates a brief discussion of the fundamental principles of genetics.

Genetics is the study of how traits are transmitted from one generation to the next. Because physical anthropologists are concerned with human evolution, adaptation, and variation, they must have a thorough understanding of the factors that lie at the very root of these phenomena. Indeed, although many physical anthropologists do not actually specialize in genetics, it is genetics that ultimately links or influences many of the various subdisciplines of biological anthropology.

The discipline of genetics is largely a twentieth-century development, and much of our present knowledge has been acquired within the last 50 years. Today, insights into the numerous aspects of inheritance are increasing at an exponential rate, with new discoveries being made virtually every day. Moreover, as genetic technologies develop and increasingly come into use, they assume an ever greater role in the lives of us all.

It is therefore more important than ever that, as people living at the beginning of the twenty-first century, we achieve a basic understanding of the factors that influence our lives. Also, from an anthropological perspective, it is only through the further elucidation of genetic principles that we can hope to understand fully the evolutionary mechanisms that have permitted humans to become the species we are today.

The Cell

To discuss genetic and evolutionary principles, we must first have a fundamental understanding of cell function. Cells are the basic units of life in all living organisms. In some forms, such as bacteria, a single cell constitutes the entire organism. However, more complex *multicellular* forms, such as plants, insects, birds, and mammals, are composed of billions of cells. Indeed, an adult human is made up of perhaps as many as 1,000 billion (1,000,000,000,000) cells, all functioning in complex ways that ultimately promote the survival of the individual.

Life on earth can be traced back at least 3.7 billion years, in the form of *prokaryotic* cells. Prokaryotes are single-celled organisms, represented today by bacteria and blue-green algae. Structurally more complex cells appeared approximately 1.2 billion years ago, and these are referred to as *eukaryotic* cells. Because eukaryotic cells are found in all multicellular organisms, they are the focus of the remainder of this discussion. In spite of the numerous differences between various life forms and the cells that constitute them, it is important to understand that the cells of all living organisms share many similarities as a result of their common evolutionary past.

In general, a eukaryotic cell is a three-dimensional entity composed of *carbohydrates, lipids (fats), nucleic acids,* and *proteins.* It contains a variety of structures called *organelles* within the *cell membrane* (Fig. 3–1). One of these organelles is the **nucleus** (*pl.,* nuclei), a discrete unit surrounded by a thin nuclear membrane. Within the nucleus are two nucleic acids that contain the genetic information that controls the cell's functions. These two critically important **molecules** are **deoxyribonucleic acid (DNA)** and **ribonucleic acid (RNA).** (In prokaryotic cells, genetic information is not contained within a walled nucleus.) Surrounding the

Nucleus
A structure (organelle) found in all eukaryotic cells. The nucleus contains chromosomes (nuclear DNA).

Molecules
Structures made up of two or more atoms. Molecules can combine with other molecules to form more complex structures.

Deoxyribonucleic acid (DNA)
The double-stranded molecule that contains the genetic code. DNA is a main component of chromosomes.

Ribonucleic acid (RNA)
A single-stranded molecule, similar in structure to DNA. The three forms of RNA are essential to protein synthesis.

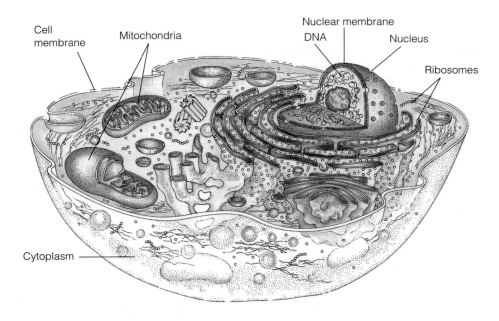

Cell
membrane

Mitochondria

Nuclear membrane
DNA
Nucleus

Ribosomes

Cytoplasm

CHAPTER 3

FIGURE 3–1
Structure of a generalized eukaryotic cell, illustrating the cell's three-dimensional nature. Although various organelles are shown, for the sake of simplicity only those we discuss are labeled.

nucleus is the **cytoplasm**, which contains numerous other types of organelles involved in various activities, such as breaking down nutrients and converting them to other substances (*metabolism*), storing and releasing energy, eliminating waste, and manufacturing **proteins (protein synthesis).**

Two of these organelles—**mitochondria** and **ribosomes**—require further mention. The mitochondria (*sing.,* mitochondrion) are responsible for energy production in the cell and are thus the "engines" that drive the cell. Mitochondria are round or oval structures enclosed within a folded membrane, and they contain their own distinct DNA, called mitochondrial DNA (mtDNA), which directs mitochondrial activities. Mitochondrial DNA has the same molecular structure and function as nuclear DNA, but it is organized somewhat differently. In recent years, mtDNA has attracted much attention because of particular traits it influences and because it has significance for studies of certain evolutionary processes. For these reasons, mitochondrial inheritance will be discussed in more detail in Chapters 4 and 13. Ribosomes are roughly spherical in shape and are the most common type of cytoplasmic organelle. They are made up partly of RNA and are essential to the synthesis of proteins (see p. 46).

There are basically two types of cells: **somatic cells** and **gametes.** Somatic cells are the cellular components of body tissues, such as muscle, bone, skin, nerve, heart, and brain. Gametes, or sex cells, are specifically involved in reproduction and are not important as structural components of the body. There are two types of gametes: *ova* (*sing.,* ovum), or egg cells, produced in the ovaries in females; and *sperm* cells, which develop in male testes. The sole function of a sex cell is to unite with a gamete from another individual to form a **zygote,** which has the potential of developing into a new individual. In this way, gametes transmit genetic information from parent to offspring.

DNA Structure

As already mentioned, cellular functions are directed by DNA. If we are to understand these functions and how characteristics are inherited, we must first know something about the structure and function of DNA.

Cytoplasm
The portion of the cell contained within the cell membrane, excluding the nucleus. The cytoplasm consists of a semifluid material and contains numerous structures involved with cell function.

Proteins
Three-dimensional molecules that serve a wide variety of functions through their ability to bind to other molecules.

Protein synthesis
The assembly of chains of amino acids into functional protein molecules. The process is directed by DNA.

Mitochondria
(*sing.,* mitochondrion) Structures contained within the cytoplasm of eukaryotic cells that convert energy, derived from nutrients, into a form that is used by the cell.

Ribosomes
Structures composed of a specialized form of RNA and protein. Ribosomes are found in the cell's cytoplasm and are essential to the manufacture of proteins.

Somatic cells
Basically, all the cells in the body except those involved with reproduction.

Gametes
Reproductive cells (eggs and sperm in animals) developed from precursor cells in ovaries and testes.

Zygote
A cell formed by the union of an egg and a sperm cell. It contains the full complement of chromosomes (in humans, 46) and has the potential of developing into an entire organism.

The Biological Basis of Life

The exact physical and chemical properties of DNA were unknown until 1953, when at Cambridge University, an American researcher named James Watson and three British scientists, Francis Crick, Maurice Wilkins, and Rosalind Franklin, developed a structural and functional model of DNA (Watson and Crick, 1953a, 1953b). The importance of their achievement cannot be overstated, for it completely revolutionized the fields of biology and medicine and forever altered our understanding of biological and evolutionary mechanisms.

The DNA molecule is composed of two chains of even smaller molecules called **nucleotides.** A nucleotide, in turn, is made up of three components: a sugar molecule (deoxyribose), a phosphate unit, and one of four nitrogenous bases (Fig. 3–2). In DNA, nucleotides are stacked upon one another to form a chain that is bonded along its bases to another **complementary** nucleotide chain. Together the two twist to form a spiral, or helical, shape. The resulting DNA molecule, then, is two-stranded and is described as forming a *double helix* that resembles a twisted ladder. If we follow the twisted ladder analogy, the sugars and phosphates represent the two sides, while the bases and the bonds that join them form the rungs.

The secret of how DNA functions lies within the four bases. These bases are *adenine, guanine, thymine,* and *cytosine,* and they are frequently referred to by their initial letters, A, G, T, and C. In the formation of the double helix, it is possible for one type of base to pair, or bond, with only one other type: Base pairs can form *only* between adenine and thymine and between guanine and cytosine (see Fig. 3–2). This specificity is essential to the DNA molecule's ability to **replicate,** or make an exact copy of itself, and DNA is the only molecule known to have this capacity.

Nucleotides
Basic units of the DNA molecule, composed of a sugar, a phosphate, and one of four DNA bases.

Complementary
Referring to the fact that DNA bases form base pairs in a precise manner. For example, adenine can bond only to thymine. Thus, these two bases are said to be *complementary* because one requires the other to form a complete DNA base pair.

Replicate
To duplicate. The DNA molecule is able to make copies of itself.

FIGURE 3–2
Part of a DNA molecule. The illustration shows the two DNA strands with the sugar and phosphate backbone and the bases extending toward the center.

DNA Replication

Growth and development of organisms and tissue repair following injury or disease are among the crucial processes made possible by cell division. Cells multiply by dividing in such a way that each new cell receives a full complement of genetic material. This is a crucial point, since a cell cannot function properly without the appropriate amount of DNA. For new cells to receive the essential amount of DNA, it is first necessary for the DNA to replicate.

Prior to cell division, specific **enzymes** break the bonds between bases simultaneously at numerous locations in the DNA molecule, leaving the two previously joined strands of nucleotides with their bases exposed (Fig. 3–3). The exposed bases

Enzymes
Specialized proteins that initiate and direct chemical reactions in the body.

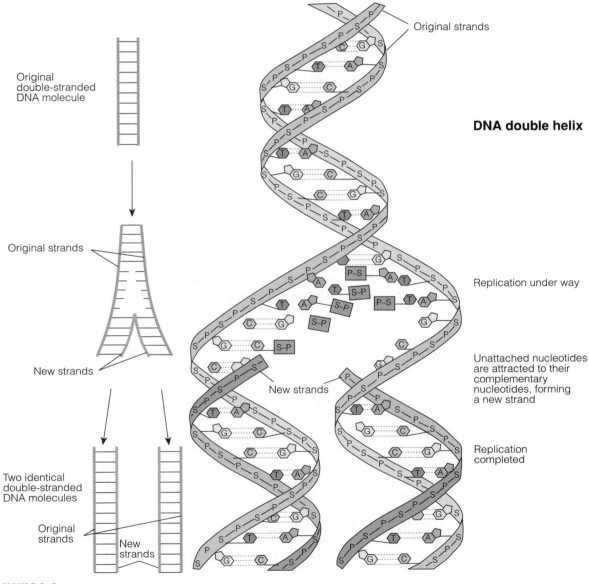

FIGURE 3–3

DNA replication. During DNA replication, the two strands of the DNA molecule are separated, and each strand serves as a template for the formation of a new strand. When replication is complete, there are two DNA molecules. Each molecule consists of one new and one original DNA strand.

then attract unattached DNA nucleotides, which are already present in the cell nucleus. Because one base can be joined to only one other, the attraction between bases occurs in a complementary fashion. Thus, the two previously joined parental nucleotide chains serve as models for the formation of new strands of nucleotides. As each new strand is formed, its bases are joined to the bases of an original strand. When the process is completed, there are two double-stranded DNA molecules exactly like the original one, and each newly formed molecule consists of one original nucleotide chain joined to a newly formed chain (see Fig. 3–3).

Protein Synthesis

One of the most important functions of DNA is that it directs protein synthesis within the cell. Proteins are complex, three-dimensional molecules that function through their ability to bind to other molecules. For example, the protein **hemoglobin**, found in red blood cells, is able to bind to oxygen and serves to transport oxygen to cells throughout the body.

Proteins function in myriad ways. Some are structural components of tissues. Collagen, for example, is the most common protein in the body and is a major component of all connective tissues. Aside from minerals, collagen is the most abundant structural material in bone. Enzymes are also proteins, and their function is to initiate and enhance chemical reactions. An example of a digestive enzyme is *lactase,* which breaks down *lactose,* or milk sugar, into two simpler sugars. Another class of proteins includes many types of **hormones.** Specialized cells produce and release hormones into the bloodstream to circulate to other areas of the body, where they produce specific effects in tissues and organs. A good example of this type of protein is *insulin,* produced by cells in the pancreas. Insulin causes cells in the liver and certain types of muscle tissue to absorb essential energy-producing glucose (sugar) from the blood. (Enzymes and hormones will be discussed in more detail in Chapter 16.)

As you can see, proteins make us what we are. Not only are they the major constituents of all body tissues, but they also direct and perform physiological and cellular functions. It is therefore critical that protein synthesis occur accurately, for if it does not, physiological development and activities can be disrupted or even prevented.

Proteins are composed of chains of smaller molecules called **amino acids.** In all, there are 20 amino acids, 8 of which must be obtained from dietary sources (see Chapter 16). The remaining 12 are produced in cells. These 20 amino acids are combined in different amounts and sequences to produce potentially millions of proteins. What makes proteins different from one another is the number of amino acids involved and the *sequence* in which they are arranged. For a protein to function properly, its amino acids must be arranged in the proper sequence.

DNA serves as a recipe for making a protein, for it is the sequence of DNA bases that ultimately determines the order of amino acids in a protein molecule. In the DNA instructions, a *triplet,* or group of three bases, specifies a particular amino acid. For example, if a triplet consists of the base sequence cytosine, guanine, and adenine (CGA), it specifies the amino acid *alanine.* If the next triplet in the chain consists of the sequence guanine, thymine, and cytosine (GTC), it refers to another amino acid—*glutamine.* Therefore, a DNA recipe might look like this: AGA CGA ACA ACC TAC TTT TTC CTT AAG GTC, and so on (Table 3–1).

Protein synthesis is a little more complicated than the preceding few sentences would imply. For one thing, protein synthesis occurs outside the nucleus at specialized structures in the cytoplasm called *ribosomes* (see p. 43). A logistics problem

---

Virtual Lab 2, section II, presents an example of protein synthesis.

Hemoglobin
A protein molecule that occurs in red blood cells and binds to oxygen molecules.

Hormones
Substances (usually proteins) that are produced by specialized cells and that travel to other parts of the body, where they influence chemical reactions and regulate various cellular functions.

Amino acids
Small molecules that are the components of proteins.

TABLE 3–1   The Genetic Code

Amino Acid Symbol	Amino Acid	mRNA Codon	DNA Triplet
Ala	Alanine	GCU, GCC, GCA, GCG	CGA, CGG, CGT, CGC
Arg	Arginine	CGU, CGC, CGA, CGG, AGA, AGG	GCA, GCG, GCT, GCC, TCT, TCC
Asn	Asparagine	AAU, AAC	TTA, TTG
Asp	Aspartic acid	GAU, GAC	CTA, CTG
Cys	Cysteine	UGU, UGC	ACA, ACG
Gln	Glutamine	CAA, CAG	GTT, GTC
Glu	Glutamic acid	GAA, GAG	CTT, CTC
Gly	Glycine	GGU, GGC, GGA, GGG	CCA, CCG, CCT, CCC
His	Histidine	CAU, CAC	GTA, GTG
Ile	Isoleucine	AUU, AUC, AUA	TAA, TAG, TAT
Leu	Leucine	UUA, UUG, CUU, CUC, CUA, CUG	AAT, AAC, GAA, GAG, GAT, GAC
Lys	Lysine	AAA, AAG	TTT, TTC
Met	Methionine	AUG	TAC
Phe	Phenylalanine	UUU, UUC	AAA, AAG
Pro	Proline	CCU, CCC, CCA, CCG	GGA, GGG, GGT, GGC
Ser	Serine	UCU, UCC, UCA, UCG, AGU, AGC	AGA, AGG, AGT, AGC, TCA, TCG
Thr	Threonine	ACU, ACC, ACA, ACG	TGA, TGG, TGT, TGC
Trp	Tryptophan	UGG	ACC
Tyr	Tyrosine	UAU, UAC	ATA, ATG
Val	Valine	GUU, GUC, GUA, GUG	CAA, CAG, CAT, CAC
Terminating triplets		UAA, UAG, UGA	ATT, ATC, ACT

arises because the DNA molecule is not capable of traveling outside the cell's nucleus. Thus, the first step in protein synthesis is to copy the DNA message into a form that can pass through the nuclear membrane into the cytoplasm. This process is accomplished through the formation of a molecule similar to DNA called ribonucleic acid, or RNA. RNA is different from DNA in three important ways:

1. It is single-stranded.
2. It contains a different type of sugar.
3. It contains the base uracil as a substitute for the DNA base thymine. (Uracil is attracted to adenine, just as thymine is.)

The RNA molecule forms on the DNA template in much the same manner as new DNA molecules are assembled. As in DNA replication, the two DNA strands separate, but only partially, and one of these strands attracts free-floating RNA nucleotides (also produced in the cell), which are joined together on the DNA template. This new RNA nucleotide chain is called **messenger RNA (mRNA)**, and its formation is called *transcription* because, in fact, it is transcribing, or copying, the DNA code (Fig. 3–4). But the resulting mRNA segment is actually a complement, rather than an identical copy, of the DNA strand on which it is formed. If, for example, the DNA triplet reads CTA, then the corresponding mRNA triplet, or **codon**, will be GAU. (Remember that in RNA, the base uracil replaces thymine; see Table 3–1.) The

Messenger RNA (mRNA)
A form of RNA that is assembled on a sequence of DNA bases. It carries the DNA code to the ribosome during protein synthesis.

Codon
A triplet of messenger RNA bases that refers to a specific amino acid during protein synthesis.

The Biological Basis of Life

process continues until a section of DNA called a terminator region (composed of one of three DNA triplets) is reached and transcription stops (see Table 3–1). At this point, the mRNA strand, comprising anywhere from 5,000 to perhaps as many as 200,000 nucleotides, peels away from the DNA model and a portion of it travels through the nuclear membrane to the ribosome. Meanwhile, the bonds between the DNA bases are reestablished, and the DNA molecule is once more intact.

As the mRNA strand arrives at the ribosome, the message it contains is translated. (This stage of the process is called *translation* because at this point, the genetic instructions are actually being decoded and implemented.) Just as each DNA triplet specifies one amino acid, mRNA codons also serve this function. Therefore, the mRNA strand is "read" in codons, or groups of three bases taken together (see Table 3–1).

Another form of RNA, **transfer RNA (tRNA)**, is essential to the actual assembly of a protein. Each molecule of tRNA has the ability to bind to one specific amino acid. A particular tRNA molecule carrying the amino acid matching the mRNA codon being translated arrives at the ribosome and deposits its amino acid (Fig. 3–5). As a second amino acid is deposited, the two are joined in the order dictated by the sequence of mRNA codons. In this way, series of amino acids are linked together to form a structure that will eventually function as a protein.

What Is a Gene?

The entire sequence of DNA bases responsible for the synthesis of a protein or, in some cases, a portion of a protein is referred to as a **gene**. Or, put another way, a gene is a segment of DNA that specifies the sequence of amino acids in a particular protein. Even more precisely, a gene codes for the production of a **polypeptide chain**. Those proteins composed of only a single polypeptide chain are produced through the action of a single gene. However, some proteins (collagen and hemoglobin, for example) are made up of two or more polypeptide chains, each of which results from the action of a different gene. Thus, while some proteins result from the action of only one gene, others are produced by two or more.

A gene may comprise only a few hundred bases, or it may be composed of thousands. If the sequence of DNA bases is altered through **mutation** (a change in the DNA), the manufacture of some proteins may not occur, and the cell (or indeed the organism) may not function properly (if it functions at all).

This definition of a gene is a functional one and is technically correct. But it is important to understand that gene action is an incredibly complex phenomenon that is only partly understood. For example, the DNA segments that are transcribed into mRNA and therefore code for specific amino acids are termed *exons*. But the vast majority of nucleotide sequences in a gene are not expressed during protein synthesis. In fact, some sequences, called *introns,* are initially transcribed but subsequently eliminated (see Box 3–1, p. 50). Thus, introns are not represented in the

FIGURE 3–4
Transcription. The two DNA strands have partly separated. Free messenger RNA (mRNA) nucleotides have been drawn to the template strand, and a strand of mRNA is being made. Note that the mRNA strand will exactly complement the DNA template strand, except that uracil (U) replaces thymine (T).

Transfer RNA (tRNA)
The type of RNA that binds to specific amino acids and transports them to the ribosome during protein synthesis.

Gene
A sequence of DNA bases that specifies the order of amino acids in an entire protein or, in some cases, a portion of a protein. A gene may be made up of hundreds or thousands of DNA bases.

DNA template strand

mRNA

a gene includes both the sequences which are translated (exons), and those which are NOT translated (introns)

FIGURE 3–5
Assembly of an amino acid chain in protein synthesis.

(a)
As the ribosome binds to the mRNA, tRNA brings a particular amino acid, specified by the mRNA codon, to the ribosome.

(b)
The tRNA binds to the first codon while a second tRNA–amino acid complex arrives at the ribosome.

(c)
The ribosome moves down the mRNA, allowing a third amino acid to be brought into position by another tRNA molecule. Note that the first two amino acids are now joined together.

newly formed mRNA segment and they are not translated into amino acid sequences. But while introns are not instrumental in protein synthesis, they are indeed a part of the DNA molecule, and it is the combination of introns and exons, interspersed along a strand of DNA, that comprises the unit we call a gene.

Although we usually think of genes as coding for the production of structural proteins, some genes function primarily to control the expression of other genes. Basically, these *regulatory genes* produce enzymes and other proteins that either switch on or turn off other segments of DNA. Consequently, this mechanism is critical for individual organisms and also has important evolutionary implications.

All somatic cells contain the same genetic information, but in any given cell, only a fraction of the DNA contained within exons is actually involved in protein synthesis. For example, bone cells carry the same DNA that codes for the production of digestive enzymes, as do the cells of the stomach lining. But bone cells do not produce digestive enzymes. Instead, they manufacture collagen, the major organic component of bone. Bone cells produce collagen and not digestive enzymes because of the differentiation of cell lines early in embryonic

Polypeptide chain
A sequence of amino acids that may act alone or in combination with others as a functional protein.

Mutation
A change in DNA. Technically, mutation refers to changes in DNA bases (specifically called point mutations); also refers to changes in chromosome number and/or structure.

BOX 3–1   A CLOSER LOOK

What's All That Junk?

It is a fact that, in all fields of inquiry, important discoveries always raise new questions that eventually lead to further revelations. Probably, there is no statement that could be more aptly applied to the field of genetics. For example, in 1977, it was recognized that during protein synthesis (p. 46) the initially formed mRNA molecule contained many more nucleotides than were represented in the proteins that were subsequently produced. This finding led to the discovery of *introns,* those portions of genes that do not code for, or specify, proteins because they are deleted from the mRNA molecule before amino acids are assembled into proteins (p. 48). Then, in the 1980s researchers learned that only about 1.5 percent of the roughly 3 billion DNA bases in the human genome is contained within *exons* or sequences that actually code for the production of protein. Therefore, while an estimated 28 percent of human DNA is comprised of genes (including introns and exons), only 5 percent of the DNA within the genes is actually composed of coding sequences (Baltimore, 2001). The remaining 23 percent is made up of introns, which in some cases contain thousands of bases. And, we also know that a human gene can specify the production of as many as three different proteins by using different combinations of the exons interspersed within it (Pennisi, 2001).

If introns seem complicated, consider this: there are other forms of noncoding DNA. Almost half of all human DNA consists of noncoding segments, not included in genes, that are *repeated over and over.* In fact, humans have more noncoding DNA than any other species so far studied (Vogel, 2001), and approximately 40 percent of the noncoding sequences fall into a category that is present only in primates. Invertebrates and some vertebrates have only small amounts of noncoding sequences and yet they are fully functional organisms. So, just what do all those noncoding segments do in humans?

The noncoding DNA that makes up about 98 percent of the human genome used to be called "junk DNA" because its functions were not known. But researchers are beginning to investigate some of its possible functions and also its origins. For example, it appears that repeated segments near the ends of chromosomes contain genes that may be involved in many of the activities of the telomeres, crucial structures at the ends of chromosomes that, among other things, influence cellular aging and the regulation of cell cycles (Reithman, et al., 2001). Indeed, the telomeres themselves are all composed of the same sequence of apparently noncoding DNA.

Some noncoding regions may also act as promotor sequences that switch on and off other genes, and others may act as regulators by influencing the activities of other genes. And, theoretically, introns and other noncoding sequences may provide additional genetic material that is advantageous in the course of evolution.

Some researchers speculate that so-called junk DNA has been inherited as obsolete, deactivated material inherited from earlier ancestors. Or perhaps it resulted from the duplication of large segments of the evolving human genome over the course of several million years. Also puzzling is the recent discovery that the human genome contains more than 200 genes shared in common with certain bacteria. The fact that these genes are not shared with more closely related invertebrate species such as worms or flies leads to the supposition that the ancient vertebrate genome took on bacterial genes after splitting away from the invertebrates. Of course it is not known if the transmission of these genes was from bacteria to vertebrates or vice versa. The sequencing of the human genome stands as a remarkable achievement but, as you can see, the myriad questions it has raised will require years to answer. But, when those questions are answered, we will have an understanding of biological and evolutionary processes that was inconceivable even 20 years ago.

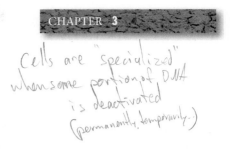

development. During this process, cells undergo changes in form, their functions become specialized, and most of their DNA is permanently deactivated through the action of regulatory genes. In other words, they become specific types of cells. (See Issue, pp. 68–69.)

Cells are "specialized" when some portion of DNA is deactivated (permanently, temporarily...)

Gene regulation also means that some genes are expressed only at certain times during the life cycle. An example of this type of control is the production of hemoglobin in human development. As mentioned, hemoglobin is the protein molecule contained in red blood cells that is responsible for transporting oxygen molecules to body cells and tissues. But humans produce three different varieties of hemoglobin at different developmental stages, depending on the availability of oxygen. Consequently, the hemoglobin produced in an early embryo differs from that in a 6-month fetus, which is again different from the hemoglobin of a 6-month-old infant. The existence of embryonic, fetal, and adult hemoglobin results from genes being turned off and on at various developmental stages by regulatory genes.

On a larger scale, alterations in the behavior of regulatory genes that influence the activities of the structural genes involved in growth and development may be responsible for some of the physical differences between closely related species. For example, some of the anatomical differences between humans and chimpanzees, who share 98 percent of their DNA, may be the results of evolutionary changes in regulatory genes in one or both lineages.

A final point is that the genetic code is *universal* (Box 3–2); that is, DNA is the genetic material in all forms of life (at least on earth). This means that the DNA of all organisms, from bacteria to oak trees to human beings, is composed of the same molecules using the same kinds of instructions. These similarities imply biological

---

BOX 3–2   A CLOSER LOOK

Characteristics of the DNA Code

1. **The Code is universal.** In other words, the same basic messages apply to all life forms on the planet, from bacteria to humans. The same triplet code, specifying each amino acid, thus applies to all life on earth. This commonality is the basis for the methods used in recombinant DNA technology.

2. **The Code is triplet.** Each amino acid is specified by a sequence of three bases in the mRNA (the codon), which in turn is coded for by three bases in the DNA.

3. **The Code is continuous—without pauses.** There are no pauses or other delimiters separating one codon from another. Thus, if a base should be deleted, the entire frame would be moved, drastically altering the message downstream for successive codons. Such a gross alteration is termed a *frame-shift mutation*. Note that although the code lacks "commas," it does contain "periods"; that is, three specific codons act to stop translation.

4. **The Code is redundant.** While there are 20 amino acids, there are 4 DNA bases and 64 possible triplets or MRNA codons. Even considering the three "stop" messages, that still leaves 61 codons specifying the 20 amino acids. Thus, many amino acids are specified by more than one codon (see Table 3–1). For example, leucine and serine are each coded for by six different codons. In fact, only two amino acids (methionine and tryptophan) are coded for by a single codon. Redundancy is useful. For one thing, it serves as a safety net of sorts by helping to reduce the likelihood of severe consequences if there is a change, or *mutation,* in a DNA base. For example, four different DNA triplets—CGA, CGG, CGT, and CGC—code for the amino acid alanine. If, in the codon CGA, A mutates to G, the resulting triplet, CGG, will still specify alanine; thus, there will be no functional change.

relationships among, and ultimately a common ancestry for, all forms of life. What makes oak trees distinct from humans is not differences in the basic DNA material, but differences in how that material is arranged.

Mutation: When a Gene Changes

Probably the best way to envision how genetic material is organized and functions is to see what happens when it changes, or mutates. The first clearly elucidated example of a molecular mutation in humans concerned a portion of the hemoglobin molecule. Normal adult hemoglobin is made up of four polypeptide chains (two *alpha* chains and two *beta* chains) that are direct products of gene action. Each beta chain is in turn composed of 146 amino acids.

There are several hemoglobin disorders with genetic origins, and perhaps the best known of these is **sickle-cell anemia**, which results from a defect in the beta chain. Individuals with sickle-cell anemia inherit a variant of a gene from *both* parents that contains the substitution of one amino acid (*valine*) for the normally occurring *glutamic acid*. This single amino acid substitution at the sixth position of the beta chain results in the production of an altered and less efficient form of hemoglobin called hemoglobin S (Hb^S). The normal form is called hemoglobin A (Hb^A). In situations where the availability of oxygen is reduced, such as high altitude, or when oxygen requirements are increased through exercise, red cells bearing Hb^S collapse, roughly assuming a sickle shape. What follows is a cascade of events, all of which result in severe anemia and its consequences. Briefly, these events include impaired circulation from blocked capillaries, red blood cell destruction, oxygen deprivation to vital organs (including the brain), and, without treatment, death.

Individuals who inherit the altered form of the gene from only one parent have what is termed *sickle-cell trait;* because only about 40 percent of their hemoglobin is abnormal, they are much less severely affected and usually have a normal life span.

The cause of all the serious problems associated with sickle-cell anemia is a change in the Hb gene. Remember that both normal hemoglobin and the sickle-cell variety have 146 amino acids, 145 of which are identical. Moreover, to emphasize further the importance of a seemingly minimal alteration, consider that triplets of DNA bases are required to specify amino acids. Therefore, it takes 438 bases (146 × 3) to produce the chain of 146 amino acids forming the adult hemoglobin beta chain. But a change in only one of these 438 bases produces the cascade of life-threatening complications seen in sickle-cell anemia.

Figure 3–6 shows a possible DNA base sequence and the resulting amino acid products for both normal and sickling hemoglobin. As can be seen, a single base substitution (from CTC to CAC) can result in an altered amino acid sequence, from

. . . proline—*glutamic acid*—glutamic acid . . .

to

. . . proline—*valine*—glutamic acid . . .

Such a change in the genetic code is referred to as a **point mutation**, and in evolution, it is the most common and most important source of new genetic variation in populations. Point mutations, like that for the Hb gene, probably occur relatively frequently during cell division. But a new mutation will have evolutionary significance only if it is passed on to offspring through the gametes. Once such a

---

Virtual Lab 2, section III, presents the example of sickle-cell anemia in human populations.

Sickle-cell anemia
A severe inherited hemoglobin disorder that results from inheriting two copies of a mutant allele. This allele results from a single base substitution at the DNA level.

Point mutation
A chemical change in a single base of a DNA sequence.

POINT MUTATION

Normal Hemoglobin			Sickling Hemoglobin	
DNA sequence	Amino acid		Amino acid	DNA sequence
•	#1		#1	•
•				•
•				•
•				•
T G A	#4 threonine		#4 threonine	T G A
G G A	#5 proline		#5 proline	G G A
C **T** C	**#6 glutamic acid**		**#6 valine**	C **A** C
C T C	#7 glutamic acid		#7 glutamic acid	C T C
T T T	#8 lysine		#8 lysine	T T T
•	•		•	•
•	•		•	•
•	•		•	•
•	#146		#146	• #1652
#1652 (including intron sequences)				

FIGURE 3–6
Substitution of one base at position #6 produces sickling hemoglobin.

mutation has occurred, its fate in the population will depend on the other evolutionary forces, especially natural selection. In fact, sickle-cell anemia is the best-demonstrated example of natural selection acting on human beings, a point that will be considered in more detail in Chapter 4.

oh-so-chill

Chromosomes

Much of a cell's existence is spent in **interphase**, the portion of its life cycle during which the cell is involved with metabolic processes and other activities. During interphase, the cell's DNA exists as an uncoiled, granular substance called **chromatin**. (Incredibly, there are an estimated 6 feet of DNA in the nucleus of every one of your somatic cells!) However, at various times in the life of most types of cells, interphase is interrupted, activities cease, and the cell divides.

Cell division results in the production of new cells, and it is during this process that the chromatin becomes tightly coiled and is visible under a light microscope as a set of discrete structures called **chromosomes** (Fig. 3–7). A chromosome is composed of a DNA molecule and associated proteins (Fig. 3–8). During normal cell function, if chromosomes were visible, they would appear as single-stranded structures. However, during the early stages of cell division, they are made up of two strands, or two DNA molecules, joined together at a constricted area called the **centromere**. There are two strands simply because the DNA molecules have *replicated* during interphase, and one strand of a chromosome is an exact copy of the other.

Chromosomes only visible in cell division

Interphase
The portion of a cell's cycle during which metabolic processes and other cellular activities occur. Chromosomes are not visible as discrete structures at this time. DNA replication occurs during interphase.

Chromatin
The loose, diffuse form of DNA seen during interphase. When condensed, chromatin forms into chromosomes.

Chromosomes
Discrete structures composed of DNA and protein found only in the nuclei of cells. Chromosomes are only visible under magnification during certain phases of cell division.

Centromere
The constricted portion of a chromosome. After replication, the two strands of a double-stranded chromosome are joined at the centromere.

FIGURE 3-7
Scanning electron micrograph of human chromosomes during cell division. Note that these chromosomes are composed of two strands, or two DNA molecules.

Biophoto Associates/Science Source/Photo Researchers

Homologous
Referring to members of chromosome pairs. Homologous chromosomes carry loci that govern the same traits. During meiosis, homologous chromosomes pair and exchange segments of DNA. They are alike with regard to size, position of centromere, and banding pattern.

Locus
(*pl.,* loci) (lo´-kus, lo-sigh´) The position on a chromosome where a given gene occurs. The term is sometimes used interchangeably with *gene,* but this usage is technically incorrect.

Alleles
Alternate forms of a gene. Alleles occur at the same locus on homologous chromosomes and thus govern the same trait. However, because they are different, their action may result in different expressions of that trait. The term is sometimes used synonymously with *gene.*

Autosomes
All chromosomes except the sex chromosomes.

Sex chromosomes
In mammals, the X and Y chromosomes.

Every species is characterized by a specific number of chromosomes in somatic cells (Table 3–2). In humans, there are 46. Chimpanzees and gorillas possess 48. This difference in chromosome number does not necessarily indicate that humans possess less DNA than chimpanzees and gorillas. The DNA is simply packaged differently in the three species.

In eukaryotic species, chromosomes generally occur in pairs. Thus, human somatic cells contain 23 pairs. One member of each pair is inherited from the father (paternal), while the other member is inherited from the mother (maternal).

Members of chromosomal pairs are said to be **homologous** in that they are alike in size and position of the centromere and they carry genetic information influencing the same *traits.* This does not imply that homologous chromosomes are genetically identical. It simply means that the characteristics they govern are the same. For example, on both of a person's ninth chromosomes, there is a **locus,** or gene position, that determines which of the four ABO blood types (A, B, AB, or O) he or she will have. However, the two ninth chromosomes might not have identical DNA segments at the ABO locus. In other words, at numerous genetic loci, there may be more than one possible form of a gene, and these molecularly different forms are called **alleles.** Thus, alleles are alternate forms of a gene that can direct the cell to produce slightly different forms of the same protein and, ultimately, different expressions of traits. At the ABO locus, there are three possible alleles: *A, B,* and *O.* (However, since individuals only possess two ninth chromosomes, only two alleles are present in any one person.) It is the allelic variation at the ABO locus that is responsible for the variation among humans in ABO blood type. Moreover, the potential variation that exists at specific loci in homologous chromosomes (as illustrated by the ABO example) explains how members of a chromosome pair may influence the same traits and yet not be genetically identical. (This point is covered in more detail in Chapter 4.)

There are two basic types of chromosomes: **autosomes** and **sex chromosomes.** Autosomes carry genetic information that governs all physical characteristics except primary sex determination. The two sex chromosomes are the X and Y chromosomes. In mammals, the Y chromosome carries genetic information directly

22 autosomes
1 sex chromosome

FIGURE 3–8
A model of a human chromosome, illustrating the relationship of chromosomes to DNA.

(a) Each of the more than 1 trillion somatic cells in the body consists of a cell membrane, cytoplasm, and a nucleus.

(b) Each somatic cell nucleus contains 46 chromosomes— 23 contributed by the mother and 23 by the father. The chromosomes consist of protein and DNA.

(c) Each set of chromosomes contains 50,000 to 100,000 genes carried in 3 billion nucleotide pairs of DNA.

(d) To form the chromosome, the DNA is coiled into higher and higher levels of organization.

(e) The DNA is coiled around specialized proteins, providing structure to the chromosome.

(f) A specific sequence of nucleotide base pairs constitutes a gene.

TABLE 3–2 Standard Chromosomal Complement in Various Organisms

Organism	Chromosome Number in Somatic Cells	Chromosome Number in Gametes
Human (*Homo sapiens*)	46	23
Chimpanzee (*Pan troglodytes*)	48	24
Gorilla (*Gorilla gorilla*)	48	24
Dog (*Canis familiaris*)	78	39
Chicken (*Gallus domesticus*)	78	39
Frog (*Rana pipiens*)	26	13
Housefly (*Musca domestica*)	12	6
Onion (*Allium cepa*)	16	8
Corn (*Zea mays*)	20	10
Tobacco (*Nicotiana tabacum*)	48	24

Source: Cummings, 1991, p. 16.

involved with determining maleness. The X chromosome, although termed a "sex chromosome," is larger and functions more like an autosome in that it is not actually involved in primary sex determination but does influence a number of other traits.

Among mammals, all genetically normal females have two X chromosomes (XX); they are female simply because the Y chromosome is not present. All genetically normal males have one X and one Y chromosome (XY). In other classes of animals, such as birds or insects, primary sex determination is governed by differing chromosomal mechanisms.

It is extremely important to note that *all* autosomes occur in pairs. Normal human somatic cells have 22 pairs of autosomes and one pair of sex chromosomes. It should also be noted that abnormal numbers of autosomes are almost always fatal to the individual, usually soon after conception. Although abnormal numbers of sex chromosomes are not usually fatal, they may result in sterility and frequently have other consequences as well (see p. 62 for further discussion). Therefore, to function normally, it is essential for a human cell to possess both members of each chromosomal pair, or a total of 46 chromosomes.

Karyotyping Chromosomes

One method frequently used to examine chromosomes in an individual is to produce what is termed a **karyotype.** (An example of a human karyotype is shown in Fig. 3–9.) Chromosomes used in karyotypes are obtained from dividing cells. (You will remember that chromosomes are visible as discrete entities only during cell division.) For example, white blood cells, because they are easily obtained, may be cultured, chemically treated, and microscopically examined to identify those that are dividing. These cells are then photographed through a microscope to pro-

Karyotype
The chromosomal complement of an individual or that which is typical for a species. Usually displayed in a photomicrograph, the chromosomes are arranged in pairs and according to size and position of the centromere.

FIGURE 3–9
A karyotype of a male, with the chromosomes arranged by size and position of the centromere, as well as by the banding patterns.

Ifti Ahmed

duce *photomicrographs* of intact, double-stranded chromosomes. Homologous chromosomes are then matched up, and the entire set is arranged in descending order by size so that the largest (number 1) appears first.

In addition to overall size, position of the centromere also aids in identification of individual chromosomes, since the position of the centromere is characteristic of each chromosome. Moreover, with the development of special techniques to highlight DNA segments that differentially take up various colored stains, it is now possible to identify every chromosome on the basis of specific *banding patterns*.

Karyotyping has numerous practical applications. Physicians and genetic counselors routinely use karyotypes to aid in the diagnosis of chromosomal disorders in patients. Moreover, karyotypes are often employed in the prenatal diagnosis of chromosomal abnormalities in developing fetuses.

Karyotypes have also proved extremely useful in comparing the chromosomes of different species. Indeed, karyotype analysis has revealed marked chromosomal similarities shared by different primate species, including humans. The similarities in overall karyotype, as well as the marked biochemical and DNA similarities indicated by banding patterns (discussed in Chapter 5), point to close *genetic* relationships especially between humans and the African great apes.

Cell Division

Mitosis

Cell division in somatic cells is called **mitosis**. Mitosis occurs during growth of the individual. It also acts to promote healing of injured tissues and to replace older cells with newer ones. In short, it is the way somatic cells reproduce.

In the early stages of mitosis, a human somatic cell possesses 46 double-stranded chromosomes. As the cell begins to divide, the chromosomes line up in random order along the center of the cell (Fig. 3–10c). The chromosomes then split apart at the centromere, so that the strands are separated. Once the two strands are apart, they pull away from each other and move to opposite ends of the dividing cell (Fig. 3–10d). At this point, each strand is now a distinct chromosome, *composed of one DNA molecule*. Following the separation of chromosome strands, the cell membrane pinches in and becomes sealed, so that two new cells are formed, each with a full complement of DNA, or 46 chromosomes. Most biology textbooks subdivide the continuous process of mitotic cell division into four phases: *prophase, metaphase, anaphase,* and *telophase*.

Mitosis is referred to as "simple cell division" because a somatic cell divides one time to produce two daughter cells that are genetically identical to each other and to the original cell. In mitosis, the original cell possesses 46 chromosomes, and each new daughter cell inherits an exact copy of all 46. This arrangement is made possible by the ability of the DNA molecule to replicate. Thus, it is DNA replication that ensures that the quantity and quality of the genetic material remain constant from one generation of cells to the next.

Meiosis

While mitosis produces new cells, **meiosis** may lead to the development of new individuals, since it produces reproductive cells, or gametes. Although meiosis is another form of cell division and is in some ways similar to mitosis, it is a more complicated process.

During meiosis, specialized cells in male testes and female ovaries divide and develop, eventually to become sperm and egg cells. Initially, these cells contain the

Mitosis
Simple cell division; the process by which somatic cells divide to produce two identical daughter cells.

Meiosis
Cell division in specialized cells in ovaries and testes. Meiosis involves two divisions and results in four daughter cells, each containing only half the original number of chromosomes. These cells can develop into gametes.

(a) The cell is involved in metabolic activities. DNA replication occurs, but chromosomes are not visible.

(b) The nuclear membrane disappears, and double-stranded chromosomes are visible.

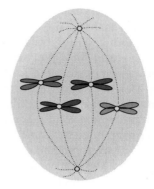

(c) The chromosomes align themselves at the center of the cell.

(d) The chromosomes split at the centromere, and the strands separate and move to opposite ends of the dividing cell.

(e) The cell membrane pinches in as the cell continues to divide. The chromosomes begin to uncoil (not shown here).

(f) After mitosis is complete, there are two identical daughter cells. The nuclear membrane is present, and chromosomes are no longer visible.

FIGURE 3–10
Mitosis.

Diploid
Referring to the full complement of chromosomes in a somatic cell—two of each pair.

Haploid
Referring to a half set of chromosomes, one member of each pair. Haploid sets are found in gametes.

full complement of chromosomes (46 in humans) and are referred to as **diploid** cells. (The number of chromosomes forming a complete set in a somatic cell is called the diploid number.) Meiosis is characterized by two divisions that result in four daughter cells, each of which contains 23 chromosomes, or half the original number. Because each of these newly formed cells receives only one member of each chromosomal pair, they are said to be **haploid** cells containing a haploid number of chromosomes.

Reduction of chromosome number is a critical feature of meiosis, because the resulting gamete, with its 23 chromosomes, may ultimately unite with another gamete, which also carries 23 chromosomes. The product of this union, the *zygote*, or fertilized egg, reestablishes the diploid number of chromosomes (46). In other

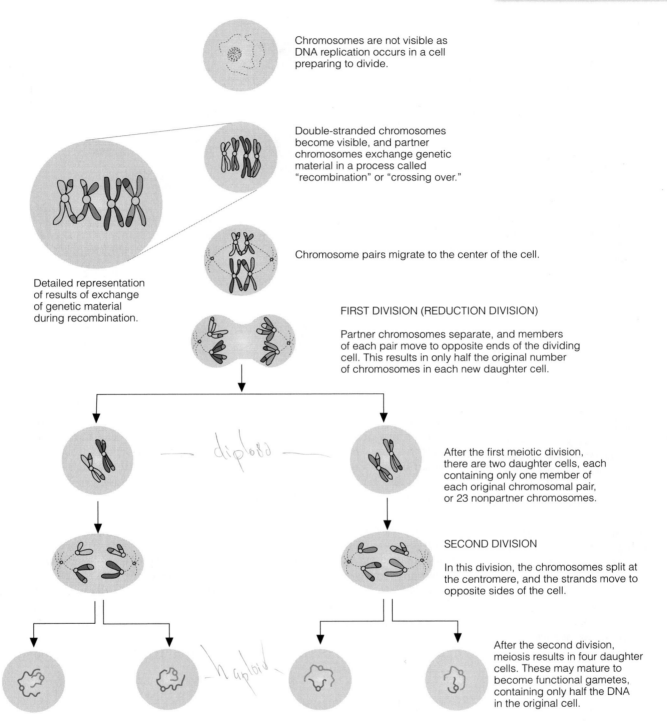

Chromosomes are not visible as DNA replication occurs in a cell preparing to divide.

Double-stranded chromosomes become visible, and partner chromosomes exchange genetic material in a process called "recombination" or "crossing over."

Detailed representation of results of exchange of genetic material during recombination.

Chromosome pairs migrate to the center of the cell.

FIRST DIVISION (REDUCTION DIVISION)

Partner chromosomes separate, and members of each pair move to opposite ends of the dividing cell. This results in only half the original number of chromosomes in each new daughter cell.

After the first meiotic division, there are two daughter cells, each containing only one member of each original chromosomal pair, or 23 nonpartner chromosomes.

SECOND DIVISION

In this division, the chromosomes split at the centromere, and the strands move to opposite sides of the cell.

After the second division, meiosis results in four daughter cells. These may mature to become functional gametes, containing only half the DNA in the original cell.

words, the zygote inherits the full complement of DNA it needs (half from each parent) to develop and function normally. If it were not for *reduction division* (the first division) in meiosis, it would not be possible to maintain the correct number of chromosomes from one generation to the next.

During the first meiotic division, partner chromosomes come together, forming pairs of double-stranded chromosomes. In this way, pairs of chromosomes line up along the cell's center (Fig. 3–11). Pairing of homologous chromosomes is highly

FIGURE 3–11
Meiosis.

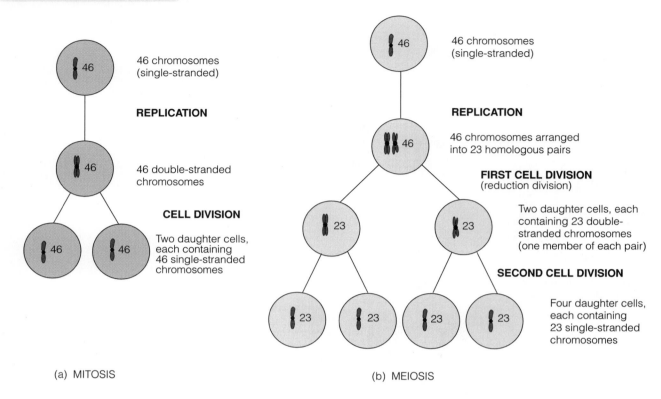

(a) MITOSIS

(b) MEIOSIS

FIGURE 3–12
Mitosis and meiosis compared. In mitosis, one division produces two daughter cells, each of which contains 46 chromosomes. Meiosis is characterized by two divisions. After the first, there are two cells, each containing only 23 chromosomes (one member of each original chromosome pair). Each daughter cell divides again, so that the final result is four cells, each with only half the original number of chromosomes.

Recombination (crossing over)
The exchange of genetic material between homologous chromosomes during meiosis.

significant, for while they are together, members of pairs exchange genetic information in a process called **recombination**, or **crossing over.** Pairing is also important because it facilitates the accurate reduction of chromosome number by ensuring that each new daughter cell will receive only one member of each pair.

As the cell begins to divide, the chromosomes themselves remain intact (i.e., double-stranded), but *members of pairs* separate and migrate to opposite ends of the cell. After the first division, there are two new daughter cells, but they are not identical to each other or to the parental cell because each contains only one member of each chromosome pair and therefore only 23 chromosomes, each of which still has two strands (see Fig. 3–11). Moreover, because of crossing over, each chromosome now contains some genetic variations it did not have previously.

The second meiotic division proceeds in much the same way as in mitosis (Fig. 3–12). In the two newly formed cells, the 23 double-stranded chromosomes align themselves at the cell's center and, as in mitosis, the strands of each chromosome separate at the centromere and move apart. Once this second division is completed, there are four daughter cells, each with 23 single-stranded chromosomes (i.e., 23 DNA molecules).

The Evolutionary Significance of Meiosis

Meiosis occurs in all sexually reproducing organisms, and it is a highly important evolutionary innovation, since it increases genetic variation in populations at a faster rate than mutation alone can do in asexually reproducing species. Individual members of sexually reproducing species are not genetically identical clones of other individuals. Rather, they result from the contribution of genetic information from two parents. From any one human mating, an enormous number of possible offspring can result. From just the random arrangements of chromosome pairs lining up along the center of the cell during the first division of meiosis, each parent can produce 8 million genetically different gametes. And given the joint probability accounting for both parents, the total number of possible genetic combinations for any human mating is about 70 trillion. It should be noted that this staggering number is the result solely of the paired arrangements (called **random assortment**) and does not even take into account the many more combinations resulting from crossing over.

Genetic diversity is therefore considerably enhanced by meiosis. As was mentioned in Chapter 2, natural selection acts on genetic variation in populations. (You will recall that Charles Darwin emphasized this point.) In all species, *mutation* is the only source of *new* genetic variation. But in sexually reproducing species, recombination produces new *arrangements* of genetic information, which potentially provide additional material for natural selection to act on.

Genetic variation is essential if species are to adapt to changing selective pressures. If all individuals were genetically identical, natural selection would have nothing to act on and evolution could not occur. It has been argued that this influence on variation is the principal adaptive advantage of sexual reproduction. Therefore, although reproduction has been strictly asexual for most of the time life has existed on this planet, sexual reproduction and meiosis are of major evolutionary importance because they contribute to the role of natural selection in populations.

Sexual reproduction is an adaptation bc it increases diversity

Problems with Meiosis

For meiosis to ensure a reasonably good opportunity for normal fetal development, the process must be exact. The two-stage division must produce a viable gamete with exactly 23 chromosomes—that is, with only one member of each chromosome pair present. Superficially, it appears that the process works quite well, since more than 98 percent of newborns have the correct number of chromosomes. However, this statistic is misleading. It has been estimated that as many as half of all pregnancies naturally terminate early as spontaneous abortions (miscarriages). An estimated 70 percent of these miscarriages are caused by an improper number of chromosomes (Cummings, 2000). Thus, it appears that during meiosis, there are frequent errors with quite serious consequences.

If chromosomes or chromosome strands fail to separate during either of the two meiotic divisions, serious problems can arise. This failure to separate is called **nondisjunction**. The result of nondisjunction is that one of the daughter cells receives two copies of the affected chromosome, while the other daughter cell receives none. If such an affected gamete unites with a normal gamete containing 23 chromosomes, the resulting zygote will have either 45 or 47 chromosomes. Having only one member of a chromosome pair is referred to as *monosomy*. The term *trisomy* refers to the presence of three copies of a particular chromosome.

The far-reaching effects of an abnormal number of chromosomes can be appreciated only by remembering that the zygote will faithfully reproduce itself through mitosis. Thus, every cell in the developing body will also have the abnormal chromosome number. Most situations of this type involving autosomes are lethal, and the embryo is spontaneously aborted, frequently before the pregnancy is even recognized.

One example of an abnormal number of autosomes is *Down syndrome*, more properly called *trisomy 21,* where there are three copies of the twenty-first chromosome. This is the only example of an abnormal number of autosomes being compatible with life beyond the first few months after birth. Trisomy 21, which occurs in approximately 1 out of every 1,000 live births, is associated with a number of developmental and health problems. These problems include congenital heart defects (seen in about 40 percent of affected newborns), increased susceptibility to

Random assortment
The chance distribution of chromosomes to daughter cells during meiosis; along with recombination, the source of variation resulting from meiosis.

Nondisjunction
The failure of homologous chromosomes or chromosome strands to separate during cell division.

TABLE 3–3 Examples of Nondisjunction in Sex Chromosomes

Chromosomal Complement	Condition	Estimated Incidence	Manifestations
XXX	Trisomy X	1 per 1,000 female births	Affected women are usually clinically normal, but there is a slight increase in sterility and mental retardation compared to the general population. In cases with more than three X chromosomes, mental retardation can be severe.
XYY	XYY syndrome	1 per 1,000 male births	Affected males are fertile and tend to be taller than average.
XO	Turner syndrome	1 per 10,000 female births	Affected females are short-statured, have broad chests and webbed necks, and are sterile. There is usually no mental retardation, but concepts relating to spatial relationships, including mathematics, can pose difficulties. Between 95 and 99 percent of affected fetuses die before birth.
XXY	Klinefelter syndrome	1 per 1,000 male births	Symptoms are noticeable by puberty: reduced testicular development, reduced facial and body hair, some breast development in about half of all cases, and reduced fertility or sterility. Some individuals exhibit lowered intelligence. Additional X chromosomes (XXXY) are associated with mental retardation.

respiratory infections, and leukemia. However, the most widely recognized effect of trisomy 21 is mental retardation, which is variably expressed and ranges from mild to severe.

Trisomy 21 is partly associated with advanced maternal age. For example, the risk of a 20-year-old woman giving birth to an affected infant is just 0.05 percent (5 in 10,000). However, 3 percent of babies born to mothers 45 and older are affected (a 60-fold increase). Actually, most affected infants are born to women under the age of 35, but this statistic is due to the fact that the majority of babies are born to women in this age category. The increase in incidence with maternal age is thought to be related to the early initiation of meiosis in females and the presumed age changes in the gametic cell lines, resulting in increased risk of nondisjunction. Indeed, a number of conditions related to nondisjunction of chromosomes are thought to be influenced, in part, by increased maternal age.

Nondisjunction may also occur in sex chromosomes, producing individuals who, for example, are XXY (47 chromosomes), XO (45 chromosomes), XXX (47 chromosomes), or XYY (47 chromosomes). While these conditions do not always result in death or mental retardation, some are associated with impaired mental function and/or sterility (Table 3–3). Moreover, still greater numbers of X chromosomes, such as XXXX or XXXY, result in marked mental retardation. And some nondisjunctions of sex chromosomes are lethal. While it is possible to survive without a Y chromosome (roughly half of all humans do), it is not possible to live without an X chromosome. Indeed, the evidence suggests that embryos that possess only a Y chromosome are spontaneously aborted before a pregnancy is even recognized.

Clearly, the importance of accuracy during meiosis cannot be overstated. If normal development is to occur, it is essential that the correct number of both autosomes and sex chromosomes be present.

New Frontiers

Since the discovery of DNA structure and function in the 1950s, the field of genetics has revolutionized biological science and reshaped our understanding of inheritance, genetic disease, and evolutionary processes. For example, a technique developed in 1986 called **polymerase chain reaction (PCR)** now enables scientists to produce multiple copies of DNA, making it possible to analyze segments of DNA as small as one molecule. This ability is critically important because samples of DNA, such as those obtained at crime scenes or from fossils, are frequently too small to permit reliable analysis of nucleotide sequences.

In PCR, the two strands of a DNA sample are separated, and an enzyme synthesizes complementary strands on the exposed bases, as in DNA replication. Because this process can be repeated many times, it is possible to produce over a million copies of the original DNA material! Thus, scientists have been able to identify nucleotide sequences in, for example, fossils (including Neandertals), Egyptian mummies, and members of the Russian royal family murdered in 1918. As you can imagine, PCR has limitless potential for many disciplines, including forensic science, medicine, and evolutionary biology.

Over the last two decades, using the techniques of **recombinant DNA technology**, scientists have been able to transfer genes from the cells of one species into those of another. The most common method has been to insert human genes that direct the production of various proteins into bacterial cells, thus causing the altered bacteria to produce human gene products. There are numerous commercial applications for this technology, many of which are aimed at treating genetic disease in humans. For example, until the early 1980s, diabetic patients relied on insulin derived from nonhuman animals. However, this insulin was not plentiful, and some patients developed allergies to it. But since 1982, abundant supplies of human insulin, produced by bacteria, have been available; and bacteria-derived insulin does not cause allergic reactions in patients.

Human genes may also be inserted into the fertilized eggs of some nonhuman animals. The eggs are then implanted into the uteri of females who subsequently give birth to genetically altered offspring. These offspring serve as a source of various substances needed in medical practice. For example, genetically altered female sheep can carry a human gene that causes them to produce an enzyme that is present in most people and which prevents a serious form of emphysema. This enzyme is produced in the sheep's milk, and once extracted and purified, it can be administered to people who do not normally produce it.

Genetic transfer techniques have also been used in efforts to improve crops in a variety of ways. For instance, genetically altered strawberries are able to withstand temperatures of 10–12°F below freezing without being damaged. Likewise, some tomatoes can be ripened on the vine before being shipped because they carry a gene that inhibits the potentially damaging softness that normally develops during ripening.

In recent years, genetic manipulation has become increasingly controversial owing to questions related to product safety, environmental concerns, and animal welfare, among others. For example, the insertion of bacterial DNA into certain crops has made them toxic to leaf-eating insects, thus reducing the need for pesticide use. And cattle and pigs are commonly treated with genetically engineered growth hormone to increase growth rates. Although there is no current evidence that humans are susceptible to the insect-repelling bacterium or adversely affected by the consumption of meat and dairy products from animals treated with growth hormone, there are serious concerns over the unknown effects of such long-term exposure. In fact, tremendous opposition to genetically modified foods has resulted in greatly increased demand for organically grown produce and hormone-free meats, especially in Europe.

Regardless of how contentious these new techniques may be, nothing has generated as much controversy as cloning. The controversy escalated with the birth of Dolly, a **clone** of a female sheep, in 1997 (Wilmut et al., 1997). Actually, cloning is

Polymerase chain reaction (PCR)
A method of producing thousands of copies of a DNA segment using the enzyme DNA polymerase.

Recombinant DNA technology
A process in which genes from the cell of one species are transferred to somatic cells or gametes of another species.

Clone
An organism that is genetically identical to another organism. The term may also be used to refer to genetically identical DNA segments and molecules.

Human Genome Project
An international effort aimed at sequencing and mapping the entire human genome.

Genome
The entire genetic makeup of an individual or species. In humans, it is estimated that each individual possesses approximately 3 billion DNA nucleotides.

not as new as you might think. Anyone who has ever taken a cutting from a plant and rooted it to grow a new plant has produced a clone. In the 1950s, plant biologists developed methods of cloning carrots by culturing cells taken from mature plants. In the 1960s, an African toad became the first animal to be cloned, but for a number of reasons, cloning a mammal remained an elusive goal. Then, in 1981, a Swiss team of geneticists successfully produced cloned mice, and these experiments were followed by cloned cattle and sheep. So, you might ask, why was Dolly such a big deal? The furor was partly due to the fact that earlier cloning results had not been well publicized, and this report raised fears that the research would lead to human cloning. But in parts of the scientific community, there was excitement over the techniques that were used.

The Dolly research was unique because the donor nucleus was derived not from an undifferentiated embryonic cell (standard practice) but from a cell of a *mature* animal (see Issue, pp. 68–69). This demonstrated that DNA derived from a specialized somatic cell is capable of returning to an embryonic state, where it can direct cell division and ultimately orchestrate the development of an entire organism. Until now, this ability had been questioned.

Since the original reports of the Dolly experiment were published, it has emerged that the donor cell for Dolly may inadvertently have been a fetal cell and not one taken from an adult sheep after all. But teams of Japanese scientists have now reported cloning cattle and mice using donor cells from adult animals (Wakayama et al., 1998). Thus, while it is possible that Dolly was not derived from an adult somatic cell, other animals have been.

As exciting as these innovations are, probably the single most important advance in genetics has been the progress made by the **Human Genome Project**. The goal of this international effort, begun in 1990, has been the sequencing of the entire human **genome**, which consists of some 3 billion bases comprising approximately 30,000 genes. In February 2001, two rival teams of researchers simultaneously announced they had revealed a virtually complete sequence of human DNA. As phenomenal as this achievement is, scientists are still several years away from sorting out which DNA segments operate as functional genes and which do not. It will also be years before the identity and function of many of the proteins produced by these newly identified genes are ascertained. Put another way, it is one thing to know the chemical makeup of a gene but quite another to know what that gene does. Nevertheless, the magnitude and importance of the achievement cannot be overstated, because it will ultimately transform biomedical and pharmaceutical research and will change forever how many human diseases are diagnosed and treated.

Moreover, at the same time scientists were sequencing human genes, the genomes of other organisms were also being studied. As of September 2000, the genomes of over 600 species (mostly microorganisms) had been either partially or completely identified. This research has enormous implications not only for biomedical research but also for studies of evolutionary relationships among species. We already know that humans share many genes with other organisms, but just how many and which ones will partly be clarified by upcoming projects aimed at sequencing nonhuman primate (especially chimpanzee) genomes. Eventually, comparative genome analysis should provide a thorough assessment of genetic similarities and differences, and thus the evolutionary relationships, between humans and other primates. Indeed, it would not be an exaggeration to say that this is the most exciting time in the history of evolutionary biology since Darwin published *On the Origin of Species*.

SUMMARY

The topics covered in this chapter relate almost entirely to discoveries made after Darwin and Wallace described the fundamentals of natural selection. But all the issues presented here are basic to an understanding of biological evolution, adaptation, and human variation.

It has been shown that cells are the fundamental units of life and that there are basically two types of cells. Somatic cells make up body tissues, while gametes (eggs and sperm) are reproductive cells that transmit genetic information from parent to offspring.

Genetic information is contained in the DNA molecule, found in the nuclei of cells. The DNA molecule is capable of replication, or making copies of itself, and it is the only molecule known to have this ability. Replication makes it possible for daughter cells to receive a full complement of DNA (contained in chromosomes).

DNA also controls protein synthesis by directing the cell to arrange amino acids in the proper sequence for each particular type of protein. Also involved in the process of protein synthesis is another, similar molecule called RNA. Not all the DNA in a gene codes for the production of a protein. Segments called introns are deleted after the formation of messenger RNA, and it is the remaining segments called exons that actually direct protein synthesis. There are also genes that control the function of other genes. These regulatory genes are crucial to growth and development, and they have evolutionary significance as well. The DNA code for all life is universal and triplet, the latter meaning that amino acids are coded for by DNA bases occurring in groups of three.

Cells multiply by dividing, and during cell division, DNA is visible under a microscope in the form of chromosomes. In humans, there are 46 chromosomes (23 pairs). If the complement is not precisely distributed to succeeding generations of cells, severe consequences will follow.

Somatic cells divide during growth or tissue repair or to replace old, worn-out cells. Somatic cell division is called mitosis. A cell divides one time to produce two daughter cells, each possessing a full and identical (diploid) set of chromosomes.

Sex cells are produced when specialized cells in the ovaries and testes divide during meiosis. Unlike mitosis, meiosis is characterized by two divisions that produce four nonidentical daughter cells, each containing only half (haploid) the amount of DNA (23 chromosomes) as that carried by the original cell.

QUESTIONS FOR REVIEW

1. Genetics is the study of what?
2. What components of a eukaryotic cell are discussed in this chapter?
3. What are the two basic types of cells in individuals? Give an example of each.
4. What are nucleotides?
5. Name the four DNA bases. Which pairs with which?
6. What is DNA replication, and why is it important?
7. What are proteins? Give two examples.
8. What are enzymes?
9. What are the building blocks of protein? How many different kinds are there?
10. What is the function of DNA in protein synthesis?
11. What is the function of mRNA?
12. What is the function of tRNA?

13. Does the entire DNA molecule code for the manufacture of proteins? Explain.
14. Does all of the DNA in a gene code for the production of a protein? Explain.
15. What is the role of regulatory genes? Give an example.
16. Define gene, allele, and locus.
17. Define chromosome.
18. What are homologous chromosomes?
19. What is polymerase chain reaction (PCR), and why is it important?
20. How many cell divisions occur in mitosis? In humans, how many chromosomes does each new cell have?
21. How many cell divisions occur in meiosis? How many daughter cells are produced when meiosis is complete? In humans, how many chromosomes does each new cell contain?
22. Why is reduction division important?
23. What is recombination, and why is it important? When does it occur?
24. Why is the genetic code said to be universal? Why is it said to be redundant?
25. What are the two sex chromosomes? Which two do males have? Which two do females have?
26. Why is meiosis important to the process of natural selection?
27. How does meiosis in females differ from meiosis in males?
28. Why is the study of genetics important to physical anthropology?

SUGGESTED FURTHER READING

"The Business of the Human Genome." 2000. *Scientific American* 283(1): 48–69. Special Report.

Brown, Kathryn. 2001. "Seeds of Concern." *Scientific American,* 284(4): 52–57.

Collins, Francis S., and Karin G. Jegalian. 1999. "Deciphering the Code of Life." *Scientific American* 281(6): 86–91.

Cummings, Michael R. 2000. *Human Heredity.* 4th ed. Belmont, CA: Brooks/Cole.

Hopkin, Karen. 2001. "The Risks on the Table." *Scientific American,* 284(4): 60–61.

Moxon, E. Richard and Christopher Wills, 1999. "DNA Microsatellites: Agents of Evolution?" *Scientific American,* 280(1): 94–99.

Pedersen, Roger A. 2001. "Embryonic Stem Cells for Medicine." *Scientific American,* 280(4): 68–73.

Wallace, Douglas C. 1997. "Mitochondrial DNA in Aging and Disease." *Scientific American,* 277(2): 40–47.

See entire issue of *Scientific American,* vol. 253(4) (October 1985), for numerous articles pertaining to molecular genetics and evolution.

RESOURCES ON THE INTERNET

Wadsworth Anthropology Resource Center
http://anthropology.wadsworth.com

The companion website for this text includes a range of enrichment material focused on the chapter's topic. While online you can enhance your understanding of the chapter by exploring one of the several additional Internet exercises, by researching topics, and by accessing full articles on InfoTrac College Edition. You can also reinforce the concepts by taking online practice exams.

Internet Exercises

The subject of genetics is well represented on the Internet. Use your search engine to do a word search for *genetics*. See if you can find the original 1953 article by Watson and Crick that describes the structure of the DNA molecule. Read this very short Nobel Prize–winning article and make a list of facts that are not presented in Chapter 3. What is your overall impression of the Watson and Crick paper?

InfoTrac College Edition
http://www.infotrac-college.com/wadsworth

Conduct a subject search for *DNA*. Choose at least one article, read it, and write a short summary. In your summary, discuss some aspect of the article that pertains to one of the topics discussed in Chapter 3.

Stem Cell Research: Promise and Controversy

Stem cells are undifferentiated, or unspecialized, cells that can divide and replicate indefinitely, and depending on their origins (and given the right circumstances), they can give rise to many, if not all, the specialized cells that make up an organism.

Adult stem cells are found in specialized tissues, such as bone marrow, skin, and the gastrointestinal tract. They are able to replicate themselves throughout the life of the organism and can also give rise to all the specialized types of cells *that make up the tissue in which they are found*. For example, stem cells in bone marrow give rise to all the cells that comprise blood, including oxygen-transporting red cells and all the white cells involved in the immune response. In short, adult stem cells replace certain types of cells that have lived out their life span or have been lost through disease or trauma.

For years, one type of adult stem cell, hematopoietic (blood-producing) stem cells (HSCs) have been transplanted into patients with immune disorders and various forms of cancer, especially leukemias. These procedures, called bone marrow transplants, require the painful extraction of bone marrow cells from a donor (usually from the pelvis) and then their transplantation into a recipient. Nowadays, bone marrow transplants are beginning to be replaced by injections of hematopoietic stem cells extracted directly from the donor's circulating blood. Stem cell transfer, as the procedure is now called, is dangerous, particularly in the treatment of cancer,

because the patient's cancerous blood-producing cells and immune system are virtually destroyed by chemotherapy or radiation prior to the stem cell transfer; thus, there is a risk of death due to infection or graft-versus-host immune reactions. But success rates are increasing, and in many cases, the stem cells give rise to healthy white and red blood cells in a patient whose cancer has been eradicated or at least put into remission.

By the late 1980s, researchers recognized that HSCs are also present in the approximately 3 ounces of blood contained in umbilical cords. Since 1988, HSCs derived from cord blood have been used to treat thousands of children with various forms of leukemia. In one highly publicized case, the parents of a daughter with a type of leukemia conceived a second child, in part to provide HSCs derived from the cord blood of a close relative. In this case, several embryos were produced through *in vitro* fertilization (i.e., in a test tube or culture dish). The embryo chosen for implantation into the mother's uterus was shown not to be affected by the leukemia. In the press, considerable outrage was expressed over the notion that parents would deliberately conceive a child to provide donor cells to treat their daughter. However, a team of bioethicists had ruled that this course of action was indeed ethical, since the resulting infant would in no way be harmed by the procedure and, importantly, the parents wanted another child. Subsequently, a son was born and the daughter received a transplant of normal HSCs from her new

brother's umbilical cord blood, and she is currently in remission.

Human embryonic stem cells are, as the name implies, derived from 5-day-old embryos consisting of 200 to 250 cells. Most of these embryos are the unused products of *in vitro* fertilization of eggs at fertility clinics and are donated by patients. In some cases, embryos resulting from therapeutic abortions have also been used. At this stage, the embryo consists of two portions: one that becomes the placenta, and the other, an inner cell mass consisting of about 40 cells, that develops into the fetus. Those cells comprising the inner cell mass are the undifferentiated embryonic stem cells that have the potential of giving rise to the more than 200 types of cells found in mammals. It is this potential that makes embryonic stem cells so attractive to researchers, because it is doubtful that adult stem cells have this same capacity.

Work with embryonic stem cells is still in the early stages, but when such cells are exposed to certain chemicals, they give rise to specialized cells that produce substances (proteins) potentially capable of curing symptoms related to disease or trauma. For example, exposing mouse embryonic stem cells to a derivative of vitamin A stimulates genes that cause the cells to produce nerve cells (neurons). Furthermore, embryonic stem cells transplanted into mouse brains have give rise to neurons that produce an enzyme necessary for the synthesis of dopamine, the neurochemical lacking in patients with Parkinson's disease. These findings have led researchers to

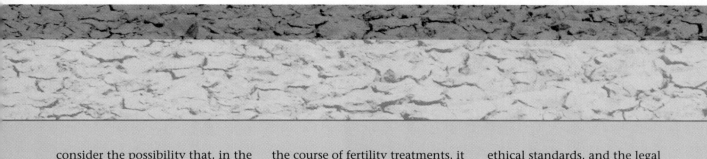

consider the possibility that, in the future, embryonic stem cells can be implanted into patients with Alzheimer's disease or those with brain and spinal cord injuries to replace damaged or destroyed neurons. It is also hoped that nonfunctioning pancreatic cells in diabetic patients can be replaced with stem cells that will produce healthy, insulin-producing cells. Or perhaps it will be possible to replace damaged cardiac muscle cells in patients with heart disease—and even skin cells in burn victims.

But there are many ethical objections to the use of embryonic stem cells and many technical problems to overcome. The strongest objections are raised by abortion opponents and those who believe that any fertilized egg, with the potential to develop into a human being if implanted into a woman's uterus, should not be destroyed. It is this objection that has led, in the United States, to a presidential executive order that limits federal funding for embryonic stem cell research to the approximately 60 cell lines already established by the summer of 2001. (Privately funded research remains unaffected by this decision.) There is also a funding ban on all projects that create embryos solely for research, and, as of this writing, the U.S. Congress is considering a total ban on all nonreproductive cloning of human embryos.

Although in general agreement with the guidelines, the scientific community has questioned the suitability of some of the existing cell lines for certain types of research. Another point made by the scientific community is that in the course of fertility treatments, it is necessary to create more embryos than will actually be used, so that fertility clinics destroy thousands of surplus embryos every year. It is these surplus embryos that have been used in research, and scientists argue that it is far better to use them for the benefits they may provide than to destroy them. At the same time, many abortion opponents are unhappy with the executive order because they believe that although the existing cell lines no longer possess the potential for human life, *any* use of human embryos in research is wrong. Moreover, there are concerns that the ruling may leave the door open for future use of embryos. Consequently, neither side of the debate is completely happy with the current state of affairs.

Funding limitations similar to those in the United States exist in some other countries, including Germany. But in Britain, public funds are available for embryonic stem cell studies, even those that include nonreproductive cloning and the creation of embryos for research purposes.

In addition to funding constraints, there are other concerns the scientific community must address. First, the potential of stem cells to produce malignant (i.e., constantly replicating) cell lines is not known. Second, there is the problem of tissue rejection in patients receiving stem cell transplants that are recognized as foreign by their own immune systems. These two problems alone will require years of investigation to solve.

This discussion illustrates the conflicts between technology, ethical standards, and the legal system. The questions raised by developing technologies challenge traditionally held views about fundamental aspects of life. In the past, people with hereditary disorders frequently died. They still do. But now there are treatments, however costly, for some conditions. How we come to view these new discoveries and how we come to terms with the ethical and legal issues surrounding our new technologies will increasingly become social, religious, and ultimately political concerns. Solutions will not come easily, and they will not please everyone.

Critical Thinking Questions

1. What do you see as the most disturbing aspect of stem cell research? What do you think is the most positive? Explain your answers.

2. Do you approve of the non-reproductive cloning of human embryos for stem cell research? Why or why not?

3. Do you approve of the decision of the parents to conceive a second child partly to provide donor cells for their daughter? Why or why not? What would you do in their position?

Sources

Kline, Ronald M. "Whose Blood Is It, Anyway?" *Scientific American* 284(4): 42–49.

Stem Cells: Scientific Progress and Future Research Directions. Report from the National Institutes of Health to Secretary of Health and Human Services, Tommy G. Thompson, February 2001. Internet version obtained from the NIH website: **www.nih.gov/news/stemcell/scireport/htm.**

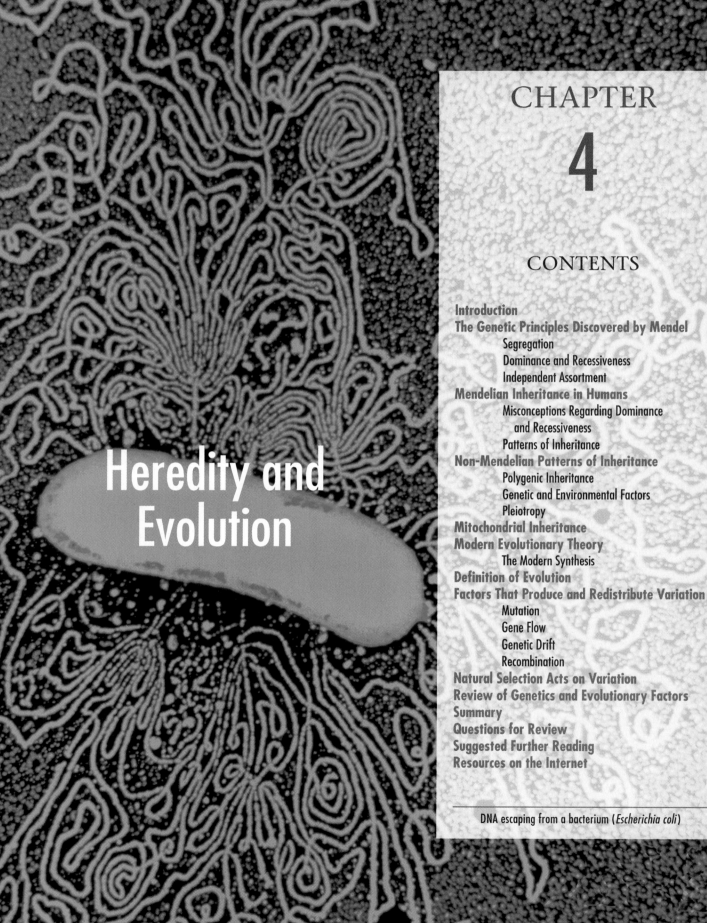

CHAPTER

4

CONTENTS

Heredity and Evolution

DNA escaping from a bacterium (*Escherichia coli*)

Introduction

This chapter is roughly divided into two parts. In the first, we continue with the discussion of genetic principles we began in Chapter 3. That chapter dealt with the structure and function of DNA within the cell. In this chapter, we shift to a somewhat broader perspective and focus on the principles that guide the transmission of traits from parent to offspring. These principles, first elucidated by Gregor Mendel, form much of the basis of modern genetics, and we cover them in some detail because of their relevance to the evolutionary process. The second part of this chapter integrates the basics of DNA function and Mendelian patterns of inheritance into a comprehensive theory of the forces that guide biological evolution.

For at least 10,000 years, beginning with the domestication of plants and animals, people have attempted to explain how traits are passed from parents to offspring. Although most theories have been far from accurate, farmers and herders have known for millennia that they could enhance the frequency and expression of desirable attributes through selective breeding. However, exactly why desirable traits were often seen in the offspring of carefully chosen breeding stock remained a mystery. It was equally curious when offspring did not show the traits their human owners had hoped for.

From the time ancient Greek philosophers considered the problem until well into the nineteenth century, one predominant belief was that characteristics of offspring resulted from the *blending* of parental traits. Blending was supposedly accomplished by means of particles that existed in every part of the body. These so-called *pangenes* contained miniatures of the body part (limbs, organs, etc.) from which the particles derived, and they traveled through the blood to the reproductive organs and blended with particles of another individual during reproduction. There were variations on the theme of *pangenesis,* and numerous scholars, including Charles Darwin, adhered to some aspects of the theory.

The Genetic Principles Discovered by Mendel

It was not until Gregor Mendel (1822–1884) addressed the question of heredity that it began to be resolved (Fig. 4–1). Mendel was a monk living in an Augustinian abbey at Brno in what is now the Czech Republic. At the time he began his research, he had already acquired scientific expertise in botany, physics, and mathematics at the University of Vienna and had conducted various experiments in the monastery gardens. These experiments led him to explore the various ways in which physical traits, such as color or height, could be expressed in plant **hybrids.** He hoped that by making crosses between two strains of *purebred* plants and examining their progeny, he could determine (and predict) how many different forms of hybrids there were, arrange the forms according to generation, and evaluate the proportion of each type in each generation.

Mendel chose to work with common garden peas, and he focused on seven different traits, each of which could be expressed in two ways (Table 4–1). Because the genetic principles Mendel discovered apply to humans as well as to peas (and all other biological organisms), we discuss his work in some detail to illustrate the basic rules of inheritance.

Segregation

The plants Mendel used in the first cross were designated the *parental,* or *P,* generation, and all were either tall or short. The hybrid offspring of the P generation were designated the F_1 (first filial) generation, and as they matured, they were not

See the following sections of the CD-ROM for topics covered in this chapter: Virtual Lab 2, sections II and III.

Courtesy, Dept. of Library Services, American Museum of Natural History

FIGURE 4–1
Gregor Mendel.

Hybrids
Offspring of individuals that differ with regard to certain traits or certain aspects of genetic makeup; heterozygotes.

Heredity and Evolution

TABLE 4–1   The Seven Garden Pea Characteristics Studied by Mendel

Characteristic	Dominant Trait	Recessive Trait
1. Form of ripe seed	Smooth	Wrinkled
2. Color of seed albumen	Yellow	Green
3. Color of seed coat	Gray	White
4. Form of ripe pods	Inflated	Constricted
5. Color of unripe pods	Green	Yellow
6. Position of flowers on stem	Axial	Terminal
7. Length of stem	Tall	Short

intermediate in height, as blending theories of inheritance would have predicted. To the contrary, they were all tall (Fig. 4–2).

Next, Mendel allowed the F_1 plants to self-fertilize and produce a second generation of plants (the F_2 generation). But this time, only approximately $3/4$ of the offspring were tall, and the remaining $1/4$ were short. One expression of the trait completely disappeared in the F_1 generation and reappeared in the F_2 generation. Moreover, the expression that was present in the F_1 generation was more common in the F_2 plants, occurring in a ratio of approximately 3:1.

These results suggested that different expressions of a trait were controlled by discrete *units,* which occurred in pairs, and that offspring inherited one unit from each parent. Mendel correctly concluded that the members of a pair of units controlling a trait somehow separated into different sex cells and were again united with another member during fertilization of the egg. This is Mendel's *first principle of inheritance,* known as the **principle of segregation.**

Today we know that meiosis explains Mendel's principle of segregation. You will remember that during meiosis, paired chromosomes, and the genes they carry, separate from one another and are distributed to different gametes. However, in the zygote, the full complement of chromosomes is restored, and both members of each chromosome pair are present in the offspring.

Dominance and Recessiveness

Mendel also recognized that the expression that was absent in the F_1 plants had not actually disappeared at all. It had remained present, but somehow it was masked and could not be expressed. To describe the trait that seemed to be lost, Mendel used the term **recessive**; the trait that was expressed was said to be **dominant**. Thus, the important principles of *dominance* and *recessiveness* were formulated, and they remain today as important concepts in the field of genetics.

You will recall that a *gene* is a segment of DNA that directs the production of a specific protein or part of a protein. Furthermore, the location of a gene on a chromosome is its *locus (pl.,* loci). At numerous genetic loci, however, there is more than one possible form of the gene, and these variations of genes at specific loci are called *alleles.* Therefore, alleles are alternate forms of a gene that can direct the cell to produce slightly different forms of the same protein and, ultimately, different expressions of traits.

As it turns out, plant height in garden peas is controlled by two different alleles at one genetic locus. The allele that determines that a plant will be tall is dominant

Principle of segregation
Genes (alleles) occur in pairs (because chromosomes occur in pairs). During gamete production, the members of each gene pair separate, so that each gamete contains one member of each pair. During fertilization, the full number of chromosomes is restored, and members of gene or allele pairs are reunited.

½ alleles is passed

Recessive
Describing a trait that is not expressed in heterozygotes; also refers to the allele that governs the trait. For a recessive allele to be expressed, there must be two copies of the allele (i.e., the individual must be homozygous).

Dominant
Describing a trait governed by an allele that can be expressed in the presence of another, different allele (i.e., in heterozygotes). Dominant alleles prevent the expression of recessive alleles in heterozygotes. (This is the definition of *complete* dominance.)

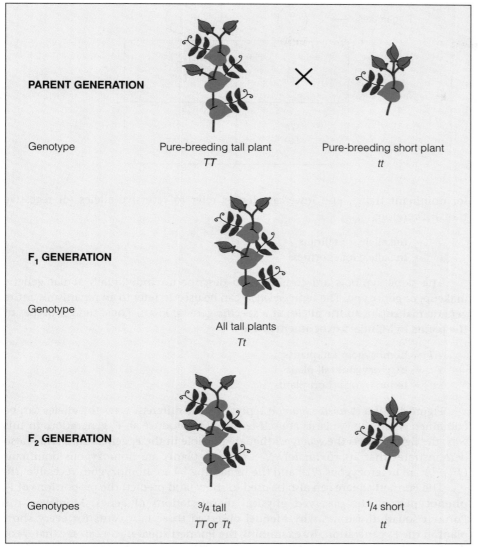

FIGURE 4–2
Results of crosses when only one trait at a time is considered.

PARENT GENERATION

Genotype

Pure-breeding tall plant
TT

×

Pure-breeding short plant
tt

F₁ GENERATION

Genotype

All tall plants
Tt

F₂ GENERATION

Genotypes

³/₄ tall
TT or *Tt*

¹/₄ short
tt

to the allele for short. (It is worth mentioning that height is not governed in this manner in all plants.)

In Mendel's experiments, all the parent (P) plants had two copies of the same allele, either dominant or recessive, depending on whether they were tall or short. When two copies of the same allele are present, the individual is said to be **homozygous.** Thus, all the tall P plants were homozygous for the dominant allele, and all the short P plants were homozygous for the recessive allele. (This homozygosity explains why tall plants crossed with tall plants produced only tall offspring, and short plants crossed with short plants produced all short offspring; i.e., they were "pure lines" and lacked genetic variation at this locus.) However, all the F₁ plants (hybrids) had inherited one allele from each parent plant; therefore, they all possessed two different alleles at specific loci. Individuals that possess two different alleles at a locus are **heterozygous.**

Figure 4–2 illustrates the crosses that Mendel initially performed. Geneticists use standard symbols to refer to alleles. Uppercase letters refer to dominant alleles

Homozygous
Having the same allele at the same locus on both members of a chromosome pair.

Heterozygous
Having different alleles at the same locus on members of a chromosome pair.

FIGURE 4–3
Punnett square representing possible genotypes and phenotypes and their proportions in the F₂ generation. The circles across the top and at the left of the Punnett square represent the gametes of the F₁ parents. The four squares illustrate that ¼ of the F₂ plants can be expected to be homozygous tall (*TT*); another ½ also can be expected to be tall but will be heterozygous (*Tt*); and the remaining ¼ can be expected to be short (*tt*). Thus, ¾ can be expected to be tall and ¼ to be short.

 See Virtual Lab 2, section II for a Punnett square exercise.

Genotype
The genetic makeup of an individual. Genotype can refer to an organism's entire genetic makeup or to the alleles at a particular locus.

(or dominant traits), and lowercase letters refer to recessive alleles (or recessive traits). Therefore,

T = the allele for tallness
t = the allele for shortness

The same symbols are combined to describe an individual's actual genetic makeup, or **genotype.** The term *genotype* can be used to refer to an organism's entire genetic makeup or to the alleles at a specific genetic locus. Thus, the genotypes of the plants in Mendel's experiments were

TT = homozygous tall plants
Tt = heterozygous tall plants
tt = homozygous short plants

Figure 4–3 is a *Punnett square.* It represents the different ways the alleles can be combined when the F₁ plants are self-fertilized to produce an F₂ generation. In this way, the figure shows the *genotypes* that are possible in the F₂ generation, and it also demonstrates that approximately ¼ of the F₂ plants are homozygous dominant (*TT*); ½ are heterozygous (*Tt*); and the remaining ¼ are homozygous recessive (*tt*).

The Punnett square can also be used to show (and predict) the proportions of F₂ **phenotypes**, or the observed physical manifestations of genes. Moreover, the Punnett square illustrates why Mendel observed three tall plants for every short plant in the F₂ generation. By examining the Punnett square, you can see that ¼ of the F₂ plants are tall because they have the *TT* genotype. Furthermore, an additional ½, which are heterozygous (*Tt*), will also be tall because *T* is dominant to *t* and will therefore be expressed in the phenotype. The remaining ¼ are homozygous recessive (*tt*), and they will be short because no dominant allele is present. It is important to note that the *only* way a recessive allele can be expressed is if it occurs with another recessive allele, that is, if the individual is homozygous recessive at the particular locus in question.

In conclusion, ¾ of the F₂ generation will express the dominant phenotype, and ¼ will show the recessive phenotype. This relationship is expressed as a **phenotypic ratio** of 3:1 and typifies all **Mendelian traits** (characteristics governed by only one genetic locus) when only two alleles are involved, one of which is completely dominant to the other.

Phenotypes
The observable or detectable physical characteristics of an organism; the detectable expressions of genotypes.

Phenotypic ratio
The proportion of one phenotype to other phenotypes in a group of organisms. For example, Mendel observed that there were approximately three tall plants for every short plant in the F₂ generation. This is expressed as a phenotypic ratio of 3:1.

Mendelian traits
Characteristics that are influenced by alleles at only one genetic locus. Examples include many blood types, such as ABO. Many genetic disorders, including sickle-cell anemia and Tay-Sachs disease, are also Mendelian traits.

Independent Assortment

Mendel also made crosses in which two traits were considered simultaneously to see if they tended to be inherited together. Figure 4–4 illustrates that the recessive traits disappeared in the F₁ generation and reappeared in the F₂ plants, but the combinations of characteristics occurred in different proportions because plant height and

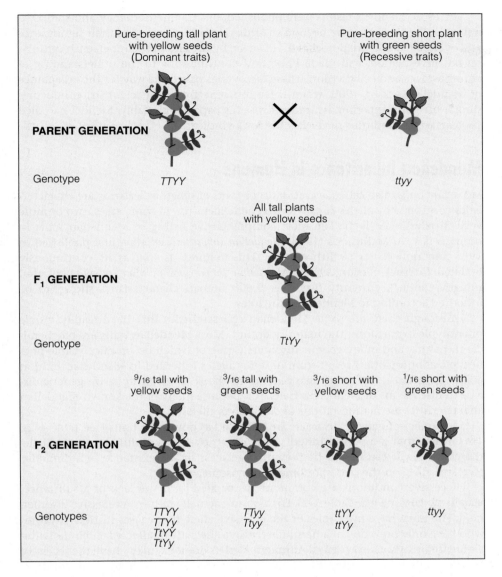

Pure-breeding tall plant
with yellow seeds
(Dominant traits)

Pure-breeding short plant
with green seeds
(Recessive traits)

PARENT GENERATION

Genotype

TTYY

ttyy

All tall plants
with yellow seeds

F₁ GENERATION

Genotype

TtYy

9/16 tall with
yellow seeds

3/16 tall with
green seeds

3/16 short with
yellow seeds

1/16 short with
green seeds

F₂ GENERATION

Genotypes

TTYY
TTYy
TtYY
TtYy

TTyy
Ttyy

ttYY
ttYy

ttyy

FIGURE 4–4
Results of crosses when two traits are considered simultaneously. Stem length and seed color are independent of each other. Also shown are the genotypes associated with each phenotype. Note that the ratio of tall plants to short plants is $^3/_4$ to $^1/_4$, or 3:1, the same as in Figure 4–2. The ratio of yellow to green seeds is also 3:1. Note that the phenotypic ratios in the F_2 generation are 9:3:3:1.

seed color are independent of each other. In other words, there is nothing to dictate that a tall plant must have yellow (or green) seeds, because the allele for tallness has a 50-50 chance of ending up with the allele for either green or yellow seeds.

Mendel stated this relationship as the **principle of independent assortment,** which says that the genes that code for different traits assort independently of each other during gamete formation. Today we know that this occurs because the genetic loci controlling these two characteristics are located on different chromosomes, and during meiosis, chromosomes travel to newly forming cells independently of one another. But if Mendel had used just *any* two traits, his results might have been quite different. For example, if the two traits in question had been influenced by **linked** genes (i.e., genes located on the same chromosome), Mendel's results would have been considerably altered. Because linked genes usually remain together during meiosis, they are not independent of one another; therefore, the traits they influence do not conform to the ratios predicted by independent assortment. While Mendel did not know about linkage, he was certainly aware that all characteristics did not sort out independently of one another in the F_2 generation. He therefore reported only on those traits that did in fact illustrate independent assortment.

Principle of independent assortment
The distribution of one pair of alleles into gametes does not influence the distribution of another pair. The genes controlling different traits are inherited independently of one another.

unless...

Linked
Describing genetic loci or genes located on the same chromosome.

In 1866, Mendel's results were published, but the methodology and statistical nature of the research were beyond the thinking of the time, and their significance was overlooked and unappreciated. However, by the end of the nineteenth century, several investigators had made important contributions to the understanding of chromosomes and cell division. These discoveries paved the way for the acceptance of Mendel's work by 1900, when three different groups of scientists, conducting similar breeding experiments, came across his paper. Regrettably, Mendel had died 16 years earlier and thus never saw his work vindicated.

Mendelian Inheritance in Humans

Mendelian traits, also called *discrete traits* or traits *of simple inheritance,* are characteristics controlled by alleles at only one genetic locus (or, in some cases, two or more very closely linked loci). The most comprehensive listing of Mendelian traits in humans is V. A. McKusick's (1998) *Mendelian Inheritance in Man,* first published in 1965 and now in its twelfth edition. This volume, as well as its continuously updated Internet version, *Online Mendelian Inheritance in Man* (www3.ncbi.nlm. nih.gov/Omim/), currently lists over 9,600 human characteristics shown to be inherited according to Mendelian principles.

Although there are some Mendelian characteristics that have readily visible phenotypic expressions, the majority do not. Most Mendelian traits are biochemical in nature, and many genetic disorders (some of which do produce visible phenotypic abnormalities) result from harmful alleles inherited in Mendelian fashion (Table 4–2). Thus, if it seems like genetics textbooks overly emphasize genetic disease in discussions of Mendelian traits, it is because many of the known Mendelian characteristics are manifestations of deleterious alleles.

A number of genetic disorders are inherited as dominant traits (see Table 4–2). This means that if a person inherits only one copy of a harmful, dominant allele, the condition it causes will be present, regardless of the existence of a different, recessive allele on the corresponding chromosome.

Recessive conditions are commonly associated with the lack of a substance, usually an enzyme (see Table 4–2). For a person actually to have a recessive disorder, he or she must have *two* copies of the recessive allele that causes it. Heterozygotes who have only one copy of a harmful recessive allele are unaffected. Such individuals are frequently called *carriers.* Although carriers do not actually have the recessive condition they carry, they can pass the allele that causes it to their children. (Remember, half their gametes will carry the recessive allele.) If their mate is also a carrier, then it is possible for them to have a child who will be homozygous for the allele, and that child will be affected. In fact, in a mating between two carriers, the risk of having an affected child is 25 percent (refer back to Fig. 4–3).

Among the best examples of nondeleterious human Mendelian traits are the blood groups, such as the ABO system. The ABO system is governed by three alleles, *A, B,* and *O,* found at the ABO locus on the ninth chromosome. These alleles determine which ABO blood type an individual has by coding for the production of substances called **antigens** on the surface of red blood cells. If only antigen A is present, the blood type (phenotype) is A; if only B is present, the blood type is B; if both are present, the blood type is AB; and when neither is present, the blood type is O.

Dominance and recessiveness are clearly illustrated by the ABO system. The *O* allele is recessive to both *A* and *B;* therefore, if a person has type O blood, he or she must be homozygous for (have two copies of) the *O* allele. However, since both *A* and *B* are dominant to *O,* an individual with blood type A can actually have one of two genotypes: *AA* or *AO.* The same is true of type B, which results from the genotypes *BB* and *BO* (Table 4–3). However, type AB presents a slightly different situation and is an example of **codominance.**

See Virtual Lab 2, section II for an example of human blood groups.

ABO is Mendelian

Antigens
Large molecules found on the surface of cells. Several different loci governing antigens on red and white blood cells are known. (Foreign antigens provoke an immune response in individuals.)

Codominance
The expression of two alleles in heterozygotes. In this situation, neither allele is dominant or recessive, thus both influence the phenotype.

TABLE 4–2   Some Mendelian Traits in Humans

Dominant Traits		Recessive Traits	
Condition	**Manifestations**	**Condition**	**Manifestations**
Achondroplasia	Dwarfism due to growth defects involving the long bones of the arms and legs; trunk and head size usually normal.	Cystic fibrosis	Among the most common genetic (Mendelian) disorders among European Americans; abnormal secretions of the exocrine glands, with pronounced involvement of the pancreas; most patients develop obstructive lung disease. Until the recent development of new treatments, only about half of all patients survived to early adulthood.
Brachydactyly	Shortened fingers and toes.		
Familial hyper-cholesterolemia	Elevated cholesterol levels and cholesterol plaque deposition; a leading cause of heart disease, with death frequently occurring by middle age.		
Neurofibromatosis	Symptoms range from the appearance of abnormal skin pigmentation to large tumors resulting in gross deformities; can, in extreme cases, lead to paralysis, blindness, and death.	Tay-Sachs disease	Most common among Ashkenazi Jews; degeneration of the nervous system beginning at about 6 months of age; lethal by age 2 or 3 years.
		Phenylketonuria (PKU)	Inability to metabolize the amino acid phenylalanine; results in mental retardation if left untreated during childhood; treatment involves strict dietary management and some supplementation.
Marfan syndrome	The eyes and cardiovascular and skeletal systems are affected; symptoms include greater than average height, long arms and legs, eye problems, and enlargement of the aorta; death due to rupture of the aorta is common. (Abraham Lincoln may have had Marfan syndrome.)	Albinism	Inability to produce normal amounts of the pigment melanin; results in very fair, untannable skin, light blond hair, and light eyes; may also be associated with vision problems. (There is more than one form of albinism.)
Huntington disease	Progressive degeneration of the nervous system accompanied by dementia and seizures; age of onset variable but commonly between 30 and 40 years.	Sickle-cell anemia	Abnormal form of hemoglobin (Hb^S) that results in collapsed red blood cells, blockage of capillaries, reduced blood flow to organs, and, without treatment, death.
Camptodactyly	Malformation of the hands whereby the fingers, usually the little finger, is permanently contracted.	Thalassemia	A group of disorders characterized by reduced or absent alpha or beta chains in the hemoglobin molecule; results in severe anemia and, in some forms, death.
Hypodontia of upper lateral incisors	Upper lateral incisors are absent or only partially formed (peg-shaped). Pegged incisors are a partial expression of the allele.	Absence of permanent dentition	Failure of the permanent dentition to erupt. The primary dentition is not affected.
Cleft chin	Dimple or depression in the middle of the chin; less prominent in females than males.		
PTC tasting	The ability to taste the bitter substance phenylthiocarbamide (PTC). Tasting thresholds vary, suggesting that alleles at another locus may also exert an influence.		

Codominance is seen when two different alleles occur in heterozygous condition, but instead of one having the ability to mask the expression of the other, the products of *both* are expressed in the phenotype. Therefore, when both *A* and *B* alleles are present, both A and B antigens can be detected on the surface of red blood cells.

Heredity and Evolution

TABLE 4–3 ABO Genotypes and Associated Phenotypes

Genotype	Antigens on Red Blood Cells	ABO Blood Type (Phenotype)
AA, AO	A	A
BB, BO	B	B
AB	A and B	AB
OO	None	O

Misconceptions Regarding Dominance and Recessiveness

Traditional methods of teaching genetics have led to some misunderstanding of dominance and recessiveness. Perhaps the most glaring misunderstanding of this type is one that is still perpetuated in some high school biology textbooks, namely that eye color is a Mendelian characteristic and that brown eyes are dominant to blue eyes. However, eye color is not a Mendelian trait. In fact, it is influenced by alleles occurring at two or perhaps three loci. Interestingly, however, it does appear that at one of these loci, the allele for blue eye color is recessive to that for brown eye color; and at another locus, the allele for blue is recessive to that for green eye color.

Virtually all introductory students (and most people in general) also have the impression that dominance and recessiveness are all-or-nothing situations. This misconception especially pertains to recessive alleles, and the general view is that when these alleles occur in heterozygotes (i.e., carriers), they have absolutely no effect on the phenotype—that is, they are completely inactivated by the presence of another (dominant) allele. Certainly, this is how it appeared to Gregor Mendel and, until the last two or three decades, to most geneticists.

However, various biochemical techniques, unavailable in the past but in wide use today, have demonstrated that recessive alleles do indeed exert some influence on phenotype, although these effects are not usually detectable through simple observation. Indeed, it is now clear that our *perception* of recessive alleles greatly depends on one important factor: whether we examine them at the directly observable phenotypic level or the biochemical level.

Scientists now know of several recessive alleles that do indeed produce detectable phenotypic effects in heterozygotes. Consider Tay-Sachs disease, a lethal condition that results from the inability to produce the enzyme hexosaminidase A (see Table 4–2). This inability, seen in people who are homozygous for a recessive allele (*ts*) on chromosome 15, invariably results in death by early childhood. Carriers do not have the disease, and practically speaking, they are unaffected. However, in 1979, it was shown that Tay-Sachs carriers, although functionally normal, have only about 40 to 60 percent of the amount of the enzyme seen in normal people. In fact, there are now voluntary tests to screen carriers in populations at risk for Tay-Sachs disease.

Similar misconceptions also relate to dominant alleles. The majority of people see dominant alleles as somehow "stronger" or "better," and there is always the mistaken notion that dominant alleles are more common in populations. These misconceptions undoubtedly stem partly from the label "dominant" and the connotations that the term carries. But in genetic usage, those connotations are somewhat misleading. If dominant alleles were always more common, then a majority of people would be affected by such conditions as achondroplasia and Marfan syndrome (see Table 4–2).

Clearly, the relationships between recessive and dominant alleles and their functions are more complicated than they would appear at first glance. Previously held views of dominance and recessiveness were guided by available technologies; as genetic technologies continue to change, new theories may emerge, and our perceptions will be further altered. In fact, it is possible that one day the concepts of dominance and recessiveness, as traditionally taught, will be obsolete.

Patterns of Inheritance

It is of obvious importance to be able to establish the pattern of inheritance of genetic traits, especially those that result in serious disease. Equally important, particularly in families with a history of inherited disorders, is the ability to determine an individual's risk of inheriting deleterious alleles or expressing symptoms. But because humans cannot be used in experimental breeding programs, as were Mendel's peas, a more indirect approach must be used to demonstrate patterns of inheritance. The principal technique traditionally used in human genetic studies has been the construction of a **pedigree chart**, a diagram of matings and offspring in a family over the span of a few generations.

Pedigree analysis helps determine if a trait is indeed Mendelian in nature. It also helps establish the mode of inheritance. From considerations of whether the locus that influences a particular trait is located on an autosome or sex chromosome and whether it is dominant or recessive, six different modes of Mendelian inheritance have been recognized in humans: *autosomal dominant, autosomal recessive, X-linked recessive, X-linked dominant, Y-linked,* and *mitochondrial.* We shall discuss the first three of these in some detail.

Standardized symbols are used in the construction of pedigree charts. Squares and circles represent males and females, respectively. Horizontal lines connecting individuals indicate matings, and offspring are connected to horizontal mating lines by vertical lines. Siblings are joined to one another by a horizontal line to which they are connected by vertical lines (Fig. 4–5).

Autosomal Dominant Traits   As the term implies, autosomal dominant traits are governed by loci on autosomes (i.e., any chromosomes except X or Y). One example of an autosomal dominant trait is brachydactyly, a condition characterized by malformed hands and shortened fingers (see Table 4–2).

Because brachydactyly is caused by a dominant allele, anyone who inherits just one copy will express the trait. (For purposes of this discussion, we will use the symbol *B* to refer to the dominant allele that causes the condition, and *b* for the recessive, normal allele.) Since the allele is rare, virtually everyone who has brachydactyly is a heterozygote (*Bb*). (Generally speaking, individuals who are homozygous dominant for rare, deleterious alleles are uncommon. Mutant alleles that produce abnormalities in heterozygotes cause such extreme defects in homozygotes that affected fetuses frequently abort prior to reaching full term.) Unaffected individuals are homozygous recessive (*bb*).

Figure 4–6 is a partial pedigree for brachydactyly. It is apparent from this pedigree that all affected members have at least one affected parent; thus, the abnormality does not skip generations. This pattern is true of all autosomal dominant traits. Another characteristic of autosomal dominant traits is that there is no sex bias, and males and females are more or less equally affected.

One other fact illustrated by Figure 4–6 is that approximately half the offspring of affected parents are also affected. This proportion is what we would predict for an autosomal dominant trait where only one parent is affected, and it is explained by events in meiosis as well as by Mendel's principle of segregation (Fig. 4–7).

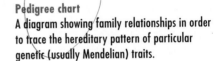

Pedigree chart
A diagram showing family relationships in order to trace the hereditary pattern of particular genetic (usually Mendelian) traits.

Parents

Offspring (siblings)

FIGURE 4–5
Typical symbols used in pedigree charts.

FIGURE 4–6
Inheritance of an autosomal dominant trait: a human pedigree for brachydactyly. Why are individuals 5, 11, 14, 15, and 17 unaffected? What is the genotype of all affected individuals?

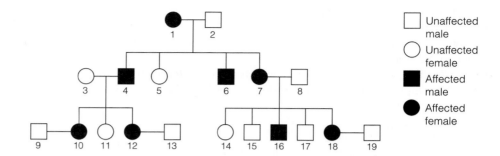

Unaffected male

Unaffected female

Affected male

Affected female

FIGURE 4–7
The pattern of inheritance of autosomal dominant traits is the direct result of the distribution of chromosomes, and the alleles they carry, into gametes during meiosis. (a) Diagrammatic representation of possible gametes produced by two parents, one with brachydactyly and another with normal hands and fingers. The brachydactylous individual can produce two types of gametes: half with the dominant allele (*B*) and half with the recessive allele (*b*). All the gametes produced by the normal parent will carry the recessive allele. (b) A Punnett square depicting the possible genotypes in the offspring of one parent with brachydactyly (*Bb*) and one with normal hands and fingers (*bb*). Statistically speaking, half the offspring would be expected to have the *Bb* genotype and thus brachydactyly. The other half would be homozygous recessive (*bb*) and would be normal.

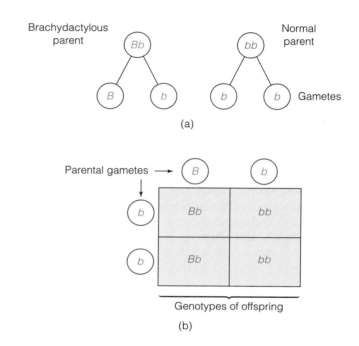

Autosomal Recessive Traits   Autosomal recessive traits are also influenced by loci on autosomes but show a different pattern of inheritance. A good example is shown in Figure 4–8, a pedigree for albinism, a metabolic disorder causing deficient production of a skin pigment called melanin (see Chapter 15). This disorder is phenotypically expressed as very light skin, hair, and iris of the eyes.

Actually, albinism is a group of genetic disorders, each influenced by different loci. Some forms affect only the eyes, while others also involve skin and hair. The most widely known variety of albinism does influence eye, skin, and hair pigmentation and is caused by an autosomal recessive allele. The frequency of this particular form of albinism varies widely among populations, with an incidence of about 1 in 37,000 in American whites but a much higher frequency, approaching 1 in 200, among Hopi Indians. How populations have come to be so different in the frequencies of various alleles (such as those for albinism) will be a major focus of Chapter 14.

Pedigrees for autosomal recessive traits show obvious differences from those for autosomal dominant characteristics. For one thing, recessive traits often appear to skip generations, so that an affected offspring is produced by two phenotypically normal parents. In fact, most affected individuals have unaffected parents. In addition, the proportion of affected offspring from most matings is less than the 50 percent so

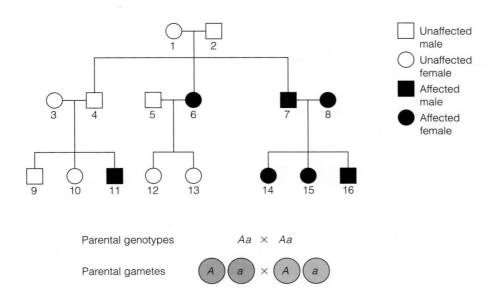

FIGURE 4–8
Partial pedigree for albinism, an autosomal recessive trait. Why are some of the offspring of affected individuals unaffected? Individuals 6 and 7, children of unaffected parents, are affected. Why? Four individuals are *definitely* unaffected carriers. Which ones are they? Does the pattern of inheritance in this chart conform to the *expected* ratios shown in Figure 4–9?

FIGURE 4–9
A cross between two phenotypically normal parents, both of whom are carriers of the albinism allele. From a mating such as this between two carriers, we would expect the following possible proportions of genotypes and phenotypes in the offspring: homozygous dominants (*AA*) with normal phenotype, 25 percent; heterozygotes, or carriers (*Aa*), with normal phenotype, 50 percent; and homozygous recessives (*aa*) with albinism, 25 percent. This yields the phenotypic ratio of three normal to one albino.

frequently seen in pedigrees for autosomal dominant traits. However, when both parents have the trait, all the offspring will be affected. As in the pattern for autosomal dominant traits, males and females are equally affected.

As Figure 4–9 illustrates, the Mendelian principle of segregation explains the pattern of inheritance of autosomal recessive traits. In fact, this pattern is the very one first elucidated by Mendel in his pea experiments (refer back to Fig. 4–3). Unaffected parents who produce an albino child *must* both be carriers, and their child is homozygous for the recessive allele that causes the abnormality. The Punnett square in Figure 4–9 shows how such a mating produces both unaffected and affected offspring in predictable proportions—the typical phenotypic ratio of 3:1.

Sex-Linked Traits Sex-linked traits are controlled by loci on sex chromosomes; the term *sex-linked* simply refers to the fact that these loci are located on the X or Y chromosome. (Almost all such loci have no role in primary sex determination.) Of the more than 240 traits suspected to result from this form of inheritance, almost all are controlled by loci on the X chromosome (Table 4–4). Only recently have any traits been traced to regions on the Y chromosome, where at least four loci have been identified. One is involved in determining maleness (the TDF locus), and one other may be involved with sperm production (the H-Y locus). Because of the scarcity of known Y-linked traits, they are not dealt with here.

The best known of the sex-linked traits is hemophilia, caused by a recessive allele at a locus on the X chromosome. This type of condition is thus said to be *X-linked recessive*. Hemophilia results from the lack of a clotting factor in the blood (factor VIII), and affected individuals suffer bleeding episodes and may hemorrhage to death from incidents that most of us would consider trivial.

TABLE 4–4   Some Mendelian Disorders Inherited as X-Linked Recessive Traits in Humans

Condition	Manifestations
G-6-PD (glucose-6-phosphate dehydrogenase) deficiency	Lack of an enzyme (G-6-PD) in red blood cells; produces severe, sometimes fatal anemia in the presence of certain foods (e.g., fava beans) and/or drugs (e.g., the antimalarial drug primaquin). (See p. 385 for further discussion relating to a possible link with malaria as a selective agent.)
Muscular dystrophy	One form; other forms can be inherited as autosomal recessives. Progressive weakness and atrophy of muscles beginning in early childhood; continues to progress throughout life; some female carriers may develop heart problems.
Red-green color blindness	Actually, there are two separate forms, one involving the perception of red and the other affecting only the perception of green. About 8 percent of European males have an impaired ability to distinguish green.
Lesch-Nyhan disease	Impaired motor development noticeable by 5 months; progressive motor impairment, diminished kidney function, self-mutilation, and early death.
Hemophilia	There are three forms; two (hemophilia A and B) are X-linked. In hemophilia A, a clotting factor is missing; hemophilia B is caused by a defective clotting factor. Both produce abnormal internal and external bleeding from minor injuries; severe pain is a frequent accompaniment; without treatment, death usually occurs before adulthood.
Ichthyosis	There are several forms; one is X-linked. A skin condition due to lack of an enzyme; characterized by scaly, brown lesions on the extremities and trunk. In the past, people with this condition sometimes were exhibited in circuses and sideshows as "the alligator man."

The most famous pedigree documenting this malady is that of Queen Victoria and her descendants (shown in Fig. 4–10). The most striking feature shown by this pattern of inheritance is that usually only males are affected. To understand this pattern, once again we must refer to the principle of segregation, but with one additional stipulation: We are now dealing with *sex chromosomes*.

Because they possess two X chromosomes, females show the same pattern of expression of X-linked traits as for autosomal traits. That is, the only way an X-linked recessive allele can be phenotypically expressed in a female is when she is homozygous for it. Therefore, heterozygous females are unaffected. In cases where female heterozygotes express an X-linked trait, it is an X-linked dominant.

On the other hand, since males are XY and have only one X chromosome, they possess only one copy of an X-linked gene. With only one X chromosome, males can never be homozygous or heterozygous for X-linked loci and are thus referred to as **hemizygous.** Moreover, males do not exhibit dominance or recessiveness for X-linked traits because *any* allele located on their X chromosome, even a recessive one, will be expressed. In fact, any time a recessive allele occurs in a hemizygous state, it is expressed.

The difference between males and females in number of X chromosomes is directly related to the incidence of hemophilia seen in Figure 4–10. Females who have one copy of the hemophilia allele are carriers for the trait. Although they may have some tendency toward bleeding, they are not severely affected. On the other hand, males who have the allele on their *only* X chromosome are severely afflicted, and prior to the availability of recent therapy, they faced short and painful lives.

when only one trait is genetically occurrent but phenotypically present

Hemizygous
(*hemi*, meaning "half") Having only one member of a pair of alleles. Because males have only one X chromosome, all their X-linked alleles are hemizygous. All recessive alleles on a male's X chromosome are expressed in the phenotype.

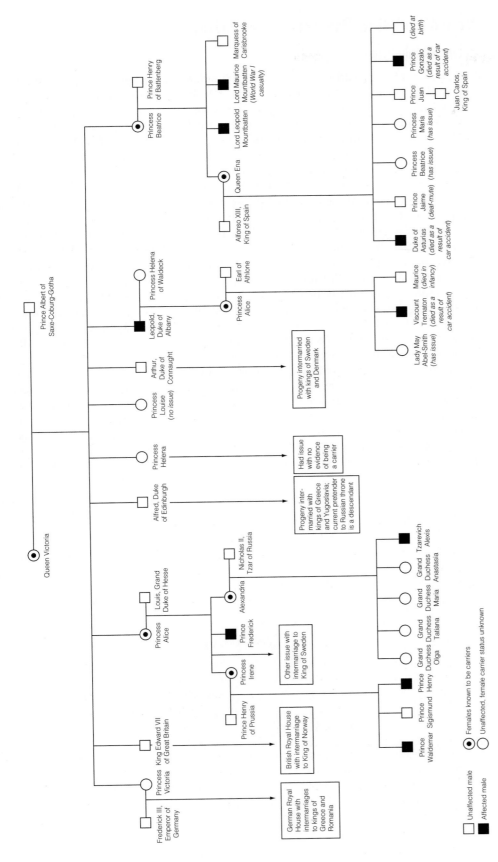

FIGURE 4–10
Pedigree for Queen Victoria and some of her descendants, showing inheritance of hemophilia, an X-linked recessive trait in humans.

Non-Mendelian Patterns of Inheritance

Polygenic Inheritance

Mendelian traits are said to be *discrete,* or *discontinuous,* because their phenotypic expressions do not overlap; rather, they fall into clearly defined categories (Fig. 4–11a). For example, Mendel's pea plants were either short or tall, but none was intermediate in height. In the ABO system, the four phenotypes are completely distinct from one another; that is, there is no intermediate form between type A and type B to represent a gradation between the two. In other words, Mendelian traits do not show *continuous* variation.

However, many traits do have a wide range of phenotypic expressions that form a graded series. These are called **polygenic,** or *continuous,* traits (Fig. 4–11b). While Mendelian traits are governed by only one genetic locus, polygenic characteristics are influenced by alleles at two or more loci, with each locus making a contribution to the phenotype. For example, one of the most frequently cited instances of polygenic inheritance in humans is skin color. The single most important factor influencing skin color is the amount of the pigment melanin present.

Melanin production is believed to be influenced by between three and six genetic loci, with each locus having at least two alleles, neither of which is dominant. Individuals having only alleles for more melanin production (i.e., they are homozygous at all loci) have the darkest skin. Those having only alleles that code for reduced melanin production have very fair skin.

As there are perhaps six loci and at least 12 alleles, there are numerous ways in which these alleles can combine in individuals. If an individual inherits 11 alleles coding for maximum pigmentation and only one for reduced melanin production, skin color will be very dark. A person who inherits a higher proportion of reduced pigmentation alleles will have lighter skin color. This is because in this system, as in some other polygenic systems, there is an *additive effect.* This means that each allele that codes for melanin production makes a contribution to

Polygenic
Referring to traits that are influenced by genes at two or more loci. Examples of such traits are stature, skin color, and eye color. Many polygenic traits are also influenced by environmental factors.

FIGURE 4–11
(a) This histogram shows the discontinuous distribution of a Mendelian trait (ABO blood type) in a hypothetical population. The expression of the trait is described in terms of frequencies.
(b) This histogram represents the continuous expression of a polygenic trait (height) in a large group of people. Note that the percentage of extremely short or tall individuals is low; the majority of people are closer to the mean, or average, height, represented by the vertical line at the center of the distribution.

(a)

(b)

increased melanization (although for some characteristics the contributions of the alleles are not all equal). Likewise, each allele coding for reduced melanin production contributes to reduced pigmentation. Therefore, the effect of multiple alleles at several loci, each making a contribution to individual phenotypes, is to produce continuous variation from very dark to very fair skin within the species. (Skin color is also discussed in Chapter 15.)

Polygenic traits actually account for most of the readily observable phenotypic variation seen in humans, and they have traditionally served as a basis for racial classification (see Chapter 15). In addition to skin color, polygenic inheritance in humans is seen in hair color, weight, stature, eye color (Fig. 4–12), shape of face, shape of nose, and fingerprint pattern. Because they exhibit continuous variation, most polygenic traits can be measured on a scale composed of equal increments. For example, height (stature) is measured in feet and inches (or meters and centimeters). If one were to measure height in a large number of individuals, the distribution of measurements would continue uninterrupted from the shortest extreme to the tallest. That is what is meant by *continuous traits*.

Because polygenic traits usually lend themselves to metric analysis, biologists, geneticists, and physical anthropologists treat them statistically. Although statistical analysis can be complicated, the use of simple summary statistics, such as the *mean* (average) or *standard deviation* (a measure of within-group variation), permits basic descriptions of, and comparisons between, populations. For example, one might be interested in average height in two different populations

© Corbis

Lynn Kilgore

© Corbis

Lynn Kilgore

Lynn Kilgore

Lynn Kilgore

FIGURE 4–12
Examples of the continuous variation seen in human eye color.

and whether or not differences between the two are significant, and if so, why. Or a researcher might determine that in the same geographical area, one group shows significantly more variation in skin color than another, and it would be useful to explain this variability. (You should also note that *all* physical traits measured and statistically treated in fossils are polygenic in nature.)

These particular statistical manipulations are not possible with Mendelian traits simply because those traits cannot be measured in the same manner. They are either present or they are not; they are expressed one way or another and can be described in terms of frequencies. But just because Mendelian traits are not amenable to the same types of statistical tests as polygenic traits does not mean that Mendelian traits are less worthy of study or less informative of genetic processes. It simply means that scientists must approach the study of these two types of inheritance from different perspectives.

Mendelian characteristics can be described in terms of frequency within populations, yielding between-group comparisons regarding incidence. Moreover, these characteristics can also be analyzed for mode of inheritance (dominant or recessive) from pedigree data. Finally, for many Mendelian traits, the approximate or exact position of genetic loci has been identified, making it possible to examine the mechanisms and patterns of inheritance at these loci.

Because polygenic characters are influenced by several loci, they cannot as yet be traced to specific genes on specific chromosomes; therefore, such analysis is currently not possible.

Genetic and Environmental Factors

From the preceding discussion, it might appear that phenotype is solely the expression of the genotype, but this is not true. (Here we use the terms *genotype* and *phenotype* in a broader sense to refer to an individual's *entire* genetic makeup and *all* observable or detectable characteristics.) The genotype sets limits and potentials for development, but it also interacts with the environment, and many aspects of phenotype are influenced by this genetic-environmental interaction. For many traits, scientists have developed statistical methods for calculating what proportion of phenotypic variation is due to genetic or environmental factors. However, it is usually not possible to identify the *specific* environmental components that influence the phenotype.

Many polygenic traits are quite obviously influenced by environmental conditions. Adult stature is strongly affected by the individual's nutritional status during growth and development. One study showed that children of Japanese immigrants to Hawaii were, on average, 3 to 4 inches taller than their parents. This dramatic difference, seen in one generation, was attributed to environmental alteration—specifically to a change in diet (Froelich, 1970).

Other important environmental factors include exposure to sunlight, altitude, temperature, and, unfortunately, increasing levels of exposure to toxic waste and airborne pollutants. All these and many more contribute in complex ways to the continuous phenotypic variation seen in characteristics governed by multiple loci.

Mendelian traits are less likely to be influenced by environmental factors. For example, ABO blood type is determined at fertilization and remains fixed throughout the individual's lifetime, regardless of diet, exposure to ultraviolet radiation, temperature, and so forth.

Mendelian and polygenic inheritance produce different kinds of phenotypic variation. In the former, variation occurs in discrete categories, while in the latter, it is continuous. However, it is important to understand that even for polygenic characteristics, Mendelian principles still apply at individual loci. In other words, if a trait is influenced by seven loci, each one of those loci may have two or more alleles, with some perhaps being dominant to others or with the alleles being codominant. It is the combined action of the alleles at all seven loci, interacting with the environment, that results in observable phenotypic expression.

Pleiotropy

Pleiotropy
A situation whereby several seemingly unrelated phenotypic effects are influenced by the action of a single gene.

Whereas polygenic traits are governed by the actions of several genes, **pleiotropy** is a situation where a single gene influences more than one phenotypic expression. Although this might seem unusual, pleiotropic effects are probably the rule rather than the exception.

The autosomal recessive disorder phenylketonuria (PKU) provides one example of pleiotropy (see Table 4–2). Individuals who are homozygous for the PKU allele do not produce phenylketonurase, the enzyme involved in the initial conversion of the amino acid phenylalanine to another amino acid, tyrosine. Because of this block in the metabolic pathway, phenylalanine breaks down into substances that accumulate in the central nervous system, and without dietary management, they lead to mental retardation. And there are several additional consequences. Because tyrosine is ultimately converted into several other substances, including the pigment melanin, numerous other systems can also be affected. Consequently, one additional manifestation of PKU, owing to a diminished ability to produce melanin, is that affected people usually have blue eyes, fair skin, and light hair.

There are many known examples of pleiotropic genes, including the allele that causes sickle-cell anemia. Although it is not necessary to include a detailed discussion here, it is clear that gene action may exert an influence over a number of seemingly unrelated phenotypic expressions.

Mitochondrial Inheritance

There is another component of inheritance that has gained much attention in recent years, and it involves organelles called *mitochondria* (see p. 43). All cells contain several hundred of these oval-shaped structures that convert energy (derived from the breakdown of nutrients) into a form that can be used by the cell.

Each mitochondrion contains several copies of a ring-shaped DNA molecule, or chromosome. While **mitochondrial DNA (mtDNA)** is distinct from the DNA found within cell nuclei, its molecular structure and functions are the same. The entire molecule has been sequenced and is known to contain around 40 genes that direct the conversion of energy within the cell.

Mitochondrial DNA is subject to mutations just like nuclear DNA, and such mutations can lead to certain genetic disorders, some of which have been traced to specific loci. In general, these disorders result from impaired energy conversion and can produce a wide range of symptoms. Importantly, mitochondrial DNA is transmitted to offspring only from the mother; it is thus the mother who transmits all mitochondrial traits to her offspring of both sexes. This is so because mitochondria occur in cellular cytoplasm, and while egg cells retain their cytoplasm, sperm cells lose theirs prior to fertilization.

Mitochondrial mutation rates have been used as a basis for constructing evolutionary relationships between species. They have also been used, with much controversy, to establish ancestral relationships within the human lineage (see Chapter 13). While these techniques are still being refined and remain the topic of debate, it is clear that we have much to learn from mitochondrial DNA.

Mitochondrial DNA (mtDNA)
DNA found in the mitochondria that is inherited only from the mother.

Modern Evolutionary Theory

By the beginning of the twentieth century, the essential foundations for evolutionary theory had already been developed. Darwin and Wallace had articulated the key principle of natural selection 40 years earlier, and the rediscovery of Mendelian genetics in 1900 contributed the other major component—a mechanism for inheritance. We might expect that these two basic contributions would have been joined rather quickly into a consistent theory of evolution. However, such was not the case. For the first 30 years of the twentieth century, rival explanations emphasized mutation *or* natural selection as the prime mover of evolutionary change. A *synthesis* of these two views was not achieved until the mid-1930s, and we owe much of our current view of the evolutionary process to this intellectual development (see Box 4–1).

BOX 4–1   A CLOSER LOOK

Development of Modern Evolutionary Theory

Our understanding of the evolutionary process came about through contributions of biologists in the United States, Great Britain, and Russia.

While "mutationists" were arguing with "selectionists" about the single primary mechanism in evolution, several population geneticists began to realize that both small genetic changes and natural selection were necessary ingredients in the evolutionary formula.

These population geneticists were largely concerned with mathematical reconstructions of evolution—in particular, measuring those small accumulations of genetic changes in populations over just a few generations. Central figures in these early theoretical developments included Ronald Fisher and J.B.S. Haldane in Great Britain, Sewall Wright in the United States, and Sergei Chetverikov in Russia.

While the work of these scientists often produced brilliant insights (see particularly Fisher's *The Genetical Theory of Natural Selection*, 1930), their conclusions were largely unknown to most evolutionary biologists, especially in North America. It remained, therefore, for someone to transcend these two worlds: the mathematical jargon of the population geneticists and the general constructs of theoretical evolutionary biologists. The scientist who performed this task (and who is credited as the first true synthesizer) was Theodosius Dobzhansky. In his *Genetics and the Origin of Species* (1937), Dobzhansky skillfully integrated the mathematics of population genetics with overall evolutionary theory. His insights then became the basis for a period of tremendous activity in evolutionary thinking that directly led to major contributions by George Gaylord Simpson (who brought paleontology into the synthesis), Ernst Mayr,* and others. In fact, the Modern Synthesis produced by these scientists stood basically unchallenged for an entire generation as *the* explanation of the evolutionary process. In recent years, however, some aspects of this theory have been brought under serious question (see Chapter 8).

---

*For an interesting discussion of the intellectual developments concerning the formulation of modern evolutionary theory, see Ernst Mayr and William B. Provine (eds.), *The Evolutionary Synthesis* (Cambridge, MA.: Harvard University Press, 1980).

The Modern Synthesis

Biologists working on mathematical models of evolutionary change in the late 1920s and early 1930s came to realize that mutational and selective processes were not opposing themes, but that a comprehensive explanation of organic evolution required *both*. Small new changes in the genetic material transmitted from parent to offspring are, in fact, the fuel for natural selection. The two major foundations of the biological sciences had thus been brought together in what Julian Huxley termed the Modern Synthesis.

From such a "modern" (i.e., the middle of the twentieth century onward) perspective, we define evolution as a two-stage process. These two stages are:

Variation (genetic)
Inherited differences between individuals; the basis of all evolutionary change.

1. The production and redistribution of **variation** (inherited differences between individuals)
2. *Natural selection* acting on this variation (whereby inherited differences, or variation, among individuals differentially affect their ability to reproduce successfully)

Definition of Evolution

As discussed in Chapter 2, Darwin saw evolution as the gradual unfolding of new varieties of life from previous forms over long periods of time. This depiction is what most of us think of as evolution, and it is indeed the end result of the evolutionary process. But these long-term effects can come about only by the accumulation of many small genetic changes occurring every generation. To understand how the process of evolution works, we must study these short-term events. Today, we study evolutionary changes occurring between generations in various organisms (including humans) and are able to demonstrate how evolution works. From such a modern genetic perspective, we define **evolution** as *a change in **allele frequency** from one generation to the next.*

Allele frequencies are indicators of the genetic makeup of an interbreeding group of individuals known as a **population.** (We will return to this topic in more detail in Chapter 14.) Let us illustrate the way allele frequencies change (i.e., how evolution occurs) through a simplified example. First of all, we must look at a physical trait that is inherited—in this case, human blood types. The best known of the human blood types is ABO (see pp. 76–78). There are, however, many similar blood type systems controlled by different loci that determine genetically transmitted properties of the red blood cells.

Let us assume that your present class of students represents a population, an interbreeding group of individuals, and that we have ascertained the ABO blood type of each member. (To be considered a population, individuals must choose mates more often from *within* the group than from outside it. Of course, the individuals in your class will not meet this requirement, but for the sake of our example, we will overlook this stipulation.) The proportions of the *A, B,* and *O* alleles are the allele frequencies for this trait. For example, suppose we find that 50 percent of all the ABO alleles in your class are *A,* 40 percent are *B,* and 10 percent are *O.* Then the frequencies of these alleles are *A* = .50, *B* = .40, and *O* = .10.*

Since the frequencies for these genes represent only proportions of a total, it is obvious that allele frequencies can refer only to groups of individuals—that is, populations. Individuals do not have an allele frequency; they have either *A, B,* or *O* (or a combination of these). Nor can individuals change alleles. From conception onward, the genetic composition of an individual is fixed. If you start out with blood type A, you will remain type A. Therefore, an individual cannot evolve: Only a group of individuals—a population—can evolve over time.

What happens when a population evolves? Evolution is not an unusual or mysterious process. In fact, it is incredibly commonplace and may occur between every generation for every group of organisms in the world, including humans. Assume that 25 years from now, we calculate the frequencies of the ABO alleles for the children (offspring) of our classroom population and find the following: *A* = .30, *B* = .40, and *O* = .30.

We can see that the relative proportions have changed: *A* has decreased, *O* has increased, and *B* has remained the same. Such a simple, apparently minor change is what we call evolution. Over the short run of just a few generations, such changes in inherited traits may be only very small, but if further continued and elaborated, the results can and do produce spectacular kinds of adaptation and whole new varieties of life.

Evolution
(modern genetic definition) A change in the frequency of alleles from one generation to the next.

Allele frequency
In a population, the percentage of all the alleles at a locus accounted for by one specific allele.

Population
Within a species, a community of individuals where mates are usually found.

---

*This is a simplified example. Because the ABO system is governed by three alleles, calculating allele frequencies is more complicated than for a two-allele system. The way allele frequencies are calculated for a simple two-allele locus will be shown in Chapter 14.

Microevolution
Small changes occurring within species, such as a change in allele frequencies.

Macroevolution
Changes produced only after many generations, such as the appearance of a new species.

Whether we are talking about the short-term effects (as in our classroom population) from one generation to the next, which is sometimes called **microevolution**, or the long-term effects through time (speciation), sometimes called **macroevolution**, the basic evolutionary mechanisms are similar. As we will discuss in Chapter 8, however, they are not identical.

The question may be asked, How do allele frequencies change? Or, to put it another way, what causes evolution? The modern theory of evolution isolates general factors that can produce alterations in allele frequencies. As we have noted, evolution is a two-stage process. Genetic variation must first be produced and distributed before it can be acted on by natural selection.

Factors That Produce and Redistribute Variation

Mutation

Virtual Lab 2, section III illustrates mutation, gene flow, genetic drift, and recombination.

You have already learned that a molecular alteration in genetic material is one type of mutation. A genetic locus may take one of several alternative forms, which we have defined as alleles (*A, B,* or *O* for example). If one allele changes to another—that is, if the gene itself is altered—a mutation has occurred. In fact, alleles are the results of mutation. For such changes to have evolutionary significance, they must occur in the sex cells, which are passed between generations. Evolution is a change in allele frequencies *between* generations. If mutations do not occur in gametes (either the egg or sperm), they will not be transmitted to the next generation, and no evolutionary change can result. If, however, a genetic change does occur in the sperm or egg of one of the individuals in our classroom (*A* mutates to *B,* for instance), the offspring's blood type also will be altered, causing a minute shift in allele frequencies of that generation. In Chapter 3, we showed how a change in a single DNA base, a *point mutation,* could cause a change in hemoglobin structure (from normal to sickle-cell). Other mutations that produce phenotypic effects (as discussed earlier in this chapter) include the albinism allele, the allele producing brachydactyly, and the alteration causing Tay-Sachs disease.

Actually, it would be rare to see evolution occurring by mutation alone. Mutation rates for any given trait are quite low; thus, mutations would rarely be seen in such a small population as our class. In larger populations, mutations might be observed (1 individual in 10,000, say), but would by themselves have very little impact on shifting allele frequencies. However, when mutation is coupled with natural selection, evolutionary changes not only can occur, but can occur more rapidly.

It is important to remember that mutation is the basic creative force in evolution because it is the *only* way to produce new genetic variation either in the form of new genetic material or in new arrangements of it. Its key role in the production of variation represents the first stage of the evolutionary process. Darwin was not aware of the nature of mutation. Only in the twentieth century, with the spectacular development of molecular biology, have the secrets of genetic structure been revealed.

Gene Flow

Gene flow
Exchange of genes between populations.

The exchange of genes between populations is called **gene flow.** The term *migration* is frequently used instead, but strictly speaking, migration means movement of

mutation must happen in sex cells

people, whereas gene flow refers to the exchange of *genes* between groups, and this can occur only if the migrants interbreed. Moreover, it should be remembered that even if individuals move temporarily and interbreed within the new population (thus leaving a genetic contribution), they need not remain as part of the population. For example, the offspring of U.S. soldiers and Vietnamese women represent gene flow, even though their fathers may have returned to their native population. Even more exotic avenues for gene flow are possible with the advent of new genetic technologies. For generations, frozen sperm (and more recently, frozen eggs) have been routinely transported long distances in commercial farming (e.g., dairy cattle). The same technologies could be used to further disseminate human genes, although this potential hardly seems necessary.

In humans, social rules more than any other factor determine mating patterns, and cultural anthropologists must work closely with physical anthropologists to isolate and measure this aspect of evolutionary change. Population movements (particularly in the last 500 years) have reached enormous proportions, and few breeding isolates remain. It should not, however, be assumed that significant population movements did not occur prior to modern times. Our hunting and gathering ancestors probably lived in small groups that were both mobile and flexible in membership. Early farmers also were probably mobile, expanding into new areas as land wore out and human population size increased. Intensive, highly sedentary agricultural communities came later, but even then, significant migration was still possible. From the Near East, one of the early farming centers, populations spread very gradually in a "creeping occupation of Europe, India, and northern and eastern Africa" (Bodmer and Cavalli-Sforza, 1976, p. 563).

Migration between populations has been a consistent feature of hominid evolution since the first dispersal of our genus and gene flow between populations (even though sometimes limited) helps explain why in the last million years speciation has been rare. Of course, migration patterns are a manifestation of human cultural behavior, once again emphasizing the essential biocultural nature of human evolution.

An interesting example of how gene flow influences microevolutionary changes in modern human populations is seen in African Americans. African Americans in the United States are largely of West African descent, but there has also been considerable genetic admixture with European Americans. By measuring allele frequencies for specific genetic loci (e.g., Rh and Duffy blood groups, discussed in Chapter 14), we can estimate the amount of migration of European alleles into the African American gene pool. Data from northern and western U.S. cities (including New York, Detroit, and Oakland) have shown the migration rate (i.e., the proportion of *non*-African genes in the African American gene pool) at 20 to 25 percent (Cummings, 1997). However, more restricted data from the southern United States (Charleston and rural Georgia) have suggested a lower degree of gene flow (4 to 11 percent). The most consistent of these studies employ new genetic techniques, especially those involving direct DNA comparisons (discussed in Chapter 14).

It would be a misconception to think that gene flow can occur only through such large-scale movements of whole groups. In fact, significant alterations in allele frequencies can come about through long-term patterns of mate selection whereby members of a group obtain mates from one or more other groups. If exchange of mates consistently moved in one direction over a long period of time, allele frequencies would ultimately be altered.

Transportation plays a crucial role in determining the potential radius for finding mates. Today, highly efficient mechanized forms of transportation make the potential radius of mate choice worldwide, but actual patterns are obviously

[handwritten note in margin: 20-25% of African genes are European]

somewhat more restricted. For example, data from Ann Arbor, Michigan, indicate a mean marital distance (the average distance between birthplaces of partners) of about 160 miles, which obviously includes a tremendous number of potential marriage partners.

Genetic Drift

Genetic drift

Evolutionary changes—that is, changes in allele frequencies—produced by random factors. Genetic drift is a result of small population size.

Founder effect

Also called the *Sewall Wright effect*, a type of genetic drift in which allele frequencies are altered in small populations that are taken from, or are remnants of, larger populations.

small populations

Genetic drift is the purely chance factor in evolution and is tied directly to population size. The term *drift* is used because, as a completely random process, the allele frequencies can change in any direction. A particular kind of drift seen in modern population is called **founder effect.** Founder effect operates when an unusually small number of individuals contributes genes to the next generation. This phenomenon can occur when a small migrant band of "founders" colonizes a new and separate area away from the parent group. Small founding populations may also be left as remnants when famine, war, or other disasters ravage a normally large group. In these situations, the reduced group is called a population bottleneck, and the process is sometimes designated as a type of drift called the *bottleneck effect.* In reality, as we can see, each generation is the founder of all succeeding generations in any population. Consequently, many researchers (e.g., Ridley, 1993) do not draw a distinction between founder effect and bottleneck effect.

Many examples of genetic drift in human populations have been documented by researchers working on small, usually isolated, populations (e.g., island groups or small agricultural villages in New Guinea or South America. Populations which originated from fairly small groups of founders can still show the effects of genetic drift many generations later, even after the population has expanded greatly in size. The French Canadians are an excellent example of this process. While currently numbering close to six million individuals, the French Canadian population of Quebec derives from only about 8,500 founders who migrated during the sixteenth and seventeenth centuries.

Since the initial founders represented a nonrandom sample of the French population from which they came, they, by chance, carried a number of alleles in different frequencies. Among these genetic disparities are the increased prevalence of several harmful alleles (a number of which are discussed earlier in this chapter, including those that cause cystic fibrosis, a variety of Tay Sachs, thalassemia, PKU, and familial hypercholesterolemia; see Table 4–2) (Scriver, 2001). Moreover, internal migrations within Quebec during the last three centuries have further produced unusual clusters of genes, again largely the result of drift acting on small populations (Heyer, 1999). As both cultural and genetic factors have influenced the current population structure of Quebec, it is crucial to understand the complex biocultural interactions that have influenced this group (Scriver, 2001).

Genetic drift has probably played an important role in human evolution, influencing genetic changes in small isolated groups. From studies of recent hunter-gatherers in Australia, we know that the range of potential mates is limited to the linguistic tribe usually consisting of around 500 members. Given this small population size, drift could act significantly, particularly if drought or disease should reduce the population even further.

Much insight concerning the evolutionary factors that have acted in the past can be gained by understanding how such mechanisms continue to operate on human populations today. In small populations, drift plays a major evolutionary role. Fairly sudden fluctuations in allele frequency can and do occur owing to the small population size. Likewise, throughout a good deal of human evolution (at least the last 4–5 m.y.*), hominids probably lived in small groups, and drift would have had significant impact.

Joseph Birdsell, a physical anthropologist who has worked extensively in Australia, has postulated general models for human evolution from his Australian data. He suggests that population size during most of the Pleistocene was comparable to the 500 figure seen in Australia. Moreover, when people adopted agriculture and became sedentary and isolated in small villages, the effects of drift may have been even greater. Indications of such a phenomenon are still operative in Melanesia, where individuals often spend their entire lives within just a few miles of their birthplace.

While drift has been a factor producing evolutionary change in certain circumstances, the effects have been irregular and nondirectional (for drift is *random* in nature). Certainly, the pace of evolutionary change could have been accelerated if many small populations were isolated and thus subject to drift. By modifying such populations, drift can provide significantly greater opportunities for the truly directional force in evolution—natural selection.

It is important to emphasize that natural selection need not be the inevitable and *only* prime mover of evolutionary change. As we have seen, both gene flow and genetic drift can produce some evolutionary changes by themselves. However, these changes are usually *microevolutionary* ones; that is, they produce changes within species over the short term. To yield the kind of evolutionary changes that ultimately result in entire new groups (e.g., the diversification of the first primates, the appearance of the hominids), natural selection most likely would play the major role. Remember, however, that natural selection does not and cannot operate independently of the other evolutionary factors—mutation, gene flow, and genetic drift. All four factors (sometimes called the "four forces of evolution") work interactively.

Additional insight concerning the relative influences of the different evolutionary factors has emerged in recent studies of the early dispersal of modern *Homo sapiens* (discussed in Chapter 13). New evidence suggests that in the last 100,000 to 200,000 years, our species experienced a genetic bottleneck, which considerably influenced the pattern of genetic variation seen in all human populations today. In this sense, modern humans can be seen as the fairly recent product of a form of genetic drift (founder effect) acting on a somewhat grand scale. Such evolutionary changes could be potentially significant over tens of thousands of years and could cause substantial genetic shifts within species.

Recombination

Since in any sexually reproducing species both parents contribute genes to offspring, the genetic information is inevitably reshuffled every generation. Such recombination does not in itself change allele frequencies (i.e., cause evolution). However, it does produce the whole array of genetic combinations, which natural selection can then act upon. In fact, we have shown how the reshuffling of chromosomes during meiosis can produce literally trillions of gene combinations, making every human being genetically unique.

*The abbreviation m.y. stands for "million years."

Natural Selection Acts on Variation

The evolutionary factors just discussed—mutation, gene flow, genetic drift, and recombination—interact to produce variation and to distribute genes within and between populations. But there is no long-term *direction* to any of these factors. How, then, do populations adapt? The answer is natural selection. Natural selection provides directional change in allele frequency relative to *specific environmental factors.* If the environment changes, then the selection pressures change as well. Such a functional shift in allele frequencies is what we mean by *adaptation.* If there are long-term environmental changes in a consistent direction, then allele frequencies should also shift gradually each generation. If sustained for many generations, the results may be quite dramatic.

In Chapter 2, we discussed the general principles underlying natural selection and gave several nonhuman examples. Physical anthropology is, of course, centrally concerned with human evolution, and it is thus most relevant to show how natural selection operates in *human* populations. However, demonstrating clear-cut examples in our species is not an easy task. In fact, the best documented example of natural selection in humans involves hemoglobin S, an altered form of hemoglobin that results from a point mutation in the gene that produces the hemoglobin beta chain (see p. 52). As you have already learned, if an individual inherits this allele (Hb^S) from both parents, he or she will suffer the severe manifestations of sickle-cell anemia. Even with aggressive medical treatment, life expectancy in the United States today is less than 45 years for patients with sickle-cell anemia. Worldwide, sickle-cell anemia causes an estimated 100,000 deaths each year, and in the United States, approximately 40,000 to 50,000 individuals, mostly of African descent, suffer from this disease.

Apparently, Hb^S is a mutation that occurs occasionally in all human populations, but the allele usually remains relatively rare. In some populations, however, Hb^S is more common, and this is especially true in western and central Africa, where its frequency approaches 20 percent. The frequency of the allele is also moderately high in parts of Greece and India (Fig. 4–13). Given the devastating effects of Hb^S in homozygotes, how do we explain its higher prevalence in some populations? The answer to this question lies in malaria, a serious infectious disease that has exerted enormous selective pressures in the past and continues to do so today. Malaria currently kills an estimated 1 to 3 million people worldwide annually. It is caused by one of several protozoan parasites belonging to the genus *Plasmodium.* These parasites are in turn transmitted to humans by mosquitoes.

Very briefly, after an infected mosquito bite, plasmodial parasites invade red blood cells, where they obtain the oxygen they need for reproduction. The consequences of this infection to the human host include fever, chills, headache, nausea, vomiting, and, frequently, death. In parts of western and central Africa, where malaria is always present, the burden of the disease is borne by children, with as many as 50 to 75 percent of 2- to 9-year-olds being afflicted.

The geographical correlation between malaria and the distribution of the sickle-cell allele is indirect evidence of a biological relationship (Figs. 4–13 and 4–14). Further confirmation was provided by British biologist A. C. Allison in the 1950s. Volunteers from the Luo tribe of East Africa with known hemoglobin phenotypes and genotypes were injected with the malarial parasite. It goes without saying that the ethics concerning human subjects would, and should, preclude such experimentation today. The results of this study showed that those subjects with one Hb^S allele (i.e., those with sickle-cell trait) and thus some hemoglobin S had greater resistance

FIGURE 4–13
A frequency map of the sickle-cell distribution in the Old World.

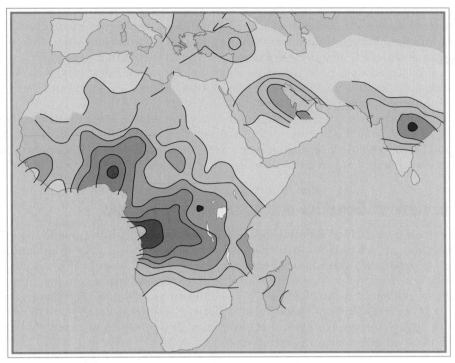

Frequencies of the sickle-cell allele:

- Greater than .14
- .12–.14
- .10–.12
- .08–.10
- .06–.08
- .04–.06
- .02–.04
- .00–.02

FIGURE 4–14
Malaria distribution in the Old World.

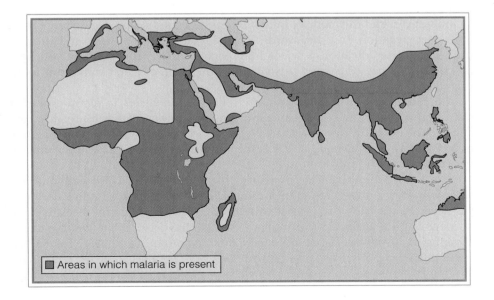

Areas in which malaria is present

to malaria than the homozygous "normals." It was subsequently demonstrated that heterozygotes resist infection because their red blood cells provide a less conducive environment for the parasite to reproduce. Thus, in environments where the prevalence of malaria is always high, individuals with sickle-cell trait have higher reproductive success than those with normal hemoglobin. Those afflicted with sickle-cell anemia, of course, have the lowest reproductive success, since without treatment, most die before reaching adulthood.

The relationship between malaria and hemoglobin S provides the best example we have of natural selection in contemporary humans. In this case, natural selection has favored the heterozygous phenotype, thus increasing the frequency of Hb^S, an allele that in homozygotes causes severe disease and early death.

Review of Genetics and Evolutionary Factors

Beginning in Chapter 3 with a discussion of the molecular and cellular bases of heredity, we proceeded in this chapter to show how such genetic information is passed from individuals in one generation to those in the next. In this chapter, we also have reviewed evolutionary theory and its current applications, emphasizing the crucial role of natural selection. These different levels—molecular, cellular, individual, and populational—are different aspects of evolution, and they are all related and highly integrated in a way that can eventually produce evolutionary change. A step-by-step example will make this clear.

We begin with a situation in which everyone in the population has the same hemoglobin type; therefore, initially no variation for this trait exists, and without some source of new variation, evolution is not possible. How does this gene change? We have seen that a substitution of a single base in the DNA sequence can alter the code significantly enough to alter the protein product and ultimately the whole phenotype of the individual. Consider that in each generation such an incident occurs in one or a few individuals. For a mutated allele to be passed on to succeeding offspring, the gametes must carry the alteration. Any new mutation, therefore, must be transmitted during sex cell formation.

mutation in sex cell

Once the mutation has occurred in the DNA, it will be packaged into chromosomes, and these chromosomes in turn will assort during meiosis to be passed to offspring. The results of this process are seen by looking at phenotypes (traits) in individuals, and the mode of inheritance is described simply by Mendel's principle of segregation. In other words, if our initial individual has a mutation in only one paired allele on a set of homologous chromosomes, there will be a 50 percent chance of passing this chromosome (with the new mutation) to an offspring.

Mendelian reproduction of variation

But what does all this activity have to do with *evolution*? To repeat an earlier definition, evolution is a change in allele frequency in a *population* from one generation to the next. The key point here is that we are now looking at an entire group of individuals, a population, and it is the population that will or will not change over time.

We know whether allele frequencies have changed in a population where sickle-cell hemoglobin is found by ascertaining the percentage of individuals with the sickling allele (Hb^S) versus those with the normal allele (Hb^A). If the relative proportions of these alleles alter with time, evolution has occurred. In addition to discovering that evolution has occurred, it is important to know why. Several possibilities arise. First, we know that the only way the new allele Hb^S could have arisen is by mutation, and we have shown how this process can happen in a single individual. This change, however, is not yet really an evolutionary one, for in a relatively large population, the alteration of one individual's genes will not significantly alter allele frequencies of the entire population. Somehow, this new allele must *spread* in the population.

One way this could happen is in a small population, where mutations in one or just a few individuals and their offspring may indeed alter the overall frequency quite quickly. This case would be representative of genetic drift. As discussed, drift acts in small populations, where random factors may cause significant changes in allele frequency. With a small population size, there is not likely to be a balance of factors affecting individual survival or reproduction. Consequently, some alleles may be completely removed from the population, while others may become established as the only allele present at that particular locus (and are said to be "fixed" in the population).

In the course of human evolution, drift may have played a significant role at times, and it is important to remember that at this microevolutionary level, drift and/or gene flow can (and will) produce evolutionary change, even in the absence of natural selection. However, directional evolutionary trends could only have been sustained by *natural selection*. The way this has worked in the past and still operates today (as in sickle-cell) is through differential reproduction. That is, individuals who carry a particular allele or combination of alleles produce more offspring. By producing more offspring than other individuals with alternative alleles, such individuals cause the frequency of the new allele in the population to increase slowly from generation to generation. When this process is compounded over hundreds of generations for numerous loci, the result is significant evolutionary change. The levels of organization in the evolutionary process are summarized in Table 4–5.

TABLE 4–5 Levels of Organization in the Evolutionary Process

Evolutionary Factor	Level	Evolutionary Process	Technique of Study
Mutation	DNA	Storage of genetic information; ability to replicate; influences phenotype by production of proteins	Biochemistry, electron microscope, recombinant DNA
Mutation	Chromosomes	A vehicle for packaging and transmitting genetic material (DNA)	Light or electron microscope
Recombination (sex cells only)	Cell	The basic unit of life that contains the chromosomes and divides for growth and for production of sex cells	Light or electron microscope
Natural selection	Organism	The unit, composed of cells, that reproduces and which we observe for phenotypic traits	Visual study, biochemistry
Drift, gene flow	Population	A group of interbreeding organisms; changes in allele frequencies between generations; it is the population that evolves	Statistical analysis

SUMMARY

We have seen how Gregor Mendel discovered the principles of segregation, independent assortment, and dominance and recessiveness by conducting experiments on garden peas. Although the field of genetics has progressed dramatically in the twentieth century, the concepts first put forth by Gregor Mendel remain the basis of our current knowledge on how traits are inherited.

Basic Mendelian principles are applied to the study of the various modes of inheritance we are familiar with today. We have presented three of these in some detail: autosomal dominant, autosomal recessive, and X-linked recessive. The most important factor in all the Mendelian modes of inheritance is the role of segregation of chromosomes, and the alleles they carry, during meiosis. Although our understanding of human inheritance has virtually exploded in the last 50 years, the very foundation of our knowledge rests in the basic rules as set forth by Gregor Mendel almost 150 years ago.

Building on fundamental nineteenth-century contributions by Charles Darwin and his contemporaries and the rediscovery in 1900 of Mendel's work, further refinements later in the twentieth century added to contemporary evolutionary thought. In particular, the combination of natural selection with Mendel's principles of inheritance and experimental evidence concerning the nature of mutation have all been synthesized into a modern understanding of evolutionary change, appropriately termed the Modern Synthesis. In this, the central contemporary theory of evolution, evolutionary change is seen as a two-stage process. The first stage is the production and redistribution of variation. The second stage is the process whereby natural selection acts on the accumulated genetic variation.

Crucial to all evolutionary change is mutation, the only source of completely new genetic variation. In addition, the factors of gene flow, genetic drift, and recombination function to redistribute variation within individuals (recombination), within populations (genetic drift), and between populations (gene flow).

Natural selection is the central determining factor influencing the long-term direction of evolutionary change. How natural selection works can best be explained as differential reproductive success—in other words, how successful individuals are in leaving offspring to succeeding generations. To more fully illustrate the mechanics of evolutionary change through natural selection, comprehensive and well-understood examples from other organisms are most helpful. The detailed history of the evolutionary spread of the sickle-cell allele provides the best-documented example of natural selection among recent human populations. It must be remembered that evolution is an integrated process, and this chapter concluded with a discussion of how the various evolutionary factors can be integrated into a single, comprehensive view of evolutionary change.

QUESTIONS FOR REVIEW

1. What is Mendel's principle of segregation?
2. How does meiosis explain the principle of segregation?
3. What is Mendel's principle of independent assortment?
4. Explain dominance and recessiveness.
5. Define allele.
6. What is a phenotype, and what is its relationship to a genotype?
7. Why were all of Mendel's F_1 pea plants phenotypically the same?

8. Explain what is meant by a phenotypic ratio of 3:1 in the F_2 generation.

9. What is codominance? Give an example.

10. If two people who have blood type A (both with the *AO* genotype) have children, what proportion of their children would be expected to have the O blood type? Why?

11. Can the two parents in question 10 have a child with AB blood? Why or why not?

12. Explain why X-linked recessive traits are more common in males than in females.

13. In a cross between two carriers for a recessive trait, why would ³/₄ of the offspring be expected *not* to show the recessive characteristic?

14. Explain how natural selection works. Illustrate through an example in humans.

15. What is polygenic inheritance? How does it differ from Mendelian inheritance?

16. What is pleiotropy? Give an example.

17. Explain why natural selection has acted to increase the frequency of *Hb^S*, the allele that causes sickle-cell anemia, in heterozygotes in some populations.

18. What is the Modern Synthesis? Explain how the major components of this theory explain evolutionary change.

19. What is genetic drift? Illustrate through an example for human populations.

20. Define gene flow. Give an example in human populations.

21. What role does variation play in the evolutionary process? Where does variation come from? (*Hint:* You may wish to discuss the source of variation as completely new to a species or as it is introduced into a population *within* a species.)

22. Discuss how evolutionary change occurs as an integrated process. Illustrate through an example.

SUGGESTED FURTHER READING

Cummings, Michael R. 2000. *Human Heredity. Principles and Issues*. 5th ed., Pacific Grove, CA: Brooks/Cole.

Heim, Werner G. 1991. "What is a Recessive Allele?" *The American Biology Teacher* 53(2): 94–97.

Little, Peter. 1999. "The Book of Genes." *Nature* 402: 467–468.

Ridley, Mark. 1993. *Evolution*. Cambridge, MA: Blackwell Scientific.

Wake, David B. 2001. "Evolution: Speciation in the Round." *Nature* 409: 299–300.

RESOURCES ON THE INTERNET

 Wadsworth Anthropology Resource Center
http://anthropology.wadsworth.com

The companion website for this text includes a range of enrichment material focused on the chapter's topic. While online you can enhance your understanding of the chapter by exploring one of the several additional Internet exercises, by researching topics, and by accessing full articles on InfoTrac College Edition. You can also reinforce the concepts by taking online practice exams.

Internet Exercises

1. While the terminology used at this site is very technical, online Mendelian Inheritance in Man (OMIM) is the most comprehensive website dealing with Mendelian and many non-Mendelian traits. To appreciate the complexity of such characteristics, go to **http://www3.ncbi.nlm.nih.gov/Omim**, click on "search the OMIM database," and enter the name of one of the conditions listed in Table 4.2 in the search field. (We suggest albinism.) Then click on #203100, the catalog number for albinism; then click on "description." Read this entry and make a list of three facts not included in the chapter. What kinds of information have you found that you think would be useful to your classmates?

2. Pedigrees and karyotypes are two tools often used in genetic research. The Genetic Analysis site (**http://library.thinkquest.org/18258/ped-karyo.htm**) provides more explanation about how to use these tools. It also offers the Pedigree Quiz.

InfoTrac College Edition

http://www.infotrac-college.com/wadsworth

Use InfoTrac College Edition and search for *human genetics*. Is there any information in recent articles about dominant and recessive traits in humans? Read one of the articles and write a short summary indicating how this article relates to anthropological questions regarding human evolution and behavior.

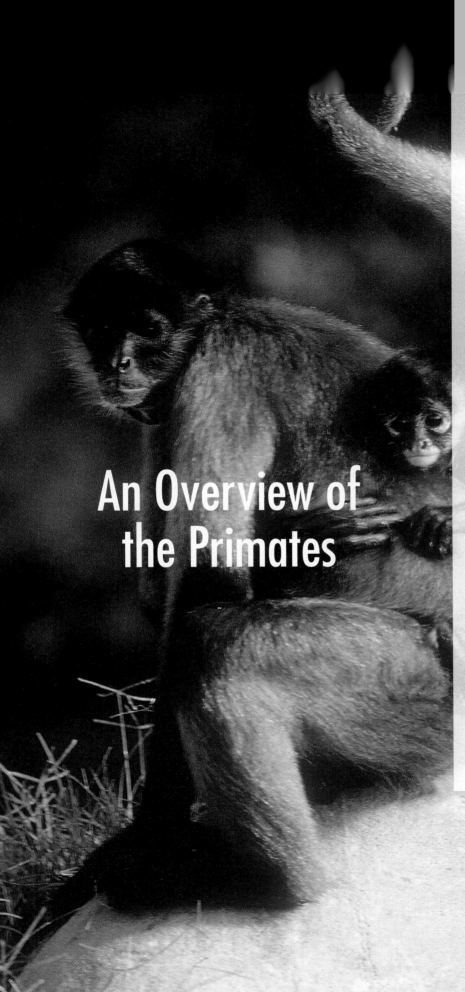

An Overview of the Primates

CHAPTER

5

CONTENTS

Female spider monkey with infant

Introduction

See the following sections of the CD-ROM for topics covered in this chapter: Virtual Lab 1, sections II and III; Virtual Lab 3; and Virtual Lab 4.

Prosimians
Members of a suborder of Primates, the *Prosimii* (pronounced "pro-sim´-ee-eye"). Traditionally, the suborder includes lemurs, lorises, and tarsiers.

Anthropoids
Members of a suborder of Primates, the *Anthropoidea* (pronounced "ann-throw-poid´-ee-uh"). Traditionally, the suborder includes monkeys, apes, and humans.

Mammalia
The technical term for the formal grouping (class) of mammals.

Thus far, we have presented the basic biological background for understanding evolutionary processes and, specifically, human evolution and adaptation. Evolution has produced a continuum of life forms, as demonstrated genetically, anatomically, and behaviorally. To gain an understanding of any organism, it is necessary, whenever possible, to compare its anatomy and behavior with those of other, closely related forms. This comparative approach helps elucidate the significance of physiological and behavioral systems as adaptive responses to various selective pressures throughout the course of evolution. This statement applies to *Homo sapiens* just as surely as to any other species, and if we are to identify the components that have shaped hominid evolution, the starting point must be a systematic comparison between humans and our closest living relatives, the approximately 230 species of nonhuman primates (**prosimians**, monkeys, and apes). (Groves, 2001b, suggests there may be as many as 350 primate species.) This chapter describes the physical characteristics that define the order Primates, gives a brief overview of the major groups of living primates, and introduces some methods of comparing living primates through genetic data. (For a detailed comparison of human and nonhuman skeletons, see Appendix A.) This chapter and the one that follows concentrate on various anatomical and behavioral features that characterize primates.

Before proceeding further, we once again call attention to a few common misunderstandings about evolutionary processes. Evolution is not a goal-directed process; thus, the fact that prosimians evolved before **anthropoids** does not mean that prosimians "progressed," or "advanced," to become anthropoids. Living primate species are in no way "superior" to their evolutionary predecessors or to one another. Consequently, in discussions of major groupings of contemporary nonhuman primates, there is no implied superiority or inferiority of any of these groups. Each grouping (lineage, or species) has come to possess unique qualities that make it better suited than others to a particular habitat and lifestyle. Given that all contemporary organisms are "successful" results of the evolutionary process, it is best to avoid altogether the use of such loaded terms as "superior" and "inferior."

Finally, you should not make the mistake of thinking that contemporary primates (including humans) necessarily represent the final stage or apex of a lineage. Remember, the only species that represent final evolutionary stages of particular lineages are those that become extinct.

Primates as Mammals

The order *Primates* is a subgroup of a larger group of organisms, the mammals (technically, the class **Mammalia**). Today there are over 4,000 species of mammals, which can be further subdivided into three major subgroups: (1) the egg-laying mammals, (2) the pouched mammals (i.e., marsupials), and (3) the placental mammals. We will discuss mammalian evolution in more detail in Chapter 8. For the moment, you should recognize that primates are members of the placental subgroup, by far the most common of living mammals (and including other common orders such as rodents and carnivores). Placental mammals today are distributed over most of the world in a wide variety of forms. In fact, biologists recognize more than 20 orders of mammals, including flying, swimming, and burrowing varieties and a host of other adaptations as well. Sizes range from the tiny dwarf shrews (just a few grams) to the whales, the largest animals ever to inhabit the earth.

Characteristics of Primates

All primates possess numerous characteristics they share in common with other placental mammals. Such traits include body hair; a relatively long gestation period followed by live birth; mammary glands (thus the term *mammal*); different types of teeth (incisors, canines, premolars, and molars); the ability to maintain a constant internal body temperature through physiological means (*homeothermy*); increased brain size; and a considerable capacity for learning and behavioral flexibility. Therefore, to differentiate primates, as a group, from other mammals, we must describe those characteristics that, taken together, set primates apart from other mammalian groups.

Identifying single traits that define the primate order is not a simple task, for among mammals, primates have remained quite *generalized*. That is, primates have retained many **primitive** mammalian traits that some other mammalian species have lost over time. In response to particular selective pressures, many mammalian groups have become increasingly **specialized**. For example, through the course of evolution, horses and cattle have undergone a reduction of the number of digits (fingers and toes) from the primitive pattern of five to one and two, respectively. Moreover, these species have developed hard, protective coverings over their feet in the form of hooves. While this type of limb structure is adaptive in prey species, whose survival depends on speed and stability, it restricts the animal to only one type of locomotion. Moreover, limb function is limited entirely to support and movement, while the ability to manipulate objects is completely lost.

Primates, precisely because they are *not* so specialized, cannot be simply defined by one or even two traits they share in common. As a result, biologists have pointed to a group of characteristics that, taken together, more or less characterize the entire order. Keep in mind that these are a set of *general* tendencies and are not all equally expressed in all primates. Indeed, this is what we would expect in a group of related but diverse animals. Moreover, while some of these traits are unique to primates, many others are retained primitive mammalian characteristics. These latter are useful in contrasting the generalized primates with the more specialized varieties of other placental mammals.

Thus, the following list is intended to give an overall structural and behavioral picture of that kind of animal we call "primate," focusing on those characteristics that tend to set primates apart from other mammals. Concentrating on certain retained (ancestral) mammalian traits, along with more specific ones, has been the traditional approach of **primatologists**. Some contemporary primatologists (Fleagle, 1999) feel that it is useful to enumerate all these features to better illustrate primate adaptations. Thus, a common evolutionary history with adaptations to similar environmental challenges is seen to be reflected in the limbs and locomotion, teeth and diet, senses, brain, and behaviors of those animals that make up the primate order.

A. *Limbs and Locomotion*
1. *A tendency toward erect posture (especially in the upper body).* Shown to some degree in all primates, this tendency is variously associated with sitting, leaping, standing, and, occasionally, bipedal walking.
2. *A flexible, generalized limb structure, permitting most primates to engage in a number of locomotor behaviors.* Primates have retained some bones (e.g., the clavicle, or collarbone) and certain abilities, (e.g., rotation of the forearm) that have been lost in some more specialized mammals. Various aspects of hip and shoulder **morphology** also provide primates with a wide range of limb movement and function. Thus, by maintaining a generalized

See Virtual Lab 1, section II for a discussion of primate characteristics.

Primitive
Referring to a trait or combination of traits present in an ancestral form.

Specialized
Evolved for a particular function; usually refers to a specific trait (e.g., incisor teeth), but may also refer to the entire way of life of an organism.

Primatologists
Scientists who study the evolution, anatomy, and behavior of nonhuman primates. Those who study behavior in noncaptive animals are usually trained as physical anthropologists.

Morphology
The form (shape, size) of anatomical structures; can also refer to the entire organism.

Overview of the Primates

FIGURE 5–1
Primate (macaque) hand.

Prehensility
Grasping, as by the hands and feet of primates.

Omnivorous
Having a diet consisting of many food types (i.e., plant materials, meat, and insects).

Diurnal
Active during the day.

Nocturnal
Active during the night.

Stereoscopic vision
The condition whereby visual images are, to varying degrees, superimposed on one another. This provides for depth perception, or the perception of the external environment in three dimensions. Stereoscopic vision is partly a function of structures in the brain.

Binocular vision
Vision characterized by overlapping visual fields provided by forward-facing eyes; essential to depth perception.

locomotor anatomy, primates are not restricted to one form of movement, as are many other mammals. Primate limbs are also used for activities other than locomotion.

3. *Hands and feet with a high degree of **prehensility** (grasping ability).* All primates use the hands, and frequently the feet, to grasp and manipulate objects (Fig. 5–1). This capability is variably expressed and is enhanced by a number of characteristics, including:

   a. *Retention of five digits on hands and feet.* This varies somewhat throughout the order, with some species showing marked reduction of the thumb or second digit.

   b. *An opposable thumb and, in most species, a divergent and partially opposable big toe.* Most primates are capable of moving the thumb so that it comes in contact (in some fashion) with the second digit or the palm of the hand.

   c. *Nails instead of claws.* This characteristic is seen in all primates except some New World monkeys. All prosimians also possess a claw on one digit.

   d. *Tactile pads enriched with sensory nerve fibers at the ends of digits.* This trend serves to enhance the sense of touch.

B. *Diet and Teeth*

  1. *Lack of dietary specialization.* This is typical of most primates, who tend to eat a wide assortment of food items.

  2. *A generalized dentition.* The teeth are not specialized for processing only one type of food, a pattern correlated with the lack of dietary specialization. In general, primates are **omnivorous**.

C. *The senses and the brain.* Primates (**diurnal** ones in particular) rely heavily on the visual sense and less on the sense of smell, especially compared to many other mammals. This emphasis is reflected in evolutionary changes in the skull, eyes, and brain.

  1. *Color vision.* This is characteristic of all diurnal primates. **Nocturnal** primates lack color vision.

  2. *Depth perception.* **Stereoscopic vision**, or the ability to perceive objects in three dimensions, is made possible through a variety of mechanisms, including:

   a. *Eyes positioned toward the front of the face (not to the sides).* This configuration provides for overlapping visual fields, or **binocular vision** (Fig. 5–2).

   b. *Visual information from each eye transmitted to visual centers in both hemispheres of the brain.* In nonprimate mammals, most optic nerve fibers cross to the opposite hemisphere through a structure at the base of the brain. In primates, about 40 percent of the fibers remain on the same side (see Fig. 5–2).

   c. *Visual information organized into three-dimensional images by specialized structures in the brain itself.* The capacity for stereoscopic vision is dependent on each hemisphere of the brain having received visual information from both eyes and from overlapping visual fields.

  3. *Decreased reliance on the sense of smell (olfaction).* This trend is seen in an overall reduction in the size of olfactory structures in the brain. Corresponding reduction of the entire olfactory apparatus has also resulted in decreased size of the snout. (In some species, such as baboons, the large muzzle is not related to olfaction, but to the presence of large teeth, especially the canines; see Box 5–1.)

  4. *Expansion and increased complexity of the brain.* This is a general trend among placental mammals, but it is especially true of primates. In primates, this

FIGURE 5–2
Simplified diagram showing overlapping visual fields (binocular vision) in primates (and some predators) with eyes positioned at the front of the face. (The green shaded area represents the area of overlap.) Stereoscopic vision (three-dimensional vision) is provided in part by binocular vision and in part by the transmission of visual stimuli from each eye to *both* hemispheres of the brain. (In nonprimate mammals, most, if not all, visual information crosses over to the hemisphere opposite the eye in which it was initially received.)

Primary receiving area for visual information

expansion is most evident in the visual and association areas of the neocortex (portions of the brain where information from different sensory modalities is integrated). Expansion in regions involved with the hand (both sensory and motor) is seen in many species, particularly humans.

D. *Maturation, learning, and behavior*

1. *A more efficient means of fetal nourishment, longer periods of gestation, reduced numbers of offspring (with single births the norm), delayed maturation, and extension of the entire life span.*

2. *A greater dependence on flexible, learned behavior.* This trend is correlated with delayed maturation and consequently longer periods of infant and child dependency on the parent. As a result of both these trends, parental investment in each offspring is increased, so that although fewer offspring are born, they receive more intense and efficient rearing.

3. *The tendency to live in social groups and the permanent association of adult males with the group.* Except for some nocturnal forms, primates tend to associate with other individuals. The permanent association of adult males with the group is uncommon in mammals but widespread in primates.

4. *The tendency to diurnal activity patterns.* This is seen in most primates; only one monkey species and some prosimians are nocturnal.

BOX 5-1   A CLOSER LOOK

Primate Cranial Anatomy

Several significant anatomical features of the primate cranium help us distinguish primates from other mammals. The mammalian trend toward increased brain development has been further emphasized in primates, as shown by a relatively enlarged braincase. In addition, the primate emphasis on vision is reflected in generally large eye sockets; and the decreased dependence on olfaction is indicated by reduction of the snout and corresponding flattening of the face (Fig. 1).

Here are some of the specific anatomical details seen in modern and most fossil primate crania:

1. The primate face is shortened, and the size of the braincase, relative to that of the face, is enlarged compared to other mammals (Fig. 1).

2. Eye sockets are enclosed at the sides by a ring of bone called the *postorbital bar* (see Fig. 1). In most other mammals, there is no postorbital bar. In addition, in anthropoids and tarsiers, there is a plate of bone at the back of the eye orbit called the *postorbital plate*. The postorbital plate is not present in prosimians. The functional significance of these structures has not been thoroughly explained, but it may be related to stresses on the eye orbits imposed by chewing (Fleagle, 1999).

3. The region of the skull that contains the structures of the middle ear is completely encircled by a bony structure called the *auditory bulla*. In primates, the floor of the auditory bulla is derived from a segment of the temporal bone (Fig. 2). Of the skeletal structures, most primate paleontologists consider the postorbital bar and the derivation of the auditory bulla to be the two best diagnostic traits of the primate order.

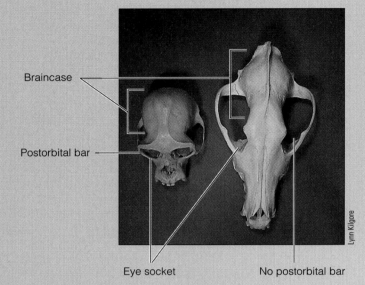

Braincase

Postorbital bar

Eye socket   No postorbital bar

Lynn Kilgore

FIGURE 1

The skull of a gibbon (left) compared to that of a red wolf (right). Note that the absolute size of the braincase in the gibbon is slightly larger than that of the wolf, even though the wolf (at about 60 to 80 pounds) is four times the size of the gibbon (about 15 pounds).

4. The base of the skull in primates is somewhat flexed, so that the muzzle (mouth and nose) is positioned lower relative to the braincase (Fig. 3). This arrangement provides for the exertion of greater force during chewing, particularly as needed for the crushing and grinding of tough vegetable fibers, seeds, and hard-shelled fruits.

Primate Adaptations

Evolutionary Factors

Arboreal
Tree-living: adapted to life in the trees.

Adaptive niche
The entire way of life of an organism: where it lives, what it eats, how it gets food, how it avoids predators, etc.

Traditionally, the suite of characteristics shared by primates has been explained as the result of adaptation to **arboreal** living. While other placental mammals were adapting to various ground-dwelling lifestyles and even marine environments, the primates found their **adaptive niche** in the trees. Indeed, some other mammals were also adapting to arboreal living, but while many of these species nested in trees, they continued to come to the ground to forage for food. But throughout the

Portion of temporal bone enclosing auditory bulla

External opening to ear (external auditory meatus)

FIGURE 2
The base of an adolescent chimpanzee skull. Note that in an adult animal, the bones of the skull would be fused together and would not appear as separate elements as shown here.

FIGURE 3
The skull of a male baboon (a) compared to that of a red wolf (b). The angle at the base of the baboon skull is due to flexion. The corresponding area of the wolf skull is flat. Note the forward-facing position of the eye orbits above the snout in the baboon. Also, be aware that in the baboon, the enlarged muzzle does *not* reflect a heavy reliance on the sense of smell. Rather, it serves to support very large canine teeth, the roots of which curve back through the bone for as much as 1½ inches.

(a)

(b)

course of evolution, primates came increasingly to exploit foods (leaves, seeds, fruits, nuts, insects, and small mammals) found in the branches themselves. The exploitation of these varied foods enhanced the general trend toward *omnivory* in primates and toward the primate generalized dentition.

We can also see this adaptive process reflected in the primate reliance on vision. In a complex, three-dimensional environment with uncertain footholds, acute color vision with depth perception is extremely beneficial. The presence of grasping hands and feet is also an indicator of the adaptation to living in the trees. Climbing can be accomplished by either digging in with claws (as in many species,

Intelligence
Mental capacity; the ability to learn, reason, or comprehend and interpret information, facts, relationships, meanings, etc.; the capacity to solve problems, whether through the application of previously acquired knowledge or through insight.

Arboreal hypothesis
The traditional view that primate characteristics can be explained as a consequence of primate diversification into arboreal habitats.

such as squirrels or raccoons) or grasping around branches with prehensile hands and feet. Primates adopted this latter strategy, which allowed a means of moving about, sometimes very rapidly, on small, unstable surfaces, and grasping abilities were further enhanced by the appearance of flattened nails instead of claws.

Finally, increased **intelligence** may be, in part, a primate solution to coping with the complexities of an arboreal habitat. In such an environment, there are varied and seasonal food resources, and predators can appear from above (eagles), in the trees (snakes), and from below (leopards). Jerison (1973) also suggested that the crucial development of increased behavioral flexibility in primates may have been further stimulated by a shift from nocturnal (nighttime) to diurnal (daytime) activity patterns.

An alternative to this traditional **arboreal hypothesis**, called the *visual predation hypothesis* (Cartmill, 1972, 1992), points out that forward-facing eyes are characteristic not only of primates, but also of predators, such as cats and owls, that prey on small animals. Furthermore, the most significant primate trends (forward-facing eyes, grasping hands and feet, and the presence of nails instead of claws) may *not* have arisen as adaptive advantages in a purely arboreal environment. According to the visual predation hypothesis, primates may first have adapted to shrubby forest undergrowth and the lowest tiers of the forest canopy, where they exploited insects and other small prey that they captured primarily through stealth.

A third scenario (Sussman, 1991) proposes that the basic primate traits developed in conjunction with another major evolutionary occurrence, the rise of the *angiosperms* (flowering plants). Flowering plants provided numerous resources, including nectar, seeds, and fruits, and their appearance and diversification were accompanied by the appearance of ancestral forms of major groups of modern birds and mammals. Sussman argues that visual predation is not common among modern primates and that forward-facing eyes, grasping extremities, and omnivory may have arisen in response to the demand for fine visual and tactile discrimination, necessary when feeding on small food items such as fruits, berries, and seeds among branches and stems.

These hypotheses are not mutually exclusive. The complex of primate characteristics might well have begun in nonarboreal settings and certainly may have been stimulated by the new econiches provided by evolving angiosperms. But one thing is certain. At some point, the primates did take to the trees, and that is where the vast majority of nonhuman primates still live today. Whereas the basic primate structural complexes may have been adapted for visual predation and/or omnivory in shrubby undergrowth and terminal branches, they became ideally suited for the arboreal adaptations that followed. We would say, then, that the early primates were "preadapted" for arboreal living and that those early adaptations have served them long and well in the trees.

Geographical Distribution and Habitats

With just a couple of exceptions, primates are found in tropical or semitropical areas of the New and Old Worlds. In the New World, these areas include southern Mexico, Central America, and parts of South America. Old World primates are found in Africa, India, Southeast Asia (including numerous islands), and Japan (see Fig. 5–4 on pp. 110–111).

The majority of primates are, as we have discussed, mostly arboreal and live in forest or woodland habitats. However, some Old World monkeys (e.g., baboons) have, to varying degrees, adapted to life on the ground in areas where trees are sparsely distributed. Moreover, among the apes, gorillas and chimpanzees spend a considerable amount of time on the ground in forested and wooded habitats. Nevertheless, no nonhuman primate is adapted to a fully terrestrial lifestyle, and all spend some time in the trees.

Diet and Teeth

As noted, primates are generally *omnivorous*. Indeed, the tendency toward omnivory is one example of the overall lack of specialization in primates. Although the majority of primate species tend to emphasize some food items over others, most eat a combination of fruit, leaves and other plant materials, and insects. Many obtain animal protein from birds and amphibians as well. Some (baboons and especially chimpanzees) occasionally kill and eat small mammals, including other primates. Others, such as African colobus monkeys and the leaf-eating monkeys (langurs) of India and Southeast Asia, have become more specialized and subsist primarily on leaves. Such an array of choices is highly adaptive, even in fairly predictable environments.

Like the majority of other mammals, most primates have four kinds of teeth: incisors and canines for biting and cutting and premolars and molars for chewing. Biologists use a device called a *dental formula* to describe the number of each type of tooth that typifies a species. A dental formula indicates the number of each tooth type in each quadrant of the mouth (Fig. 5–3). For example, all Old World *anthropoids* have two incisors, one canine, two premolars, and three molars on each side of the **midline** in both the upper and lower jaws, or a total of 32 teeth. This is represented as a dental formula of

2.1.2.3. (upper)
2.1.2.3. (lower)

The dental formula for a generalized placental mammal is 3.1.4.3. (three incisors, one canine, four premolars, and three molars). Primates have fewer teeth than this ancestral pattern because there has been a general evolutionary trend toward reduction of the number of teeth in many mammal groups. Consequently, the number of each type of tooth may vary between lineages. For example, in the majority of New World monkeys, the dental formula is 2.1.3.3. (two incisors, one canine, three premolars, and three molars). Humans, apes, and all Old World monkeys have the same dental formula: 2.1.2.3. (Note that there is one less premolar than in some New World monkeys.)

Correlated with an overall lack of dietary specialization in primates is a lack of specialization with regard to the size and shape of the teeth because tooth form is directly related to diet. For example, carnivores typically have premolars and molars with high pointed **cusps** adapted for tearing meat, while the premolars of herbivores, such as cattle and horses, have broad, flat surfaces suited to chewing tough grasses and other plant materials. Most primates possess premolars and molars that have low, rounded cusps, a molar morphology that enables them to process most types of foods. Thus, throughout their evolutionary history, the primates have developed a dentition adapted to a varied diet, and the capacity to exploit many foods has contributed to their overall success during the last 50 million years.

Midline
An anatomical term referring to a hypothetical line that divides the body into right and left halves.

Cusps
The elevated portions (bumps) on the chewing surfaces of premolar and molar teeth.

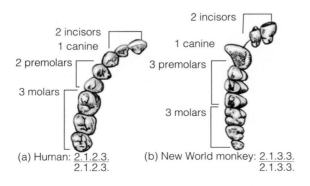

2 incisors
2 incisors
1 canine
1 canine
2 premolars
3 premolars
3 molars
3 molars

(a) Human: 2.1.2.3.
2.1.2.3.

(b) New World monkey: 2.1.3.3.
2.1.3.3.

FIGURE 5–3
Dental formulae. The number of each kind of tooth is given for one-quarter of the mouth.

Overview of the Primates

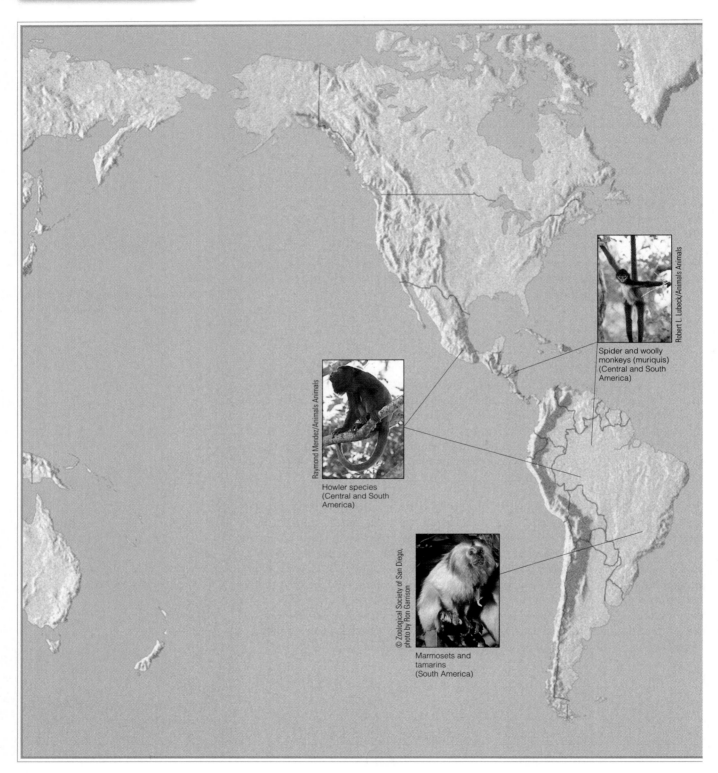

Spider and woolly
monkeys (muriquis)
(Central and South
America)

Robert L. Lubeck/Animals Animals

Raymond Mendez/Animals Animals

Howler species
(Central and South
America)

© Zoological Society of San Diego,
photo by Ron Garrison

Marmosets and
tamarins
(South America)

FIGURE 5–4
Geographical distribution of living nonhuman
primates. Much original habitat is now very
fragmented.

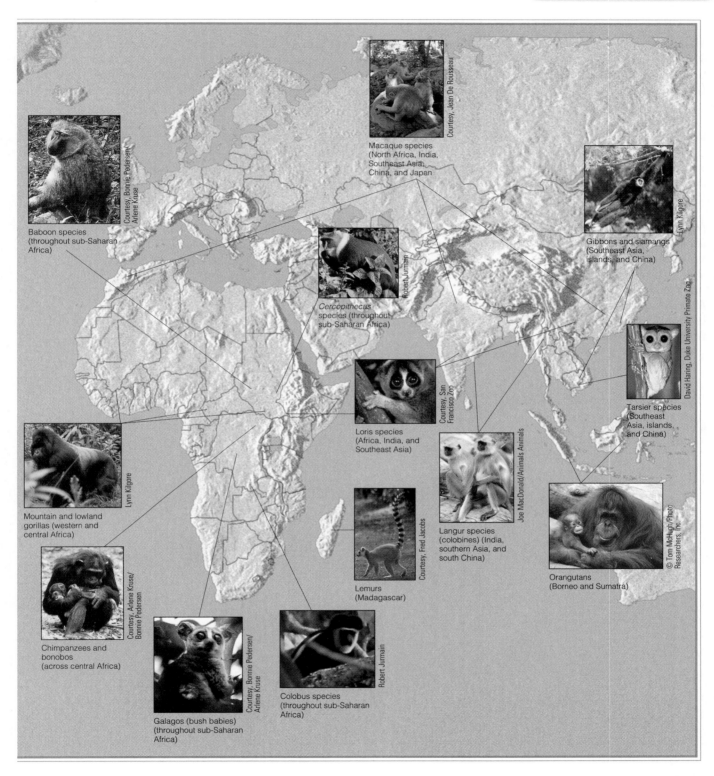

Macaque species
(North Africa, India,
Southeast Asia,
China, and Japan

Baboon species
(throughout sub-Saharan
Africa)

Gibbons and siamangs
(Southeast Asia,
islands, and China)

Cercopithecus
species (throughout
sub-Saharan Africa)

Tarsier species
(Southeast
Asia, islands,
and China)

Loris species
(Africa, India, and
Southeast Asia)

Mountain and lowland
gorillas (western and
central Africa)

Langur species
(colobines) (India,
southern Asia, and
south China)

Lemurs
(Madagascar)

Orangutans
(Borneo and Sumatra)

Chimpanzees and
bonobos
(across central Africa)

Galagos (bush babies)
(throughout sub-Saharan
Africa)

Colobus species
(throughout sub-Saharan
Africa)

Locomotion

Quadrupedal
Using all four limbs to support the body during locomotion; the basic mammalian (and primate) form of locomotion.

Almost all primates are, at least to some degree, **quadrupedal**, meaning they use all four limbs to support the body during locomotion. However, to describe most primate species in terms of only one or even two forms of locomotion would be to overlook the wide variety of methods they may use to move about. Many primates employ more than one form of locomotion, and they owe this important ability to their generalized structure.

Macaques
(muh-kaks´) Group of Old World monkeys comprising several species, including rhesus monkeys.

Although the majority of quadrupedal primates are arboreal, terrestrial quadrupedalism is fairly common and is displayed by some lemurs, baboons, and **macaques**. Typically, the limbs of terrestrial quadrupeds are approximately of equal length, with forelimbs being 90 percent (or more) as long as hind limbs (Fig. 5–5a).

FIGURE 5–5a–d
Differences in skeletal anatomy and limb proportions reflect differences in locomotor patterns. (Redrawn by Stephen Nash from original art in John G. Fleagle, *Primate Adaptation and Evolution*, copyright 1988, Elsevier Science [USA], reproduced by permission of the publisher.)

 See Virtual Labs 3 and 4 for discussions of primate locomotion.

(a) Skeleton of a terrestrial quadruped (savanna baboon).

(b) Skeleton of an arboreal New World monkey (bearded saki).

In arboreal quadrupeds, forelimbs are shorter and may be only 70 to 80 percent as long as hind limbs (Fig. 5–5b).

Quadrupeds are also characterized by a relatively long and flexible *lumbar spine* (lower back). This lumbar flexibility permits the animal to bend the body during running, thus positioning the hind limbs and feet well forward under the body and enhancing their ability to propel the animal forward. (Watch for this the next time you see slow-motion footage of cheetahs or lions on television.)

Another form of locomotion is *vertical clinging and leaping*, seen in many prosimians. As the term implies, vertical clingers and leapers support themselves vertically by grasping onto trunks of trees while their knees and ankles are tightly flexed (Fig. 5–5c). Forceful extension of their long hind limbs allows them to spring powerfully away in either a forward or backward direction. Once in midair, the body rotates so that the animal lands feet first on the next vertical support.

Yet another type of primate locomotion is **brachiation**, or arm swinging, where the body is alternatively supported under either forelimb. Because of anatomical modifications at the shoulder joint, apes and humans are capable of true brachiation. However, only the small gibbons and siamangs of Southeast Asia use this form of locomotion almost exclusively (Fig. 5–5d).

Brachiation is seen in species characterized by arms longer than legs, a short stable lumbar spine, long curved fingers, and reduced thumbs. Because these are traits seen in all the apes, it is believed that although none of the great apes (orangutans, gorillas, bonobos, and chimpanzees) habitually brachiates today, they most likely inherited these characteristics from brachiating or perhaps climbing ancestors.

Brachiation
A form of locomotion in which the body is suspended beneath the hands and support is alternated from one forelimb to the other; arm swinging.

(c) Skeleton of a vertical clinger and leaper (indri).

(d) Skeleton of a brachiator (gibbon).

Some monkeys, particularly New World monkeys, are termed *semibrachiators*, as they practice a combination of leaping with some arm swinging. In a few New World species, arm swinging and other suspensory behaviors are enhanced by use of a *prehensile tail*, which in effect serves as a marvelously effective grasping fifth "hand." It should be noted that prehensile tails are strictly a New World phenomenon and are not seen in any Old World primate species.

Primate Taxonomy

The living primates are commonly categorized into their respective subgroups as shown in Figure 5–6. This taxonomy is based on the system originally established by Linnaeus. (Remember that the primate order, which includes a diverse array of approximately 190 species, belongs to a larger group, the class *Mammalia*.)

In any taxonomic system, organisms are organized into increasingly specific categories. For example, the order *Primates* includes *all* primates. However, at the next level down—the *suborder*—the primates have conventionally been divided into two large categories, Prosimii (all the prosimians: lemurs, lorises, and, customarily, the tarsiers) and Anthropoidea (all the monkeys, apes, and humans). Therefore, the suborder distinction is more specific and more precise than the order.

At the level of the suborder, the prosimians are distinct as a group from all the other primates, and this classification makes the biological and evolutionary statement that all the prosimian species are more closely related to one another than they are to any of the anthropoids. Likewise, all anthropoid species are more closely related to one another than to the prosimians.

At each succeeding level (infraorder, superfamily, family, subfamily, genus, and species), finer distinctions are made between categories until, at the species level, only those animals that can interbreed and produce viable offspring are included. In this manner, taxonomies not only organize diversity into categories, but also illustrate evolutionary and genetic relationships between species and groups of species.

The taxonomy presented in Figure 5–6 is the traditional one and is based on physical similarities between species and lineages. However, since the goal of any classification system is to clarify biological and evolutionary relationships between groups of organisms, this technique can be problematic. For example, two primate species that superficially resemble each other (e.g., some New and Old World monkeys) may in fact not be closely related at all. Using external morphology alone overlooks the unknown effects of separate evolutionary history. But evidence such as biochemical data avoids these pitfalls and indeed shows Old and New World monkeys to be genetically and evolutionarily quite distinct.

This relatively new perspective has enormous potential for clarifying taxonomic problems by making between-species comparisons of chromosomes and amino acid sequences in proteins. Direct comparisons of proteins (products of DNA) are excellent indicators of shared evolutionary history. If two primate species are similar with regard to protein structure, we know that their DNA sequences are also similar. It also follows that if two species share similar DNA, it is highly probable that both inherited their blueprint from a common ancestor.

Primate Chromosomes, Proteins, and DNA

One way to make genetic comparisons between organisms is to study their karyotypes, identifying similarities and differences in chromosome shape, size, number, and banding patterns. The more closely two species are related, the more alike their karyotypes should be. Among the large-bodied **hominoids**, the orangutan karyotype

Hominoids
Members of the superfamily Hominoidea. This group includes apes (chimpanzees, bonobos, gorillas, orangutans, gibbons, and siamangs) and humans.

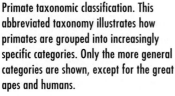

FIGURE 5–6
Primate taxonomic classification. This abbreviated taxonomy illustrates how primates are grouped into increasingly specific categories. Only the more general categories are shown, except for the great apes and humans.

Overview of the Primates

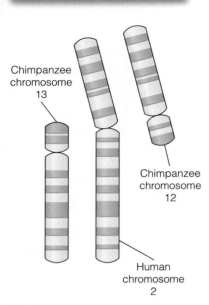

FIGURE 5–7
Human chromosome 2 has banding patterns that correspond to those of chimpanzee chromosomes 12 and 13. These similarities suggest that human chromosome 2 resulted from the fusion of these two ape chromosomes during the course of hominid evolution.

is the most conservative, with humans and the African apes displaying more recently evolved features. But within the African hominoids (gorillas, chimpanzees, bonobos, and humans), there is considerable uniformity in the structural arrangement and banding patterns of almost all the chromosomes. Consequently, the chromosomal evidence would support reclassifying orangutans, perhaps by placing them into a separate family from the African apes.

Comparisons of banding patterns of chimpanzee and human chromosomes have revealed a number of intriguing results. As you know, humans have 46 chromosomes, and chimpanzees have 48. Interestingly, the banding patterns of human chromosome 2 correspond to those of two much smaller chimpanzee chromosomes (chromosomes 12 and 13). This finding has led to speculation that in an ancestral hominoid, these two chromosomes fused to produce what became, in some populations, human chromosome 2 (Fig. 5–7).

The exact sequence of evolutionary relationships among humans and the African great apes is still in some dispute. Some tentative chromosomal data have suggested that humans and chimpanzees share a more recent ancestry after separating from gorillas (Yunis and Prakash, 1982). A more controlled study, however, with consideration of within-species variation of karyotypes (Stanyon and Chiarelli, 1982) supported the more traditional branching order, in which the human lineage diverged from the African great ape lineages, which in turn separated later.

Another method that has been used to identify genetic relationships between species is to examine the sequence of amino acids that make up specific proteins. This approach is based on the fact that proteins evolve. Consequently, while proteins serve the same functions in different species, they may vary somewhat in structure. The more closely related two species are, the more structurally similar their proteins will be. Comparisons between humans and African apes for the approximately half dozen proteins studied show striking similarities. For example, chimpanzees and humans differ with regard to only one amino acid in the series of 146 amino acids that make up the hemoglobin beta chain. However, comparisons between human hemoglobin and that of various Old World monkey species revealed differences in 4 to 9 amino acids, and the even more distantly related tarsiers differ by 15 amino acid substitutions.

Another technique called DNA hybridization matches DNA strands from two species to determine what percentage of bases match. The higher the percentage, the closer the genetic relationship between the two. The results of this technique show that 98.4 percent of the human and chimpanzee DNA base sequences examined are identical.

As useful as they are, these techniques are *indirect* methods of examining the DNA code. But today there are procedures that make it possible to sequence the nucleotides *directly* from the DNA molecule. However, the technologies of *DNA sequencing* used in the Human Genome Project (see p. 64) have not been extensively used to compare the DNA of nonhuman species. But there is strong support for such research, and once this approach is more widely applied, it will be possible to ascertain even more clearly the precise genetic and evolutionary relationships among the primates (McConkey and Vavki, 2000).

At present, amino acid sequencing and DNA hybridization, as well as other techniques, have reaffirmed the basic tenets of traditional primate classification. Moreover, they have shown how genetically close humans and the African great apes are. A systematic application of DNA hybridization (Sibley and Ahlquist, 1984) demonstrated that humans and chimpanzees are closer genetically than either is to the gorilla. For that matter, chimpanzees and humans share more genetic similarities than do zebras and horses or goats and sheep. On the basis of these results, it would be entirely consistent to classify humans and chimpanzees (perhaps gorillas

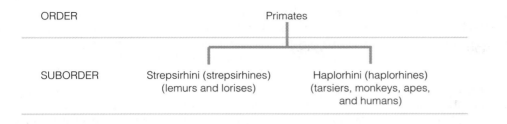

ORDER	Primates	
SUBORDER	Strepsirhini (strepsirhines) (lemurs and lorises)	Haplorhini (haplorhines) (tarsiers, monkeys, apes, and humans)

FIGURE 5–8
Revised partial classification of the primates. In this system, the terms *Prosimii* and *Anthropoidea* have been replaced by *Strepsirhini* and *Haplorhini*, respectively. The tarsier is included in the same suborder with monkeys, apes, and humans to reflect a closer relationship with these species than with lemurs and lorises. (Compare with Fig. 5–6.)

as well) within the same genus. Humans would continue to be called *Homo sapiens*, whereas chimpanzees would be classed as *Homo troglodytes*.

We have presented the traditional system of primate classification here, even though we acknowledge the need for modification. At present, not all anthropologists and biologists have completely accepted the revised terminology. Until consensus is reached and new designations are formally adopted, we think it appropriate to use the standard taxonomy along with discussion of some proposed changes. It is also important to point out that while specific details and names have not yet been worked out, the vast majority of experts do accept the evolutionary implications of the revised groupings.

Another area where modifications have been suggested concerns tarsiers (see p. 119). Tarsiers are highly specialized animals that display several unique physical characteristics. Because they possess a number of prosimian traits, tarsiers traditionally have been classified as prosimians (with lemurs and lorises); but they also share certain anthropoid features. Moreover, biochemically, tarsiers are more closely related to anthropoids than to prosimians (Dene et al., 1976); but with regard to chromosomes and several anatomical traits, they are distinct from both groups.

Today, most primatologists recognize tarsiers as more closely related to anthropoids than to prosimians. But instead of simply moving them into the suborder Anthropoidea, one proposed scheme places lemurs and lorises in a new suborder, Strepsirhini (instead of Prosimii), and includes tarsiers with monkeys, apes, and humans in another new suborder, Haplorhini (Szalay and Delson, 1979) (Fig. 5–8). Thus, in this classification, the conventionally named suborders Prosimii and Anthropoidea are replaced by Strepsirhini and Haplorhini, respectively. As yet, this designation has not been universally accepted, but the terminology has become common, especially in technical publications.

A Survey of the Living Primates

Prosimians (Lemurs and Lorises)

The most primitive of the primates are the lemurs and lorises. (We do not include tarsiers here, because their status is not as clear.) By "primitive" we mean that prosimians, taken as a group, are more similar anatomically to their earlier mammalian ancestors than are the other primates (monkeys, apes, and humans). Therefore, they tend to exhibit certain more ancestral characteristics, such as a more pronounced reliance on *olfaction* (sense of smell). Their greater olfactory capabilities (compared to other primates) are reflected in the presence of a moist, fleshy pad (**rhinarium**) at the end of the nose and in a relatively long snout. Moreover, prosimians mark territories with scent in a manner not seen in many other primates.

There are numerous other characteristics that distinguish lemurs and lorises from the anthropoids, including somewhat more laterally placed eyes, differences in reproductive physiology, and shorter gestation and maturation periods. Lemurs and lorises also possess a dental specialization known as the "dental comb." The

Rhinarium
(rine-air′-ee-um) The moist, hairless pad at the end of the nose seen in most mammalian species. The rhinarium enhances an animal's ability to smell.

Overview of the Primates

FIGURE 5–9
Prosimian dental comb, formed by forward-projecting incisors and canines.

Modern lemurs

FIGURE 5–10
Geographical distribution of modern lemurs.

dental comb is formed by forward-projecting lower incisors and canines, and together these modified teeth are used in both grooming and feeding (Fig. 5–9). One other characteristic that sets lemurs and lorises apart from anthropoids is the retention of a claw (called a "grooming claw") on the second toe.

Lemurs Lemurs are found only on the island of Madagascar and adjacent islands off the east coast of Africa (Fig. 5–10). As the only nonhuman primates on Madagascar, which comprises some 227,000 square miles, lemurs diversified into numerous and varied ecological niches without competition from monkeys and apes. Thus, the approximately 60 surviving species of lemurs, today restricted to Madagascar, represent an evolutionary pattern that has vanished elsewhere.

Lemurs range in size from the small mouse lemur, with a body length (head and trunk) of only 5 inches, to the indri, with a body length of a little over 2 feet (Napier and Napier, 1985). While the larger lemurs are diurnal and exploit a wide variety of dietary items, such as leaves, fruit, buds, bark, and shoots, the smaller forms (mouse and dwarf lemurs) are nocturnal and insectivorous.

Lemurs display considerable variation regarding numerous other aspects of behavior. While many are primarily arboreal, others, such as the ring-tailed lemur (Fig. 5–11), are more terrestrial. Some arboreal species are quadrupeds, and others (sifakas and indris) are vertical clingers and leapers (Fig. 5–12). Socially, several species (e.g., ring-tailed lemurs and sifakas) are gregarious and live in groups of 10 to 25 animals composed of males and females of all ages. Others (the indris) live in monogamous family units, and several nocturnal forms are mostly solitary.

Lorises Lorises (Fig. 5–13), which are similar in appearance to lemurs, were able to survive in mainland areas by adopting a nocturnal activity pattern at a time when most other prosimians became extinct. In this way, they were (and are) able to avoid competition with more recently evolved primates (the diurnal monkeys).

There are at least eight loris species, all of which are found in tropical forest and woodland habitats of India, Sri Lanka, Southeast Asia, and Africa. Also included in the same general category are six to nine (Bearder, 1987) galago species (Fig. 5–14), which are widely distributed throughout most of the forested and woodland savanna areas of sub-Saharan Africa.

Locomotion in lorises is a slow, cautious climbing form of quadrupedalism, and flexible hip joints permit suspension by hind limbs while the hands are used in feeding. All galagos, however, are highly agile and active vertical clingers and leapers. Some lorises and galagos are almost entirely insectivorous; others supplement their

Courtesy, Fred Jacobs

FIGURE 5–11
Ring-tailed lemur.

Courtesy, Fred Jacobs

FIGURE 5–12
Sifakas in their native habitat in Madagascar.

FIGURE 5–13
Slow loris.

FIGURE 5–14
Galago, or "bush baby."

diet with various combinations of fruit, leaves, gums, and slugs. Lorises and galagos frequently forage for food alone (females leave infants behind in nests until they are older). However, ranges overlap, and two or more females occasionally forage together or share the same sleeping nest.

Lemurs and lorises represent the same general adaptive level. Both groups exhibit good grasping and climbing abilities and a fairly well developed visual apparatus, although vision is not completely stereoscopic, and color vision may not be as well developed as in anthropoids. Most lemurs and lorises also have prolonged life spans as compared to most other small-bodied mammals, averaging about 14 years for lorises and 19 years for lemurs.

Tarsiers

There are three recognized tarsier species (Fig. 5–15), all restricted to island areas in Southeast Asia (Fig. 5–16), where they inhabit a wide range of forest types, from tropical forest to backyard gardens. Tarsiers are nocturnal insectivores, leaping onto prey (which may also include small vertebrates) from lower branches and shrubs. They appear to form stable pair bonds, and the basic tarsier social unit is a mated pair and their young offspring (MacKinnon and MacKinnon, 1980).

As we have already mentioned, tarsiers present a complex blend of characteristics not seen in other primates. Moreover, they are unique in that their enormous eyes, which dominate much of the face, are immobile within their sockets. To compensate for this inability to move the eyes, tarsiers are able to rotate their heads 180° in a decidedly owl-like manner.

Anthropoids (Monkeys, Apes, and Humans)

Although there is much variation among anthropoids, there are certain features that, when taken together, distinguish them as a group from prosimians (and other placental mammals). Here is a partial list of these traits:

1. Generally larger body size
2. Larger brain (in absolute terms and relative to body weight)
3. Reduced reliance on the sense of smell, indicated by absence of rhinarium and other structures
4. Increased reliance on vision, with forward-facing eyes placed at front of face
5. Greater degree of color vision
6. Back of eye socket formed by a bony plate
7. Blood supply to brain different from that of prosimians

FIGURE 5–15
Tarsier.

Tarsiers

FIGURE 5–16
Geographical distribution of tarsiers.

8. Fusion of the two sides of the mandible at the midline to form one bone (in prosimians and tarsiers they are joined by fibrous tissue)
9. Less specialized dentition, as seen in absence of dental comb and some other features
10. Differences with regard to female internal reproductive anatomy
11. Longer gestation and maturation periods
12. Increased parental care
13. More mutual grooming

Approximately 70 percent of all primates are monkeys. It is frequently impossible to give precise numbers of species because the taxonomic status of some primates remains in doubt, and primatologists are still making new discoveries. (In fact, between 1990 and 2001, 22 species and subspecies of monkeys were discovered and described.) Monkeys are divided into two groups separated by geographical area (New World and Old World), as well as by several million years of separate evolutionary history.

New World Monkeys   The New World monkeys exhibit a wide range of size, diet, and ecological adaptation. In size, they vary from the tiny marmosets and tamarins (about 12 ounces) to the 20-pound howler monkey (Figs. 5–17 and 5–18). New World monkeys are almost exclusively arboreal, and some never come to the ground. Like Old World monkeys, all except one species (the douroucouli, or owl monkey) are diurnal. Although confined to the trees, New World monkeys can be found in a wide range of arboreal environments throughout most forested areas in southern Mexico and Central and South America (Fig. 5–19).

One of the characteristics distinguishing New World monkeys from those found in the Old World is shape of the nose. New World forms have broad noses with outward-facing nostrils. Conversely, Old World monkeys have narrower noses with downward-facing nostrils. This difference in nose form has given rise to the terms *platyrrhine* (flat-nosed) and *catarrhine* (downward-facing nose) to refer to New and Old World anthropoids, respectively.

New World monkeys have traditionally been divided into two families: **Callitrichidae** (marmosets and tamarins) and **Cebidae** (all others). Some authors have suggested that molecular data along with recently reported fossil evidence indicate that a major regrouping of New World monkeys is in order (Fleagle, 1999).*

Callitrichidae
(kal-eh-trick´-eh-dee)

Cebidae
(see´-bid-ee)

FIGURE 5–17
A pair of golden lion tamarins.

FIGURE 5–18
Howler monkeys.

Marmosets and tamarins are the most primitive of monkeys, retaining claws instead of nails and usually giving birth to twins instead of one infant. They are mostly insectivorous, although marmoset diet includes gums from trees, and tamarins also rely heavily on fruit. Locomotion is quadrupedal, and their claws aid in climbing vertical tree trunks, much in the manner of squirrels. Moreover, some tamarins employ vertical clinging and leaping as a form of travel. Socially, these small monkeys live in family groups composed usually of a mated pair, or a female and two adult males, and their offspring. Indeed, marmosets and tamarins are among the few primate species in which males are heavily involved in infant care.

There are at least 30 cebid species, ranging in size from the squirrel monkey (body length 12 inches) to the howler (body length 24 inches). Diet varies, with most relying on a combination of fruit and leaves supplemented, to varying degrees, by insects. Most cebids are quadrupedal, but some—for example, the spider monkey (Fig. 5–20)—are semibrachiators. Some cebids, including the spider and howler, also possess powerful prehensile tails that are used not only in locomotion but also for suspension under branches while feeding on leaves and fruit. Socially, most cebids are found either in groups of both sexes and all age categories or in monogamous pairs with subadult offspring.

Old World Monkeys Except for humans, Old World monkeys are the most widely distributed of all living primates. They are found throughout sub-Saharan Africa and southern Asia, ranging from tropical jungle habitats to semiarid desert and even to seasonally snow-covered areas in northern Japan (Fig. 5–21).

Most Old World monkeys are quadrupedal and primarily arboreal, but some (e.g., baboons) are also adapted to life on the ground. Whether in trees or on the ground, these monkeys spend a good deal of time sleeping, feeding, and grooming while sitting with their upper bodies held erect. Usually associated with this

FIGURE 5–19
Geographical distribution of modern New World monkeys.

Robert L. Lubeck/Animals Animals

FIGURE 5–20
Spider monkey. Note the prehensile tail.

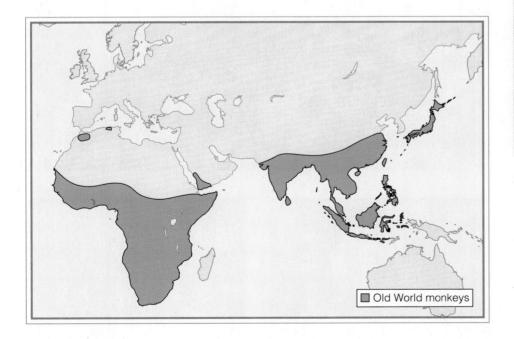

FIGURE 5–21
Geographical distribution of modern Old World monkeys.

*One possibility is to include spider monkeys, howler monkeys, and muriquis (woolly spider monkeys) in a third family, Atelidae (see taxonomic chart, p. 115). Another is to eliminate the family Callitrichidae altogether and include marmosets and tamarins as a subfamily within the family Cebidae.

Overview of the Primates

Ischial callosities
Patches of tough, hard skin on the buttocks of Old World monkeys and chimpanzees.

Cercopithecidae
(serk-oh-pith´-eh-sid-ee)

Cercopithecines
(serk-oh-pith´-eh-seens) The subfamily of Old World monkeys that includes baboons, macaques, and guenons.

Colobines
(kole´-uh-beans) The subfamily of Old World monkeys that includes the African colobus monkeys and Asian langurs.

universal sitting posture are areas of hardened skin on the buttocks (**ischial callosities**) that serve as sitting pads.

Within the entire group of Old World monkeys there is only one recognized taxonomic family: **Cercopithecidae**. This family, in turn, is divided into two subfamilies: the **cercopithecines** and **colobines**.

The cercopithecines are the more generalized of the two groups, showing a more omnivorous dietary adaptation and cheek pouches for storing food. As a group, the cercopithecines eat almost anything, including fruit, seeds, leaves, grasses, tubers, roots, nuts, insects, birds' eggs, amphibians, small reptiles, and small mammals (the last seen in baboons).

The majority of cercopithecine species, such as the mostly arboreal guenons (Fig. 5–22) and the more terrestrial savanna (Fig. 5–23) and hamadryas baboons are found in Africa. However, the several species of macaque, which include the well-known rhesus monkey, are widely distributed in southern Asia and India.

Colobine species are more limited dietarily, specializing on mature leaves, a behavior that has led to their designation as "leaf-eating monkeys." The colobines are found mainly in Asia, but both the red colobus and the black-and-white colobus are exclusively African (Fig. 5–24). Other colobines include several species of Asian langur and the proboscis monkey of Borneo.

Locomotor behavior among Old World monkeys includes arboreal quadrupedalism in guenons, macaques, and langurs; terrestrial quadrupedalism in baboons, patas, and macaques; and semibrachiation and acrobatic leaping in colobus monkeys.

FIGURE 5–22
Adult male sykes monkey, one of several guenon species.

Robert Jurmain

FIGURE 5–23
Savanna baboons. (a) Male. (b) Female.

Courtesy, Bonnie Pedersen/Arlene Kruse

Courtesy, Bonnie Pedersen/Arlene Kruse

(a)

(b)

Robert Jurmain

FIGURE 5–24
Black-and-white colobus monkey.

Marked differences in body size or shape between the sexes, referred to as **sexual dimorphism**, are typical of some terrestrial species and are particularly pronounced in baboons and patas. In these species, male body weight (up to 80 pounds in baboons) may be twice that of females.

Females of several species (especially baboons and some macaques) exhibit pronounced cyclical changes of the external genitalia. These changes, including swelling and redness, are associated with **estrus**, a hormonally initiated period of sexual receptivity in female nonhuman mammals correlated with ovulation.

Several types of social organization characterize Old World monkeys, and there are uncertainties among primatologists regarding some species. In general, colobines tend to live in small groups, with only one or two adult males. Savanna baboons and most macaque species are found in large social units comprising several adults of both sexes and offspring of all ages. Monogamous pairing is not common in Old World monkeys, but is seen in a few langurs and possibly one or two guenon species.

Old and New World Monkeys: A Striking Case of Homoplasy We have mentioned several differences between Old World monkeys and New World monkeys, but the fact remains that they are all monkeys. That is, they all are adapted to a similar (primarily arboreal) way of life. With the exception of the South American owl monkey, they are diurnal, and all are social, usually fairly omnivorous, and quadrupedal, though with variations of this general locomotor pattern.

These similarities are all the more striking when we consider that Old and New World monkeys have gone their separate evolutionary paths for at least 30 million years. It was once believed that both lineages evolved independently from separate prosimian ancestors. The current consensus among researchers, however, disputes this claim (Hoffstetter, 1972; Ciochon and Chiarelli, 1980) and postulates that both Old and New World monkeys arose in Africa from a common monkey ancestor and later reached South America by "rafting" over on chunks of land that had broken away from mainland areas.

There have been various reports of large "floating islands" of vegetation and trees on the open ocean, but there are few accounts of vertebrates being transported across large bodies of water. However, over-water dispersal hypotheses recently gained support in a report by Censky et al. (1998) that describes the probable

Sexual dimorphism
Differences in physical characteristics between males and females of the same species. For example, humans are slightly sexually dimorphic for body size, with males being taller, on average, than females of the same population.

Estrus
(ess´-truss) Period of sexual receptivity in female mammals (except humans), correlated with ovulation. When used as an adjective, the word is spelled "estrous."

introduction, in 1995, of a species of iguana to an island in the Caribbean. The dispersal of this species to new habitats was attributed to ocean currents and, more specifically, to two hurricanes that struck the region about one month prior to the appearance of the lizards on the island.

A number of conditions that existed 50–30 million years ago could have facilitated such a trans-Atlantic crossing from Africa to South America. South America and Africa were somewhat closer together than they are today, and it is believed that prevailing ocean currents would have been favorable. In fact, it is believed that a voyage of around 600 miles could have been accomplished in less than three weeks. In addition, a series of large volcanic islands that existed in the Caribbean and South Atlantic may have served as "stepping stones" for would-be immigrants.

Whether the last common ancestor shared by New and Old World monkeys was a prosimian or a monkey-like animal, what is most remarkable is that the two forms have not diverged more than they have over the last 30 million years or so. The diverse arboreal adaptations we see in the living monkeys of both hemispheres are the result of parallel adaptation in geographically distinct populations responding to similar selective pressures in tropical arboreal environments. This process is called **homoplasy** (see Chapter 8 for further discussion). The result is that the primates we recognize as monkeys evolved in both the New and Old Worlds.

Hominoids (Apes and Humans)

The other large grouping of anthropoids, the hominoids, includes apes and humans. The superfamily **Hominoidea** includes the "lesser" apes in the family **Hylobatidae** (gibbons and siamangs); the great apes in the family **Pongidae** (orangutans, gorillas, bonobos, and chimpanzees); and humans in the family Hominidae.

Apes and humans differ from monkeys in numerous ways:

1. Generally larger body size, except for gibbons and siamangs
2. Absence of a tail
3. Shortened trunk (lumbar area shorter and more stable)
4. Differences in position and musculature of the shoulder joint (adapted for suspensory locomotion)
5. More complex behavior
6. More complex brain and enhanced cognitive abilities
7. Increased period of infant development and dependency

Gibbons and Siamangs   The 14 gibbon species and the closely related siamang are today found in the southeastern tropical areas of Asia (Fig. 5–25). These animals are the smallest of the apes, with a long, slender body weighing 13 pounds in the gibbon (Fig. 5–26) and 25 pounds in the larger siamang.

The most distinctive structural feature of gibbons and siamangs is related to an adaptation for brachiation. They have extremely long arms, long, permanently curved fingers, short thumbs, and powerful shoulder muscles. These highly specialized locomotor adaptations may be related to feeding behavior while hanging beneath branches. The diet of both species is largely composed of fruit. Both (especially the siamang) also eat a variety of leaves, flowers, and insects.

The basic social unit of gibbons and siamangs comprises an adult male and female with dependent offspring. Although these small apes have been described as monogamous, in reality they sometimes do mate with other individuals. As in marmosets and tamarins, male gibbons and siamangs are very much involved in rearing their young. Both males and females are highly territorial and protect their territories with elaborate whoops and sirenlike "songs."

Homoplasy
(*homo*, meaning "same," and *plasy*, meaning "growth") The separate evolutionary development of similar characteristics in different groups of organisms.

Hominoidea
The formal designation for the superfamily of anthropoids that includes apes and humans.

Hylobatidae
(high-lo-baht´-id-ee)

Pongidae
(ponj´-id-ee)

FIGURE 5–25
Geographical distribution of modern Asian apes.

FIGURE 5–26
White-handed gibbon.

Orangutans   Orangutans (*Pongo pygmaeus*) (Fig. 5–27) are represented by two sub-species found today only in heavily forested areas on the Indonesian islands of Borneo and Sumatra (see Fig. 5–25). Due to poaching by humans and continuing habitat loss on both islands, orangutans are threatened by extinction in the wild.

Orangutans are slow, cautious climbers whose locomotor behavior can best be described as "four-handed," referring to the tendency to use all four limbs for grasping and support. Although they are almost completely arboreal, orangutans do sometimes travel quadrupedally on the ground. Orangutans are also very large animals with pronounced sexual dimorphism (males may weigh 200 pounds or more and females less than 100 pounds).

In the wild, orangutans lead largely solitary lives, although adult females are usually accompanied by one or two dependent offspring. They are primarily **frugivorous**, but bark, leaves, insects, and meat (on rare occasions) may also be eaten.

Frugivorous
(fru-give´-or-us) Having a diet composed primarily of fruit.

FIGURE 5–27
Female orangutan.

Gorillas   The largest of all living primates, gorillas (*Gorilla gorilla*) are today confined to forested areas of western and eastern equatorial Africa (Fig. 5–28). There are three generally recognized subspecies, although molecular data suggest that one of these, the western lowland gorilla (Fig. 5–29), is perhaps sufficiently genetically distinct to warrant designation as a separate species (Ruvolo et al., 1994; Garner and Ryder, 1996). The western lowland gorilla is found in several countries of western central Africa and is the most numerous of the three subspecies, with a population size of perhaps 110,000 (Doran and McNeilage, 1998). The eastern lowland gorilla is found near the eastern border of the Democratic Republic of the Congo (DRC—formerly Zaire) and numbers about 12,000. Mountain gorillas (Fig. 5–30), the most extensively studied of the three subspecies, are found in the mountainous areas of central Africa in Rwanda, the DRC, and Uganda. Mountain gorillas have probably never been very numerous, and today they are among the more endangered primates, numbering only about 600.

Gorillas exhibit marked sexual dimorphism, with males weighing up to 400 pounds and females around 150 to 200 pounds. Because of their weight, adult gorillas, especially males, are primarily terrestrial and adopt a semiquadrupedal (knuckle-walking) posture on the ground.

Mountain gorillas live in groups consisting of one (or sometimes two) large *silverback* males, a variable number of adult females, and their subadult offspring. The term *silverback* refers to the saddle of white hair across the back of full adult (at least 12 or 13 years of age) male gorillas. Additionally, the silverback male may tolerate the presence of one or more young adult *blackback* males, probably his sons. Typically, but not always, both females and males leave their natal group as young adults. Females join other groups, and males, who appear to be less likely to emigrate, may live alone for a while, or they may join an all-male group before eventually forming their own group.

Systematic studies of free-ranging western lowland gorillas were not initiated until the mid-1980s; thus, our knowledge of their social structure and behavior is still in its infancy. In general, it appears that their social structure is similar to that of mountain gorillas, but groups are smaller and somewhat less cohesive.

All gorillas are almost exclusively vegetarian. Mountain gorillas concentrate primarily on leaves, pith, and stalks. These foods are also important for western

FIGURE 5–28
Geographical distribution of modern African apes.

- ☐ Chimpanzees
- ☐ Bonobos
- ☐ Gorillas

(a) (b)

FIGURE 5–29
Western lowland gorillas. (a) Male. (b) Female.

(a)   (b)

lowland gorillas, but western lowland gorillas also eat considerably more fruit, depending on seasonal availability. Recent studies also report that western lowland gorillas, unlike mountain gorillas (which avoid water), frequently wade through swamps while foraging on aquatic plants.

Perhaps because of their large body size and enormous strength, gorillas have long been considered ferocious monsters; but in reality, they are shy and gentle. This is not to imply that gorillas are never aggressive. Indeed, male-male competition for females can be extremely violent. Moreover, when threatened, males will attack, and they will certainly defend their group from any perceived danger, whether it be another male gorilla or a human hunter. Still, the reputation of gorillas as murderous beasts is the result of uninformed myth making and little else.

Chimpanzees   Chimpanzees are probably the best known of all nonhuman primates (Fig. 5–31). Often misunderstood because of zoo exhibits, circus acts, television shows, and movies, the true nature of chimpanzees did not become known until years of fieldwork with wild groups provided a reliable picture. Today, chimpanzees are found in equatorial Africa, stretching in a broad belt from the Atlantic Ocean in the west to Lake Tanganyika in the east. Their range, however, is patchy within this large geographical area, and with further habitat destruction, it is becoming even more so.

Chimpanzees are in many ways structurally similar to gorillas, with corresponding limb proportions and upper-body shape. This similarity is due to commonalities in locomotion when on the ground (quadrupedal knuckle walking). However, the ecological adaptations of chimpanzees and gorillas differ, with chimpanzees spending more time in the trees. Moreover, whereas gorillas are typically placid and quiet, chimpanzees are highly excitable, active, and noisy.

Chimpanzees are smaller than orangutans and gorillas, and although they are sexually dimorphic, sex differences are not as pronounced as in these other species. While male chimpanzees may weigh over 100 pounds, females may weigh at least 80.

In addition to quadrupedal knuckle walking, chimpanzees (particularly youngsters) may brachiate while in the trees. When on the ground, they frequently walk bipedally for short distances when carrying food or other objects. One adult male at Jane Goodall's study area in Tanzania frequently walked bipedally because one arm was paralyzed by polio (Goodall, 1986).

FIGURE 5–30
Mountain gorillas. (a) Male. (b) Female.

(a)

(b)

FIGURE 5–31
Chimpanzees. (a) Male. (b) Female.

Chimpanzees eat an amazing variety of items, including fruit, leaves, insects, nuts, birds' eggs, berries, caterpillars, and small mammals. Moreover, both males and females occasionally take part in group hunting efforts to kill such small mammals as red colobus, young baboons, bushpigs, and antelope. When hunts are successful, the prey is shared by the group members.

Chimpanzees live in large, fluid communities of as many as 50 individuals or more. At the core of a chimpanzee community is a group of bonded males. Although relationships between them are not always peaceful or stable, these males nevertheless act as a group to defend their territory and are highly intolerant of unfamiliar chimpanzees, especially nongroup males.

Even though chimpanzees are said to live in communities, there are few times, if any, when all members are together. Indeed, it is the nature of chimpanzees to come and go, so that the individuals they encounter vary from day to day. Moreover, adult females tend to forage either alone or in the company of their offspring. The latter foraging group could comprise several chimpanzees, as females with infants sometimes accompany their own mothers and their younger siblings. A female may also leave her community, either permanently to join another community or temporarily while she is in estrus. This behavioral pattern may reduce the risk of mating with close male relatives, because males apparently never leave the group in which they were born.

Chimpanzee social behavior is complex, and individuals form lifelong attachments with friends and relatives. Indeed, the bond between mothers and infants can remain strong until one or the other dies. This may be a considerable period, because many wild chimpanzees live into their mid-30s and a few into their 40s.

Bonobos Bonobos (*Pan paniscus*) are found only in an area south of the Zaire River in the Democratic Republic of the Congo (see Fig. 5–28). Not officially recognized by European scientists until the 1920s, they remain among the least studied of the great apes. Although ongoing field studies have produced much information (Susman, 1984; Kano, 1992), research has been periodically hampered by political unrest. There are no accurate counts of bonobos, but their numbers are believed to be between 10,000 and 20,000 (IUCN, 1996), and these are threatened by human hunting, warfare, and habitat loss.

Because bonobos bear a strong resemblance to chimpanzees but are somewhat smaller, they have been called "pygmy chimpanzees." However, differences in body size are not sufficient to warrant this designation, and in fact, bonobos exhibit several anatomical and behavioral differences from chimpanzees. Physically, they have a more linear body build, longer legs relative to arms, a relatively smaller head, a dark face from birth, and tufts of hair at the side of the face (Fig. 5–32).

Bonobos are more arboreal than chimpanzees, and they appear to be less excitable and aggressive. While aggression is not unknown, it appears that physical violence both within and between groups is uncommon. Like chimpanzees, bonobos live in geographically based, fluid communities, and they exploit many of the same foods, including occasional meat derived from killing small mammals (Badrian and Malinky, 1984). But bonobo communities are not centered around a group of closely bonded males. Rather, male-female bonding is more important than in chimpanzees (and most other nonhuman primates), and females are not peripheral to the group (Badrian and Badrian, 1984). This may be related to bonobo sexuality, which differs in expression from that of other nonhuman primates in that copulation is frequent and occurs throughout a female's estrous cycle.

Bonobos are relatively late to arrive on the scene of primate research. But it is crucial that studies of this intriguing species be allowed to progress. Not only do bonobos have the potential of providing information about human behavior and

Courtesy, Ellen Ingmanson

FIGURE 5–32
Female bonobos with young.

evolution, but they are of considerable interest in their own right and they are highly endangered. In fact, without research and protection, they, like so many other nonhuman primates, are very much in danger of extinction.

Humans

Humans are the only living representatives of the family Hominidae (genus *Homo*, species *sapiens*). Our primate heritage is evident in our overall anatomy and genetic makeup and in many aspects of human behavior. With the exception of reduced canine size, human teeth are typical primate teeth; indeed, in overall morphology, they very much resemble ape teeth. The human dependence on vision and decreased reliance on olfaction, as well as flexible limbs and grasping hands, are rooted in our primate, arboreal past. Humans can even brachiate, and playgrounds often accommodate this ability in children.

Humans in general are omnivorous, although all societies observe certain culturally based dietary restrictions. Nevertheless, as a species with a rather generalized digestive system, we are physiologically adapted to digest an extremely wide assortment of foods. Perhaps to our detriment, given how humans tend to go to extremes, we also share with our relatives a fondness for sweets that originates from the importance of high-energy fruits in the diets of many nonhuman primates.

But quite obviously, humans are unique among primates and indeed among all animals. For example, no member of any other species has the ability to write or think about issues such as how they differ from other life forms. This ability is rooted in the fact that human evolution, during the last 800,000 years or so, has been characterized by dramatic increases in brain size and other neurological changes.

Humans are also completely dependent on culture. Without cultural innovation, it would have been impossible for us to have ever left the tropics. As it is, humans inhabit every corner of the planet with the exception of Antarctica, and we have even established outposts there. And lest we forget, a fortunate few have even walked on the moon. None of the technologies (indeed, none of the other aspects of culture) that humans have developed over the last several thousand years would have been possible without the highly developed cognitive abilities we alone possess. Nevertheless, the neurological basis for intelligence is rooted in our evolutionary

See Virtual Lab 1, section III for a contrast between the geographical ranges of nonhuman primates versus humans.

past, and it is something we share with other primates. Indeed, research has demonstrated that several nonhuman primate species—most notably chimpanzees, bonobos, and gorillas—display a level of problem solving and insight that most people would have considered impossible 25 years ago (see Chapter 7).

Humans are uniquely predisposed to use spoken language, and for the last 5,000 years or so, we have used written language as well. This ability exists because human evolution has modified certain neurological and anatomical structures in ways not observed in any other animal. But while nonhuman primates are not anatomically capable of producing speech, research has demonstrated that to varying degrees, the great apes are able to communicate through the use of symbols. And basically, that is a foundation for language that humans and the great apes (to a limited degree) have in common.

Aside from cognitive abilities, the one other trait that sets humans apart from other primates is our unique (among mammals) form of *habitual* bipedal locomotion. This particular trait appeared early in the evolution of our lineage, and over time, we have become more efficient at it because of related changes in the musculoskeletal anatomy of the pelvis, leg, and foot (see Chapter 10). But for whatever reasons, early hominids increasingly adopted bipedalism because they were already preadapted for it. That is, as primates, and especially as ape-like primates, they were already behaviorally predisposed to, and anatomically capable of, at least short-term bipedal walking before they adopted it wholeheartedly.

Thus, while it is certainly true that human beings are unique intellectually, and in some ways anatomically, we are still primates. In fact, it is quite reasonable to say that fundamentally, humans are exaggerated primates.

Endangered Primates

In September 2000, scientists announced that a subspecies of red colobus, named Miss Waldron's red colobus, had officially been declared extinct. This announcement came after a six-year search for the 20-pound monkey that had not been seen for 20 years (Oates, et al., 2000). Thus, this species, indigenous to the West African countries of Ghana and the Ivory Coast, has the distinction of being the first nonhuman primate to be declared extinct in the twenty-first century. But it will certainly not be the last. In fact, as of this writing, over half of all nonhuman primate species are now in jeopardy, and some face almost immediate extinction in the wild (Table 5–1).

Population estimates of free-ranging primates are difficult to obtain, but some species (hapalemur, diadem sifaka, aye-aye, lion tamarin, muriqui, red colobus subspecies, lion-tailed macaque, and mountain gorilla) now number only in the hundreds. Others are believed to be represented in the wild by a few thousand (agile mangabey, mentawi langur, red colobus subspecies, moloch gibbon, Kloss' gibbon, orangutan, lowland gorilla, chimpanzee, and bonobo).

There are three basic reasons for the worldwide depletion of nonhuman primates: habitat destruction, hunting for food, and live capture for export or local trade. Underlying these three causes is one major factor: unprecedented human population growth, which is occurring at a faster rate in developing countries than in the developed world. The developing nations of Africa, Asia, and Central and South America are home to over 90 percent of all nonhuman primate species, and these countries, aided in no small part by the industrialized countries of Europe and the United States, are cutting their forests at a rate of about 30 million acres per year (Fig. 5–33). In Brazil, the Atlantic rain forest originally covered some 385,000 square miles. Today, an estimated 7 percent is all that remains of what was once home to countless New World monkeys and thousands of other species.

TABLE 5–1   African Primates in Danger of Extinction

Species/ Subspecies Common Name	Location	Estimated Size of Remaining Population	Species/ Subspecies Common Name	Location	Estimated Size of Remaining Population
Barbary macaque	North Africa	23,000	Preuss' red colobus	Cameroon	8,000
Tana River mangabey	Tana River, Kenya	800–1,100	Bouvier's red colobus	Congo Republic	?
Sanje mangabey	Uzungwa Mts., Tanzania	1,800–3,000	Tana River red colobus	Tana River, Kenya	200–300
Drill	Cameroon, Bioko	?	Uhehe red colobus	Uzungwa Mts., Tanzania	10,000
Preuss' guenon	Cameroon, Bioko	?	Zanzibar red colobus	Zanzibar	1,500
White-throated guenon	Southwest Nigeria	?	Mountain gorilla	Virunga Volcanoes (Rwanda, Uganda, and Democratic Republic of the Congo) and Impenetrable Forest (Uganda)	550–650
Pennant's red colobus	Bioko	?			

Much of the motivation behind the devastation of the rain forests is, of course, economic: the short-term gains from clearing forests to create immediately available (but poor) farmland or ranchland; the use of trees for lumber and paper products; and large-scale mining operations (with their necessary roads, digging, etc., all of which cause habitat destruction). Regionally, the loss of rain forest ranks as a national disaster for some countries. For example, the West African nation Sierra Leone had an estimated 15,000 square miles of rain forest early in the twentieth century. Today, less than 530 square miles remain, and most of this destruction has occurred since World War II. People in many developing countries are also short of fuel and frequently use whatever firewood is obtainable And, of course, the demand for tropical hardwoods (e.g., mahogany, teak, and rosewood) in the United States, Europe, and Japan continues unabated, creating an enormously profitable market for rain forest products.

Primates have also been captured live for zoos, biomedical research, and the exotic pet trade. Live capture has declined since the implementation of the Convention on Trade in Endangered Species of Wild Flora and Fauna (CITES) in 1973. Currently, 87 countries have signed this treaty, agreeing not to allow trade in species listed by CITES as being endangered. However, even some CITES members are still occasionally involved in the illegal primate trade (Japan and Belgium, among others).

In most areas, habitat loss has been, and continues to be, the single greatest cause of declining numbers of nonhuman primates. But in parts of western and central Africa, human hunting for food now poses an even greater threat. This tragic turn of events occurred rather quickly, but during the 1990s, primatologists became increasingly aware of the immense scope of the slaughter, which now accounts for the loss of thousands of nonhuman primates and other species annually (see Issue, pp. 135–138).

But the problem extends well beyond Africa. In South America, for example, hunting nonhuman primates for food is common. And one report documents that in less than two years, one family of Brazilian rubber tappers killed almost 500 members of various large-bodied species, including spider monkeys, woolly monkeys, and howler monkeys (Peres, 1990). Moreover, live capture and (illegal) trade

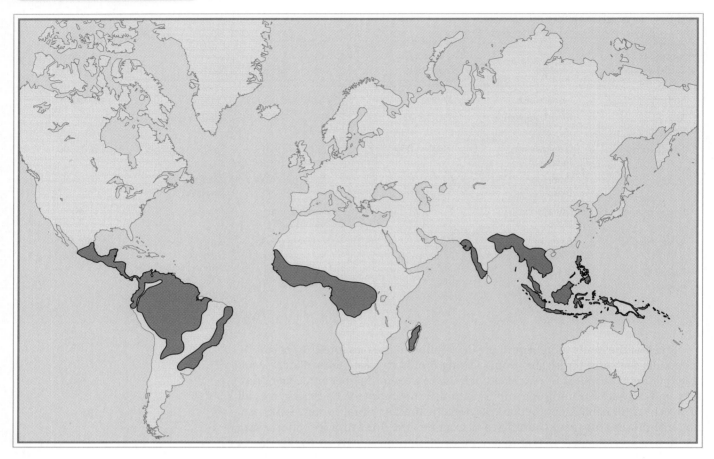

FIGURE 5–33
Tropical rain forests of the world (distribution before recent massive destruction).

in endangered primate species continues unabated in China and Southeast Asia, where nonhuman primates are eaten and also funneled into the exotic pet trade. But perhaps most important is the fact that primate body parts also figure prominently in traditional medicines, and with increasing human population size, the enormous demand for these products (and products from other, nonprimate species, such as tigers) has placed many species in extreme jeopardy.

Fortunately, steps are being taken to ensure the survival of some species. Many developing countries, such as Costa Rica and the Malagasy Republic (Madagascar), are designating national parks and other reserves for the protection of natural resources, including primates. There are also now several private international efforts aimed at curbing the bush meat trade. It is only through such practices and through educational programs that many primate species have a chance of escaping extinction, at least in the immediate future.

If you are in your 20s or 30s, you will live to hear of the extinction of some of our marvelously unique and clever cousins. Many more will undoubtedly slip away unnoticed. Tragically, this will occur, in most cases, before we have even had the opportunity to get to know them.

Each species on earth is the current result of a unique set of evolutionary events that, over millions of years, has produced a finely adapted component of a diverse ecosystem. When it becomes extinct, that adaptation and that part of biodiversity is lost forever. What a tragedy it will be if, through our own mismanagement and greed, we awaken to a world without chimpanzees, mountain gorillas, or the tiny, exquisite lion tamarin. When this day comes, we truly will have lost a part of ourselves, and we will be the poorer for it.

SUMMARY

In this chapter, we have introduced you to the primates, the mammalian order that includes humans. As a group, the primates are generalized in terms of diet and loco-motor patterns, and these behavioral generalizations are reflected in the morphology of the teeth and limbs.

We have also discussed some of the anatomical similarities and differences between the major groupings of primates: prosimians, monkeys (New and Old World), and hominoids. In the next chapter, we will turn our attention to primate social behavior and cognitive abilities. These are extremely important topics, for it is through better understanding nonhuman primate behavior that we can make more general statements about human behavior. Moreover, increasing our knowledge is essential if we are to prevent many of these uniquely adapted and marvelous relatives of ours from being lost forever.

QUESTIONS FOR REVIEW

1. Discuss why primates are said to be "generalized mammals."
2. Summarize the major characteristics of primates.
3. How does adaptation to an arboreal environment help explain primate evolution?
4. What is the geographical distribution of the nonhuman primates?
5. What are the two major subdivisions of the order Primates?
6. Which major groups of primates are included within the anthropoids?
7. What is a dental formula? What is the dental formula of all the Old World anthropoids?
8. What are quadrupedalism, vertical clinging and leaping, and brachiation? Name at least one primate species that is characterized by each of these.
9. What are the major differences between prosimians and anthropoids?
10. What are at least three anatomical differences between monkeys and apes?
11. Name the two major categories (subfamilies) of Old World monkeys. In general, what is the geographical distribution of each?
12. Explain how a taxonomic classification scheme reflects biological relationships.
13. Where are lemurs and lorises found today?
14. In general, which primates have prehensile tails?
15. What are the two family divisions of New World monkeys? Name at least one species for each.
16. In which taxonomic family have the great apes traditionally been placed?
17. Define estrus.
18. Describe the type of social organization seen in chimpanzees (*Pan troglodytes*) and gorillas.
19. How do bonobos (*Pan paniscus*) differ from "common" chimpanzees (*Pan troglodytes*)?
20. What are the major problems that threaten the survival of many nonhuman primate species today?

SUGGESTED FURTHER READING

Fleagle, John. 1999. *Primate Adaptation and Evolution*. New York: Academic Press.

Mittermeier, Russell A., Ian Tattersall, William R. Konstant, David M. Meyers, and Roderick B. Mast. 1994. *Lemurs of Madagascar*. Washington, DC: Conservation International.

Napier, J. R., and P. H. Napier. 1985. *The Natural History of the Primates*. Cambridge, MA: MIT Press.

Sussman, Robert W. 1991. "Primate Origins and the Evolution of the Angiosperms." *American Journal of Primatology* 23: 209–223.

RESOURCES ON THE INTERNET

 ### Wadsworth Anthropology Resource Center
http://anthropology.wadsworth.com

The companion website for this text includes a range of enrichment material focused on the chapter's topic. While online you can enhance your understanding of the chapter by exploring one of the several additional Internet exercises, by researching topics, and by accessing full articles on InfoTrac College Edition. You can also reinforce the concepts by taking online practice exams.

Internet Exercises

Because many primate species are endangered, conservation is a major topic. To learn more about conservation, visit Primate Info Net (**www.primate.wisc.edu/pin**). Under "Resources in Primatology," go to "Conservation," and choose one of the conservation links. Read the link and write a short summary. What species and its habitat is discussed at the link? What can we do, or what can you do, to improve the chances of survival for this species?

 ### InfoTrac College Edition
http://www.infotrac-college.com/wadsworth

Search InfoTrac College Edition for a nonhuman primate species. You will probably find more references if you search for *chimpanzee, gorilla, orangutan*, or *baboon*, but you need not limit your search to these. Does the article you found contain much of the information presented in Chapter 5? If so, list the topics the two share. Also list those topics not included in the chapter.

The Bushmeat Trade: Just When We Thought Things Couldn't Get Any Worse...

For at least two decades, habitat loss was considered the single greatest threat to wild populations of nonhuman primates, and indeed, this remains true in many parts of the world. However, many primatologists and conservationists were taken off guard when, in the 1990s, they became aware of the devastating effects of a rapidly developing trade in *bushmeat* (meat derived from wild animals) in West and central Africa. Actually, as early as the 1960s and '70s, primatologists began reporting that monkeys in many West African forests were becoming scarce because of a developing commercial trade in monkey meat (Oates, 1999). But the slaughter that is occurring now is unprecedented.

Wherever they occur, nonhuman primates have traditionally been an important source of food for people. In the past, subsistence hunting by indigenous peoples, armed with snares and bows and arrows, did not usually constitute a serious threat to nonhuman primate populations, and certainly not to entire species. But in the past 20 to 30 years, hunters have had greater access to firearms and are now armed with shotguns and sometimes automatic weapons, with which they can wipe out an entire group of monkeys, gorillas, or chimpanzees in minutes.

Numerous factors have combined to produce the current bushmeat catastrophe. Most fundamental is human population growth. The current human population of West and central Africa (approximately 24 million) increases at an annual rate of 2 to 4 percent, and most of this increase is due to childbirth, not immigration. Traditionally, the people of these regions were not pastoralists, and although households may keep a few cattle, goats, and chickens, the primary dietary source of animal protein has always been meat derived from wild animals. Today, approximately 80 percent of animal protein in the diet of people living in the Congo basin is provided by wild animals.

Another key factor in the rapidly developing bushmeat trade is logging, which occurs because of the high demand for tropical hardwoods in Europe and the United States. (We encourage you to consider this issue the next time you are tempted to buy anything made of wood from any tropical area.) The construction of logging roads, mainly by French, German, and Belgian lumber companies, has opened up vast tracts of forest that, until recently, were inaccessible to local hunters. Once the roads are cut, logging trucks provide transportation for hunters who can travel distances that now take only a few hours instead of days. (Of course, the truck drivers receive a fee, ultimately derived from the sale of bushmeat.) Logging trucks are also used to carry meat out of the forest, and this capacity, in turn, allows hunters to kill more and larger animals because they no longer have to carry the meat themselves. Lastly, the loggers themselves consume bushmeat. In one logging camp in Gabon, 1,200 logging company employees consumed an estimated 80 tons of bushmeat in just one year! In another camp in Congo, over 8,000 animals were consumed. What has emerged is a profitable trade in bushmeat, a trade in which logging company employees and local government officials participate and profit from along with local hunters, villagers, market vendors, and smugglers who cater to growing overseas markets.

As you can see, the hunting of wild animals for food, particularly in Africa, has shifted rather quickly from being a subsistence activity to a commercial enterprise of international scope. The carcasses of primates and other species are common sights in local African markets (Fig. 1). Gorilla and chimpanzee meat is seen as a delicacy in the restaurants of some West African cities, and the trade extends beyond Africa. Wildlife carcasses are smuggled into European countries to be illegally sold at high prices, and chimpanzee and gorilla meat is reportedly sometimes served in some Belgian and French restaurants. And in Great Britain, the Agriculture Ministry has become alarmed by the possibility that smuggled bushmeat might inadvertently be a source of disease, such as foot and mouth, that could spread to agricultural animals. Indeed, in the year 2000, British customs officials confiscated over 2,000 pounds of smuggled bushmeat destined for specialty markets on just one flight from Ghana to London.

The Bushmeat Trade: Just When We Thought Things Couldn't Get Any Worse...

Courtesy, J. Oates

FIGURE 1
Red-eared guenons (with red tails) and Preuss's guenons for sale in bushmeat market, Malabo, Equatorial Guinea.

With unprecedented access to the forests, and armed with modern weapons, hunters currently take over 1 million metric tons of meat (equivalent to over 4 million cattle) from the forest annually. Most of this meat comes from elephants, duikers (small forest antelopes), monkeys, porcupines, reptiles, and rodents. About 1 percent comes from great ape carcasses, but much more comes from monkeys. Given the very slow reproductive rate of primates, and great apes in particular, this level of hunting far exceeds the replacement capacity of these species and also of many nonprimate species. In fact, in many areas, most bushmeat is now derived from rodents because the more desirable, larger animals have disappeared.

It is not possible to know how many animals (primate and nonprimate) are slaughtered each year. But estimates for monkeys and apes are in the thousands. In addition to those killed, hundreds of infants are orphaned and sold in the markets as pets. Although a few of these traumatized orphans make it to sanctuaries, most die of injury, starvation, disease, and neglect within days or weeks of capture.

The solutions to the problems of overhunting are difficult, and if they are to come about, they will need to focus on the needs of millions of people living in poverty and facing hunger, if not starvation. At the local level, it is nearly impossible to convince a poor farmer not to kill monkeys he can sell in the market for a higher price than his crops will bring. While prices vary, a monkey carcass can sell for $5 and a dead gorilla for $40 (McRae, 1997), substantial figures for the average farmer or market vendor. But selling primate carcasses represents only short-term gain because there can be no long-term profit.

Conservation organizations are encouraging logging companies to set aside unlogged refuges for threatened species. Logging companies are also being urged to stop employees from transporting hunters and dead animals and to provide employees with sources of protein other than bushmeat. So far, one company has agreed to cooperate. Some governments are also considering ways to practice sustainable management of natural resources, including wildlife.

Locally, efforts are being directed at encouraging people to eat meat from domestic animals, but this is not a traditional practice in many of these cultures, and the transition will not be easy. Also, there are education programs that teach people about the substantial health risks associated with bushmeat (Fig. 2). HIV infection and ebola, for example, are two such health risks (see p. 411).

There are numerous other efforts under way, and we can only hope that they will succeed and that the funding they require will be forthcoming. Some observers have likened the killing of primates and other species in parts of Africa to the slaying of the American bison in the nineteenth century (Strier, 1999). The probable extinction of a red colobus species (p. 130) undoubtedly occurred, in part, as a result of the bushmeat trade, which has now escalated to an unsustainable level. Unless the slaughter of nonhuman primates for meat is slowed, this red colobus species will be only the first of many to disappear. In fact, many primatologists and conservationists fear that many primate species, certainly gorillas, chimpanzees, and bonobos, could well be exterminated from West and central Africa by the year 2010.

Critical Thinking Questions

1. Can you suggest ways in which the bushmeat trade might be slowed? How would you suggest that the needs of the people be addressed while encouraging them not to kill or sell nonhuman primates and other animals?

2. How have industrialized nations contributed to the development of the bushmeat trade?

3. What are some things you can do that might help stop the bushmeat trade?

4. Can you think of other examples of trade in endangered species, including primates, in other parts of the world? Can you suggest ways in which these activities can be curtailed?

Sources

"Bushmeat. A Wildlife Crisis in West and Central Africa and Around the World." Bushmeat Crisis Task Force (BCTF). Online version at **www.bushmeat.org**.

"Bushmeat Factsheet." The Jane Goodall Institute. Online version at **www.janegoodall.org/**.

Hearn, Josephine. 2001. "Unfair Game. The Bushmeat Trade Is Wiping Out Large African Mammals." *Scientific American* June: 24–26.

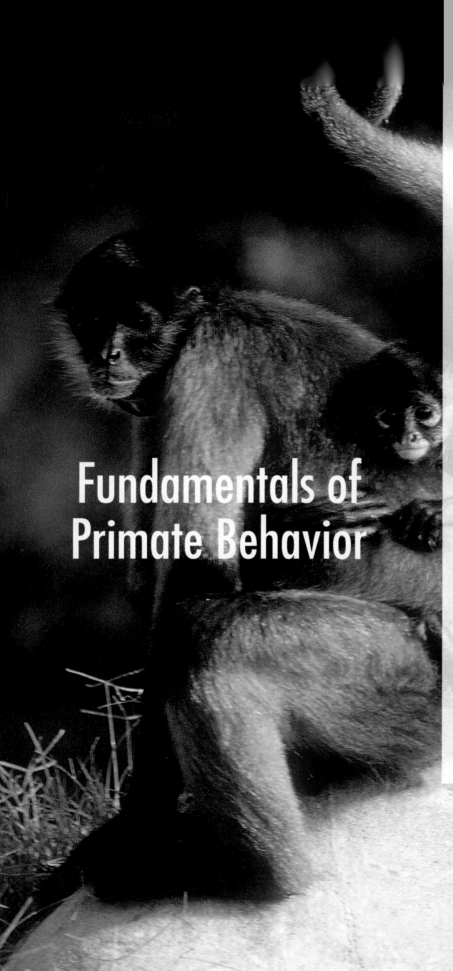

CHAPTER

6

CONTENTS

Fundamentals of
Primate Behavior

Female spider monkey with infant

Introduction

In the preceding chapter, you were introduced to the primate order. In that chapter, we discussed primate anatomical characteristics and primate taxonomy, and we provided a brief overview of the major primate groups to acquaint you with those species most closely related to ourselves.

In this chapter, discussion shifts to various aspects of nonhuman primate behavior. These are extremely important topics for anthropologists because one method of gaining a fuller understanding of human and early hominid behavior is to become more familiar with the behavior and intellectual capacities of nonhuman primates. As a group, primates exhibit a wide array of behavioral responses to environmental challenges. Because these responses have been shaped, in part, by natural selection, understanding them can help elucidate general principles that pertain to the interactions between behavior and ecology. This approach can ultimately help us understand the behavioral and environmental components that may have shaped the evolution of our own lineage (a topic we will address more fully in Chapter 7).

In addition to studying nonhuman primates to learn more about ourselves, it is just as important to learn more about them in their own right. Only within the past four decades have they been systematically studied, and we still have much to learn. Indeed, many species, especially arboreal monkeys, have scarcely been studied at all. The beginning of the twenty-first century is an especially critical time for much of life on our planet. If we hope to save even some of the many threatened and endangered species from extinction, we must understand their needs (space, diet, group organization, etc.) in the wild. Without this knowledge, we can neither preserve sufficient natural habitat for their survival in the wild nor re-create it in captivity.

See the following sections of the CD-ROM for topics covered in this chapter: Virtual Lab 2, section I; Virtual Lab 5, section I; and Virtual Lab 6.

Primate Field Studies

While other disciplines, such as psychology and zoology, have long been concerned with nonhuman primates, the study of these animals in their *natural habitats* has primarily become a focus of anthropology. Early work—that done before World War II—was especially stimulated through the influence of the American psychologist Robert Yerkes, who in the late 1920s and 1930s sent students out to the field to study gorillas, chimpanzees, and howler monkeys. It was the last of these studies by Clarence Ray Carpenter (along with his work on gibbons) that stands out particularly as a hallmark of early primate field investigations. Other such studies followed. Japanese scientists began their pioneering work with Japanese macaques in 1948 (Sugiyama, 1965). In 1960, Jane Goodall began her now-famous (and ongoing) field study of chimpanzees at Gombe National Park, Tanzania. Since that time, primatologists have studied, and continue to study, over 100 nonhuman primate species.

The primary goal of these field studies is to collect information on **free-ranging** animals. Free-ranging animals are not necessarily uninfluenced by human activities. With the exception of populations in a recently explored forest in the Democratic Republic of the Congo, it is highly unlikely that there is a single group of nonhuman primates in the world that has not experienced some human interference. Nevertheless, if we are to understand the adaptations and behavior of nonhuman primates, it is necessary to study them in their natural habitats, where human disturbance is reduced and where they feed, travel, mate, and so forth, with minimal human constraints.

Free-ranging
Pertaining to noncaptive animals living in their natural habitat, largely free from constraints imposed by humans.

FIGURE 6–1
Black-and-white colobus monkeys high up in the forest canopy. Can you spot the animals? Imagine trying to recognize them as individuals!

Courtesy, John Oates

Courtesy, Jean De Rousseau

FIGURE 6–2
Rhesus macaques, part of the large colony on Cayo Santiago Island.

Life history traits
Characteristics or developmental stages that influence reproductive rates of individuals in a species. Examples include age at sexual maturity or longevity.

Because of the problems inherent to the study of arboreal primates that move swiftly through dense vegetation (Fig 6–1), the most systematic information thus far collected on free-ranging animals comes from species that spend considerable time on the ground (including langurs, gorillas, and chimpanzees) and most especially those species that travel and feed frequently in open country (e.g., macaques, baboons, vervets, and patas monkeys). Fortunately, more data are now being collected on many arboreal species, including colobus, some guenons, howlers, capuchins, muriquis, spider monkeys, marmosets, and tamarins.

Another approach taken by some anthropologists involves studying primates in large provisioned colonies, where at least some movement, group dynamics, and so on, are possible. Probably the best example of this type of research is the long-term study of rhesus macaques (Fig 6–2) conducted on Cayo Santiago Island off the coast of Puerto Rico. First established in 1938, the island population now totals close to 1,000 individuals (Richard, 1985).

Despite significant gaps in our knowledge about many aspects of primate behavior, we presently have more information than ever before about nonhuman primate behavior. Indeed, in addition to the famous Gombe chimpanzees, there are groups of many species that have now been studied more or less continuously for 20 to 30 years. Because of the longevity of primates, these long-term studies are essential to a fuller understanding of primate adaptation and behavior, in part because they provide essential data on **life history traits**. Life history traits are characteristics or developmental stages that typify members of a given species and that affect potential reproductive rates. Examples of life history traits include age at sexual maturity, length of pregnancy, the length of time between pregnancies (interbirth interval), and life expectancy. The emphasis on life history data is one of many aspects of primatology that has emerged since the early 1980s, but it is only one example of how this important discipline has evolved. And this evolution would not have been possible without the advent of studies of free-ranging primates.

The Evolution of Behavior

Scientists who study behavior in free-ranging primates do so within an **ecological** and evolutionary framework, focusing on the relationship between behaviors (including social behavior), the natural environment, and numerous factors related to the biology of the species in question. This approach is called **behavioral ecology**, and it is based on the premise that all the various interrelated components of an ecological system evolved together.

Briefly, the cornerstone of this perspective is that *behaviors have evolved through the operation of natural selection*. That is, natural selection acts on behavior in the same way that it acts on physical characteristics. Thus, behavior constitutes a phenotype, and those individuals whose genotypes influence behavioral phenotypes that lead to greater reproductive success will be more fit and should pass on their genes at a faster rate than others.

Superficially, such an explanation implies the existence of genes that code for specific behaviors (e.g., a gene for aggression, another for cooperation). Such conclusions result, in part, from misinterpretation because behavior is a complex trait and approaching behavioral studies from an evolutionary perspective does not imply a one gene–one behavior scenario.

Much of the behavior of insects and other invertebrates, as well as that of lower vertebrates, is largely under genetic control. In other words, most behavioral patterns in these species are *innate*, not learned. However, in many vertebrates, particularly birds and mammals, the proportion of behavior that is due to *learning* is substantially increased. Accordingly, the proportion that is under genetic influence is reduced. This phenomenon is especially true of primates; and in humans, who are so much a product of culture, most behavior results from learning. Nevertheless, it is also clear that in higher organisms, some behaviors are partly influenced by certain gene products, (e.g., hormones). For example, numerous studies have shown that increased levels of testosterone increase aggressive behavior in many nonhuman species.

Behavior is a highly complex trait and must be seen not only as being influenced by specific gene products, but also as the product of *interactions between genetic and environmental factors* that are not yet fully elucidated. Indeed, the ability to learn is ultimately based in the genome inherited by individuals of any species. Between species, there is considerable variation in the limits and potentials for learning and behavioral **plasticity**. But for any given species, those limits and potentials are ultimately influenced by genetic factors that have been shaped by the evolutionary history of that species. The evolutionary history of any species is shaped by the ecological setting, not only of that species, *but of ancestral species as well*. (In fact, some current behaviors that we view as adaptive in living species may in fact not be as beneficial now as they were in that species' ancestors.) Thus, behaviors are viewed as adaptations to environmental circumstances, and it is important to note that behavioral flexibility is also a form of adaptation.

A problem arises when trying to establish the actual mechanics of behavioral evolution in complex social animals such as primates. There is a need to determine which primate behaviors have a genetic basis and how these behaviors influence reproductive success. To accomplish these goals, we must learn considerably more about genotype-phenotype interactions in complex traits. We also need accurate data on reproductive success in primate groups, and so far, such long-term data are almost completely lacking. Thus, rather than offering precise explanations, an evolutionary approach provides a set of hypotheses for explaining primate behavior, and it remains for these hypotheses to be tested.

As a theoretical framework, behavioral ecology grew out of two different approaches to the study of animal behavior: *socioecology* and **sociobiology**.

Ecological
Pertaining to the relationship between organisms and all aspects of their environment (temperature, predators, other animals, vegetation, availability of food and water, types of food, etc.)

Behavioral ecology
The study of the evolution of behavior, emphasizing the role of ecological factors as agents of natural selection. Behaviors and behavioral patterns have been selected for because they increase reproductive fitness in individuals (i.e., they are adaptive) in specific ecological contexts.

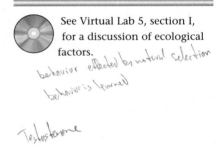

See Virtual Lab 5, section I, for a discussion of ecological factors.

behavior effected by natural selection
behavior is learned

Testosterone

Plasticity
The capacity to change; in a physiological context, the ability of systems or organisms to make alterations in order to respond to differing conditions.

how much behavior is genetic?

Sociobiology
The study of the relationship between natural selection and behavior. Unlike the approach of behavioral ecology, sociobiological theory does not strongly emphasize ecological factors.

FIGURE 6–3
Hanuman langurs.

[handwritten margin note] killing male babies of last being is self-interest (but why was he want "self-interest"? that is not a rational concept)

Socioecology, which is the study of animals and their habitats, attempts to establish patterns of relationship between the external environment and social behavior. Sociobiology, as a major theoretical concept, appeared on the scene in 1975 and, like behavioral ecology, emphasizes the role of natural selection on behavior. But the focus of sociobiology is narrower, and while it primarily concerns the relationship between natural selection and behavior, it does not strongly emphasize ecological factors.

One of the best, and certainly most famous, primate examples of sociobiological theory is the explanation of male infanticide in the Hanuman langurs of India (Hrdy, 1977). Hanuman langurs (Fig. 6–3) typically live in social groups composed of one adult male, several females, and their offspring. Other males without mates associate in "bachelor" groups. These peripheral males occasionally attack and defeat a reproductive male and drive him from his group. Sometimes, following such takeovers, the group's infants (fathered by the previous male) are attacked and killed by the new male.

It would certainly seem that such behavior is counterproductive, especially from the species' perspective. However, individuals act to maximize their *own* reproductive success, no matter what the effect may be on the population or ultimately the species. Ostensibly, that is exactly what the male langur is doing, albeit unknowingly. While a female is lactating, she does not come into estrus, and therefore she is not sexually available. But when an infant dies, its mother ceases to lactate, and within two or three months, she resumes cycling and becomes sexually receptive. Therefore, by killing the infants, the male avoids a two- to three-year wait until they are weaned. This could be especially advantageous to him, as chances are good that his tenure in the group will not even last two or three years. Moreover, he does not expend energy and put himself at risk defending infants who do not carry his genes.

Hanuman langurs are not the only primates that engage in infanticide. Indeed, infanticide has been observed (or surmised) in many primate species, such as redtail monkeys, red colobus, blue monkeys, savanna baboons, howlers, orangutans, gorillas, chimpanzees (Struhsaker and Leyland, 1987), and humans. It also occurs in numerous nonprimate species, including rodents and cats. In the majority of nonhuman primate examples, infanticide occurs in conjunction with the transfer of a new male into a group or, as in chimpanzees, an encounter with an unfamiliar female and infant.

Numerous objections to this explanation of infanticide have been raised. Alternative explanations have included competition for resources (Rudran, 1973), aberrant behaviors related to human-induced overcrowding (Curtin and Dohlinow, 1978), and inadvertent killing during aggressive episodes, where it was not clear that the infant was actually the target animal (Bartlett et al., 1993). Sussman and colleagues (1995), as well as others, have questioned the actual prevalence of the practice, arguing that although it does occur, it is not particularly common. These authors have also postulated that if indeed male fitness is increased through the practice, such increases are negligible. Yet others (Struhsaker and Leyland, 1987; Hrdy, 1995) maintain that the incidence and patterning of infanticide by males are not only significant, but consistent with the assumptions established by theories of behavioral evolution. And the debate continues.

Hrdy's explanation of infanticide illustrates the emphasis sociobiology places on genes and individual reproductive success. But while primatologists still emphasize the importance of individual reproductive success, the focus of *behavioral ecology* has broadened to include ecological interactions that have been largely ignored by sociobiology. For example, to understand the function of one particular behavioral element, such as the **social structure** of a given species, it is necessary to determine how that behavior is influenced by numerous interrelated factors, including:

Social structure
The composition, size, and sex ratio of a group of animals. Social structures, in part, are the result of natural selection in specific habitats, and they function to guide individual interactions and social relationships.

*[image credit, vertical]* Joe MacDonald/Animals Animals

1. Diet: quantity and quality of different kinds of foods (caloric value, digestive energy required, net value to the animal)
2. Distribution of food resources (dense, scattered, clumps, or seasonal availability)
3. Body size
4. Basal metabolic rate
5. Distribution of water
6. Distribution and types of predators
7. Distribution of sleeping sites
8. Activity patterns (nocturnal, diurnal)
9. Relationships with other (nonpredator) species, both primate and nonprimate
10. Impact of human activities (a more recent phenomenon)

As you can see, the topic of primate behavior is very complicated. Primatologists must consider an animal's relative brain size, metabolism, and reproductive physiology in addition to such ecological factors as the distribution of food resources and the nutritional value of foods and how they are selected and processed. (See Fleagle, 1999, and Strier, 1999, for a good discussion of these factors.) Moreover, the variability in ecological adaptations exhibited between closely related species (and even *within* the same species) must be understood. Also, the way primates relate to surrounding biological communities, especially to other species of primates, must be described. Indeed, it is a common phenomenon for many prosimian and monkey species to travel and interact with other primate species. (It is important to determine if they eat different foods and how efficiently they divide their habitat.) Lastly, it is of interest to study why primates select certain foods and avoid others. (What is the nutritional value of insects, fruits, leaves, nuts, gums, small mammals, etc., that are available to them? What toxins exist in certain plant foods that could cause harm?)

Unfortunately, the relationships among ecological variables, social structure, and behavior have not yet been thoroughly worked out; but numerous factors certainly suggest a relationship between, for example, group size and problems of obtaining food and avoiding predators. Indeed, average group size and group composition can be viewed as adaptive responses to these problems (Pulliam and Caraco, 1984).

For example, groups composed of several adult males and females (multimale-multifemale groups) have traditionally been viewed as advantageous in areas where predation pressure is high, particularly in mixed woodlands and on open savannas, where there are a number of large predators (e.g., hyenas, leopards, and lions). Where members of prey species occur in larger groups, there is increased likelihood of early predator detection and thus predator avoidance. Moreover, large-bodied males in such groups are capable of joining forces to chase and even attack predators.

These principles are supported by a report that groups of red colobus monkeys and Diana monkeys (a guenon species) form interspecific aggregations in response to predation by chimpanzees in the Tai National Park in the Ivory Coast (see Chapter 7). Normally, these two species do not form close associations with each other. However, when chimpanzee predation increases, new groupings develop and preexisting ones remain intact for longer than normal durations. This reaction was also seen to occur when human observers played recordings of chimpanzee vocalizations (Noe and Bshary, 1997).

Savanna baboons have long been cited as an example of these principles. They are found in semiarid grassland and broken woodland habitats throughout sub-Saharan Africa. To avoid nocturnal predators, savanna baboons sleep in trees; however, they spend much of the day on the ground foraging for food. In the presence

Fundamentals of Primate Behavior

of nonhuman predators, baboons flee to the safety of trees. However, if they are at some distance from safety, or if a predator is nearby, adult males may join forces to chase an intruder away. The effectiveness of male baboons in this regard should not be underestimated, for baboons have been known to kill domestic dogs and even to attack leopards and lions (Altmann and Altmann, 1970).

But as you have already learned, not all primates are found in large groups. Solitary foraging is seen in a number of species, and it is probably related to diet and distribution of resources. In the case of the small, slow-moving, insectivorous loris, for example, solitary feeding reduces competition, which allows for less distance traveled (and thus less expenditure of energy) in the search for prey. Moreover, because insects usually do not appear in dense patches but are scattered, they are more efficiently exploited by widely dispersed individuals rather than by groups. Solitary foraging may also be related to predator avoidance in species that rely chiefly on concealment for protection, rather than on escape. Again, the loris serves as a good example.

Foraging alone or with offspring is also seen in females of some diurnal anthropoid species (e.g., orangutans, chimpanzees). These females, being relatively large-bodied, have little to fear from predators, and by feeding alone or with only one or two youngsters, they maximize their access to food, free from competition with others. In the case of the orangutan, this may be particularly important, as the female is effectively removing herself from competition with males who may be twice her size.

The various solutions that primate species have developed to deal with the problems of survival differ in complicated ways. Closely related species living in proximity to one another and exploiting many of the same resources can have very different types of social structure. It is only through continued research that primatologists will be able to sort out the intricate relationships between society and the natural environment.

Five Monkey Species in the Kibale Forest, Uganda

One of the most detailed and controlled studies of primate behavioral ecology was undertaken in the Kibale Forest (Fig. 6–4) of western Uganda (Struhsaker and Leyland, 1979). The five species studied are all varieties of Old World monkeys and include the black-and-white colobus (*Colobus guereza*), red colobus (*Colobus badius*), mangabey (*Cercocebus albigena*), blue monkey (*Cercopithecus mitus*), and redtail monkey (*Cercopithecus ascanius*). In addition to these five, there are also in the Kibale Forest two other monkey species as well as pottos, two species of galago, and chimpanzees (for a discussion of the latter, see Ghiglieri, 1984). Altogether there are 11 different nonhuman primate species at Kibale, and they display the greatest number of individuals and highest primate biomass for any site yet described (Waser, 1987). In the study undertaken by Struhsaker and Leyland (1979), all species were sampled using similar methodologies, avoiding the pitfall of making comparisons across highly variable research strategies (a problem usually unavoidable in cross-species comparisons). Moreover, the research at Kibale is important because this region is probably the least disturbed habitat where primates have been studied long-term.

Although these species are **sympatric**, they differ with regard to anatomy, behavior, and dietary preference. Body weights vary considerably (3 to 4 kg for redtails and up to 7 to 10 kg for the mangabey and colobus species). Diet also differs, with the two colobus species primarily eating leaves (i.e., they are folivorous) and the other three species showing more concentration on fruits supplemented by insects.

Several aspects of social organization also vary among the five species. For example, the red colobus and mangabey have several adult males in the group,

Sympatric
Living in the same area; pertaining to two or more species whose habitats partly or largely overlap.

FIGURE 6–4
Kibale Forest habitat, Uganda.

Courtesy, John Oates

while only one fully adult male is typically present in the other species. Furthermore, all five species occasionally have solitary males moving independently of the bisexual groups, but bachelor groups do not typically form. Even among the mostly multimale-multifemale species, there is a marked difference. In mangabeys, females constitute the permanent core of the group, with males transferring out. In red colobus, it is the females who transfer (with the males remaining the long-term residents) (Struhsaker and Leyland, 1987). Indeed, there is so much variability that Struhsaker and Leyland could find little correlation between social organization and feeding ecology.

More detailed analysis of feeding patterns showed even further differences. For instance, while both colobus species eat mostly leaves, they nevertheless exploit different resources. Black-and-white colobus eat mature leaf blades, some high in protein. Red colobus, on the other hand, eat a wider variety of leaves, but usually not mature ones, as well as fruits and shoots. Perhaps correlated with these dietary differences are the observations that black-and-white colobus spend less time feeding but more time resting; in contrast, red colobus range farther and live in higher density (i.e., higher biomass). In addition, some species show dramatic variability from month to month. Among redtail monkeys, the proportion of fruit in the monthly diet varies from as low as 13 percent to as much as 81 percent (Richard, 1985).

Ecological patterns and social ramifications are unquestionably complicated. In the same forest at Kibale, the closely related colobus species show marked differences in social organization. (Black-and-white colobus are found in one-male groups, red colobus in multimale-multifemale groups; see Box 6–1.) Yet in another area (the Tana River Forest of Kenya), red colobus live in one-male groups (like black-and-white colobus at Kibale), and *both* males and females transfer (unlike either colobus species at Kibale) (Richard, 1985). The distinct impression one gathers from attempts to find correlations is that many primate species are exceedingly flexible regarding group composition, a fact that makes generalizing an extremely tentative undertaking at best.

Still, the highly controlled nature of the Kibale study makes some comparisons and provisional generalizations possible:

wide variety of social patterns among sympatric primates

BOX 6–1   A CLOSER LOOK

Types of Nonhuman Primate Social Groups*

1. *Single-male multifemale.* A single adult male, several adult females, and their offspring. This is the most common primate mating structure, in which only one male actively breeds (Jolly, 1985). Usually formed by a male joining a kin group of females. Females usually form the permanent nucleus of the group. Examples: guenons, gorillas, some pottos, some spider monkeys, patas, some langurs, some colobus.

2. *Multimale-multifemale.* Several adult males, several adult females, and their young. Several of the males reproduce. The presence of several males in the group may lead to tension and to a dominance hierarchy. Examples: some lemurs, macaques, mangabeys, savanna baboons, vervets, squirrel monkeys, some spider monkeys, chimpanzees.

3. *Monogamous pair.* A mated pair and its young (although extra-pair matings do sometimes occur). Usually arboreal, minimal sexual dimorphism, frequently territorial. Adults usually do not tolerate other adults of the same sex. Not found among great apes, and least common of the breeding

structures among nonhuman primates. Examples: gibbons, indris, titis, sakis, owl monkeys, pottos.

4. *Polyandry.* One female and two males. Seen only in some New World monkeys (marmosets and tamarins).

5. *Solitary.* Individual forages for food alone. Seen in some nocturnal prosimians (aye-ayes, lorises, galagos). In some species, adult females may forage in pairs or may be accompanied by offspring. Also seen in orangutans.

Sources
Jolly, 1985; Napier and Napier, 1985.

---

*These are called breeding groups by Jolly and permanent groupings by Napier and Napier. There are also other groupings, such as foraging groups, hunting groups, all female or male groups, and so on. Like humans, nonhuman primates do not always maintain one kind of group; single-male multifemale groups may sometimes form multimale-multifemale groups and vice versa. Hamadryas baboons, for example, are described as living in one-male groups but "form herds of 100 or more at night when they move towards the safety of the steep cliffs where they sleep" (Napier and Napier, 1985, p. 61). Also, variability is seen in other forms, for example, red colobus monkeys.

1. The omnivores (mangabeys, redtail and blue monkeys) move about more than the folivores (the two colobus species).
2. Among the omnivores there is an inverse relationship between body size and group size (i.e., the smaller the body size, the larger the group tends to be); also among the omnivores, there is a direct relationship between body size and **home range.**
3. Omnivores are spatially more dispersed than folivores.
4. Female sexual swelling (see p. 153) is obvious only in those species (red colobus and mangabeys) that live in multimale-multifemale groups.
5. Feeding, spacing, group residency, dispersal, and reproductive strategies may be very different for males and females of the same species. These considerations have become a central focus of ecological and evolutionary research.

Home range
The area exploited by an animal or social group; usually given for one year—or for the entire lifetime—of an animal.

Primate Social Groups

As you have seen, many different patterns of social groupings exist among the primates (see Box 6–1). Most typically, primate social groups include members of all ages and of both sexes, a composition that does not vary significantly during the annual cycle. This situation differs from that of most mammals, among whom adult males and females associate only during the breeding season and the young of either sex do not usually remain with the adults after reaching puberty.

Since many mammalian species do not live in permanent social groups, one might ask why most primates do. In addition to helping avoid predation, group living permits more effective defense of resources from other animals, especially members of the same species. Groups of related females may tolerate the presence of one or more males because of the role males frequently play in defending against predators or protecting food resources. And males tolerate females because of the reproductive opportunities they offer.

[margin note: why social: ① protects predation ② defend resources]

But there are disadvantages to group living. For one thing, permanent association with other animals increases the likelihood of intragroup competition for resources; consequently, there are more opportunities for violence. Therefore, for the predation hypothesis to be correct, the risks of predation must outweigh the costs of intragroup competition and aggression.

[margin note: why bad ① more chances for internal conflict]

We have already mentioned that the makeup of social groups is influenced by several factors, such as diet, body size, activity patterns (diurnal/nocturnal), availability of resources, and mating patterns. In addition to these, one other important consideration is dispersal. As is true of most mammals (and indeed, most vertebrates), members of one sex leave the group in which they were born (their natal group) about the time they reach puberty. There is considerable variability within and between species regarding which sex leaves, but male dispersal is the most common pattern in primates (e.g., ring-tailed lemurs, vervets, and macaques, to name a few). Female dispersal is seen in some colobus species, hamadryas baboons, chimpanzees, and mountain gorillas.

Dispersal may have more than one outcome. Typically, when females leave, they join another group. Males may do likewise, but in some species they may remain solitary for a time, or they may temporarily join an all-male "bachelor" group until they are able to establish a group of their own. But one common theme that emerges is that those individuals who disperse usually find mates outside their natal group. This commonality has led primatologists to conclude that the most valid explanations for dispersal are probably related to two major factors: reduced competition for mates (particularly between males) and, perhaps even more important, decreased likelihood of close inbreeding.

[margin note: males leave b/c ① less competition ② no inbreeding]

Members of the **philopatric** sex enjoy certain advantages. Individuals (of either sex) who remain in their natal group are able to establish long-term bonds with relatives and other animals, with whom they cooperate to protect resources or enhance their position within the social structure. This is well illustrated by chimpanzee males who permanently reside in their natal groups (see further discussion in Chapter 7).

[margin note: Philopatric = home-body]

Philopatric Remaining in one's natal group or home range as an adult. In most species, members of one sex disperse from their natal group as young adults, and members of the philopatric sex remain. In the majority of nonhuman primate species, the philopatric sex is female.

Because some individuals remain together over a long period of time, members of a primate group get to know each other well. They learn—as they must—how to respond to a variety of actions that may be threatening, friendly, or neutral. In such social groups, individuals must be able to evaluate a situation before acting. Evolutionarily speaking, this would have placed selective pressure on social intelligence, which in turn would select for brains that could assess such situations and store the information. One of the results of such selection would be the evolution of proportionately larger and more complex brains, especially among the higher primates (i.e., anthropoids).

See Virtual Lab 6, section II, for a discussion of ethograms or catalogs of behavior.

Primate Social Behavior

Because primates solve their major adaptive problems in a social context, we might expect them to participate in a number of activities to reinforce the integrity of the group. The better known of these activities are described in the sections that follow. Bear in mind that all these behaviors have evolved as adaptive responses over 50 million years of primate evolution.

[margin note: behavior that enforces the necessity to live in groups]

Virtual Lab 6, section IV, includes several video exercises about baboon behavior.

Dominance

A number of primate societies are organized into **dominance hierarchies.** Dominance hierarchies impose a certain degree of order within groups by establishing parameters of individual behavior. Although aggression is frequently a means of increasing one's status, dominance usually serves to reduce the amount of actual physical violence. Not only are lower-ranking animals unlikely to attack or even threaten a higher-ranking one, but dominant animals are also frequently able to exert control simply by making a threatening gesture.

Individual rank or status may be measured by access to resources, including food items and mating partners. Dominant individuals are given priority by others, and they usually do not give way in confrontations.

Many (but not all) primatologists postulate that the primary benefit of dominance is the increased reproductive success of the individual. This observation would be true if it could be demonstrated that dominant males compete more successfully for mates than do subordinate males. However, there is also good evidence that lower-ranking males of some species successfully mate; they just do so surreptitiously. Likewise, increased reproductive success can be postulated for high-ranking females, who have greater access to food than subordinate females. High-ranking females are provided with more energy for offspring production and care (Fedigan, 1983), and presumably their reproductive success is greater. Altmann et al. (1988) reported that while dominant female yellow baboons in one study group did not have higher birthrates than lower-ranking females, they did reach sexual maturity earlier (presumably because of their enhanced nutritional status), thus increasing their potential number of offspring throughout the course of their lives. In another example, during a drought in Kenya, dominant female vervets in two groups prevented a third group from gaining access to their water hole. The deprived third group resorted to licking dew from tree trunks, but the lower-ranking members of this group were again denied access by higher-ranking members. Consequently, over half of this group died, and all of those were either adolescents or low-ranking adults (Cheney et al., 1988).

An individual's rank is not permanent and changes throughout life. It is influenced by many factors, including sex, age, level of aggression, amount of time spent in the group, intelligence, perhaps motivation, and sometimes the mother's social position (particularly true of macaques).

In species organized into groups containing a number of females associated with one or several adult males, the males are generally dominant to females. Within such groups, males and females have separate hierarchies, although very high ranking females can dominate the lowest-ranking males (particularly young males). There are exceptions to this pattern of male dominance. Among many lemur species, females are the dominant sex. Moreover, among species that form monogamous pairs (e.g., indris, gibbons), males and females are codominant.

All primates *learn* their position in the hierarchy. From birth, an infant is carried by its mother, and it observes how she responds to every member of the group. Just as important, it sees how others react to her. Dominance and subordination are indicated by gestures and behaviors, some of which are universal throughout the primate order (including humans), and this gestural repertoire is part of every youngster's learning experience.

Young primates also acquire social rank through play with age peers. As they spend more time with play groups, their social interactions widen. Competition and rough-and-tumble play allow them to learn the strengths and weaknesses of peers, and they carry this knowledge with them throughout their lives. Thus, through early contact with the mother and subsequent exposure to peers, young primates learn to negotiate their way through the complex web of social interactions that make up their daily lives.

CHAPTER 6

Communication

Communication is universal among animals and includes scents and unintentional, **autonomic** responses and behaviors that convey meaning. Such attributes as body posture convey information about an animal's emotional state. For example, a crouched position indicates a certain degree of insecurity or fear, while a purposeful striding gait implies confidence. Moreover, autonomic responses to threatening or novel stimuli, such as raised body hair (most species) or enhanced body odor (gorillas), indicate excitement.

Many intentional behaviors also serve as communication. In primates, these include a wide variety of gestures, facial expressions, and vocalizations, some of which we humans share. Among many primates, a mild threat is indicated by an intense stare, and indeed, we humans find prolonged eye contact with strangers very uncomfortable. For this reason, people should avoid eye contact with captive primates. Other threat gestures are a quick yawn to expose canine teeth (baboons, macaques) (Fig. 6–5); bobbing back and forth in a crouched position (patas monkeys); and branch shaking (many monkey species). High-ranking baboons *mount* the hindquarters of subordinates to express dominance (Fig. 6–6). Mounting may also serve to defuse potentially tense situations by indicating something like, "It's okay, I accept your apology, I know you didn't intend to offend me."

There is also a variety of behaviors that indicate submission, reassurance, or amicable intentions. Submission is indicated by a crouched position (most primates) or presenting the hindquarters (baboons). Reassurance takes the form of touching, patting, and, in chimpanzees, hugging and holding hands. Grooming also serves in a number of situations to indicate submission or reassurance.

A wide variety of facial expressions indicating emotional state is seen in chimpanzees and, especially, in bonobos (Fig. 6–7). These include the well-known play face (also seen in several other primate and nonprimate species), associated with play behavior, and the fear grin (seen in *all* primates) to indicate fear and submission.

Communication
Any act that conveys information, in the form of a message, to another individual. Frequently, the result of communication is a change in the behavior of the recipient. Communication may not be deliberate but may be the result of involuntary processes or a secondary consequence of an intentional action.

Autonomic
Pertaining to physiological responses not under voluntary control. An example in chimpanzees would be the erection of body hair during excitement. An example in humans is blushing. Both convey information regarding emotional states, but neither is a deliberate behavior, and communication is not intended.

FIGURE 6–5
Adolescent male savanna baboon threatens photographer with a characteristic "yawn" that shows the canine teeth. Note also that the eyes are closed briefly to expose light, cream-colored eyelids. This has been termed the "eyelid flash."

FIGURE 6–6
One young male savanna baboon mounts another as an expression of dominance.

Relaxed

Relaxed with dropped lip

Horizontal pout face
(distress)

Fear grin
(fear/excitement)

Full play face

FIGURE 6–7

Chimpanzee facial expressions. (Adapted with permission of the publishers from *The Chimpanzees of Gombe* by Jane Goodall, Cambridge, Mass.: Harvard University Press, © 1986 by the President and Fellows of Harvard College.)

Displays
Sequences of repetitious behaviors that serve to communicate emotional states. Nonhuman primate displays are most frequently associated with reproductive or agonistic behavior.

Ritualized behaviors
Behaviors removed from their original context and sometimes exaggerated to convey information.

Primates also use a wide array of vocalizations for communication. Some, such as the bark of a baboon that has just spotted a leopard, are unintentional startled reactions. Others, such as the chimpanzee food grunt, are heard only in specific contexts. Nevertheless, both serve the same function: They inform others, although not necessarily deliberately, of the possible presence of predators or food.

Primates (and other animals) also communicate through **displays**, which are more complicated, frequently elaborate combinations of behaviors. For example, the exaggerated courtship dances of many male birds, often enhanced by colorful plumage, are displays. Common gorilla displays are chest slapping and the tearing of vegetation to indicate threat. Likewise, an angry chimpanzee, with hair bristling, may charge an opponent while screaming, waving its arms, and tearing vegetation.

By describing a few communicative behaviors shared by many primates (including humans), we do not intend to convey that these gestures are dictated solely by genetic factors. Indeed, if primates are not reared within a relatively normal social context, such behaviors may not be performed appropriately, because the contextual manifestations of communicatory actions are *learned*. But the underlying *predisposition* to learn and use them and the motor patterns involved in their execution are genetically influenced, and these factors do have adaptive significance. Therefore, theories about how such expressive devices evolved focus on motor patterns and the original context in which they occurred.

Over time, certain behaviors and motor patterns that originated in specific contexts have assumed increasing importance as communicatory signals. For example, crouching (seen also in many nonprimate species, such as dogs) initially aided in avoiding physical attack. But this behavior also conveyed that the individual was fearful, submissive, and nonaggressive. Thus, crouching became valuable not only for its primary function, but for its role in communication as well, and natural selection increasingly favored it for this secondary role. In such a manner, over time, the expressions of specific behaviors may thus become elaborated or exaggerated because of their value in enhancing communication. Moreover, many complex displays incorporate various combinations of **ritualized behaviors.**

Mounting, as seen in baboons, is a good example of a ritualized behavior. Higher-ranking individuals mount the hindquarters of more subordinate animals in the manner of copulation, not to mate, but to express dominance. (It should be noted that when mounting serves a communicatory function, mounters and mountees may be members of the same sex.) In most anthropoid species characterized by one-male or multimale groups, males (the mounters in the mating context) are socially dominant to females. Thus, in the context of communication, the mounter assumes the male reproductive role. Likewise, presentation of the hindquarters in solicitation of mounting indicates submission or subordination by the mountee. As communication, these behavior patterns are entirely removed from their original reproductive context, and they function instead to reinforce and clarify the respective social roles of individuals in specific interactions.

All nonhuman animals employ various vocalizations, body postures, and, to some degree, facial expressions that transmit information. However, the array of communicative devices is much richer among nonhuman primates, even though they do not use language in the manner of humans. Communication is important, for it truly is what makes social living possible. Through submissive gestures, aggression is reduced and physical violence is less likely. Likewise, friendly intentions and relationships are reinforced through physical contact and grooming. Indeed, it is in the familiar methods of nonverbal communication that we humans can see ourselves in other primate species most clearly.

Aggressive and Affiliative Interactions

Within primate societies, there is an interplay between **affiliative** behaviors, which promote group cohesion, and aggressive behaviors, which can lead to group disruption. Conflict within a group frequently develops out of competition for resources, including mating partners and food items. Instead of actual attacks or fighting, most intragroup aggression occurs in the form of various signals and displays, frequently within the context of a dominance hierarchy. The majority of such situations are resolved through various submissive and appeasement behaviors.

But, conflict is not always resolved peacefully, and it can have serious consequences. For example, high-ranking female macaques frequently intimidate, harass, and even attack lower-ranking females, particularly to restrict their access to food. High-ranking females consistently chase subordinates away from food and have even been observed to take food from their mouths; these behaviors can result in weight loss and poorer nutrition in low-ranking females. Even more important, these females exhibit lower reproductive success because they are less able to successfully rear offspring to maturity, in part because of their inability to obtain desired food items (Dittus, 1979).

Competition between males for mates frequently results in injury and occasionally in death. In species that have a distinct breeding season (e.g., squirrel monkeys), conflict between males is most common during that time. Male squirrel monkeys form coalitions to compete with other males, and when outright fighting occurs, injuries can be severe. In species not restricted to a mating season, competition between males can be an ongoing process. As you have seen, one-male social groups are common in primates, and a male who gains control of a group of females must constantly protect his own interests against the interests of other males attempting to overthrow him. While a majority of conflicts do not result in death, it does occur. In one well-known example, Dian Fossey once found the skull of an adult male mountain gorilla in which was embedded a canine tooth of another male gorilla!

Even though conflict can be destructive, a certain amount of aggression is useful in maintaining order within groups and protecting either individual or group resources. Fortunately, to reinforce bonds between individuals, promote group cohesion, minimize actual violence, and defuse potentially dangerous situations, there is an array of affiliative, or friendly, behaviors that serve to reinforce bonds between individuals and enhance group stability.

Common affiliative behaviors include reconciliation, consolation, and simple amicable interactions between friends and relatives. Most such behaviors involve various forms of physical contact, such as touching, hand holding, hugging, and, among chimpanzees, kissing. In fact, physical contact is one of the most important factors in primate development and is crucial in promoting peaceful relationships in many primate social groups.

Affiliative
Pertaining to amicable associations between individuals. Affiliative behaviors, such as grooming, reinforce social bonds and promote group cohesion.

most fighting for sex

Grooming

Picking through fur to remove dirt, parasites, and other materials that may be present. Social grooming is common among primates and reinforces social relationships.

set,
peace,
hygeine

FIGURE 6–8

Grooming primates. (a) Patas monkeys; female grooming male. (b) Longtail macaques. (c) Savanna baboons. (d) Chimpanzees.

Grooming is one of the most important affiliative behaviors in many primate species. Although grooming occurs in other animal species, social grooming is mostly a primate activity, and it plays an important role in day-to-day life (Fig. 6–8). Because grooming involves using the fingers to pick through the fur of another individual (or one's own) to remove insects, dirt, and other materials, it serves hygienic functions. But it is also an immensely pleasurable activity that individuals of some species (especially chimpanzees) engage in for considerable periods of time.

Grooming occurs in a variety of contexts. Mothers groom infants. Males groom sexually receptive females. Subordinate animals groom dominant ones, sometimes to gain favor. Friends groom friends. In general, grooming is comforting. It restores peaceful relationships between animals who have quarreled and provides reassurance during tense situations. In short, grooming reinforces social bonds and consequently helps to maintain and strengthen the structure of the group.

Conflict resolution through reconciliation is another important aspect of primate social behavior. Following a conflict, chimpanzee opponents frequently

(a)   Robert Jurmain

(b)   Courtesy, Meredith Small

(c)   Lynn Kilgore

(d)   Courtesy, Arlene Kruse/Bonnie Pedersen

move, within minutes, to reconcile (de Waal, 1982). Reconciliation takes many forms, including hugging, kissing, and grooming. Even uninvolved individuals may take part, either grooming one or both participants or forming their own grooming parties. In addition, bonobos are unique in their use of sex to promote group cohesion, restore peace after conflicts, and relieve tension within the group (de Waal, 1987, 1989).

Social relationships are crucial to nonhuman primates, and the bonds between individuals can last a lifetime. These relationships serve a variety of functions. Individuals of many species form alliances in which one supports another against a third. Alliances, or coalitions, as they are also called, can be used to enhance the status of members. For example, at Gombe, the male chimpanzee Figan achieved alpha status because of support from his brother (Goodall, 1986, p. 424). In fact, chimpanzees so heavily rely on coalitions and are so skillful politically that an entire book, appropriately titled *Chimpanzee Politics* (de Waal, 1982), is devoted to the topic.

Reproduction and Reproductive Strategies

In most primate species, sexual behavior is tied to the female's reproductive cycle, with females sexually receptive to males only when they are in estrus. Estrus is characterized by behavioral changes that indicate a female is receptive. In Old World monkeys and apes that live in multimale groups, estrus is also accompanied by swelling and changes in color of the skin around the genital area. These changes serve as visual cues of a female's readiness to mate (Fig. 6–9).

Permanent bonding between males and females is not common among nonhuman primates. However, male and female savanna baboons sometimes form mating *consortships*. These temporary relationships last while the female is in estrus, and the two spend most of their time together, mating frequently. Moreover, lower-ranking baboon males often form "friendships" (Smuts, 1985) with females and

FIGURE 6–9
Estrous swelling of genital tissues in a female chimpanzee.

Lynn Kilgore

occasionally may mate with them, although they may be driven away by high-ranking males when the female is most receptive.

Mating consortships are sometimes seen in chimpanzees and are particularly common among bonobos. In fact, a male and female bonobo may spend several weeks primarily in each other's company. During this time, they mate often, even when the female is not in estrus. These relationships of longer duration are not typical of chimpanzee (*Pan troglodytes*) males and females.

Such a male-female bond may result in increased reproductive success for both sexes. For the male, there is the increased likelihood that he will be the father of any infant the female conceives. At the same time, the female potentially gains protection from predators or others of her group and perhaps assistance in caring for offspring she may already have.

Reproductive Strategies

Reproductive strategies, and especially how they differ between the sexes, have been a primary focus of primate research. The goal of such strategies is to produce and successfully rear to adulthood as many offspring as possible.

Primates are among the most **K-selected** of mammal species. By this we mean that individuals produce only a few young, in whom they invest a tremendous amount of parental care. Contrast this pattern with **r-selected** species, where individuals produce large numbers of offspring but invest little or no energy in parental care. Good examples of r-selected species include insects, most fish, and, among mammals, mice and rabbits.

When we consider the degree of care required by young, growing primate offspring, it is clear that enormous investment by at least one parent is necessary, and it is usually the mother who carries most of the burden both before and after birth. Primates are totally helpless at birth. They develop slowly and are thus exposed to expanded learning opportunities within a *social* environment. This trend has been elaborated most dramatically in great apes and humans, and especially in the latter. Thus, what we see in ourselves and our close primate kin (and presumably in our more recent ancestors as well) is a strategy wherein a few "high-quality," slowly maturing offspring are produced through extraordinary investment by at least one parent, usually the mother.

Finding food and mates, avoiding predators, and caring for and protecting dependent young are difficult challenges for nonhuman primates. Moreover, in most species, males and females employ different strategies to meet these challenges.

Female primates spend almost all their adult lives either pregnant, lactating, and/or caring for offspring, and the resulting metabolic demands are enormous. A pregnant or lactating female, although perhaps only half the size of her male counterpart, may require about the same number of calories per day. Even if these demands are met, her physical resources may be drained. For example, analysis of chimpanzee skeletons from Gombe National Park, in Tanzania, shows significant loss of bone and bone mineral in older females (Sumner et al., 1989).

Given these physiological costs, a female's best strategy is to maximize the amount of resources available to her and her offspring. Indeed, females of many primate species (gibbons, marmosets, and macaques, to name a few) are viciously competitive with other females and aggressively protect resources and territories. In other species, as we have seen, females distance themselves from others to avoid competition.

Males, however, face a separate set of challenges. Having little investment in the rearing of offspring (except in the case of monogamous pairs), it is to the male's advantage to secure as many mates and produce as many offspring as possible. By

Reproductive strategies
The complex of behavioral patterns that contributes to individual reproductive success. The behaviors need not be deliberate, and they often vary considerably between males and females.

K-selected
Pertaining to an adaptive strategy whereby individuals produce relatively few offspring, in whom they invest increased parental care. Although only a few infants are born, chances of survival are increased for each individual because of parental investments in time and energy. Examples of nonprimate K-selected species are birds and canids (e.g., wolves, coyotes, and dogs).

r-selected
Pertaining to an adaptive strategy that emphasizes relatively large numbers of offspring and reduced parental care (compared to K-selected species). (*K-selection* and *r-selection* are relative terms; e.g., mice are r-selected compared to primates but K-selected compared to many fish species.)

 See Virtual Lab 2, section I, for a discussion of reproductive strategies.

so doing, he is effectively increasing his genetic contribution to the next generation relative to other males. *why does he care?*

One outcome of different mating strategies is **sexual selection**, a phenomenon first described by Charles Darwin. Sexual selection is a type of natural selection that operates on only one sex, usually males, whereby the selective agent is male competition for mates and, in some species, mate choice in females. The long-term effect of sexual selection is to increase the frequency of those traits that lead to greater success in acquiring mates.

In the animal kingdom there are numerous male attributes that result from sexual selection. In some bird species, for example, males are much more brightly colored than females. For various reasons, female birds find those males with more vividly colored plumage more attractive as mates; thus, selection has increased the frequency of alleles that influence brighter coloration in males. However, not all bird species exhibit color dimorphism. Moreover, in some species, such as phalaropes, females compete for males, and it is the males who sit on developing eggs. In phalaropes, sexual selection acts on females, who are more brightly colored than males. This example also illustrates the fact that given the necessity for predator avoidance, it is beneficial for those responsible for hatching the eggs to be as inconspicuous as possible.

Sexual selection in primates is most important in species in which mating is polygynous and male competition for females is prominent. In these species, sexual selection produces dimorphism with regard to a number of traits, most noticeably body size. The males of many primate species are considerably larger than females (indeed, male gorillas and orangutans can be twice as large), and males also have larger canine teeth. Males of multimale-multifemale societies also have relatively larger testes than males of other types of groups, presumably because of the potential need to produce greater numbers of sperm, which may ultimately compete with the sperm of other males when females mate with more than one individual.

in a group - bigger balls for more sperm to compete with other sperm

Conversely, in species that live in pairs (e.g., gibbons) or where male competition is reduced, sexual dimorphism in canine and body size is either reduced or nonexistent, and relative testis size is smaller. For these reasons, the presence or absence of sexually dimorphic traits in a species can be a reasonably good indicator of mating structure.

pairs → not so sexy

Mothers and Infants

The basic social unit among all primates is the female and her infants (Fig. 6–10). Except in those species in which monogamy or **polyandry** occurs, males do not participate greatly in the rearing of offspring. Observations both in the field and in captivity suggest that the mother-offspring core provides the social group with its stability.

The mother-infant bond, one of the most basic themes running throughout primate social relations, begins at birth. Although the exact nature of the bonding process is not fully known, there appear to be predisposing innate factors that strongly attract the female to her infant, so long as she herself has had sufficiently normal experience with her own mother. This does not mean that primate mothers possess innate knowledge of how to care for an infant. Indeed, they do not. Monkeys and apes raised in captivity without contact with their own mothers not only do not know how to care for a newborn infant, but may also be afraid of it and attack and kill it. Thus, learning is also critically important in the establishment of a mother's attraction to her infant.

motherhood is learned

The crucial role of bonding between primate mothers and infants was clearly demonstrated by the Harlows (1959), who raised infant monkeys with surrogate

Sexual selection
A type of natural selection that operates on only one sex within a species. It is the result of competition for mates, and it can lead to sexual dimorphism with regard to one or more traits.

 Virtual Lab 1, section IV, presents a discussion of sexual dimorphism.

Polyandry
A mating system wherein a female continuously associates with more than one male (usually two or three) with whom she mates. Among non-human primates, this pattern is seen only in marmosets and tamarins.

Courtesy, David Haring, Duke University Primate Center

(a)

Courtesy, Arlene Kruse/Bonnie Pedersen

(b)

Robert Jurmain

(c)

© Tom McHugh/Photo Researchers, Inc.

(d)

Robert Jurmain

(e)

FIGURE 6–10

Primate mothers with young. (a) Mongoose lemurs. (b) Chimpanzees. (c) Patas monkeys. (d) Orangutans. (e) Sykes monkeys.

mothers fashioned from wire or a combination of wire and cloth. Other monkeys were raised with no mothers at all. In one experiment, infants retained an attachment to their cloth-covered surrogate mother (Fig. 6–11). But those raised with no mother were incapable of forming lasting affectional ties. These deprived monkeys sat passively in their cages and stared vacantly into space. None of the motherless males ever successfully copulated, and those females who were (somewhat artificially) impregnated either paid little attention to offspring or reacted aggressively toward them (Harlow and Harlow, 1961). The point is that monkeys reared in isolation were denied opportunities to *learn* the rules of social and maternal behavior. Moreover, and just as essential, they were denied the all-important physical contact so necessary for normal primate psychological and emotional development.

The importance of a normal relationship with the mother is demonstrated by field studies as well. From birth, infant primates are able to cling to their mother's fur, and they are in more or less constant physical contact with her for several months. During this critical period, the infant develops a closeness with the mother that does not always end with weaning. This closeness is often maintained throughout life (especially among some Old World monkeys). It is reflected in grooming behavior that continues between mother and offspring even after the young reach adulthood and have infants of their own.

In later studies, Suomi and colleagues emphasized that social isolation initiated early in life could have devastating effects on subsequent development and behavior for many species of primates. The primate deprivation syndrome that results from early isolation is characterized by displays of abnormal self-directed behavior, such as hugging oneself or rocking back and forth, and by gross deficits in all aspects of social behavior (Suomi et al., 1983, p. 190).

Although infants are mainly cared for by the mother, in some species adult males are also known to take more than a casual interest. This phenomenon has frequently been noted among male hamadryas and savanna baboons (Fig. 6–12). Male gibbons and siamangs are directly involved in the care of offspring, and among marmosets and tamarins, the males provide most of the direct infant care, only transferring them back to their mother for nursing.

What may be an extension of the mother-infant relationship has been called **alloparenting**. This type of behavior occurs in many animal species but is most richly expressed in primates, and some researchers believe that it is found among all social primates. Usually, alloparents crowd around an infant and attempt to groom, hold, or touch it. Some species, like the common langur, are well known for their "aunts," and as many as eight females may hold an infant during its first day of life. Occasionally, rough treatment by inexperienced or aggressive animals can result in injury or death to the infant. For this reason, mothers may attempt to shield infants from overly attentive individuals.

Several functions are suggested for alloparenting. If the mother dies, the infant stands a chance of being adopted by an alloparent or other individual of the group. Moreover, the practice may bind together the adults of the group. Also, it may simply be convenient for the mother to leave her infant occasionally with another female. Finally, the practice of alloparenting may assist in the training of young females for motherhood.

FIGURE 6–11
Infant macaque clinging to cloth mother.

Alloparenting
A common behavior in many primate species whereby individuals other than the parent(s) hold, carry, and in general interact with infants.

FIGURE 6–12
Male savanna baboon carrying an infant. This is an example of alloparenting.

SUMMARY

We have discussed many aspects of nonhuman primate behavior, such as social structure and dominance hierarchies, communication, aggression, affiliation, reproduction, reproductive strategies, and mother-infant relationships. We have also discussed sexual selection and its role in influencing sexual dimorphism. These behaviors have been treated, to considerable extent, from an ecological perspective; specifically, we have attempted to show what features of the environment are most likely to be important in shaping primate social behavior.

Group size and composition are influenced by such environmental components as resource availability and predators. Moreover, many behaviors are seen as the result of natural selection; that is, they promote increased likelihood of survival and reproduction. Consequently, individuals should behave in ways that will maximize their own reproductive success relative to others. Although this does not imply that in mammals, and especially primates, there are genes for specific behaviors, it does suggest that genes may have mediating effects on behavior and that behavioral attributes have evolved in response to demands imposed by numerous ecological factors.

In the next chapter, we will explore how nonhuman primate behaviors, and the evolutionary factors that have shaped them, can provide information about early hominid behavior. These factors can also illuminate various aspects of behavior in modern humans.

QUESTIONS FOR REVIEW

1. What factors should be considered if one approaches the study of nonhuman primate behavior from an ecological perspective?
2. What are some of the environmental factors believed to influence group size and social organization? Give two examples.
3. How could multimale-multifemale groupings be advantageous to species living in areas where predation pressure is high?
4. How may solitary foraging be advantageous to primates? Discuss two examples.
5. Define behavioral ecology. What is the main premise of this approach?
6. How may genetic factors influence behavior?
7. Discuss a primate behavior that has traditionally been used as an example of sociobiology. What is one argument against it?
8. What are reproductive strategies, and what is their basic benefit?
9. Primates are said to be K-selected. What does this mean? What is r-selection? Give an example of r-selection.
10. Explain male and female differences with regard to parental investment.
11. What are dominance hierarchies? What is their function in primate groups?
12. What is believed to be the primary benefit of being a high-ranking individual? What are three factors that influence an individual's rank in a group?
13. What is grooming? Why is it so important in many primate species; that is, what functions does it serve?
14. Discuss three ways nonhuman primates can communicate information to other group members. Name at least two "threat gestures."
15. Name two ways in which nonhuman primates communicate reassurance.
16. What is seen as the basic social unit among all primates? Why is it so important?

SUGGESTED FURTHER READING

Cartmill, Matt. 1990. "Human Uniqueness and Theoretical Content in Paleoanthropology." *International Journal of Primatology* 11(3): 173–192.

Cheney, Dorothy L., and Robert M. Seyfarth. 1990. *How Monkeys See the World.* Chicago: University of Chicago Press.

Goodall, Jane. 1986. *The Chimpanzees of Gombe*. Cambridge, MA: The Belknap Press of Harvard University Press.

King, Barbara J. 1994. *The Information Continuum: Social Information Transfer in Monkeys, Apes, and Hominids*. Santa Fe: SAR Press.

Napier, J. R., and P. H. Napier. 1985. *The Natural History of the Primates*. Cambridge, MA: The MIT Press.

Packer, C., and A. E. Pusey. 1997. "Divided We Fall: Cooperation Among Lions." *Scientific American* 276(5): 52–59.

Smuts, Barbara B., Dorothy L. Cheney, Robert M. Seyfarth, Richard W. Wrangham, and Thomas T. Struhsaker (eds.). 1987. *Primate Societies*. Chicago: University of Chicago Press.

Strier, Karen B. 2000. *Primate Behavioral Ecology*. Boston: Allyn Bacon.

RESOURCES ON THE INTERNET

Wadsworth Anthropology Resource Center
http://anthropology.wadsworth.com

The companion website for this text includes a range of enrichment material focused on the chapter's topic. While online you can enhance your understanding of the chapter by exploring one of the several additional Internet exercises, by researching topics, and by accessing full articles on InfoTrac College Edition. You can also reinforce the concepts by taking online practice exams.

Internet Exercises

Living Links is a website at the Yerkes Regional Primate Research Center dedicated to research on the great apes. Visit this site at **www.emory.edu/LIVING_LINKS/** and explore the various topics presented there. Topics include behavior, communication, and conservation, to name a few. There are also audios of some nonhuman primate vocalizations. Choose any topic and, after reading the available information, make a list of facts you have learned.

InfoTrac College Edition
http://www.infotrac-college.com/wadsworth

Do a search for *primatology* and go to *primates,* then the subdivision behavior. Select an article from this list of references that relates to some aspect of primate behavior. Do any of the behaviors described in this article reflect the approach of behavioral ecology? If so, how?

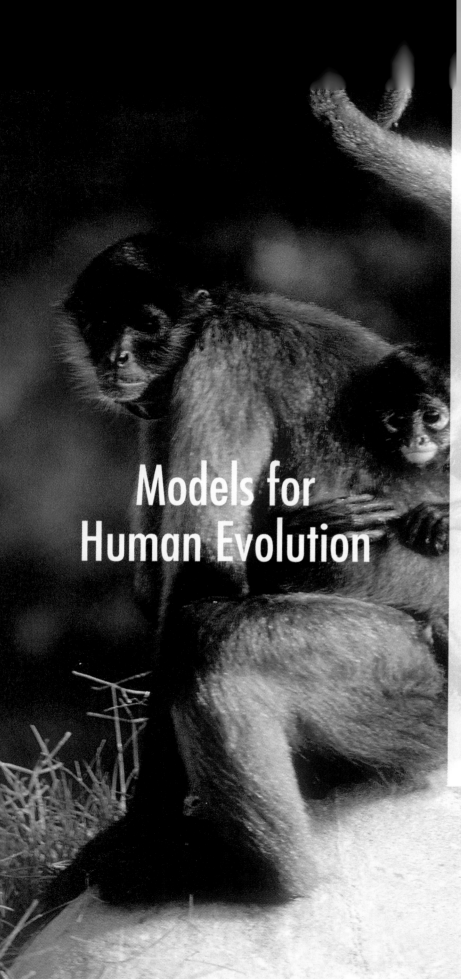

CHAPTER

7

CONTENTS

Models for
Human Evolution

Female spider monkey with infant

Introduction

As you learned in Chapter 5, one characteristic that distinguishes primates, as a group, from most other mammals is increased neurological complexity. Such physiological development is directly reflected in behavioral complexity or, to put it simply, *intelligence*. But while primatologists have documented hundreds of examples of primate intelligence, the question of why primates are so clever remains unanswered. One hypothesis is that the predilection to live in social groups was one of several factors that provided selective pressures favoring intelligence, especially *social* intelligence, as an adaptive strategy for primates.

Primates exhibit a propensity for forming long-term social bonds that frequently include complex alliances and friendships. This predisposition for complex social life provided a foundation for the evolution of the earliest hominids. One of the hallmarks of later hominid evolution is increased relative brain size, but the foundations of neurological complexity were laid long before bipedal hominids began making stone tools. Those foundations are still evident today in behavioral patterns shared by human and nonhuman primates.

Within the social sciences, human behavior has traditionally been considered separately from that of all other organisms, even other primates. This perspective has consistently avoided biological explanations for human behavior, emphasizing that most (if not all) of human behavior is *learned.*

Certainly, human behavior *is* predominantly learned. But the *ability to learn* and behave in complex ways is ultimately rooted in biological (genetic) factors, and natural selection has favored increased learning capacities and behavioral modification in the human lineage.

In the last two decades, there has been a growing consensus, particularly among primatologists, that certain human predispositions reflect patterns also seen in other primates (Cartmill, 1990; King, 1994; de Waal, 1996). Moreover, because we do share an evolutionary history with other primates, a useful approach in developing a better understanding of the evolution of human behavior is to identify in other species those factors that also produced specific patterns in humans. This approach places human behavior, although unarguably unique, within a biological and evolutionary context.

A biological perspective does not assume that all human abilities and behavioral patterns are genetically determined or unalterable. Rather, such an approach aids in explaining *how* certain patterns may have come about and what their adaptive significance might be. Within this framework, the plasticity of human behavior is clearly recognized and emphasized.

As Hinde (1987, p. 413) warns, "Attempting to draw parallels in behavior between human and nonhuman species is a dangerous pastime." Hinde proceeds to caution that owing to the number and diversity of primate species and human cultures, it is not difficult to find comparable behaviors in nonhuman and human primates. Once shared behavioral patterns have been identified, it is easy to support almost any hypothesis one develops, regardless of its validity. However, as Hinde further emphasizes, if one recognizes the risks and limitations of drawing comparisons between species, investigations of shared behavioral *patterns* and principles can be a fruitful endeavor.

The examples presented in this chapter to illustrate the evolution of behavior in primates (including humans) ultimately have their origins in the evolution and physiology of the brain. Because these behaviors and abilities have developed as a function of natural selection, they must be viewed within the framework of behavioral ecology and as components of *life history*.

See the following sections of the CD-ROM for topics covered in this chapter: Virtual Labs 1 and 9–12.

Models for Human Evolution

Behavior and Human Origins

Virtual Labs 9–12 discuss the evolution of many human traits.

What does it mean to be human? There are several physical characteristics, such as adaptations for bipedal locomotion and an enlarged brain, that characterize humans and, to varying degrees, our hominid ancestors. But from a structural point of view, humans are not really that unique when compared with other primates, especially the great apes.

Clearly, it is behavioral attributes that most dramatically set humans apart, and long ago, culture became our strategy for coping with life's challenges. No other primate even comes close to the human ability to modify the environment. Communication through symbolic language is yet another uniquely human trait. In addition, several other features differentiate humans from the majority of other primates, as summarized in the following list. Keep in mind that any one of these traits may be found in one or more other primate species, but only humans can claim them all:

1. Humans are bipedal. (Some apes occasionally walk bipedally, but they do not do so habitually.)
2. Humans live in permanent bisexual social groups with males often bonded to one or more females.
3. Humans have large brains relative to body weight, and they are capable of complex learning. (All primates learn, as do all mammals, but none has the capacity for learning to the degree shown by humans.)
4. Partly as a consequence of neurological reorganization, humans can think symbolically, and they use language, a communication system that is symbolic in nature.
5. Also related to neurological reorganization, *culture* has become the fundamental hominid adaptive strategy.
6. Humans obtain food through some male-female division of labor. Moreover, food is actively transported back to a base camp (home) for purposes of sharing.
7. There is a relaxation of the estrous cycle and concealed ovulation in humans, so that females are sexually receptive throughout the year.

These traits are characteristic of all modern humans. Moreover, much of this complex is a reasonable theoretical framework within which we can investigate the early stages of hominid emergence. In fact, behavioral reconstructions are often central to theories that explain how hominids came to be hominids in the first place.

According to most experts, modern African apes and humans last shared a common ancestor somewhere between 8 and 5 m.y.a. Researchers believe that since that time, ape behavior has indeed changed, but these changes have not been as dramatic as those that occurred in hominids, who developed culture as a major adaptive strategy. Therefore, if we are interested in what hominid behavior might have been like before culture became a significant factor, and if we wish to know what behaviors may have led hominids to become dependent on culture, we must search for clues in the behavior of our closest relatives.

Aspects of Life History and Body Size

In the last decade, primatologists have become increasingly interested in broad generalizations regarding primate lifestyles, maturation, and reproduction, topics that are all subsumed under the category of life history. A crucial factor that crosscuts all these aspects of life history is body size. By body size we mean some overall measure of body mass, sometimes given as a linear measure, such as stature, or (more critically) some estimate of weight. In modeling significant features of human evolution, a broad comparative perspective using data from other primates can be useful. We can obtain rough estimates of the body size of ancient hominids from preserved skeletal evidence, especially through extrapolation from joint size. In those rare instances where partial (or even mostly complete) skeletons are preserved, details concerning limb proportions, relative brain size, and so forth, can also be tentatively determined. As we will see in succeeding chapters, there are two quite famous partial skeletons (both from East Africa) now available for such reconstruction. (A third such discovery, in South Africa, was announced in December 1998, but this fossil has not yet been analyzed.)

Virtual Lab 1, section IV, presents a discussion of several life history variables.

Among living primates, body size is extraordinarily diverse, ranging from the tiny mouse lemur (66 g, or 2.4 ounces) to the massive gorilla (117 kg, or 258 pounds). And, of course, there is an array of species in between. Several critical features of primate life history are correlated with variation in adult body size. For example, small-bodied species tend to specialize in insectivorous diets, while only larger-bodied species are leaf eaters (i.e., folivorous). It should be noted that almost *all* species eat some fruit, but how this component is supplemented varies considerably and is correlated with body size. Supplementing a diet made up largely of fruits is necessary, for while they are high in calories, fruits lack protein. Primates thus acquire protein from other sources—insects, young buds, leaves, and shoots. In addition, some highly specialized species exploit exudates, that is, tree gums.

Small animals have very high energy needs (per unit of body mass), and for them, insects are an extremely efficient source of calories and protein. However, an animal can capture only so many insects per day, thus placing an upper limit on body size for species that rely heavily on insects to supplement their diet.

On the other hand, to process leaves (especially mature leaves containing cellulose), an animal needs a specialized gut with elongated intestines and/or a multi-chambered stomach. These physiological adaptations are necessary to digest large amounts of low-energy food, giving microorganisms (bacteria) the opportunity to break down cellulose and neutralize plant toxins. Primates that emphasize leaves in their diets (e.g., colobus monkeys and langurs) have larger overall body size than those that are primarily insectivorous (e.g., tarsiers and lorises).

Tied closely to these dietary factors, body size is also correlated with metabolic rate. The larger an animal is, the more efficient its thermal control will be (see Bergmann's rule, Chapter 15), and consequently, its metabolic rate will be lower than that of a smaller animal. "Thus large animals expend less energy and consequently need fewer calories per unit of body weight than small animals. Put more simply, two 5-kg (11-pound) monkeys require more food than a single 10-kg (22-pound) monkey" (Fleagle, 1999, p. 284). The content of the diet also frequently correlates with metabolism (usually measured as basal metabolic rate). On average, folivores have a lower metabolism than other primates—an especially relevant factor when comparing animals of roughly equal body size.

Locomotion and habitat preference, too, are partly correlated with overall body size. Most arboreal primates are small and practice some leaping. Larger arboreal primates tend to exhibit more suspensory behavior. And the largest primates of all tend to be at least partly terrestrial. Monkeys that weigh over 10 kg (22 pounds) are almost always *primarily* terrestrial in their habitat preference. These relationships, however, are not quite this simple. Adaptive solutions such as locomotor behavior are always compromises among competing requirements. While large size may facilitate a more efficient metabolism, it hinders arboreal locomotion and might therefore preclude access to some of the most nutritious food items, located at the ends of small terminal branches. On the ground, larger size might, in some cases, discourage predators, but it will also make the animal more conspicuous.

Body Size and Brain Size

Body size is closely correlated with brain size. Clearly, an animal the size of a chimpanzee 45 kg (100 pounds) has a larger brain than a squirrel monkey (adult weight, almost 1 kg or 2 pounds). However, in making such a superficial comparison of *absolute* brain size, one is ignoring the more important consideration of *proportional brain size.*

It has been known for some time that in mammals in general, not only is brain size tied directly to body size, but the relationship is not completely linear. In other words, in cross-species comparisons, as body weight increases, brain size does not necessarily increase at the same rate.

The predictable relationship between body and brain size has been called the index of **encephalization** (Jerison, 1973). The degree of encephalization can be a very powerful analytical tool, as it provides a gauge of the expected brain size for any given body size. Most primates fall close to the predicted curve, but there is one notable exception: *Homo sapiens.* Modern humans have a brain size well beyond that expected for a primate of similar body weight. It is this degree of encephalization that must be explained as a unique and central component of recent human evolution. Using these same analytical perspectives as applied to the fossil materials in the next several chapters, you will see that earlier members of genus *Homo* as well as more primitive hominids (*Australopithecus*) were not nearly as encephalized as modern *H. sapiens.*

Timing of growth also provides an interesting contrast. In nonhuman primates, the most rapid period of brain development occurs either before or immediately after birth. In humans, rapid growth occurs prior to and after birth—so that already large-brained neonates continue to show considerable brain expansion for at least the first year after birth. The metabolic costs of such rapid and sustained neurological growth are enormous, requiring more than 50 percent of the infant's metabolic output (Aiello, 1992).

Carefully controlled comparisons are essential in making cross-species generalizations regarding animals of differing sizes (a point to keep in mind when we discuss early hominids, most of which varied notably from *Homo sapiens* in body size). Such controls relate to considerations of what is called *scaling,* or (more technically) **allometry.** These allometric comparisons have now become increasingly important in understanding contemporary primate life history variables and adaptations. Moreover, similar approaches, as directly borrowed from these primate models, are now also routinely applied to interpretation of the primate/hominid fossil record.

Language Capabilities

One of the most significant events in human evolution was the development of language. Indeed, the use of language is one trait that does distinguish humans from the rest of the animal kingdom. In the previous chapter, we described several behaviors and autonomic responses that convey information among primates. But although we emphasized the importance of communication to nonhuman primate social life, we also stated that nonhuman primates do not use language in the way that humans do.

The view traditionally held by most linguists and behavioral psychologists has been that nonhuman communication consists of mostly involuntary vocalizations and actions that convey information solely about the emotional state of the animal (anger, fear, etc.). Nonhuman animals have not been considered capable of com-

Encephalization
The proportional size of the brain relative to some other measure, usually some estimate of overall body size. More precisely, the term refers to increases in brain size beyond that which would be expected given the body size of a particular species.

Allometry
Also called "scaling," the differential proportion among various anatomical structures. For example, the relative size of the brain changes during the development of an individual. Moreover, scaling effects must also be considered when comparing species.

municating about external events, objects, or other animals, either in close proximity or removed in space or time. For example, when a startled baboon barks, other group members know only that it is startled. They do not know what elicited the bark, and this they can only ascertain by looking around. In general, then, it has been assumed that nonhuman animals, including primates, use a *closed system* of communication, where the use of vocalizations and other modalities does not include references to specific external phenomena.

In recent years, these views have been challenged (Steklis, 1985; King, 1994). For example, it is now known that vervet monkeys (Fig. 7–1) use specific vocalizations to refer to particular categories of predators, such as snakes, birds of prey, and leopards (Struhsaker, 1967; Seyfarth, Cheney, and Marler, 1980a, 1980b). When researchers made tape recordings of various vervet alarm calls and played them back within hearing distance of free-ranging vervets, they observed differing responses to various calls. In response to leopard-alarm calls, the monkeys climbed trees; eagle-alarm calls caused them to look upward and run into bushes; and snake-alarm calls elicited visual searching of nearby grass.

These results demonstrate that vervets use distinct vocalizations to refer to specific components of the external environment. These calls are not involuntary, and they do not refer solely to the emotional state (alarm) of the individual, although this information is also conveyed. While these findings dispel certain long-held misconceptions about nonhuman communication (at least for some species), they also indicate certain limitations. Vervet communication is restricted to the present; as far as we know, no vervet can communicate about a predator it saw yesterday or one it might see in the future.

Other studies have demonstrated that numerous nonhuman primates, including cottontop tamarins (Cleveland and Snowdon, 1982), Goeldi's monkeys (Masataka, 1983), red colobus (Struhsaker, 1975), and gibbons (Tenaza and Tilson, 1977), produce distinct calls that have specific references. There is also growing evidence that many birds and some nonprimate mammals use specific predator alarm calls (Seyfarth, 1987).

In contrast, humans use *language*, a set of written and/or spoken symbols that refer to concepts, other people, objects, and so on. This set of symbols is said to be

FIGURE 7–1
Group of free-ranging vervets.

arbitrary in that the symbol itself has no inherent relationship with whatever it stands for. For example, the English word for *flower* when written or spoken neither looks, sounds, smells, nor feels like the thing it represents. Moreover, humans can recombine their linguistic symbols in an infinite number of ways to create new meanings, and we can use language to refer to events, places, objects, and people far removed in both space and time. For these reasons, language is described as an *open system* of communication, based on the human ability to think symbolically.

Language, as distinct from other forms of communication, has always been considered a uniquely human achievement, setting humans apart from the rest of the animal kingdom. But work with captive apes has raised doubts about certain aspects of this supposition. Although many people were skeptical about the capacity of nonhuman primates to use language, reports from psychologists, especially those who work with chimpanzees, leave little doubt that apes can learn to interpret visual signs and use them in communication. No mammal other than humans has the ability to speak. However, the fact that apes cannot speak has less to do with lack of intelligence than to differences in the anatomy of the vocal tract and *language-related structures in the brain*.

Because of failed attempts by others to teach young chimpanzees to speak, psychologists Beatrice and Allen Gardner designed a study to test language capabilities in chimpanzees by teaching an infant female named Washoe to use ASL (American Sign Language for the deaf). Beginning in 1966, the Gardners began teaching Washoe signs in the same way parents would instruct a deaf human infant. In just over three years, Washoe acquired at least 132 signs. "She asked for goods and services, and she also asked questions about the world of objects and events around her" (Gardner et al., 1989, p. 6).

Years later, an infant chimpanzee named Loulis was placed in Washoe's care. Psychologist Roger Fouts and colleagues wanted to know if Loulis would acquire signing skills from Washoe and other chimpanzees in the study group. Within just eight days, Loulis began to imitate the signs of others. Moreover, Washoe also deliberately *taught* Loulis some signs. For example, instructing him to sit, "Washoe placed a small plastic chair in front of Loulis, and then signed CHAIR/SIT to him several times in succession, watching him closely throughout" (Fouts et al., 1989, p. 290).

There have been other chimpanzee language experiments. The chimp Sara, for instance, was taught by David Premack to recognize plastic chips as symbols for various objects. The chips did not resemble the objects they represented. For example, the chip that represented an apple was neither round nor red. Sara's ability to associate chips with concepts and objects to which they bore no visual similarity implies some degree of symbolic thought.

At the Yerkes Regional Primate Research Center in Atlanta, Georgia, another chimp, Lana, worked with a specially designed computer keyboard with chips attached to keys. After six months, Lana recognized symbols for 30 words and was able to ask for food and answer questions through the machine (Rumbaugh, 1977). Also at Yerkes, two male chimpanzees, Sherman and Austin, have learned to communicate using a series of lexigrams, or geometric symbols, imprinted on a computer keyboard (Savage-Rumbaugh, 1986).

Dr. Francine Patterson, who taught ASL to Koko, a female lowland gorilla, reports that Koko uses more than 500 signs. Furthermore, Michael, an adult male gorilla who was also involved in the study until his death in 2000 had a considerable sign vocabulary, and the two gorillas communicated with each other via signs.

In the late 1970s, a two-year-old male orangutan named Chantek (also at Yerkes) began to use signs after one month of training. Eventually, he acquired approximately 140 signs, which were sometimes used to refer to objects and persons not present. Chantek also invented signs and recombined them in novel ways, and he appeared to understand that his signs were *representations* of items, actions, and people (Miles, 1990).

Questions have been raised about this type of experimental work. Do the apes really understand the signs they learn, or are they merely imitating their trainers? Do they learn that a symbol is a name for an object or simply that executing a symbol will produce that object? Other unanswered questions concern the apes' use of grammar, especially when they combine more than just a few "words" to communicate.

Partly in an effort to address some of these questions and criticisms, psychologist Sue Savage-Rumbaugh taught the two chimpanzees Sherman and Austin to use symbols to categorize *classes* of objects, such as "food" or "tool." This was done in recognition of the fact that in previous studies, apes had been taught symbols for *specific* items. Savage-Rumbaugh reasoned that simply to use a symbol as a label is not the same thing as understanding the *representational value* of the symbol.

Sherman and Austin were taught to recognize familiar food items, for which they routinely used symbols, as belonging to a broader category referred to by yet another symbol, "food." They were then introduced to unfamiliar food items, for which they had no symbols, to see if they would place them in the food category. The fact that they both had perfect or nearly perfect scores further substantiated that they could categorize unfamiliar objects. More importantly, it was clear that they were capable of assigning to unknown objects symbols that denoted membership in a broad grouping. This ability was a strong indication that the chimpanzees understood that the symbols were being used referentially.

However, subsequent work with Lana, who had different language experiences, did not prove as successful. Although Lana was able to sort actual objects into categories, she was unable to assign generic symbols to novel items (Savage-Rumbaugh and Lewin, 1994). Thus, it became apparent that the manner in which chimpanzees are introduced to language influences their ability to understand the representational value of symbols.

Throughout the relatively brief history of ape language studies, one often repeated assertion was that young chimpanzees must be *taught* to use symbols. This pattern was contrasted with the ability of human children to learn language spontaneously, through exposure, without being deliberately taught. Therefore, it was significant when Savage-Rumbaugh and her colleagues reported that Kanzi, an infant male bonobo, was *spontaneously* acquiring and using symbols at the age of $2^1/2$ years (Savage-Rumbaugh et al., 1986) (Fig. 7–2). Kanzi's younger half-sister also began to use symbols spontaneously at 11 months of age. Both animals had been exposed to the use of lexigrams when they accompanied their mother to training sessions, but neither had received instruction and in fact were not involved in these sessions.

While the abilities shown by Kanzi and his sister reveal a remarkable degree of cognitive complexity, it nevertheless remains evident that apes do not acquire and use language in the same way humans do. Moreover, it appears that not all signing apes understand the referential relationship between symbol and object, person, or action. Nonetheless, there is abundant evidence that humans are not the only species capable of some degree of symbolic thought and complex communication.

In nonhuman primates, vocalizations are not completely controlled by the **motor cortex.** However, some of the regions of the brain involved in human speech production *are* located in the motor cortex, and they direct movement of the mouth, larynx, and tongue, but *only as those movements pertain to language.*

Motor cortex
That portion of the cortex pertaining to outgoing signals involved in muscle use. (The *cortex* of the brain, the outer layer, is composed of nerve cells, or neurons.)

Models for Human Evolution

FIGURE 7–2
The bonobo Kanzi, as a youngster, using lexigrams to communicate with human observers. (Photograph by Elizabeth Pugh.)

Courtesy, Rose A. Sevcik, Language Research Center, Georgia State University; photo by Elizabeth Pugh

Damage to these neural tracts does not cause paralysis, as damage to other areas will do, but it will disturb speech, demonstrating that these structures are adapted to movements related specifically to speech production. However, human speech involves much more than simply the motor control of specific muscle groups.

In most humans, language function is located primarily in the left hemisphere of the brain, especially the left temporal lobe (Fig. 7–3). In particular, two regions, *Wernicke's area* (in the temporal lobe) and *Broca's area* (located in the frontal lobe) are directly involved in the perception and production (respectively) of spoken language. But the perception and production of speech involves much more than these two areas, and the use of written language requires still other neurological structures.

Association areas, composed of thousands of neural connections, integrate information sent from various parts of the cerebral cortex. Information relating to visual, olfactory, tactile, and auditory stimuli is first combined and then relayed to Broca's area, where it is translated for speech production. This remarkable human ability depends on interconnections between receiving areas for all sensory stimuli. While the brains of other species have such association areas, they do not have the ability to transform this information for the purpose of using language.

However, Cantalupo and Hopkins (2001) report that magnetic resonance imaging of chimpanzee, bonobo, and gorilla brains has demonstrated that, as in humans, a portion of Broca's area is larger on the left side than on the right. In humans, this area is involved in some of the motor aspects of speech production and the report suggests that it also may have been important to the development of gestural language. The authors further note that in captive great ape studies, gestures are preferentially made by the right hand (controlled by the left hemisphere) and this preference is greater when gestures are combined with vocalizations. Thus, as these authors suggest, it is possible that the anatomical basis for the development of left hemisphere dominance in speech production was present in hominoids prior to the divergence of the hominid lineage.

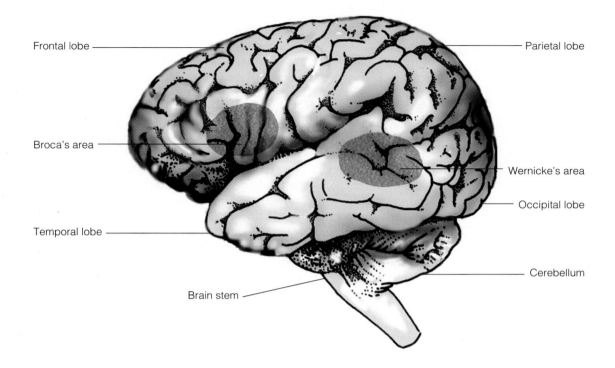

Frontal lobe

Parietal lobe

Broca's area

Wernicke's area

Occipital lobe

Temporal lobe

Cerebellum

Brain stem

In discussions of human evolution, much emphasis is placed on increased brain size, both in relative and absolute terms. While increased brain size is certainly important, it was the *reorganization* of neurological structures that permitted the development of language. Although the study of comparative brain structure is still in its infancy, much current evidence suggests that *new* structures and novel connections *have not been the basis for neurological differences among species.* Rather, systematic reorganization, elaboration, and/or reduction of existing structures, as well as shifts in the proportions of existing connections, have been far more important (Deacon, 1992).

From an evolutionary perspective, the ape language experiments may suggest clues to the origins of human language. It is quite likely that the last common ancestor that hominids shared with the African great apes possessed communication capabilities similar to those we now see in these species. If so, we need to elucidate the factors that enhanced the adaptive significance of these characteristics in our own lineage. It is equally important to explore why these pressures did not operate to the same degree in gorillas, chimpanzees, and bonobos.

For reasons we do not yet fully understand, communication became increasingly important during the course of human evolution, and natural selection favored anatomical and neurological changes that enhanced our ancestors' ability to use spoken language. However, this trend would not have been possible if early hominids had not already been predisposed to language development.

Some researchers argue that language capabilities appeared late in human evolution (i.e., with the wide dispersal of modern *Homo sapiens* some 100,000 to 30,000 years ago). Others postulate a much earlier origin, possibly with the appearance of the genus *Homo* some 2 m.y.a. Whichever scenario is true, language came about as complex and efficient forms of communication gained selective value in our lineage.

FIGURE 7-3
Left lateral view of the human brain, showing major regions and areas involved in speech.

See Virtual Lab 11, section I, for a discussion of tool use in chimpanzees.

Primate Cultural Behavior

One important trait that makes primates, and especially chimpanzees and bonobos, attractive as models for behavior in early hominids may be called *cultural behavior*. Although many cultural anthropologists and others prefer to use the term *culture* to refer specifically to human activities, most biological anthropologists consider it appropriate to use the term in discussions of nonhuman primates as well (McGrew, 1992, 1998; de Waal, 1999; Whiten et. al., 1999).

Undeniably, there are many aspects of culture that are uniquely human, and one must be cautious when interpreting nonhuman animal behavior. But again, since humans are products of the same evolutionary forces that have produced other species, they can be expected to exhibit some of the same *behavioral patterns* seen in other species, particularly other primates. However, because of increased brain size and learning capacities, humans express many characteristics to a greater degree. We would argue that the *aptitude for culture* as a means of adapting to the natural environment is one such characteristic.

Among other things, cultural behavior is *learned;* it is passed from generation to generation not biologically, but through learning. Whereas humans deliberately teach their young, free-ranging nonhuman primates (with the exception of a few reports) do not appear to do so. But at the same time, like young nonhuman primates, human children also acquire a tremendous amount of knowledge not from instruction, but through observation. Nonhuman primate infants, through observing their mothers and others, learn about food items, appropriate behaviors, and how to use and modify objects to achieve certain ends. In turn, their own offspring will observe their activities. What emerges is a *cultural tradition* that may eventually come to typify an entire group or even a species.

A famous example of cultural behavior was seen in a study group of Japanese macaques on Koshima Island. In 1952, Japanese researchers began provisioning the 22-member troop with sweet potatoes. The following year, a young female named Imo began washing her potatoes in a freshwater stream prior to eating them. Within three years, several monkeys had adopted the practice, but they had switched from using the stream to taking their potatoes to the ocean nearby. Perhaps they liked the salt seasoning!

The researchers proposed that dietary habits and food preferences are learned and that potato washing was an example of nonhuman culture. Because the practice arose as an innovative solution to a problem and gradually spread through the troop until it became a tradition, it was seen as containing elements of human culture.

Among chimpanzees, we see more elaborate examples of cultural behavior in the form of *tool use*. This point is very important, for traditionally, tool use (along with language) was said to set humans apart from other animals.

Chimpanzees insert twigs and grass blades into termite mounds in a practice called "termite fishing" (Fig. 7–4). When termites seize the twig, the chimpanzee withdraws it and eats the attached insects. Chimpanzees modify some of their stems and twigs by stripping the leaves—in effect, manufacturing a tool from the natural material. To some extent, chimpanzees even alter objects to a "regular and set pattern" and have been observed preparing objects for later use at an out-of-sight location (Goodall, 1986, p. 535). For example, a chimpanzee will very carefully select a piece of vine, bark, twig, or palm frond and modify it by removing leaves or other extraneous material, then break off portions until it is the proper length. Chimpanzees have also been seen making these tools even before the termite mound is in sight.

All this preparation has several implications. First, the chimpanzees are engaged in an activity that prepares them for a future (not immediate) task at a somewhat distant location, and this action implies planning and forethought. Second, attention

(a)

(b)

to the shape and size of the raw material indicates that chimpanzee toolmakers have a preconceived idea of what the finished product needs to be in order to be useful. To produce a tool, even a simple tool, based on a concept is an extremely complex behavior. Scientists previously believed that such behavior was the exclusive domain of humans, but now we must question this very basic assumption.

Chimpanzees also crumple and chew handfuls of leaves, which they dip into the hollow of a tree where water has accumulated. Then they suck the water from their newly made "leaf sponges," water that otherwise would have been inaccessible to them. Leaves are also used to wipe substances from fur; twigs are sometimes used as toothpicks; stones may be used as weapons; and various objects, such as branches and stones, may be dragged or rolled to enhance displays. Lastly, sticks or leaves are used as aids in processing mammalian prey, but with one exception these practices appear to be incidental. The one exception, observed in chimpanzees in the Tai Forest (Ivory Coast), is the frequent use of sticks to extract marrow from long bones (Boesch and Boesch, 1989).

Chimpanzees in numerous West African study groups use hammerstones with platform stones to crack nuts and hard-shelled fruits (Boesch et al, 1994). However, it is important to note that neither the hammerstone nor the platform stone was deliberately manufactured.* Wild capuchin monkeys use leaves to extract water from cavities in trees (Phillips, 1998) and also smash objects against stones (Izawa and Mizuno, 1977), and their use of stones in captivity (both as hammers and anvils) has been reported (Visalberghi, 1990). (Stones serve as anvils when fruit or other objects are bashed against the rock surface.) In nature, chimpanzees are the only nonhuman animal to use stones both as hammers and anvils to obtain food.

FIGURE 7–4
(a) Female chimpanzee using a tool to "fish" for termites at Gombe National Park, Tanzania. (b) A chimpanzee at the Sacramento Zoo also uses a tool in the same manner as free-ranging animals.

---

*Observers of nonhuman primates rarely distinguish natural objects used as tools from modified objects deliberately manufactured for specific purposes. The term *tool* is usually employed in both cases.

171

They are the only nonhuman primate that consistently and habitually makes and uses tools (McGrew, 1992).

Importantly, chimpanzees exhibit regional variation regarding both the types and methods of tool use. Use of stone hammers and platforms is confined to West African groups. And at central and eastern African sites, termites are obtained by means of stems and sticks, while at some West African locations, it appears that no tools are used in this context (McGrew, 1992).

Regional dietary preferences are also noted for chimpanzees (Nishida et al., 1983; McGrew, 1992, 1998). For example, oil palms are exploited for their fruit and nuts at many locations, including Gombe, but even though they are present in the Mahale Mountains, they are not utilized by the chimpanzees there. Such regional patterns in tool use and food preferences that are not related to environmental variation are reminiscent of the cultural variations characteristic of humans.

McGrew (1992) presents eight criteria for cultural behaviors in nonhuman species (Table 7–1). Of these, the first six were established by the pioneering cultural anthropologist Alfred Kroeber (1928); the last two were added by McGrew and Tutin (1978). McGrew (1992) demonstrates that Japanese macaques meet the first six criteria. However, all the macaque examples have developed, in some way, from human interference (which is not to say they all resulted directly from human intervention). To avoid this difficulty, the last two criteria were added.

Chimpanzees unambiguously meet the first six criteria, although not all groups meet the last two because most study groups have had to be at least minimally provisioned. However, all criteria are met by at least some chimpanzees in some instances (McGrew, 1992). While it is obvious that chimpanzees do not possess human culture, we cannot overlook the implications that tool use and local traditions of learned behavior have for early hominid evolution.

Using sticks, twigs, and stones enhances chimpanzees' ability to exploit resources. Learning these behaviors occurs during infancy and childhood, partly as a function of prolonged contact with the mother. Also important in this regard is the continued exposure to others provided by living in social groupings. These statements also apply to early hominids. While sticks and unmodified stones do not remain to tell tales, our early ancestors surely used these same objects as tools in much the same manner as chimpanzees still do today.

While chimpanzees in the wild have not been observed modifying the stones they use, the male bonobo Kanzi (see p. 167) has learned to strike two stones together to produce sharp-edged flakes. In a study conducted by Sue Savage-Rumbaugh and archaeologist Nicholas Toth, Kanzi was allowed to watch as Toth produced stone flakes, which were then used to open a transparent plastic food

TABLE 7–1 Criteria for Cultural Acts in Other Species

Innovation	New pattern is invented or modified.
Dissemination	Pattern is acquired (through imitation) by another from an innovator.
Standardization	Form of pattern is consistent and stylized.
Durability	Pattern is performed without presence of demonstrator.
Diffusion	Pattern spreads from one group to another.
Tradition	Pattern persists from innovator's generation to the next.
Nonsubsistence	Pattern transcends subsistence.
Naturalness	Pattern is shown in absence of direct human influence.

Source: Adapted from Kroeber, 1928, and McGrew and Tutin, 1978. In McGrew, 1992.

container (Savage-Rumbaugh and Lewin, 1994). Although bonobos apparently do not commonly use objects as tools in the wild, Kanzi readily appreciated the utility of the flakes in obtaining food. Moreover, he was able to master the basic technique of producing flakes without having been taught the various components of the process, even though his initial progress was slow. Eventually, Kanzi realized that he could overcome his difficulties by throwing a stone onto a hard floor, causing it to shatter, thus providing an abundance of cutting implements. Although his solution was not necessarily the one that Savage-Rumbaugh and Toth expected, it nevertheless provided an excellent example of bonobo insight and problem-solving ability. Moreover, Kanzi did eventually learn to produce flakes by striking two stones together, and these flakes were then used to obtain food. Not only is this behavior an example of tool manufacture and tool use, albeit in a captive situation; it is also a very sophisticated goal-directed activity.

Human culture has become the environment in which modern *Homo sapiens* lives. Quite clearly, use of sticks in termite fishing and hammerstones to crack nuts is hardly comparable to modern human technology. However, modern human technology had its beginnings in these very types of behaviors we observe in other primates. This does not mean that nonhuman primates are "on their way" to becoming human. Remember, evolution is not goal directed, and if it were, there is nothing to dictate that modern humans necessarily constitute an evolutionary goal. Such a conclusion is a purely **anthropocentric** view, and it has no validity in discussions of evolutionary processes.

Anthropocentric
Viewing nonhuman phenomena in terms of human experience and capabilities; emphasizing the importance of humans over everything else.

Moreover, nonhuman primates have probably been capable of certain cultural behaviors for millions of years. As we have stated, the common ancestor that humans share with chimpanzees undoubtedly used sticks and stones to exploit resources and, perhaps, even as weapons. These behaviors are not newly developed in our close relatives simply because we have only recently discovered and documented them. Thus, we must continue to study these capabilities in nonhuman primates in their social and ecological context so that we may eventually understand more clearly how cultural traditions emerged in our own lineage.

Aggressive Interactions Between Groups

Interactions between groups of **conspecifics** can be just as revealing as those that take place within groups. For many primate species, especially those whose ranges are small, contact with one or more other groups of the same species is a daily occurrence, and the nature of these encounters can vary from species to species.

Conspecifics
Members of the same species.

Between groups, aggression is used to protect resources through defense of **territories.** Primate groups are associated with a *home range* where they remain permanently. (Although individuals may leave their home range and join another community, the groups themselves remain in a particular area.) Within the home range is a portion called the **core area.** This area contains the highest concentration of predictable resources, and it is where the group most frequently may be found. Although portions of the home range may overlap with the home range of one or more other groups, core areas of adjacent groups do not overlap. The core area can also be said to be a group's territory, and it is the portion of the home range defended against intrusion. However, in some species, other areas of the home range may also be defended. Whatever area is defended is termed the *territory.*

Territories
Portions of an individual's or group's home range actively defended against intrusion, particularly by conspecifics.

Core area
The portion of a home range containing the highest concentration and most reliable supplies of food and water. The core area is frequently the area that will be defended.

Not all primates are territorial. In general, territoriality is associated with species whose ranges are sufficiently small to permit patrolling and protection (e.g., gibbons and vervets). Among many species (e.g., squirrel monkeys, rhesus macaques, and baboons), group encounters are usually nonaggressive. Nonterritorial tree dwellers use vocalizations to avoid other groups, spacing themselves throughout the forest canopy with minimal contact.

Male chimpanzees in particular are highly intolerant of unfamiliar chimpanzees, especially other males and will fiercely defend their territories and resources. Therefore, intergroup interactions are almost always characterized by aggressive displays, chasing, and frequently actual fighting.

Members of chimpanzee communities frequently travel to areas where their range borders or overlaps that of another community. These peripheral areas are not entirely safe, and before entering them, chimpanzees usually hoot and display to determine if other animals are present. They then remain silent, listening for a response. If members of another community should appear, some form of aggression will ensue until one group retreats.

Male chimpanzees (sometimes accompanied by one or two females) commonly patrol borders. During patrols, party members travel silently in compact groupings. They stop frequently to sniff, look around, or climb tall trees, where they may sit for an hour or more surveying the region. During such times, individuals are tense, and a sudden sound, such as a snapping twig, causes them to touch or embrace in reassurance (Goodall, 1986). It is most apparent from their tension and very uncharacteristic silence that the chimpanzees are quite aware that they have ventured into a potentially dangerous situation.

If a border patrol happens upon one or two strangers, the patrollers most surely will attack. However, if they encounter a group larger than their own, they themselves may be attacked, or at least chased.

Recent discussion among primatologists has focused on aggression between groups of the same species and whether the primary motivation is solely territoriality (i.e., protection of resources in a given area) or whether other factors are also involved (Cheney, 1987; Manson and Wrangham, 1991; Nishida, 1991). Much of this discussion has centered on intergroup aggression and lethal raiding in chimpanzees and has emphasized implications for the evolution of human aggressive behavior as well.

Beginning in 1974, Jane Goodall and her colleagues witnessed at least five unprovoked and extremely brutal attacks by groups of chimpanzees (usually, but not always, males) upon lone individuals. To explain these attacks, it is necessary to point out that by 1973, the original Gombe community had divided into two distinct groups, one located in the north and the other in the south of what had once been the original group's home range. In effect, the southern splinter group had denied the others access to part of their former home range.

By 1977, all seven males and one female of the splinter group were either known or suspected to have been killed. All observed incidents involved several animals, usually adult males, who brutally attacked lone individuals. Although it is not possible to know exactly what motivated the attackers, it was clear that they intended to incapacitate their victims (Goodall, 1986).

Goodall (1986) has suggested that the attacks strongly imply that although chimpanzees do not possess language and do not wage war as we know it (i.e., armed conflict between nations), they do exhibit behaviors that, if present in early hominids, could have been precursors to war.

A situation similar to that at Gombe has been reported for a group of chimpanzees in the Mahale Mountains south of Gombe. Over a 17-year period, all the males of a small community disappeared. Although no attacks were actually observed, there was circumstantial evidence that most of these males met the same fate as the Gombe attack victims (Nishida et al., 1985, 1990).

Lethal, unprovoked aggression between groups of conspecifics is *known* to occur in only two mammalian species: humans and chimpanzees. Prior to its discovery in chimpanzees, such lethal aggression was thought to be an exclusively human endeavor, motivated by territoriality. In the past few years, a number of researchers have posed various questions within the theoretical framework that specific aggressive patterns may be explained by similar factors operating in both species. According to Manson and Wrangham (1991, p. 370), "These similarities between chimpanzees and humans suggest a common evolutionary background. Thus, they indicate that lethal male raiding could have had precultural origins and might be elicited by the same set of conditions among humans as among chimpanzees."

In chimpanzees and most traditional human cultures, males are *philopatric* and form lifelong bonds within their social group. Indeed, the core of a chimpanzee community is a group of closely bonded males who, because of their long-term association, act cooperatively in various endeavors, including hunting and attack. In most other primate species, females are the philopatric sex, and in some species (notably macaques and baboons), females may cooperate in aggressive encounters against females from other groups. (Usually these conflicts develop as contests for resources, and they do not result in fatalities.) Generally, then, conflicts between groups of conspecifics involve members of the philopatric sex. In fact, Manson and Wrangham (1991) suggest that in chimpanzees, lethal aggression is a male activity *because* males are the philopatric sex.

Efforts to identify the social and ecological factors that predispose human and chimpanzee males to engage in lethal attacks have led to hypotheses that attempt to explain the function and adaptive value of these activities. In this context, the benefits and costs of extreme aggression must be identified. The principal benefit to aggressors is acquisition of mating partners and food. Costs include risk of injury or death and loss of energy expended in performing aggressive acts.

Although the precise motivation of chimpanzee intergroup aggression may never be fully elucidated, it is clear that a number of interrelated factors are involved ((Nishida et al., 1985, 1990; Goodall, 1986; Manson and Wrangham, 1991; Nishida, 1991). Moreover, although chimpanzees do not meet all the criteria developed for true territorial behavior (Goodall, 1986), it appears that various aspects of resource acquisition and protection are involved. Through careful examination of shared aspects of human and chimpanzee social life, we can develop hypotheses regarding how intergroup conflict may have arisen in our own lineage.

Cultural anthropologist Napoleon Chagnon (1979, 1988) has argued that among the Yanomamo Indians of Brazil, competition for mates between males is the motivation behind warfare between groups. Among the Yanomamo over 30 percent of male deaths are attributed to violence, and Chagnon believes that the majority of hostilities either *within* or *between* villages (with raids leading to deaths, then revenge raids leading to more fatalities) are caused initially by competition for females. These phenomena are explained as functions of some of the same evolutionary principles that operate in chimpanzees, in full recognition of the obvious differences between the two species regarding weaponry, language, and mating systems (Manson and Wrangham, 1991). Chagnon (1988, p. 986) states that "men who demonstrate their willingness to act violently and exact revenge for the deaths of kin may have higher marital and reproductive success."

Early hominids and chimpanzees may well have inherited from a common ancestor the predispositions that have resulted in shared patterns of strife between populations. It is not possible to draw direct comparisons between chimpanzee conflict and modern human warfare owing to later human elaborations of culture, use of symbols (e.g., national flags), and language. But it is important and intriguing to speculate on the fundamental issues that may have led to the development of similar patterns in both species.

Affiliation, Altruism, and Cooperation

In Chapter 6, we briefly discussed affiliative behaviors and the role they play in maintaining group cohesion by reinforcing bonds between individuals. There are also behaviors that indicate just how important such bonds are, and some of them can perhaps be said to be examples of caregiving, or compassion.

When discussing nonhuman animal (or indeed, human) behavior, it is impossible to know with certainty what an individual's motivation is. Thus, the use of the term *compassion* is a bit risky, because in humans, compassion is motivated by empathy for another. Whether nonhuman primates can empathize with the suffering or misfortune of another is not known, but certainly there are numerous examples, mostly from chimpanzee studies, of caregiving actions that resemble compassionate behavior in humans. Examples include protection of others during attacks, helping younger siblings, and staying near ill or dying relatives or friends.

In a poignant example from Gombe, the young adult female Little Bee brought food to her mother on at least two occasions while the latter lay dying of wounds inflicted by attacking males (Goodall, 1986). When chimpanzees have been observed sitting near a dying relative, they were seen occasionally to shoo flies away or groom the other, as if attempting to assist in some way.

Altruism

Altruism
Behaving in a manner that benefits another individual but at some potential risk or cost to oneself.

Altruism, behavior that benefits another while involving some risk or sacrifice to the performer, is common in many primate species, and altruistic acts sometimes contain elements of compassion and cooperation. The most fundamental of altruistic behaviors, the protection of dependent offspring, is ubiquitous among mammals and birds, and in the majority of species, altruistic acts are confined to this context. However, among primates, recipients of altruistic acts may include individuals who are not offspring and who may not even be closely related to the performer. Chimpanzees routinely come to the aid of relatives and friends; female langurs join forces to protect infants from infanticidal males; and male baboons cooperate to chase predators. In fact, the primate literature abounds with examples of altruistic acts, whereby individuals place themselves at some risk to protect others from attacks by conspecifics or predators.

Adoption of orphans is a form of altruism that has been reported for macaques and baboons, and it is common in chimpanzees. When chimpanzee youngsters are orphaned, they are routinely adopted, usually by older siblings who are solicitous and highly protective. Adoption is crucial to the survival of orphans, who would certainly not survive on their own. In fact, it is extremely rare for a chimpanzee orphan less than three years of age to survive even if it is adopted.

Evolutionary explanations of altruism are based on the premise that risky or self-sacrificing behaviors are more likely to be performed for the benefit of a relative, who shares genes with the performer. According to this hypothesis, known as *kin selection,* an individual's reproductive success may be enhanced by saving the life of a relative, with whom genes are shared. Even if the performer's life is lost as a result of the act, the relative may survive to reproduce and pass on genes that both individuals share.

Cooperation

The formation of alliances, coalitions, and even grooming partnerships are all cooperative behaviors whereby the participants may achieve some benefit through their combined actions. Chimpanzees form alliances to increase their status within the group or to gain protection from others. At Gombe, one low-ranking and partially disabled female named Gilka had such an alliance with her higher-ranking brother Jomeo. When Jomeo was not present, Gilka was submissive to others and generally kept to herself. But in her brother's protective presence, she became more assertive and sociable.

Another example of cooperation among primates is chimpanzee hunting behavior. Chimpanzees hunt small mammals, including bushpigs and small antelopes, but their favorite prey is the red colobus monkey. The first person to document chimpanzees successfully hunting and killing a red colobus monkey was Jane Goodall at Gombe National Park in the early 1960s. Numerous accounts now exist, and it appears that all chimpanzee groups hunt, although they may use somewhat different strategies.

Chimpanzees are not the only primates that hunt, nor are they the only mammals that hunt cooperatively. Killing and eating prey animals is seen in many primate species (in addition to nocturnal insectivores), but it is sporadic and opportunistic and does not involve cooperation between individuals. And, as anyone who has ever watched nature programs on television knows, social carnivores such as lions, wolves, African wild dogs, hyenas, and orcas (killer whales) all cooperate in highly complex ways to chase and kill prey animals that are frequently much larger than themselves.

In chimpanzees, hunting is not always a cooperative effort. But when it is, it frequently begins with two or more individuals, usually males, who may simply come upon a group of monkeys in a tree or see them at a distance. The actual form of the hunt depends on a number of social and ecological circumstances, and certain aspects vary from one locality to another (Boesch and Boesch, 1989; Boesch, 1994). But generally, if there are a number of hunters, the chimpanzees may silently move to block their intended prey's escape routes before they begin their pursuit. This is a highly goal-directed activity that requires assessment of the situation and planning. Sometimes, other chimpanzees may watch the hunt from the ground, apparently anticipating that a monkey may fall, as often happens.

Kills are made amid great excitement, with participants and nonparticipants alike screaming and charging about. Afterward, some of the meat is usually shared, even with those who did not take part in the hunt but who nevertheless beg for a share with outstretched hands.

From a chimpanzee perspective, hunting is a successful enterprise in terms of numbers of prey animals killed. Stanford et al. (1994) report that over a 10-year period at Gombe, 52 percent of all colobus hunts resulted in at least one monkey being killed. In all, 350 monkeys are known to have been taken, and the actual total is probably much higher.

There is some debate over the role of hunting in human evolution. Hunting has long been considered a factor in the development of human food sharing, cooperation, division of labor between the sexes, and the use of base camps. While the environmental contexts of early hominids and modern chimpanzees are quite different, the patterns of cooperative hunting in chimpanzees may provide insights into how this important behavior developed over time in the human lineage.

The Primate Continuum

It is an unfortunate fact that humans generally view themselves as separate from the rest of the animal kingdom. This perspective is, in no small measure, due to a prevailing lack of knowledge of the behavior and abilities of other species. Moreover, these notions are continuously reinforced through exposure to advertising, movies, television, and other forms of media (Fig. 7–5).

For decades, behavioral psychology taught that animal behavior represents nothing more than a series of conditioned responses to specific stimuli. (This

Models for Human Evolution

FIGURE 7–5
This unfortunate advertising display is a good example of how humans misunderstand and thus misrepresent our closest relatives.

Lynn Kilgore

Biological continuum
Refers to the fact that organisms are related through common ancestry and that behaviors and traits seen in one species are also seen in others to varying degrees. (When expressions of a phenomenon continuously grade into one another so that there are no discrete categories, they are said to exist on a continuum. Color is such a phenomenon.)

perspective is very convenient for those who wish to exploit nonhuman animals, for whatever purposes, and remain free of guilt.) Fortunately, this attitude has begun to change in recent years to reflect a growing awareness that humans, although in many ways unquestionably unique, are nevertheless part of a **biological continuum.** Indeed, we are also a part of a behavioral continuum.

Where do humans fit, then, in this biological continuum? Are we at the top? The answer depends on the criteria used. Certainly, we are the most intelligent species if we define intelligence in terms of problem-solving abilities and abstract thought. However, if we look more closely, we recognize that the differences between ourselves and our primate relatives, especially chimpanzees and bonobos, are primarily quantitative and not qualitative.

Although human brains are absolutely and relatively larger, neurological processes are functionally the same. The necessity of close bonding with at least one parent and the need for physical contact are essentially the same. Developmental stages and dependence on learning are strikingly similar. Indeed, even in the capacity for cruelty and aggression combined with compassion, tenderness, and altruism exhibited by chimpanzees, we see a close parallel to the dichotomy between "evil" and "good" so long recognized in ourselves. The main difference between how chimpanzees and humans express these qualities (and therefore the dichotomy) is one of degree. Humans are much more adept at cruelty and compassion, and humans can reflect on their behavior in ways that chimpanzees cannot. While chimpanzees may not understand the suffering they inflict on others, humans do. Likewise, while an adult chimpanzee may sit next to and protect a dying relative or friend, it does not appear to feel intense grief and a sense of loss to the extent a human normally does.

To arrive at any understanding of what it is to be human, it is vastly important to recognize that many of our behaviors are but elaborate extensions of those of our hominid ancestors and close primate relatives. The fact that so many of us prefer to bask in the warmth of the "sun belt" with literally millions of others reflects our heritage as social animals adapted to life in the tropics. And the "sweet tooth" seen in so many humans is a direct result of our earlier primate ancestors' predilection for high-energy sugar contained in desirably sweet, ripe fruit. Thus, it is important to recognize our primate heritage as we explore how humans came to be and how we continue to adapt.

SUMMARY

Various aspects of nonhuman primate behavior and adaptation have been discussed as they pertain to modern humans and to human evolution. Such capacities as efficient communication (including language), affiliation, intergroup aggression, and cultural behavior are explained within an evolutionary framework. Although this does not imply that in mammals, and especially primates, there are genes for specific behaviors, it does suggest that genes may have mediating effects on behavior. Moreover, these capabilities and the similarity of their expression in many primate species argue for their adaptive significance in complex social settings.

Language and tool use, like most human capacities, can be seen as elaborations of patterns observed in many nonhuman primates. Humans reflect their evolutionary heritage as primates and stand as one component of a biological continuum. It is this evolutionary relationship, then, that accounts for many of the behaviors we have in common with prosimians, monkeys, and apes.

QUESTIONS FOR REVIEW

1. How can aspects of human behavior be explained in terms of biological evolution without necessarily postulating that complex behaviors are under *strict* genetic control?
2. How does human language differ from most nonhuman communication? What is the evidence to suggest that some nonhuman primates exhibit certain language abilities seen in humans?
3. Briefly discuss neurological changes that occurred in human evolution that relate to language function.
4. Discuss an example of between-group aggression. What is thought to have motivated the violence between two groups of chimpanzees at Gombe?
5. Discuss two examples of nonhuman primate cultural behavior. Why is our discovery of these behaviors important to studies of early human evolution?
6. Discuss the language acquisition studies using chimpanzees, bonobos, and gorillas. What are the implications of this research?
7. What do we mean when we state that humans are a part of a biological continuum? How does the view expressed in this statement differ from traditional views expressed by most people?
8. Why are anthropologists interested in cooperative hunting in chimpanzees?

SUGGESTED FURTHER READING

Cartmill, Matt. 1990. "Human Uniqueness and Theoretical Content in Paleoanthropology: *International Journal of Primatology* 11(3): 173–192.
Cheney, Dorothy L., and Robert M. Seyfarth. 1990. *How Monkeys See the World.* Chicago: University of Chicago Press.
de Waal, Frans B. M. (ed.) 2001. *Tree of Origin. What Primate Behavior Can Tell Us about Human Social Evolution.* Cambridge, MA: Harvard University Press.
Fouts, Roger (with Stephen Tukel Mills). 1997. *Next of Kin. What Chimpanzees Have Taught Me About Who We Are.* New York: Morrow.
Goodall, Jane. 1986. *The Chimpanzees of Gombe.* Cambridge, MA. The Belknap Press of Harvard University Press.

King, Barbara J. 1994. *The Information Continuum: Social Information Transfer in Monkeys, Apes, and Hominids*. Santa Fe: SAR Press.

McGrew, W. C. 1992. *Chimpanzee Material Culture*. Cambridge, England: Cambridge University Press.

Savage-Rumbaugh, S., and Roger Lewin. 1994. *Kanzi: The Ape at the Brink of the Human Mind*. New York: Wiley.

Stanford, Craig. 2001. *Significant Others. The Ape-Human Continuum and the Quest for Human Nature*. New York: Basic Books.

Wrangham, R. W. and D. Peterson. 1996. *Demonic Males: Apes and the Evolution of Human Aggression*. Boston: Houghton Mifflin.

RESOURCES ON THE INTERNET

Wadsworth Anthropology Resource Center
http://anthropology.wadsworth.com

The companion website for this text includes a range of enrichment material focused on the chapter's topic. While online you can enhance your understanding of the chapter by exploring one of the several additional Internet exercises, by researching topics, and by accessing full articles on InfoTrac College Edition. You can also reinforce the concepts by taking online practice exams.

Internet Exercises

Go to **www.primate.wisc.edu/pin/behavior.html** and under the heading "Cognition and Intelligence," choose one article to read. Write a short summary of the article and include in your discussion your own thoughts as to how it relates to the material discussed in this chapter.

InfoTrac College Edition
http://www.infotrac-college.com/wadsworth

Do an author search for Craig Stanford and find the article, "Culture: the anthropologists' account," *The Sciences*, May 2000, vol. 40, p. 38. Based on what you have read in this chapter, what is your reaction to this article? Do you think it is appropriate to use the term *culture* when discussing nonhuman primate behavior? Why or why not?

Primates in Biomedical Research: Ethics and Concerns

The use of nonhuman animals for experimentation is an established practice, long recognized for its benefits to human beings as well as to nonhuman animals. Currently, an estimated 17 to 22 million animals are used annually in the United States for the testing of new vaccines and other methods of treating or preventing disease, as well as for the development of innovative surgical procedures. Nonhuman animals are also used in psychological experimentation and in the testing of consumer products.

Because of biological and behavioral similarities shared with humans, nonhuman primates are among those species most desired for biomedical research. According to figures from the United States Department of Agriculture (USDA), 42,620 primates were used in laboratory studies in 1991. On average, about 50,000 are used annually, with approximately 3,000 being involved in more than one study. The most commonly used primates are baboons, vervets, various macaque species, squirrel monkeys, marmosets, and tamarins. Because they are more costly than other species (such as mice, rats, rabbits, cats, and dogs), primates are usually reserved for medical and behavioral studies and not for the testing of consumer goods such as cosmetics or household cleaners. (It should be noted that many cosmetic companies assert that they no longer perform tests on animals.)

Although work with primates has certainly benefited humankind, these benefits are expensive, not only monetarily but in terms of suffering and animal lives lost. The development of the polio vaccine in the 1950s serves as one example of the costs involved. Prior to the 1950s, polio had killed and crippled millions of people worldwide. Now the disease is almost unheard of, at least in developed nations. But included in the price tag for the polio vaccine were the lives of 1.5 *million* rhesus macaques, mostly imported from India.

Unquestionably, the elimination of polio and other diseases is a boon to humanity, and such achievements are part of the obligation of medical research to promote the health and well-being of humans. But at the same time, serious questions have been raised about medical advances made at the expense of millions of nonhuman animals, many of whom are primates. Indeed, one well-known primatologist, speaking at a conference some years ago, questioned whether we can morally justify depleting populations of threatened species solely for the benefit of a single, highly overpopulated one.

This question will seem extreme, if not absurd, to many readers, especially in view of the fact that the majority of people would argue that *whatever* is necessary to promote human health and longevity is justified.

Leaving the broader ethical issues aside for a moment, one area of controversy regarding laboratory primates is housing. Traditionally, lab animals have been kept in small metal cages, usually one or two per cage. Cages are usually bare, except for food and water, and they are frequently stacked one on top of another, so that their inhabitants find themselves in the unnatural situation of having animals above and below them, as well as on each side.

The primary reason for small cage size is simple. Small cages are less expensive than large ones and they require less space (space is also costly). Moreover, sterile, unenriched cages (i.e., lacking objects for manipulation or play) are easier and therefore cheaper to clean. But for such curious, intelligent animals as primates, these easy-to-maintain facilities result in a deprivation that leads to depression, neurosis, and psychosis. (The application of these terms to a nonhuman context is criticized as being anthropomorphic by many who believe that nonhuman animals, including primates, cannot be said to have psychological needs.)

Chimpanzees, reserved primarily for AIDS and hepatitis B research, probably suffer more than any other species from inadequate facilities. In 1990, Jane Goodall published a description of conditions she encountered in one lab she visited in Maryland. In this facility, she saw two- and three-year-old chimpanzees housed, two together, in cages measuring 22 inches square and 24 inches high. Obviously, movement for these youngsters was virtually impossible, and they had been housed in this manner for over three months. At this same lab and others, adult chimps, infected with HIV or hepatitis, were confined alone for several years in small isolation chambers, where they rocked back and forth, seeing little and hearing nothing of their surroundings.

Fortunately, conditions are improving. There has been increased public awareness of existing conditions; and there is, among some members of the biomedical community, a growing sensitivity toward the special requirements of primates.

In 1991, amendments to the Animal Welfare Act were enacted to require all labs to provide minimum standards for the humane care of all "warm-blooded" animals. (For some reason, birds and rodents were not included in this category.) These minimum standards provide specific requirements for cage size based on weight of the animal. For example, primates weighing less than 2.2 pounds must have 1.6 square feet of floor space per animal, and the cage must be at least 20 inches high. Those weighing more than 55 pounds are allotted at least 25.1 square feet of floor space per animal and at least 84 inches (7 feet) of vertical space.

Clearly, the enclosures described above are not sufficiently large for normal locomotor activities, and this could certainly contribute to psychological stress. One method of reducing such stress is to provide cages with objects and climbing structures (even part of a dead branch is a considerable improvement and costs nothing). Several facilities are now implementing such procedures. Also, many laboratory staffs are now

trained to provide enrichment for the animals in their care. Moreover, the Maryland lab that Dr. Goodall observed no longer maintains chimpanzees in isolation chambers. Rather, they are now housed with other animals in areas measuring 80 cubic feet and are provided with enrichment devices.

Aside from the treatment of captive primates, there continues to be concern over the depletion of wild populations in order to provide research animals. Actually, the number of wild-caught animals used in research today is small compared to the numbers lost to habitat destruction and hunting for food. However, in the past, particularly in the 1950s and 1960s, the numbers of animals captured for research were staggering. In 1968, for example, 113,714 primates were received in the United States alone!

Fortunately, the number of animals imported into the United States has declined dramatically since the Convention on Trade in Endangered Species (CITES) was ratified in 1973 (see p. 131). In 1984, for example, the United States imported 13,148 primates (Mittermeier and Cheney, 1987). On average, the United States annually imports some 20,000 (some from breeding colonies in the country of origin). Although it would be best if no free-ranging primates were involved, at least these figures represent a substantial improvement since the 1960s.

It is important to note that biomedical research accounts for only a small part of the demand for primates captured in the wild. The

exotic pet trade provides a much greater share of the market, both locally and internationally. But even more important is the hunting or live capture of primates for human consumption. This is especially true in parts of West Africa and Asia. Moreover, in several Asian countries there is a growing demand for animal (including primate) products (body parts such as bones or brain tissue) for medicinal purposes (see pp. 131–132; 135–138).

In response to concerns for diminishing wild populations and regulations to protect them, a number of breeding colonies have been established in the United States and other countries to help meet demands for laboratory animals. Additionally, in 1986, the National Institutes of Health established the National Chimpanzee Breeding Program to provide chimpanzees primarily for AIDS and hepatitis B research.

Furthermore, in 1989, the United States Fish and Wildlife Service upgraded the status of wild chimpanzees from "threatened" to "endangered." The endangered status was not applied to animals born in captivity; the upgrade was intended to provide additional protection for free-ranging populations. Unfortunately, even with all the policies now in place, there is no guarantee that some wild-born chimpanzees will not find their way into research labs.

The animal rights movement has been described by many in the scientific community as "anti-science," or "anti-intellectual."

Certainly, there are extremists in the animal rights movement for whom these labels are appropriate. But to categorize in this manner all who have concern for animals and, in this case, primates is unjustified. There are many concerned members of the biomedical and scientific communities, including the authors of this text, to whom these labels do not apply.

It is neither antiscience nor anti-intellectual to recognize that humans who derive benefits from the use of nonhuman species have an obligation to reduce suffering and provide adequate facilities for highly intelligent, complex animals. This obligation does not necessitate laboratory break-ins. But improvement does mean that individual members of the biomedical community must become yet more aware of the requirements of captive primates. Moreover, those involved in primate testing, as well as the granting agencies that fund them, should be kept well informed as to the status of wild primate populations. Lastly, and perhaps most importantly, existing laws that regulate the capture, treatment, and trade of wild-caught animals *must* be more strictly enforced.

Undoubtedly, humankind has much to gain by using nonhuman primates for experimentation. But we also have a moral obligation to ensure their survival in the wild, as well as to provide them with humane treatment and enriched captive environments. But most of all, we owe them respect as complex, intelligent, and sensitive animals that are not so different from ourselves. If we grant them this, the rest should follow.

Critical Thinking Questions

1. What do you see as the benefits derived from using nonhuman primates in biomedical research? Have you personally benefited from this type of research? If so, how?

2. Do you personally have concerns regarding the use of nonhuman primates in biomedical research? Explain your views.

3. Delineate the issues surrounding habitat enrichment for laboratory primates. Do you think enrichment is an important concern? Why or why not? If so, how would you address this issue, bearing in mind that there are constraints on funding?

4. What do you see as solutions to the problem of depletion of wild populations of nonhuman primates? Your answer should be practical and should take into consideration the needs of humans and limited financial resources.

Sources

Goodall, Jane. 1990. *Through a Window*. Boston: Houghton-Mifflin.

Holden, Constance. 1988. "Academy Explores Use of Laboratory Animals." *Science* 242 (October): 185.

Mittermeier, R. A., and D. Cheney. 1987. "Conservation of Primates in their Habitats," in Smuts, B., et al., eds., *Primate Societies*, pp. 477–496. Chicago: University of Chicago Press.

United States Department of Agriculture. Subchapter A—Animal Welfare. Washington, DC: U.S. Government Printing Office, Publication Number 311-364/60638, 1992.

Note: We would like to express special appreciation to Dr. Shirley MacGreal, President, International Primate Protection League, and to Dr. Thomas L. Wolfle, Director, Institute of Laboratory Animal Resources, for providing information for this issue.

CHAPTER

8

CONTENTS

Trail of hominid footprints fossilized in volcanic ash at
Laetoli, Tanzania (approximate age, 3.7 million years)

Processes of Macroevolution: Mammalian/Primate Evolutionary History

Introduction

In the three preceding chapters, we surveyed the structure, ecology, and social behavior of *living* primates. In this chapter, we shift our focus to primate evolution. To place primates, and more specifically, hominids, in their proper evolutionary context, we first give a brief summary of vertebrate and mammalian evolution.

In addition to the broad trends of evolutionary history, we also discuss some contemporary issues relating to evolutionary theory. In particular, we emphasize concepts that relate to large-scale evolutionary processes, that is, *macroevolution* (in contrast to the microevolutionary focus of Chapter 4). The fundamental perspectives reviewed here concerning geological history, principles of classification, and modes of evolutionary change will serve as a basis for topics covered throughout much of the remainder of the text.

 See the following sections of the CD-ROM for topics covered in this chapter: Virtual Lab 7, sections I, II, and III.

The Human Place in the Organic World

There are millions of species living today; if we were to include microorganisms, the total would surely exceed tens of millions. And if we then added in the vast multitudes of species that are now extinct, the total would be staggering—perhaps hundreds of millions!

How do biologists cope with all this diversity? As is typical for *Homo sapiens*, scientists approach complexity through simplification. Thus, biologists group life forms together; that is, they construct a **classification.** For example, today there are probably more than 15 million species of animals, most of them insects. No one knows exactly how many species there are, because more than 90 percent have yet to be scientifically described or named. Nevertheless, even with the tens of thousands of species that biologists do know something about, there is still too much diversity to handle conveniently—indeed, too many names for the human brain to remember. Thus, the solution is to organize the diversity into groups to (1) reduce the complexity and (2) indicate evolutionary relationships.

Organisms that move about and ingest food (but do not photosynthesize, as do plants) are called animals. More precisely, the multicelled animals are placed within the group called the **Metazoa** (Fig. 8–1). Within the Metazoa there are more than 20 major groups termed *phyla* (*sing.*, phylum). One of these phyla is the **Chordata,** animals with a nerve cord, gill slits (at some stage of development), and a stiff supporting cord along the back called a *notochord.* Most chordates today are **vertebrates,** in which the notochord has become a vertebral column (which gives its name to the group); in addition, vertebrates have a developed brain and paired sensory structures for sight, smell, and balance.

The vertebrates themselves are subdivided into six classes: bony fishes, cartilaginous fishes, amphibians, reptiles, birds, and mammals. We will discuss mammal classification later in this chapter.

Classification
In biology, the ordering of organisms into categories, such as phyla, orders, and families, to show evolutionary relationships.

Metazoa
Multicellular animals; a major division of the animal kingdom.

Chordata
The phylum of the animal kingdom that includes vertebrates.

Vertebrates
Animals with bony backbones; includes fishes, amphibians, reptiles, birds, and mammals.

Principles of Classification

Before we go any further, it would be useful to discuss the bases of animal classification. The field that specializes in delineating the rules of classification is called *taxonomy*. As mentioned in Chapter 5, organisms are classified first, and most traditionally, on the basis of physical similarities. Such was the basis of the first systematic classification devised by Linnaeus in the eighteenth century (see Chapter 2).

Today, basic physical similarities are still considered a good starting point in postulating schemes of organic relationships. For similarities to be useful, however,

FIGURE 8–1

Classification chart, modified from Linnaeus. All animals are placed in certain categories based on structural similarities. Not all members of categories are shown. For example, there are up to 20 orders of placental mammals (8 are depicted). A more comprehensive classification of the primate order was presented in Chapter 5.

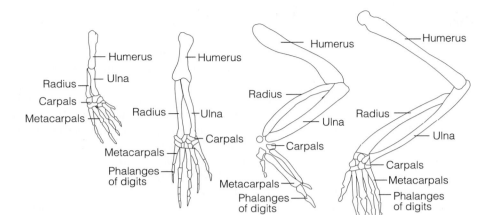

FIGURE 8–2
Homologies. The similarities in the bones of these animals can be most easily explained by descent from a common ancestor.

FROG (amphibian) LIZARD (reptile) BIRD HUMAN

they *must* reflect evolutionary descent. For example, the bones of the forelimb of all terrestrial air-breathing vertebrates (tetrapods) are so similar in number and form (Fig. 8–2) that the obvious explanation for the striking resemblance is that all four kinds of air-breathing vertebrates ultimately derived their forelimb structure from a common ancestor.

Structures that are shared by species on the basis of descent from a common ancestor are called **homologies**. Homologies alone are reliable indicators of evolutionary relationship. But we must be careful not to draw hasty conclusions from superficial similarities.

For example, both birds and butterflies have wings, but they should not be grouped together on the basis of this single characteristic; butterflies (as insects) differ dramatically from birds in a number of other, even more fundamental ways. (For example, birds have an internal skeleton, central nervous system, and four limbs; insects do not.).

What has happened in evolutionary history is that from quite distant ancestors, both butterflies and birds have developed wings *independently*. Thus, their (superficial) similarities are a product of separate evolutionary response to roughly similar functional demands; such similarities, based on independent functional adaptation and *not* on shared evolutionary descent, are called **analogies**. The process that leads to the development of analogies (also called analogous structures) such as wings in birds and butterflies is termed **homoplasy**. In the case of butterflies and birds, the homoplasy has occurred in evolutionary lines that share only very remote ancestry. Here, homoplasy has produced analogous structures separately from any homology. In some cases, however, homoplasy can occur in lineages that are more closely related (and which thus share considerable homology as well). Examples of homoplasy in closely related lineages are evident among the primates (e.g., among New and Old World monkeys and also among the great apes; see Chapter 5).

Constructing Classifications and Interpreting Evolutionary Relationships

There are two major approaches, or "schools," by which evolutionary biologists interpret evolutionary relationships and thus produce classifications. The first of these, called **evolutionary systematics**, is a more traditional approach, whereas the

Homologies
Similarities between organisms based on descent from a common ancestor. *common structure different function*

Analogies *common function different structure*
Similarities between organisms based strictly on common function with no assumed common evolutionary descent.

Homoplasy
(*homo*, meaning "same," and *plasy*, meaning "growth") The separate evolutionary development of similar characteristics in different groups of organisms.

Evolutionary systematics
A traditional approach to classification (and evolutionary interpretation) in which presumed ancestors and descendants are traced in time by analysis of homologous characters.

Cladistics
An approach to classification that seeks to make rigorous evolutionary interpretations based solely on analysis of certain types of homologous characters (those considered derived characters).

 See Virtual Lab 7, section II, for a discussion of taxonomy and classification.

Ancestral (primitive)
Referring to characters inherited by a group of organisms from a remote ancestor and thus not diagnostic of groups (lineages) branching subsequent to the time the character first appeared.

Derived (modified)
Referring to characters that are modified from the ancestral condition and thus *are* diagnostic of particular evolutionary lineages.

second approach, called **cladistics**, has emerged primarily in the last two decades. While aspects of both approaches are still utilized by most evolutionary biologists, in recent years cladistic methodologies have predominated among anthropologists. Indeed, one noted primate evolutionist recently commented that "virtually all current studies of primate phylogeny involve the methods and terminology" of cladistics (Fleagle, 1998, p. 1).

Before drawing distinctions between these two approaches, it is first helpful to note features shared by both evolutionary systematics and cladistics. First, both schools are interested in tracing evolutionary relationships and constructing classifications that reflect these relationships. Second, both schools recognize that organisms must be compared for specific features (called *characters*) and that some of these characters are more informative than others. And third (and deriving directly from the previous two points), both approaches focus exclusively on homologies.

However, there are also significant differences between these approaches in terms of how characters are chosen, which groups are compared, and how the results are interpreted and eventually incorporated into evolutionary schemes and classifications. The primary difference is that cladistics more explicitly and more rigorously defines the kinds of homologies that yield the most useful information. For example, at a very basic level, all life (except for some viruses) shares DNA as the molecule underlying all organic processes. However, beyond inferring that all life most likely derives from a single origin (a most intriguing point), the presence of DNA tells us nothing further regarding more specific relationships among different kinds of life forms. To draw further conclusions, we need to look at particular characters that are shared by certain groups as the result of more recent ancestry.

This perspective emphasizes an important point: Some homologous characters are much more informative than others. We saw earlier that all terrestrial vertebrates share homologies in the number and basic arrangement of bones in the forelimb. Thus, while these similarities are broadly useful in showing that these large evolutionary groups (amphibians, reptiles, birds, and mammals) are all related through a distant ancestor, they do not provide any usable information by which to distinguish one from another (a reptile from a mammal, for example). Such characters (also called traits) that are shared through such remote ancestry are said to be **primitive**, or **ancestral**. We prefer the term *ancestral* because it does not carry a negative connotation regarding the evolutionary value of the character in question. In physical anthropology, the term *primitive* or *ancestral* simply means that a character seen in two organisms is derived in both of them from a distant ancestor.

In most circumstances, analysis of ancestral characters does not provide enough information to make accurate evolutionary interpretations regarding relationships between different groups. In fact, misinterpretation of ancestral characters can easily lead to quite inaccurate evolutionary conclusions! The traits that cladistics focuses on, and which are far more informative, are those that distinguish particular evolutionary lineages. Such characters are said to be **derived**, or **modified**. Thus, while the general ancestral bony pattern of the forelimb in land animals with backbones does not allow us to distinguish among them, the further modification in certain groups (as hooves, flippers, or wings, for instance) does.

A simplified example might help clarify the basic principles used in cladistic analysis. Figure 8–3a shows a hypothetical "lineage" of passenger vehicles. All of the "descendant" vehicles share a common ancestor, the prototype passenger vehicle. The first major division (I) is that differentiating passenger cars from trucks. The second split (i.e., diversification) is between luxury cars and sports cars (you could, of course, imagine many other subcategories). Modified (derived) traits that distinguish trucks from cars might include type of frame, suspension, wheel size, and, in some forms, an open cargo bed. Derived characters that might distinguish sports

(a)

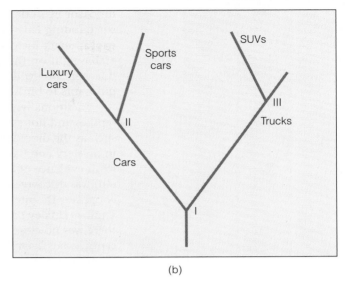

(b)

From a common ancestor of all passenger vehicles, the first major divergence is that between cars and trucks (I). A later divergence also occurs between luxury cars and sports cars (II). Derived features of each grouping ("lineage") appear only after its divergence from other groups (e.g., cargo beds are found only in trucks, cushioned suspension only in cars; likewise, only sports cars have a decorative racing stripe).

In this "tree," SUVs diverge from trucks, but like sports cars, they have a decorative racing stripe. This feature is a homoplasy and does *not* make SUVs sports cars. The message is that classifications based on just one characteristic that can appear independently in different groups can lead to an *incorrect* conclusion.

cars from luxury cars could include engine size and type, wheel base size, and a decorative racing stripe.

Now let us assume that you are presented with an "unknown" vehicle (i.e., one as yet unclassified). How do you decide what kind of vehicle it is? You might note such features as four wheels, a steering wheel, and a seat for the driver, but these are *ancestral* characters of all passenger vehicles (and ones found in the common ancestor). If, however, you note that the vehicle lacks a cargo bed and raised suspension (i.e., is not a truck) but has a racing stripe, you might conclude that it is a car, and more than that, a sports car (since it has a derived feature presumably of *only* that group).

All this seems fairly obvious, and you probably have noticed that this simple type of decision making characterizes much of human mental organization. Still, there are frequently complications that are not so obvious. What if you are presented with a sports utility vehicle (SUV) with a racing stripe (Fig. 8–3b)? SUVs are basically trucks, but the presence of the racing stripe could be seen as a homoplasy with sports cars. The lesson here is that we need to be careful, to look at several traits, to decide which are ancestral and which are derived, and finally to try to recognize the complexity (and confusion) introduced by homoplasy.

The preceding example is useful up to a point. Because it concerns human inventions, the groupings possess characters that humans can add and delete in almost any combination. Naturally occurring organic systems are more limited in this respect. Any species can only possess characters that have been inherited from its ancestor or that have been subsequently modified (derived) from those shared with the ancestor. Thus, any modification in *any* species is constrained by that species' evolutionary legacy—that is, what the species starts out with.

Another example, one drawn from paleontological (fossil) evidence of actual organisms, can help clarify these points. Most people know something about

FIGURE 8–3
Evolutionary "trees" showing development of passenger vehicles.

189

dinosaur evolution, and some of you may know about the recent controversies surrounding this topic. There are a number of intriguing issues concerning the evolutionary history of dinosaurs, and recent fossil discoveries have shed considerable light on them. We will mention some of these issues later in the chapter, but here we will consider one of the more fascinating: the relationship of dinosaurs to birds.

Traditionally, it had been thought that birds were a quite distinct group from reptiles and not especially closely related to any of them (including extinct forms, such as the dinosaurs) (Fig. 8–4a). However, the early origins of birds were clouded in mystery and have been much debated for more than a century. In fact, the first fossil evidence of a very primitive bird (now known to be about 150 million years old) was discovered in 1861, just two years following Darwin's publication of *Origin of Species*. Despite some initial and quite remarkably accurate interpretations by Thomas Huxley linking these early birds to dinosaurs, most experts concluded that there was no close relationship. This view persisted through most of the twentieth century, but events of the last two decades have swung the consensus back to the hypothesis that birds *are* closely related to some dinosaurs. Two developments in particular have influenced this change of opinion: the remarkable discoveries in the 1990s from China, Madagascar, and elsewhere and the application of cladistic methods to the interpretation of these and other fossils.

Recent finds from Madagascar of chicken-size very primitive birds dated to 70–65 million years ago (m.y.a.) show an elongated second toe (similar, in fact, to that in the dinosaur *Velociraptor*, made infamous in the film *Jurassic Park*). Indeed, these primitive birds from Madagascar show many other similarities to *Velociraptor* and its close cousins, which together comprise a group of small- to medium-sized ground-living, carnivorous dinosaurs called **theropods**. Even more extraordinary finds have been unearthed recently in China, where embossed in fossilized sediments are traces of what were once *feathers*! For many researchers, these new finds have finally solved the mystery of bird origins, leading some experts to conclude that this evidence "shows that birds are not only *descended* from dinosaurs, they *are* dinosaurs (and reptiles)—just as humans are mammals, even though people are as different from other mammals as birds are from other reptiles" (Padian and Chiappe, 1998, p. 43) (Fig. 8–4b).

Theropods
Small- to medium-sized ground-living dinosaurs, dated to approximately 150 m.y.a. and thought to be related to birds.

FIGURE 8–4
Evolutionary relationships of birds and dinosaurs. (a) Traditional view, showing no close relationship. (b) Revised view, showing common ancestry of birds and dinosaurs.

(a)

(b)

There are some doubters who remain concerned that the presence of feathers in dinosaurs (145–125 m.y.a.) might simply be a homoplasy (i.e., these creatures developed the trait independently from its appearance in birds). Certainly, the possibility of homoplasy must always be considered, as it can add considerably to the complexity of what seems like a straightforward evolutionary interpretation. Indeed, strict cladistic analysis assumes that homoplasy is not a common occurrence; if it were, perhaps no evolutionary interpretation could be very straightforward! In the case of the proposed relationship between some (theropod) dinosaurs and birds, the presence of feathers looks like an excellent example of a shared derived characteristic, which therefore *does* link the forms. Moreover, cladistic analysis emphasizes that several characteristics should be examined, since homoplasy might muddle an interpretation based on just one or two shared traits. In the bird-dinosaur case, several other characteristics further suggest their evolutionary relationship.

As we already noted, dinosaur paleontology continues to be a hotbed, fueled by dramatic new discoveries, reinterpretations, and ongoing disputes. Another spectacular new analysis (using ultraviolet light) of a 100 m.y.a. Italian theropod has revealed the presence of internal organs, including the intestines, liver, trachea, and some muscles (Ruben et al., 1999). Initial analysis has suggested that this theropod dinosaur had a breathing mechanism quite different from that of birds but in some ways similar to that of living crocodiles. Some researchers have thus argued that this new evidence casts some doubt on the theropod-bird link. For the moment, however, the overall cladistic analysis of several other traits (following Padian and Chiappe, 1998) argues for a fairly close theropod-bird evolutionary relationship. (*Note:* To falsify this hypothesis, a great deal of homoplasy in theropods and birds would have had to take place.)

One last point needs to be mentioned. Traditional phylogenetic systematics illustrates the hypothesized evolutionary relationships using a *phylogeny,* more properly called a **phylogenetic tree.** Strict cladistic analysis, however, shows relationships in a **cladogram** (Fig. 8–5). If you examine these charts, you will see some obvious differences. A phylogenetic tree incorporates the dimension of time, shown approximately in Figure 8–4. (Numerous other examples can be found in this and subsequent chapters.) A cladogram does not indicate time; all forms (fossil and modern) are indicated along one dimension. Phylogenetic trees usually attempt to make some hypotheses regarding ancestor-descendant relationships (e.g., theropods are ancestral to modern birds). Cladistic analysis (through cladograms)

Phylogenetic tree
A chart showing evolutionary relationships as determined by phylogenetic systematics. It contains a time component and implies ancestor-descendant relationships.

Cladogram
A chart showing evolutionary relationships as determined by cladistic analysis. It is based solely on interpretation of shared derived characters. No time component is indicated, and ancestor-descendant relationships are *not* implied.

FIGURE 8–5
Cladogram showing relationships of birds, dinosaurs, and other terrestrial vertebrates. Note that no time scale is utilized, and both living and fossil forms are shown along the same dimension (i.e., there is *no* indication of ancestor-descendant relationships).

makes no attempt whatsoever to discern ancestor-descendant relationships. In fact, strict cladists are quite skeptical that the evidence really permits such specific evolutionary hypotheses to be scientifically confirmed (since there are many more extinct species than living ones).

In practice, most physical anthropologists (and other evolutionary biologists) utilize cladistic analysis to identify and assess the utility of traits and to make testable hypotheses regarding the relationships of groups of organisms. Moreover, they frequently extend this basic cladistic methodology to further hypothesize likely ancestor-descendant relationships shown relative to a time scale (i.e., in a phylogenetic tree). In this way, aspects of both traditional evolutionary systematics and cladistic analyses are combined to produce a more complete picture of evolutionary history.

Definition of Species

Whether biologists are doing a cladistic or more traditional phylogenetic analysis, they are comparing groups of organisms—that is, different species, genera*, families, orders, and so forth. Fundamental to all these levels of classification is the most basic, the species.

It is appropriate, then, to ask, How do biologists define species? We addressed this issue briefly in Chapter 1 and there applied the most common definition, one that emphasizes interbreeding and reproductive isolation. While not the only definition of species (others will be discussed shortly), this view, called the **biological species concept** (Mayr, 1970), is the one preferred by most zoologists.

The best way to understand what species are is to consider how they come about in the first place—what Darwin called "origin of species." This most fundamental of macroevolutionary processes is today called **speciation**. According to the biological species concept, the way new species are first produced involves some form of isolation. Picture a single species (baboons, for example) composed of several populations distributed over a wide geographical area. Gene exchange between populations (gene flow) will be limited if a geographical barrier, such as an ocean or mountain range, effectively separates these populations. This extremely important form of isolating mechanism is called *geographical isolation*.

If one baboon population (A) is separated from another baboon population (B) by a mountain range, individual baboons of population A will not mate with individuals from B (Fig. 8–6). As time passes (several generations), genetic differences

Biological species concept
A depiction of species as groups of individuals capable of fertile interbreeding, but reproductively isolated from other such groups.

Speciation
The process where a new species evolves from a prior species. Speciation is the most basic process in macroevolution.

FIGURE 8–6
A speciation model.

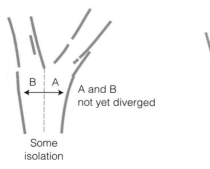

B | A
A and B not yet diverged
Some isolation

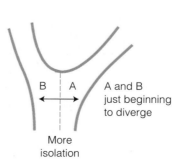

B | A
A and B just beginning to diverge
More isolation

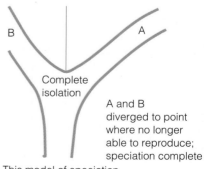

B   A
Complete isolation
A and B diverged to point where no longer able to reproduce; speciation complete
This model of speciation is called branching evolution, or cladogenesis.

*Plural of *genus*.

will accumulate in both populations. If population size is small, we can predict that genetic drift will cause allele frequencies to change in both populations. Moreover, since drift is *random* in nature, we would not expect the effects to be the same. Consequently, the two populations will begin to diverge.

As long as gene exchange is limited, the populations can only become more genetically different with time. Moreover, further difference can be expected if the baboon groups are occupying slightly different habitats. These additional genetic differences would be incorporated through the process of natural selection. Certain individuals in population A would be most reproductively fit in their own environment, but would show less reproductive success in the environment occupied by population B. Thus, allele frequencies will shift further, and the results, again, will be divergent in the two groups.

With the cumulative effects of genetic drift and natural selection acting over many generations, the result will be two populations that—even if they were to come back into geographical contact—could no longer interbreed. More than just geographical isolation might now apply. There may, for instance, be behavioral differences interfering with courtship—what we call *behavioral isolation*. Using our *biological* definition of species, we now would recognize two distinct species where initially only one existed.

Another related process that can contribute to the further differentiation of populations into incipient species concerns mate recognition. Sometimes called the **recognition species concept,** the crucial process again concerns reproduction (i.e., who is mating with whom) (Ridley, 1993).

Assume in our baboon example that some isolation has already occurred and that phenotypic (and genotypic) differences have started to be established between two populations. In this situation, coloration patterns of faces or the size, location, coloration, or even smell of the estrous swelling might vary from group to group. If so, then a female from population A might not recognize a male from population B as an appropriate mate (and vice versa, of course). Natural selection would quickly favor such discrimination if hybrids were less reproductively successful than within-population crosses. Indeed, once such "selective breeding" became established, speciation would be accelerated considerably.

Another definition of species focuses primarily on natural selection and emphasizes that speciation is the result of influences of varied habitats. Called the **ecological species concept**, a species is here defined as a group of organisms exploiting a single niche.

For each population, initially the habitats will vary slightly, and different genotypes will be slightly more advantageous in each. It is assumed that there is an adaptive "gap" separating the ecological zones, so that intermediate genotypes (and intermediate environmental adaptations) would not occur. For example, one population might be more arboreal and another more terrestrial; but there would not be an intermediate population equally successful on the ground and in the trees.

In recent years, the ecological species concept has attracted support from a number of evolutionary biologists, especially among physical anthropologists. While the biological species concept emphasizes gene flow and reproductive isolation, the ecological species concept stresses the role of natural selection. Clearly, our approach in this text has been to focus on the evolutionary contribution of natural selection; thus, the ecological species concept has much to offer here. Nevertheless, our understanding of species need not entail an either/or choice between the biological species concept and the ecological species concept. Some population isolation could indeed *begin* the process of speciation. The process might then be reinforced by natural selection through habitat differentiation as well as mate recognition.

Recognition species concept
A depiction of species where the key aspect is the ability of individuals to identify members of their own species for purposes of mating (and to avoid mating with members of other species). In theory, this type of selective mating is a component of a species concept emphasizing mating and is therefore compatible with the biological species concept.

Ecological species concept
The concept that a species is a group of organisms exploiting a single niche. This view emphasizes the role of natural selection in separating species from one another.

Processes of Speciation

Now that we have seen how species can be defined in somewhat varied ways, what are some of the more specific theories that evolutionary biologists have developed to account for *how* species originate? First, you should recognize that these hypotheses are quite abstract and thus difficult to test doing conventional field biology on contemporary species. No one has actually observed an animal species speciate and become two different species. In fact, some biologists estimate that it takes between 1.5 and 3.5 million years for a new species of fruit fly (*Drosophila*) to evolve; mammal species would presumably take longer to fully speciate.

Given the constraints of field testing in such a slowly occurring phenomenon, biologists have hypothesized that speciation could occur in three different ways: by **allopatric** speciation, *parapatric* speciation, or *sympatric* speciation.

By far, the most widely accepted view of speciation emphasizes an allopatric pattern. This model requires complete reproductive isolation within a population, leading to the formation of an incipient species separated (geographically) from its ancestral population.

In parapatric speciation, only *partial* reproductive isolation is required, so that the ranges of the populations may be partially overlapping. In this situation, a hybrid zone would form in an area between the two partially separated populations. More complete separation could then occur through reinforcement of mate recognition and selective breeding.

Interestingly, in some areas of East Africa, there is good evidence that parapatric speciation might be currently (and slowly) taking place between populations of savanna baboons and hamadryas baboons. Long-term research by Jane Phillips-Conroy and Clifford Jolly has carefully documented hybrid individuals produced by the mating of savanna baboons with hamadryas baboons. Traditionally, these two types of baboons have been placed in separate species (savanna as *Papio cynocephalus* and hamadryas as *Papio hamadryas*). Yet, the hybrids appear quite functional and are *fertile* (Phillips-Conroy et al., 1992; Jolly, 1993). Thus, what we are likely seeing here is speciation in process—and probably following a parapatric pattern. Thus, we might regard these two types of baboons as incipient species. It is also possible that some mate recognition differentiation may be operating as well, since male-female interactions differ considerably between savanna and hamadryas baboons.

The third type of speciation proposed, sympatric speciation, is theorized to occur completely within one population with *no* necessary reproductive isolation. However, this form of speciation, while possible, is not well supported by contemporary evidence and is thus considered the least significant of the three models.

A fourth type of speciation has also been recognized and may have played a role in the evolution of certain species. In this pattern, called *instantaneous speciation*, chromosomal rearrangements occur (by chromosomal mutation), producing reproductive barriers immediately. As well documented in plants, this type of speciation can be very rapid, with varieties emerging with completely different numbers of chromosomes. Here, the process is one of multiplication of chromosome sets (due to mistakes in meiosis), producing a condition called *polyploidy* (see Chapter 3). While common in plants, such drastic reorganization of chromosome number is not a factor in speciation of animals, where polyploidy is always lethal. However, somewhat less dramatic chromosomal alterations, such as inversions and translocations (including fusions; see p. 116), could accelerate speciation in animals. Certainly, chromosomal alterations may be important in speciation, and some researchers have even suggested that such processes may be a central factor in macroevolution.

Allopatric
A model of speciation emphasizing complete (or nearly complete) reproductive isolation of divergent populations from their ancestral population.

*parapatric—
one element of hybrid zone.
i.e. produce fertile offspring*

Nevertheless, demonstration in animals of the systematic influence of such large-scale mutation has been difficult. Indeed, theoretical models suggest that major mutational change could not *by itself* produce speciation in animals, but would require some further mechanism to help "fix" the genetic changes within populations. Inbreeding within small population segments has been suggested by some investigators as a possible mechanism that could reinforce rapid speciation by chromosomal mutation. Moreover, some theoretical support for this process (from data concerning relative amounts of within-species chromosomal variation) has been found in those species divided into small social groupings. And, perhaps of greatest interest, the best evidence of this type of patterning has been shown in species of horses and primates.

Interpretation of Species and Other Groups in the Fossil Record

Later in this chapter and throughout the next several chapters, we will be using a variety of taxonomic terms for fossil primates (including fossil hominids); you will be introduced to such terms as *Proconsul, Sivapithecus, Australopithecus,* and *Homo.* Of course, *Homo* is still a living primate, as are several others we have discussed in the previous three chapters (e.g., *Pan, Papio, Pongo,* and *Cebus*). But it is especially complex to make these types of designations from remains of animals that are long dead (and only partially preserved as skeletal remains). In these contexts, what do such names mean in evolutionary terms?

Our goal when applying species, genus, or other taxonomic labels to groups of organisms is to make meaningful biological statements about the variation that is present. When looking at populations of living or long-extinct animals, we are assuredly going to see variation. The situation is true of *any* sexually reproducing organism because of the factors of recombination (see Chapter 3). As a result of recombination, each individual organism is a unique combination of genetic material, and the uniqueness is usually reflected to some extent in the phenotype.

In addition to such *individual variation,* we see other kinds of systematic variation in all biological populations. *Age changes* certainly alter overall body size as well as shape in many mammals. One pertinent example for fossil hominoid studies is the great change in number, size, and shape of teeth from deciduous (milk) teeth (only 20 present) to the permanent dentition (32 present). It would be an obvious error to differentiate fossil forms solely on the basis of such age-dependent criteria. If one individual were represented just by milk teeth and another (seemingly very different) individual were represented just by adult teeth, they easily could be different-aged individuals from the *same* population. Variation due to sex also plays an important role in influencing differences among individuals observed in biological populations. Differences in structural traits between males and females of the same population are called *sexual dimorphism* and can result in marked variance in body size and proportions in adults of the same species.

Keeping in mind all the types of variation present within interbreeding groups of organisms, the minimum biological category we would like to define in fossil primate samples is the *species*. As already defined (according to the biological species concept), a species is a group of interbreeding or potentially interbreeding organisms that is reproductively isolated from other such groups. In modern organisms, this concept is theoretically testable by observations of reproductive behavior. In animals long dead, such observations are obviously impossible. Therefore, to get a handle on the interpretation of variation seen in fossil groups, we must refer to living animals.

Intraspecific
Within species; refers to variation seen within the same species.

Interspecific
Between species; refers to variation beyond that seen within the same species to include additional aspects seen between two different species.

Paleospecies
Species defined from fossil evidence, often covering a long time span.

Genus
A group of closely related species

We know without doubt that variation is present. The question is, What is its biological significance? Two immediate choices occur: Either the variation is accounted for by individual, age, and sex differences seen within every biological species (it is **intraspecific**) or the variation represents differences between reproductively isolated groups (it is **interspecific**). How do we decide which alternative is at work? We clearly must refer to already defined groups where we can observe reproductive behavior—in other words, contemporary species.

If the amount of morphological variation observed in fossil samples is comparable to that seen today *within species of closely related forms,* then we should not "split" our sample into more than one species. We must, however, be careful in choosing modern analogues, for rates of morphological evolution vary widely among different groups of mammals. In interpreting past primates, we do best when comparing them with well-known species of modern primates.

Nevertheless, studies of such living groups have shown that delimiting exactly where species boundaries begin and end is often difficult. In dealing with extinct species, the uncertainties are even greater. In addition to the overlapping patterns of variation *over space,* variation also occurs *through time.* In other words, even more variation will be seen in such **paleospecies**, since individuals may be separated by thousands or even millions of years. Applying strict Linnaean taxonomy to such a situation presents an unavoidable dilemma. Standard Linnaean classification, designed to take account of variation present at any given time, describes a static situation. However, when we deal with paleospecies, the time frame is expanded, and the situation can be dynamic (i.e., later forms might be different from earlier ones). In such a dynamic situation, taxonomic decisions (where to draw species boundaries) are ultimately going to be somewhat arbitrary.

The next level of formal taxonomic classification, the **genus**, presents another problem. To have more than one genus, we obviously must have at least two species (reproductively isolated groups), and the species of one genus must differ in a basic way from the species of another genus. A genus is therefore defined as a group of species composed of members more closely related to each other than they are to species from any other genus.

Grouping species together into genera is largely a subjective procedure wherein the degree of relatedness becomes a relative judgment. One possible test for contemporary animals is to check for results of hybridization between individuals of different species—rare in nature but quite common in captivity. If two normally separate species interbreed and produce live, though not necessarily fertile, offspring, they probably are not too different genetically and should therefore be grouped together in the same genus. A well-known example of such a cross is horses with donkeys (*Equus callabus* × *Equus asinus*), which normally produces live, sterile offspring (mules).

As previously mentioned, we cannot perform breeding experiments with extinct animals, but another definition of genus becomes highly relevant. Species that are members of the same genus share the same broad adaptive zone. What this represents is a general ecological lifestyle more basic than the narrower ecological niches characteristic of individual species. This ecological definition of genus can be an immense aid in interpreting fossil primates. Teeth are the most frequently preserved parts, and they often can provide excellent general ecological inferences. Moreover, cladistic analysis (see pp. 188–192) also provides assistance in making judgments about evolutionary relationships. That is, members of the *same* genus should all share derived characters not seen in members of other genera.

As a final comment, we should point out that classification by genus is not always a straightforward decision. Indeed, the argument among primatologists over whether the chimpanzee and gorilla represent one genus (*Pan troglodytes, Pan gorilla*) or two different genera (*Pan troglodytes, Gorilla gorilla*) demonstrates that even with living, breathing animals, the choices are not always clear. For that matter, many current researchers, pointing to the very close genetic similarities between humans and chimpanzees, would place both in the same genus (*Homo sapiens, Homo troglodytes*). When it gets this close to home, it is even more difficult to remain objective!

Vertebrate Evolutionary History: A Brief Summary

In addition to the staggering array of living and extinct life forms, biologists must also contend with the vast amount of time that life has been evolving on earth. Again, scientists have devised simplified schemes—but in this case to organize *time*, not organic diversity.

Geologists have formulated the **geological time scale** (Fig. 8–7), in which very large time spans are organized into eras and periods. Periods, in turn, can be broken

Geological time scale
The organization of earth history into eras, periods, and epochs; commonly used by geologists and paleoanthropologists.

FIGURE 8–7
Geological time scale.

 See Virtual Lab 7, section I, for a discussion of geological time.

ERA	PERIOD	(Began m.y.a.)	EPOCH	(Began m.y.a.)
CENOZOIC	Quaternary	1.8	Holocene Pleistocene	0.01 1.8
	Tertiary	65	Pliocene Miocene Oligocene Eocene Paleocene	5 23 34 55 65
MESOZOIC	Cretaceous	136		
	Jurassic	190		
	Triassic	225		
PALEOZOIC	Permian	280		
	Carboniferous	345		
	Devonian	395		
	Silurian	430		
	Ordovician	500		
	Cambrian	570		
PRE-CAMBRIAN				

down into epochs (as we will do later in our discussion of primate evolution). For the time span encompassing vertebrate evolution, there are three eras: the Paleozoic, the Mesozoic, and the Cenozoic. The first vertebrates are present in the fossil record dating to early in the Paleozoic 500 m.y.a. and probably go back considerably further. It is the vertebrate capacity to form bone that accounts for their more complete fossil record *after* 500 m.y.a.

During the Paleozoic, several varieties of fishes (including the ancestors of modern sharks and bony fishes), amphibians, and reptiles appeared. In addition, at the end of the Paleozoic, close to 250 m.y.a., several varieties of mammal-like reptiles were also diversifying. It is widely thought that some of these forms gave rise to the mammals.

The evolutionary history of vertebrates and other organisms during the Paleozoic and Mesozoic was profoundly influenced by geographical events. We know that the positions of the earth's continents have dramatically shifted during the last several hundred million years. This process, called **continental drift**, is explained by the geological theory of *plate tectonics,* which views the earth's crust as a series of gigantic moving and colliding plates. Such massive geological movements can induce volcanic activity (as, for example, all around the Pacific rim), mountain building (e.g., the Himalayas), and earthquakes. Living on the edge of the Pacific and North American plates, residents of the Pacific coast of the United States are acutely aware of some of these consequences, as illustrated by the explosive volcanic eruption of Mt. St. Helens or the frequent earthquakes in Alaska and California.

Geologists, in reconstructing the earth's physical history, have established the prior (significantly altered) positions of major continental landmasses. During the late Paleozoic, the continents came together to form a single colossal landmass called *Pangea*. In actuality, the continents had been drifting on plates, coming together and separating, long before the end of the Paleozoic (c. 225 m.y.a.), and to be more precise, the large landmass at this time should be called Pangea II. During the early Mesozoic, the southern continents (South America, Africa, Antarctica, Australia, and India) began to split off from Pangea, forming a large southern continent called *Gondwanaland* (Fig. 8–8a). Similarly, the northern continents (North America, Greenland, Europe, and Asia) were consolidated into a northern landmass called *Laurasia*. During the Mesozoic, Gondwanaland and Laurasia continued to

Continental drift
The movement of continents on sliding plates of the earth's surface. As a result, the positions of large landmasses have shifted dramatically during the earth's history.

FIGURE 8–8
Continental drift. Changes in positions of the continental plates from late Paleozoic to the early Cenozoic. (a) The positions of the continents during the Mesozoic (c. 125 m.y.a.). Pangea is breaking up into a northern landmass (Laurasia) and a southern landmass (Gondwanaland). (b) The positions of the continents at the beginning of the Cenozoic (c. 65 m.y.a.).

	PALEOZOIC						MESOZOIC		
Cambrian	Ordovician	Silurian	Devonian	Carbon-iferous	Permian		Triassic	Jurassic	Cretaceous
Trilobites abundant; also brachiopods, jellyfish, worms, and other invertebrates	First fishes; trilobites still abundant; graptolites and corals become plentiful; possible land plants	Jawed fishes appear; first air-breathing animals; definite land plants	Age of Fish; first amphibians; first forests	First reptiles; radiation of amphibians; modern insects diversify	Reptile radiation; mammal-like reptiles	Major extinction event	Reptiles further radiate; first dinosaurs; egg-laying mammals	Great Age of Dinosaurs; flying and swimming dinosaurs; first toothed birds	Placental and marsupial mammals appear; first modern birds	Major extinction event

570 m.y.a   500 m.y.a   430 m.y.a   395 m.y.a   345 m.y.a   280 m.y.a   225 m.y.a   190 m.y.a   136 m.y.a   65 m.y.a

drift apart and to break up into smaller segments. By the end of the Mesozoic (c. 65 m.y.a.), the continents were beginning to assume their current positions (Fig. 8–8b).

The evolutionary ramifications of this long-term continental drift were profound. Groups of land animals became effectively isolated from each other by large water boundaries, and the distribution of reptiles and mammals was significantly influenced by continental movements. Although not producing such dramatic continental realignments, the process continued into the Cenozoic. The more specific effects of continental drift on early primate evolution are discussed later in this chapter.

During most of the Mesozoic, reptiles were the dominant land vertebrates, and they exhibited a broad expansion into a variety of **ecological niches**, which included aerial and marine habitats. No doubt, the most famous of these highly successful Mesozoic reptiles were the dinosaurs, which themselves evolved into a wide array of sizes and lifestyles. Dinosaur paleontology, never a boring field, has advanced several startling notions in recent years: that many dinosaurs were warm-blooded; that some varieties were quite social and probably also engaged in considerable parental care; that many forms became extinct as the result of major climatic changes to the earth's atmosphere from collisions with comets or asteroids; and finally, as previously discussed, that not all dinosaurs became entirely extinct, with many descendants still living today (i.e., all modern birds). (See Figure 8–9 for a summary of major events in early vertebrate evolutionary history.)

The earliest mammals are known from fossil traces fairly early in the Mesozoic, but the first *placental* mammals cannot be positively identified until quite late in the Mesozoic, approximately 70 m.y.a. This highly successful mammalian adaptive radiation is thus almost entirely within the most recent era of geological history, the Cenozoic.

The Cenozoic is divided into two periods, the Tertiary (about 63 million years duration) and the Quaternary, from about 1.8 m.y.a. up to and including the present. Because this division is rather imprecise, paleontologists more frequently refer to the next level of subdivision within the Cenozoic, the **epochs**. There are seven epochs within the Cenozoic: the Paleocene, Eocene, Oligocene, Miocene, Pliocene, Pleistocene, and Holocene, the last often referred to as the Recent (see Box 8–1).

FIGURE 8–9
Time line of major events in early vertebrate evolution.

Ecological niches
The positions of species within their physical and biological environments, together making up the *ecosystem*. A species' ecological niche is defined by such components as diet, terrain, vegetation, type of predators, relationships with other species, and activity patterns, and each niche is unique to a given species.

Epochs
Categories of the geological time scale; subdivisions of periods. In the Cenozoic, epochs include the Paleocene, Eocene, Oligocene, Miocene, Pliocene (from the Tertiary), and the Pleistocene and Holocene (from the Quaternary).

BOX 8-1   A CLOSER LOOK

Deep Time

The vast expanse of time during which evolution has occurred on earth staggers the imagination. Indeed, this fundamental notion of what John McPhee has termed "deep time" is not really understood or, in fact, widely believed. Of course, as we have emphasized beginning in Chapter 1 (see Issue, pp. 19–20), *belief*, as such, is not part of science. But observation, theory building, and testing are. Nevertheless, in a world populated mostly by nonscientists, the concept of deep time, crucial as it is to geology and anthropology, is resisted by many people. This situation is really not surprising; as an idea that can be truly understood (i.e., internalized and given some personal meaning), deep time is in many ways counterintuitive. As individuals, human beings measure their existence in months, years, or in the span of human lifetimes.

But what are these durations, measured against geological or galactic phenomena? In a real sense, these vast time expanses are beyond human comprehension. We can reasonably fathom the reaches of human history, stretching to about 5,000 years ago. In a leap of imagination, we can perhaps even begin to grasp the stretch of time back to the cave painters of France and Spain, approximately 17,000 to 25,000 years ago. How do we relate, then, to a temporal span 10 times this, back to 250,000 years ago (about the time of the earliest modern *Homo sapiens*)—or to 10 times this span to 2,500,000 years ago (about the time of the appearance of our genus, *Homo*)? We surely can respond that any

of these time blocks are vast—and then *more* vast. But multiply this last duration another 1,000 times (to 2,500,000,000), and we are back to a time of fairly early life forms. And we would still have to reach further into earth's past another 1.5 billion years to approach the *earliest* documented life.

The dimensions of these intervals are humbling, to say the least. The discovery in the nineteenth century of deep time (as we documented in Chapter 2) in what Stephen Jay Gould, of the American Museum of Natural History in New York City, calls "geology's greatest contribution to human thought" plunged one more dagger into humanity's long-cherished special view of itself. Astronomers had previously established how puny our world was in the physical expanse of space, and then geologists showed that even on our own small planet, we were but residues dwarfed within a river of time "without a vestige of a beginning or prospect of an end" (from James Hutton, a founder of modern geology and one of the discoverers of deep time). It is no wonder that there is resistance to the concept of deep time; it not only stupefies our reason, but implies a sense of collective meaninglessness and reinforces our individual mortality.

Geologists, astronomers, and other scholars have struggled for over a century, with modest success, to translate the tales told in rocks and hurtling stars in terms that can be understood by everyone. Various analogies have been attempted—metaphors, really—drawn from common experience. Among the most suc-

Mammalian Evolution

See Virtual Lab 7, section II, for a discussion of placental mammal relationships.

Following the extinction of dinosaurs and many other Mesozoic forms (at the end of the Mesozoic), there was a wide array of ecological niches open for the rapid expansion and diversification of mammals. The Cenozoic was an opportunistic time for mammals, and it is known as the Age of Mammals. Mesozoic mammals were small animals, about the size of mice, which they resembled superficially. The wide diversification of mammals in the Cenozoic saw the rise of the major lineages of all modern mammals. Indeed, mammals, along with birds, replaced reptiles as the dominant terrestrial vertebrates.

How do we account for the rapid success of the mammals? Several characteristics relating to learning and general flexibility of behavior are of prime importance. To process more information, mammals were selected for larger brains than those typically found in reptiles. In particular, the cerebrum became generally enlarged, cessful of these attempts is a "cosmic calendar" devised by eminent astronomer Carl Sagan in his book *Dragons of Eden* (1977). In this version of time's immensity, Sagan likens the passage of geological time to that of one calendar year. The year begins on January 1 with the "Big Bang," the cosmic explosion marking the beginning of the universe and the beginning of time. In this version, the Big Bang is set at 15 billion years ago.* with some of the major events in the geological past as follows:

*Recent evidence gathered by the Hubble Space Telescope has questioned the established date for the Big Bang. However, even the most recent data are somewhat contradictory, suggesting a date from as early as 16 billion years ago (indicated by the age of the oldest stars) to as recent as 8 billion years ago (indicated by the rate of expansion of the universe). Here, we will follow the conventional dating of 15 billion years; if you apply the most conservative approximation (8 billion years), the calibrations shift as follows: 1 day = 22,000,000 years; 1 hour = 913,000 years; 1 minute = 15,000 years. Using these calculations, for example, the first hominids appear on Dec. 31 at 7:37 P.M., and modern *Homo sapiens* are on the scene at 11:42 P.M.

Time Unit Conversions Using the Cosmic Calendar:

1 year = 15,000,000,000 years	1 hour = 1,740,000 years		*December 31 Events*
1 month = 1,250,000,000 years	1 minute = 29,000 years	Appearance of early hominoids apes and humans)	12:30 P.M.
1 day = 14,000,000 years	1 second = 475 years	First hominids	9:30 P.M.
Big Bang	January 1	Extensive cave painting in Europe	11:59 P.M.
Formation of the earth	September 14	Invention of agriculture	11:59:20 P.M.
Origin of life on earth (approx.)	September 25	Renaissance in Europe; Ming Dynasty in China; emergence of scientific method	11:59:59 P.M.
Significant oxygen atmosphere begins to develop	December 1		
Precambrian ends; Paleozoic begins; invertebrates flourish	December 17	Widespread development of science and technology; emergence of a global culture; first steps in space exploration	NOW: the first second of the New Year
Paleozoic ends and Mesozoic begins	December 25		
Cretaceous period: first flowers; dinosaurs become extinct	December 28		
Mesozoic ends; Cenozoic begins; adaptive radiation of placental mammals	December 29		

especially the outer covering, the neocortex, which controls higher brain functions (Fig. 8–10). In some mammals, the cerebrum expanded so much that it came to comprise the majority of brain volume; moreover, the number of surface convolutions increased, creating more surface area and thus providing space for even more nerve cells (neurons). As we have already seen (in Chapter 5), this is a trend even further emphasized among the primates.

For such a large and complex organ as the mammalian brain to develop, a longer, more intense period of growth is required. Slower development can occur internally (*in utero*) as well as after birth. While internal fertilization and internal development are not unique to mammals, the latter is a major innovation among terrestrial vertebrates. Other forms (birds, most fishes, and reptiles) incubate their young externally by laying eggs (i.e., they are oviparous), while mammals, with very few exceptions, give birth to live young and are thus said to be **viviparous.** Even among mammals, however, there is considerable variation among the major

Viviparous
Giving birth to live young.

FIGURE 8–10

Lateral view of the brain. The illustration shows the increase in the cerebral cortex of the brain. The cerebral cortex integrates sensory information and selects responses.

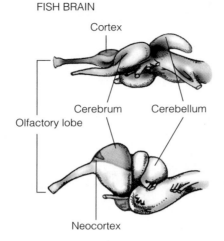

FISH BRAIN

Cortex

Cerebrum   Cerebellum

Olfactory lobe

Neocortex

REPTILE BRAIN

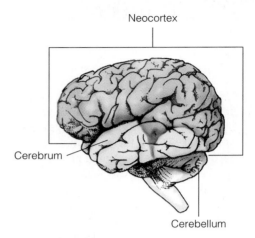

Neocortex

Cerebrum

Cerebellum

PRIMATE BRAIN

REPTILIAN (alligator): homodont

MAMMALIAN: heterodont

Incisors

Canine

Premolars   Molars

Cheek teeth

FIGURE 8–11

Reptilian and mammalian teeth.

Heterodont

Having different kinds of teeth; characteristic of mammals, whose teeth consist of incisors, canines, premolars, and molars.

Endothermic

(*endo*, meaning "within" or "internal")

Able to maintain internal body temperature through the production of energy by means of metabolic processes within cells; characteristic of mammals, birds, and perhaps some dinosaurs.

groups in how mature the young are at birth. As you will see, it is in mammals like ourselves, the *placental* forms, where development *in utero* goes the furthest.

Another distinctive feature of mammals is seen in the dentition. While living reptiles consistently have similarly shaped teeth (called a *homodont* dentition), mammals have differently shaped teeth (Fig. 8–11). This varied pattern, termed a **heterodont** dentition, is reflected in the primitive (ancestral) mammalian array of dental elements, which includes 3 incisors, 1 canine, 4 premolars, and 3 molars for each quarter of the mouth. Since the upper and lower jaws are usually the same and are symmetrical for both sides, the "dental formula" is conventionally illustrated by dental quarter (see p. 109 for a more complete discussion of dental patterns as they apply to primates). Thus, with 11 teeth per quarter segment, the primitive (i.e., ancestral) mammalian dental complement includes a total of 44 teeth. Such a heterodont arrangement allows mammals to process a wide variety of foods. Incisors can be used for cutting, canines for grasping and piercing, and premolars and molars for crushing and grinding.

A final point regarding teeth relates to their disproportionate representation in the fossil record. As the hardest, most durable portion of a vertebrate skeleton, teeth have the greatest likelihood of becoming fossilized (i.e., mineralized). As a result, the vast majority of the available fossil data for most vertebrates, including primates, consists of teeth.

Another major adaptive complex that distinguishes contemporary mammals from reptiles is the maintenance of a constant internal body temperature. Also colloquially (and incorrectly) called warm-bloodedness, this central physiological adaptation is also seen in contemporary birds (and was also perhaps characteristic of many dinosaurs as well). In fact, many contemporary reptiles are able to approximate a constant internal body temperature through behavioral means (especially by regulating activity and exposing the body to the sun). In this sense, reptiles (along with birds and mammals) could be said to be *homeothermic*. Thus, the most important distinction in contrasting mammals (and birds) with reptiles is how the energy to maintain body temperature is produced and channeled. In reptiles, this energy is obtained directly from exposure (externally) to the sun; reptiles are thus said to be *ectothermic*. In mammals and birds, however, the energy is generated *internally* through metabolic activity (by processing food or by muscle action); mammals and birds are hence referred to as **endothermic.**

Major Mammalian Groups

As briefly mentioned in Chapter 5, there are three major subgroups of living mammals: the egg-laying mammals, or monotremes (Fig. 8–12), the pouched mammals, or marsupials (Fig. 8–13), and the placental mammals. The monotremes are extremely primitive and are considered more distinct from marsupials or placentals than these latter are from each other.

The most notable distinction differentiating the marsupials from the placentals is the type of fetal development. In marsupials, the young are born extremely immature and must complete development in an external pouch. It has been suggested (Carroll, 1988) that such a reproductive strategy is more energetically costly than retaining the young for a longer period *in utero*. In fact, the latter is exactly what placental mammals have done through a more advanced placental connection (from which the group gets its popular name). But perhaps even more basic than fetal nourishment are the means to allow the mother to *tolerate* her young internally over an extended period. Marsupial young are born so quickly after conception that there is little chance for the mother's system to recognize and have an immune rejection of the fetal "foreign" tissue. But in placental mammals, such an immune response would occur were it not for the development of a specialized tissue that isolates the fetus from the mother's immune detection, thus preventing tissue rejection. Quite possibly, this innovation is the central factor in the origin and initial rapid success of placental mammals (Carroll, 1988).

In any case, with a longer gestation period, the central nervous system could develop more completely in the fetus. Moreover, after birth, the "bond of milk" between mother and young also would allow more time for complex neural structures to form. It should also be emphasized that from a *biosocial* perspective, this dependency period not only allows for adequate physiological development, but also provides for a wider range of learning stimuli. That is, the young mammalian brain receives a vast amount of information channeled to it through observation of the mother's behavior and through play with age-mates. It is not sufficient to have evolved a brain capable of learning. Collateral evolution of mammalian social systems has ensured that young mammal brains are provided with ample learning opportunities and are thus put to good use.

FIGURE 8–12
The spiny anteater (a monotreme).

FIGURE 8–13
A wallaby with an infant in the pouch (marsupials).

See Virtual Lab 7, section III, for a detailed discussion of early primate evolution.

Doug Wechsler/Animals Animals

FIGURE 8–14
Colugo.

Early Primate Evolution

The roots of the primate order go back to the beginnings of the placental mammal radiation circa 65 m.y.a. Thus, the earliest primates were diverging from quite early primitive placental mammals. We have seen (in Chapter 5) that strictly defining living primates using clear-cut derived features is not an easy task. The further back we go in the fossil record, the more primitive and, in many cases, the more generalized the fossil primates become. Such a situation makes classifying them all the more difficult.

As a case in point, the earliest identifiable primates were long thought to be a Paleocene group known as the plesiadapiforms. You must remember, however, that much of our understanding, especially of early primates, is based on quite fragmentary evidence, mostly jaws and teeth. In just the last few years, much more complete remains of plesiadapiforms from Wyoming have been discovered, including a nearly complete skull and elements of the hand and wrist.

As a result of this more complete information, the plesiadapiforms have been removed from the primate order altogether. From distinctive features (shared derived characteristics) of the skull and hands, these Paleocene mammals are now thought to be closely related to the colugo (Fig. 8–14). The colugo is sometimes called a "flying lemur," a misnomer, really, as it is not a lemur, nor does it fly (it glides). This group of unusual mammals is probably closely linked to the roots of primates, but apparently was already diverged by Paleocene times.

Given these new and major reinterpretations, we are left with extremely scarce traces of the beginnings of primates. Scholars have suggested that some other recently discovered bits and pieces from North Africa *may* be those of a very small primitive primate. Until more evidence is found, and remembering the lesson of the plesiadapiforms, we will just have to wait and see.

A large array of fossil primates from the Eocene (55–34 m.y.a.) have been discovered and now total more than 200 recognized species. Unlike the available Paleocene forms, those from the Eocene display distinctive primate features. Indeed, primatologist Elwyn Simons (1972, p. 124) has called them "the first primates of modern aspect." These animals have been found primarily in sites in North America and Europe (which were then still connected). It is important to recall that the landmasses that connect continents, as well as the water boundaries that separate them, have obvious impact on the geographical distribution of such terrestrially bound animals as primates.

Some interesting late Eocene forms have also been found in Asia, which was joined to Europe by the end of the Eocene epoch. Looking at the whole array of Eocene primates, it is certain that they were (1) primates, (2) widely distributed, and (3) mostly extinct by the end of the Eocene. What is less certain is how any of them might be related to the living primates. Some of these forms are probably ancestors of the *prosimians*—the lemurs and lorises.* Others are probably related to the tarsier. New evidence of *anthropoid* origins has also recently been discovered in several sites from North Africa, the Persian Gulf, and China. These newly discovered fossils of late Eocene anthropoids have now shown that anthropoid origins were well established by 35 m.y.a.

Some new discoveries of very small primates from China are particularly interesting. These 45-million-year-old fossils have been suggested as representing early anthropoids (Gebo et al., 2000), but this hypothesis is still very tentative (there are, as yet, no cranial remains discovered, and the traits that are present are primitive rather than derived in the anthropoid direction). The most intriguing aspect of this recent discovery is the extremely small body size estimated for these primates, considerably smaller, in fact, than any living primate (see Box 8–2).

---

*In strict classification terms, especially from a cladistic point of view, lemurs and lorises should be referred to as strepsirhines (see p. 117).

BOX 8–2

A CLOSER LOOK

Telling It Like It Isn't

The discovery of new fossil primates often provokes dramatic media coverage. As we will see in subsequent chapters, when the fossils are hominids, public interest is even keener. When in spring 2000, the discovery of two tiny species of primates from China was first published (Gebo et al., 2000), it quickly received national coverage in the news media. The scientific publication (in a professional journal) provided photographs of the fossils (two small ankle bones) and quantitative estimates of the likely size of the animals. Appropriately, given the very incomplete nature of the remains (Figs. 1 and 2), no visual reconstructions of the new species were attempted. However, newspapers, magazines, and Internet sources are not as constrained by scientific considerations. Indeed, a widely published and speculative full-body reconstruction was reproduced in many of these popular news sources (Fig. 3). Interestingly, images of the actual fossil finds were usually omitted, so the average reader would easily conclude that the reconstruction derived from reasonable scientific inference. Apparently, the popular media generally assume that the average reader is too unsophisticated to be concerned with actual fossils and is content merely to see what the animal looked like ("in the flesh"). We think this attitude underestimates the intelligence of many readers. We ask you to compare Figures 1 and 2 with Figure 3 and draw your own conclusions.

The most conservative scientific conclusion here would be that no such complete reconstruction is attainable. What is perhaps even more startling than the baseless attempt to depict such a reconstruction is that in almost every significant detail (body proportions, size of head, position of eyes, length of snout, length of tail), it is almost certainly wildly inaccurate, as evidenced from what is actually known from other fossils already discovered. It seems that some illustrator decided simply to draw a little monkey (one, in fact, very reminiscent of a modern squirrel monkey).

FIGURE 1
Actual size
(left) 4.5 mm ($^3/_{16}$")
(right) 4.1 mm ($^5/_{32}$")

FIGURE 2
Enlargement of fossil ankle bones shown in Figure 1 (magnification approximately 500% of actual size).

FIGURE 3
Reconstruction of fossil primate (from fossil bones shown in Figure 1). This reconstruction was widely used by popular media (shown to approximate size).

FIGURE 8–15
Location of the Fayum, an Oligocene primate site in Egypt.

The Oligocene (34–23 m.y.a.) has yielded numerous additional fossil remains of several different species of early anthropoids. Most of these forms are *Old World anthropoids,* all discovered at a single locality in Egypt, the Fayum (Fig. 8–15). In addition, from North and South America, there are a few known bits that relate only to the ancestry of New World monkeys. By the early Oligocene, continental drift had separated the New World (i.e., the Americas) from the Old World (Africa and Eurasia). Some of the earliest Fayum forms, nevertheless, *may* potentially be close to the ancestry of both Old and New World anthropoids. It has been suggested that late in the Eocene or very early in the Oligocene, the first anthropoids (primitive "monkeys") arose in Africa and later reached South America by "rafting" over the water separation on drifting chunks of vegetation. What we call "monkey," then, may have a common Old World origin, but the ancestry of New and Old World varieties remains separate after about 35 m.y.a. Our closest evolutionary affinities after this time are with other Old World anthropoids, that is, with Old World monkeys and apes.

The possible roots of anthropoid evolution are illustrated by different forms from the Fayum; one is the genus *Apidium.* Well known at the Fayum, *Apidium* is represented by several dozen jaws or partial dentitions and more than 100 specimens from the limb and trunk skeleton. Because of its primitive dental arrangement, some paleontologists have suggested that *Apidium* may lie near or even before the evolutionary divergence of Old and New World anthropoids. As so much fossil material of teeth and limb bones of *Apidium* has been found, some informed speculation regarding diet and locomotor behavior is possible. It is thought that this small, squirrel-sized primate ate mostly fruits and some seeds and was most likely an arboreal quadruped, adept at leaping and springing (Table 8–1).

The other genus of importance from the Fayum is *Aegyptopithecus.* This genus, also well known, is represented by several well-preserved crania and abundant jaws and teeth. The largest of the Fayum anthropoids, *Aegyptopithecus* is roughly the size of a modern howler monkey (13 to 20 pounds) (Fleagle, 1983) and is thought to have been a short-limbed, slow-moving arboreal quadruped (see Table 8–1). *Aegyptopithecus* is important because, better than any other known form, it bridges the gap between the Eocene fossils and the succeeding Miocene hominoids.

Nevertheless, *Aegyptopithecus* is a very primitive Old World anthropoid, with a small brain and long snout and not showing any derived features of either Old World monkeys or hominoids. Thus, it may be close to the ancestry of *both* major groups of living Old World anthropoids. Found in geological beds dating to 35–33 m.y.a., *Aegyptopithecus* further suggests that the crucial evolutionary divergence of hominoids from other Old World anthropoids occurred *after* this time (Fig. 8–16).

TABLE 8–1 Inferred General Paleobiological Aspects of Oligocene Primates

	Weight Range	Substratum	Locomotion	Diet
Apidium	750–1,600 g (2–3 lb)	Arboreal	Quadruped	Fruit, seeds
Aegyptopithecus	6,700 g (15 lb)	Arboreal	Quadruped	Fruit, some leaves?

Source: After Fleagle, 1999.

EOCENE	OLIGOCENE	MIOCENE

Sivapithecus

Apidium

Dryopithecus

Aegyptopithecus

Proconsul

Early anthropoid radiation

Hominoid radiation

Earliest anthropoids

Earliest hominoids

Prosimian radiation

Earliest definite primates

55 m.y.a   34 m.y.a   23 m.y.a   5 m.y.a

FIGURE 8–16
Major events in early primate evolution.

See Virtual Lab 7 glossary, for a phylogeny and pronunciation guide of primate fossils.

Miocene Fossil Hominoids

During the approximately 18 million years of the Miocene (23–5 m.y.a.), a great deal of evolutionary activity took place. In Africa, Asia, and Europe, a diverse and highly successful group of hominoids emerged (Fig. 8–17). Indeed, there were many more forms of hominoids from the Miocene than are found today (now represented by the highly restricted groups of apes and one species of humans). In fact, the Miocene could be called "the golden age of hominoids." Many thousands of fossils have been found from dozens of sites scattered in East Africa, southwest Africa, southwest Asia, into western and southern Europe, and extending into southern Asia and China.

During the Miocene, significant transformations relating to climate and repositioning of landmasses took place. By 23 m.y.a., *major* continental locations approximated those of today (except that North and South America were separate). Nevertheless, the movements of South America and Australia further away from Antarctica significantly altered ocean currents. Likewise, the continued impact of the South Asian plate into Asia produced the Himalayan Plateau. Both of these paleogeographical modifications had significant impact on the climate, and the early Miocene was considerably warmer than the preceding Oligocene. Moreover, by 16 m.y.a., the Arabian Plate (which had been separate) "docked" with northeastern Africa. As a result, migrations of animals from Africa directly into southwest Asia (and in the other direction as well) became possible. Among the earliest transcontinental migrants (soon after 16 m.y.a.) were African hominoids who colonized Asia and later Europe.

FIGURE 8–17
Miocene hominoid distribution, from fossils thus far discovered.

Processes of Macroevolution: Mammalian/Primate Evolutionary History

 See Virtual Lab 7, section III, for a discussion of Miocene hominoid fossils.

A problem arises in any attempt to simplify the complex evolutionary situation regarding Miocene hominoids. For example, for many years paleontologists tended to think of these fossil forms as either "apelike" or "humanlike" and used modern examples as models. But as we have just noted, there are very few hominoids remaining. We should not rashly generalize from the living forms to the much more diverse fossil forms; otherwise, we obscure the evolutionary uniqueness of these animals. In addition, we should not expect all fossil forms to be directly or even particularly closely related to living varieties. Indeed, we should expect the opposite; that is, most lines vanish without descendants.

Over the last three decades, the Miocene hominoid assemblage has been interpreted and reinterpreted. As more fossils are found, the evolutionary picture grows more complicated. The vast array of fossil forms has not yet been completely studied, so conclusions remain tenuous. Given this uncertainty, it is probably best, for the present, to group Miocene hominoids geographically:

1. *African forms (23–14 m.y.a.)* Known especially from western Kenya, these include quite generalized, in many ways primitive, hominoids. The best-known genus is *Proconsul* (Fig. 8–18). In addition to the well-known East African early Miocene hominoids, a more recent discovery (in 1992) from Namibia has further extended by over 1,800 miles the known range of African Miocene hominoids (Conroy et al., 1992).

2. *European forms (13–11 m.y.a.)* Known from widely scattered localities in France, Spain, Italy, Greece, Austria, and Hungary, most of these forms are quite derived. However, this is a varied and not well understood lot. The best known of the forms are placed in the genus *Dryopithecus;* the Hungarian and Greek fossils are usually assigned to other genera. The Greek fossils are called *Ouranopithecus* and remains date to sites 9 to 10 million years of age. Evolutionary relationships are uncertain, but several researchers have suggested a link with the African ape/hominid group.

3. *Asian forms (16–7 m.y.a.)* The largest and most varied group from the Miocene fossil hominoid assemblage, geographically dispersed from Turkey through India/Pakistan and east to the highly prolific site Lufeng, in southern China, most of these forms are *highly* derived. The best-known genus is *Sivapithecus* (known from Turkey and Pakistan). The Lufeng material (now totaling more than 1,000 specimens) is usually placed in a separate genus from *Sivapithecus* (and is referred to as *Lufengpithecus*).

FIGURE 8–18
Proconsul africanus skull (from early Miocene deposits on Rusinga Island, Kenya).

Robert Jurmain

Four general points are certain concerning Miocene hominoid fossils: They are widespread geographically; they are numerous; they span a considerable portion of the Miocene, with *known* remains dated between 23 and 6 m.y.a.; and at present, they are poorly understood. However, we can reasonably draw the following conclusions:

1. These are hominoids—more closely related to the ape-human lineage than to Old World monkeys.
2. Moreover, they are mostly **large-bodied hominoids,** that is, more akin to the lineages of orangutans, gorillas, chimpanzees, and humans than to smaller-bodied apes (i.e., gibbons).
3. Most of the Miocene forms thus far discovered are so derived as to be improbable ancestors of *any* living form.
4. One lineage that appears well established relates to *Sivapithecus* from Turkey and Pakistan. This form shows some highly derived facial features similar to the modern orangutan, suggesting a fairly close evolutionary link (Fig. 8–19).

Large-bodied hominoids
Those hominoids including the great apes (orangutans, chimpanzees, gorillas) and hominids, as well as all ancestral forms back to the time of divergence from small-bodied hominoids (i.e., the gibbon lineage).

5. As of yet, there are no fully documented, *definite* **hominids** found at any Miocene-dated locale. However, some very recently discovered materials, dating as old as 6 m.y.a. (i.e. the very end of the Miocene), *may* turn out to be the earliest hominids yet discovered (see pp. 249–251).

Courtesy, David Pilbeam

FIGURE 8–19

Comparison of *Sivapithecus* cranium (center) with that of modern chimpanzee (left) and orangutan (right). The *Sivapithecus* fossil is specimen GSP 15000 from the Potwar Plateau, Pakistan, c. 8 m.y.a.

Processes of Macroevolution

As noted earlier, evolution operates at both microevolutionary and macroevolutionary levels. We discussed evolution primarily from a microevolutionary perspective in Chapter 4; in this chapter, our focus is on macroevolution. Macroevolutionary mechanisms operate more on the whole species than on individuals or populations and take much longer than microevolutionary processes to have a noticeable impact.

Adaptive Radiation

The potential capacity of a group of organisms to multiply is practically unlimited; its ability to increase its numbers, however, is regulated largely by the available resources of food, shelter, and space. As the size of a population increases, its food supply, shelter, and space decrease, and the environment will ultimately prove inadequate. Depleted resources engender pressures that will very likely induce some members of the population to seek an environment in which competition is considerably reduced and the opportunity for survival and reproductive success increased. This evolutionary tendency to exploit unoccupied habitats may eventually produce an abundance of diverse species.

A good example of the evolutionary process known as **adaptive radiation** is seen in the divergence of the stem reptiles into the profusion of different forms of the late Paleozoic and especially those of the Mesozoic. It is a process that has taken place many times in evolutionary history when a life form has rapidly taken advantage, so to speak, of the many newly available ecological niches.

The principle of evolution illustrated by adaptive radiation is fairly simple, but important. It may be stated thus: *A species, or group of species, will diverge into as many variations as two factors allow: (1) its adaptive potential and (2) the adaptive opportunities of the available zones.*

In the case of reptiles, there was little divergence in the very early stages of evolution, when the ancestral form was little more than one among a variety of amphibian water dwellers. In reptiles, a more efficient egg than that of amphibians (i.e., one that could incubate out of water) had developed, but although it had great adaptive potential, there were few zones to invade. However, once reptiles became fully terrestrial, there was a sudden opening of available zones—ecological niches—accessible to them.

This new kind of egg provided the primary adaptive trait that freed reptiles from their attachment to water. The adaptive zones for reptiles were not limitless; nevertheless, continents were now open to them with no serious competition from any other animal. The reptiles moved into the many different ecological niches on land (and to some extent in the air and sea), and as they adapted to these areas, they diversified into a large number of species. This spectacular radiation burst forth with such evolutionary rapidity that it may well be termed an adaptive explosion.

Hominids
Colloquial term for members of the family Hominidae, which includes all bipedal hominoids back to the divergence from African great apes.

Adaptive radiation
The relatively rapid expansion and diversification of life forms into new ecological niches.

The rapid expansion of placental mammals at the beginning of the Cenozoic and the diversification of lemurs in Madagascar are other good examples of adaptive radiation. This latter (primate) example is particularly instructive. As we noted in Chapter 5, the contemporary array of 61 lemur species shows considerable diversity, both in size and in lifestyle (diet, degree of arboreality, etc.). Indeed, if we also include several other species that have become extinct in the last 1,000 years (following intensive human occupation of the island), the degree of lemur biodiversity was even greater—even including a ground-living form the size of a gorilla! The diversification of so many different kinds of lemur in Madagascar is explained by their adaptive radiation from a common ancestor, beginning up to 50 m.y.a. Without competition from other types of mammals, the lemurs fairly rapidly diversified and expanded into a number of varied niches in their isolated island home.

Generalized and Specialized Characteristics

Another aspect of evolution closely related to adaptive radiation involves the transition from generalized characteristics to specialized characteristics. These two terms refer to the adaptive potential of a particular trait. A trait that is adapted for many functions is said to be generalized; a trait that is limited to a narrow set of ecological functions is said to be specialized.

For example, a generalized mammalian limb has five fairly flexible digits adapted for many possible functions (grasping, weight support, digging). In this respect, our hands are still quite generalized. On the other hand (or foot), there have been many structural modifications in our feet suited for the ecologically specialized function of stable weight support in an upright posture.

The terms *generalized* and *specialized* are also sometimes used when speaking of the adaptive potential of whole organisms. For example, the aye-aye of Madagascar is a highly specialized animal structurally adapted in its dentition for an ecologically narrow rodent/woodpecker-like niche—digging holes with prominent incisors and removing insect larvae with an elongated finger.

The notion of adaptive potential is a relative judgment and can estimate only crudely the likelihood of one form evolving into one or more other forms. Adaptive radiation is a related concept, for only a generalized ancestor can provide the flexible evolutionary basis for such rapid diversification. Only a generalized species with potential for adaptation into varied ecological niches can lead to all the later diversification and specialization of forms into particular ecological niches.

An issue that we have already raised also bears on this discussion: the relationship of ancestral and derived characters. While not always the case, ancestral characters *usually* tend to be more generalized than specialized. And specialized characteristics are almost always also derived ones.

Modes of Evolutionary Change

Until recently, the general consensus among evolutionary biologists was that microevolutionary mechanisms could be translated directly into the larger-scale macroevolutionary changes, especially the most central of all macroevolutionary processes, speciation (also called *transspecific evolution*). A smooth gradation of change was assumed to run directly from microevolution into macroevolution. A representative view was expressed by a leading synthesist, Ernst Mayr: "The proponents of the synthetic theory maintain that all evolution is due to accumulation of small genetic changes, guided by natural selection, and that transspecific evolution is nothing but an extrapolation and magnification of events that take place within populations and species" (Mayr, 1970, p. 351).

In the last two decades, this view has been seriously challenged. Many theorists now believe that macroevolution cannot be explained solely in terms of accumulated microevolutionary changes. Consequently, these researchers are convinced that macroevolution is only partly understandable through microevolutionary models.

Gradualism vs. Punctuated Equilibrium   The traditional view of evolution has emphasized that change accumulates gradually in evolving lineages—the idea of phyletic gradualism. Accordingly, the complete fossil record of an evolving group (if it could be recovered) would display a series of forms with finely graded transitional differences between each ancestor and its descendant. The fact that such transitional forms are only rarely found is attributed to the incompleteness of the fossil record, or, as Darwin called it, "a history of the world, imperfectly kept, and written in changing dialect."

For more than a century, this perspective dominated evolutionary biology, but in the last 25 years, some biologists have called this notion into serious question. The evolutionary mechanisms operating on species over the long run are often not continuously gradual. In some cases, species persist for thousands of generations basically unchanged. Then, rather suddenly, at least in evolutionary terms, a "spurt" of speciation occurs. This uneven, nongradual process of long stasis and quick spurts has been termed **punctuated equilibrium** (Gould and Eldredge, 1977).

What the advocates of punctuated equilibrium are disputing are the tempo (rate) and mode (manner) of evolutionary change as commonly understood since Darwin's time. Rather than a slow, steady tempo, this alternate view postulates long periods of no change punctuated only occasionally by sudden bursts. From this observation, it was concluded that the mode of evolution, too, must be different from that suggested by classical Darwinists. Rather than gradual accumulation of small changes in a single lineage, advocates of punctuated equilibrium believe that an additional evolutionary mechanism is required to push the process along. They thus postulate *speciation* as the major influence in bringing about rapid evolutionary change.

How well does the paleontological record agree with the predictions of punctuated equilibrium? Indeed, considerable fossil data show long periods of stasis punctuated by occasional quite rapid changes (on the order of 10,000 to 50,000 years). The best supporting evidence for punctuated equilibrium has come from the fossilized remains of marine invertebrates. Intermediate forms are rare, not so much because the fossil record is poor, but because the speciation events and longevity of these transitional species were so short that we should not expect to find them very often.

How well, then, does the primate fossil record fit the punctuated equilibrium model? In studies of Eocene primates, rates of evolutionary change were shown to be quite gradual (Gingerich, 1985; Brown and Rose, 1987; Rose, 1991). In another study, here of Paleocene plesiadapiforms, evolutionary changes were also quite gradual. Although no longer considered primates, these forms show a gradual tempo of change in another, closely related group of mammals. The predictions consistent with punctuated equilibrium have thus far not been substantiated in those evolving lineages of primates for which we have adequate data to test the theory.

It would, however, be a fallacy to assume that evolutionary change in primates or in any other group must therefore be of a completely gradual tempo. Such is clearly not the case. In all lineages, the pace assuredly speeds up and slows down as a result of factors that influence the size and relative isolation of populations. In addition, environmental changes that influence the pace and direction of natural selection must also be considered. Nevertheless, in general accordance with the Modern Synthesis, microevolution and macroevolution need not be "decoupled," as some evolutionary biologists have recently suggested.

Punctuated equilibrium
The concept that evolutionary change proceeds through long periods of stasis punctuated by rapid periods of change.

SUMMARY

This chapter has surveyed the basics of mammalian/primate evolution, emphasizing a macroevolutionary perspective. Given the huge amount of organic diversity displayed, as well as the vast time involved, two major organizing perspectives prove indispensable: schemes of formal classification to organize organic diversity and the geological time scale to organize geological time. The principles of classification were reviewed in some detail, contrasting two differing approaches: evolutionary systematics and cladistics. Because primates are vertebrates and, more specifically, mammals, these broader organic groups were briefly reviewed, emphasizing major evolutionary trends. The fossil history of primates was taken up in more detail with surveys of earliest traces from the Paleocene and Eocene epochs. The beginnings of anthropoid radiation can be traced to the end of the Eocene and to the Oligocene (the Fayum in Egypt), and the broad, complex radiation of hominoids during the Miocene is even more central to understanding human evolution.

Theoretical perspectives relating to contemporary understanding of macroevolutionary processes (especially the concepts of species and speciation) are crucial to interpreting any long-term aspect of evolutionary history, be it mammalian, primate, hominoid, or hominid. As genus and species designation is the common form of reference for both living and extinct organisms (and will be used frequently throughout the next five chapters), its biological significance was discussed in depth. From a more general theoretical perspective, evolutionary biologists have postulated two different modes of evolutionary change: gradualism and punctuated equilibrium. At present, the available primate evolutionary record does not conform to the predictions of punctuated equilibrium, but one should not conclude that evolutionary tempo was necessarily strictly gradual (which it certainly was not).

QUESTIONS FOR REVIEW

1. What are the two primary goals of organic classification?
2. What are the six major groups of vertebrates?
3. What are the two main approaches to the classification of organisms? Compare them.
4. What are the major eras of geological time over which vertebrates have evolved?
5. What primary features distinguish mammals—especially placental mammals—from other vertebrates?
6. What is meant by a homology? Contrast with analogy, using examples.
7. Why do evolutionary biologists concentrate on derived features rather than primitive ones? Give an example of each.
8. What is the biological species concept? Contrast this with another definition of species.
9. Why is it difficult to identify very early primates from other primitive placental mammals?
10. How diversified and geographically widespread were hominoids in the Miocene?
11. Humans are Old World anthropoids. What other groups are also Old World anthropoids?

12. Contrast the gradualist view of evolutionary change with that of punctuated equilibrium. Give an example from primate evolution that supports one view or the other.
13. How are species and genus defined? Discuss how the definitions apply to both living and fossil groups.

SUGGESTED FURTHER READING

Carroll, Robert L. 1988. *Vertebrate Paleontology and Evolution*. New York: Freeman.
Conroy, G. C. 1990. *Primate Evolution*. New York: Norton.
Fleagle, John. 1999. *Primate Adaptation and Evolution*. 2nd ed. New York: Academic Press.
Ridley, Mark. 1993. *Evolution*. Boston: Blackwell Scientific Publications.

RESOURCES ON THE INTERNET

Wadsworth Anthropology Resource Center
http://anthropology.wadsworth.com

The companion website for this text includes a range of enrichment material focused on the chapter's topic. While online you can enhance your understanding of the chapter by exploring one of the several additional Internet exercises, by researching topics, and by accessing full articles on InfoTrac College Edition. You can also reinforce the concepts by taking online practice exams.

Internet Exercises

Visit the University of California Museum of Paleontology (**http://www.ucmp.berkeley.edu/**). This site provides extensive online exhibits on geology, phylogeny, and mammalian evolution. Explore the site and see what you can find to supplement the information in the text on mammalian evolution. When did mammals first appear? When did they begin to differentiate into the modern orders? When and where did primates first appear?

InfoTrac College Edition
http://www.infotrac-college.com/wadsworth

On InfoTrac College Edition, search for the keywords *evolution* and *mammals*. Choose one of the articles found by this search and read through it. What does this research reveal about evolution?

CHAPTER

9

CONTENTS

Trail of hominid footprints fossilized in volcanic ash at
Laetoli, Tanzania (approximate age, 3.7 million years)

Paleoanthropology: Reconstructing Early Hominid Behavior and Ecology

Introduction

In the last four chapters, we have seen how humans are classed as primates, both structurally and behaviorally, and how our evolutionary history coincides with that of other mammals and, specifically, with other primates. However, we are a unique kind of primate, and our ancestors have been adapted to a particular lifestyle for several million years. Some primitive hominoid may have begun this process more than 7 m.y.a., but there is much more definite hominid fossil evidence from Africa shortly after 5 m.y.a. The hominid nature of these remains is revealed by more than the morphological structure of teeth and bones; we know that these animals are hominids also because of the way they behaved—emphasizing once again the *biocultural* nature of human evolution. In this chapter, we will discuss the methods scientists use to explore the secrets of early hominid behavior and ecology, and we will demonstrate these methods through the example of the best-known early hominid site in the world: Olduvai Gorge in East Africa.

Definition of Hominid

If any of the Miocene hominoid fossils represent the earliest stages of hominid diversification, our definition of them as hominid must primarily be a *dental* one, for teeth and jaws are most of what we have of these Miocene forms. In fact, as we have seen in the previous chapter, excepting perhaps some new finds from the end of the Miocene, none of the fossils discovered thus far from this epoch is clearly hominid. Dentition is not the only way to describe the special attributes of our particular evolutionary radiation, and it certainly is not the most distinctive characteristic of its later stages. Modern humans and our hominid ancestors are distinguished from our closest living relatives (the great apes) by more obvious features than proportionate tooth and jaw size. For example, various scientists have pointed to such hominid characteristics as large brain size, bipedal locomotion, and toolmaking behavior as being significant (at some stage) in defining what makes a hominid a hominid (as opposed to a pongid or anything else).

It must be emphasized that not all these characteristics developed simultaneously. Quite the opposite, in fact, has been apparent in hominid evolution over the last 5 million years. This pattern, in which different physiological systems (and behavioral correlates) evolve at different rates, is called **mosaic evolution.** As we first pointed out in Chapter 1 and will discuss in more detail in Chapter 10, the most defining characteristic for all of hominid evolution is *bipedal locomotion.* Certainly for the earliest stages of the hominid lineage, skeletal evidence of bipedal locomotion is the only truly reliable indicator of hominid status. However, in later stages of hominid evolution, other features, especially those relating to neurology and behavior, do become highly significant (Fig. 9–1).

These behavioral aspects of hominid emergence—particularly toolmaking capacity—is what we wish to emphasize in this chapter. The important structural attributes of the hominid brain, teeth, and especially locomotor apparatus will be discussed in the next chapter, where we investigate early hominid anatomical adaptations in greater detail.

Biocultural Evolution: The Human Capacity for Culture

When compared with other animals, the most distinctive behavioral feature of humans is our extraordinary elaboration of and dependence on culture. Certainly, other primates, and many other animals for that matter, modify their environments.

See the following sections of the CD-ROM for topics covered in this chapter: Virtual Lab 7, sections I and II; Virtual Lab 8, section I, and Virtual Lab 11.

Mosaic evolution
A pattern of evolution in which the rate of evolution in one functional system varies from that in other systems. For example, in hominid evolution, the dental system, locomotor system, and neurological system (especially the brain) all evolved at markedly different rates.

See Virtual Lab 11 for a discussion of the archaeological record.

	Locomotion	Brain	Dentition	Toolmaking Behavior
(Modern *Homo sapiens*)	Bipedal: shortened pelvis; body size larger; legs longer; fingers and toes not as long	Greatly increased brain size—highly encephalized	Small incisors; canines further reduced; molar tooth enamel caps thick	Stone tools found after 2.5 m.y.a.; increasing trend of cultural dependency apparent in later hominids
(Early hominid)	Bipedal: shortened pelvis; some differences from later hominids, showing smaller body size and long arms relative to legs; long fingers and toes; probably capable of considerable climbing	Larger than Miocene forms, but still only moderately encephalized	Moderately large front teeth (incisors); canines somewhat reduced; molar tooth enamel caps very thick	In earliest stages unknown; no stone tool use prior to 2.5 m.y.a.; probably somewhat more oriented toward tool manufacture and use than chimpanzees
(Miocene, generalized hominoid)	Quadrupedal: long pelvis; some forms capable of considerable arm swinging, suspensory locomotion	Small compared to hominids, but large compared to other primates; a fair degree of encephalization	Large front teeth (including canines); molar teeth variable, depending on species; some have thin enamel caps, others thick enamel caps	Unknown—no stone tools; probably had capabilities similar to chimpanzees

Time scale markers: 0.5 m.y.a., 1 m.y.a., 2 m.y.a., 3 m.y.a., 4 m.y.a., 20 m.y.a.

FIGURE 9–1
Mosaic evolution of hominid characteristics: a postulated time line.

As we saw in Chapter 7, chimpanzees especially are known for such behaviors as using termite sticks and sponges and even transporting rocks to crush nuts. Given such observations, it becomes tenuous to draw sharp lines between hominid toolmaking behavior and that exhibited by other animals.

Another point to remember is that human culture, at least as it is defined in contemporary contexts, involves much more than toolmaking capacity. For humans, culture integrates an entire adaptive strategy involving cognitive, political, social, and economic components. The *material culture*, the tools and other items humans use, is but a small portion of this cultural complex.

Nevertheless, when examining the archaeological record of earlier hominids, what is available for study is almost exclusively certain remains of material culture, especially residues of stone tool manufacture. Thus, it is extremely difficult to learn anything about the earliest stages of hominid cultural development prior to the regular manufacture of stone tools. As you will see, this most crucial cultural development has been traced to approximately 2.5 m.y.a. Yet, hominids undoubtedly were using other kinds of tools (such as sticks) and displaying a whole array of other cultural behaviors long before this time. However, without any "hard" evidence preserved in the archaeological record, the development of these nonmaterial cultural components remains elusive.

The fundamental basis for human cultural elaboration relates directly to cognitive abilities. Again, we are not dealing with an absolute distinction, but a relative one. As you have learned, some other primates possess some of the symboling capabilities exhibited by humans. Nevertheless, modern humans display these abilities in a complexity several orders of magnitude beyond that of any other animal. Moreover, only humans are so completely dependent on symbolic communication and its cultural by-products that contemporary *Homo sapiens* could not survive without them.

When did the unique combination of cognitive, social, and material cultural adaptations become prominent in human evolution? We must be careful to recognize the manifold nature of culture and not expect it always to contain the same elements across species (as when compared with nonhuman primates) or through time (when trying to reconstruct ancient hominid behavior). Richard Potts (1993) has critiqued this overly simplistic perspective and suggests a more dynamic approach, one that incorporates many subcomponents (including aspects of behavior, cognition, and social interaction).

We know that the earliest hominids almost certainly did *not* regularly manufacture stone tools (at least, none that has been found!). The earliest members of the hominid lineage, perhaps dating back to approximately 7–5 m.y.a., could be referred to as **protohominids**. These protohominids may have carried objects such as naturally sharp stones or stone flakes, parts of carcasses, and pieces of wood. At minimum, we would expect them to have displayed these behaviors to at least the same degree as living chimpanzees.

Protohominids
The earliest members of the hominid lineage, as yet basically unrepresented in the fossil record; thus, their structure and behavior are reconstructed hypothetically.

Moreover, as you will see in the next chapter, by at least 4 m.y.a., hominids had developed one crucial advantage: They were bipedal and could therefore much more easily carry all manner of objects from place to place. Ultimately, the efficient exploitation of resources widely distributed in time and space would most likely have led to using "central" spots where key components, especially stone objects, were cached (Potts, 1991).

What is certain is that over a period of several million years, during the formative stages of hominid emergence, numerous components interacted, but not all developed simultaneously. As cognitive abilities developed, more efficient means of communication and learning resulted. Largely as a result of such neural reorganization, more elaborate tools and social relationships also emerged. These, in turn, selected for greater intelligence, which in turn selected for further neural elaboration. Quite clearly, then, these mutual dynamics are at the very heart of what we call hominid *biocultural* evolution.

The Strategy of Paleoanthropology

To understand human evolution adequately, we obviously need a broad base of information. The task of recovering and interpreting all the clues left by early hominids is the work of paleoanthropologists. Paleoanthropology is defined as the study of ancient humans. As such, it is a diverse *multidisciplinary* pursuit seeking to reconstruct every possible bit of information concerning the dating, structure, behavior, and ecology of our hominid ancestors. In the last few decades, the study of early humans has marshaled the specialized skills of many different kinds of scientists. Included in this growing and exciting adventure are geologists, archaeologists, physical anthropologists, and **paleoecologists** (Table 9–1).

Paleoecologists
(*paleo*, meaning "old," and *ecology*, meaning "environmental setting") Scientists who study ancient environments.

TABLE 9–1   Subdisciplines of Paleoanthropology

Physical Sciences	Biological Sciences	Social Sciences

Geology
  Stratigraphy
  Petrology
    (rocks, minerals)
  Pedology (soils)
Geomorphology
Geophysics
Chemistry
Taphonomy
	Physical anthropology
	Paleoecology
	  Paleontology (fossil
	    animals)
	  Palynology (fossil pollen)
	Primatology
		Archaeology
		Ethnoarchaeology
		Cultural anthropology
		  Ethnography
		Psychology

Artifacts
Material traces of hominid behavior. Very old ones are usually made of stone or, occasionally, bone.

Geologists, usually working with anthropologists, do the initial surveys to locate potential early hominid sites. Many sophisticated techniques can aid in this search, including aerial and satellite photography. Paleontologists are usually involved in this early survey work, for they can help find fossil beds containing faunal remains. Where conditions are favorable for the preservation of bone from such species as pigs and elephants, conditions may also be favorable for the preservation of hominid remains. In addition, paleontologists can (through comparison with known faunal sequences) give fairly quick estimates of the approximate age of fossil sites without having to wait for the more expensive and time-consuming analyses. In this way, fossil beds of appropriate geological ages (i.e., where hominid finds are most likely) can be identified.

Once potential early hominid localities have been found, much more extensive surveying begins. At this point, at least for some sites postdating 2.5 m.y.a., archaeologists take over in the search for hominid "traces." We do not necessarily have to find remains of early hominids themselves to know that they consistently occupied a particular area. Preserved material clues, or **artifacts**, also inform us directly and unambiguously about early hominid activities. Modifying rocks according to a consistent plan or simply carrying them around from one place to another (over fairly long distances) is characteristic of no other animal but a hominid. Therefore, when we see such behavioral evidence at a site, we know absolutely that hominids were present.

Because organic materials such as sticks and bones do not usually preserve in the archaeological record, we have no solid evidence of the earliest stages of hominid cultural modifications. On the other hand, our ancestors at some point showed a veritable fascination with stones, for these provided not only easily accessible and transportable materials (to use as convenient projectiles to throw or to hold down objects, such as skins and windbreaks) but also the most durable and sharpest cutting edges available at that time. Luckily for us, stone is almost indestructible, and some early hominid sites are strewn with thousands of stone artifacts. The earliest artifact sites now documented are from the Gona and Bouri areas in northeastern Ethiopia, dating to 2.5 m.y.a. (Semaw et al., 1997; de Heinzelin et al., 1999). Other contenders for the "earliest" stone assemblage come from the adjacent Hadar and Middle Awash areas, immediately to the south in Ethiopia, dated 2.5–2.0 m.y.a.

If an area is clearly demonstrated to be a hominid site, much more concentrated research will then begin. We should point out that a more mundane but very significant aspect of paleoanthropology not shown in Table 9–1 is the financial one. Just the initial survey work in usually remote areas costs many thousands of dollars, and mounting a concentrated research project costs several hundred thousand dollars. Therefore, for such work to go on, massive financial support is required from government agencies and private donations. A significant amount of a paleoan-thropologist's efforts and time is necessarily devoted to writing grant proposals or speaking on the lecture circuit to raise the required funds for this work.

Once the financial hurdle has been cleared, a coordinated research project can commence. Usually headed by an archaeologist or physical anthropologist, the field crew will continue to survey and map the target area in great detail. In addi-tion, field crew members will begin to search carefully for bones and artifacts erod-ing out of the soil, take pollen and soil samples for ecological analysis, and carefully recover rock samples for use in various dating techniques. If, in this early stage of exploration, members of the field crew find a fossil hominid, they will feel very lucky indeed. The international press usually considers human fossils the most exciting kind of discovery, a situation that produces wide publicity, often ensuring future financial support. More likely, the crew will accumulate much information on geological setting, ecological data (particularly faunal remains), and, with some luck, archaeological traces (hominid artifacts).

After long and arduous research in the field, even more time-consuming and detailed analysis is required back in the laboratory. Archaeologists must clean, sort, label, and identify all artifacts, and paleontologists must do the same for all faunal remains. Knowing the kinds of animals represented, whether forest browsers, woodland species, or open-country forms, will greatly help in reconstructing the local *paleoecological* settings in which early hominids lived. In addition, analysis of pollen remains by a palynologist will further aid in a detailed environmental recon-struction. All these paleoecological analyses can assist in reconstructing the diet of early humans. Also, the **taphonomy** of the site must be worked out in order to understand its depositional history—that is, whether the site is part of a *primary* or *secondary* **context**.

In the concluding stages of interpretation, the paleoanthropologist will draw together the following essentials:

1. *Dating*
   geological
   paleontological
   geophysical
2. *Paleoecology*
   paleontology
   palynology
   geomorphology
   taphonomy
3. *Archaeological traces of behavior*
4. *Anatomical evidence from hominid remains*

From all this information, scientists will try to "flesh out" the kind of animal that may have been our direct ancestor, or at least a very close relative. In this final analysis, still further comparative scientific information may be needed. Primatologists may assist here by showing the detailed relationships between the anatomical structure and behavior of humans and that of contemporary nonhuman primates (see Chapters 5 through 7). Cultural anthropologists may contribute ethnographic information concerning the varied nature of human behavior, partic-ularly ecological adaptations of those contemporary hunter-gatherer groups exploit-ing roughly similar environmental settings as those reconstructed for a hominid site.

The end result of years of research by dozens of scientists will (we hope) pro-duce a more complete and accurate understanding of human evolution—how we came to be the way we are. Both biological and cultural aspects of our ancestors per-tain to this investigation, each process developing in relation to the other.

Taphonomy
(*taphos,* meaning "dead") The study of how bones and other materials came to be buried in the earth and preserved as fossils. A taphono-mist studies the processes of sedimentation, the action of streams, preservation properties of bone, and carnivore disturbance factors.

Context
The environmental setting where an archaeologi-cal trace is found. A *primary* context is a setting in which an archaeological trace was originally deposited. A *secondary* context is one to which it has been moved (e.g., by the action of a stream).

Paleoanthropology: Reconstructing Early Hominid Behavior and Ecology

FIGURE 9–2
Major paleoanthropological projects.

See Virtual Lab 7, section 1, for a discussion of geological processes.

Paleoanthropology in Action—Olduvai Gorge

Several paleoanthropological projects of the scope just discussed have recently been pursued in diverse places in the Old World (Fig. 9–2). The most important of these include David Pilbeam's work in the Miocene beds of the Potwar Plateau of western Pakistan (circa 13–7 m.y.a.); Don Johanson's projects at Hadar and other areas of Ethiopia (circa 3.7–1.6 m.y.a.), sponsored by the Institute of Human Origins; a recently intensified effort just south of Hadar in Ethiopia in an area called the Middle Awash (circa 5–4 m.y.a.), led by Berkeley paleoanthropologists Tim White and Desmond Clark; a now completed research project along the Omo River of southern Ethiopia (circa 4–1.5 m.y.a.), directed by F. Clark Howell; Richard and Meave Leakey's fantastically successful research near Lake Turkana (formerly Lake Rudolf) in northern Kenya (circa 4.2–1.5 m.y.a.); Mary Leakey's famous investigations at Olduvai Gorge in northern Tanzania (circa 1.85 m.y.a. to present); and finally the recent exploration by Phillip Tobias of hominid localities in southern Africa (the most important being Swartkrans, discussed in Chapter 10).

Of all these localities, the one that has yielded the finest quality and greatest abundance of paleoanthropological information concerning the behavior of early hominids has been Olduvai Gorge. First "discovered" in the early twentieth century by a German butterfly collector, Olduvai was soon scientifically surveyed and its wealth of paleontological evidence recognized. In 1931, Louis Leakey made his first trip to Olduvai Gorge and almost immediately realized its significance for studying early humans. From 1935, when she first worked there, until she retired in 1984, Mary Leakey directed the archaeological excavations at Olduvai.

Located in the Serengeti Plain of northern Tanzania, Olduvai is a steep-sided valley resembling a miniature version of the Grand Canyon. A deep ravine cut into an almost mile-high grassland plateau of East Africa, Olduvai extends more than 25 miles in total length. Climatically, the semiarid pattern of present-day Olduvai is believed to be similar to what it has been for the last 2 million years. The surrounding countryside is a grassland savanna broken occasionally by scrub bushes and acacia trees.

Geographically, Olduvai is located on the eastern branch of the Great Rift Valley of Africa. The geological processes associated with the formation of the Rift Valley make Olduvai (and other East African sites) extremely important to paleoanthropological investigation. Three results of geological rifting are most significant:

1. Faulting, or earth movement, exposes geological beds near the surface that are normally hidden by hundreds of feet of accumulated overburden.
2. Active volcanic processes cause rapid sedimentation, which often yields excellent preservation of bone and artifacts that normally would be scattered by carnivore activity and erosion forces.
3. Volcanic activity provides a wealth of radiometrically datable material.

As a result, Olduvai is the site of superb preservation of ancient hominids, portions of their environment, and their behavioral patterns in datable contexts, all of which are readily accessible.

The greatest contribution Olduvai has made to paleoanthropological research is the establishment of an extremely well documented and correlated *sequence* of geological, paleontological, archaeological, and hominid remains over the last 2 million years. At the very foundation of all paleoanthropological research is a well-established geological context. At Olduvai, the geological and paleogeographical situation is known in minute detail. Olduvai is today a geologist's delight, containing sediments in some places 350 feet thick, accumulated from lava flows (basalts), tuffs (windblown or waterborne fine deposits from nearby volcanoes), sandstones,

Robert Jurmain

FIGURE 9–3
View of the main gorge at Olduvai. Note the clear sequence of geological beds. The discontinuity to the right is a major fault line.

claystones, and limestone conglomerates, all neatly stratified (Fig. 9–3). A hominid site can therefore be accurately dated relative to other sites in the Olduvai Gorge by cross-correlating known marker beds. At the most general geological level, the stratigraphic sequence at Olduvai is broken down into four major beds (Beds I–IV).

Paleontological evidence of fossilized animal bones also has come from Olduvai in great abundance. More than 150 species of extinct animals have been recognized, including fish, turtles, crocodiles, pigs, giraffes, horses, and many birds, rodents, and antelopes. Careful analysis of such remains has yielded voluminous information concerning the ecological conditions of early human habitats. In addition, the precise analysis of bones directly associated with artifacts can sometimes tell us about the diets and bone-processing techniques of early hominids. (There are some reservations, however; see pp. 228–229.)

The archaeological sequence is also well documented for the last 2 million years. Beginning at the earliest hominid site (circa 1.85 m.y.a.), there is already a well-developed stone tool kit, including chopping tools and some small flake tools (Leakey, 1971). Such a tool industry is called *Oldowan* (after Olduvai), and it continues into later beds with some small modifications, where it is called *Developed Oldowan*.

Finally, partial remains of several fossilized hominids have been found at Olduvai, ranging in time from the earliest occupation levels to fairly recent *Homo sapiens*. Of the more than 40 individuals represented, many are quite fragmentary, but a few are excellently preserved. While the center of hominid discoveries has now shifted to other areas of East Africa, it was the initial discovery by Mary Leakey of the *Zinjanthropus* skull at Olduvai in July 1959 that focused the world's attention on this remarkably rich area (Fig. 9–4). "Zinj" provides an excellent example of how financial ramifications directly result from hominid fossil discoveries. Prior to 1959, the Leakeys had worked sporadically at Olduvai on a financial shoestring, making marvelous paleontological and archaeological discoveries. Yet, there was little support available for much needed large-scale excavations. However, following the discovery of "Zinj," the National Geographic Society funded the Leakeys' research, and within a year, more than twice as much dirt had been excavated than during the previous 30 years!

Harry Nelson

FIGURE 9–4
Zinjanthropus skull, discovered by Mary Leakey at Olduvai Gorge in 1959. The skull and reconstructed jaw depicted here are casts at the National Museums of Kenya, Nairobi. As we will see in Chapter 10, this fossil is now included as part of the genus *Australopithecus*.

Dating Methods

One of the essentials of paleoanthropology is placing sites and fossils into a chronological framework. In other words, we want to know how old they are. How, then, do we date sites—or, more precisely, the geological strata in which sites are found? The question is both reasonable and important, so let us examine the dating techniques used by paleontologists, geologists, paleoanthropologists, and archaeologists.

Scientists use two kinds of dating for this purpose: relative dating and **chronometric dating** (also known as *absolute dating*). Relative dating methods tell us that something is older or younger than something else, but not by how much. If, for example, a cranium is found at a depth of 50 feet and another cranium at 70 feet at the same site, we usually assume that the specimen discovered at 70 feet is older. We may not know the date (in years) of either one, but we would know that one is older (or younger) than the other. Although this may not satisfy our curiosity about the actual number of years involved, it would give some idea of the evolutionary changes in cranial morphology (structure), especially if a number of crania at different levels are found and compared.

This method of relative dating is based on **stratigraphy** and was one of the first techniques to be used by scholars working with the vast period of geological time. Stratigraphy, in turn, is based on the law of superposition, which states that a lower stratum (layer) is older than a higher stratum. Given the fact that much of the earth's crust has been laid down by layer after layer of sedimentary rock, much like the layers of a cake, stratigraphy has been a valuable aid in reconstructing the history of the earth and the life upon it.

Stratigraphic dating does, however, have a number of problems. Earth disturbances, such as volcanic activity, river activity, and mountain building, may shift strata and the objects within them, and the chronology of the material may be difficult or even impossible to reconstruct. Furthermore, the time period of a particular stratum—that is, the length of time it took to accumulate—is not possible to determine with much accuracy.

Another method of relative dating is *fluorine analysis,* which applies only to bones (Oakley, 1963). Bones in the earth are exposed to the seepage of groundwater that usually contains fluorine. The longer a bone lies in the earth, the more fluorine it will incorporate during the fossilization process. Therefore, bones deposited at the same time in the same location should contain the same amount of fluorine. The use of this technique by Professor Oakley of the British Museum in the early 1950s exposed the Piltdown (England) hoax by demonstrating that a human skull was considerably older than the jaw (ostensibly also human) found with it (Weiner, 1955). A discrepancy in fluorine content led Oakley and others to a closer examination of the bones, and they found that the jaw was not that of a hominid at all but of a young adult orangutan! (See Issue, p. 240.)

Unfortunately, fluorine is useful only with bones found at the same location. Because the amount of fluorine in groundwater is based on local conditions, it varies from place to place. Also, some groundwater may not contain any fluorine. For these reasons, comparing bones from different localities by fluorine analysis is impossible.

In both stratigraphy and fluorine analysis, the actual age of the rock stratum and the objects in it is impossible to calculate. To determine the age in years, scientists have developed a variety of chronometric techniques based on the phenomenon of radioactive decay. The theory is quite simple: Certain radioactive isotopes of elements are unstable, disintegrate, and form an isotopic variation of another element. Since the rate of disintegration follows a definite mathematical

Chronometric dating
(*chrono,* meaning "time," and *metric,* meaning "measure") A dating technique that gives an estimate in actual numbers of years.

Stratigraphy
Study of the sequential layering of deposits.

See Virtual Lab 7, section I, for a discussion of dating methods.

pattern, the radioactive material forms an accurate geological time clock. By measuring the amount of disintegration in a particular sample, scientists can calculate the number of years it took for that amount of decay to accumulate. Chronometric techniques have been used for dating the immense age of the earth as well as artifacts less than 1,000 years old. Several techniques have been employed for a number of years and are now quite well known.

Uranium-238 (^{238}U) decays with a *half-life* of 4.5 billion years to form lead. That is, one-half of the original amount of ^{238}U is lost in 4.5 billion years and through various processes becomes lead. Therefore, if a sample of rock containing this element is analyzed and one-half of the uranium has been converted to lead, the age of that rock is 4.5 billion years. In another 4.5 billion years, half the remaining ^{238}U will have decayed. The isotope ^{238}U has proved a useful tool in dating the age of the formation of the earth.

Another chronometric technique involves potassium-40 (^{40}K), which has a half-life of 1.25 billion years and produces argon-40 (^{40}Ar). Known as the K/Ar or potassium-argon method, this procedure has been extensively used by paleoanthropologists in dating materials in the 1- to 5-million-year range, especially in East Africa. In addition, a variant of this technique, the ^{40}Ar/^{39}Ar method, has recently been used to date a number of hominid localities. The ^{40}Ar/^{39}Ar method allows analysis of smaller samples (even single crystals), reduces experimental error, and is more precise than standard K/Ar dating. Consequently, it can be used to date a wide chronological range—indeed, the entire hominid record, even up to modern times. Recent applications have provided excellent dates for several early hominid sites in East Africa (discussed in Chapter 10) as well as somewhat later sites in Java (discussed in Chapter 11). In fact, the technique was recently used to date the famous Mt. Vesuvius eruption of A.D. 79 (which destroyed the city of Pompeii). Remarkably, the midrange date obtained by the ^{40}Ar/^{39}Ar technique was A.D. 73, just six years from the known date (Deino et al., 1998)! Organic material, such as bone, cannot be measured by these techniques, but the rock matrix in which the bone is found can be. K/Ar was used to provide a minimum date for the deposit containing the *Zinjanthropus* cranium by dating a volcanic layer above the fossil.

Rocks that provide the best samples for K/Ar and ^{40}Ar/^{39}Ar are those heated to an extremely high temperature, such as that generated by volcanic activity. When the rock is in a molten state, argon, a gas, is driven off. As the rock cools and solidifies, potassium-40 continues to break down to argon, but now the gas is physically trapped in the cooled rock. To obtain the date of the rock, it is reheated and the escaping gas measured.

A well-known radiometric method popular with archaeologists makes use of carbon-14 (^{14}C), with a half-life of 5,730 years. Carbon-14 has been used to date material from less than 1,000 years to as old as 75,000 years, although the probability of error rises rapidly after 40,000 years. Since this technique applies to the latter stages of hominid evolution, its applications relate to material discussed in Chapters 12 and 13. In addition, other dating techniques (thermoluminescence and electron spin resonance) that are used for calibrating these latter time periods will be discussed in Chapter 12.

We should stress that none of these methods is precise, and each is beset with problems that must be carefully considered during laboratory measurement and the collection of material to be analyzed. Because the methods are imprecise, approximate dates are given as probability statements with a plus or minus factor. For example, a date given as 1.75 ± 0.2 million years should be read as having a 67 percent chance that the actual date lies somewhere between 1.55 and 1.95 million years (see Box 9–1).

BOX 9–1   A CLOSER LOOK

Chronometric Dating Estimates

Chronometric dates are usually determined after several geological samples are tested. The dates that result from such testing are combined and expressed statistically. For example, say that five different samples are used to give the K/Ar date 1.75 6 0.2 m.y. for a particular geological bed. The individual results from all five samples are totaled together to give an average date (here, 1.75 m.y.), and the standard deviation is calculated (here, 0.20 m.y.; that is, 200,000 years). The dating estimate is then reported as the mean plus or minus (±) one standard deviation. For those of you who have taken statistics,

you realize that (assuming a normal distribution) 67 percent of a distribution of dates is included within 1 standard deviation (±) of the mean. Thus, the chronometric results, as shown in the reported range, is simply a probability statement that 67 percent of the dates from all the samples tested fell within the range of dates from 1.55 to 1.95 m.y.a. You should carefully read chronometric dates and study the reported ranges. The smaller the range, probably the more samples that were analyzed. Smaller ranges mean more precise estimates; better laboratory controls will also increase precision.

There are, then, two ways in which the question of age may be answered. We can say that a particular fossil is x number of years old, a date determined usually either by K/Ar or ^{14}C chronometric dating techniques. Or we can say that fossil X lived before or after fossil Y, a relative dating technique.

Application of Dating Methods: Examples from Olduvai

Olduvai has been a rich proving ground for materials datable by numerous techniques, and as a result, it has some of the best-documented chronology for any hominid site in the Lower or Middle Pleistocene.

The potassium-argon (K/Ar) method is an extremely valuable tool for dating early hominid sites and has been widely used in areas containing suitable volcanic deposits (mainly in East Africa). At Olduvai, K/Ar has given several reliable dates of the underlying basalt and several tuffs in Bed I, including the one associated with the "Zinj" find (now dated at 1.79 ± 0.03 m.y.a.). When dating relatively recent samples (from the perspective of a half-life of 1.25 billion years for K/Ar, *all* paleoanthropological material is relatively recent), the amount of radiogenic argon (that argon produced by disintegration of a potassium isotope) is going to be exceedingly small. Experimental errors in measurement can therefore occur as well as the thorny problem of distinguishing the atmospheric argon normally clinging to the outside of the sample from the radiogenic argon. In addition, the initial sample may have been contaminated or argon leakage may have occurred while it lay buried.

Due to the potential sources of error, K/Ar dating must be cross-checked using other independent methods. Once again, the sediments at Olduvai provide some of the best examples of the use of many of these other dating techniques.

Fission-track dating is one of the most important techniques for cross-checking K/Ar determinations. The key to fission-track dating is that uranium-238 (^{238}U) decays regularly by spontaneous fission. By counting the proportion of uranium atoms that have fissioned (shown as microscopic tracks caused by explosive fission of ^{238}U nuclei), we can ascertain the age of a mineral or natural glass sample. One of the earliest applications of this technique was on volcanic pumice from Olduvai, giving a date of 2.30 (±0.28 m.y.a.)—in good accord with K/Ar dates. Fission-track dating has also been used to date baked earth and pottery from contexts as recently as 5,000 years ago from a site in Iran (Wagner, 1996).

Another important means of cross-checking dates is called **paleomagnetism.** This technique is based on the constantly shifting nature of the earth's magnetic pole. Of course, the earth's magnetic pole is now oriented in a northerly direction, but this has not always been so. In fact, the orientation and intensity of the geomagnetic field have undergone numerous documented changes in the last few million years. From our present point of view, we call a northern orientation "normal" and a southern one "reversed." Major epochs (also called "*chrons*") of recent geomagnetic time are:

0.7 m.y.a.–present	Normal
2.6–0.7 m.y.a.	Reversed
3.4–2.6 m.y.a.	Normal
?–3.4 m.y.a.	Reversed

Paleomagnetic dating is accomplished by carefully taking samples of sediments that contain magnetically charged particles. Since these particles maintain the magnetic orientation they had when they were consolidated into rock (many thousands or millions of years ago), we have a kind of "fossil compass." Then the paleomagnetic *sequence* is compared against the K/Ar dates to check if they agree. Some complications may arise, for during an epoch, a relatively long period of time can occur when the geomagnetic orientation is the opposite of what is expected. For example, during the reversed epoch from 2.6 to 0.7 m.y.a. (the Matuyama epoch), there was an *event* lasting about 210,000 years when orientations were normal. (Because this phenomenon was first conclusively demonstrated at Olduvai, it is appropriately called the *Olduvai event*.) However, once these oscillations in the geomagnetic pole are worked out, the sequence of paleomagnetic orientations can provide a valuable cross-check for K/Ar and fission-track age determinations.

A final dating technique employed in the Lower Pleistocene beds at Olduvai and other African sites is based on the regular evolutionary changes in well-known groups of mammals. This technique, called *faunal correlation* or **biostratigraphy,** provides yet another means of cross-checking the other methods. Animals that have been widely used in biostratigraphic analysis in East and South Africa are fossil pigs (suids), elephants (proboscids), antelopes (bovids), rodents, and carnivores. From areas where dates are known (by K/Ar, for instance), approximate ages can be extrapolated to other lesser-known areas by noting which genera and species are present.

All these methods—potassium-argon, fission-track, paleomagnetism, and biostratigraphy—have been used in dating sites at Olduvai. So many different dating techniques are necessary because no single one is perfectly reliable by itself. Sampling error, contamination, and experimental error can all introduce ambiguities into our so-called "absolute" dates. However, the sources of error are different for each technique; therefore, cross-checking among several independent methods is the most reliable way of authenticating the chronology for early hominid sites.

Excavations at Olduvai

Because the vertical cut of the Olduvai Gorge provides a ready cross section of 2 million years of earth history, sites can be excavated by digging "straight in" rather than first having to remove tons of overlying dirt (Fig. 9–5). In fact, sites are usually discovered by merely walking the exposures and observing what bones, stones, and so forth, are eroding out.

Paleomagnetism
Dating method based on the shifting magnetic pole.

Biostratigraphy
Dating method based on evolutionary changes within an evolving lineage.

FIGURE 9–5
Excavations in progress at Olduvai. This site, more than 1 million years old, was located when a hominid ulna (arm bone) was found eroding out of the side of the gorge.

Robert Jurmain

See Virtual Lab 11, section III, for a discussion of the factors that influence the development of archaeological localities.

Several dozen hominid sites (at a minimum, they are bone and tool scatters) have been surveyed at Olduvai, and Mary Leakey extensively excavated close to 20 of these. An incredible amount of paleoanthropological information has come from these excavated areas, data that can be generally grouped into three broad categories of site types, depending on implied function:

1. *"Butchering" localities*, areas containing one or only a few individuals of a single species of large mammal associated with a scatter of archaeological traces. Two "butchering" sites, one containing an elephant and another containing a *Deinotherium* (a large extinct relative of the elephant), have been found at levels approximately 1.7 m.y.a. Both sites contain only a single animal, and it is impossible to ascertain whether the hominids actually killed these animals or exploited them (either for meat or, perhaps, to extract marrow) after they were already dead. A third butchering locality dated at approximately 1.2 m.y.a. shows much more consistent and efficient exploitation of large mammals by this time. Remains of 24 *Pelorovis* individuals (a giant extinct relative of the buffalo, with horn spans more than 10 feet across!) have been found here, and Louis Leakey suggested they were driven into a swamp by a band of hominids and then systematically slaughtered (Leakey, 1971). (*Note:* This is an interpretation that is no longer widely accepted.)

2. *Quarry localities*, areas where early hominids extracted their stone resources and initially fashioned their tools. At such sites, thousands of small stone fragments of only one type of rock are found, usually associated with no or very little bone refuse. At Olduvai, a 1.6- to 1.7-million-year-old area was apparently a chert (a rock resembling flint) factory site, where hominids came repeatedly to quarry this material.

3. *Multipurpose localities* (also called "campsites"), general-purpose areas where hominids possibly ate, slept, and put the finishing touches on their tools. The accumulation of living debris, including broken bones of many animals of several different species and many broken stones (some complete tools, some waste flakes), is a basic human pattern. As Glynn Isaac noted:

The fact that discarded artifacts tend to be concentrated in restricted areas is itself highly suggestive. It seems likely that such patches of material reflect the

Robert Jurmain

FIGURE 9–6
A dense scatter of stone and some fossilized animal bone from a site at Olduvai, dated at approximately 1.6 m.y.a. Some of these remains are the result of hominid activities.

organization of movement around a camp or home base, with recurrent dispersal and reuniting of the group at the chosen locality. Among living primates this pattern in its full expression is distinctive of man. The coincidence of bone and food refuse with the artifacts strongly implies that meat was carried back—presumably for sharing. (Isaac, 1976, pp. 27–28)

(See Box 9–2, pp. 228–229 for a different interpretation.)

Several multipurpose areas have been excavated at Olduvai, including one that is over 1.8 million years old. This site has a circle of large stones forming what at one time was thought to be a base for a windbreak; however, this interpretation is now considered unlikely. Whatever its function, without the meticulous excavation and recording of modern archaeological techniques, the presence of such an archaeological feature would never have been recognized. This point requires further emphasis. Many people assume that archaeologists derive their information simply from analysis of objects (stone tools, gold statues, or whatever). However, it is the *context* and **association** of objects (i.e., precisely where the objects are found and what is found associated with them) that give archaeologists the data they require to understand the behavioral patterns of ancient human populations. Once pot hunters or looters pilfer a site, proper archaeological interpretation is never again possible.

Association
What an archaeological trace is found with.

The types of activities carried out at these multipurpose sites remain open to speculation (Fig. 9–6). Archaeologists had thought, as the quote by Glynn Isaac indicates (and as also argued by Mary Leakey), that the sites functioned as "campsites." Lewis Binford has forcefully critiqued this view and has alternatively suggested that much of the refuse accumulated is the result of nonhominid (i.e., predator) activities. Another possibility, suggested by Richards Potts (1984), postulates that these areas served as collecting points (caches) for some tools. This last interpretation has received considerable support from other archaeologists in recent years.

A final interpretation, incorporating aspects of the hypotheses proposed by Binford and Potts, has been suggested by Robert Blumenschine. He argues that early hominids were gatherers and scavengers, and the bone and stone scatters reflect these activities (Blumenschine, 1986; Blumenschine and Cavallo, 1992; see pp. 228–229).

BOX 9-2   A CLOSER LOOK

Who Was Doing What at Olduvai and other Plio-Pleistocene Sites?

The long-held interpretation of the bone refuse and stone tools discovered at Olduvai has been that most, if not all, of these materials are the result of hominid activities. More recently, however, a comprehensive reanalysis of the bone remains from Olduvai localities has challenged this view (Binford 1981, 1983). Archaeologist Lewis Binford criticizes those drawn too quickly to the conclusion that these bone scatters are the remnants of hominid behavior patterns while simultaneously ignoring the possibility of other explanations.

From information concerning the kinds of animals present, which body parts were found, and the differences in preservation among these skeletal elements, Binford has concluded that much of what is preserved could be explained by carnivore activity. This conclusion has been reinforced by certain details observed by Binford himself in Alaska—details on animal kills, scavenging, the transportation of elements, and preservation that are the result of wolf and dog behaviors. Binford describes his approach thus:

I took as "known," then, the structure of bone assemblages produced in various settings by animal predators and scavengers; and as "unknown" the bone deposits excavated by the Leakeys at Olduvai Gorge. Using mathematical and statistical techniques I considered to what degree the finds from Olduvai Gorge could be accounted for in terms of the results of predator behavior and how much was "left over." (Binford, 1983, pp. 56–57)

Binford is not arguing that all of the remains found at Olduvai have resulted from nonhominid activity. In fact, he recognizes that "residual material" was consistently found on surfaces with high tool concentration "which could not be explained by what we know about African animals" (Binford 1983).

Support for the idea that at least some of the bone refuse was utilized by early hominids has come from a totally different perspective. Researchers have analyzed (both macroscopically and microscopically) the cut marks left on fossilized bones. By experimenting with modern materials, they have further been able to delineate clearly the differences between marks left by stone tools and those left by animal teeth (or other factors) (Bunn, 1981; Potts and Shipman, 1981). Analysis of bones from several early localities at Olduvai have shown unambiguously that these specimens were utilized by hominids, who left telltale cut marks from stone tool usage. The sites thus far investigated reveal a somewhat haphazard cutting and chopping, apparently unrelated to deliberate disarticulation. It has thus been concluded (Shipman, 1983) that hominids scavenged carcasses (probably of carnivore kills) and did *not* hunt large animals themselves.

Following and expanding on the experimental approaches pioneered by Binford, Bunn, and others, more detailed analysis of the Olduvai material has recently been done by Robert Blumenschine of Rutgers University. Like his predecessors, Blumenschine has

Experimental Archaeology

Flake   Core

FIGURE 9–7
Flake and core.

Simply classifying artifacts into categories and types is scientifically insufficient. We can learn considerably more about our ancestors by understanding how they made and used their tools. It is, after all, the artifactual traces of prehistoric tools of stone (and, to a lesser degree, bone) that constitute our primary information concerning early human behavior. Tons of stone debris litter archaeological sites worldwide. A casual walk along the bottom of Olduvai Gorge could well be interrupted every few seconds by tripping over prehistoric tools!

Archaeologists are thus presented with a wealth of information revealing at least one part of human material culture. What do these artifacts tell us about our ancestors? How were these tools made? In which ways were they used? To answer these questions, contemporary archaeologists have attempted to reconstruct prehistoric techniques of stone toolmaking, butchering, and so forth. In this way, experimental archaeologists are, in a sense, trying to re-create the past.

also concluded that the cut marks on animal bones are the result of hominid processing (Blumenschine, 1995). Moreover, Blumenschine and colleagues have surmised that most meat acquisition (virtually all from large animals) was the result of scavenging (from remains of carnivore kills or from animals who died from natural causes). In fact, these researchers suggest that scavenging was a critically important adaptive strategy for early hominids and considerably influenced their habitat usage, diet, and stone tool utilization (Blumenschine and Cavallo, 1992; Blumenschine and Peters, 1998). Of notable scientific merit, Blumenschine and colleagues have developed a model detailing how scavenging and other early hominid adaptive strategies integrate into patterns of land use (i.e., differential utilization of various niches in and around Olduvai). From this model they have formulated specific hypotheses concerning the predicted distribution of artifacts and animal remains in different areas at Olduvai. Ongoing excavations at Olduvai are now aimed specifically at *testing* these hypotheses.

If early hominids (close to 2 m.y.a.) were not hunting consistently, what did they obtain from scavenging the kills of other animals? One obvious answer is, whatever meat was left behind. However, the position of the cut marks suggests that early hominids were often hacking at non-meat-bearing portions of the skeletons. Perhaps they were after bone marrow and brain, substances not fully exploited by other predators and scavengers (Binford, 1981; Blumenschine and Cavallo, 1992).

Exciting new discoveries from the Bouri Peninsula of the Middle Awash of Ethiopia provide the best evidence yet for meat and marrow exploitation by early hominids. Dated to 2.5 m.y.a. (i.e., as old as the oldest known artifacts), antelope and horse fossils from Bouri show telltale incisions and breaks indicating that bones were smashed to extract marrow and also cut, ostensibly to retrieve meat (de Heinzelin et al., 1999). The researchers who analyzed these materials have suggested that the greater dietary reliance on animal products may have been important in stimulating brain enlargement in the lineage leading to genus *Homo*.

Another new research twist relating to the reconstruction of early hominid diets has come from biochemical analysis of hominid teeth from South Africa (dating to about the same time range as hominids from Olduvai—or perhaps slightly earlier). In an innovative application of stable carbon isotope analysis (see p. 233), Matt Sponheimer of Rutgers University and Julia Lee-Thorp of the University of Cape Town found that these early hominid teeth revealed telltale chemical signatures relating to diet (Sponheimer and Lee-Thorp, 1999). In particular, the proportions of stable carbon isotopes indicated that these early hominids either ate grass products (such as seeds) or ate meat/marrow from animals that in turn had eaten grass products (i.e., the hominids might well have derived a significant portion of their diet from meat or other animal products). This evidence comes from an exciting new perspective, for it provides a more *direct* indicator of early hominid diets. While it is not clear how much meat these early hominids consumed, these new data do suggest they were consistently exploiting more open regions of their environment.

Stone Tool (Lithic) Technology

Since stone is by far the most common residue of prehistoric cultural behavior, archaeologists have long been keenly interested in this material.

When struck properly, certain types of stone will fracture in a controlled way. The smaller piece struck off is called a **flake**, while the larger remaining chunk is called a **core** (Fig. 9–7). The obvious result is that both core and flake now possess sharp edges useful for cutting, sawing, or scraping. The earliest hominid cultural inventions probably employed nondurable materials that did not survive archaeologically (such as a digging stick or an ostrich eggshell used as a watertight container). Still, a basic human invention was the recognition that stone can be fractured to produce sharp edges.

For many years it has been assumed that in the earliest known stone tool industry (i.e., the Oldowan), both core and flake tools were deliberately manufactured as final, desired products. Such core implements as "choppers," "polyhedrons," and

Flake
Thin-edged fragment removed from a core.

Core
Stone reduced by flake removal, and not necessarily a "tool" itself.

Lithic
(*lith*, meaning "stone") Referring to stone tools.

Knappers
Those who flake stone tools.

Direct percussion
Striking a core or flake with a hammerstone.

FIGURE 9–8
Direct percussion.

FIGURE 9–9
Pressure flaking.

Microliths
(*micro*, meaning "small," and *lith*, meaning "stone") Small stone tools usually produced from narrow blades punched from a core; found especially in Africa during the latter part of the Pleistocene.

Pressure flaking
A method of removing flakes from a core by pressing a pointed implement (e.g., bone or antler) against the stone.

"discoids" were thought to be central artifactual components of these early **lithic** assemblages (indeed, the Oldowan has often been depicted as a "chopping tool industry"). However, recent detailed reevaluation of these artifacts by Richard Potts of the Smithsonian Institution has thrown these traditional assumptions into doubt. From careful statistical analysis of the attributes of Oldowan artifacts from Bed I at Olduvai, Potts (1991, 1993) has concluded that the so-called core tools were really not tools after all. He suggests rather that what early hominids were deliberately producing were flake tools, and the various stone nodules (discoids, polyhedrons, choppers, etc.) were simply "incidental stopping points in the process of removing flakes from cores" (Potts, 1993, p. 60). Potts summarizes his reevaluation: "The flaked stones of the Oldowan thus cannot be demonstrated to constitute discrete target designs, but can be shown to represent simple by-products of the repetitive act of producing sharp flakes" (Potts, 1993, pp. 60–61).

Breaking rocks by bashing them together is one thing. Producing consistent results, even apparently simple flakes, is quite another. It takes years of practice before modern stone **knappers** learn the intricacies of the type of rock to choose, the kind of hammer to employ, the angle and velocity with which to strike, and so on. Such experience allows us to appreciate how skilled in stoneworking our ancestors truly were.

Flakes can be removed from cores in a variety of ways. The object in making a tool, however, is to produce a usable cutting surface. By reproducing results similar to those of earlier stoneworkers, experimental archaeologists can infer which kinds of techniques *might* have been employed.

For example, the nodules (now thought to be blanks) found in sites in Bed I at Olduvai (circa 1.85–1.2 m.y.a.) are flaked on one side only (i.e., *unifacially*). It is possible, although by no means easy, to produce such implements by hitting one stone—the hammerstone—against another—the core—in a method called **direct percussion** (Fig. 9–8).

In Bed IV sites (circa 400,000 y.a.*), however, the majority of tools are flaked on both sides (i.e., *bifacially*) and have long sinuous edges. Such a result cannot be reproduced by direct percussion with just a hammerstone. The edges must have been straightened ("retouched") with a "soft" hammer, such as bone or antler.

To reproduce implements similar to those found in later stages of human cultural development, even more sophisticated techniques are required. Tools such as the delicate **microliths** found in the uppermost beds at Olduvai (circa 17,000 y.a.), the superb Solutrean blades from Europe (circa 20,000 y.a.), and the expertly crafted Folsom projectile points from the New World (circa 10,000 y.a.) all require a mastery of stone matched by few knappers today.

Reproducing implements such as those mentioned above requires removal of extremely thin flakes, possible only through **pressure flaking**—for example, using a pointed piece of bone, antler, or hard wood and pressing firmly against the stone (Fig. 9–9).

Once the tools were manufactured, the ways our ancestors used them can be inferred through further experimentation. For example, archaeologists from the Smithsonian Institution successfully butchered an entire elephant (which had died in a zoo) using stone tools they had made for that purpose (Park, 1978). Others have cut down trees using stone axes they had made.

Ancient tools themselves may carry telltale signs of how they were used. In his graduate work at Oxford University, Lawrence Keeley, now at the University of Illinois, Chicago, performed a series of experiments in which he manufactured flint

---

*y.a. stands for "years ago."

tools and then used them in diverse ways—whittling wood, cutting bone, cutting meat, and scraping skins (Keeley, 1980). Viewing those implements under a microscope at fairly high magnification revealed patterns of polishes, striations, and other kinds of **microwear** (Fig. 9–10). What is most intriguing is that these patterns vary, depending on how the implement was used and which material was worked. For example, Keeley was able to distinguish among implements used on bone, antler, meat, plant materials, and hides. In the latter case, he was even able to determine if the hides were fresh or dried! In addition, orientations of microwear markings are also indicative of the way in which the tool was used (e.g., for cutting or scraping). Evidence of microwear polish has been examined on even the extremely early hominid stone tools from Koobi Fora (East Lake Turkana), in Kenya (Keeley and Toth, 1981).

Recent advances in tool use studies include the application of scanning electron microscopy (SEM). Working at 10,000× magnification, researchers have found that the working edges of stone implements sometimes retain plant fibers and amino acids, as well as nonorganic residues, including **phytoliths.** Because phytoliths produced by different plant species are morphologically distinctive, there is good potential for identifying the botanical materials that came in contact with the tool during use (Rovner, 1983). Such work is most exciting, since for the first time, we may be able to make definite statements concerning the uses of ancient tools.

Analysis of Bone

Experimental archaeologists are also interested in the ways bone is altered by human and natural forces. Other scientists are vitally concerned with this process as well; in fact, it has engendered an entire new branch of paleoecology—taphonomy. In recent years, taphonomists have carried out comprehensive research on how natural factors influence bone deposition and preservation. In South Africa, C. K. Brain has collected data on contemporary African butchering practices, carnivore (dog) disturbances, and so forth, and has correlated these factors with the kinds and numbers of elements usually found in bone accumulations (Brain, 1981). In this way, he has been able to account for the accumulation of most (if not all) of the bones in South African cave sites. Likewise, in East African game parks, observations have been made on decaying animals to measure the effects of weathering, predator chewing, and trampling (Behrensmeyer et al., 1979).

Further insight into the many ways bone is altered by natural factors has come from experimental work in the laboratory (Boaz and Behrensmeyer, 1976). In an experiment conducted at the University of California, Berkeley, human bones were put into a running-water trough. Researchers observed how far different pieces were transported and how much damage was done. Application of such information is extremely useful in interpreting early hominid sites. For example, the distribution of hominid fossils at Olduvai suggests that less active water transport was prevalent there than in the Omo River Valley.

Detailed examination of bones may also provide evidence of butchering and bone breakage by hominids, including cut marks and percussion marks left by stone tools. Great care must be taken to distinguish scars left on bone by carnivore or rodent gnawing, weathering processes, hoof marks, or even normal growth. High magnification of a cut made by a stone tool may reveal a minutely striated and roughened groove scored into the bone's surface. Many such finds have been recognized at early hominid sites, including Olduvai Gorge (Bunn et al., 1980; Bunn, 1981; Potts and Shipman, 1981) (see pp. 228–229).

Microwear
Polishes, striations, and other diagnostic microscopic changes on the edges of stone tools.

Phytoliths
(*phyto*, meaning "hidden," and *lith*, meaning "stone") Microscopic silica structures formed in the cells of many plants, particularly grasses.

Courtesy, Larry Keeley

FIGURE 9–10
Microwear: the polish left on an experimental flint implement by scraping wood for 10 minutes. Bright, smooth areas are the microwear polish; dark, grainy areas are the unworn flint surface. Arrows indicate implement edge. (Magnification 200×)

Reconstruction of Early Hominid Environments and Behavior

Now that we have reviewed the various methods used by paleoanthropologists to *collect* their varied data, we will turn to the intriguing ways this information is *interpreted*. We must caution that much of this interpretation is quite speculative and not as amenable to scientific verification as are more concrete sources of data (e.g., that relating to dating, geology, or hominid anatomy). (In Chapter 1, we discussed how hypotheses are developed and tested by scientists, noting the requirement that *scientific* explanations be falsifiable.)

However, paleoanthropologists are keenly interested in not just *how* early hominids evolved, but also *why* the process occurred in the manner that it did. Accordingly, the data available are frequently used as a basis for broad, speculative **scenarios** seeking to explain both early hominid adaptations to a changing environment and the new behaviors that these hominids adopted. Such scenarios are fascinating, and paleoanthropologists enjoy constructing them (and certainly many in the general public enjoy reading them). Without doubt, for scientists and laypersons alike, our curiosity inevitably leads to intriguing and sweeping generalizations. Nevertheless, in the following discussion, we will attempt, wherever possible, to focus on what is *known* from the paleoanthropological record itself and to separate that from the more speculative conclusions. You, too, should evaluate these explanations with a critical eye and attempt to discern the empirical basis for each type of reconstruction. It is important to go beyond accepting views merely because they are appealing (often because they are simple) or just because they seem *plausible*. We always need to ask ourselves what kinds of evidence support a particular contention, how generally the explanation fits the evidence (i.e., how consistent it is with different types of data from varied sources), and what types of *new* evidence might either help verify or potentially falsify the interpretation.

Environmental Explanations for Hominid Origins

As we saw in Chapter 8, there are no *definite* hominid remains yet discovered from any Miocene-dated context. From what we presently know, the earliest hominids did not appear until early in the Pliocene (4–5 m.y.a.). What were the environmental conditions at this time and immediately prior to it? Can these general ecological patterns help explain the origins of the first hominids (as they diversified from other kinds of hominoids)?

Before continuing, we should provide one further caution. A common misconception that many students have is that a single large environmental change is related clearly to a major adaptive change in a type of organism (in other words, environmental change X produced adaptation Y in a particular life form). This oversimplification is a form of **environmental determinism**, and it grossly underestimates the true complexity of the evolutionary process. It is clear that the environment does influence evolutionary change, as seen in the process of natural selection. But organisms are highly complex systems, composed of thousands of genes, and any adaptive shift to changing environmental circumstances is likely to be a compromise, balancing several selective factors simultaneously (such as temperature requirements, amount and distribution of food and water, predators, and safe sleeping sites). Our discussion of the socioecological dynamics of nonhuman primate adaptations in Chapter 6 made this same point.

There is some evidence that at about the same time the earliest hominids were diverging, there *may* have been some major ecological changes occurring in Africa. Could these ecological and evolutionary changes be related to each other? As we

Scenarios
General, speculative reconstructions derived from various scientific data. In paleoanthropology, scenarios are usually presented as imaginative reconstructions of early hominid behavior. Such interpretations are broader than typical scientific hypotheses and theories and are not as rigorously amenable to verification.

Environmental determinism
An interpretation that links simple environmental changes directly to a major evolutionary shift in an organism. Such explanations tend to be extreme oversimplifications of the evolutionary process.

will see, there is much debate regarding such a sweeping generalization. For most of the Miocene, Africa was generally tropical, with heavy rainfall persisting for most of the year; consequently, most of the continent was heavily forested. However, beginning later in the Miocene and intensifying up to the end of the epoch (about 5 m.y.a.), the climate became cooler, drier, and more seasonal.

We should mention as well that there were other regions of the world where paleoecological evidence reveals a distinct cooling trend at the end of the Miocene. However, our focus is on Africa, particularly East Africa, for it is from this region that we have the earliest evidence of hominid diversification. As already noted, one method used by paleoanthropologists to reconstruct environments is to analyze animal (faunal) remains and fossilized pollen. In addition, an innovative technique also studies the chemical pathways utilized by different plants. In particular, **stable carbon isotopes** are produced by plants in differing proportions, depending partly on temperature and aridity (plants adapted to warmer, wetter climates, such as most trees, shrubs, and tubers, versus plants requiring hotter, drier conditions, as typified by many types of grasses). Animals eat the plants, and the differing concentrations of the stable isotopes of carbon are incorporated into their bones and teeth, thus providing a "signature" of the general type of environment in which they lived.

It is from a combination of these analytical techniques that paleoecologists have gained a reasonably good handle on worldwide and continentwide environmental patterns of the past. For example, one model postulates that as climates grew cooler in East Africa 12–5 m.y.a., forests became less continuous. As a result, forest "fringe" habitats and transitional zones between forests and grasslands became more widespread. It is hypothesized that in such transitional environments, some of the late Miocene hominoids may have exploited more intensively the drier grassland portions of the fringe (these would be the earliest hominids); conversely, other hominoids concentrated more on the wetter portions of the fringe (these presumably were the ancestors of African great apes). In the incipient protohominids, further adaptive strategies would have followed, including bipedalism, increased tool use, dietary specialization (perhaps on hard items such as seeds and nuts), and changes in social organization.

Such assertions concerning interactions of habitat, locomotion, dietary changes, and social organization are not really testable (since we do not know which changes came first). Still, some of the more restricted contentions of this "climatic forcing" theory are amenable to testing; in fact, some of the more basic predictions of the model have not been verified. Most notably, further analyses using stable carbon isotopes from several East African localities suggest that during the late Miocene, environments across the area were consistently quite densely forested (i.e., grasslands never predominated, except perhaps at a local level).

You should be aware that there can be wide fluctuations at the local level pertaining to such factors as temperature, rainfall, vegetation, and the animals exploiting the vegetation. For example, local uplift can produce a rain shadow, dramatically altering rainfall and temperature in a region. River and related lake drainages also have major impacts in some areas, and these topographical features are often influenced by highly localized geological factors. To generalize about climates in Africa, good data from several regions are required.

It would thus appear, given current evidence and available analytical techniques, that our knowledge of the factors influencing the appearance of the *earliest* hominids is very limited. Considering the constraints, most hypotheses relating to potential factors are best kept restricted in scope and directly related to actual data. In this way, their utility can be more easily evaluated and they can be modified and built upon.

Stable carbon isotopes
Isotopes of carbon that are produced in plants in differing proportions, depending on environmental conditions. Through analyzing the proportions of the isotopes contained in fossil remains of animals (who ate the plants), it is possible to reconstruct aspects of ancient environments (particularly temperature and aridity).

Changing Environments and Later Hominid Diversifications

From the Pliocene and early Pleistocene, we have much more data relating to hominids and the environments in which they lived. One innovative explanation has sought to link periods of hominid and other mammalian diversification (when new species appear) with regular shifts in the African environment. From her research in both South and East Africa, Elizabeth Vrba, of Yale University, noticed that the appearance of new species of antelope as well as hominids was correlated with three periods of increased aridity (at 2.5, 1.8, and 1.0 m.y.a.) (Vrba, 1988, 1995). Could the environment have played a significant role in stimulating mammalian (including hominid) evolution at several crucial stages? This view has come to be called the **evolutionary pulse theory** and has been supported from data in Africa and other regions.

However, more recent and highly detailed analyses of more than 400 paleontological sites located around Lake Turkana (in northern Kenya and southern Ethiopia) have cast doubt on some aspects of the evolutionary pulse theory. Anna Behrensmeyer and colleagues from the Smithsonian Institution collected data from more than 10,000 specimens from contexts dated to 4.4 m.y.a. to the present to see if any "spikes" in rates of extinction or appearance of new species were evident (Behrensmeyer et al., 1997). The key period pointed to by many proponents of the evolutionary pulse theory is around 2.5 m.y.a., since this is a time of considerable activity in the hominid lineage (including the first documented evidence of the genus *Homo*). Was there a general evolutionary pulse at 2.5 m.y.a. associated with climate change that impacted a wide variety of African mammals? The evidence for this time period from the Lake Turkana region does not support any such rapid evolutionary event. In fact, species turnover between 3 and 2 million years ago in this area was quite gradual, with no indication of a pulse. Some species associated with drier habitats persisted throughout this million-year time period.

Vrba's hypothesis suggested a series of rapid, continentwide environmental changes, which then stimulated accelerated evolutionary changes in various animals (including hominids) around 2.5 m.y.a. This view is intriguing and was initially bolstered by some paleontological data, especially those from South Africa. However, for the Turkana area, "the absence of a pulse from the best calibrated, fossil-rich deposits from this time period weakens the case for rapid climatic forcing of continent scale ecological change and faunal turnover" (Behrensmeyer et al., 1997, p. 1593). Nevertheless, this region is only one segment of Africa and may not indicate broad climatic trends occurring elsewhere on the continent. The evolutionary pulse theory is thus not yet clearly established, but the proposal has stimulated innovative further research. In this way, we can see scientific methodology working at its best. Better data analyzed with better controls *should* yield better explanations. Indeed, Vrba has suggested two other periods of evolutionary pulses, one of these occurring at 1.8 m.y.a. These periods of increased speciation and extinction are again thought to be associated with significant evolutionary changes among the hominids. Interestingly, the data from the Turkana region lends support to fairly rapid turnover in mammalian species at 1.8 m.y.a. Thus, there may have been a significant role played by broad climatic influences, at least during some stages of hominid evolution.

We should not, however, assume that for any period, environmental explanations can be simply applied. What we should conclude is that such broad environmental changes probably were just one factor among many influencing the evolution of early African hominids at different times and in different regions of the continent.

Evolutionary pulse theory
A view that postulates a correlation of periods of hominid diversification during the Pliocene and early Pleistocene with major shifts in several African mammalian species. These changes in mammalian evolution, in turn, are thought to be related to periodic episodes of aridity.

Why Did Hominids Become Bipedal?

As we have noted several times, the adaptation of hominids to bipedal locomotion was *the* most fundamental adaptive shift among the early members of our family. But what were the factors that initiated this crucial change? Ecological theories, similar to some of those just discussed, have long been thought to be central to the development of bipedalism. Clearly, however, environmental influences would have to occur *before* documented evidence of well-adapted bipedal behavior. In other words, the major shift would have been at the end of the Miocene or beginning of the Pliocene. Although the evidence indicates that no *sudden* wide ecological change took place at this time, locally forests probably did become patchier as rainfall became more seasonal. Given the changing environmental conditions, did hominids come to the ground to seize the opportunities offered in these more open habitats? Did bipedalism then quickly ensue, stimulated by this new way of life? At a very general level, the answer to these questions is yes. Obviously, hominids did at some point become bipedal, and this adaptation took place on the ground. Likewise, hominids are more adapted to mixed and open-country habitats than are our closest ape cousins. Successful terrestrial bipedalism probably made possible the further adaptation to more arid, open-country terrain. Still, this rendition simply tells us *where* hominids found their niche, not *why*.

As always, one must be cautious when speculating about causation in evolution. It is all too easy to draw superficial conclusions. For example, it is often surmised that the mere fact that ground niches were available (and perhaps lacked direct competitors) inevitably led the earliest hominids to terrestrial bipedalism. But consider this: There are plenty of mammalian species, including some nonhuman primates, that also live mostly on the ground in open country—and they are not bipedal. Clearly, beyond such simplistic environmental determinism, some more complex explanation for hominid bipedalism is required. There must have been something *more* than just an environmental opportunity to explain this adaptation to such a unique lifestyle.

Another issue sometimes overlooked in the discussion of early hominid bipedal adaptation is that these creatures did not suddenly become *completely* terrestrial. We know, for example, that all terrestrial species of nonhuman primates (e.g., savanna baboons, hamadryas baboons, patas monkeys; see Chapter 7) regularly seek out "safe sleeping sites" off the ground. These safe havens help protect against predation and are usually found in trees or on cliff faces. Likewise, early hominids almost certainly sought safety at night *in the trees,* even after they became well adapted to terrestrial bipedalism during daytime foraging. Moreover, the continued opportunities for feeding in the trees would most likely have remained significant to early hominids, well after they were also utilizing ground-based resources.

A variety of hypotheses to explain why hominids initially became bipedal have been suggested and are summarized in Table 9–2. The primary influences claimed to have stimulated the shift to bipedalism include the ability to carry objects (and offspring); hunting on the ground; gathering of seeds and nuts; feeding from bushes; better view of open country (to spot predators); long-distance walking; and provisioning by males of females with dependent offspring.

These are all creative scenarios, but once again are not very conducive to rigorous testing and verification. Nevertheless, two of the more ambitious scenarios proposed by Clifford Jolly (1970) and Owen Lovejoy (1981) deserve further mention. Both of these views sought to link several aspects of early hominid ecology, feeding, and social behavior, and both utilized models derived from studies of contemporary nonhuman primates.

TABLE 9–2   Possible Factors Influencing the Initial Evolution of Bipedal Locomotion in Hominids

Factor	Speculated Influence	Comments
Carrying (objects, tools, weapons, infants)	Upright posture freed the arms to carry various objects (including offspring)	Charles Darwin emphasized this view, particularly relating to tools and weapons; however, evidence of stone tools is found much later in record than first evidence of bipedalism.
Hunting	As correlated with above theory, carrying weapons made hunting more efficient; in addition, long-distance walking may have been more energetically efficient (see below)	Systematic hunting is now thought not to have been practiced until after the origin of bipedal hominids (see Issue, Chapter 11)
Seed and nut gathering	Feeding on seeds and nuts occurred while standing upright	Model initially drawn from analogy with gelada baboons (see text)
Feeding from bushes	Upright posture provided access to seeds, berries, etc., in lower branches; analogous to adaptation seen in some specialized antelope	Climbing adaptation already existed as prior ancestral trait in earliest hominids (i.e., bush and tree feeding already was established prior to bipedal adaptation)
Visual surveillance	Standing up provided better view of surrounding countryside (view of potential predators as well as other group members)	Behavior seen occasionally in terrestrial primates (e.g., baboons); probably a contributing factor, but unlikely as "prime mover"
Long-distance walking	Covering long distances was more efficient for a biped than for a quadruped (during hunting or foraging); mechanical reconstructions show that bipedal walking is less energetically costly than quadrupedalism (this is not the case for bipedal *running*)	Same difficulties as with hunting explanation; long-distance foraging on ground also appears unlikely adaptation in *earliest* hominids
Male provisioning	Males carried back resources to dependent females and young	Monogamous bond suggested; however, most skeletal data appear to falsify this part of the hypothesis (see text)

Jolly's seed-eating hypothesis used the feeding behavior and ecology of gelada baboons as an analogy for very early hominids. In this view, early hominids are hypothesized to have adapted to open country and bipedalism as consequences of their *primary* adaptation to eating seeds and nuts (found on the ground). The key assumption is that early hominids were eating seeds acquired in similar ecological conditions to those of contemporary gelada baboons.

Lovejoy, meanwhile, has combined *presumed* aspects of early hominid ecology, feeding, pair bonding, infant care, and food sharing to devise his creative scenario. This view hinges on the following assumptions: (1) that the earliest hominids had offspring at least as K-selected (see p. 154) as other large-bodied hominoids; (2) that hominid males ranged widely and provisioned females and their young, who remained more tied to a "home base"; and (3) that males were paired *monogamously* with females.

As we have noted, while not strictly testable, such scenarios do make certain predictions (which can be verified). Accordingly, aspects of each scenario can be evaluated in light of more specific data (obtained from the paleoanthropological record). As pertaining to the seed-eating hypothesis, predictions relating to size of the back teeth in most early hominids are met; however, the proportions of the front teeth in many forms are not what would be expected in a committed seed eater. Moreover, the analogy with gelada baboons is not as informative as once thought, since these animals actually do not eat that many seeds. Finally, many of the characteristics suggested by Jolly to be restricted to hominids (and geladas) are also found in several late Miocene hominoids (who were not hominids). Thus, regarding the seed-eating hypothesis, the proposed dental and dietary adaptations do not appear to be linked specifically to hominid origins or bipedalism.

Similarly, further detailed analyses of data have questioned crucial elements of Lovejoy's male-provisioning scenario. The evidence that appears to most contradict this view is that *all* early hominids were quite sexually dimorphic. According to Lovejoy's model (and analogies with contemporary monogamous nonhuman primates such as gibbons), there should not be such dramatic differences in body size between males and females. Moreover, the notions of food sharing (presumably including considerable meat), home bases, and long-distance provisioning are questioned by more controlled interpretations of the archaeological record (see Box 9–2).

Another imaginative view is also relevant to this discussion of early hominid evolution, since it relates the adaptation to bipedalism (which was first) to increased brain expansion (which came later). This interpretation, proposed by Dean Falk, of the State University of New York at Albany, suggests that an upright posture put severe constraints on brain size (since blood circulation and drainage would have been altered and thus cooling would have been more limited than in quadrupeds). Falk thus hypothesizes that new brain-cooling mechanisms must have coevolved with bipedalism, articulated in what she calls the "radiator theory" (Falk, 1990). Falk further surmises that the requirements for better brain cooling would have been particularly marked as hominids adapted to open-country ground living on the hot African savanna. Another interesting pattern observed by Falk concerns two different cooling adaptations found in different early hominid species. She thus suggests that the type of "radiator" adapted in the genus *Homo* was particularly significant in reducing constraints on brain size—which presumably limited some other early hominids. The radiator theory works well, since it not only helps explain the relationship of bipedalism to later brain expansion, but also explains why only some hominids became dramatically encephalized.

The radiator theory, too, has been criticized by some paleoanthropologists. Most notably, the presumed species distinction concerning varying cooling mechanisms is not so obvious as suggested by the hypothesis. Both types of venous drainage systems can be found in contemporary *Homo sapiens* as well as within various early hominid species (i.e., the variation is intraspecific, not just interspecific). Indeed, in some early hominid specimens, both systems can be found in the *same* individual (expressed on each side of the skull). Moreover, as Falk herself has noted, the radiator itself did not lead to larger brains; it simply helped reduce constraints on increased encephalization among hominids. It thus requires some *further* mechanism (prime mover) to explain why, in some hominid species, brain size increased in the manner it did.

As with any such ambitious effort, it is all too easy to find holes. Falk aptly reminds us that "the search for such 'prime movers' is highly speculative and these theories do not lend themselves to hypothesis testing" (Falk, 1990, p. 334). Nevertheless, the attempt to interrelate various lines of evidence, the use of contemporary primate models, and predictions concerning further evidence obtained from paleoanthropological contexts all conform to sound scientific methodology. All the views discussed here have contributed to this venture—one not just aimed at understanding our early ancestors, but one also seeking to refine its methodologies and scientific foundation.

SUMMARY

The biocultural nature of human evolution requires that any meaningful study of human origins examine both biological and cultural information. The multidisciplinary approach of paleoanthropology is designed to bring together varied scientific specializations to reconstruct the anatomy, behavior, and environments of early hominids. Such a task is centered around the skills of the geologist, paleontologist, paleoecologist, archaeologist, and physical anthropologist.

Much of what we know about the origins of human culture between 2 and 1 m.y.a. comes from archaeological excavations by Mary Leakey at Olduvai Gorge, in East Africa. Olduvai's well-documented stratigraphic sequence, its superior preservation of remains, and the varied dating techniques possible there have made it an information bonanza for paleoanthropologists. Excavated sites have yielded a wealth of bones of fossil animals, as well as artifact traces of hominid behavior. Ecological reconstructions of habitat and dietary preferences are thereby possible and inform us in great detail concerning crucial evolutionary processes affecting early hominid populations.

Archaeologists are better able to interpret the "bones and stones" of earlier populations through experimentation. In recent years, much new light has been shed on the techniques of making stone tools as well as the factors affecting preservation of bone.

Broader interpretations, leading to several speculative scenarios, have also been attempted to help us understand the environmental influences and behavioral adaptations exhibited by early hominids. Most notably, attempts have been made to link the earliest origins of hominids as well as somewhat later diversifications to general ecological changes in Africa. Finally, many researchers have speculated concerning the factors influencing that most fundamental of all early hominid adaptations, the development of bipedal locomotion. In the next chapter, we will survey the fossil hominid evidence in South and East Africa that informs us directly about human origins during the Plio-Pleistocene.

QUESTIONS FOR REVIEW

1. Why are cultural remains so important in the interpretation of human evolution?
2. How are early hominid sites found, and what kind of specialist is involved in the excavation and analysis of paleoanthropological data?
3. What kinds of paleoanthropological information have been found at Olduvai Gorge? Why is this particular locality so rich in material?
4. What techniques have been used to date early hominid sites at Olduvai? Why is more than one technique necessary for accurate dating?
5. Why are context and association so important in the interpretation of archaeological remains?
6. What different activities can be inferred from the different kinds of sites at Olduvai? Discuss alternative views in the interpretation of these "sites."
7. How do archaeologists determine the functions of ancient stone tools?
8. What is a scenario? How does it differ from a scientific hypothesis? Give an example.

9. What environmental factors have been postulated as important in influencing the origins of the first hominids? How satisfactory are these explanations?

10. What are some of the factors thought to be important in influencing the early evolution of bipedal locomotion?

SUGGESTED FURTHER READING

Binford, Lewis. 1981. *Bones: Ancient Men and Myths.* New York: Academic Press.

Leakey, Mary. 1984. *Disclosing the Past. An Autobiography.* Garden City, NJ: Doubleday.

Leakey, Richard. 1981. *The Making of Mankind.* New York: Dutton.

Rasmussen, D. T. (ed.). 1993. *The Origin and Evolution of Humans and Humanness.* Boston: Jones and Bartlett.

Willis, Delta. 1989. *The Hominid Gang: Behind the Scenes in the Search for Human Origins.* New York: Viking.

RESOURCES ON THE INTERNET

 Wadsworth Anthropology Resource Center
http://anthropology.wadsworth.com

The companion website for this text includes a range of enrichment material focused on the chapter's topic. While online you can enhance your understanding of the chapter by exploring one of the several additional Internet exercises, by researching topics, and by accessing full articles on InfoTrac College Edition. You can also reinforce the concepts by taking online practice exams.

Internet Exercises

The Institute for Human Origins is one of the major research institutes in paleoanthropology. At their website (**http://www.asu.edu/clas/iho**) you can view pictures of some of their field research as well as some of the fossils they have found. Read through the science section and look at the photography section. In particular, spend some time looking at the pictures of the fieldwork at Hadar and Swartkrans. What different fieldwork methods were used at these two sites?

 InfoTrac College Edition
http://www.infotrac-college.com/wadsworth

Search InfoTrac College Edition for *bipedalism*. What hypotheses are offered in these articles for the origins of bipedalism? Do you find any single hypothesis more convincing than the others? Why or why not?

The Piltdown Caper: Who Dunnit?

When first announced to the world in 1912, *Eoanthropus dawsoni* (Dawson's Dawn Man) created an anthropological sensation. Found during 1911 in Sussex in the south of England by Charles Dawson, a lawyer and amateur geologist, this "fossil" was to bewilder two generations of anthropologists. "Piltdown man," as he popularly came to be called, was composed of a fragmented skull and parts of a lower jaw. The enigma of the fossil from the very beginning was the combination of a large *sapiens*-like partial skull with an apelike lower jaw.

Most tantalizing of all, Piltdown was apparently extremely ancient, associated with long extinct fauna, such as mastodon, hippo, and rhino, all suggesting a date of early Pleistocene. A puzzling feature was the presence of these early fossils mixed in with clearly late Pleistocene fauna. The prevailing consensus, however, was that Piltdown was indeed ancient, "the earliest known representative of man in western Europe."

Despite its seeming incongruities, Piltdown was eagerly accepted by British scientists, including A. Keith, G. Elliot Smith, and A. Smith Woodward (all later knighted). What made the fossil such a delectable treat was that it confirmed just what had been expected, a combination of *modern* ape and *modern* human characteristics—a true "missing link." We, of course, know that no ancestral fossil form is a 50-50 compromise between modern ones, but represents its own unique adaptation.

Besides inciting enthusiasm for a missing link, the fossil also represented a "true man" as opposed to the obviously primitive beasts (Java "man," Neandertals) found elsewhere. Such a fervently biased desire to find an "ancient modern" in the human lineage has obscured evolutionary studies for decades and still causes confusion in some circles.

While generally accepted in England, experts in France, Germany, and the United States felt uneasy about Piltdown. Many

FIGURE 1
The Piltdown skull.

Robert Jurmain

critics, however, were silenced when a second fragmentary find was announced in 1917 (actually found in 1915) in an area 2 miles away from the original site. The matter stood in limbo for years, with some scientists as enthusiastic supporters of the Piltdown man and others remaining doubters. The uneasiness continued to fester as more hominid material accumulated in Java, China, and (particularly in regard to australopithecines) South Africa. None of these hominids showed the pecu-

liar combination of a human cranium with an apelike jaw seen in Piltdown, but actually indicated the reverse pattern.

The final proof of the true nature of the Dawn Man came in the early 1950s, when British scientists began an intensive reexamination of the Piltdown material. In particular, fluorine analysis performed by Kenneth Oakley showed both the skull and jaw to be relatively recent. Later, more extensive tests showed the jaw to be younger than the skull and *very* recent in date. Now a much more critical eye was turned to all the material. The teeth, looking initially as though they had been worn down flat in the typical hominid fashion, were apparently ape teeth filed down deliberately to give that impression. The mixed bag of fauna had apparently been acquired from all manner of places (a fossil elephant came from Tunisia in North Africa), and the fossils had been chemically stained so that they were all the same color. Finally, some "tools" found at Piltdown had also met the hand of a forger, for the bone implements showed modifications that apparently could have been made only by a metal knife.

The "fossil" itself had probably been purchased from local dealers. The skull probably came from a moderately ancient grave (a few thousand years old), and the jaw was a specially broken, filed, and stained mandible of a fairly recently deceased adolescent orangutan! The evidence was indisputable: a deliberate hoax. But who did it?

Just about everyone connected with the "crime" has at one time or another been implicated, beginning with Piltdown's discoverer, Charles Dawson. Yet Dawson was an amateur and thus may have lacked the expertise to carry out the admittedly crafty job of anatomical modification.

In addition, at various times, suspicions have been cast toward neuroanatomist Sir Grafton Elliot Smith, geologist W. J. Sollas, anatomist Sir Arthur Keith, and French philosopher and archaeologist Father Pierre Teilhard de Chardin. Even the legendary mystery writer and physician, Sir Arthur Conan Doyle (creator of Sherlock Holmes), was at one time suspected (Winslow and Meyer, 1983).

An unsolved mystery is always an irresistible temptation; so the Piltdown "affair" has remained a challenge to several generations of amateur sleuths (especially those otherwise employed as academics). It seemed, however, that there was little hope of solving the mystery, as the forgery had been perpetrated 90 years ago (and its demonstration as a hoax announced 50 years ago). Without some new clues, the case seemed unsolvable and the trail stone cold.

Enter, however, Professor Brian Gardinier of King's College, London, and a startling piece of new evidence. First, the evidence: While cleaning the attic at London's Natural History Museum, workers came across a trunk with the initials of Martin Hinton, a curator of zoology at the museum

at the time of the fraud. Contained within the trunk were several pieces of artificially carved and chemically stained fossil bones. The trunk was found in the mid-1970s, but its contents required meticulous analysis and corroboration. Here is where Professor Gardinier comes in. His own investigations had led him to circumstantial evidence implicating Hinton. The contents of the trunk, however, proved to be the final conclusive evidence—as the fossils had been deliberately modified employing exactly the same combination of chemicals as that used on the Piltdown material (it seems that the pieces in the trunk were used in "trial runs" by the forger—Hinton—to practice his technique). Hinton's motives are now difficult to establish, but there is some reason to believe he had a grudge against Smith Woodward, who had been his supervisor at the museum. If, indeed, the goal was to embarrass Smith Woodward, Hinton did succeed spectacularly—since Smith Woodward spent most of his professional career (he died in 1944) in a spirited defense of the significance and validity of the Piltdown find.

After years of study, Professor Gardinier was prepared to announce his findings—which he did in 1996 to much fanfare and media attention. Has the mystery finally been solved? Since the riddle has survived for nine decades, it is difficult now for some to abandon the hunt. There are still a great number of sleuths out there yearning to keep the mystery alive!

Critical Thinking Questions

1. Why do you think hoaxes are occasionally perpetrated in science?
2. Why are such hoaxes inevitably discovered, even if it is years later?
3. More importantly, *how* are such further discoveries made?
4. If you had suspicions regarding the authenticity of a scientific study, how would you check it?

Sources

Gee, Henry. 1996. "Box of Bones 'Clinches' Identity of Piltdown Palaeontology Hoaxer." *Nature* 381: 261–262

Spencer, Frank. 1990. *Piltdown: A Scientific Forgery.* New York: Oxford University Press.

Weiner, J. W. 1955. *The Piltdown Forgery.* London: Oxford University Press.

Winslow, John Hathaway, and Alfred Meyer. 1983. "The Perpetrator at Piltdown." *Science '83* (September): 33–43.

CHAPTER

10

CONTENTS

Trail of hominid footprints fossilized in volcanic ash at Laetoli, Tanzania (approximate age, 3.7 million years)

Hominid Origins

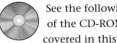

Introduction

In Chapter 9, we discussed the techniques used by paleoanthropologists to collect and interpret basic background data relating to the evolution of early hominids. Such geological, ecological, and archaeological information helps us understand the environments and behaviors of the earliest members of the hominid family.

In this chapter, we turn to the physical evidence of the hominid fossils themselves. From the Pliocene epoch and the first half of the Pleistocene, a very large fossil collection of these early hominids has been found in Africa. Comprising the time span of 5–1 m.y.a., this period is usually referred to as the **Plio-Pleistocene**. These fossil hominids are a rich and varied lot, and their discovery has stimulated a great deal of interest among both the scientific community and the general public. Given these circumstances, it is perhaps no great surprise that the interpretation of these finds has also generated considerable controversy. Thus, in addition to reviewing the anatomical details revealed directly in the fossil material, we will also attempt to sort out the complex and frequently conflicting interpretations concerning the evolutionary patterns of Plio-Pleistocene hominids.

The Bipedal Adaptation

In our overview of behavioral reconstructions in early hominids, we highlighted several hypotheses that attempt to explain *why* bipedal locomotion first evolved in the hominids. Here we turn to the specific anatomical (i.e., **morphological**) evidence that shows us when, where, and how hominid bipedal locomotion evolved.

In our discussion of primate anatomical trends in Chapter 5, we noted that there is a general tendency in all primates for erect body posture and some bipedalism. However, of all living primates, efficient bipedalism as the primary form of locomotion is seen *only* in hominids. Functionally, the human mode of locomotion is most clearly shown in our striding gait, where weight is alternately placed on a single fully extended hind limb. This specialized form of locomotion has developed to a point where energy levels are used to near peak efficiency. Such is not the case in nonhuman primates, who move bipedally with hips and knees bent and maintain balance in a clumsy and inefficient manner.

Our mode of locomotion is indeed extraordinary, involving as it does an activity in which "the body, step by step, teeters on the edge of catastrophe" (Napier, 1967, p. 56). The problem is to maintain balance on the "stance" leg while the "swing" leg is off the ground. In fact, during normal walking, both feet are simultaneously on the ground only about 25 percent of the time, and as speed of locomotion increases, this figure becomes even smaller.

To maintain a stable center of balance in this complex form of locomotion, many drastic structural/anatomical alterations in the basic primate quadrupedal pattern are required. The most dramatic changes are seen in the pelvis. The pelvis is composed of three elements: two *ossa coxae* (*sing.*, os coxae) joined at the back to the sacrum (Fig. 10–1). In a quadruped, the ossa coxae are elongated bones positioned along each side of the lower portion of the spine and oriented more or less parallel to it. In hominids, the pelvis is comparatively much shorter and broader and extends around to the side (Fig. 10–2). This configuration helps to stabilize the line of weight transmission, in a bipedal posture, from the lower back to the hip joint (Fig. 10–3).

A number of consequences resulted from the remodeling of the pelvis during early hominid evolution. Broadening the two sides and extending them around to the side and front of the body produced a basin-shaped structure that helps support the abdominal organs (indeed, *pelvis* means "basin" in Latin). Moreover, these

See the following sections of the CD-ROM for topics covered in this chapter: Virtual Lab 7, sections I; Virtual Lab 8, section I; Virtual Labs 9 and 10; and Virtual Lab 12, section I.

Plio-Pleistocene
Pertaining to the Pliocene and first half of the Pleistocene, a time range of 5–1 m.y.a. For this time period, the earliest fossil hominids have been found in Africa.

Morphological
Pertaining to the form and structure of organisms.

Left os coxae
Right os coxae
Sacrum

FIGURE 10–1
The human pelvis: various elements shown on a modern skeleton.

FIGURE 10–2

The human os coxae, composed of three bones (right side shown).

Ilium

Pubis

Ischium

FIGURE 10–3

Ossa coxae. (a) *Homo sapiens.* (b) Early hominid (*Australopithecus*) from South Africa. (c) Great ape. Note especially the length and breadth of the iliac blade and the line of weight transmission (shown in red).

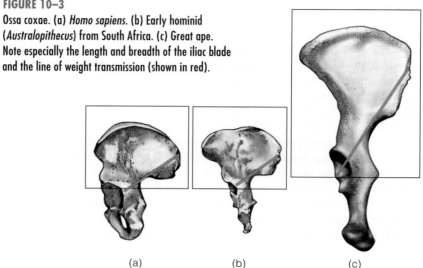

(a)   (b)   (c)

Foramen magnum

The opening at the base of the skull through which the spinal cord passes as it enters the body to descend through the vertebral column. In quadrupeds, it is located more to the rear of the skull, while in bipeds, it is located farther beneath the skull.

alterations repositioned the attachments of several key muscles that act on the hip and leg, changing their mechanical function. Probably the most important of these altered relationships is that involving the *gluteus maximus*, the largest muscle in the body, which in humans forms the bulk of the buttocks. In quadrupeds, the gluteus maximus is positioned to the side of the hip and functions to pull the thigh to the side, away from the body. But in humans, this muscle acts, along with the hamstrings, to extend the thigh, pulling it to the rear during walking and running (Fig 10–4). Indeed, the gluteus maximus is a powerful extensor of the thigh and provides additional force, particularly during running and climbing.

Modifications also occurred in other parts of the skeleton as a result of the shift to bipedalism. The most significant of these are summarized in Box 10–1 on page 246 and include (1) repositioning of the **foramen magnum**, the opening at the base of the skull through which the spinal cord emerges; (2) the addition of

FIGURE 10–4

Comparisons of important muscles that act to extend the hip. Note that the attachment surface (origin, shown in red) of the gluteus maximus in humans (a) is farther in back of the hipbone than in a chimpanzee standing bipedally (b). Conversely, in chimpanzees, the hamstrings are farther in back of the knee.

 See Virtual Lab 9, section I, for a discussion of the evolution of bipedalism.

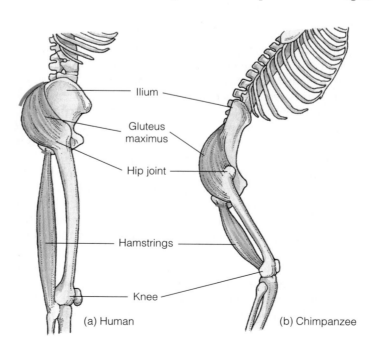

Ilium

Gluteus maximus

Hip joint

Hamstrings

Knee

(a) Human   (b) Chimpanzee

spinal curves that facilitate the transmission of the weight of the upper body to the hips in an upright posture; (3) shortening and broadening of the pelvis and the stabilization of weight transmission (discussed earlier); (4) lengthening of the hind limb, thus increasing stride length; (5) angling of the femur (thighbone) inward to bring the knees and feet closer together under the body; and (6) several structural changes in the foot, including the development of a longitudinal arch and realignment of the big toe in parallel with the other toes (i.e., it was no longer divergent).

As you can appreciate, the evolution of hominid bipedalism required complex anatomical reorganization. For natural selection to produce anatomical change of the magnitude seen in hominids, the benefits of bipedal locomotion must have been significant indeed. We mentioned in Chapter 9 several possible adaptive advantages that bipedal locomotion *may* have conferred upon early hominids. However, these all remain hypotheses (even more accurately, they could be called scenarios), and we lack adequate data with which to test the various proposed alternatives.

Still, given the anatomical alterations that efficient bipedalism necessitated, there must have been some major behavioral stimuli influencing its development. In the interpretation of evolutionary history, biologists are fond of saying that form follows function. In other words, during evolution, organisms do not undergo significant reorganization in structure *unless* these changes (over many generations) assist individuals in some functional capacity (and, in so doing, increase their reproductive success). Such changes did not necessarily occur all at once, but probably evolved over a fairly long period of time. Nevertheless, once behavioral influences initiated certain structural modifications, the process gained momentum and proceeded irreversibly.

We say that hominid bipedalism is *habitual* and *obligate*. By habitual, we mean that hominids, unlike any other primate, move bipedally as their standard and most efficient mode of locomotion. By obligate, we mean that hominids are committed to bipedalism and cannot locomote efficiently in any other manner. For example, the loss of grasping ability in the foot makes climbing much more difficult for humans (although by no means impossible). The central task, then, in trying to understand the earliest members of the hominid family is to identify anatomical features that indicate bipedalism and to interpret to what degree these organisms were committed to this form of locomotion (i.e., was it habitual and was it obligate?).

What structural patterns are observable in early hominids, and what do they imply regarding locomotor function? All the major structural changes required for bipedalism are seen in early hominids from East and South Africa (at least insofar as the evidence has thus far been comprehensively reported). In particular, the pelvis, as clearly documented by several excellently preserved specimens, was dramatically remodeled to support weight in a bipedal stance (see Fig. 10–3b).

In addition, other structural changes shown in even the earliest definitive hominid postcranial remains further confirm the pattern seen in the pelvis. For example, the vertebral column (as known from specimens in East and South Africa) shows the same curves as in modern hominids. The lower limbs were also elongated and were apparently proportionately about as long as in modern humans (although the arms were longer). Further, the carrying angle of weight support from the hip to the knee was also very similar to that seen in *Homo sapiens*.

Fossil evidence of early hominid foot structure has come from two sites in South Africa, and especially important are some recently announced new fossils from Sterkfontein (Clarke and Tobias, 1995). These specimens, consisting of four articulating elements from the ankle and big toe, indicate that the heel and longitudinal arch were both well adapted for a bipedal gait. However, the paleoanthropologists (Ron Clarke and Phillip Tobias) who analyzed these remains also suggest that the large toe was *divergent*, unlike the hominid pattern shown in Box 10–1. If the large toe really did possess this anatomical position, it most likely would have aided the foot in grasping. In turn, this grasping ability (as in other primates) would

BOX 10-1   A CLOSER LOOK

Major Features of Bipedal Locomotion

During hominid evolution, several major structural features throughout the body have been reorganized (from that seen in other primates) to facilitate efficient bipedal locomotion. These are illustrated here, beginning with the head and progressing to the foot: (a) The foramen magnum (shown in red) is repositioned farther underneath the head, so that the head is more or less balanced on the spine (and thus requires less robust neck muscles to hold the head upright). (b) The spine has two distinctive curves—a backward (thoracic) one and a forward (lumbar) one—that keep the trunk

have enabled early hominids to more effectively exploit arboreal habitats. Finally, since anatomical remodeling is always constrained by a set of complex functional compromises, a foot highly capable of grasping and climbing is *less* capable as a stable platform during bipedal locomotion. Some researchers therefore see early hominids as not necessarily obligate bipeds. Further investigation of the cave site in 1998 revealed a remarkable find, the remains of a nearly complete skeleton belonging to the same individual from which the foot came (see p. 265).

Further evidence for evolutionary changes in the foot skeleton comes from Olduvai Gorge in Tanzania, where a nearly complete hominid foot is preserved (Fig. 10–5), and from Hadar in Ethiopia, where numerous foot elements have been (and weight) centered above the pelvis. (c) The pelvis is shaped more in the form of a basin to support internal organs; moreover, the ossa coxae (specifically, iliac blades) are shorter and broader, thus stabilizing weight transmission. (d) Lower limbs are elongated, as shown by the proportional lengths of various body segments (e.g., in humans the thigh comprises 20 percent of body height, while in gorillas it comprises only 11 percent). (e) The femur is angled inward, keeping the legs more directly under the body; modified knee anatomy also permits full extension of this joint. (f) The big toe is enlarged and brought in line with the other toes; in addition, a distinctive longitudinal arch (shown in red) forms, helping absorb shock and adding propulsive spring.

recovered. As in the remains from South Africa, the East African fossils suggest a well-adapted bipedal gait. The arches are developed, but some differences in the ankle also imply that considerable flexibility was possible (again, suggested for continued adaptation to climbing). As we will see, some researchers have recently concluded that many early forms of hominids probably spent considerable time in the trees. Moreover, they may not have been quite as efficient bipeds as has previously been suggested. Nevertheless, to this point, *all* the early hominids that have been identified from Africa are thought by most researchers to have been both habitual and obligate bipeds (notwithstanding the new evidence from South Africa and the earliest traces from East Africa, all of which will require further study).

FIGURE 10–5
A nearly complete hominid foot (OH 8) from Olduvai Gorge, Tanzania.

FIGURE 10–6
The East African Rift Valley system and locations of major hominid sites.

Early Hominids in the Plio-Pleistocene

The beginnings of hominid differentiation almost certainly have their roots in the late Miocene (circa 10–5 m.y.a.). Sometime during the period between 7 and 5 m.y.a., hominids began to adapt more fully to their peculiar ground-living niche, and fossil evidence from this period would be most illuminating, particularly any remains indicating a bipedal adaptation. However, only incomplete information is presently available concerning the course of hominid evolution during this 2-million-year period—although new finds are beginning to fill in this crucial gap. Somewhat later in the fossil record, beginning around 4.5 m.y.a., the evidence picks up considerably. We now have a wealth of fossil hominid material from the Pliocene and the earliest stages of the Pleistocene (5–1 m.y.a.), and as noted, this whole span is usually referred to as the Plio-Pleistocene.

The East African Rift Valley

Stretching along a more than 1,200-mile trough extending through Ethiopia, Kenya, and Tanzania from the Red Sea in the north to the Serengeti Plain in the south is the eastern branch of the Great Rift Valley of Africa (Fig. 10–6). This massive geological feature has been associated with active mountain building, faulting, and vulcanism over the last several million years.

Because of these gigantic earth movements, earlier sediments (normally buried under hundreds of feet of earth and rock) were literally thrown to the surface, where they became exposed to the trained eye of the paleoanthropologist. Such earth movements have exposed Miocene beds at sites in Kenya, along the shores of Lake Victoria, where abundant remains of early fossil hominoids have been found. In addition, Plio-Pleistocene sediments are also exposed all along the Rift Valley, and paleoanthropologists in recent years have made the most of this unique opportunity.

More than just exposing normally hidden deposits, rifting has stimulated volcanic activity, which in turn has provided a valuable means of chronometrically dating many sites in East Africa. Unlike the sites in South Africa (see pp. 263–271), those along the Rift Valley are *datable* and have thus yielded much crucial information concerning the precise chronology of early hominid evolution.

The Earliest East African Hominids

The site that focused attention on East Africa as a potential paleoanthropological gold mine was Olduvai Gorge in northern Tanzania. As discussed in great detail in Chapter 9, this site has offered unique opportunities because of the remarkable preservation of geological, paleontological, and archaeological records. Following Mary Leakey's discovery of "Zinj" in 1959 (and the subsequent dating of its site at 1.75 m.y.a.), numerous other areas in East Africa have been surveyed and several intensively explored. We will review the fossil discoveries from these sites and briefly discuss their chronological and geological context, beginning with the earliest.

See Virtual Lab 8, section I, for a discussion of the fossil evidence for the earliest hominids.

Earliest Traces

Exciting new discoveries, dating to late in the Miocene or early in the Pliocene from several localities in Kenya and Ethiopia, are shedding light on the earliest stages of hominid evolution (see Box 10–2 on page 250).

Tugen Hills   The oldest of these finds come from sites in the Tugen Hills of central Kenya, near Lake Baringo (Pickford and Senut, 2001; Senut et al., 2001). Good radiometric determinations place the age of the remains at close to 6 m.y.a.

The fossil remains are a mixed assortment, with a couple of pieces of lower jaw and several isolated teeth. Most intriguing, however, are a few limb bone pieces, including two excellently preserved femora (Table 10–1). From these latter fossils especially, French paleontologist Brigitte Senut (of the Museum of Natural History in Paris) and her colleagues are convinced that these 6-million-year-old primates walked *bipedally* and are thus hominids. However, there are also some unusual aspects of the teeth, mostly suggesting a primitive, apelike morphology. This curious combination of features has led the French scientists to assign the remains to a completely new genus and species (*Orrorin tugenensis*).

Since the Tugen Hills fossils were first discovered in 2000, the popular press has dubbed this form "Millennium Man." The initial reports, published early in 2001, were rather sketchy and did not initially receive much support from other scholars. To establish satisfactorily whether "Millennium Man" is indeed the earliest hominid yet found will require further study. Nevertheless, the well-preserved lower limb bones should help considerably in determining clearly whether (or not) these animals moved about bipedally. Moreover, the French team has announced additional discoveries made in 2001, but as of this writing, these new fossils have not been described.

Middle Awash   Coming from a few hundred miles north of the Tugen Hills, in the Middle Awash region of Ethiopia, another group of quite early fossils was also first described in 2001. Yohannes Haile-Selassie, an anthropology graduate student at the University of California, Berkeley, discovered the first remains in 1997, with further discoveries extending to 2001 (Haile-Selassie, 2001). Well-controlled radiometric dating determinations place the fossils in the late Miocene (at 5.8–5.2 m.y.a.),

BOX 10–2   A CLOSER LOOK

Something Old, Something New: Recent Finds of Hominids in East Africa

Paleoanthropologists Martin Pickford and Brigitte Senut with specimens of *Orrorin tugenensis*, discovered at the Tugen Hills, Kenya. Dating to 6.0 million years ago, these are perhaps the oldest hominids yet discovered.

Paleoanthropologist, Yohannes Hailie-Selassie, holds a tooth of *Ardipithecus ramidus*. This specimen from the Middle Awash, Ethiopia, dated at 5.8–5.2 m.y., is potentially among the earliest hominids ever found.

Professor Tim White of the University of California, Berkeley, shown excavating at Bouri, Ethiopia. Nearby, a cranium of *Australopithecus garhi* (dated 2.5 m.y.) was discovered.

Meave Leakey and Kenyan colleagues, shown at Kanapoi holding some of their *Australopithecus anamensis* fossil discoveries (dated at 4.2–3.9 m.y.).

New hominid discoveries from Aramis, dated at 4.4 m.y. Alemayehu Asfaw is holding his discovery of an upper arm bone (humerus). In the background, team members search for other fragments; parts of all three bones of the upper appendage of one *Ardipithecus ramidus* individual were discovered.

TABLE 10–1 Discoveries of Earliest Hominid* Fossil Remains

Site	Dates (m.y.a.)	Taxonomic Designation	Fossil Sample
Belohdelie (Ethiopia)	3.9–3.8	*Australopithecus afarensis*	5 pieces of cranium
Allia Bay (East Turkana) (Kenya)	3.9	*Australopithecus anamensis*	13 specimens
Kanapoi (Kenya)	4.2–3.9	*Australopithecus anamensis*	9 specimens
Aramis (Ethiopia)	4.4	*Ardipithecus ramidus*	Up to 50 individuals
Tabarin (Kenya) (Chemeron Beds)	5.0	Uncertain	1 specimen (partial mandible)
Mabaget (Kenya) (Chemeron Beds)	5.1–5.0	Uncertain	1 specimen (partial subadult humerus)
Lothagam (Kenya)	5.8–5.6	Uncertain (possibly *Ardipithecus*)	1 specimen (partial mandible)
Middle Awash (five localities)	5.8–5.2	*Ardipithecus ramidus*	11 specimens (minimum of 5 individuals), including teeth, one jaw fragment, and a few limb bones (most notably, a complete toe bone)
Tugen Hills (Kenya) (Lukeino Beds, four localities)	6.0	*Orrorin tugenensis*	13 specimens (minimum of 5 individuals), including teeth, jaw fragments, and quite complete limb bones

*Note: In some cases, hominid status is not yet well established.

just a little later than the Tugen Hills finds. These latter fossil remains are quite fragmentary, including mostly teeth, a jaw fragment, and just a few pieces of the limb skeleton, the latter including one toe bone, a phalanx from the middle of the foot (see Appendix A, Fig. A–8). From suggestive clues seen in this toe bone, Haile-Selassie concludes that this primate was a well-adapted *biped* (once again, the best supporting evidence of hominid status).

There are other, more complete remains from the Middle Awash area discovered at the Aramis site (discussed shortly), originating a little later in time. These remains have been assigned to the genus *Ardipithecus,* and for the moment, Haile-Selassie has determined that the earlier fossils from this same region should be placed in this same genus. Nevertheless, like the Tugen Hills finds, these very early Ethiopian fossils will require more intensive examination to confirm their hominid status (see Table 10–1 for further details).

Other Early Discoveries In addition to the reasonably complete remains from the Tugen Hills and the Middle Awash, there are several scattered finds of what many researchers think may be other very early hominids. In the time range 5–4 m.y.a., there are three additional localities (two from central Kenya and one from Ethiopia). However, none of this further material is particularly informative (or diagnostic), since only a single (fragmentary) specimen has been recovered from each locality (see Table 10–1 for a complete listing).

Ardipithecus from Aramis (Ethiopia)

The Middle Awash sites are in one of the most exciting areas for future research in East Africa, the Afar Triangle of northeastern Ethiopia, where the Red Sea, Rift Valley, and Gulf of Aden all intersect. From this area have come many of the most important recent discoveries bearing on human origins. Several areas have yielded

Aramis
(air´-ah-miss)

(a)

(b)

FIGURE 10–7
Position of the foramen magnum in (a) a human and (b) a chimpanzee. Note the more forward position in the human cranium.

Australopithecus
An early hominid genus, known from the Plio-Pleistocene of Africa, characterized by bipedal locomotion, a relatively small brain, and large back teeth.

fossil remains in recent decades, and many potentially very rich sites are currently being explored. One of these sites quite recently discovered, located in the Middle Awash (along the banks of the Awash River), is called **Aramis.** Initial radiometric dating of the sediments places the hominid remains at 4.4 m.y.a., making this the earliest substantial *collection* of hominids yet discovered.

Fossil remains from Aramis were excavated between 1992 and 1995 and include up to 50 different individuals (Wolpoff, 1999). This crucial and quite large fossil assortment includes several dental specimens as well as an upper arm bone (humerus) and some fragmentary cranial remains. Most exciting of all, in 1995, 40 percent of a skeleton was discovered; however, the bones are all encased in limestone matrix, thus requiring a long and tedious process to remove the fossils intact from the cementlike material surrounding them. In fact, as of this writing, the Aramis remains (including the skeleton) have not yet been fully scientifically described. Nevertheless, details from initial reports are highly suggestive that these remains are, in fact, very early hominids (if not the earliest; see earlier discussion).

First of all, in an Aramis partial cranium, the *foramen magnum* is positioned farther forward in the base of the skull than is the case in quadrupeds (Fig. 10–7). Second, features of the humerus also differ from those seen in quadrupeds, indicating that the Aramis humerus did not function in locomotion to support weight (i.e., the upper limbs were free). From these two features, the provisional interpretation by Tim White, of the University of California, Berkeley, and his colleagues was that the Aramis individuals were *bipedal.* Moreover, initial interpretation of the partial skeleton (while not yet fully cleaned and reported) also suggests obligate bipedalism (Wolpoff, 1999).

Nevertheless, these were clearly quite primitive hominids, displaying an array of characteristics quite distinct from other members of our family. These primitive characteristics include flattening of the cranial base and relatively thin enamel caps on the molar teeth. From measurements of the humerus head, Wolpoff (1999) estimates a body weight of 42 kg (93 pounds); if this humerus comes from a male individual, this weight estimate is very similar to that hypothesized for other Plio-Pleistocene hominids (see Table 10–3, p. 268).

Thus, current conclusions (which will be either unambiguously confirmed or falsified as the skeleton is fully cleaned and studied) interpret the Aramis remains as among the earliest hominids yet known. These individuals from Aramis, although very primitive hominids, were apparently bipedal, although not necessarily in the same way that later hominids were.

Tim White and colleagues have recently argued (White et al., 1995) that the fossil hominids from Aramis are so primitive and so different from other early hominids that they should be assigned to a new genus (and, necessarily, a new species as well): *Ardipithecus ramidus.* Most especially, the thin enamel caps on the molars are in dramatic contrast to all other confirmed early hominids, who show quite thick enamel caps. These other early hominid forms (all somewhat later than *Ardipithecus*) are placed in the genus **Australopithecus.** Moreover, White and his associates have further suggested that as the earliest and most primitive hominid yet discovered, *Ardipithecus* may possibly be the root species for all later hominids. This view does not take into account the recently discovered Tugen Hills finds, which are provisionally assigned to the new genus *Orrorin.* However, this interpretation does encompass the earlier remains from the Middle Awash—which, for the moment, are also included within *Ardipithecus.*

Another intriguing aspect of all these late Miocene/early Pliocene locales (i.e., Tugen Hills, early Middle Awash sites, and Aramis) relates to the ancient environments associated with the suggested earliest of hominids. Rather than the more open grassland savanna habitats so characteristic of most later hominid sites, the environments at these early locales is more heavily forested. Perhaps we are seeing at Aramis and these other ancient sites the very beginnings of hominid divergence, very soon after the division from the African apes!

Australopithecus from East Africa

Several sites in Ethiopia, Kenya, and Tanzania have yielded remains of somewhat later hominids than the *Ardipithecus* remains from Aramis. Dating from 4.2 m.y.a. to approximately 1.4 m.y.a., most of these later East African fossils are included in the genus *Australopithecus*.* Note, however, that in the later half of this time span, some other specimens are placed in the genus *Homo*.

The earliest members of *Australopithecus* found to date come from two sites near Lake Turkana in northern Kenya (Allia Bay and Kanapoi). Like the other sites we have been reviewing, these localities have only recently been fully explored, with the majority of discoveries coming during 1994 and 1995 (Leakey et al., 1995). Not as many specimens have been found at these two sites as at Aramis (see Table 10–1), but from what has been discovered, Meave Leakey and her colleagues have detected some interesting patterns. First, as with the Aramis specimens, limb bones indicate that these individuals were bipedal. Moreover, the molar teeth have thick enamel, like other members of *Australopithecus*.

However, there are also some primitive characteristics in these still quite early hominid specimens (dated 4.2–3.9 m.y.a.). For example, Leakey and colleagues point to such primitive features as a large canine, a **sectorial** lower first premolar (Fig. 10–8), and a small opening for the ear canal. Since these particular *Australopithecus* individuals have initially been interpreted as more primitive than all the later members of the genus, Meave Leakey and associates have provisionally assigned them to a separate species (*Australopithecus anamensis*). Further study and (with some luck) additional more complete remains will help decide whether such a distinction is warranted.

Slightly later and much more complete remains of *Australopithecus* have come from the sites of Hadar (in Ethiopia) and Laetoli (in Tanzania) (see Fig. 10–6). Much of this material has been known for some time (since the mid-1970s), and the fossils have been very well studied; indeed, in certain instances, they are quite famous. For example, the Lucy skeleton was discovered at Hadar in 1974, and the Laetoli footprints were first found in 1978.

Literally thousands of footprints have been found at Laetoli, representing more than 20 different kinds of animals (Pliocene elephants, horses, pigs, giraffes, antelope, hyenas, and an abundance of hares). Several hominid footprints have also been found, including a trail more than 75 feet long, made by at least two—and perhaps three—individuals (Leakey and Hay, 1979) (Fig 10–9). Such discoveries of well-preserved hominid footprints are extremely important in furthering our understanding of human evolution. For the first time, we can make *definite* statements regarding the locomotor pattern and stature of early hominids. Analyses of these Pliocene footprints suggests a stature of about 4 feet 9 inches for the larger individual and 4 feet 1 inch for the smaller individual.

Studies of these impression patterns clearly show that the mode of locomotion of these hominids was bipedal (Day and Wickens, 1980). As we have discussed, the development of bipedal locomotion is the most important defining characteristic of

Sectorial
Adapted for cutting or shearing; among primates, refers to the compressed (side-to-side) first lower premolar, which functions as a shearing surface with the upper canine.

Sectorial lower first premolar

FIGURE 10–8
Left lateral view of the teeth of a male patas monkey. Note how the large upper canine shears against the elongated surface of the *sectorial* lower first premolar.

---

*Moreover, some paleoanthropologists place portions of the *Australopithecus* sample into another genus designated *Paranthropus* (see p. 277).

FIGURE 10-9
Hominid footprint from Laetoli, Tanzania. Note the deep impression of the heel and the large toe (arrow) in line (adducted) with the other toes.

FIGURE 10-10
"Lucy," a partial hominid skeleton, discovered at Hadar in 1974. This individual is assigned to *Australopithecus afarensis*.

early hominid evolution. Some researchers, however, have concluded that these early hominids were not bipedal in quite the same way that modern humans are. From detailed comparisons with modern humans, estimates of stride length, cadence, and speed of walking have been ascertained, indicating that the Laetoli hominids moved in a slow-moving ("strolling") fashion with a rather short stride (Chateris et al., 1981).

Two extraordinary discoveries at Hadar are most noteworthy. First, there is the Lucy skeleton (Fig. 10–10), found by Don Johanson eroding out of a hillside. This fossil is scientifically designated as Afar Locality (AL) 288-1, but is usually just called Lucy (after the Beatles' song "Lucy in the Sky with Diamonds"). Representing almost 40 percent of a skeleton, this is one of the three most complete individuals from anywhere in the world for the entire period before about 100,000 years ago.*

The second find, a phenomenal discovery, came to light in 1975 at another Hadar locality. Don Johanson and his amazed crew found dozens of hominid bones scattered along a hillside. These bones represented at least 13 individuals, including 4 infants. Possibly members of one social unit, it has been argued that the members of this group died at about the same time, thus representing a "catastrophic" assemblage (White and Johanson, 1989). However, the precise deposition of the site has not been completely explained, so this assertion must be viewed as quite tentative. (In geological time, an "instant" could represent many decades or centuries.) Considerable cultural material has been found in the Hadar area, mostly washed into stream channels, but some stone tools have been reported in context at a site dated at 2.5 m.y.a., potentially making the findings among the oldest cultural evidence yet discovered.

Because the Laetoli area was covered periodically by ashfalls from nearby volcanic eruptions, accurate dating is possible and has provided dates of 3.7–3.5 m.y.a. Dating from the Hadar region has not proved as straightforward; however, more complete dating calibration, using a variety of techniques (see Chapter 9), has determined a range of 3.9–3.0 m.y.a. for the hominid discoveries from this area (see Table 10–1).

---

*The others are a specimen from Sterkfontein in South Africa (see p. 265) and a *H. erectus* skeleton from west of Lake Turkana, Kenya (see p. 301). Also note that the crushed and embedded skeleton from Aramis may be nearly as complete as Lucy.

Australopithecus afarensis from Laetoli and Hadar

Several hundred specimens, representing a minimum of 60 individuals (and perhaps as many as 100), have been removed from Laetoli and Hadar. At present, these materials represent the largest *well-studied* collection of early hominids. Moreover, it has been suggested that fragmentary specimens from other locales in East Africa are remains of the same species as that found at Laetoli and Hadar. Most scholars refer to this species as *Australopithecus afarensis*.

Without question, *A. afarensis* is more primitive than any of the other **australopithecine** fossils from South or East Africa (discussed subsequently), although the recently described materials from Kanapoi and Allia Bay (*Australopithecus anamensis*) are even more primitive yet. By "primitive," we mean that *A. afarensis* is less evolved in any particular direction than are later occurring hominid species. That is, *A. afarensis* shares more primitive features with other early homin*oids* and with living pongids than do later hominids, who display more derived characteristics.

For example, the teeth of *A. afarensis* are quite primitive. The canines are often large, pointed teeth. Moreover, the lower first premolar is semisectorial (i.e., it provides a shearing surface for the upper canine), and the tooth rows are parallel, even converging somewhat toward the back of the mouth (Fig. 10–11).

The cranial portions that are preserved, including a more recently discovered specimen, also display several primitive hominoid characteristics, including a compound crest in the back as well as several primitive features of the cranial base. Cranial capacity estimates for *A. afarensis* show a mixed pattern when compared to later hominids. A provisional estimate for the one partially complete cranium—apparently a large individual—gives a figure of 500 cm^3, but another, even more fragmentary cranium is apparently quite a bit smaller and has been estimated at about 375 cm^3 (Holloway, 1983). Thus, for some individuals (males?), *A. afarensis* is well within the range of other australopithecine species (see Box 10–3), but others (females?) may have a significantly smaller cranial capacity. However, a detailed depiction of cranial size for *A. afarensis* is not possible at this time; this part of the skeleton is unfortunately too poorly represented. One thing is clear: *A. afarensis* had a small brain, probably averaging for the whole species not much over 420 cm^3.

On the other hand, a large assortment of postcranial pieces has been found at Hadar. Initial impressions suggest that relative to lower limbs, the upper limbs are longer than in modern humans (also a primitive hominoid condition). (This statement does not mean that the arms of *A. afarensis* were longer than the legs.) In addition, the wrist, hand, and foot bones show several differences from modern

Australopithecine
(os-tra-loh-pith´-e-seen) The colloquial name for members of the genus *Australopithecus*. The term was first used as a subfamily designation, but it is now most commonly used informally.

 See Virtual Lab 8, section I, for a discussion of *Australopithecus afarensis*.

(a)

(b)

FIGURE 10–11
Jaws of *Australopithecus afarensis*. (a) Maxilla, AL 200-1a, from Hadar, Ethiopia. (Note the parallel tooth rows and large canines.) (b) Mandible, LH 4, from Laetoli, Tanzania. This fossil is the type specimen for the species *Australopithecus afarensis*.

BOX 10-3	A CLOSER LOOK

Cranial Capacity

Cranial capacity, usually reported in cubic centimeters, is a measure of brain size, or volume. The brain itself, of course, does not fossilize. However, the space once occupied by brain tissue (the inside of the cranial vault) does sometimes preserve, at least in those cases where fairly complete crania are recovered.

For purposes of comparison, it is easy to obtain cranial capacity estimates for contemporary species (including humans) from analyses of skeletonized specimens in museum collections. From studies of this nature, estimated cranial capacities for modern hominoids have been determined as follows (Tobias, 1971, 1983):

	Range (cm³)	Average (cm³)
Human	1150–1750*	1325
Chimpanzee	285–500	395
Gorilla	340–752	506
Orangutan	276–540	411
Bonobo	—	350

*The range of cranial capacity for modern humans is very large—in fact, even greater than that shown (which approximates cranial capacity for the *majority* of contemporary *H. sapiens*).

These data for living hominoids can then be compared with those obtained from early hominids:

	Average (cm³)
Ardipithecus	Not presently known
Australopithecus anamensis	Not presently known
Australopithecus afarensis	438
Later australopithecines	410–530
Early members of genus *Homo*	631

As the tabulations indicate, cranial capacity estimates for australopithecines fall within the range of most modern great apes, and gorillas actually average slightly more than *A. afarensis*. It must be remembered, however, that gorillas are very large animals, whereas australopithecines probably weighed on the order of 100 pounds (see Table 10–3). Since brain size is partially correlated with body size, comparing such different-sized animals cannot be justified. Compared to living chimpanzees (most of which are slightly larger than early hominids) and bonobos (which are somewhat smaller), australopithecines had *proportionately* about 10 percent bigger brains, and we would therefore say that these early hominids were more *encephalized.*

See Virtual lab 10, section IV, for a discussion of the evolution of hominid brain size.

humans (Susman et al., 1985). Stature can now be confidently estimated: *A. afarensis* was a short hominid. From her partial skeleton, Lucy is figured to be only 3½ to 4 feet tall. However, Lucy—as demonstrated by her pelvis—was probably a female, and at Hadar and Laetoli, there is evidence of larger individuals as well. The most economical hypothesis explaining this variation is that *A. afarensis* was quite sexually dimorphic: The larger individuals are male and the smaller ones, such as Lucy, are female. Estimates of male stature can be approximated from the larger footprints at Laetoli, inferring a height of not quite 5 feet. If we accept this interpretation, *A. afarensis* was a very sexually dimorphic form indeed. In fact, for overall body size, this species may have been as dimorphic as *any* living primate (i.e., as much as gorillas, orangutans, or baboons).

In a majority of dental and cranial features, *A. afarensis* is clearly more primitive than later hominids. In fact, from the neck up, *A. afarensis* is so primitive that without any evidence from the limbs, one would be hard-pressed to call it a hominid at all (although the back teeth are large and heavily enameled, unlike pongids, and the position of the foramen magnum indicates an upright posture).

What, then, makes *A. afarensis* a hominid? The answer is revealed by its manner of locomotion. From the abundant limb bones recovered from Hadar and those beautiful footprints from Laetoli, we know unequivocally that *A. afarensis* walked bipedally when on the ground. Whether Lucy and her contemporaries still spent considerable time in the trees and just how efficiently they walked, have become topics of some controversy. Most researchers, however, agree that *A. afarensis* was an efficient habitual biped while on the ground. These hominids were also clearly obligate bipeds, which would have hampered their climbing abilities but would not necessarily have precluded arboreal behavior altogether. As one physical anthropologist has surmised: "One could imagine these diminutive early hominids making maximum use of *both* terrestrial and arboreal resources in spite of their commitment to exclusive bipedalism when on the ground. The contention of a mixed arboreal and terrestrial behavioral repertoire would make adaptive sense of the Hadar australopithecine forelimb, hand, and foot morphology without contradicting the evidence of the pelvis" (Wolpoff, 1983b, p. 451).

See Virtual Lab 9, section V, for a discussion of the locomotion of *A. afarensis*.

Another East African Hominid

The pace of hominid discoveries in East Africa has dramatically intensified in recent years, and many of these new discoveries have revealed a different combination of anatomical features from those recognized in remains discovered previously. Among the most distinctive and intriguing of these new finds is a cranium unearthed in 1999 on the west side of Lake Turkana in northern Kenya (Leakey et al., 2001).

Dated to 3.5 m.y.a., this fossil hominid is thus contemporaneous with *Australopithecus afarensis*. Yet, it shows a quite distinctive combination of facial and dental features (most especially, a flat lower face and fairly small molar teeth). In these respects, this newly discovered Kenyan hominid is different from *A. afarensis*, and, in fact, from *all* known australopithecines. Because the skull has been severely distorted, cranial capacity is difficult to establish clearly. However, the best estimates suggest that the cranial capacity is similar to that of *Australopithecus* (i.e., in the range of 400–500 cm^3.).

Because of its unusual anatomical features, Meave Leakey and her colleagues have proposed an entirely new hominid genus (*Kenyanthropus*) for this exceptional cranium. Whether this designation will be substantiated by further, more detailed analysis remains to be seen. At minimum, this and all the other discoveries from recent years are forcing a major reassessment of the early stages of hominid evolution (see Box 10–4 on page 274).

Later East African Australopithecine Finds

An assortment of fossil hominids, including many specimens of later members of the genus *Australopithecus*, has been recovered from geological contexts with dates after 3 m.y.a. at several localities in East Africa. Up to 10 different such sites are now known (in the time range of 3–1 m.y.a.), but here we will concentrate on the three most significant ones: East Lake Turkana, West Lake Turkana (both in northern Kenya), and Olduvai Gorge (in northern Tanzania) (Table 10–2).

A significant new hominid discovery from another site in East Africa was announced in 1999 (Asfaw et al., 1999). Behane Asfaw, Tim White, and colleagues have discovered several fossils, dated to 2.5 m.y.a., of what they suggest may be yet another species of *Australopithecus*, termed *A. garhi*, *garhi* meaning "surprise" in the

TABLE 10–2 Summary of Later East African Hominid Discoveries

Site Name	Location	Age (m.y.a.)	Hominids
Olduvai	N. Tanzania	1.85–1.0	48 specimens; australopithecines; early *Homo*
Turkana	N. Kenya (eastern side of Lake Turkana)	1.9–1.3	More than 150 specimens; many australopithecines; several early *Homo*
	West side of Lake Turkana	3.5–1.6	2 nearly complete crania (1 australopithecine), the other assigned to *Kenyanthropus**); 3 jaw fragments, isolated teeth, and one cranial fragment (also *Kenyanthropus?*); 1 nearly complete skeleton (*H. erectus*)
Middle Awash (Bouri)	N.E. Ethiopia	2.5	5 hominids; 1 cranium; parts of limb skeleton (*A. garhi*)
Hadar	N.E. Ethiopia	3.9–3.0	Minimum of 40 individuals (maximum of 65); early australopithecines (*A. afarensis*)
Laetoli	N. Tanzania	3.7–3.5	24 hominids; early australopithecines (*A. afarensis*)

*The genus *Kenyanthropus* is a provisional designation and has not yet been accepted by all paleoanthropologists.

FIGURE 10–12
Reconstructed cranium of *Australopithecus garhi* from Bouri, Ethiopia; estimated date, 2.5 m.y.a.

© David L. Brill/Atlanta

Afar language (Fig. 10–12). These important new finds come from the Bouri site also in the Middle Awash region of Ethiopia, just south of Aramis. The hominid fossils, including an incomplete cranium and much of the limb skeleton (from another individual), are in several ways quite different from any other Plio-Pleistocene hominid. For example, the cranium combines a projecting face, fairly large front teeth, and very large back teeth. The limb proportions are also unusual, with long forelimbs (as in *A. afarensis*) but also with quite long hind limbs (as in *Homo*). Finally, the hominids at Bouri were found close to animal bones displaying clear signs of butchering (see p. 229).

Located very near the considerably older Allia Bay site on the east shore of Lake Turkana is Koobi Fora (Fig. 10–13). This latter locality, with sediments dating to 1.8–1.3 m.y.a., has provided specimens representing at least 100 individuals, and this fine sample includes several complete crania, many jaws, and an assortment of postcranial bones. Next to Olduvai, Koobi Fora has yielded the most information concerning the behavior of early hominids. More than 20 archaeological sites have been discovered, and excavation or testing has been done at 10 localities.

Across the lake, on the west side of Lake Turkana, are other deposits that recently have yielded new and very exciting discoveries—including the earlier *Kenyanthropus* finds (discussed earlier). In addition, Olduvai Gorge (discussed in detail in Chapter 9) has also yielded a considerable collection of early hominid fossils (see Table 10–2).

National Museums of Kenya

Australopithecines from Olduvai and Lake Turkana

Most fossil hominids from Olduvai, West Lake Turkana, and especially Koobi Fora are later in time than the *A. afarensis* remains from Laetoli and Hadar (by at least 500,000 years). It is thus not surprising that they are more derived, in some cases dramatically so. Also, these later hominids are considerably more diverse. Most researchers accept the interpretation that all the hominids from Laetoli and Hadar are members of a single taxon, *A. afarensis*. However, it is clear that the remains from the Turkana area and Olduvai collectively represent multiple taxa—two different genera and perhaps up to five or six different species. Current discussion on how best to sort this complex material is among the most vehement in paleoanthropology. Here we summarize the broad patterns of physical morphology. At the end of this chapter, we will take up the various schemes that attempt to interpret the fossil remains in a broader evolutionary context.

Following 2.5 m.y.a., later (and more derived) representatives of *Australopithecus* are found in East Africa. This is a most distinctive group that has popularly been known for some time as "robust" australopithecines. By "robust" it had generally been meant that these forms—when compared to other australopithecines—were larger in body size. However, more recent and better controlled studies (Jungers, 1988; McHenry, 1988, 1992) have shown that all the species of *Australopithecus* overlapped considerably in body size. As you will see shortly, "robust" australopithecines have also been found in South Africa.

As a result of these new weight estimates, many researchers have either dropped the use of the term *robust* (along with its opposite, *gracile*) or presented it in quotation marks to emphasize its conditional application. We believe that the term *robust* can be used in this latter sense, as it still emphasizes important differences in the scaling of craniodental traits. In other words, even if they are not larger overall, robust forms are clearly robust in the skull and dentition.

Dating to approximately 2.5 m.y.a., the earliest representative of this robust group comes from northern Kenya on the west side of Lake Turkana. A complete cranium (WT 17000—"the black skull") was unearthed there in 1985 and has

FIGURE 10–14

The "black skull," WT 17000, discovered at West Lake Turkana in 1985. This specimen is provisionally assigned to *Australopithecus aethiopicus*. It is called the "black skull" owing to the dark color from the fossilization (mineralization) process.

Reproduced with permission of the National Museums of Kenya, copyright reserved, courtesy of Alan Walker

Sagittal crest
Raised ridge along the midline of the cranium where the temporal muscle (which closes the jaw) is attached.

See Virtual Lab 10 for a discussion of the evolution of the genus *Homo*.

proved to be a most important discovery (Fig. 10–14). This skull, with a cranial capacity of only 410 cm³, has the smallest definitely ascertained brain volume of any hominid yet found and has other primitive traits reminiscent of *A. afarensis*. For example, there is a compound crest in the back of the skull, the upper face projects considerably, the upper dental row converges in back, and the cranial base is extensively pneumatized—that is, it possesses air pockets (Kimbel et al., 1988).

What makes the black skull so fascinating, however, is that mixed with this array of distinctively primitive traits are a host of derived ones linking it to other members of the robust group (including a broad face, a very large palate, and a large area for the back teeth). This mosaic of features seems to place skull WT 17000 between earlier *A. afarensis* on the one hand and the later robust species on the other. Because of its unique position in hominid evolution, WT 17000 (and the population it represents) has been placed in a new species, *Australopithecus aethiopicus*.

Around 2 m.y.a., different varieties of even more derived members of the robust lineage were on the scene in East Africa. As well documented by finds at Olduvai and Koobi Fora, robust australopithecines have relatively small cranial capacities (ranging from 510 to 530 cm³) and very large, broad faces with massive back teeth and lower jaws. The larger (probably male) individuals also show a raised ridge, called a **sagittal crest**, along the midline of the cranium. The first find of a recognized Plio-Pleistocene hominid in East Africa, in fact, was of a nearly complete robust australopithecine cranium, discovered in 1959 by Mary Leakey at Olduvai Gorge (see p. 221). As a result of Louis Leakey's original naming of the fossil (as *Zinjanthropus*), this find is still popularly referred to as "Zinj." However, it and other members of the same species in East Africa are now usually classified as *Australopithecus boisei*.

Early *Homo*

In addition to the robust australopithecine remains in East Africa, there is another contemporaneous Plio-Pleistocene hominid that is quite distinctive. In fact, as best documented by fossil discoveries from Olduvai and Koobi Fora, these materials have been assigned to the genus *Homo*—and thus are different from all species assigned to *Australopithecus*.

The earliest appearance of genus *Homo* in East Africa may be as ancient as that of the robust australopithecines. (As we have discussed, the black skull from West Turkana has been dated to approximately 2.5 m.y.a.) Recent reinterpretations of a temporal fragment from the Lake Baringo region of central Kenya have suggested that early *Homo* may also be close to this same antiquity (estimated age of 2.4 m.y.a) (Hill et al., 1992). More diagnostic remains of a lower jaw of early *Homo* have also recently been reported from Hadar, in Ethiopia, and are dated to 2.3 m.y.a. (Kimbel et al., 1996). Given that the robust australopithecine lineage was probably diverging at this time, it is not surprising to find the earliest representatives of the genus *Homo* also beginning to diversify.

The presence of a Plio-Pleistocene hominid with a significantly larger brain than seen in *Australopithecus* was first suggested by Louis Leakey in the early 1960s on the basis of fragmentary remains found at Olduvai Gorge. Leakey and his colleagues gave a new species designation to these fossil remains, naming them **Homo habilis**.

The *Homo habilis* material at Olduvai ranges in time from 1.85 m.y.a. for the earliest to about 1.6 m.y.a. for the latest. Due to the fragmentary nature of the fossil remains, interpretations have been difficult and much disputed. The most immediately obvious feature distinguishing the *H. habilis* material from the australopithecines is cranial size. For all the measurable *H. habilis* skulls, the estimated average cranial capacity is 631 cm^3, compared to 520 cm^3 for all measurable robust australopithecines and 442 cm^3 for the less robust species (McHenry, 1988) (see Box 10–2). *Homo habilis*, therefore, shows an increase in cranial size of about 20 percent over the larger of the australopithecines and an even greater increase over some of the smaller-brained forms (from South Africa, discussed shortly). In their initial description of *H. habilis*, Leakey and his associates also pointed to differences from australopithecines in cranial shape and in tooth proportions (larger front teeth relative to back teeth and narrower premolars).

The naming of this fossil material as *Homo habilis* ("handy man") was meaningful from two perspectives. First of all, Leakey inferred that members of this group were the early Olduvai toolmakers. If true, how do we account for a robust australopithecine like "Zinj" lying in the middle of the largest excavated area known at Olduvai? What was he doing there? Leakey suggested that he was the remains of a *habilis* meal! Excepting those instances where cut marks are left behind (see pp. 228–229), we must point out again that there is no clear way archaeologically to establish the validity of such a claim. However, the debate over this assertion serves to demonstrate that cultural factors as well as physical morphology must be considered in the interpretation of hominids as biocultural organisms. Secondly, and most significantly, by calling this group *Homo*, Leakey was arguing for at least *two separate branches* of hominid evolution in the Plio-Pleistocene. Clearly, only one could be on the main branch eventually leading to *Homo sapiens*. By labeling this new group *Homo* rather than *Australopithecus*, Leakey was guessing that he had found our ancestors.

Because the initial evidence was so fragmentary, most paleoanthropologists were reluctant to accept *H. habilis* as a valid taxon distinct from *all* australopithecines. Later discoveries, especially from Lake Turkana, of better-preserved fossil material have shed further light on early *Homo* in the Plio-Pleistocene. The most important of this additional material is a nearly complete cranium (ER 1470) discovered at Koobi Fora (Fig. 10–15). With a cranial capacity of 775 cm^3, this individual is well outside the known range for australopithecines and actually overlaps the lower boundary for *Homo erectus*. In addition, the shape of the skull vault is in many respects unlike that of australopithecines. However, the face is still quite robust (Walker, 1976), and the fragments of tooth crowns that are preserved indicate that the back teeth in this individual were quite large. Dating of the Koobi Fora early *Homo* material places it contemporaneous with the Olduvai remains—that is, about 1.8–1.6 m.y.a.

On the basis of evidence from Olduvai and particularly from Koobi Fora, we can reasonably postulate that one or more species of early *Homo* were present in East Africa probably by 2.4 m.y.a., developing in parallel with at least one line of australopithecines (Fig. 10–16). These two hominid lines lived contemporaneously for a minimum of 1 million years, after which the australopithecine lineage apparently disappeared forever. At the same time, probably the early *Homo* line was evolving into a later form, *Homo erectus*, which in turn developed into *H. sapiens*.

Homo habilis
(hab´-ih-liss) A species of early *Homo*, well known from East Africa but perhaps also found in other regions.

(a)

(b)

FIGURE 10–15

A nearly complete early *Homo* cranium from East Lake Turkana (ER 1470), one of the most important single fossil hominid discoveries from East Africa. (a) frontal view; (b) lateral view.

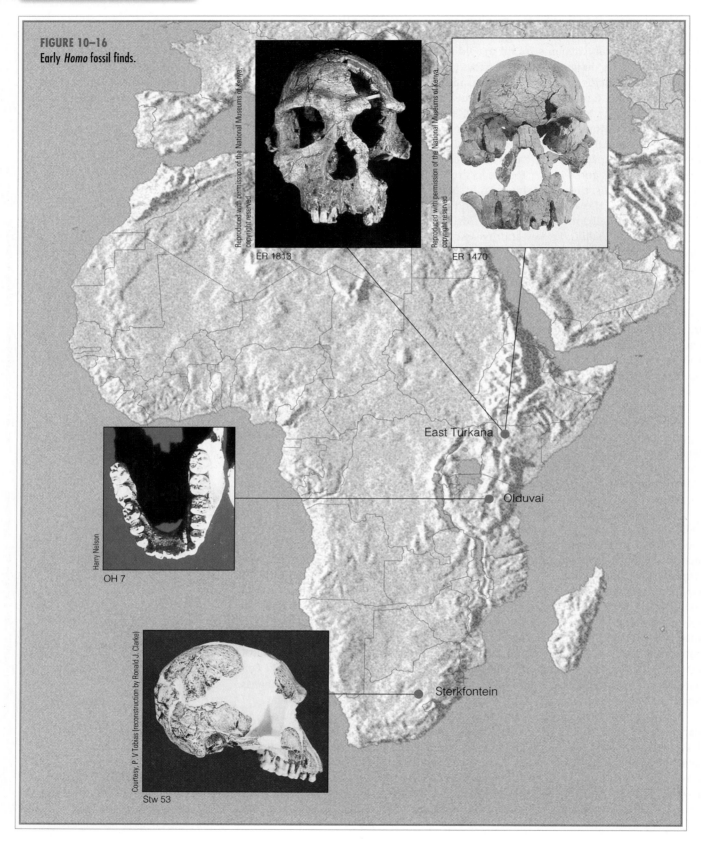

FIGURE 10–16
Early *Homo* fossil finds.

ER 1813

ER 1470

East Turkana

Olduvai

OH 7

Stw 53

Sterkfontein

Central Africa

In 1995, another new early hominid discovery was announced from a rather surprising location—Chad, in central Africa (Brunet et al., 1995) (see Fig. 10–6). From an area called the Bahr el Ghazal (Arabic for "River of the Gazelles"), a partial hominid mandible was discovered in association with faunal remains tentatively dated to 3.5–3.0 m.y.a. (Further confirmation will have to await chronometric dating, assuming that appropriate materials become available.) The preliminary analysis suggests that this fossil is an australopithecine with closest affinities to *A. afarensis*. What makes this find remarkable is its geographical location, more than 1,500 miles west of the previously established range of early hominids!

South African Sites

Earliest Discoveries

The first quarter of the twentieth century saw the discipline of paleoanthropology in its scientific infancy. Informed opinions considered the likely origins of the human family to be in Asia, where fossil forms of a primitive kind of *Homo* had been found in Indonesia in the 1890s. Europe was also considered a center of hominid evolution, for spectacular discoveries there of archaic *Homo sapiens* (including the famous Neandertals) and millions of stone tools had come to light, particularly in the early 1900s.

Few scholars would have given much credence to Darwin's prediction:

> In each region of the world the living mammals are closely related to the extinct species of the same region. It is, therefore, probable that Africa was formally inhabited by extinct apes closely allied to the gorilla and chimpanzee, and as these two species are now man's nearest allies, it is somewhat more probable that our early progenitors lived on the African continent than elsewhere. (Darwin, *The Descent of Man*, 1871)

Moreover, it would be many more decades before the East African discoveries would come to light. It was in such an atmosphere of preconceived biases that the discoveries of a young Australian-born anatomist were to jolt the foundations of the scientific community in the 1920s. Raymond Dart (Fig. 10–17) arrived in South Africa in 1923 at the age of 30 to take up a teaching position in Johannesburg. Fresh from his evolution-oriented training in England, Dart had developed a keen interest in human evolution. Consequently, he was well prepared when startling new evidence began to appear at his very doorstep.

The first clue came in 1924, when Dart received a shipment of fossils from the commercial limeworks quarry at Taung (200 miles southwest of Johannesburg). He immediately recognized something that was quite unusual, a natural **endocast** of a higher primate. The endocast fit into another limestone block containing the fossilized front portion of the skull, face, and lower jaw (Fig. 10–18). However, these were difficult to see clearly, for the bone was hardened into a cemented limestone matrix. Dart patiently chiseled away for weeks, later describing the task:

> No diamond cutter ever worked more lovingly or with such care on a precious jewel—nor, I am sure, with such inadequate tools. But on the seventy-third day, December 23, the rock parted. I could view the face from the front, although the right side was still imbedded. . . . What emerged was a baby's face, an infant with a full set of milk teeth and its permanent molars just in the process of erupting. I doubt if there was any parent prouder of his offspring than I was of my Taung baby on that Christmas. (Dart, 1959, p. 10)

FIGURE 10-17
Raymond Dart, shown working in his laboratory.

Endocast
A solid impression of the inside of the skull, often preserving details relating to the size and surface features of the brain.

FIGURE 10–18
The Taung child discovered in 1924. The endocast is in back, with the fossilized bone mandible and face in front.

Hominid Origins

 See Virtual lab 8, section I, for a discussion of South African early hominids.

Australopithecus africanus
(os-tral-oh-pith′-e-kus af-ri-kan′-us)

As indicated by the formation and eruption of the teeth, the Taung child was probably about three to four years old. Interestingly, the rate of development of this and many other Plio-Pleistocene hominids was more like that of apes than of modern *Homo* (Bromage and Dean, 1985). Dart's initial impression that this form was a hominoid was confirmed when he could observe the face and teeth more clearly. However, as it turned out, it took considerably more effort before the teeth could be seen completely, since Dart worked for four years to separate the upper and lower jaws.

But Dart was convinced long before he had an unimpeded view of the dentition that this discovery was a remarkable one, an early hominoid from South Africa. The question was, What kind of hominoid? Dart realized that it was extremely improbable that this specimen could have been a forest ape, for South Africa has had a relatively dry climate for millions of years. Even though the climate at Taung may not have been as dry as Dart initially speculated (Butzer, 1974), it was still a very unlikely spot to find an ape!

If not an ape, then what was it? Features of the skull and teeth of this small child held clues that Dart seized on almost immediately. The entrance of the spinal cord into the brain (the *foramen magnum* at the base of the skull; see Fig. 10–8) was farther forward in the Taung skull than in modern great apes, though not as much as in modern humans. From this fact Dart concluded that the head was balanced *above* the spine, indicating erect posture. In addition, the slant of the forehead was not as receding as in apes, the milk canines were exceedingly small, and the newly erupted permanent molars were very large, broad teeth. In all these respects, the Taung fossil was more akin to hominids than to apes. There was, however, a disturbing feature that was to confuse many scientists for several years: The brain was quite small. More recent studies have estimated the Taung child's brain size at approximately 405 cm^3 (which translates to a full adult estimate of 440 cm^3), not very large (for a hominid) when compared to modern great apes (see Box 10–3).

The estimated cranial capacity of the Taung fossil falls within the range of modern great apes, and gorillas actually average about 10 percent greater. It must, however, be remembered that gorillas are very large animals, whereas the Taung specimen derives from a population where adults may have averaged less than 80 pounds. Since brain size is partially correlated with body size, comparing such differently sized animals is unjustified. A more meaningful comparison would be with the bonobo (*Pan paniscus*), whose body weight is comparable. Bonobos have adult cranial capacities averaging 356 cm^3 for males and 329 cm^3 for females, and thus the Taung child, versus a *comparably sized* ape, displays a 25 percent increase in cranial capacity.

Despite the relatively small size of the brain, Dart saw that it was no ape. Realizing the immense importance of his findings, Dart promptly reported them in the British scientific weekly *Nature* on February 7, 1925—a bold venture, since Dart, only 32, was presumptuously proposing a whole new view of human evolution. The small-brained Taung child was christened by Dart *Australopithecus africanus* (southern ape of Africa), which he saw as a kind of halfway "missing link" between modern apes and humans. This concept of a single "missing link" was a fallacious one, but Dart correctly emphasized the hominid-like features of the fossil.

Not all scientists were ready for such a theory from such an "unlikely" place. Hence, Dart's report was received with indifference, disbelief, and even caustic scorn. Dart realized that more complete remains were needed. The skeptical world would not accept the evidence of one partial immature individual, no matter how suggestive the clues. Most scientists in the 1920s regarded this little Taung child as an interesting aberrant form of ape. Clearly, more fossil evidence was needed, particularly adult crania (since these would show more diagnostic features). Not an experienced fossil hunter himself, Dart sought further assistance in the search for more australopithecines.

Further Discoveries of South African Hominids

Soon after publication of his controversial theories, Dart found a strong ally in Robert Broom (Fig. 10–19). A Scottish physician and part-time paleontologist, Broom's credentials as a fossil hunter had been established earlier with his highly successful paleontological work on early mammal-like reptiles in South Africa.

Although interested, Broom was unable to participate actively in the search for additional australopithecines until 1936. From two of Dart's students, Broom learned of another commercial limeworks site, called **Sterkfontein,** not far from Johannesburg. Here, as at Taung, the quarrying involved blasting out large sections with dynamite, leaving piles of debris that often contained fossilized remains. Accordingly, Broom asked the quarry manager to keep his eyes open for fossils, and when Broom returned to the site in August 1936, the manager asked, "Is this what you are looking for?" Indeed it was, for Broom held in his hand the endocast of an adult australopithecine—exactly what he had set out to find! Looking further over the scattered debris, Broom was able to find most of the rest of the skull of the same individual.

Such remarkable success, just a few months after beginning his search, was not the end of Broom's luck, for his magical touch was to continue unabated for several more years. In the 1930s and 1940s, Broom discovered two further hominid sites, including **Swartkrans,** the most prolific of all South African Plio-Pleistocene locales (it has since yielded hundreds of fossils). In the 1940s, Raymond Dart discovered another hominid site, bringing the total to five.

Numerous extremely important discoveries came from these additional sites, discoveries that would eventually swing the tide of intellectual thought to the views that Dart expressed back in 1925. Particularly important was a nearly complete cranium and pelvis, both found at Sterkfontein in 1947. As the number of discoveries accumulated, it became increasingly difficult to simply write the australopithecines off as aberrant apes.

By 1949, at least 30 hominid individuals were represented from five South African sites, and leading scientists were coming to accept the australopithecines as hominids. With this acceptance also came the necessary recognition that hominid brains had their greatest expansion *after* earlier changes in teeth and locomotor systems. In other words, once again we see that the rate of evolution in one functional system of the body varies from that of other systems, thus displaying the *mosaic* nature of human evolution.

Since the 1950s, exploration of the South African hominid sites has continued, and numerous important discoveries were made in the 1970s and 1980s. The most spectacular new find was made in 1998 at Sterkfontein, where the remains of a virtually complete australopithecine skeleton were found by Ron Clarke and his associates from the University of Witwatersrand. Most of the remains are still embedded in the surrounding limestone matrix and may require years for removal, cleaning, and reconstruction.

As we will discuss in more detail shortly, dating of all the South African Plio-Pleistocene sites has proved most difficult; estimates for the Sterkfontein australopithecine skeleton are between 3.6 and 2.5 m.y.a. Even before the remains have been fully excavated, this is still recognized as an unusual and highly significant find. Because such complete individuals are so rare in the hominid fossil record, this discovery has tremendous potential to shed more light on the precise nature of early hominid locomotion. For example, will the rest of the skeleton confirm what foot bones of the same individual have implied regarding arboreal climbing in this bipedal hominid (see p. 246)? Moreover, relative proportion of brain size compared to body size, better estimates of overall body size, relative proportions of the limbs, and much more can be more accurately assessed from such a completely preserved skeleton.

Wide World

FIGURE 10–19
Robert Broom.

Sterkfontein
(sterk´-fon-tane)

Swartkrans
(swart´-kranz)

FIGURE 10–20

A gracile australopithecine cranium from Sterkfontein (Sts 5). Discovered in 1947, this specimen is the best-preserved gracile skull yet found in South Africa.

Transvaal Museum, South Africa

Review of Hominids from South Africa

The Plio-Pleistocene hominid discoveries from South Africa are most significant. First, they were the initial hominid discoveries in Africa and helped point the way to later finds in East Africa. Second, morphology of the South African hominids shows broad similarities to the forms in East Africa, but with several distinctive features, which argues for separation at least at the species level. Finally, there is a large assemblage of hominid fossils from South Africa, and exciting discoveries are still being made (Fig. 10–20).

Further discoveries are also coming from entirely new sites. In the 1990s, the site known as Drimolen was found in South Africa, very near to Sterkfontein and Swartkrans (Keyser, 2000). While only provisionally published thus far, we do know that up to 80 specimens have been recovered—including the most complete *Australopithecus* cranium found anywhere in Africa.

A truly remarkable collection of early hominids, the remains from South Africa exceed 1,500 (counting all teeth as separate items), and the number of individuals is now more than 200. From an evolutionary point of view, the most meaningful remains are those of the pelvis, which now include portions of nine ossa coxae (see p. 244). Remains of the pelvis are so important because, better than any other area of the body, this structure displays the unique requirements of a bipedal animal (as in modern humans *and* in our hominid forebears).

"Robust" Australopithecines In addition to the discoveries of *A. aethiopicus* and *A. boisei* in East Africa, there are also numerous finds of robust australopithecines in South Africa. Like their East African cousins, the South African robust forms also have small cranial capacities. (The only measurable specimen equals 530 cm^3; the Drimolen cranium is smaller and might come from a female, but no cranial measurements have as yet been published.) They also possess large broad faces and very large premolars and molars (although not as massive as in East Africa). Owing to the differences in dental proportions, as well as important differences in facial architecture (Rak, 1983), most researchers now agree that there is a species-level difference between the later East African robust variety (*A. boisei*) and the South African group (*A. robustus*).

Despite these differences, all members of the robust lineage appear to be specialized for a diet made up of hard food items, such as seeds and nuts. For many years, paleoanthropologists (e.g., Robinson, 1972) had speculated that robust australopithecines concentrated their diet on heavier vegetable foods than those seen in the diet of other early hominids. More recent research that included examining microscopic polishes and scratches on the teeth (Kay and Grine, 1988) has confirmed this view.

"Gracile" Australopithecines Another variety of australopithecine (also small-brained, but not as large-toothed as the robust varieties) is known from Africa. However, while the robust lineage is represented in both East and South Africa, this other (gracile) australopithecine form is known only from the southern part of the continent. First named *A. africanus* by Dart for the single individual at Taung, this australopithecine is also found at other sites, especially Sterkfontein (Fig. 10–21).

Traditionally, it had been thought that there was a significant variation in body size between the gracile and robust forms. But as mentioned earlier and shown in Table 10–3, there is not much difference in body size among the australopithecines. In fact, most of the differences between the robust and gracile forms are found in the face and dentition.

The facial structure of the gracile australopithecines is more lightly built and somewhat dish-shaped compared to the more vertical configuration seen in robust

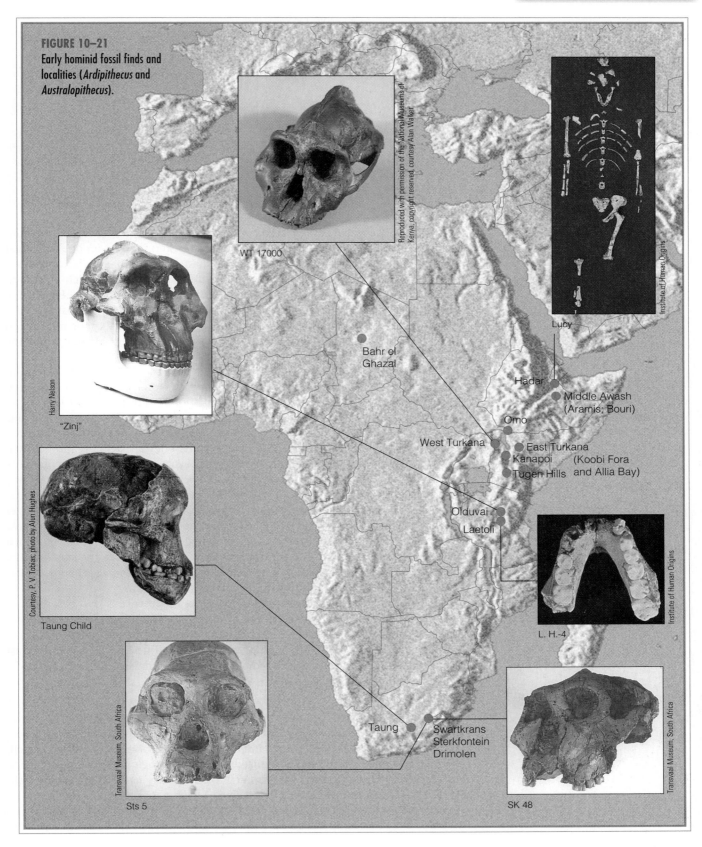

FIGURE 10–21
Early hominid fossil finds and localities (*Ardipithecus* and *Australopithecus*).

WT 17000

Lucy

"Zinj"

Bahr el Ghazal

Hadar

Middle Awash (Aramis; Bouri)

Omo

West Turkana

East Turkana (Koobi Fora and Allia Bay)

Kanapoi

Tugen Hills

Olduvai

Laetoli

L. H.-4

Taung Child

Sts 5

Taung

Swartkrans Sterkfontein Drimolen

SK 48

(a) Hominid (robust australopithecine)

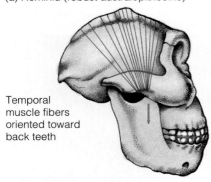

Temporal muscle fibers oriented toward back teeth

(b) Pongid (male gorilla)

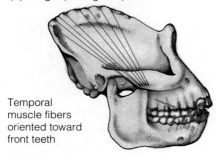

Temporal muscle fibers oriented toward front teeth

FIGURE 10–22
Sagittal crests and temporal muscle orientations. Hominid compared to pongid. (Line of greatest muscle force is shown in red.)

See Virtual Lab 10, section III, for a discussion of the methods used to estimate body mass in early hominids.

TABLE 10–3 Estimated Body Weights and Stature in Plio-Pleistocene Hominids

	Body Weight		Stature	
	Male	**Female**	**Male**	**Female**
A. afarensis	45 kg (99 lb)	29 kg (64 lb)	151 cm (59 in.)	105 cm (41 in.)
A. africanus	41 kg (90 lb)	30 kg (65 lb)	138 cm (54 in.)	115 cm (45 in.)
A. robustus	40 kg (88 lb)	32 kg (70 lb)	132 cm (52 in.)	110 cm (43 in.)
A. boisei	49 kg (108 lb)	34 kg (75 lb)	137 cm (54 in.)	124 cm (49 in.)
H. habilis	52 kg (114 lb)	32 kg (70 lb)	157 cm (62 in.)	125 cm (49 in.)

Source: After McHenry, 1992.

specimens. As we noted earlier, in robust individuals, a raised ridge along the midline of the skull is occasionally observed. Indeed, at Sterkfontein, among the larger individuals (males?), a hint of such a sagittal crest is also seen. This structure provides additional attachment area for the large temporal muscle, which is the primary muscle operating the massive jaw below. Such a structure is also seen in some modern apes, especially male gorillas and orangutans; however, in most australopithecines, the temporal muscle acts most efficiently on the back of the mouth and is therefore not functionally equivalent to the pattern seen in great apes, where the emphasis is more on the front teeth (Fig 10–22).

The most distinctive difference observed between gracile and robust australopithecines is in the dentition. Compared to modern humans, they both have relatively large teeth, which are, however, definitely hominid in pattern. In fact, more emphasis is on the typical back-tooth grinding complex among these early forms than is seen in modern humans; therefore, if anything, australopithecines are "hyperhominid" in their dentition. (In other words, they are dentally more *derived* than are modern humans.) Robust forms emphasize this trend to an extreme degree, showing deep jaws and much-enlarged back teeth, particularly the molars, leaving little room in the front of the mouth for the anterior teeth (incisors and canines). Conversely, the gracile australopithecines have proportionately larger front teeth compared to the size of their back teeth. The contrast is seen most clearly in the relative size of the canine compared to the first premolar: In robust individuals, the first premolar is clearly a much larger tooth than the small canine (about twice as large), whereas in gracile specimens, it only averages about 20 percent larger than the fairly good-sized canine (Howells, 1973).

These differences in the relative proportions of the teeth and jaws best define a gracile, as compared to a robust, australopithecine. In fact, most of the differences in skull shape we have discussed can be directly attributed to contrasting jaw function in the two forms. Both the sagittal crest and broad vertical face of the robust form are related to the muscles and biomechanical requirements of the heavy back-tooth chewing adaptation seen in this animal.

Early *Homo* in South Africa As in East Africa, early members of the genus *Homo* have also been found in South Africa, apparently living contemporaneously with australopithecines. At both Sterkfontein and Swartkrans, and perhaps Drimolen as well, fragmentary remains have been recognized as most likely belonging to *Homo*. In fact, Ron Clarke (1985) has shown that the key fossil of early *Homo* from Sterkfontein (Stw 53) is nearly identical to the OH 24 *Homo habilis* cranium from Olduvai.

However, a problem with both OH 24 and Stw 53 is that while most experts agree that they belong to the genus *Homo*, there is considerable disagreement as to

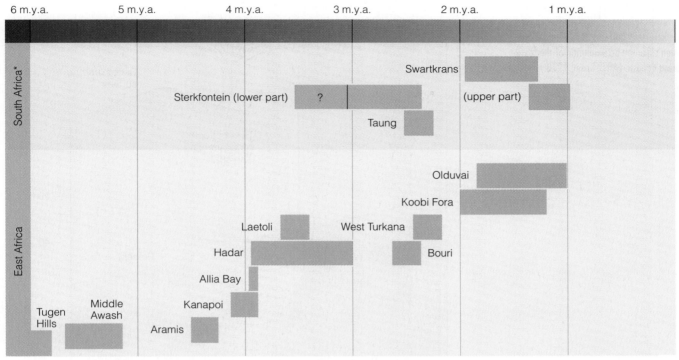

6 m.y.a.　　5 m.y.a.　　4 m.y.a.　　3 m.y.a.　　2 m.y.a.　　1 m.y.a.

*South African dates are very approximate.

whether they should be included in the species *habilis*. The relationships of the Plio-Pleistocene fossil hominids to one another and the difficulties of such genus and species interpretation will be discussed in the following sections. A time line for all the Plio-Pleistocene sites discussed in the text is shown in Figure 10–23.

FIGURE 10–23
Time line of major Plio-Pleistocene hominid sites. Note that some dates are approximations. Question marks indicate those estimates that are most tentative.

Geology and Dating Problems in South Africa

While the geological and archaeological context in East Africa is often straight-forward, the South African early hominid sites are much more complex geologi-cally. All were discovered by commercial quarrying activity, which greatly disrupted the geological picture and, in the case of Taung, completely destroyed the site.

The hominid remains are found with thousands of other fossilized bones embedded in limestone cliffs, caves, fissures, and sinkholes. The limestone was formed by millions of generations of shells of marine organisms during the Precambrian—more than 2 billion years ago—when South Africa was submerged under a shallow sea. Once deposited, the limestones were cut through by perco-lating groundwater from below and rainwater from above, forming a maze of caves and fissures often connected to the surface by narrow shafts (Fig. 10–24). Through these vertical shafts and horizontal cave openings, bones either fell or were carried in, where they conglomerated with sand, pebbles, and soil into a cementlike matrix called *breccia*.

As the cave fissures filled in, they were constantly subjected to further erosion forces from above and below, so that caves would be partially filled, then closed to the surface for a considerable time, then reopened again to commence accumula-tion thousands of years later. All this activity yields an incredibly complex geologi-cal situation that can be worked out only after the most detailed kind of paleoecological analysis.

FIGURE 10–24
Swartkrans, geological section. The upper (reconstructed) part has been removed by erosion since the accumulation of the fossil-bearing deposit. (After Brain, 1970.)

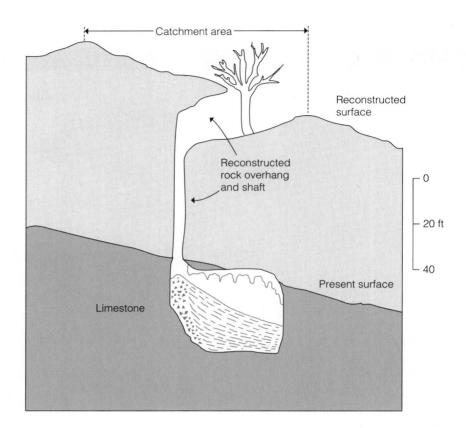

Osteodontokeratic
(*osteo*, meaning "bone," *donto*, meaning "tooth," and *keratic*, meaning "horn")

Since bones accumulated in these caves and fissures largely by accidental processes, it seems likely that none of the South African australopithecine sites are *primary* hominid localities. In other words, unlike the East African sites, these are not areas where hominids organized activities, scavenged food, and so on.

Just how did all the fossilized bone accumulate, and, most particularly, what were the ancient hominids doing there? In the case of Swartkrans and Sterkfontein, the bones probably accumulated through the combined activities of carnivorous leopards, saber-toothed cats, and hyenas (Fig. 10–24). Moreover, the unexpectedly high proportion of primate (baboon and hominid) remains suggests that these localities were the location (or very near the location) of primate sleeping sites, thus providing ready primate prey for various predators (Brain, 1981).

Raymond Dart argued enthusiastically for an alternative explanation, suggesting that the hominids regularly used bone, tooth, and horn remains as tools, which he called the **osteodontokeratic** culture complex. However, analogies with the food habits of modern African foragers indicate that the bone accumulation may be accounted for simply by hominid and carnivore eating practices.

Owing to the complex geological picture as well as a lack of appropriate material (such as volcanic deposits) for chronometric techniques, dating the South African early hominid sites has posed tremendous problems. Without chronometric dating, the best that can be done is to correlate the faunal sequences in South Africa with areas in East Africa where dates are better known (this approach is called biostratigraphy; see p. 225). Faunal sequencing of this sort on pigs, bovids such as antelope, and Old World monkeys has provided the following tenuous chronology:

Location	Age
Swartkrans	1 m.y.
Taung	2 m.y.
Sterkfontein	3 m.y.

FIGURE 10–25

Time line of Plio-Pleistocene hominids. Note that most dates are approximations. Question marks indicate those estimates that are most tentative.

Attempts at paleomagnetic dating (see p. 225) suggest an age of 3.3–2.8 m.y.a. for the oldest South African hominid (Brock et al., 1977), thus pushing the estimates to the extreme limits of those provided by biostratigraphy. In fact, some researchers believe that the paleomagnetic results are ambiguous and continue to "put their money" on the biostratigraphic data, especially those dates determined by analysis of pig and monkey fossils. From such consideration, they place the oldest South African early hominid sites at perhaps as much as half a million years later (i.e., around 2.5 m.y.a.) (White et al., 1981). This is crucial, since it places *all* the South African hominids after *Australopithecus afarensis* in East Africa (Fig. 10–25). Recent excavations at Sterkfontein have suggested that the earliest hominids *may* come from levels as early as 3.5 m.y.a. (Clarke and Tobias, 1995). However, this date, which would be as early as *A. afarensis* in East Africa, has not yet been corroborated.

Interpretations: What Does It All Mean?

By this time, it may seem that anthropologists have an almost perverse fascination in finding small scraps buried in the ground and then assigning them confusing numbers and taxonomic labels impossible to remember. We must realize that the collection of all the basic fossil data is the foundation of human evolutionary research. Without fossils, our speculations would be completely hollow. Several large, ongoing paleoanthropological projects discussed in Chapter 9 are now collecting additional data in an attempt to answer some of the more perplexing questions about our evolutionary history.

FIGURE 10–26
Morphology and variation of robust australopithecines. (Note both the typical features and the range of variation as shown in different specimens.)

ER 406 (Koobi Fora)
Superior view

Sagittal crest

WT 17000 (West Turkana)

Postorbital constriction

OH 5 ("Zinj;" Olduvai)

Small incisor and canine teeth

Broad cheekbones (zygomatics)

SK 48 (Swartkrans)

Large backwardly extending zygomatic arch

ER 732 (Koobi Fora)

Note: The size and proportions of this specimen differ from ER 406 and OH 5 (above), and this individual has been suggested as a female *A. boisei.*

Very large molar teeth

ER 729 (Koobi Fora)

The numbering of specimens, which may at times seem somewhat confusing, is an attempt to keep the designations neutral and to make reference to each individual fossil as clear as possible. The formal naming of finds as *Australopithecus*, *Homo habilis*, or *Homo erectus* should come much later, since it involves a lengthy series of complex interpretations. Assigning generic and specific names to fossil finds is more than just a convenience; when we attach a particular label, such as *A. boisei*, to a particular fossil, we should be fully aware of the biological implications of such an interpretation.

Even more basic to our understanding of human evolution, the use of taxonomic nomenclature involves interpretations of fossil relationships. For example, the two fossils "Zinj" and ER 406 (Fig. 10–26) are both usually called *A. boisei*. What we are saying here is that they are both members of one interbreeding species. These two fossils can now be compared with others, like Sts 5 from Sterkfontein (see Fig. 10–20), which is usually called *A. africanus*. What we are implying now is that "Zinj" and ER 406 are more closely related to each other than *either* is to Sts 5. Furthermore, that Sts 5 (*A. africanus*) populations were incapable of successfully interbreeding with *A. boisei* populations is a direct biological inference of this nomenclature.

We can carry the level of interpretation even further. For example, fossils such as ER 1470 (see Fig. 10–16) are called early *Homo* (*Homo habilis*). We are now making a genus-level distinction, and two basic biological implications are involved:

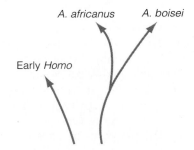

FIGURE 10–27
Phylogenetic interpretation. Early *Homo* is generically distinct from australopithecines.

1. *A. africanus* (Sts 5) and *A. boisei* ("Zinj" and ER 406) are more closely related to each other than either is to ER 1470 (Fig. 10–27).
2. The distinction between the groups reflects a basic difference in adaptive level (see Chapter 8).

From the time that fossil sites are first located to the eventual interpretation of hominid evolutionary events, several steps are necessary. Ideally, they should follow a logical order, for if interpretations are made too hastily, they confuse important issues for many years. Here is a reasonable sequence:

1. Selecting and surveying sites
2. Excavating sites and recovering fossil hominids
3. Designating individual finds with specimen numbers for clear reference
4. Cleaning, preparing, studying, and describing fossils
5. Comparing with other fossil material—in chronological framework if possible
6. Comparing fossil variation with known ranges of variation in closely related groups of living primates and analyzing ancestral and derived characteristics
7. Assigning taxonomic names to fossil material

See Box 10–4 for further discussion.

The task of interpretation is still not complete, for what we really want to know in the long run is what happened to the populations represented by the fossil remains. Indeed, in looking at the fossil hominid record, we are looking for our ancestors. In the process of eventually determining those populations that are our most likely antecedents, we may conclude that some hominids are on evolutionary side branches. If this conclusion is accurate, those hominids necessarily must have become extinct. It is both interesting and relevant to us as hominids to try to find out what influenced some earlier members of our family to continue evolving while others died out.

BOX 10–4   A CLOSER LOOK

Hominids, Hominids. How Many Hominids?

The last decade has been an exciting time for paleoanthropology. With greater political stability in parts of Africa, renewed opportunities to explore geologically rich areas have been exploited. And the results have been spectacular, with dozens of new fossils coming from 15 additional localities. Moreover, significant new discoveries have been made at sites explored previously (particularly from Kanapoi, in Kenya, and Sterkfontein, in South Africa).

As earlier and earlier fossil-bearing geological localities have been identified, the proposed date for the earliest hominid has been extended back in time. In 1995, available evidence suggested this date at close to 4 m.y.a. Then, with the first discoveries of *Ardipithecus* at Aramis, it was pushed back to 4.4 m.y.a. And, most recently, with the announcements of additional finds, the date has been stretched to 6 m.y.a. In other words, just in the last six years, the time depth of hominid emergence has been expanded by 50 percent beyond prior estimates.

All this activity accompanying claims of "the earliest hominid" has attracted intense media coverage, including front-page newspaper articles and cover stories in publications such as *Time* magazine. To scientists, accustomed to relative obscurity, this is pretty heady stuff. Moreover, as students hear about these discoveries, their interest in anthropology is piqued. And needless to say, all these recent finds are providing vast quantities of additional data, further stimulating discussion and debate among the experts.

So much for the good news. Once the initial exhilaration of novelty begins to fade, college instructors realize we now have to *explain* all this to our students. Moreover, with the data now coming in so rapidly and with so many major evolutionary realignments being proposed, there has not been adequate time to fully evaluate or test the various hypotheses. Considering the unfortunate history of interpretive excesses in hominid paleontology, this last concern is especially troublesome. Below we discuss four major considerations which pertain to current scientific perspectives within such a rapidly changing situation.

1. We know that in the past there was *much* greater diversity among hominoids (particularly large-bodied ones; see p. 208) than there is today. Indeed, with only four genera and five species, living large-bodied hominoids are among the least diverse of any group of extant primate (especially when compared to Old World monkeys, New World monkeys, or even lemurs). However, the fossil record for most of the Miocene documents many more hominoid genera and species. Thus, at some point, hominoid diversity was drastically reduced. The question is, When?

2. In the early days of hominid discoveries, poor biological methods led to an excessive number of pro-

Continuing Uncertainties—Taxonomic Issues

As previously discussed, paleoanthropologists are concerned with making biological interpretations of variation found in the hominid fossil record. Most especially, researchers endeavor to assign extinct forms to particular genera and species. We saw that for the diverse array of Miocene hominoids, the evolutionary picture is exceptionally complex. As new finds accumulate, there is continued uncertainty even as to family assignment, to say nothing of genus and species!

For the very end of the Miocene and for the Plio-Pleistocene, the situation is considerably clearer. First, there is a larger fossil sample from a more restricted geographical area (South and East Africa) and from a more concentrated time period (spanning about 5 million years, from 6 to 1 m.y.a.). Second, more complete specimens exist (e.g., Lucy), and we thus have good evidence for most parts of the body.

posed extinct genera and species. For example, in the first half of the twentieth century, up to 10 different genera of hominids were recognized. Those advocating such a perspective—that is, giving a new genus (and species) designation to every additional fossil discovery—have been referred to as "splitters." A more technical term for this trend in evolutionary interpretation is *multiplication of taxa*. By the 1970s, however, the number of widely recognized hominid genera had been reduced to only two (*Australopithecus* and *Homo*, although some researchers were comfortable adding a third genus, *Paranthropus;* see p. 277); and throughout the latter part of the twentieth century, the prior willingness to overly split hominids into many groups (taxa) was dramatically curtailed, giving the intellectual momentum to paleoanthropologists inclined to be "lumpers."

3. In the last decade, we have seen a tendency to again subdivide the hominid fossil record into more taxa. New discoveries have obviously stimulated this approach, but so, too, have new techniques and, to an even greater degree, new theoretical perspectives. The new techniques include *cladistic* methodologies (see pp. 188–192), which paleoanthropologists have almost universally adopted. (*Note:* Cladistic methods do not necessarily entail recognition of further fossil taxa, but they do help considerably in systematically identifying variation in the fossil record itself.) And, the approach of *punctuated equilibrium* (see p. 211) provides a theoretical basis for paleoanthropologists and other evolutionary biologists to identify

(indeed, expect) much greater diversity than was previously acknowledged. Are we then entering another era of hominid paleontology dominated by evolutionary splitters? In a sense, we are. But it is one based in sound evolutionary theory and clearly not as biologically flawed as the excesses of the last century.

4. Nevertheless, not everyone is pleased with the direction such interpretations are taking paleoanthropological research. There is considerable skepticism and hesitancy to accept the validity of all the recently proposed new genera. And paleoanthropologists have been most active of late. To the two (or three) genera agreed on in the early 1990s, three additional ones have since been proposed (*Ardipithecus, Orrorin,* and *Kenyanthropus*). By incorporating all three of these genera within the hominids, we would be more than doubling the number of such groups within our family.

As a final point, we should emphasize that the evolutionary process does not usually produce simple and easily interpretable results—with just a minimum of genera and species. This is certainly not the case for most animals, including most groups of primates. The extremely reduced number of recent hominoids is a most unusual exception. How paleoanthropologists cope with the increasing diversity just recently recognized (to say nothing of yet further discoveries) is bound to generate considerable debate. Some of these discussions are likely to be heated. We are certainly living in interesting times!

Accordingly, there is considerable consensus on several basic aspects of evolutionary development during the Plio-Pleistocene. For materials prior to 4 m.y.a., not all scholars are as yet convinced of clear hominid status. However, for fossils dating later than 4 m.y.a., researchers agree unanimously that these forms are hominids (members of the family Hominidae). And as support for this point, all these forms are seen as habitual, well-adapted bipeds, committed at least in part to a terrestrial niche. Moreover, researchers generally agree as to genus-level assignments for most of the forms, although *Orrorin, Ardipithecus,* and *Kenyanthropus* have all been so recently named as to not yet be fully evaluated and accepted (there is also some disagreement regarding how to group the robust australopithecines).

As for species-level designations, little consensus can be found. Indeed, as new fossils have been discovered (e.g., the "black skull"), the picture seems to muddy further. Once again, we are faced with a complex evolutionary process. In attempts to deal with it, we impose varying degrees of simplicity. In so doing, we hope that the evolutionary processes will become clearer—not just for introductory students, but for professional paleoanthropologists and textbook authors as well! Nevertheless, evolution is not a simple process, and disputes and disagreements are bound to arise, especially in making such fine-tuned interpretations as species-level designations.

Consider the following ongoing topics of interest and occasional disagreement among paleoanthropologists dealing with Plio-Pleistocene hominids. You should realize, however, that such continued debate is at the heart of scientific endeavor; indeed, it provides a major stimulus for further research. Here we raise questions regarding four areas of taxonomic interpretation. In general, there is still reasonably strong agreement on these points, and we follow, where possible, the current consensus as reflected in recent publications (Grine, 1988a; Klein, 1989; Conroy, 1997; Fleagle, 1999).

1. *Are the earliest proposed hominid finds (i.e., those prior to 4 m.y.a.) actually hominids?*

   While there is considerable fossil evidence of *Ardipithecus* (especially from Aramis), the analyses are thus far quite incomplete. This same tentative conclusion applies even more so to the very early *Orrorin* fossils from the Tugen Hills. Until more complete investigations have been done and thoroughly reviewed by a variety of scholars, the hominid status of all these remains must still be regarded as tentative. Moreover, beyond a more general designation of the specimens as "hominid," the same caution applies to the full scientific recognition of either *Orrorin* (which thus far appears particularly tenuous) or *Ardipithecus* as a separate genus from other, better-established hominid forms (most notably, *Australopithecus*).

2. *Are* Australopithecus anamensis *and* Australopithecus garhi *separate species from* Australopithecus afarensis?

   The fossil discoveries of *A. anamensis* have thus far been quite fragmentary. When we compare them with the much better known *A. afarensis* materials, the anatomical differences in the Allia Bay and Kanapoi specimens are by no means striking. Likewise, the newly discovered materials from Bouri (*A. garhi*) are still provisionally assigned to a new species. Thus, until more complete remains are discovered, it is best to be cautious and regard the new species designations (*Australopithecus anamensis* and *A. garhi*) as a tentative hypothesis and one requiring further confirmation.

3. *How many genera of australopithecines are there?*

   Many years ago, a plethora of genera was suggested by Robert Broom and others. However, in the 1960s and 1970s, most researchers agreed to "lump" all these forms into *Australopithecus*. With the discovery of early members of the genus *Homo* in the 1960s (and its general recognition in the 1970s), most researchers also recognized the presence of our genus in the Plio-Pleistocene as well (Fig. 10–28).

FIGURE 10–28
Plio-Pleistocene hominids.

A. afarensis   A. robustus   A. africanus   A. boisei   Early *Homo*

In the last decade, there has been an increasing tendency to resplit some of the australopithecines. Recognizing that the robust group (*aethiopicus*, *boisei*, and *robustus*) forms a distinct evolutionary lineage (clade), many researchers (Grine, 1988a; Wood et al., 1994) have argued that the generic term *Paranthropus* should be used to set these robust forms apart from *Australopithecus* (now used in the strict sense).

We agree that there are adequate grounds to make a genus-level distinction, given the evolutionary distinctiveness of the robust clade as well as its apparent adaptive uniqueness (see Fig 10–27). However, for *closely related taxa*, such as we are dealing with here, making this type of interpretation is largely arbitrary. (See discussion, pp. 195–197.) The single genus *Australopithecus* has been used for four decades in the wider sense (to include all robust forms), and because it simplifies terminology, we follow the current consensus and continue the traditional usage—*Australopithecus* for all small-brained Plio-Pleistocene hominids with large, thickly enameled teeth (particularly molars) and including all five recognized species: *A. afarensis*, *A. aethiopicus*, *A. africanus*, *A. robustus*, and *A. boisei*.

4. *How many species of early* **Homo** *existed?*
Here is another species-level type of interpretation that is unlikely to be resolved soon. Yet, as it strikes closer to home (our own genus) than the issue for robust australopithecines, the current debate is generating more heat.

Whether we find resolution or not, the *form* of the conflicting views is instructive. The main issue is again interpreting whether variation is *inter-* or *intraspecific*. For those anthropologists who include all the early *Homo* remains from Africa within *one* species (e.g., Tobias, 1991), the considerable variation is thought largely to be due to sexual dimorphism. However, many other researchers (a growing consensus, in fact) see too much variation among the specimens to be explained as part of just one species (even a highly variable one). These paleoanthropologists (Lieberman et al., 1988; Wood, 1992a) thus argue that there was *more than one species* of early *Homo*.* We agree that more than one species is probably represented, but for simplicity suggest referring to all the specimens as "early *Homo*."

Putting It All Together

The interpretation of our paleontological past in terms of which fossils are related to other fossils and how they are all related to modern humans is usually shown diagrammatically in the form of a **phylogeny**. Such a diagram is a family tree of fossil evolution. (Note that strict practitioners of cladistics prefer to use cladograms; see pp. 191–192.) This kind of interpretation is the eventual goal of evolutionary studies, but it is the final goal, only after adequate data are available to understand what is going on.

Another, more basic way to handle these data is to divide the fossil material into subsets. This avoids (for the moment) what are still problematic phylogenetic relationships. Accordingly, for the Plio-Pleistocene hominid material from Africa, we can divide the data into four broad groupings:

Set I. Basal hominids (6.0–4.4 m.y.a.)   The earliest (and most primitive) collection of remains that have been classified as hominids are those from the Tugen Hills and the Middle Awash, the latter area also including the site of Aramis.

Phylogeny
A schematic representation showing ancestor-descendant relationships, usually in a chronological framework.

---

*The species names *Homo habilis* and *Homo rudolfensis* are the ones most commonly used for designating two different species of early *Homo*.

These fossils have, for the moment, been assigned to either *Orrorin* or *Ardipithecus* and are hence each provisionally interpreted as being generically distinct from all the other Plio-Pleistocene forms (listed in sets II–IV). Analysis thus far indicates that at least for the latter Aramis fossils, these forms were likely bipedal, but with a primitive dentition. Brain size of *A. ramidus* is not yet known, but was almost certainly quite small.

Set II. Early, primitive *Australopithecus* (4.2–3.0 m.y.a.) This grouping comprises one well-known species, *A. afarensis*, especially well documented at Laetoli and Hadar. Slightly earlier, closely related forms (perhaps representing a distinct second species) come from two other sites and are provisionally called "*Australopithecus anamensis.*" Best known from analysis of the *A. afarensis* material, the hominids in this set are characterized by a small brain, large teeth (front and back), and a bipedal gait (probably still allowing for considerable climbing). The recently discovered *Kenyanthropus* cranium does not fit neatly in this set or within any of the others. But for the moment (and pending more complete study), it is placed here because it is contemporaneous with these other hominids and is apparently no more encephalized.

Set III. Later, more derived *Australopithecus* (2.5–1.4 m.y.a.; possibly as early as 3.5 m.y.a.) This group is composed of numerous species. (Most experts recognize at least three; some subdivide this material into five or more species.) Remains have come from several sites in both South and East Africa. All of these forms have very large back teeth and do not show appreciable brain enlargement (i.e., encephalization) compared to *A. afarensis*.

Set IV. Early *Homo* (2.4–1.8 m.y.a.) The best known specimens are from East Africa (East Turkana and Olduvai), but early remains of *Homo* have also been found in South Africa (Sterkfontein and possibly Swartkrans and Drimolen). This group is composed of possibly just one, but probably more than one, species. Early *Homo* is characterized (compared to *Australopithecus*) by greater encephalization, altered cranial shape, and smaller (especially molars) and narrower (especially premolars) teeth.

Although hominid fossil evidence has accumulated in great abundance, the fact that so much of the material has been discovered so recently makes any firm judgments concerning the route of human evolution premature. However, paleoanthropologists are certainly not deterred from making their "best guesses," and diverse hypotheses have abounded in recent years. The vast majority of the hundreds of fossils from East Africa is still in the descriptive and early analytical stages. At this time, the construction of phylogenies of human evolution is analogous to building a house with only a partial blueprint. We are not even sure how many rooms there are! Until the existing fossil evidence has been adequately studied, to say nothing about possible new finds, speculative hypotheses must be viewed with a critical eye.

In Figure 10–29, we present several phylogenies representing different and opposing views of hominid evolution. We suggest that you not attempt to memorize them, for they *all* could be out of date by the time you read this book. It will prove more profitable to look at each one and assess the biological implications involved. Also, note which groups are on the "main line" of human evolution (the one including *Homo sapiens*) and which are placed on extinct side branches.

Interpreting the Interpretations

All the schemes in Figure 10–29 postdate 1979, when *A. afarensis* was first suggested as the most likely common ancestor of all later hominids (Johanson and White, 1979). Since the early 1980s, most paleoanthropologists have accepted this view.

PHYLOGENY A
A. afarensis common ancestor theory
(after Johanson and White, 1979)

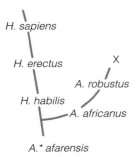

Note: Afarensis postulated as common ancestor to all Plio-Pleistocene hominids.

PHYLOGENY B
Multiple lineage early divergence
(after Senut and Tardieu, 1985)

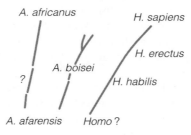

Note: Major split occurs before A. afarensis. Possible multiple lineages in Plio-Pleistocene.

PHYLOGENY C
A. africanus common ancestor theory
(after Skelton et al., 1986)

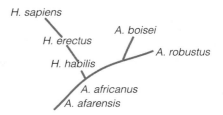

Note: Major split occurs after A. africanus. Therefore, A. africanus is seen as still in our lineage as well as that of more derived australopithecines.

PHYLOGENY D
Early robust lineage
(after Delson, 1986, 1987; Grine, 1993)

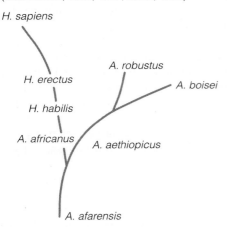

PHYLOGENY E
Ardipithecus as probable root species for later hominids (and also incorporating other recent modifications) (after Skelton and McHenry, 1992; Wolpoff, 1999)

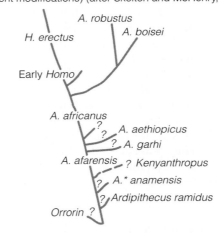

* For genus designation, the *A* in all phylogenies refers to *Australopithecus* and *H* refers to *Homo*.

One exception is shown in phylogeny B (after Senut and Tardieu, 1985), but this position—based on the premise that *A. afarensis* is actually more than one species—has not been generally supported.

We have not included evolutionary schemes prior to 1979, as they do not account for the crucial discoveries at Hadar and Laetoli of *Australopithecus afarensis*. These now-outdated models frequently postulated *A. africanus* as the common ancestor of later *Australopithecus* (robust varieties) and early *Homo*. In modified form, this view is still continued in some respects (see phylogeny C).

Probably the most intractable problems for interpretation of early hominid evolution involve what to do with *A. aethiopicus* and *A. africanus*. Carefully look at the different evolutionary reconstructions to see how various researchers deal with these complicated issues. Finally, the newest finds (*Orrorin, Ardipithecus, Kenyanthropus, Australopithecus anamensis,* and *Australopithecus garhi*) will need to be incorporated into these schemes. Phylogeny E is an initial attempt to do so, but only points up how frequently hominid evolutionary interpretations need to be reevaluated and substantially revised.

FIGURE 10–29
Phylogenies of hominid evolution.

SUMMARY

After so much detail relating to hominid evolution in the Plio-Pleistocene, you may feel frustrated by what must seem to be endlessly changing and conflicting interpretations. However, after 75 years of discoveries of early hominids in Africa, there are several general points on which most researchers agree:

1. *A. afarensis* is the earliest hominid at present with substantial definite supporting evidence. It is possible, however, that *Ardipithecus* will soon supplant *A. afarensis* for this status of earliest definite hominid. Where *"Orrorin"* fits in remains to be seen.
2. *A. afarensis* is probably ancestral to all later hominids (or is very closely related to the species that is).
3. *A. aethiopicus* is ancestral solely to the "robust" group (clade), linking it with earlier *afarensis* as well as with one (or both) later robust species.
4. All australopithecines were extinct by 1 m.y.a. (or shortly before).
5. All australopithecine species (presumably early *Homo* as well) were highly variable, showing extreme sexual dimorphism.
6. Since there is so much intraspecific variation, on average there was not much difference in body size among australopithecine species.
7. *A. africanus* was probably not the last common ancestor of the robust lineage and genus *Homo*. That is, phylogeny C is probably not entirely correct.
8. All forms (*Australopithecus*, early *Homo,* and all other proposed early hominids) were small-brained (as compared to later species of the genus *Homo*); nevertheless, all early hominids are more encephalized than apes of comparable body size.
9. Most forms (including some members of early *Homo*) had large back teeth.
10. There was substantial parallelism (homoplasy) in physical traits among early hominid lineages.
11. Given the current state of knowledge, there are several equally supportable phylogenies.

As this list makes clear, we have come a long way in reaching an understanding of Plio-Pleistocene hominid evolution. Nevertheless, a truly complete understanding is not at hand. Such is the stuff of science!

QUESTIONS FOR REVIEW

1. In East Africa, all the early hominid sites are found along the Rift Valley. Why is this significant?
2. (a) Why is postcranial evidence (particularly the lower limb) so crucial in showing the australopithecines (or other early forms) as definite hominids?
   (b) What particular aspects of the australopithecine pelvis and lower limb are hominid-like?
3. In what ways are the remains of *Ardipithecus ramidus* and *Australopithecus anamensis* primitive? How do we know that these forms are hominids?

4. Why are some Plio-Pleistocene hominids from East Africa called "early *Homo*" (or *H. habilis*)? What does this imply for the evolutionary relationships of the australopithecines?

5. What kinds of dating techniques have been used in South Africa?

6. Why is the dating control better in East Africa than in South Africa?

7. Discuss the first thing you would do if you found an early hominid fossil and were responsible for its formal description and publication. What would you include in your publication?

8. Discuss two current disputes regarding taxonomic issues concerning early hominids. Try to give support for alternative positions.

9. Why would one use the taxonomic term *Paranthropus* in contrast to *Australopithecus*?

10. What is a phylogeny? Construct one for early hominids (6.0–1 m.y.a.). Make sure you can describe what conclusions your scheme makes. Also, try to defend it.

11. Discuss at least two alternative ways that *A. africanus* is currently incorporated into phylogenetic schemes.

12. What are the most recently discovered of the Plio-Pleistocene hominid materials, and how are they, for the moment, incorporated into a phylogenetic scheme? How secure do you think this interpretation is?

SUGGESTED FURTHER READING

Agnew, Neville and Martha Demas. 1998. "Preserving the Laetoli Footprints." *Scientific American* 279(3): 44–57.

Conroy, Glenn C. 1997. *Reconstructing Human Origins. A Modern Synthesis*. New York: Norton.

Corruccini, Robert S., and Russel L. Ciochon (eds.). 1994. *Integrative Paths to the Past: Paleoanthropology Advances in Honor of F. Clark Howell*. Englewood Cliffs, NJ: Prentice Hall.

Delson, Eric (ed.). 1985. *Ancestors: The Hard Evidence*. New York: Liss.

Grine, Fred (ed.). 1988. *Evolutionary History of the Robust Australopithecines*. New York: de Gruyter.

Rak, Yoel. 1983. *The Australopithecine Face*. New York: Academic Press.

Tattersall, Ian. 2000. "Once We Were Not Alone." *Scientific American* 282(1): 56–62.

Wolpoff, Milford H. 1999. *Paleoanthropology*. 2nd ed. Boston: McGraw-Hill.

RESOURCES ON THE INTERNET

 Wadsworth Anthropology Resource Center
http://anthropology.wadsworth.com

The companion website for this text includes a range of enrichment material focused on the chapter's topic. While online you can enhance your understanding of the chapter by exploring one of the several additional Internet exercises, by researching topics, and by accessing full articles on InfoTrac College Edition. You can also reinforce the concepts by taking online practice exams.

Internet Exercises

Search the Internet for information regarding one of the early hominid sites, Aramis, Kanapoi, or Allia Bay. What information have you learned that supplements the material in this textbook? Also, search the news sites, including ScienceDaily (http://www.sciencedaily.com). What new information has come out regarding these sites or any other early hominid sites since this text was written?

 InfoTrac College Edition

http://www.infotrac-college.com/wadsworth

Review the Plio-Pleistocene hominid sites mentioned in the text. Can you find research about any of these sites on InfoTrac College Edition? (*Hint:* Use PowerTrac.) What was found at these sites? To what taxon or taxa are these finds attributed?

CHAPTER

11

CONTENTS

Homo erectus and Contemporaries

Trail of hominid footprints fossilized in volcanic ash at
Laetoli, Tanzania (approximate age, 3.7 million years)

CHAPTER 11

See the following sections
of the CD-ROM for topics
covered in this chapter: Virtual
Lab 10.

Introduction

In Chapter 10, we traced the earliest evidence of hominid evolution by reviewing the abundant fossil material from Africa that documents the origins of *Australopithecus, Homo,* and possibly earlier forms, dating from the late Miocene and extending up through the Pliocene and early Pleistocene. In this chapter, we take up what might be called the next stage of hominid evolution, the appearance and dispersal of *Homo erectus* (see Fig. 11–2).

Homo erectus was a widely distributed species and was in fact the first hominid (for which we have definite evidence) to have migrated out of Africa and to have inhabited vast new regions of the Old World. Moreover, as a species, *H. erectus* existed over an exceptionally long time, spanning well over 1 million years. If one judges species success by longevity, *H. erectus* appears to be the most successful hominid that has ever existed. How can we explain the remarkable success of this species?

In this chapter, we discuss many of the physical changes that characterized *H. erectus*, especially as compared to what came before (early *Homo*) and after (*Homo sapiens*). Certainly, some of the physical alterations, such as increased brain size, larger body size, and dental modifications, help account for the success of *H. erectus*. But that is not the whole story. As we have emphasized, hominid evolution has long been characterized by a biocultural interaction. Thus, it is only through explaining the behavioral capacities of *Homo erectus* (in concert with morphological change) that we can understand the success of this hominid species. For this reason, we also highlight some of the abundant archaeological evidence and related biocultural reconstructions that have so long occupied and fascinated paleoanthropologists.

Homo erectus: Terminology and Geographical Distribution

The discoveries of fossils now referred to as *H. erectus* go back to the nineteenth century. Later in this chapter, we will discuss in some detail the historical background of these earliest discoveries in Java and the somewhat later discoveries in China. From this work, as well as presumably related finds in Europe and North Africa, a variety of taxonomic names were suggested. The most significant of these earlier terms were *Pithecanthropus* (for the Javanese remains) and *Sinanthropus* (for the fossils from northern China). In fact, you may still see these terms in older sources or occasionally used colloquially and thus placed in quotation marks (e.g., "*Pithecanthropus*").

It is important to realize that taxonomic *splitting* (which this terminology reflects) was quite common in the early years of paleoanthropology. Only after World War II and with the incorporation of the Modern Synthesis into paleontology (see p. 88 and pp. 195–197) did more systematic biological thinking come to the fore. Following this trend, in the early 1950s all the material previously referred to as "*Pithecanthropus*," "*Sinanthropus*," and so forth, was included in a single species of genus *Homo—H. erectus*. This reclassification proved to be a most significant development on two counts:

1. It reflected the incorporation of modern evolutionary thinking into hominid paleontology.
2. The simplification in terminology, based as it was on sound biological principles, refocused research away from endless arguments regarding classification to broader populational, behavioral, and ecological considerations.

Discoveries in the last few decades have established *well-dated* finds of *H. erectus* in East Africa from geological contexts chronometrically dated as old as 1.8 m.y.a. In addition, new dates first published in 1994 by geologists from the Berkeley

Geochronology Laboratory (Swisher et al., 1994) have suggested that two localities in Java are as old as those in East Africa (with dates of 1.8 and 1.6 m.y.a.). These early dates have come as somewhat of a surprise to many paleoanthropologists, but as you will see, there is now growing evidence for an early dispersal of hominids outside of Africa—that is, one *well before* 1 m.y.a.

 See Virtual Lab 10 for an interactive map showing the distribution of *Homo erectus.*

Current interpretations thus view the first hominid dispersal out of Africa as occurring between 1.5 and 2 m.y.a. A likely route would have taken these hominids through southwestern Asia, and there are some intriguing hints from the Ubeidiya site in Israel that this route was indeed exploited quite early on. The most conclusive evidence from Ubeidiya is archaeological, including a number of stone tools dated (by paleomagnetism and faunal correlation) to 1.4–1.3 m.y.a. In addition, there are some fragmentary hominid remains, including cranial pieces and two teeth. Unfortunately, the association of these hominid remains with the tools at a date prior to 1 m.y.a. is uncertain. Consequently, there is not yet *definitive* fossil evidence of *H. erectus* (or a close relative) from southwest Asia. Nevertheless, the Ubeidiya archaeological discoveries are highly suggestive and fit with the overall emerging pattern of an early hominid dispersal from Africa.

More than likely, these first continental migrants were members of *H. erectus* or a group very closely related to *H. erectus* (although an earlier dispersal of a more primitive member of genus *Homo* cannot be ruled out). What the current evidence most economically suggests is that *Homo erectus* migrated out of East Africa, eventually to occupy South and North Africa, southern and northeastern Asia, and perhaps Europe as well. The most significant early finds of hominids in Europe (indeed perhaps the earliest finds anywhere outside of Africa) come from the Dmanisi site in the Republic of Georgia (Fig. 11–1). Dating to more than 1.7 m.y.a., these fossils (including two recently discovered crania) are similar to their African cousins and together might represent a closely related but different species from *Homo erectus* (see p. 302 for further discussion). Another recent find pushing back the antiquity of hominids in western Europe has come from the 500,000-year-old Boxgrove site in southern England, where a hominid tibia (shinbone) was unearthed in 1994. And still another recent find (1994), from the Ceprano site in central Italy, may be the best evidence yet of *H. erectus* in Europe (Ascenzi et al., 1996). Provisional dating of a partial cranium from this important site suggests a date greater than 700,000 years ago. The primary researchers, as well as Rightmire (1998), conclude that cranial morphology places this specimen quite close to *H. erectus.*

FIGURE 11–1
Dmanisi mandible.

Finally, some other fossil remains from Spain, also discovered in 1994 and announced in 1995, may well be the oldest hominids yet found in western Europe (see Fig. 11–2 for locations of these hominid sites). From the Gran Dolina site in the highly productive Atapuerca region of northern Spain, where numerous, somewhat more recent hominid fossils have also been discovered (discussed in Chapter 12), several fragments of at least four individuals have been found (Carbonell et al., 1995). The dating, based on paleomagnetic determinations (see p. 225), places the Gran Dolina hominids at approximately 780,000 y.a.* (Parés and Pérez-González, 1995). If this dating is further corroborated, these early Spanish finds would be *at least* 250,000 years older than any other hominid yet discovered in western Europe. Because all the 36 pieces thus far identified are quite fragmentary, the taxonomic assignment of these fossils still remains problematic. Initial analysis, however, suggests that most of the European fossils are *not H. erectus.* Whether any of these early European hominids, except perhaps for the Ceprano cranium, belong within the species *Homo erectus* thus still remains to be determined.

The dispersal of *Homo erectus* from Africa was influenced by climate, topography, water boundaries, and access to food and other resources. Paleoenvironmental reconstructions are thus of crucial importance in understanding the expansion of

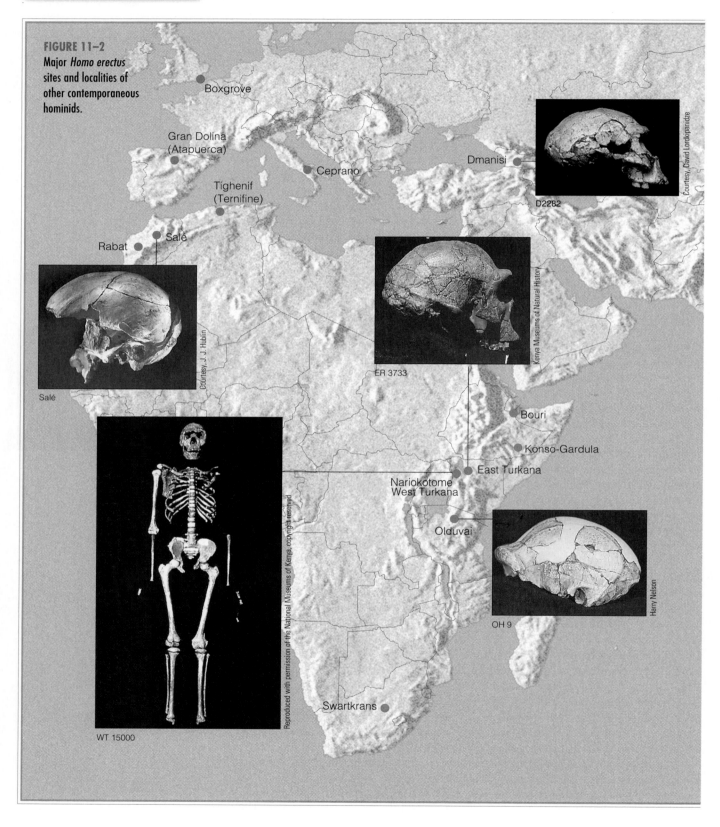

FIGURE 11–2
Major *Homo erectus* sites and localities of other contemporaneous hominids.

Boxgrove

Gran Dolina (Atapuerca)

Ceprano

Tighenif (Ternifine)

Rabat

Salé

Dmanisi

D2282

Salé

ER 3733

Bouri

Konso-Gardula

East Turkana

Nariokotome
West Turkana

Olduvai

WT 15000

Swartkrans

OH 9

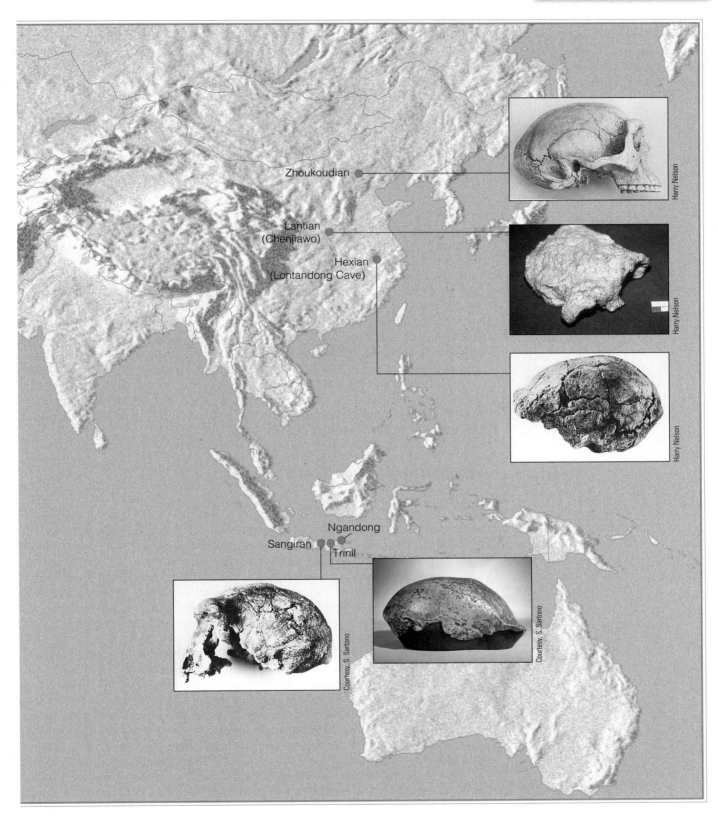

Zhoukoudian

Lantian
(Chenjiawo)

Hexian
(Lontandong Cave)

Ngandong

Sangiran

Trinil

Harry Nelson

Harry Nelson

Harry Nelson

Courtesy, S. Sartono

Courtesy, S. Sartono

Pleistocene
The epoch of the Cenozoic from 1.8 m.y.a. until 10,000 y.a. Frequently referred to as the Ice Age, this epoch is associated with continental glaciations in northern latitudes.

H. erectus to so many parts of the Old World. The long temporal span of *H. erectus* begins very early in the **Pleistocene** and extends to fairly late in that geological epoch. To comprehend the world of *Homo erectus*, we must understand how environments shifted during the Pleistocene.

The Pleistocene (1.8 m.y.a.–10,000 y.a.)

During much of the Pleistocene (also known as the Age of Glaciers or Ice Age), large areas of the Northern Hemisphere were covered with enormous masses of ice, which advanced and retreated as the temperature fell and rose. An early classification of glacial (and interglacial) Europe divided the Pleistocene into four major glacial periods. However, climatic conditions varied in different areas of Europe, and distinctive glacial periods are also now known for the North Sea, England, and eastern Europe, not to mention Asia and North America. New dating techniques have revealed a much more complex account of glacial advance and retreat, and the many oscillations of cold and warm temperatures during the Pleistocene affected both plants and animals: "The Pleistocene record shows that there were about 15 major cold periods and 50 minor advances during its [more than] 1.5-m.y. duration, or one major cold period every 100,000 years" (Tattersal et al., 1988, p. 230).

The Pleistocene, which lasted more than 1.75 million years, was a significant period in hominid evolutionary history and encompassed the appearance and disappearance of *Homo erectus*. By the end of the Pleistocene, modern humans had already appeared, dependence on culture had dramatically increased, and domestication of plants and animals—one of the great cultural revolutions of human history—was either about to commence or had already begun. Given this background on the time span in which *H. erectus* evolved and lived, let us examine more closely this predecessor of *H. sapiens*.

The Morphology of *Homo erectus*

Brain Size

Homo erectus differs in several respects from both early *Homo* and *Homo sapiens*. The most obvious feature is cranial size (which, of course, is closely related to brain size). Early *Homo* had cranial capacities ranging from as small as 500 cm³ to as large as 800 cm³. *H. erectus*, on the other hand, shows considerable brain enlargement, with a cranial capacity of 750 to 1,250 cm³ (with a mean of approximately 900 cm³). However, in making such comparisons, we must bear in mind two key questions: What is the comparative sample, and what were the overall body sizes of the species being compared?

In relation to the first question, you should recall that many scholars are now convinced that there was more than one species of early *Homo* in East Africa around 2 m.y.a. If so, only one of these could have been ancestral to *H. erectus*. (Indeed, it is possible that neither species gave rise to *H. erectus* and that perhaps we have yet to find direct evidence of the ancestral species.) Taking a more optimistic view that at least one of these fossil groups is a likely ancestor of later hominids, the question still remains—which one? If we choose the smaller-bodied sample of early *Homo* as our presumed ancestral group, then *H. erectus* shows as much as a 40 percent increase in cranial capacity. However, if the comparative sample is the larger-bodied group of early *Homo* (as exemplified by skull 1470, from East Turkana), then *H. erectus* shows a 25 percent increase in cranial capacity.

As we previously discussed, brain size is closely tied to overall body size (a relationship termed *encephalization*). We have made a point of the increase in *H. erectus* brain size; however, it must be realized that *H. erectus* was also considerably larger overall than earlier members of the genus *Homo*. In fact, when *H. erectus* is compared with the larger-bodied early *Homo* sample, *relative* brain size is about the same (Walker, 1991). Furthermore, when considering the relative brain size of *H. erectus* in comparison with *H. sapiens*, it is seen that *H. erectus* was considerably less encephalized than later members of the genus *Homo*.

See Virtual Lab 10, section III, for an interactive exercise concerning the estimation of body mass from a fossil femur.

Body Size

As we have just mentioned, another feature displayed by *H. erectus*, compared to earlier hominids, is a dramatic increase in body size. For several decades, little was known of the postcranial skeleton of *H. erectus*. However, with the discovery of a nearly complete skeleton in 1984 from **Nariokotome** (on the west side of Lake Turkana in Kenya) and its detailed analysis (Walker and Leakey, 1993), the data base is now much improved. From this specimen (and from less complete individuals at other sites), some *Homo erectus* adults are estimated to have weighed well over 100 pounds, with an average adult stature of about 5 feet 6 inches (McHenry, 1992; Ruff and Walker, 1993). Another point to keep in mind is that *Homo erectus* was quite sexually dimorphic—at least as indicated by the East African specimens. Thus, for male adult body size, weight and stature in some individuals may have been considerably greater than the average figures just mentioned. In fact, it is estimated that if the Nariokotome boy had survived, he would have attained an adult stature of over 6 feet (Walker, 1993).

Associated with the large stature (and explaining the significant increase in body weight) is also a dramatic increase in robusticity. In fact, this characteristic of very heavy body build was to dominate hominid evolution not just during *H. erectus* times, but through the long transitional era of archaic *Homo sapiens* as well. Only with the appearance of anatomically modern *H. sapiens* do we see a more gracile skeletal structure, which is still characteristic of most modern populations.

Nariokotome
(nar´-ee-oh-ko´-tow-may)

Cranial Shape

The cranium of *Homo erectus* displays a highly distinctive shape, partly as a result of increased brain size, but probably more correlated with significant body size (robusticity). The ramifications of this heavily built cranium are reflected in thick cranial bone (most notably in Asian specimens) and large browridges (supraorbital tori) in the front of the skull and a projecting **nuchal torus** at the rear (Fig. 11–4 on p. 290).

The vault is long and low, receding back from the large browridges with little forehead development. Moreover, the cranium is wider at the base compared with earlier *or* later species of genus *Homo*. The maximum breadth is below the ear opening, giving a pentagonal contour to the cranium (when viewed from behind). In contrast, both early *Homo* crania and *H. sapiens* crania have more vertical sides, and the maximum width is *above* the ear openings.

Nuchal torus
(nuke´-ul, pertaining to the neck)
A projection of bone in the back of the cranium where neck muscles attach, used to hold up the head. The nuchal torus is a distinctive feature of *H. erectus*.

Dentition

The dentition of *Homo erectus* is much like that of *Homo sapiens*, but the earlier species exhibits somewhat larger teeth. However, compared with early *Homo*, *H. erectus* does show some dental reduction.

Another interesting feature of the dentition of some *H. erectus* specimens is seen in the incisor teeth. On the back (lingual) surfaces, the teeth are scooped out in appearance, forming a surface reminiscent of a shovel. Accordingly, such teeth are referred to as "shovel-shaped" incisors, and they are also found in several modern human populations (Fig. 11–3). It has been suggested that teeth shaped in this

FIGURE 11–3
Shovel-shaped incisors, shown here in a modern *Homo sapiens* individual.

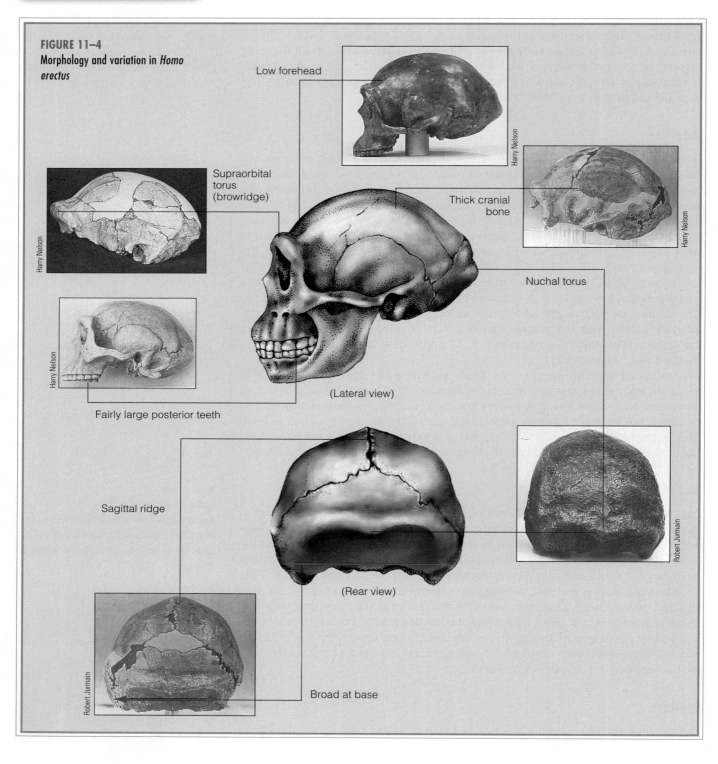

FIGURE 11–4
Morphology and variation in *Homo erectus*

Low forehead

Supraorbital torus (browridge)

Thick cranial bone

Nuchal torus

Fairly large posterior teeth

(Lateral view)

Sagittal ridge

(Rear view)

Broad at base

manner are an adaptation in hunter-gatherers for processing foods, a contention not yet proved (or really even framed in a testable manner). One thing does seem likely: Shovel-shaped incisors are probably an ancestral feature of the species *H. erectus*, as the phenomenon has been found not just in the Chinese specimens, but also in the early individual from Nariokotome.

Historical Overview of *Homo erectus* Discoveries

In our discussion of Plio-Pleistocene hominids, we traced the evolutionary developments in *chronological* order, that is, discussing the oldest specimens first. Here we take a different approach and discuss the finds in the order in which they were discovered. We believe that this approach is useful, as the discoveries cover a broad range of time—indeed, almost the entire history of paleoanthropology. Given this relatively long history of scientific discovery, the later finds were assessed in the light of earlier ones (and thus can still be best understood within a historical context).

Java

Dutch anatomist Eugene Dubois (1858–1940) (Fig. 11–5) was the first scientist to deliberately design a research plan that would take him from his anatomy lab to where fossil bones might be buried. Up until this time, embryology and comparative anatomy were considered the proper methods of studying humans and their ancestry, and the research was done in the laboratory. Dubois changed all this.

The latter half of the nineteenth century was a period of intellectual excitement. In Europe, Darwin's *On the Origin of Species* (published in 1859) provoked scientists as well as educated laypeople to take opposing sides, often with heated emotion. In 1856, an unusual skull had been recovered near Düsseldorf, Germany. This specimen is now known as Neandertal, but when a description of it was published, scientific opinion was again divided, and feelings ran high.

This stimulating intellectual climate surrounded the youthful Eugene Dubois, who left Holland for Sumatra in 1887 to search for, as he phrased it, "the missing link." Dubois went to work immediately and soon unearthed a variety of animal bones, including orangutan, gibbon, and several other mammalian species. However, his successes soon diminished, and in 1890 he switched his fieldwork to the banks of the Solo River near the town of Trinil, on the neighboring island of Java.

In October 1891, the field crew unearthed a skullcap that was to become internationally famous. The following year, a human femur was recovered about 15 yards upstream in what Dubois claimed was the same level as the skullcap. Dubois assumed that the skullcap (with a cranial capacity of slightly over 900 cm^3) and the femur belonged to the same individual.

After studying these discoveries for a few years, Dubois startled the world in 1894 with a paper provocatively titled "*Pithecanthropus erectus*, A Manlike Species of Transitional Anthropoid from Java." In 1895, Dubois returned to Europe, where his paper had received strong criticism. He countered the criticism by elaborating the points briefly covered in his original paper. He also brought along the actual fossil material, which gave scientists an opportunity to examine the evidence. As a result, many opponents became more sympathetic to his views.

However, to this day, questions about the finds remain: Does the femur really belong with the skullcap? Did the field crew dig through several layers, thus mixing the remains? Moreover, some anthropologists think that the Trinil femur is relatively recent and representative of modern *H. sapiens*, not *H. erectus*.

Despite the still-unanswered questions, there is general acceptance that Dubois was correct in identifying the skull as representing a previously undescribed species; that his estimates of cranial capacity were reasonably accurate; that "*Pithecanthropus erectus*," or *H. erectus* as we call it today, is the ancestor of *H. sapiens*; and that bipedalism preceded enlargement of the brain.

By 1930, the controversy had faded, especially in the light of important new discoveries near Peking (Beijing), China, in the late 1920s (discussed shortly). Similarities between the Beijing skulls and Dubois' "*Pithecanthropus*" were obvious,

FIGURE 11–5
Eugene Dubois, discoverer of the first *H. erectus* fossil to be found.

and scientists pointed out that the Java form was not an "apeman," as Dubois contended, but rather was closely related to modern *Homo sapiens.*

One might expect that Dubois would welcome the finds from China and the support they provided for the human status of *"Pithecanthropus,"* but Dubois would have none of it. He refused to recognize any connection between Beijing and Java and described the Beijing fossils as "a degenerate Neanderthaler" (von Koenigswald, 1956, p. 55). He also refused to accept the classification of *"Pithecanthropus"* in the same species with later finds from Java.

Homo erectus from Java

Six sites in eastern Java have yielded all the *H. erectus* fossil remains found to date on that island. The dating of these fossils has been hampered by the complex nature of Javanese geology. It has been generally accepted that most of the fossils belong in the Middle Pleistocene and are less than 800,000 years old. However, as we noted earlier, new dating estimates have suggested one find (from Modjokerto) to be close to 1.8 million years old and another fossil from the main site of Sangiran to be approximately 1.6 million years old.

At Sangiran, where the remains of at least five individuals have been excavated, the cranial capacities of the fossils range from 813 cm³ to 1,059 cm³. Another site called Ngandong has also been fruitful, yielding the remains of 12 crania (Fig. 11–6). The dating here is also confusing, but the Upper Pleistocene has been suggested, which may explain the larger cranial measurements of the Ngandong individuals as well as features that are more modern than those found on other Javanese crania. Newly published dates for the Ngandong site are very recent, remarkably so, in fact. Using two specialized dating techniques (discussed in Chapter 13; see p. 347), Swisher and colleagues from the Berkeley Geochronology Laboratory have determined from animal bones found at the site (and presumably associated with the hominids) a date ranging from about 50,000 years ago to as recently as 25,000 years ago (Swisher et al., 1996). If these dates are further confirmed, it would show a *very* late survival of *Homo erectus* in Java, long after they had disappeared elsewhere. They would thus be contemporary with *Homo sapiens*—which, by this time, had expanded widely in the Old World (see Chapter 12).

We cannot say much about the *H. erectus* way of life in Java. Very few artifacts have been found, and those have come mainly from river terraces, not from primary sites: "On Java there is still not a single site where artifacts can be associated with *H. erectus*" (Bartstra, 1982, p. 319).

Peking (Beijing)

The story of Peking *H. erectus* is another saga filled with excitement, hard work, luck, and misfortune. Europeans had known for a long time that "dragon bones," used by the Chinese as medicine and aphrodisiacs, were actually ancient mammal bones. In 1917, the Geological Survey of China decided to find the sites where these dragon bones were collected by local inhabitants (who later sold them to apothecary shops). In 1921 a Swedish geologist, J. Gunnar Andersson, was told of a potentially fruitful fossil site in an abandoned quarry near the village of **Zhoukoudian**. A villager showed Andersson's team a fissure in the limestone wall, and within a few minutes they found the jaw of a pig: "That evening we went home with rosy dreams of great discoveries" (Andersson, 1934, pp. 97–98).

A young Chinese geologist, Pei Wenshong, took over the excavation in 1929 and began digging out the sediment in one branch of the lower cave, where he found one of the most remarkable fossil skulls to be recovered up to that time. One of the Chinese workers tells the story:

FIGURE 11–6

Rear view of a Ngandong skull. Note that the cranial walls slope downward and outward (or upward and inward), with the widest breadth low on the cranium, giving it a pentagonal form.

Courtesy, S. Sartono

Zhoukoudian
(zhoh´-koh-dee´-en)

We had got down about 30 meters deep. . . . It was there the skull-cap was sighted, half of it embedded in loose earth, the other in hard clay. The sun had almost set . . . . The team debated whether to take it out right away or to wait until the next day when they could see better. The agonizing suspense of a whole day was felt to be too much to bear, so they decided to go on. (Jia, 1975, pp. 12–13)

Pei brought the skull to anatomist Davidson Black (Fig 11–7). Because the fossil was embedded in hard limestone, it took Black four months of hard, steady work to free it from its tough matrix. The result was worth the labor. The skull, that of a juvenile, was thick, low, and relatively small, but in Black's mind there was no doubt it belonged to an early hominid. The response to this discovery, quite unlike that which greeted Dubois almost 40 years earlier, was immediate and enthusiastically favorable.

Franz Weidenreich (Fig. 11–8), a distinguished anatomist well known for his work on European fossil hominids, succeeded Black. After Japan invaded China in 1933, Weidenreich decided to move the fossils from Beijing to prevent them from falling into the hands of the Japanese. Weidenreich left China in 1941, taking excellent prepared casts, photographs, and drawings of the fossil material with him. After he left, the bones were packed, and arrangements were made for the U.S. Marine Corps in Beijing to take them to the United States. The bones never reached the United States, and they have never been found. To this day, no one knows what happened to them, and their location remains a mystery.

Zhoukoudian *Homo erectus*

In their more recent analysis (1990), Jia and Huang list the total fossil remains of *H. erectus* unearthed at the Zhoukoudian Cave as of 1982 (Fig. 11–9):

14 skullcaps (only 6 relatively complete) (Fig. 11–10)
6 facial bones (including maxillae, palates, and zygomatic bone fragments)
15 mandibles (mostly one side, only one nearly complete, many fragments)
122 isolated teeth
38 teeth rooted in jaws

FIGURE 11–7
Davidson Black, responsible for the first study of the Zhoukoudian fossils.

The New York Academy of Medicine Library

FIGURE 11–8
Franz Weidenreich.

Special Collections, American Museum of Natural History

FIGURE 11–9
Zhoukoudian Cave. The grid on the wall was drawn for purposes of excavation. The entrance to the cave can be seen near the grid.

Special Collections, American Museum of Natural History

FIGURE 11–10
H. erectus (cast of specimen from Zhoukoudian). From this view, the supraorbital torus, low vault of the skull, and nuchal torus can clearly be seen.

Robert Jurmain

See Virtual Lab 10, section I, for a 3-D animation of a Zhoukoudian cranium.

3 humeri (upper arm bones, only 1 well preserved, the rest in fragments)
1 clavicle (both ends absent)
1 lunate (wrist bone)
7 femurs (only 1 well preserved)
1 tibia (shinbone, fragmentary)
(and over 100,000 artifacts)

These remains belong to upward of 40 male and female adults and children and constitute a considerable amount of evidence, the largest number of *H. erectus* specimens found at any one site. With the meticulous work by Weidenreich, the Zhoukoudian fossils have led to a good overall picture of the eastern *H. erectus* of China.

Peking *H. erectus*, like that from Java, possesses typical *H. erectus* features, including the supraorbital torus in front and the nuchal torus behind; also, the skull is keeled by a sagittal ridge, the face protrudes, the incisors are shoveled, and the molars contain large pulp cavities. Again, like the Javanese forms, the skull shows the greatest breadth near the bottom. (These similarities were recognized long ago by Black and Weidenreich.)

Cultural Remains More than 100,000 artifacts have been recovered from this vast site that was occupied intermittently for almost 250,000 years. According to the Chinese (Wu and Lin, 1983, p.86), Zhoukoudian "is one of the sites with the longest history of habitation by man or his ancestors." The occupation of the site has been divided into three cultural stages:

Earliest Stage (460,000–420,000 y.a.)* The tools are large, close to a pound in weight, and made of soft stone, such as sandstone.

Middle Stage (370,000–350,000 y.a.) Tools become smaller and lighter (under a pound), and these smaller tools comprise approximately two-thirds of the sample.

Final Stage (300,000–230,000 y.a.) Tools are still small, and the tool materials are of better quality. The coarse quartz of the earlier periods is replaced by a finer quartz, sandstone tools have almost disappeared, and flint tools increase in frequency by as much as 30 percent.

The early tools are crude and shapeless but become more refined over time. Common tools at the site are choppers and chopping tools, but retouched flakes were fashioned into scrapers, points, burins, and awls (Fig. 11–11). The way of life at Zhoukoudian has traditionally been described as that of hunter-gatherers who killed deer and horses as well as other animals and gathered fruits, berries, and ostrich eggs. Fragments of charred ostrich eggshells, the abundant deposits of hackberry seeds unearthed in the cave, and the flourishing plant growth surrounding the cave all suggest that meat was supplemented by the gathering of herbs, wild fruits, tubers, and eggs. Layers of what has long thought to be ash in the cave, over 18 feet deep at one point, suggest to some researchers the use of fire by *H. erectus*; however, whether Beijing hominids could actually make fire is unknown. Wu and Lin (1983, p. 94) state that "Peking Man was a cave dweller, a fire user, a deer hunter, a seed gatherer and a maker of specialized tools," but several questions about Zhoukoudian *H. erectus* remain unanswered.

---

*These dates should be considered tentative until more precise chronometric techniques are available.

Quartzite chopper

Flint point

Flint awl

Graver, or burin

Did *H. erectus* at Zhoukoudian use language? If by language we mean articulate speech, it is unlikely. Nevertheless, some scholars believe that speech originated early in hominid evolution; others argue that speech did not originate until up to 200,000 years later in the Upper Paleolithic, with the origin of anatomically modern humans (see Chapter 13). We agree with Dean Falk when she writes, "Unfortunately, what it is going to take to *settle* the debate about when language originated in hominids is a time machine. Until one becomes available, we can only speculate about this fascinating and important question" (1989, p. 141).

Did these hominids wear clothes? Almost surely clothing of some type, probably in the form of animal skins, was worn. Winters in Beijing are harsh today and appear to have been bitter during the Middle Pleistocene as well. Moreover, awls were found at Zhoukoudian, and one of the probable bone tools may be a needle.

What was the life span of *H. erectus* at Zhoukoudian? Apparently, not very long, and infant and childhood mortality was probably very high. Studies of the fossil remains reveal that almost 40 percent of the bones belong to individuals under the age of 14, and only 2.6 percent are estimated to be in the 50- to 60-year age-group (Jia, 1975).

This picture of Zhoukoudian life has been challenged by several researchers. Lewis Binford and colleagues (Binford and Ho, 1985; Binford and Stone, 1986a, 1986b) reject the description of Beijing *H. erectus* as hunters and argue that the evidence clearly points to them as scavengers. As we saw in Chapter 9, the controversy of early hominids as hunters or scavengers has engaged the attention of paleoanthropologists, and the matter is not yet settled.

Using techniques of taphonomy (discussed in Chapter 9), Noel Boaz and colleagues have even questioned whether the *H. erectus* remains at Zhoukoudian represent evidence of hominid habitation of the cave. By carefully comparing the types of bones as well as the damage to the bones found at Zhoukoudian with that seen in contemporary carnivore dens, Boaz and Ciochon (2001) have suggested that much of the materials in the cave likely accumulated through the activities of a giant extinct hyena. Indeed, they hypothesize that most of the *H. erectus* remains, too, are the food refuse of hyenic meals!

Boaz and his associates do recognize that the tools in the cave and possibly cut marks on some of the animal bones do provide evidence of hominid activities at Zhoukoudian. They also recognize that more detailed analysis is required to test their hypotheses and to "determine the nature and scope" of the *H. erectus* presence at Zhoukoudian.

Probably the most intriguing archaeological aspect of the presumed hominid behavior at Zhoukoudian has been the long-held assumption that *H. erectus* deliberately utilized fire inside the cave. The technological control of fire was one of the

FIGURE 11–11
Chinese tools from Middle Pleistocene sites. (Adapted from Wu and Olsen, 1985.)

BOX 11-1 A CLOSER LOOK

The Control of Fire

An important distinction exists between the *making* of fire and the *use* of fire captured from natural sources. Some very ancient methods that could have been used deliberately to make fire might have included striking hard rocks together or rubbing wood together to create sparks through friction. Without such technological innovations, earlier hominids would have been limited to obtaining and transporting fire from natural sources, such as lightning strikes and geothermal localities.

The archaeological evidence, however, may never be sufficiently complete to allow this distinction to be made with much precision. Nevertheless, *at minimum*, the consistent use of fire would have been a major technological breakthrough and could have had potentially marked influence on hominid biological evolution as well. For example, as a result of cooking, food items would have been more tender; thus, chewing stresses would have been reduced, perhaps leading to selection for reduced size of the dentition.

It is possible that australopithecines took advantage of and used naturally occurring fire, but the evidence relating to the use of fire is not always easy to interpret. At open-air sites, for example, remains suggesting an association between hominids and burning may be found. However, ashes may already have been blown away, and stones and bones blackened by fire could be the result of a natural brush fire, as could charcoal and baked earth. Furthermore, remains found on the surface of a site might be the result of a natural fire that occurred long after the hominids had left.

There are several possible advantages that controlled use of fire may have provided to earlier hominids, including:

1. Warmth
2. Cooking meat and/or plant foods, thus breaking down fibers and, in the case of many plants, neutralizing toxins
3. Fire-hardening wood, such as the end of a spear
4. Facilitating the predictable flaking of certain stone materials, thus aiding in the production of stone tools
5. Chasing competing predators (such as bears) from caves and keeping dangerous animals at bay
6. Providing illumination in caves and, more fundamentally, extending usable light into the night

This last implication of human control of fire may have had a profound effect on human sleep cycles and with it alterations in activity patterns, neurological functioning, and hormonal balance. In fact, recent experiments have suggested that humans still today can readily (and comfortably) adjust to "natural" light/dark cycles with periods of inactivity of up to 14 hours (thus simulating winter conditions *prior* to the systematic control of fire).

Since controlling fire is so important to humans, it would be useful to know who tamed the wild flames

major cultural breakthroughs of all prehistory. By providing warmth, a means of cooking, an aid to further modify tools, and so forth (see Box 11–1), controlled fire would have been a giant technological innovation. While some potential early African sites have been suggested as giving evidence of hominid control of fire, it has long been concluded that the first *definite* evidence of hominid fire use comes from Zhoukoudian.

Now, new evidence has radically altered this assumption. Much more detailed excavations at Zhoukoudian were carried out in 1996 and 1997 by biologist Steve Weiner and colleagues. These researchers also carefully analyzed the soil samples they collected for distinctive chemical signatures (which would show whether fire had occurred in the cave) (Weiner et al., 1998). Weiner and his colleagues found that only rarely was any burnt bone found associated with tools, and in most cases the burning appeared to have taken place *after* fossilization (i.e., they were not cooked). Moreover, the "ash" layers mentioned earlier are not ash at all, but rather and when, where, and how they did it. With that knowledge we could learn much more about the culture of our ancient ancestors and their evolution. Archaeologists are not certain who the first fire makers were. Two of the earliest presumed examples of fire use come from Africa, and both have been suggested as indicating deliberate hominid pyrotechnics *prior* to 1 m.y.a. At Chesowanja in southern Kenya, patches of burned clay dated at 1.4 m.y.a. were found in association with stone tools. John Gowlett and his colleague, Jack Harris, have suggested that the burned clay is the residue of ancient campfires. And recent excavations from upper levels at Swartkrans in South Africa by C. K. Brain and Andrew Sillen have recovered many pieces of burnt bone, again in association with stone tools dated at 1.3–1 m.y.a. (For a further discussion of Swartkrans, see pp. 265–268.) Both of these possible occurrences of hominid control of fire in Africa are thought to be associated with *Homo erectus*. However, neither of the early African contexts has yet to fully convince other experts.

True caves* may be a more probable source for finding human-made fire, because caves, except at the entrance, are damp, very dark, and impossible for habitation without light. Also, by the time humans began to occupy caves, they may have invented a method of making fire. It is possible, of course, to carry a natural fire into a cave, which is another snag in determining whether the fire was deliberately made or natural.

Probably the most famous cave site is Zhoukoudian (discussed in this chapter), where both Chinese and Western archaeologists have been working for more than 70 years. Evidence of supposed fire is abundant,

but this evidence (such as charred animal bones, layers of ash, charcoal, and burned stone artifacts) has led to differing interpretations and recent reassessments by archaeologists (see discussion in text).

There appears to be evidence of fire at other open sites in China and several caves in Europe, provisionally dated to about 300,000 years ago. They have yielded evidence of fire possibly made by archaic *H. sapiens*. But again, not all archaeologists are persuaded that humans were responsible.

Other prehistorians are sure that Neandertals (discussed in Chapter 12), who built hearths, were the first to make fire toward the end of the Middle Pleistocene (circa 125,000 y.a.). A deliberately built hearth is probably the best evidence for human-controlled fire. Ancient hearths are usually built with stone cobbles arranged in a circular or oval shape to constrain the fire. The presence of numerous hearths at a site (like finding a box of matches near a fire) tends to serve as proof that the fires were probably started by humans. It is the absence of identifiable hearths that is so troublesome at the older sites and which immediately signals a doubt that the fire was made (or even systematically used) by hominids. It will take the development of carefully constructed interpretive techniques to overcome the difficulties of solving the case of the first significant controllers of fire.

---

*Swartkrans was not a cave during the time of hominid archaeological accumulation, but has been shown to have been a natural fissure into which animals and other objects fell.

naturally accumulated organic sediment. This last conclusion was derived from chemical testing showing no sign whatsoever of wood burning inside the cave. Finally, the "hearths" that have figured so prominently in archaeological reconstructions of the fire control at this site are apparently not hearths at all. They simply are round depressions formed in the past by water collecting when the cave was more open to the elements.

Indeed, another provisional interpretation of the cave's geology suggests that the cave did not open in the manner of habitation sites, but had access only through a vertical shaft, leading archaeologist Alison Brooks to remark, "It wouldn't have been a shelter, it would have been a trap" (quoted in Wuethrich, 1998).

These serious doubts regarding control of fire, coupled with the suggestive evidence of bone accumulation by carnivores, have led anthropologists Noel Boaz and Russell Ciochon to conclude, "Zhoukoudian cave was neither hearth nor home" (Boaz and Ciochon, 2001).

Other Chinese Sites

More work has been done at Zhoukoudian than at any other Chinese site. Nevertheless, there are other hominid sites worth noting. Three of the more important sites, besides Zhoukoudian, are Chenjiawo and Gongwangling (both in Lantian County and sometimes referred to as Lantian) and Longtandong Cave in Hexian County (often referred to as the Hexian find) (Table 11–1).

At Chenjiawo, an almost complete mandible containing several teeth was found in 1963. It is quite similar to those from Zhoukoudian but has been provisionally dated at about 650,000 y.a. If the dating is correct, this specimen would be older than the Beijing material. The following year, a partial cranium was discovered at Gongwangling, not far from Chenjiawo. Provisionally dated to as much as 1.15 m.y.a. (Etler and Tianyuan, 1994), the Gongwangling specimen may be the oldest Chinese *Homo erectus* fossil yet known.

Perhaps the most significant find was made in 1980 at Longtandong Cave, where remains of several individuals were recovered. One of the specimens is a well-preserved cranium (with a cranial capacity of about 1,025 cm³) lacking much of its base. Dated roughly at 250,000 y.a., it is not surprising that this Hexian cranium displays several advanced features. The cranial constriction, for example, is not as pronounced as in earlier forms, and certain temporal and occipital characteristics are "best compared with the later forms of *H. erectus* at Zhoukoudian" (Wu and Dong, 1985, p. 87).

In 1993, Li Tianyuan and Dennis Etler reported that two relatively complete skulls were discovered in 1989 at a hominid site in Yunxian County. The date given for the site is 350,000 y.a., which, if correct, would make these the most complete crania of this great antiquity in China (Fig. 11–12).

TABLE 11–1 *H. erectus* Fossils from China

Designation	Site	Age* (Years Ago)	Material	Cranial Capacity (cm3)	Year Found	Remarks
Hexian	Longtandong Cave, Anhui	250,000	Calvarium, skull fragments, mandible fragments, isolated teeth	1,025	1980–81	First skull found in southern or southwest China
Zhoukoudian (Peking)	Zhoukoudian Cave, Beijing	500,000–200,000	5 adult crania, skull fragments, facial bones, isolated teeth, postcranial pieces (40+ individuals)	850–1,225; avg: 1,010	1927–ongoing	Most famous fossils in China and some of the most famous in the world
Yunxian	Longgudong Cave, Hubei	?500,000	Isolated teeth		1976–82	
Yunxian	Quyuanhekou	350,000	2 mostly complete (but crushed) crania	Undetermined	1989	The most complete crania from China, but still requiring much restoration
Lantian	Chenjiawo, Lantian	650,000	Mandible		1963	Old female
Lantian	Gongwangling, Lantian	1,150,000–800,000	Calvarium, facial bones	780	1964	Female over 30; most ancient *H. erectus* found so far in China

Sources: Atlas of Primitive Man in China (1980); Lisowski, 1984; Pope, 1984; Wu and Dong, 1985; Etler and Tianyuan, 1994.

*These are best estimates; authorities differ.

(a)

(b)

Courtesy, Denis Etler

FIGURE 11–12

(a) EV 9002 (Yunxian, China). The skull is in better shape than its companion, and its lateral view clearly displays features characteristic of *H. erectus*: flattened vault, receding forehead (frontal bone), angulated occiput, and supra-orbital torus. (b) EV 9001 (Yunxian). Unfortunately, the skull was crushed, but it preserves some lateral facial structures absent in EV 9002.

The Yunxian crania are both large and robust, considerably exceeding in size those from Zhoukoudian. In general, the Yunxian individuals fit within *Homo erectus*, but in the facial region especially they also show some interesting advanced features. A few of these features suggest to some scholars "a mid-facial morphology similar to that of modern Asians" (Etler and Tianyuan, 1994, p. 668).

Unfortunately, both skulls are still covered with a hard calcareous matrix, and critics argue that until the skulls are cleaned and the crushed parts properly put together, it is too early to make accurate assessments. In any case, these Yunxian crania will ultimately provide considerable data to help clarify hominid evolution in China and perhaps elsewhere in the Old World as well.

A number of archaeological sites have been excavated in China, and early stone tools have been found in numerous locations in widely separated areas. At present, there is little reason to believe that *H. erectus* culture in these provinces differed much from that described at Zhoukoudian.

The Asian crania from both Java and China are mainly Middle Pleistocene fossils and share many similar features, which may be explained by *H. erectus* migration from Java to China about 800,000 years ago. African *H. erectus* forms are generally older than most Asian forms and are not as similar to them as Asian forms (i.e., from Java and China) are to each other.

 See Virtual Lab 10, section I, for a 3-D animation of East African *Homo erectus* specimens.

East Africa

Olduvai Back in 1960, Louis Leakey unearthed a fossil skull at Olduvai (OH 9) that he identified as *H. erectus*. Skull OH 9 from Upper Bed II is dated at 1.4 m.y.a. and preserves a massive cranium but is faceless except for a bit of nose below the supraorbital torus. Estimated at 1,067 cm³, the cranial capacity of OH 9 is the largest of all the African *Homo erectus* specimens. The browridge is huge, the largest known for any hominid in both thickness and projection, but the vault walls are thin. This latter characteristic of fairly thin cranial vault bones is seen in most East African *H. erectus* specimens, and in this respect, they differ from Asian *H. erectus* (in which cranial vaults are thick).

East Turkana Some 400 miles north of Olduvai Gorge, on the northern boundary of Kenya, is Lake Turkana. Explored by Richard Leakey and colleagues since 1969, the eastern shore of the lake has been a virtual gold mine for australopithecine, early *Homo*, and *H. erectus* fossil remains.

The most significant *H. erectus* discovery from East Turkana is ER 3733, an almost complete skull lacking a mandible (Fig. 11–13). Discovered in 1974, the specimen has been given a firm date of close to 1.8 m.y.a. The cranial capacity is estimated at 848 cm³, at the lower end of the range for *H. erectus*, but this is not surprising considering its early date. The cranium generally resembles Asian *H. erectus* in many features (but with some important differences, discussed shortly).

Reproduced with permission of the Kenya Museums of Natural History

FIGURE 11–13
ER 3733, the most complete East Turkana *H. erectus* cranium.

Acheulian

(ash´-oo-lay-en) Pertaining to a stone tool industry of the Lower and Middle Pleistocene characterized by a large proportion of bifacial tools (flaked on both sides). Acheulian tool kits are very common in Africa, Southwest Asia, and western Europe, but are less common elsewhere. (Also spelled "Acheulean.")

FIGURE 11–14

WT 15000 from Nariokotome, Kenya: the most complete *H. erectus* specimen yet found.

Reproduced with permission of the Kenya Museums of Natural History

Not many tools have been found at *H. erectus* sites in East Turkana. Oldowan types of flakes, cobbles, and core tools have been found, and the introduction of **Acheulian** tools about 1.4 m.y.a. replaced the Oldowan tradition.

West Turkana*   In August 1984, Kamoya Kimeu, a member of Richard Leakey's team, further added to his reputation as an outstanding fossil hunter when he discovered a small piece of skull near the base camp on the west side of Lake Turkana. Leakey and his colleague, Alan Walker of Pennsylvania State University, excavated the site known as Nariokotome in 1984 and again in 1985 (see Box 11–2).

The dig was a resounding success. The workers unearthed the most complete *H. erectus* skeleton yet found (Fig. 11–14). Known properly as WT 15000, the all but complete skeleton includes facial bones and most of the postcranial bones, a rare finding indeed for *H. erectus*, since these elements are scarce at other *H. erectus* sites.

Another remarkable feature of the find is its age. Its dating is based on the chronometric dates of the geological formation in which the site is located and is set at about 1.6 million years. The skeleton is that of a boy about 12 years of age and 5 feet 3 inches tall. Had he grown to maturity, his height, it is estimated, would have been more than 6 feet, taller than *H. erectus* was heretofore thought to have been. The postcranial bones appear to be quite similar, though not identical, to those of modern humans. The cranial capacity of WT 15000 is estimated at 880 cm^3; brain growth was nearly complete, and it is estimated that the boy's adult cranial capacity would have been approximately 909 cm^3 (Begun and Walker, 1993).

Ethiopia   *Homo erectus* remains have been found at two sites in Ethiopia: Konso-Gardula (in the south) and from Bouri in the Middle Awash area (the same site that has yielded remains of *Australopithecus garhi* discussed in chapter 10). The Konso-Gardula remains are quite fragmentary, but the newly announced Bouri materials include a mostly complete cranium (with a cranial capacity of 995 cm^3) (Asfaw et al., 2002). Initial analysis of this new cranium shows similarities with other *H. erectus* fossils from Africa as well as Eurasia, strongly suggesting to the researchers that all these fossils should be included within a single species (and thus supporting the view discussed below).

Summary of East African *H. erectus*

The *Homo erectus* remains from East Africa show several differences from the fossil samples from Java and China. The African specimens (as exemplified by ER 3733, presumably a female, and WT 15000, presumably a male) are not as strongly buttressed in the cranium (by supraorbital or nuchal tori) and do not have such thick cranial bones as seen in Asian representatives of *H. erectus*. These differences, as well as others observed in the postcranial skeleton, have so impressed some researchers that they in fact argue for a *separate* species status for the African *H. erectus* remains (as distinct from the Asian samples). Bernard Wood, the leading proponent of this view, has suggested that the name *"Homo ergaster"* be used for the African remains; *H. erectus* would then be reserved solely for the Asian material (Wood, 1991). In addition, the very early dates now postulated for the dispersal of *H. erectus* into Asia (Java) would argue for a more than 1-million-year separate history for Asian and African populations.

Nevertheless, this species division has not been fully accepted, and the current consensus (reflected in this text) is to continue to refer to all these hominids as *Homo erectus* (Kramer, 1993; Conroy, 1997; Rightmire, 1998). As with the Plio-Pleistocene samples, we accordingly will have to accommodate a considerable

---

*WT is the symbol for West Turkana, that is, the west side of Lake Turkana. The east side is designated by ER—East Rudolf. Rudolf was the former name of the lake. (See p. 258.)

BOX 11–2 A CLOSER LOOK

The Nariokotome Skeleton— A Boy for All Seasons

The discovery of the spectacularly well-preserved skeleton from Nariokotome on the west side of Lake Turkana has allowed considerable new insight into key anatomical features of *Homo erectus*. Since its recovery in 1984 and 1985, detailed studies have been undertaken, and the published results (Walker, 1993; Walker and Leakey, 1993) have allowed some initial conclusions to be drawn. Moreover, the extraordinary quality of the remains has also allowed anthropologists to speculate on some major behavioral traits of *H. erectus* in Africa (and, more generally, of the entire species).

The remains comprise an almost complete skeleton, lacking only most of the small bones of the hands and feet and the unfused ends of long bones. This degree of preservation is remarkable, and this individual is the most complete skeleton of *any* fossil hominid yet found from before about 100,000 y.a. (after which deliberate burial facilitated much improved preservation). This superior preservation may well have been aided by rapid sedimentation in what is thought to have been an ancient shallow swamp. Once the individual died, his skeleton would have been quickly covered up, but some disturbance and breakage nevertheless occurred—from chewing by catfish, but most especially from trampling by large animals wading in the swamp 1.6 m.y.a.

As we have discussed, the individual was not fully grown when he died. His age (11 to 13 years—Walker, 1993) is determined by the stage of dental eruption (his permanent canines are not yet erupted) and by union of the ends of long bones. Moreover, as we have noted, this young *Homo erectus* male was quite tall (5 feet 3 inches), and using modern growth curve approximations, his adult stature would have been over 6 feet had he lived to full maturity.

More than simply tall, the body proportions of this boy's skeleton are intriguing. Reconstructions suggest that he had a linear build with long appendages, conforming to predictions of *Allen's rule* for inhabitants of hot climates (see Chapter 15). Further extrapolating from this observation, Alan Walker also suggests that *H. erectus* must have had a high sweating capacity to dissipate heat (in the modern human fashion). (See pp. 404–405 for a discussion of heat adaptation in humans.)

The boy's limb proportions suggest a quite warm mean annual temperature (90°F/30°C) in East Africa 1.6 m.y.a. Paleoecological reconstructions confirm this estimate of tropical conditions (much like the climate today in northern Kenya).

Another fascinating anatomical clue is seen in the beautifully preserved vertebrae. The opening through which the spinal cord passes (the neural canal; see Appendix A) is quite small in the thoracic elements. The possible behavioral corollaries of this reduced canal (as compared to modern *H. sapiens*) are also intriguing. Ann MacLarnan (1993) has proposed that the reduced canal argues for reduced size of the spinal cord, which in turn may suggest less control of the muscles between the ribs (the intercostals). One major function of these muscles is the precise control of breathing during human speech. From these data and inferences, Alan Walker has concluded that the Nariokotome youth (and *H. erectus* in general) was not fully capable of human articulate speech. (As an argument regarding language potential, this conclusion will no doubt spark considerable debate.)

A final interesting feature can be seen in the pelvis of this adolescent skeleton. It is very narrow and is thus correlated with a narrow bony birth canal. Walker (1993) again draws a behavioral inference from this anatomical feature. He estimates that a newborn with a cranial capacity no greater than a mere 200 cm³ could have passed through this pelvis. As we showed elsewhere, the adult cranial capacity estimate for this individual was slightly greater than 900 cm³—thus arguing for significant postnatal growth of the brain (exceeding 75 percent of its eventual size), again mirroring the modern human pattern. Walker speculates that this slow neural expansion (compared to other primates) leads to delayed development of motor skills and thus a prolonged period of infant/child dependency (what Walker terms "secondary altriciality"). Of course, as with other speculative behavioral scenarios, critics will no doubt find holes in this reconstruction. One point you should immediately note is that this specimen is the immature pelvis of a male. Thus, the crucial dimensions of an adult female *H. erectus* pelvis remain unknown. Nevertheless, they could not have departed too dramatically from the dimensions seen at Nariokotome—unless one accepts an extreme degree of sexual dimorphism in this species.

degree of intraspecific variation within this species. Wood has concluded, regarding variation within such a broadly defined *H. erectus* species, "It is a species which manifestly embraces an unusually wide degree of variation in both the cranium and postcranial skeleton" (Wood, 1992a, p. 329).

South Africa

A mandible was found among fossil remains collected at Swartkrans in South Africa in the 1940s and 1950s. This specimen, SK 15, was originally assigned to "*Telanthropus capensis,*" but is now placed within the genus *Homo* (there is, however, disagreement about its species designation). Rightmire (1990) suggests that it may be linked with *Homo erectus*, but others are not certain. If it is *H. erectus*, it would demonstrate that *H. erectus* inhabited South Africa as well as the other regions documented by other more complete fossil finds.

North Africa

With evidence from China and Java, it appears clear that *H. erectus* populations, with superior tools and weapons and presumably greater intelligence than their predecessors, had vastly expanded their habitat beyond that of early hominids. The earliest evidence for *H. erectus*, 1.8–1.6 m.y.a., comes from East Africa and Java and about 1 million years later in China. Early dispersal of *H. erectus* to Europe (prior to 1 m.y.a.) may also have occurred. It is not surprising, therefore, that *H. erectus* migrations would have taken them to northwest Africa as well.

North African remains, consisting almost entirely of mandibles (or mandible fragments) and a partial parietal bone, have been found at Ternifine (now Tighenif), Algeria, and in Morocco, at Sidi Abderrahman and Thomas Quarries. The three Ternifine mandibles and the parietal fragment are quite robust and have been dated to about 700,000 y.a. The Moroccan material is not as robust as Ternifine and may be a bit younger, at 500,000 years. In addition, an interesting cranium was found in a quarry north of Salé, in Morocco. The walls of the skull vault are thick, and several other features resemble those of *H. erectus*. Some features suggest that the Salé fossil is *H. sapiens*, but a date of 400,000 y.a. and an estimated cranial capacity of about 900 cm^3 throw doubt on that interpretation.

Europe

Recent discoveries in Europe are dramatically pushing back the time frame for earliest hominid occupation of this portion of the Old World. For several decades, it had been assumed that hominids did not reach Europe until late in the Middle Pleistocene (presumably after 400,000 y.a.) and were already identifiable as a form very similar to *Homo sapiens*. It was thus concluded that *H. erectus* (and contemporaries) never expanded there. As the new discoveries are evaluated, such assumptions are being questioned. The most exciting finds have come in just the last few years from Dmanisi in the Republic of Georgia. Beginning in the early 1990s, a few pieces were found, but the most informative specimens are two very well preserved crania discovered in 1999 (Gabunia et al., 2000) (Fig. 11–15). These specimens are important because their morphology is distinctively like *Homo erectus,* especially the African varieties. There are several anatomical similarities to the African fossils (from Olduvai, East Turkana, and Nariokotome), which have been referred to by many paleoanthropologists as "*Homo ergaster.*" These physical resemblances include fairly thin cranial bones and a higher vault and somewhat smaller browridges than are characteristic of fossils from Java or China. Moreover, the cranial capacity of the two Dmanisi skulls is quite small (650 cm^3 for the smaller individual, thought possible to be a female, and 775 cm³ for the larger, presumably male, individual). Furthermore, the early date for the finds—at 1.8–1.7 m.y.a.—is secure, with correlated results from several techniques (argon-argon, paleomagnetism, and biostratigraphy; see Chapter 9).

Finally, there are also a variety of stone tools associated with the Dmanisi fossils, and they suggest a quite simple technological tradition (very similar to the Oldowan seen at African sites prior to 1.6 m.y.a.). Taken together, the evidence suggests that *H. erectus* (or its African cousin) migrated to Eurasia *very* soon after it first evolved in East Africa. And further, these earliest African emigrants apparently managed to expand widely with only a quite basic stone tool technology.

The fossil remains from elsewhere in Europe *all* appear to be at least 1 million years later than Dmanisi, and they reflect a somewhat confusing evolutionary picture. For example, the skull from Ceprano (Italy) is the most definite *H. erectus* fossil from Europe (meaning *H. erectus* in the strict sense—to include Asian forms, but not those from Africa or Dmanisi). Yet, at a roughly contemporary time to Ceprano, the early material from Atapuerca (Spain) is different, and Spanish researchers have provisionally assigned these hominids to still another species of *Homo* (a view that has not been widely accepted). We should note that much of this early Pleistocene European fossil material is fragmentary, and all of it has been only recently found. Thus, all current interpretations are, for the moment, both tentative and controversial.

After about 400,000 y.a., the European fossil hominid record becomes increasingly abundant. Nevertheless, interpretations relating to the proper taxonomic assessment of many of these remains have been debated, in some cases for decades. In recent years, several of these somewhat later (i.e., Middle Pleistocene) specimens have been placed within a grouping of early *Homo sapiens* referred to as "archaic *Homo sapiens*." Needless to say, not everyone agrees. These enigmatic archaic *H. sapiens* specimens are discussed in Chapter 12. A time line for the *H. erectus* discoveries discussed in this chapter as well as other finds of more uncertain status is shown in Figure 11–16 on page 304.

(a)

(b)

FIGURE 11–15
Dmanisi crania discovered in 1999 and dated to 1.8–1.7 m.y. (a) Specimen 2282 and (b) Specimen 2280.

Technological and Population Trends in the Middle Pleistocene

Technological Trends

Many researchers have noted the remarkable stasis of the physical and cultural characteristics of *Homo erectus* populations, which seemed to change so little in the more than 1.5 million years of their existence. There is, however, dispute on this point. Some scholars (Rightmire, 1981) see almost no detectable changes in cranial dimensions over more than 1 million years of *H. erectus* evolution. Other paleoanthropologists (e.g., Wolpoff, 1984), who use different methodologies to date and subdivide their samples, draw a different conclusion, seeing some significant long-term morphological trends. Accepting a moderate position, we can postulate that there were some changes: The brain of later *H. erectus* was somewhat larger, the nose more protrusive, and the body not as robust as in earlier forms. Moreover, there were modifications in stone tool technology.

Expansion of the brain presumably enabled *H. erectus* to develop a more sophisticated tool kit than seen among earlier hominids. The important change in this kit was a core worked on both sides, called a *biface* (known widely as a hand axe or cleaver; Fig 11–17). The biface had a flatter core than the roundish earlier Oldowan pebble tool. And, probably even more important, this *core* tool was obviously a target design, that is, the main goal of the toolmaker. This greater focus and increased control enabled the stoneknapper to produce sharper, straighter edges, resulting in a

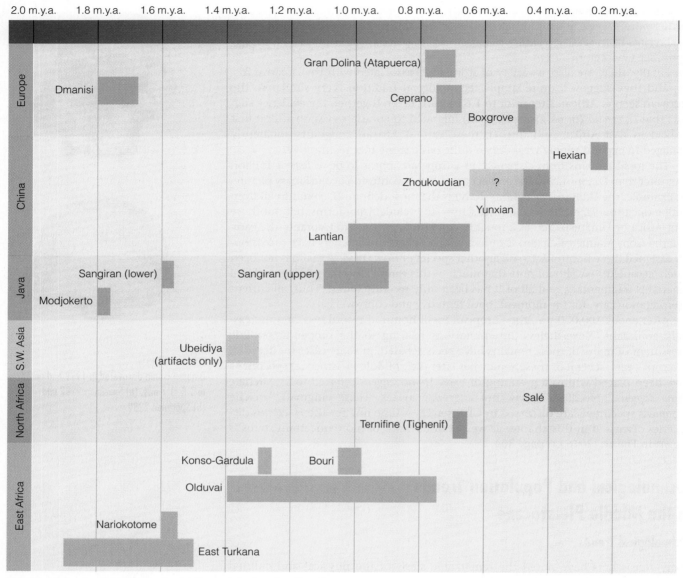

2.0 m.y.a. 1.8 m.y.a. 1.6 m.y.a. 1.4 m.y.a. 1.2 m.y.a. 1.0 m.y.a. 0.8 m.y.a. 0.6 m.y.a. 0.4 m.y.a. 0.2 m.y.a.

Europe
Dmanisi
Gran Dolina (Atapuerca)
Ceprano
Boxgrove

China
Hexian
Zhoukoudian   ?
Yunxian
Lantian

Java
Sangiran (lower)
Sangiran (upper)
Modjokerto

S.W. Asia
Ubeidiya (artifacts only)

North Africa
Salé
Ternifine (Tighenif)

East Africa
Konso-Gardula
Bouri
Olduvai
Nariokotome
East Turkana

Note: Most dates are only imprecise estimates. However, the dates from East African sites are chronometrically determined and are thus much more secure. In addition, the early dates from Java are also radiometric and are gaining wide acceptance, although some researchers (e.g., Wolpoff, 1999) suggest that they are not secure and may be later than shown.

FIGURE 11–16
Time line for *Homo erectus* discoveries and other contemporary hominids. Note that most dates are approximations.

more efficient implement. This Acheulian stone tool became standardized as the basic *H. erectus* all-purpose tool (with only minor modification) for more than a million years. It served to cut, scrape, pound, dig, and more—a most useful tool that has been found in Africa, parts of Asia, and later in western Europe. It should also be noted that Acheulian tool kits also included several types of small tools (Fig. 11–18).

For many years, it was thought that a cultural "divide" separated the Old World—with Acheulian technology found *only* in Africa, southwest Asia, and western Europe, but not elsewhere (i.e., absent in eastern Europe and most of Asia). However, newly reported excavations from more than 20 sites in the Bose Basin of southern China have forced reevaluation of this hypothesis (Yamei et al., 2000). As noted, the most distinctive tools of the Acheulian are bifaces, and they are the very tools thought lacking throughout most of the Pleistocene in eastern Europe and most of Asia. The new archaeological assemblages from southern China are securely dated at abut 800,000 y.a. and contain numerous bifaces, very similar to contemporaneous Acheulian bifaces from Africa (see Figs. 11–17 and 11–19b). It now appears likely that cultural traditions relating to stone tool technology were largely equivalent over the *full* geographical range of *H. erectus* and contemporaries.

While geographical distinctions are not so obvious, temporal changes in tool technology are evident. In early days, toolmakers employed a stone hammer (simply an ovoid-shaped stone about the size of an egg or a bit larger) to remove flakes from the core, thus leaving deep scars. Later, they used other materials, such as wood and bone. They learned to use these new materials as soft hammers, which gave them more control over flaking, thus leaving shallow scars, sharper edges, and a more symmetrical form. Toward the end of the Acheulian industry, toolmakers blocked out a core with stone hammers and then switched to wood or bone for defining the edges. This technique produced more elegant-appearing and pear-shaped implements.

Evidence of butchering is widespread at *H. erectus* sites, and in the past, such evidence has been cited in arguments for consistent hunting. For example, at the Olorgesailie site in Kenya (Fig. 11–19), dated at approximately 800,000 y.a., thousands of Acheulian hand axes have been recovered in association with remains of large animals, including giant baboons (now extinct). However, the assumption of consistent hunting has been challenged, especially by archaeologists who argue that the evidence does not prove the hunting hypothesis. Instead, they suggest that *H. erectus* was primarily a scavenger, a hypothesis that also has not yet been proved conclusively. We thus discuss *H. erectus* as a potential hunter *and* scavenger. It is crucial to remember, too, that *gathering* of wild plant foods was also practiced by *H. erectus* groups. Indeed, probably a majority of the calories they consumed came from such gathering activities.

Courtesy, The Museum of Primitive Art and Culture, Peace Dale, RI, photo by William Turnbaugh

FIGURE 11–17

Acheulian biface ("hand axe"), a basic tool of the Acheulian tradition.

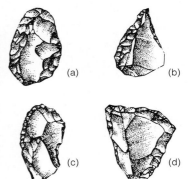

FIGURE 11–18

Small tools of the Acheulian industry. (a) Side scraper. (b) Point. (c) End scraper. (d) Burin.

FIGURE 11–19

(a) A Middle Pleistocene butchering site at Olorgesailie, Kenya, excavated by Louis and Mary Leakey, who had the catwalk built for observers. (b) A close-up of the Acheulian tools, mainly hand axes, found at the site.

Robert Jurmain

(a)

Robert Jurmain

(b)

Moreover, as we have seen, the mere *presence* of animal bones at archaeological sites does not prove that hominids were killing animals or even necessarily exploiting meat. Indeed, as was the case in the earlier South African sites (discussed in Chapter 10), the hominid remains themselves may have been the meal refuse of large carnivores! Thus, in making interpretations of early hominid sites, we must consider a variety of alternatives. As Stanford University archaeologist Richard Klein has concluded regarding Middle Pleistocene sites, the interpretations are far from clear: "In sum, the available data do not allow us to isolate the relative roles of humans, carnivores, and factors such as starvation, accidents, and stream action in creating bone assemblages. . . . Certainly, as presently understood, the sites do not tell us how successful or effective *Homo erectus* was at obtaining meat" (1989, p. 221).

Population Trends

One of the fascinating qualities of *H. erectus* was a penchant for travel. From the relatively close confines of East Africa, *H. erectus* dispersed widely in the Old World. By the time *H. sapiens* appeared a million or more years later, *H. erectus* had migrated to South and North Africa. And even earlier, some groups had moved from Africa to Asia and to Europe as well.

The life of hunter-scavengers (and still, no doubt, *primarily* gatherers) was nomadic, and the woodland and savanna that covered the southern tier of Asia would have been an excellent environment for *H. erectus* (as it was similar to the econiche of their African ancestors). As the population grew, small groups budded off and moved on to find their own resource areas. This process, repeated again and again, led *H. erectus* east, crossing to Java, arriving there, it seems, as early as the most ancient known sites in East Africa itself.

Once in Java, it had been assumed that *H. erectus* would have found it impossible to venture farther south or east, since during the Pleistocene, deep water channels presumably separated Java completely from more southerly islands and Australia. However, recent reinterpretation (and firmer chronometric dates) of stone tools found on the island of Flores, 375 miles east of Java, has prompted some paleoanthropologists to reconsider this assumption (Gibbons, 1998). With a suggested date of 750,000 y.a. for these tools, it raises a most unexpected possibility: Could ancient *H. erectus* at this *very* early period construct ocean-going vessels (rafts?) that could navigate over deep, fast-moving waters?

While initial dating of the Flores stone materials appears reasonably good, the conclusion that the finds *prove* such seemingly advanced capabilities for *H. erectus* is not yet generally accepted. A number of troublesome issues remain to be resolved, the first being whether the lithic materials from Flores are *deliberate* tools or are simply naturally fractured rock. This latter possibility would argue against *H. erectus* (or any other hominid) having expanded south or east beyond Java at such an early date. Of course, the most unambiguous evidence would be fossil discoveries of *H. erectus* itself.

When we look back at the evolution of *H. erectus*, we realize how significant this early human's achievements were. It was *H. erectus* who increased in body size with more efficient bipedalism; who embraced culture wholeheartedly as a strategy of adaptation; whose brain was reshaped and increased in size to within *H. sapiens* range; who became a more efficient scavenger and likely hunter with greater dependence on meat; and who apparently established more permanent bases. In short, it was *H. erectus*, committed to a cultural way of life, who transformed hominid evolution to human evolution; or as Foley states, "The appearance and expansion of *H. erectus* represented a major change in adaptive strategy that influenced the subsequent process and pattern of human evolution" (1991, p. 425).

SUMMARY

Homo erectus remains are found in geological contexts dating from about 1.8 million to about 200,000 years ago (and perhaps much later), a period of more than 1.5 million years. The first finds were made by Dubois in Java, and later discoveries came from China and Africa. Differences from early *Homo* are notable in *H. erectus'* larger brain, taller stature, robust build, and changes in facial structure and cranial buttressing.

The long period of *H. erectus'* existence was marked by a remarkably uniform technology over space and time. Nevertheless, compared to earlier hominids, *H. erectus* and contemporaries introduced more sophisticated tools and probably ate novel and/or differently processed foods, using these new tools and at later sites perhaps fire as well. They were also able to move into different environments and successfully adapt to new conditions.

It is generally assumed that some *H. erectus* populations evolved to *H. sapiens*, since many fossils, such as Ngandong (and others discussed in Chapter 12), display both *H. erectus* and *H. sapiens* features. There remain questions about *H. erectus* behavior (e.g., did they hunt?) and about evolution to *H. sapiens* (was it gradual or rapid, and which *H. erectus* populations contributed genes to *H. sapiens*?). The search for answers continues.

QUESTIONS FOR REVIEW

1. Describe the Pleistocene in terms of (a) relationship to glacial sequences and (b) the dating of fossil hominids.
2. Describe *Homo erectus*. How is *H. erectus* anatomically different from early *Homo*? From *H. sapiens*?
3. In what areas of the world have *Homo erectus* fossils been found?
4. In comparing *H. erectus* with earlier hominids, why is it important to specify which comparative sample is being used?
5. What was the intellectual climate in Europe in the latter half of the nineteenth century, especially concerning human evolution?
6. Why do you think there was so much opposition to Dubois' interpretation of the hominid fossils he found in Java?
7. Why do you think Zhoukoudian *H. erectus* was enthusiastically accepted, whereas the Javanese fossils were not?
8. Describe the way of life of *H. erectus* at Zhoukoudian as depicted by earlier researchers. What disagreements have been voiced about this conjecture?
9. *H. erectus* has been called the first human. Why?
10. What is the *H. erectus* evidence from Africa, and what questions of human evolution does the evidence raise?
11. Can you suggest any reason why the earliest remains of *H. erectus* have come from East Africa?
12. *H. erectus* migrated to various points in Africa and vast distances to eastern Asia and elsewhere. What does this tell you about the species?
13. What kinds of stone tools have been found at *H. erectus* sites?

SUGGESTED FURTHER READING

Day, Michael. 1986. *Guide to Fossil Man.* Chicago: University of Chicago Press.
Lewin, Roger. 1998. *Principles of Human Evolution: A Core Textbook.* New York: Blackwell Science.
Rightmire, G. P. 1990. *The Evolution of* Homo erectus. New York: Cambridge University Press.
Shapiro, Harry L. 1980. *Peking Man.* New York: Simon & Schuster.
Walker, Alan, and Richard Leakey (eds). 1993. *The Nariokotome* Homo erectus *Skeleton.* Cambridge, MA: Harvard University Press.
Wolpoff, Milford. 1984. "Evolution in *Homo erectus*: The Question of Stasis." *Paleobiology* 10: 389–406.

RESOURCES ON THE INTERNET

 Wadsworth Anthropology Resource Center
http://anthropology.wadsworth.com

The companion website for this text includes a range of enrichment material focused on the chapter's topic. While online you can enhance your understanding of the chapter by exploring one of the several additional Internet exercises, by researching topics, and by accessing full articles on InfoTrac College Edition. You can also reinforce the concepts by taking online practice exams.

Internet Exercises

Visit The Evidence for Human Evolution in China (**http://www.cruzio.com/~cscp/index.htm**). There is a great deal of information on this site about *Homo erectus* and early *Homo sapiens* in China. Go to the Interactive Timeline to view summary evidence for human evolution in China. You can click on any of the individual pictures to get more information on that specimen. Choose one feature of morphology—brain size, cranial shape, facial shape, dentition, and so on—and go through the time line. Write a short paper on how that feature of the anatomy changes through time, based on the evidence presented here.

 InfoTrac College Edition
http://www.infotrac-college.com/wadsworth

Using PowerTrac, search InfoTrac College Edition for news on *Homo erectus*. Choose one story, read it, and write a page about the contribution of this piece of research to what we know about early hominid evolution. Does this article provide any information that differs from that in the textbook? If so, write a summary of these differences.

Anthropologists have long been concerned with the behavioral evolution of our species. Accompanying changes in anatomy (limb structure, dentition, brain size and shape) were changes in mating patterns, social structure, cultural innovations, and, eventually, language. In fact, changes in these behavioral complexes are what mostly *explain* the concomitant adaptations in human biological structure.

We are, then, vitally interested in the behavioral adaptations of our early hominid ancestors. In seeking to reconstruct the behavioral patterns of these early hominids, anthropologists use inferences drawn from modern primates, social carnivores, and hunting-gathering peoples. In addition, they derive information directly from the paleoanthropological record (see Chapter 9).

Despite numerous attempts at such behavioral reconstructions, the conclusions must remain largely speculative. In point of fact, behavior does not fossilize. Accordingly, researchers must rely considerably on their imaginations in creating scenarios of early hominid behavioral evolution (see p. 232). In such an atmosphere, biases often emerge; these biased renditions, in turn, stimulate heated debates and alternative scenarios—often as narrow as those being attacked.

Among the most controversial topics in anthropology, and one that has displayed some of the most glaring biases, is the debate concerning origins of hominid gender role differences. Did early hominid males have characteristically different behavioral adaptations from their female counterparts? Did one sex dominate the frontier of early hominid cultural innovation? And if one sex did lead the way, which one?

A now well-known rendition of early hominid behavioral development was popularized in the 1960s and 1970s. According to this "man, the hunter" theory, the hunting of large animals by males was the central stimulus of hominid behavioral evolution. Such widely read works as *The Naked Ape* (1967), by Desmond Morris, and *The Hunting Hypothesis* (1976) and other books by Robert Ardrey maintain that early apish-looking forms *became* hominids as a result of a hunting way of life. As Ardrey states, "Man is man, and not a chimpanzee, because for millions upon millions of evolving years we killed for a living" (1976, p. 10).

In this reconstruction, the hunting of large, dangerous mammals by cooperating groups of males fostered the development of intelligence, language, tools, and bipedalism. In this scenario, increased intelligence accompanied by the development of weapons is also blamed for the roots of human aggressiveness, murder, and warfare.

This "man, the hunter" scenario further suggests that while the males are leading the vanguard in hominid evolution, females remain mostly sedentary, tied to the home base by the burden of dependent young. Females may have contributed some wild plant foods to the group's subsistence, but this is not seen as a particularly challenging (and certainly not a very noble) endeavor. In this situation of marked division of labor, sexual relationships quickly changed. Males, constantly away from the home base (and thus away from the females, too), could not keep a watchful eye over their mates. In order to better ensure fidelity, monogamy came into being. In this way, a male would be assured that the young in which he invested were his own. This important factor of male-female bonding as a product of differential foraging patterns has more recently been restated by Owen Lovejoy (1981) (see p. 236).

From the female's point of view, it would be beneficial to maintain a close bond with a provisioning male. Consequently, she would want to appear "attractive," and thus, through time, the female breasts and buttocks would become more conspicuous. Besides rearing their young and being attractive sex objects, females were useful to males in another way. Groups of male hunters living in the same area might occasionally come into potentially dangerous competition for the same resources. As a means of solidifying political ties between groups, the males would thus routinely exchange females (by giving or "selling" their daughters to neighboring bands).

Thus, in a single stroke, this complex of features accounts for human intelligence, sexual practices, and political organization.

Man, the Hunter; Woman, the Gatherer? (continued)

As might be expected, such a male-centered scenario did not go unchallenged. Ignoring females or relegating them to a definitely inferior role in human behavioral evolution drew sharp criticism from several quarters. As Sally Slocum notes:

So, while the males were out hunting, developing all their skills, learning to cooperate, inventing language, inventing art, creating tools and weapons, the poor dependent females were sitting back at the home base having one child after another and waiting for the males to bring home the bacon. While this reconstruction is certainly ingenious, it gives one the decided impression that only half the species—the male half—did any evolving. In addition to containing a number of logical gaps, the argument becomes somewhat doubtful in the light of modern knowledge of genetics and primate behavior. (Slocum, 1975, p. 42)

In fact, such a rigid rendering of our ancestors' behavior does not stand up to critical examination. Hunting is never defined rigorously. Does it include only large, terrestrial mammals? What of smaller mammals, sea mammals, fish, and birds? In numerous documented human societies, females actively participate in exploiting these latter resources.

Moreover, nonhuman primates do not conform to predictions derived from the "man, the hunter" model. For example, among chimpanzees, females do most of the toolmaking, not the males. Finally in most nonhuman primates (most mammals, for that matter), it is the females—not the males—who choose with whom to mate.

Granting that the hunting hypothesis does not work, what alternatives have been proposed? As a reaction to male-centered views, Elaine Morgan (1972) advanced the "aquatic hypothesis." In this rendition, females are seen as the pioneers of hominid evolution. But rather than having the dramatic changes of human emergence occur on the savanna, Morgan has them take place on the seashore. As females lead the way to bipedal locomotion, cultural innovation, and intellectual development, the poor males are seen as splashing pitifully behind.

Unfortunately, this scenario has less to back it up than the hunting hypothesis. Not a shred (even a watery one) of evidence has ever been discovered in the contexts predicted by the aquatic theory. Little is accomplished by such unsubstantiated overzealous speculation. Chauvinism—whether male or female—does not elucidate our origins and only obscures the evolutionary processes that operated on the *whole* species.

Another interesting aspect of these different behavioral "theories" has been pointed out by cultural anthropologist Misia Landau. She notes that these theories are like mythical stories with a hero emerging (from the forest) and ultimately conquering the challenges of existence (by boldly going bipedally onto the savanna). It could also be noted that in most of these myths, traditionally the hero is a male who acts to defend, provide for, and inseminate the females (who, otherwise, are not given much consideration).

What can we conclude from all these arguments? While the pattern is not as rigid as the hunting hypothesis advocates would have us believe, in the vast majority of human societies, hunting of large, terrestrial mammals is almost always a male activity. In fact, a comprehensive cross-cultural survey shows that of 179 societies, males do the hunting exclusively in 166, both sexes participate in 13, and in *no* group is hunting done exclusively by females (Murdock, 1965).

In addition, there is some incipient division of labor in foraging patterns among chimpanzees. Females tend to concentrate more on termiting, while hunting is done mostly by males. Early hominids, expanding upon such a subsistence base, eventually adapted a greater sexual division of labor than is found in any other primate. Two points, however, must be kept in mind. First, both the gathering of wild plant foods and the hunting of animals would have been indispensable components of the diet. Consequently, *both* males and females always played a significant role. Second, the strategies must always have been somewhat flexible. With a shifting, usually unpredictable resource base, nothing else would have worked. As a result, males probably always did a considerable amount of gathering, and in most foraging societies they still do. Moreover, females—while not usually engaged in the stalking and killing of large prey—nonetheless contribute significantly to meat acquisition. Once large animals have been killed, there still remain the arduous tasks of butchering and transport back to the home base. In many societies, women and men participate equally in these activities.

A balanced view of human behavioral evolution must avoid simplistic and overly rigid scenarios. As stated by Adrienne Zihlman, a researcher concerned with reconstructing early hominid behavior:

Both sexes must have been able to care for young, protect themselves from predators, make and use tools, and freely move about the environment in order to exploit available resources widely distributed through space and time. It is this range of behaviors—the overall behavioral flexibility of both sexes—that may have been the primary ingredient of early hominids' success in the savanna environment. (Zihlman, 1981, p. 97)

Following the notion developed by Landau that much of the literature on the evolution of human behavior resembles storytelling, anthropologist Linda Fedigan concluded her own comprehensive review of the topic (1986):

People will not stop wanting to hear origin stories and scientists will not cease to write scholarly tales. But we can become aware of the symbolic content of our stories, for much as our theories are not independent of our beliefs, so our behavior is not independent of our theories of human society. In these origin tales, we try to coax the material evidence into telling us about the past, but the narrative we weave about the past also tells us about the present.

Critical Thinking Questions

1. What do we mean when we say, "Behavior does not fossilize"?
2. Exactly, what is it that *does* fossilize?
3. What is meant by male (or female) chauvinism? Do you detect elements of chauvinism in any of the views discussed here?
4. Select a feature of early hominid adaptation (e.g., bipedal locomotion or sexual dimorphism, where males are considerably larger than females) and construct your own behavioral explanation of how it might have evolved. (Do so in two different ways. First, restrict yourself to only firm evidence. Then be as speculative as possible, giving full vent to your imagination. Lastly, compare your two reconstructions and evaluate the *scientific* merit of each.)

Sources

Ardrey, Robert. 1976. *The Hunting Hypothesis.* New York: Atheneum.

Dahlberg, Frances (ed.). 1981. *Woman the Gatherer.* New Haven: Yale University Press.

Fedigan, Linda. 1986. "The Changing Role of Woman in Models of Human Evolution." *Annual Review of Anthropology* 15: 25–66.

Landau, Misia. 1986. "Human Evolution as Narrative." *American Scientist* 72: 262–268.

Lovejoy, C. Owen. 1981. "The Origin of Man." *Science* 211: 341–350.

Morgan, Elaine. 1972. *The Descent of Woman.* New York: Stein and Day.

Morris, Desmond. 1967. *The Naked Ape.* New York: McGraw-Hill.

Murdock, G. P. 1965. *Culture and Society.* Pittsburgh: University of Pittsburgh Press.

Slocum, Sally. 1975. "Woman the Gatherer: Male Bias in Anthropology," *Toward an Anthropology of Women,* R. R. Reiter, ed. New York: Monthly Review Press, pp. 36–50.

Zihlman, Adrienne L. 1981. "Women as Shapers of the Human Adaptation," *Woman the Gatherer,* op. cit., pp. 75–120.

CHAPTER
12

CONTENTS

Neandertals and Other Archaic *Homo sapiens*

Trail of hominid footprints fossilized in volcanic ash at Laetoli, Tanzania (approximate age, 3.7 million years)

Introduction

In the previous chapter, we saw that *Homo erectus* (or a close relative) first evolved in East Africa and spread quickly to several other areas of the Old World. While there is some debate concerning the number of species present during the time from 1.8 m.y.a. until about 400,000 y.a., there is general recognition that all these hominids are at a stage (what is called a "grade") that comes prior to that of *Homo sapiens*.

What, then, of the next grade of human evolution, that which occurs after 400,000 y.a.? During this time period, we have considerable evidence of the emergence of *Homo sapiens,* with fossil material coming from several areas of the Old World. In the next chapter, we will discuss the origins and dispersal of modern *Homo sapiens*. However, the appearance of hominids essentially identical to ourselves (anatomically and, presumably, behaviorally as well) did not occur instantaneously.

Between 400,000 and 100,000 y.a., coming from widely scattered sites in Africa, Asia, and Europe, fossil evidence indicates that our species emerged as the result of a long and intermittent evolutionary process. In many respects, these hominids during this time period are *transitional* forms, retaining some characteristics of their immediate precursors (*Homo erectus*) as well as displaying some traits similar to their later descendants (modern *Homo sapiens*).

Paleoanthropologists do not entirely agree what name (or names) to use for this varied group of transitional Middle Pleistocene hominids, but often refer to them as **archaic Homo sapiens.** By contrast, hominids essentially identical to us are referred to as **anatomically modern Homo sapiens.**

In this chapter, we will discuss the geographical localities, anatomy, and behavior of archaic *Homo sapiens* and will divide these hominids into two chronological groups: early archaic *Homo sapiens* and late archaic *Homo sapiens* (including especially the Neandertals).

Early Archaic *H. sapiens*

Many early archaic forms show morphological changes compared with *H. erectus*. These derived changes are reflected in brain expansion; increased parietal breadth (the basal portion of the skull is no longer the widest area, and therefore, the shape of the skull as seen from the rear is no longer pentagonal); some decrease in the size of the molars; and general decrease in cranial and postcranial robusticity.

A difficulty of major significance concerns exactly how to classify all this Middle Pleistocene hominid material. Here we take a conservative taxonomic approach and classify *all* of the specimens (as archaic forms) within the species *Homo sapiens*. However, a growing number of paleoanthropologists (e.g., Stringer, 1995; Larick and Ciochon, 1996; Rightmire, 1998) disagree with this interpretation and prefer to classify most, if not all, of the individuals into other species of the genus *Homo*. In this view, some of the earlier archaic forms could be ancestral to modern humans, but the later ones most likely would not be. As in other debates of this nature discussed in previous chapters, the essential issue concerns interpretation of intra- as compared to interspecific variation. We will return to this crucial topic at the end of this chapter.

A further complication in understanding archaic *H. sapiens* is that there is considerable variation both within and between samples of these hominids. Moreover, they are geographically very widely dispersed. In fact, archaic *H. sapiens* fossils have been found on the three continents of Africa, Asia, and Europe. In Europe, the well-known Neandertals are included in this category. (Neandertals are not found anywhere *except* Europe and western Asia.)

See the following sections of the CD-ROM for topics covered in this chapter: Virtual Lab 10, section I and Virtual Lab 11.

Archaic *Homo sapiens*
Earlier forms of *Homo sapiens* (including Neandertals) from the Old World that differ from *H. erectus* but lack the full set of characteristics diagnostic of modern *H. sapiens*.

Anatomically modern *Homo sapiens*
All modern humans and some fossil forms, perhaps dating as early as 200,000 y.a.; defined by a set of derived characteristics, including cranial architecture and lack of skeletal robusticity; usually classified at the subspecies level as *Homo sapiens sapiens*.

FIGURE 12–1
Broken Hill (Kabwe). Note the very heavy supraorbital torus.

Africa did not birth Neans [handwritten]

Chinese evolved from H. erectus, not european Hu sapiens [handwritten]

Africa

In Africa, archaic *H. sapiens* fossils have been found at several sites (Figs. 12–1 and 12–2). One of the best known is Broken Hill (Kabwe). At this site in Zambia, a complete cranium, together with other cranial and postcranial elements belonging to several individuals, was discovered.

In this and other African early archaic specimens, a mixture of older and more recent traits can be seen. The skull's massive supraorbital torus (one of the largest of any hominid), low vault, and prominent occipital torus recall those of *H. erectus*. On the other hand, the occipital region is less angulated, the cranial vault bones are thinner, and the cranial base is essentially modern. Dating estimates of Broken Hill and most of the other early archaic *H. sapiens* specimens from Africa have ranged throughout the Middle and Upper Pleistocene, but recent estimates have given dates for most of the localities in the range of 150,000–125,000 y.a.

A total of eight other archaic *H. sapiens* crania from South and East Africa also show a combination of *H. erectus* and *H. sapiens* characteristics, and they are all mentioned in the literature as being similar to Broken Hill. The most important of these African finds come from the sites of Florisbad and Elandsfontein in South Africa, Laetoli in Tanzania, and Bodo in Ethiopia (see Fig. 12–2). The general similarities in all these African archaic *H. sapiens* fossils may signify a fairly close genetic relationship of hominids from East and South Africa. It is also possible—although it seems most unlikely—that several populations were evolving in a somewhat similar way from *H. erectus* to a more *H. sapiens*-looking morphology.

We should point out that the evolutionary path of these hominids did not take a Neandertal turn. It seems that there were no Neandertals in Africa—nor were there any in the Far East (Table 12–1).

Asia

China   Like their counterparts in Europe and Africa, Chinese archaic *H. sapiens** specimens also display both earlier and later characteristics. Chinese paleoanthropologists suggest that archaic *H. sapiens* traits, such as a sagittal ridge (see p. 290) and flattened nasal bones, are shared with *H. erectus,* especially those specimens from Zhoukoudian. They also point out that some of these features can be found in modern *H. sapiens* in China today, indicating substantial genetic continuity. That is, some Chinese researchers have argued that anatomically modern Chinese did not evolve from *H. sapiens* in either Europe or Africa, evolving instead specifically in China from a separate *H. erectus* lineage.

That such regional evolution occurred in many areas of the world or, alternatively, that anatomically modern migrants from Africa displaced local populations is the subject of a major ongoing debate in paleoanthropology. This important controversy will be the central focus of the next chapter.

Dali, the most complete skull of the late Middle or early Upper Pleistocene fossils in China, displays *H. erectus* and *H. sapiens* traits, but it is clearly classified as early *H. sapiens* (despite its relatively small cranial capacity of 1,120 cm³). Several other Chinese specimens also reflect both earlier and later traits and are placed in the same category as Dali. In addition, the more recently discovered (1984) partial skeleton from Jinniushan, in northeast China, has been given a provisional date of 200,000 y.a. (Tiemel et al., 1994). The cranial capacity is fairly large (approximately 1,260 cm³), and the walls of the braincase are thin—both modern features and quite unexpected in an individual this ancient (if the dating estimate does indeed hold up).

---

*Chinese anthropologists prefer the term "early *Homo sapiens*" instead of "archaic *H. sapiens.*"

TABLE 12–1   A Partial List of Archaic *Homo sapiens* (Outside of Europe)

Name	Site	Date*	Human Remains	Associated Finds	Cranial Capacity (cm³)	Comments
Africa Bodo	Awash River Valley, Ethiopia	Middle Pleistocene (600,000 y.a.?)	Incomplete skull, part of braincase	Acheulian artifacts, animal bones	1,300	Resembles Broken Hill; first evidence of scalping
Broken Hill (Kabwe)	Cave deposits near Kabwe, Zambia	Late Middle Pleistocene; (130,000 y.a. or older)	Nearly complete cranium, cranial fragments of second individual, miscellaneous postcranial bones	Animal bones and artifacts in cave, but relationship to human remains unknown	1,280	Massive browridge, low vault, prominent occipital torus; cranial capacity within range of modern *H. sapiens*
China Dali	Shaanxi Province, north China	Late Middle Pleistocene (230,000–180,000 y.a.)	Nearly complete skull	Flake tools, animal bones	1,120–1,200	Robust supra-orbital ridge, low vault, retreating forehead, canine fossa
Jinniushan	Liaoning Province, northeast China	Late Middle Pleistocene (200,000 y.a.)	Partial skeleton, including a cranium	Flake tools	1,260	Thin cranial bones
Maba	Cave near Maba village, Guangdong Province, south China	Early Upper Pleistocene (140,000–120,000 y.a.)	Incomplete skull of middle-aged male	Animal bones	Insufficient remains for measurement	Receding forehead, modest keel on frontal bone

*Also see Figure 12–3.

India In 1982, a partial skull was discovered in the Narmada Valley, in central India. Associated with this fossil were various hand axes, cleavers, flakes, and choppers. This Narmada specimen has been dated as Middle Pleistocene with a probable cranial capacity within the range of 1,155 to 1,421 cm³. K. A. R. Kennedy (1991), who made a more recent study of the fossil, suggests that Narmada should be viewed as an early example of *H. sapiens*.

Europe

Various attempts have been made to organize European archaic *H. sapiens* of the Middle and early Upper Pleistocene in the time range of 400,000–150,000 y.a. (Fig. 12–3 on p. 318). Because in many cases definite dates or adequate remains (or both) are lacking, it is difficult to be certain which fossils belong where in the evolutionary sequence. As already noted, what we find in Europe are fossils, such as those in Africa and China, whose features resemble both *H. erectus* and *H. sapiens.* You should further note that the earliest fossil finds from western Europe (including those from Boxgrove in England and Atapuerca in Spain, discussed in Chapter 11) already show some of these transitional features.

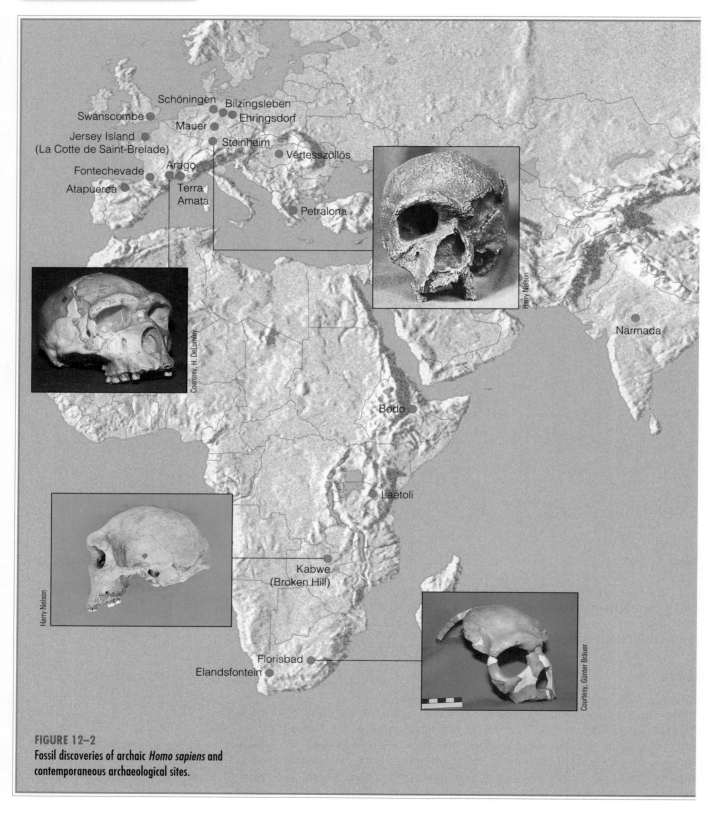

FIGURE 12–2

Fossil discoveries of archaic *Homo sapiens* and contemporaneous archaeological sites.

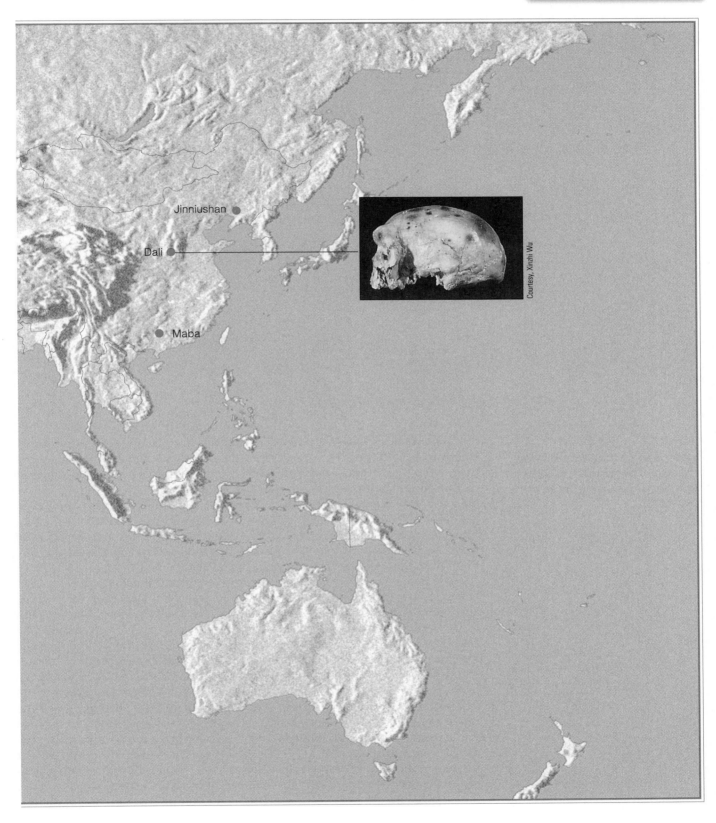

Courtesy, Xinzhi Wu

Jinniushan

Dali

Maba

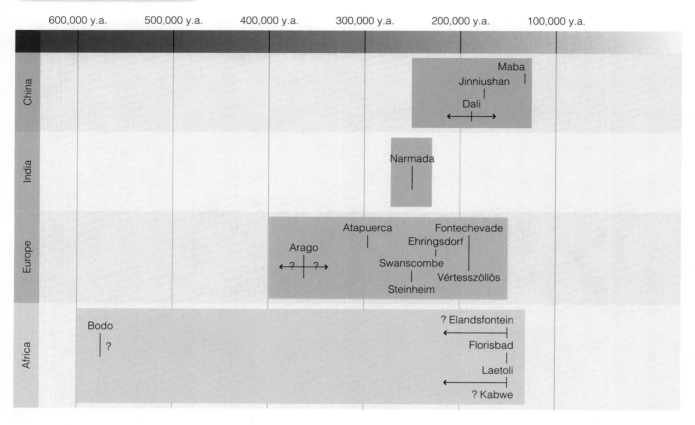

	600,000 y.a.	500,000 y.a.	400,000 y.a.	300,000 y.a.	200,000 y.a.	100,000 y.a.

China: Maba, Jinniushan, Dali ↔

India: Narmada

Europe: Atapuerca, Fontechevade, Ehringsdorf, Arago ←?|?→, Swanscombe, Vértesszöllös, Steinheim

Africa: Bodo ?, ? Elandsfontein ←, Florisbad, Laetoli ←, ? Kabwe

FIGURE 12–3

Time line of early archaic *Homo sapiens*. Note that most dates are approximations. Question marks indicate those estimates that are most tentative.

transist to Neands?

The earliest archaic *H. sapiens* representatives from Europe show some resemblance to *H. erectus* in the robusticity of the mandible, thick cranial bones, pronounced occipital torus, heavy supraorbital torus, receding frontal bone, greatest parietal breadth near the base of the skull, and large teeth. (They, of course, also have one or more *H. sapiens* characteristics.) Examples of these early archaic forms from Europe include fossils from Steinheim, Swanscombe, and Vértesszöllös (see Fig. 12–2). Later European archaic representatives also possess some *H. erectus* characteristics, but they also have one or more of the following traits: larger cranial capacity, more rounded occipital area, parietal expansion, and reduced tooth size (Table 12–2).

The later group, essentially from the latter half of the Middle Pleistocene, overlaps to some extent with the earlier group. From an evolutionary point of view, this later group may have evolved from the earlier one, and since many of these individuals display traits unique to Neandertals, they may in turn have given rise to the Neandertals. Examples of this somewhat later European transitional group include specimens from Fontechevade (France) and Ehringsdorf (Germany), as well as recent discoveries from Atapuerca, in northern Spain, in the same region as the recently discovered more ancient remains discussed in Chapter 11. This last site (called Sima de los Huesos), dated to approximately 300,000 y.a., has yielded the largest sample yet of archaic *H. sapiens* from anywhere in the world and includes the remains of at least 32 individuals (among which are several excellently preserved crania) (Arsuaga et al., 1993, 1997; Kunzig, 1997). Excavations continue at this remarkable site, where bones have somehow accumulated within a deep chamber inside a cave. There are also large numbers of carnivore remains (bear, fox), but these fossils are generally in separate locations from where the hominids were found. From initial descriptions, the hominid morphology has been interpreted as showing several indications of an early Neandertal-like pattern (arching browridges, projecting midface, and other features) (Rightmire, 1998).

TABLE 12–2 Early Archaic *Homo sapiens* in Europe

Name	Site	Date*	Human Remains	Associated Finds	Cranial Capacity (cm³)	Comments
Arago (Tautavel)	Cave site near Tautavel, Verdouble Valley, Pyrenees, southeastern France	400,000–300,000 y.a.; date uncertain	Face; parietal perhaps from same person; many cranial fragments; up to 23 individuals represented	Upper Acheulian artifacts, animal bones	1,150	Thick supra-orbital torus, pronounced alveolar prog-nathism; pari-etal resembles Swanscombe
Bilzingsleben	Quarry at Bilzingsleben, near Erfurt, Germany	425,000–200,000 y.a., probably 280,000 y.a.	Skull fragments and teeth	Flake industry, plant and animal remains	Insufficient material	Resembles *H. erectus* in some features
Atapuerca	Sima de los Huesos, northern Spain	320,000–190,000 y.a., probably 300,000 y.a.	Minimum of 32 individuals, including some nearly complete crania	Many carnivore remains, but at different levels from human remains	Highly variable; small indiv., 1,125; larger indiv., 1,390 (probably reflects sexual dimorphism)	Several resem-blances to Neandertals; oldest evidence of deliberate disposal of dead; largest sample of archaic *H. sapiens* at any site
Petralona	Cave near Petralona, Khalkidhiki, northeastern Greece	300,000–200,000 y.a.; date uncertain	Nearly complete skull	None	1,190–1,220	Mosaic; some bones resemble Neandertal, Broken Hill, and *H. erectus*
Steinheim	Gravel pit at Steinheim, Germany	Mindel-Riss Interglacial—300,000–250,000 y.a.; date uncertain	Nearly complete skull, lacking mandible	No artifacts, some animal bones	1,100	Pronounced supraorbital torus, frontal low, occipital rounded
Swanscombe	Swanscombe, Kent, England	Mindel-Riss Interglacial—300,000–250,000 y.a.; date uncertain	Occipital and parietals	Middle Acheulian artifacts, animal bones	1,325 (estimate)	Bones thick like *H. erectus*; occipital resembles Neandertal
Ehringsdorf	Fossil quarry; travertine deposits, eastern Germany	245,000–190,000 y.a.	Minimum of 9 individuals, including partial cranium	Mousterian artifacts	1,450	Resembles Neandertals in some respects
Vértesszöllös	Near village of Vértesszöllös, 30 miles west of Budapest, Hungary	210,000–160,000 y.a.; date uncertain	Adult occipital bone, fragments of infant teeth	Flake and pebble tools, animal bones	1,115–1,434 (estimate)	Occipital thick (*H. erectus* trait), but size and angulation sug-gest *H. sapiens*

*Also see Figure 12–3.

A Review of Middle Pleistocene Evolution (circa 400,000–125,000 y.a.)

erectus/sapiens mix forms are different in Asia, Africa, Europe

Like the *erectus/sapiens* mix in Africa and China, the fossils from Europe also exhibit a mosaic of traits from both species (Fig. 12–4). However, it is important to note that the fossils from each continent differ; that is, <u>the mosaic Chinese forms are not the same as those from Africa or Europe</u>. Some European fossils, assumed to be earlier, are more robust and possess more similarities to *H. erectus* than to modern *H. sapiens*. The later Middle Pleistocene European fossils appear to be more Neandertal-like, but the uncertainty of dates prevents a clear scenario of the Middle Pleistocene evolutionary sequence.

The physical differences from *H. erectus* are not extraordinary. Bones remain thick, the supraorbital torus is prominent, and vault height shows little increase. There is, however, a definite increase in brain size and a change in the shape of the skull from pentagonal to globular as seen from the rear. There is also a trend, especially with the later Middle Pleistocene forms, toward less occipital angulation. It is interesting to note that in Europe, the changes move toward a Neandertal *H. sapiens* pattern, but in Africa and Asia, toward modern *H. sapiens*.

AFRICA/ASIA
erectus
↓
modern sapien

EUROPE
erectus
↓
Neandertal sapien

Middle Pleistocene Culture

The Acheulian technology of *H. erectus* carried over into the Middle Pleistocene with relatively little change until near the end of the period, when it became slightly more sophisticated. Bone, a very useful tool material, apparently went practically unused by archaic *H. sapiens*. Stone flake tools similar to those of the earlier era persisted, perhaps in greater variety. Archaic *H. sapiens* in Africa and Europe invented a method—the Levallois technique (Fig. 12–5)—for controlling flake size and shape. Requiring several coordinated steps, this was no mean feat and suggests

(a)

(b)

Harry Nelson

FIGURE 12–4

Cast of an archaic *Homo sapiens* skull from Germany (Steinheim). (a) Frontal view showing damaged skull. (b) Basal view showing how the foramen magnum was enlarged, apparently for removal of the brain, perhaps for dietary or ritualistic purposes.

to many scholars increased cognitive abilities in late archaic *H. sapiens* compared to earlier archaic forms.

Interpretation of the distribution of artifacts during the later Middle Pleistocene has generated considerable discussion among archaeologists. We have noted (in Chapter 11) that there is a general geographical distribution characteristic of the Lower Pleistocene, with bifaces (mostly hand axes) found quite often at sites in Africa, but only rarely at sites in most of Asia, and not at all among the rich assemblage at Zhoukoudian (see p. 294). Moreover, where hand axes proliferate, the stone tool industry is referred to as Acheulian, while at localities without hand axes, various other terms are used (e.g., "chopper/chopping tool"—a misnomer, since most of the tools are actually flakes).

Acheulian assemblages have been found at many African sites as well as numerous European ones (e.g., Swanscombe in England and Arago in France). Nevertheless, the broad geographical distribution of what we call Acheulian should not blind us to the considerable intraregional diversity in stone tool industries. For example, while a variety of European sites do show a typical Acheulian complex, rich in bifacial hand axes and cleavers, other contemporaneous ones—for example, Bilzingsleben in Germany and Vértesszöllös in Hungary—do not. At these latter two sites, a variety of small retouched flake tools and flaked pebbles of various sizes were found, but no hand axes.

It thus appears that different stone tool industries coexisted in some areas for long periods. Various explanations (Villa, 1983) have been offered to account for this apparent diversity: (1) The tool industries were produced by different peoples (i.e., different cultures, perhaps hominids that also differed biologically); (2) the tool industries represent different types of activities carried out at separate locales; (3) the presence (or absence) of specific tool types—bifaces—represents the availability (or unavailability) of appropriate local stone resources.

Archaic *H. sapiens* populations continued to live both in caves and in open-air sites, but may have increased their use of caves. Did archaic *H. sapiens* control fire? Klein (1989, p. 255) suggests that these hominids did. He writes that there was a "concentration of burnt bones in depressions 50–60 cm across at Vértesszöllös" and that "fossil hearths have also been identified at Bilzingsleben and in several French caves that were probably occupied by early *H. sapiens*." Chinese archaeologists insist that many Middle Pleistocene sites in China contain evidence of human-controlled fire. However, not everyone is convinced.

That archaic *H. sapiens* built temporary structures is revealed by concentrations of bones, stones, and artifacts at several sites. Here, they manufactured artifacts and exploited the area for food. The stones may have been used to support the sides of a shelter.

In the Lazaret Cave in the city of Nice, in southern France, a shelter about 36 feet by 11 feet was built against the cave wall, and skins probably were hung over a framework of poles as walls for the shelter. The base was supported by rocks and large bones, and inside the shelter were two hearths. The hearth charcoal suggests that the hominid occupants used slow-burning oak and boxwood, which produced easy-to-rekindle embers. Very little stone waste was found inside the shelter, suggesting that they manufactured tools outside, perhaps because there was more light.

Archaeological evidence clearly alludes to the utilization of many different food sources, such as fruits, vegetables, seeds, nuts, and bird eggs, each in its own season. Marine life was also exploited. From Lazaret and Orgnac (southern France) comes evidence of freshwater fishing for trout, perch, and carp. The most detailed reconstruction of Middle Pleistocene life in Europe, however, comes from evidence at Terra Amata, on the southern coast of France (de Lumley and de Lumley, 1973;

Nodule

The nodule is chipped on the perimeter.

Flakes are radially removed from top surface.

A final blow at one end removes a large flake.

FIGURE 12–5
The Levallois technique.

Villa, 1983). From this site has come fascinating evidence relating to short-term, seasonal visits by archaic *H. sapiens* groups, who built flimsy shelters, gathered plants, exploited marine resources, and possibly hunted medium-sized and large mammals.

The hunting capabilities of these early members of *H. sapiens*, as for earlier hominids, remain open to dispute. What seems clear is that the evidence does not yet unambiguously establish widely practiced advanced abilities. In earlier professional discussions (as well as in earlier editions of our texts), archaeological evidence from Terra Amata (in France) and Torralba and Ambrona (in Spain) was used to argue for significantly advanced hunting skills for archaic *H. sapiens* in Europe. However, reconstruction of these sites by Richard Klein and others has now cast doubt on those prior conclusions. Once again, we see that application of scientific rigor (which is simply good critical thinking) makes us question assumptions. And in so doing, we frequently must conclude that other less dramatic (and less romantic) explanations fit the evidence as well as or better than those based on initial imaginative scenarios.

A possible exception to the current, much more conservative view of the hunting skills of archaic *H. sapiens* comes from an archaeological site excavated on the Channel Island of Jersey off the west coast of France (see Fig. 12–2). In a cave site called La Cotte de Saint-Brelade, many skeletal remains of large mammals (mammoth and woolly rhinoceros) were found in association with stone flakes. Unlike the remains from the sites mentioned earlier, the animals sampled at La Cotte de Saint-Brelade represent primarily subadults and adults in prime age (*not* what one would expect in naturally occurring accumulations). Moreover, the preserved elements also exhibit the kind of damage that further suggests hominid activities. Directly killing such large animals may not have been within the capabilities of the hominids (archaic *H. sapiens*?) who occupied this site. Thus, K. Scott, who led the excavations, has suggested that these early hominids may have driven their prey off a nearby cliff, bringing certain prized parts back to the cave for further butchering (Scott, 1980).

Another recent and exceptional find is also challenging assumptions regarding hunting capabilities of archaic *H. sapiens* in Europe. From the site of Schöningen in Germany, three remarkably well-preserved wooden spears were discovered in 1995 (Thieme, 1997). As we have noted before, fragile organic remains (such as wood) can rarely be preserved more than a few hundred years; yet these beautifully crafted implements are provisionally dated to 380,000–400,000 y.a.! Beyond this surprisingly ancient date, the spears are intriguing on a variety of other counts. Firstly, they are all large (about 6 feet long), very finely made, selected from hard spruce wood, and expertly balanced. Each spear would have required considerable planning, time, and skill to manufacture. Further, the weapons were most likely used as throwing spears, presumably to hunt large animals. Of interest in this context, bones of numerous horses were also recovered at Schöningen. Archaeologist Hartmut Thieme has thus concluded that "the spears strongly suggest that systematic hunting, involving foresight, planning and the use of appropriate technology, was part of the behavioural repertoire of pre-modern hominids" (1997, p. 807). Therefore, as with the remains from La Cotte de Saint-Brelade, these extraordinary spears from Schöningen make a strong case for advanced hunting skills practiced by at least some archaic *Homo sapiens* populations.

As documented by the fossil hominid remains as well as artifactual evidence from archaeological sites, the long period of transitional hominids in Europe was to continue well into the Upper Pleistocene (after 125,000 y.a.). However, the evolution of archaic *H. sapiens* was to take a unique turn with the appearance and expansion of the Neandertals.

Some advanced hunting skills.

Neandertals: Late Archaic *H. sapiens* (130,000–35,000 y.a.)

Since their discovery more than a century ago, the Neandertals have haunted the best-laid theories of paleoanthropologists. They fit into the general scheme of human evolution, and yet they are misfits. Classified as *H. sapiens*, they are like us and yet different. It is not an easy task to put them in their place.*

While Neandertal fossil remains have been found at dates approaching 130,000 y.a., in the following discussion of Neandertals, we refer to those populations that lived especially during the last glaciation, which began about 75,000 y.a. and ended about 10,000 y.a. (Fig. 12–6). We should also note that the evolutionary roots of Neandertals apparently reach quite far back in western Europe, as evidenced by the 300,000 y.a. remains from Sima de los Huesos, Atapuerca, in northern Spain. The majority of fossils have been found in Europe, where they have been most studied, and our description of Neandertals is based primarily on those specimens from western Europe, who are usually called *classic* Neandertals. Not all Neandertals—including others from eastern Europe and western Asia and those from the interglacial that preceded the last glacial—entirely conform to our description of the classic morphology. They tend to be less robust, perhaps because the climate in which they lived was not as cold as western Europe during the last glaciation.

One striking feature of Neandertals is brain size, which in these hominids actually was larger than that of *H. sapiens* today. The average for contemporary *H. sapiens* is between 1,300 and 1,400 cm³, while for Neandertals it was 1,520 cm³. The larger size may be associated with the metabolic efficiency of a larger brain in cold weather. The Inuit (Eskimo) brain also averages larger than that of other modern human populations (about the size of the Neandertal brain). It should also be pointed out that the larger brain size in both archaic and contemporary *Homo sapiens* in populations adapted to *cold* climates is partially correlated with larger body size, which has also evolved among these groups (see Chapter 15).

The classic Neandertal cranium is large, long, low, and bulging at the sides. Viewed from the side, the posterior portion of the occipital bone is somewhat bun-shaped, but the marked occipital angle typical of many *H. erectus* crania is absent. The forehead rises more vertically than that of *H. erectus*, and the browridges arch over the orbits instead of forming a straight bar (Fig. 12–7).

Compared with anatomically modern humans, the Neandertal face stands out. It projects almost as if it were pulled forward. This feature can be seen when the distance of the nose and teeth from the eye orbits is compared with that of modern *H. sapiens*. Postcranially, Neandertals were very robust, barrel-chested, and powerfully muscled. This robust skeletal structure, in fact, dominates hominid evolution from *H. erectus* through archaic *H. sapiens*. Nevertheless, the Neandertals appear particularly robust, with shorter limbs than seen in most modern *H. sapiens* populations. Both the facial anatomy and robust postcranial structure of Neandertals have been interpreted by Erik Trinkaus (of Washington University in St. Louis) to reflect adaptation to rigorous living in a cold climate.

For about 100,000 years, Neandertals lived in Europe and western Asia (see Fig. 12–11 on pp. 328–329), and their coming and going has raised more questions and

See Virtual Lab 10, section I, for a discussion of Neandertals.

***Homo sapiens neanderthalensis* is the subspecific designation for Neandertals, although not all paleoanthropologists agree with this terminology. (The subspecies for anatomically modern *H. sapiens* is designated as *Homo sapiens sapiens*.) *Thal,* meaning "valley," is the old spelling and is kept in the species designation (the "h" was always silent and not pronounced). The modern spelling is *tal* and is now used this way in Germany; we shall adhere to contemporary usage in the text with the spelling *Neandertal*.

FIGURE 12–6

Correlation of Pleistocene subdivisions with archaeological industries and hominids. Note that the geological divisions are separate and different from the archaeological stages (e.g., Upper Pleistocene is *not* synonymous with Upper Paleolithic).

(Years)	Pleistocene	GLACIAL	PALEOLITHIC	CULTURAL PERIODS (Archaeological Industries)	HOMINIDAE
10,000	UPPER PLEISTOCENE	Last glacial period	Upper Paleolithic	Magdalenian / Solutrean (20,000) / Gravettian (25,000) / Aurignacian/Perigordian / Chatelperronian	NEANDERTALS / MODERN SAPIENS
20,000					
30,000					
40,000					
50,000			Middle Paleolithic	Mousterian	
75,000					
100,000		Last interglacial period			
125,000	MIDDLE PLEISTOCENE	Earlier glacial periods	Lower Paleolithic	Acheulian	ARCHAIC H. SAPIENS / HOMO ERECTUS
700,000					
1,800,000	LOWER PLEISTOCENE			Oldowan	AUSTRALO-PITHECUS / EARLY HOMO

controversies than perhaps any other hominid group. As noted, Neandertal forebears date back to the later archaic *H. sapiens*. But these were transitional forms, and it is not until the last interglacial that Neandertals were fully recognizable.

Neandertal takes its name from the Neander Valley, near Düsseldorf, Germany. In 1856, workmen quarrying limestone caves in the valley came across some fossilized bones. The owner of the quarry believed them to be bear and gave them to a natural science teacher, who realized that they were not the remains of a cave bear, but rather the remains of an ancient human. Exactly what the bones represented

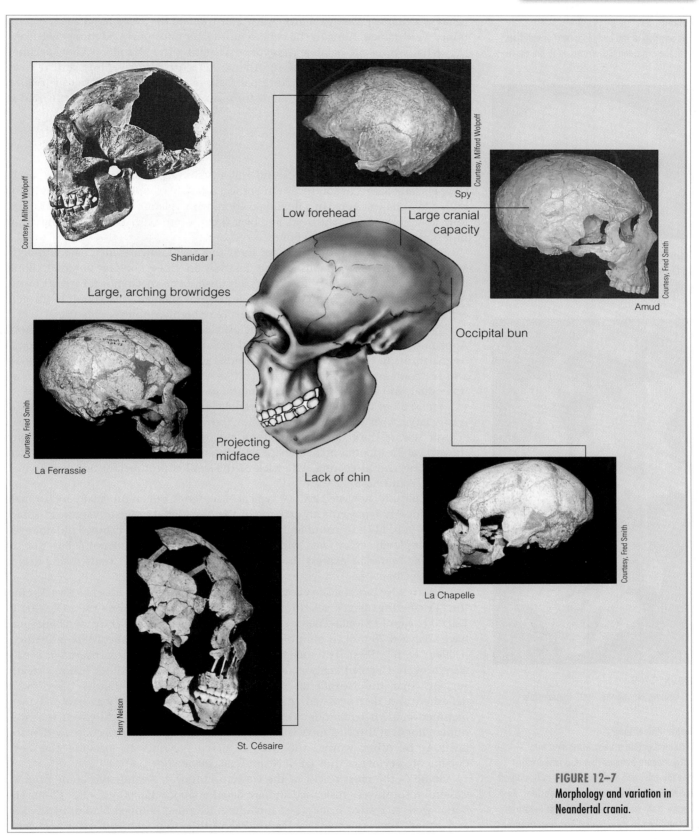

Shanidar I

Spy

Low forehead

Large cranial capacity

Amud

Large, arching browridges

Occipital bun

La Ferrassie

Projecting midface

Lack of chin

La Chapelle

St. Césaire

FIGURE 12–7
Morphology and variation in Neandertal crania.

Flexed
The position of the body in a bent orientation, with the arms and legs drawn up to the chest.

FIGURE 12–8
La Chapelle-aux-Saints. Note the occipital bun, projecting face, and low vault.

FIGURE 12–9
St. Césaire, among the "last" Neandertals.

Upper Paleolithic
A cultural period usually associated with early modern humans (but also found with Neandertals) and distinguished by technological innovation in various stone tool industries. Best known from western Europe, similar industries are also known from central and eastern Europe and Africa.

became a *cause célèbre* for many years, and the fate of "Neandertal Man," as the bones were named, hung in the balance until later finds provided more evidence.

What swung the balance in favor of accepting the Neander Valley specimen as a genuine hominid fossil were other nineteenth-century finds similar to it. What is more important, the additional fossil remains brought home the realization that a form of human different from nineteenth-century Europeans had in fact once existed.

France and Spain

One of the most important Neandertal discoveries was made in 1908 at La Chapelle-aux-Saints in southwestern France. A nearly complete skeleton was found buried in a shallow grave in a **flexed** position, with several fragments of nonhuman long bones placed over the head, and over them, a bison leg. Around the body were flint tools and broken animal bones.

The skeleton was turned over for study to a well-known French paleontologist, Marcellin Boule, who published his analysis in three copious volumes. Boule depicted the La Chapelle Neandertal as a brutish, bent-kneed, not fully erect biped. As a result of this exaggerated interpretation, some scholars, and certainly the general public, concluded that all Neandertals were highly primitive creatures.

Why did Boule draw these conclusions from the La Chapelle skeleton? Apparently, he misconstrued Neandertal posture owing to the presence of spinal osteoarthritis in this older male. In addition, and probably more important, Boule and his contemporaries found it difficult to accept fully as a human ancestor an individual who appeared to depart from the modern pattern.

The skull of this male, who was possibly at least 40 years of age when he died, is very large, with a cranial capacity of 1,620 cm³. As is typical for western European "classic" forms, the vault is low and long, the supraorbital ridges are immense, with the typical Neandertal arched shape, the forehead is low and retreating, and the face is long and projecting. The back of the skull is protuberant and bun-shaped (Figs. 12–7 and 12–8).

La Chapelle, however, is not a typical Neandertal, but an unusually robust male that "evidently represents an extreme in the Neandertal range of variation" (Brace et al., 1979, p. 117). Unfortunately, this skeleton, which Boule claimed did not even walk completely erect, was widely accepted as "Mr. Neandertal." But not all Neandertal materials express the suite of "classic Neandertal" traits to the degree seen in La Chapelle.

Another Neandertal site excavated recently in southern France has revealed further fascinating details relating to Neandertal behavior. From the 100,000- to 120,000-year-old Moula-Guercy cave site, Alban Defleur, Tim White, and colleagues have analyzed 78 broken hominid fragments representing probably six individuals (Defleur et al., 1999). The intriguing aspect of these remains concerns *how* they were broken. Detailed analysis of cut marks, pits, scars, and other features clearly suggests that the Neandertal individuals were *processed*—that is, they "were defleshed and disarticulated. After this, the marrow cavity was exposed by a hammer-on-anvil technique" (Defleur et al., 1999, p. 131). Moreover, the nonhuman bones at this site, especially the deer remains, were processed in an identical fashion. In other words, the Moula-Guercy Neandertals provide the best-documented evidence thus far of Neandertal cannibalism.

Some of the most recent of the western European Neandertals come from St. Césaire in southwestern France and are dated at about 35,000 y.a. (Fig. 12–9). The bones were recovered from a bed including discarded chipped blades, hand axes, and other stone tools of an **Upper Paleolithic** tool industry associated with Neandertals. Another site, Zafarraya Cave in southern Spain, may provide yet a

FIGURE 12–10
Time line for Neandertal (*Homo sapiens neanderthalensis*) fossil discoveries.

more recent time range for Neandertal occupation in Europe. During the 1980s and 1990s, a few pieces of hominid individuals were found at Zafarraya that have been interpreted as Neandertal in morphology. What is most interesting, however, is the *date* suggested for the site. French archaeologist Jean-Jacques Hublin, who has excavated the site, asserts that the date is close to 29,000 y.a.—a full 6,000 years later than St. Césaire.

Another site, also recently redated, is apparently about the same age as Zafarraya, but it is located in central Europe. Recent recalibration by radiocarbon dating has indicated that the later Neandertal levels at Vindija, in Croatia (discussed shortly), are about 28,000 to 29,000 years old (Smith et al., 1999). If one of these dates is further confirmed, then either Zafarraya or Vindija would gain the distinction of having the most recent Neandertals thus far discovered.

Yet a more recent site in Portugal has recently been interpreted as showing hybridization between Neandertals and modern *Homo sapiens*. (We will discuss this intriguing suggestion in more detail in Chapter 13.)

The St. Césaire, Zafarraya, and Vindija sites are fascinating for several reasons. Anatomically modern humans were living in central and western Europe by about 35,000 y.a. or a bit earlier. Therefore, it is possible that Neandertals and modern *H. sapiens* were living in close proximity for several thousand years (Fig. 12–10). How did these two groups interact? Evidence from a number of French sites (Harrold, 1989) indicates that Neandertals borrowed technological methods and tools (such as blades) from the anatomically modern populations and thereby modified their own tools, creating a new industry, the **Chatelperronian**. However, such an example of cultural diffusion does not specify *how* the diffusion took place. Did the Neandertals become assimilated into modern populations? Did the two groups interbreed? It would also be interesting to know more precisely how long the coexistence of Neandertals and modern *H. sapiens* lasted.* No one knows the answers to

Chatelperronian
Pertaining to an Upper Paleolithic tool industry found in France and Spain, containing blade tools and associated with Neandertals.

---

*For a fictionalized account of the meeting between Neandertals and anatomically modern humans, see Bjorn Kurten's *Dance of the Tiger. A Novel of the Ice Age*. Another novel on the subject is Jean M. Auel's *Clan of the Cave Bear*. Several movies and a Discovery Channel production have also been made on this theme.

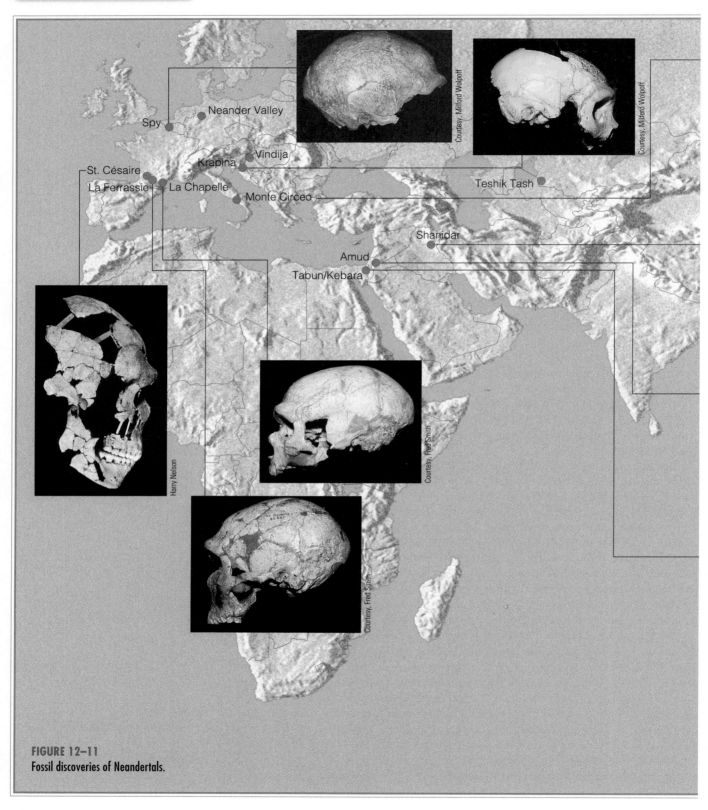

FIGURE 12–11
Fossil discoveries of Neandertals.

Monte Circeo

Courtesy, Fred Smith

Shanidar

Courtesy, Milford Wolpoff

Amud

Courtesy, Fred Smith

Tabun

Courtesy, Fred Smith

Neands died quicker

no fossil co-existence

these questions, but it has been suggested that an average annual difference of 2 percent mortality between the two populations (i.e., modern *H. sapiens* lived longer than Neandertals) would have resulted in the extinction of the Neandertals in approximately 1,000 years (Zubrow, 1989).

It should be noted that not all paleoanthropologists agree with the notion of the coexistence of Neandertals and Upper Paleolithic modern humans. For example, in a recent paper, David Frayer of the University of Kansas states: "There is still *no human fossil evidence* which supports the coexistence of Neanderthal and Upper Paleolithic forms in Europe" (emphasis added) (1992, p. 9). That is, despite the indications of cultural diffusion noted here, no European site has yet produced directly associated remains of *both* types of humans.

Central Europe

There are quite a few other European classic Neandertals, including significant finds in central Europe. At Krapina, Croatia, an abundance of bones (1,000 fragments representing up to 70 individuals) and 1,000 stone tools or flakes have been recovered (Trinkaus and Shipman, 1992). Krapina is an old site, perhaps the earliest showing the full "classic" Neandertal morphology, dating back to the last interglacial (estimated at 130,000–110,000 y.a.). Moreover, despite the relatively early date, the characteristic Neandertal features of the Krapina specimens (although less robust) are similar to the western European finds (Fig. 12–12). Krapina is also important as an intentional burial site, one of the oldest on record.

Another interesting site in central Europe is Vindija, about 30 miles from Krapina. The site is an excellent source of faunal, cultural, and hominid materials stratified in *sequence* throughout much of the Upper Pleistocene. Neandertal fossils consisting of some 35 specimens are dated between about 42,000 and 28,000 y.a. (the latter date would be among the most recent of all Neandertal discoveries). Even though some of their features approach the morphology of early modern south-central European *H. sapiens*, the overall pattern is definitely Neandertal. However, these modified Neandertal features, such as smaller browridges and slight chin development, may also be seen as an evolutionary trend toward modern *H. sapiens*.

Fred Smith, of Northern Illinois University, takes the view that variation in Vindija cranial features points to a trend continuing on to the later anatomically modern specimens found in the upper levels of the cave. Does Vindija support the proposition that the origin of *H. sapiens* could have occurred here in central Europe? Smith does not insist on this interpretation and suggests that anatomically modern *Homo sapiens* could have come from elsewhere. But he does believe that there is at least some morphological and genetic continuity between the samples found in the lower and upper levels of the cave.

(a)

(b)

Courtesy, Fred Smith

FIGURE 12–12
Krapina C. (a) Lateral view showing characteristic Neandertal traits. (b) Three-quarters view.

Western Asia

Israel   In addition to European Neandertals, there are numerous important discoveries from southwest Asia. Several specimens from Israel display some modern features and are less robust than the classic Neandertals of Europe, but again the overall pattern is Neandertal. The best known of these discoveries is from Tabun (Mugharet-et-Tabun, "Cave of the Oven") at Mt. Carmel, a short drive south from Haifa (Fig. 12–13). Tabun, excavated in the early 1930s, yielded a female skeleton, recently dated by thermoluminescence (TL) at about 120,000–110,000 y.a. If this dating proves accurate, it places the Tabun find as clearly contemporary with early modern *H. sapiens* found in nearby caves. (TL dating is discussed on p. 347.)

FIGURE 12–13
Excavation of the Tabun Cave, Mt. Carmel, Israel.

A more recent Neandertal burial, a male discovered in 1983, comes from Kebara, a neighboring cave of Tabun at Mt. Carmel. Although the skeleton is incomplete—the cranium and much of the lower limbs are missing—the pelvis, dated to 60,000 y.a., is the most complete Neandertal pelvis so far recovered. Also recovered at Kebara is a hyoid bone, the first from a Neandertal, and this find is especially important from the point of view of reconstructing language capabilities.*

Iraq   A most remarkable site is Shanidar, in the Zagros Mountains of northeastern Iraq, where partial skeletons of nine individuals—males and females, seven adults and two infants—were found, four of them deliberately buried. One of the more interesting individuals is Shanidar 1, a male who lived to be approximately 30 to 45 years old, a considerable age for a prehistoric human (Fig. 12–14). His stature is estimated at 5 feet 7 inches, his cranial capacity 1,600 cm^3. This individual shows several fascinating features:

> There had been a crushing blow to the left side of the head, fracturing the eye socket, displacing the left eye, and probably causing blindness on that side. He also sustained a massive blow to the right side of the body that so badly damaged the right arm that it became withered and useless; the bones of the shoulder blade, collar bone, and upper arm are much smaller and thinner than those on the left. The right lower arm and hand are missing, probably not because of poor preservation . . . but because they either atrophied and dropped off or because they were amputated. (Trinkaus and Shipman, 1992, p. 340)

In addition to these injuries, there was damage to the lower right leg (including a healed fracture of a foot bone). The right knee and left leg show signs of pathological involvement, and these changes to the limbs and foot may have left this man with a limping gait.

FIGURE 12–14
Shanidar 1. Does he represent an example of Neandertal compassion for the disabled?

---

*The Kebara hyoid is identical to that of modern humans, suggesting that Neandertals did not differ from *H. sapiens sapiens* in this key element.

How such a person could perform normal obligations and customs is difficult to imagine. However, both Ralph Solecki, who supervised the work at Shanidar Cave, and Erik Trinkaus, who has carefully studied the Shanidar remains, believe that to survive, he must have been helped by others: "A one-armed, partially blind, crippled man could have made no pretense of hunting or gathering his own food. That he survived for years after his trauma was a testament to Neandertal compassion and humanity" (Trinkaus and Shipman, 1992, p. 341).*

Central Asia

Uzbekistan   About 1,600 miles east of Shanidar in Uzbekistan, in a cave at Teshik-Tash, is the easternmost Neandertal discovery. The skeleton is that of a nine-year-old boy who appears to have been deliberately buried. It was reported that he was surrounded by five pairs of wild goat horns, suggesting a burial ritual or perhaps a religious cult, but owing to inadequate published documentation of the excavation, this interpretation has been seriously questioned. The Teshik-Tash individual, like some specimens from Croatia and southwest Asia, also shows a mixture of Neandertal traits (heavy browridges and occipital bun) and modern traits (high vault and definite signs of a chin).

As noted, the Teshik-Tash site represents the easternmost location presently established for Neandertals. Thus, based on current evidence, it is clear that the geographical distribution of the Neandertals extended from France eastward to central Asia, a distance of about 4,000 miles.

Culture of Neandertals

Neandertals, who lived in the cultural period known as the Middle Paleolithic, are usually associated with the **Mousterian** industry (although the Mousterian industry is not always associated with Neandertals). In the early part of the last glacial period, Mousterian culture extended across Europe and North Africa into the former Soviet Union, Israel, Iran, and as far east as Uzbekistan and perhaps even China. Moreover, in Africa, the contemporaneous Middle Stone Age industry is broadly similar to the Mousterian.

Technology

Neandertals improved on previous prepared-core techniques (i.e., the Levallois) by inventing a new variation. They trimmed a flint nodule around the edges to form a disk-shaped core. Each time they struck the edge, they produced a flake, continuing this way until the core became too small and was discarded. Thus, the Neandertals were able to obtain more flakes per core than their predecessors. They then trimmed (retouched) the flakes into various forms, such as scrapers, points, and knives (Fig.12–15).

Neandertal craftspeople elaborated and diversified traditional methods, and there is some indication of development in the specialization of tools used in skin and meat preparation, hunting, woodworking, and hafting. There is, however, still nearly a complete absence of bone tools, in strong contrast to the succeeding cultural period, the Upper Paleolithic. Nevertheless, Neandertals advanced their technology, which tended to be similar in basic tool types over considerable geographical distances, far beyond that of *H. erectus*. It is quite possible that their modifications in technology helped provide a basis for the remarkable changes of the Upper Paleolithic (discussed in the next chapter).

Mousterian
Pertaining to the stone tool industry associated with Neandertals and some modern *H. sapiens* groups; also called Middle Paleolithic. This industry is characterized by a larger proportion of flake tools than is found in Acheulian tool kits.

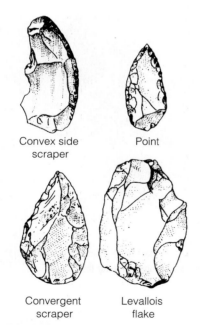

Convex side
scraper

Point

Convergent
scraper

Levallois
flake

FIGURE 12–15
Mousterian tools. (After Bordes.)

---

*K. A. Dettwyler (1991) asserts that Shanidar 1 could have survived without assistance and that there is no solid evidence that compassion explains this individual's survival.

Settlements

People of the Mousterian culture lived in a variety of open sites, caves, and rock shelters. Living in the open on the cold tundra suggests the building of structures, and there is some evidence of such structures (although the last glaciation must have destroyed many open sites). At the site of Moldova, in the Ukraine (now an independent state and neighbor of Russia), archaeologists found traces of an oval ring of mammoth bones enclosing an area of about 26 by 16 feet and which may have been used to weigh down the skin walls of a temporary hut or tent. Inside the ring are traces of a number of hearths, hundreds of tools, thousands of waste flakes, and many bone fragments, quite possibly derived from animals brought back for consumption.

Evidence of life in caves is abundant. Windbreaks of poles and skin were probably erected at the cave mouth for protection against severe weather. Fire was in general use by this time and was no doubt used for cooking, warmth, light, and keeping predators at bay.

How large were Neandertal settlements, and were they permanent or temporary? These questions are not yet answered, but Binford (1981) suggests that the settlements were used repeatedly for short-term occupation.

Subsistence

Neandertals were successful hunters, as the abundant remains of animal bones at their sites demonstrate. But while it is clear that Neandertals could hunt large mammals, they may not have been as efficient at this task as were Upper Paleolithic hunters. Inferring from his detailed work in the Middle East, Harvard anthropologist Ofer Bar-Yosef (1994) has concluded that only after the beginning of the Upper Paleolithic was the spear-thrower, or atlatl (see p. 357), invented. Moreover, shortly thereafter, the bow and arrow may have greatly facilitated efficiency (and safety) in hunting large mammals. Lacking such long-distance weaponry, and thus mostly limited to close-proximity spears, Neandertals may have been more prone to serious injury—a hypothesis recently given some intriguing support by paleoanthropologists Thomas Berger and Erik Trinkaus. Berger and Trinkaus (1995) analyzed the pattern of trauma (particularly fractures) in Neandertals and compared it with that seen in contemporary human samples. Interestingly, the pattern in Neandertals—especially the relatively high proportion of head and neck injuries—matched most closely to that seen in contemporary rodeo performers. Berger and Trinkaus thus conclude, "The similarity to the rodeo distribution suggests frequent close encounters with large ungulates unkindly disposed to the humans involved" (Berger and Trinkaus, 1995, p. 841).

Meat was, of course, not the only component of Neandertal diet. Evidence (from Shanidar, for example) indicates that Neandertals gathered as well, consuming berries, nuts, and other plants.

It is assumed that in the bitter cold of the last glacial period, Neandertals wore clothing, and they probably had developed methods of curing skins. But since there is no evidence of sewing equipment, the clothing was probably of simple design, perhaps something like a poncho.

We know much more of European Middle Paleolithic culture than of any prior period, as it has been studied longer by more scholars. In recent years, however, Africa has been a target not only of physical anthropologists (as we have seen copiously documented in earlier chapters), but also of archaeologists, who have added considerably to our knowledge of African Pleistocene hominid history. In many instances, the technology and assumed cultural adaptations in Africa were similar to those in Europe and southwest Asia. We will see in the next chapter that the African technological achievements also kept pace with (or even preceded) those in western Europe.

See Virtual Lab 11 for a discussion of dietary reconstruction.

Symbolic Behavior

can speak, but not like H. sapiens sapiens

There are a variety of hypotheses concerning the speech capacities of Neandertals. Many of these views are highly contradictory, with some scholars arguing that Neandertals were incapable of human speech. Nevertheless, the current consensus is that Neandertals were capable of articulate speech, even perhaps fully competent in the range of sounds produced by modern humans. However, this conclusion is not to argue that because Neandertals *could* speak they necessarily had the same language capacities as modern *Homo sapiens*. A major contemporary focus among paleoanthropologists is the apparently sudden expansion of modern *H. sapiens* (discussed in Chapter 13) and various explanations for the success of this group. Moreover, at the same time we are explaining how and why *H. sapiens sapiens* expanded its geographical range, we are left with the further problem of explaining what happened to the Neandertals. In making these types of interpretations, a growing number of paleoanthropologists suggest that *behavioral* differences are the key.

Upper Paleolithic *H. sapiens* is hypothesized to have possessed some significant behavioral advantages that Neandertals (and other archaic *H. sapiens*) lacked. Was it some kind of new and expanded ability to symbolize, communicate, organize social activities, elaborate technology, obtain a wider range of food resources, or care for the sick or injured, or was it some other factor? Were there, compared with *H. sapiens sapiens*, neurological differences that limited the Neandertals and thus contributed to their demise?

The direct anatomical evidence derived from Neandertal fossils is not especially helpful in specifically answering these questions. Ralph Holloway (1985) has maintained that Neandertal brains (at least as far as the fossil evidence suggests) do not differ significantly from that of modern *H. sapiens*. Moreover, Neandertal vocal tracts and other morphological features, compared with our own, do not appear seriously to have limited them. Furthermore, a recent study of the size of a small opening in the base of the skull (the hypoglossal canal; see Figure A–4 in Appendix A) has shed new insight on Neandertal speech capabilities. Richard Kay, Matt Cartmill, and Michelle Balow of Duke University measured the size of this canal in a variety of fossil hominids as well as in modern humans and great apes (Kay et al., 1998). The size of the hypoglossal canal may be particularly significant to speech production, since the main nerve supply for the tongue passes through this opening. The Duke researchers found that Neandertals (and other archaic *H. sapiens*) had hypoglossal canals as large as those seen in modern humans, arguing that Neandertal speech capabilities would not have been hampered in this respect. Interestingly, however, in earlier hominids (*Australopithecus* and early *Homo*), the hypoglossal canal was much smaller—in fact, similar in size to that seen in chimpanzees. Another recent study (DeGusta et al., 1999), however, has cast considerable doubt on all these assertions (see p. 368).

Most of the reservations about advanced cognitive abilities in Neandertals have come from archaeological data. Interpretation of Neandertal sites, when compared with succeeding Upper Paleolithic sites (especially as documented in western Europe), have led to several intriguing contrasts, as shown in Table 12–3.

Neandls replaced by moderns b/c of
culture?
or biology?

On the basis of this type of behavioral and anatomical evidence, Neandertals in recent years have increasingly been viewed as an evolutionary dead end. Whether their disappearance and ultimate replacement by anatomically modern Upper Paleolithic peoples (with their presumably "superior" culture) was solely the result of cultural differences or was also influenced by biological variation cannot at present be determined.

TABLE 12–3 Cultural Contrasts* Between Neandertals and Upper Paleolithic *Homo sapiens sapiens*

Neandertals	Upper Paleolithic *H. sapiens sapiens*
Tool Technology	
Numerous flake tools; few, however, apparently for highly specialized functions; use of bone, antler, or ivory very rare; relatively few tools with more than one or two parts	Many more varieties of stone tools; many apparently for specialized functions; frequent use of bone, antler, and ivory; many more tools comprised of two or more component parts
Hunting Efficiency and Weapons	
No long-distance hunting weapons; close-proximity weapons used (thus, more likelihood of injury)	Use of spear-thrower and bow and arrow; wider range of social contacts, perhaps permitting larger, more organized hunting parties (including game drives)
Stone Material Transport	
Stone materials transported only short distances—just "a few kilometers" (Klein, 1989)	Stone tool raw materials transported over much longer distances, implying wider social networks and perhaps trade
Art	
Artwork uncommon; usually small; probably mostly of a personal nature; some items perhaps misinterpreted as "art"; others may be intrusive from overlying Upper Paleolithic contexts; cave art absent	Artwork much more common, including transportable objects as well as elaborate cave art; well executed, using a variety of materials and techniques; stylistic sophistication
Burial	
Deliberate burial at several sites; graves unelaborated; graves frequently lack artifacts	Burials much more complex, frequently including both tools and remains of animals

*The contrasts are more apparent in some areas (particularly western Europe) than others (eastern Europe, Near East). Elsewhere (Africa, eastern Asia), where there were no Neandertals, the cultural situation is quite different (see p. 363). Moreover, even in western Europe, the cultural transformations were not necessarily abrupt, but may have developed more gradually from Mousterian to Upper Paleolithic times. For example, Straus (1995) argues that many of the Upper Paleolithic features were not consistently manifested until after 20,000 y.a.

Burials

It has been known for some time that Neandertals deliberately buried their dead. Indeed, the spectacular discoveries at La Chapelle, Shanidar, and elsewhere were the direct results of ancient burial, thus facilitating much more complete preservation. Such deliberate burial treatment extends back at least 90,000 years at Tabun. Moreover, some form of consistent "disposal" of the dead (but not necessarily below-ground burial) is evidenced at Atapuerca, Spain, where at least 32 individuals comprising more than 700 fossilized elements were found in a cave at the end of a deep vertical shaft. From the nature of the site and the accumulation of hominid remains, Spanish researchers are convinced that the site demonstrates some form of human activity involving deliberate disposal of the dead (Arsuaga et al., 1997).

The provisional 300,000-year-old age for Atapuerca suggests that Neandertals (more precisely, their immediate precursors) were, by the Middle Pleistocene, handling their dead in special ways, a behavior thought previously to have emerged only much later (in the Upper Pleistocene). And, apparently as far as current data indicate, this practice is seen in western European contexts well before it appears in Africa or in eastern Asia. For example, in the archaic *H. sapiens* sites at Laetoli, Kabwe, and Florisbad (discussed earlier), deliberate disposal of the dead is not documented. Nor is it seen in African early modern sites (e.g., Klasies River Mouth, dated at 120,000–100,000 y.a.; see p. 347).

Nevertheless, in later contexts (after 35,000 y.a.) in Europe, where anatomically modern *H. sapiens* (*H. sapiens sapiens*) remains are found in clear burial contexts, their treatment is considerably more complex than is seen in Neandertal burials. In these later (Upper Paleolithic) sites, grave goods, including bone and stone tools as well as animal bones, are found more consistently and in greater concentrations. Because many Neandertal sites were excavated in the nineteenth or early twentieth century, before the development of more rigorous archaeological methods, there are questions regarding numerous purported burials. Nevertheless, the evidence seems quite clear that deliberate burial was practiced at La Chapelle, La Ferrassie (eight graves), Tabun, Amud, Kebara, Shanidar, and Teshik-Tash (as well as at several other localities, especially in France). Moreover, in many instances, the *position* of the body was deliberately modified and placed in the grave in a flexed posture (see p. 326). Such a flexed position has been found in 16 of the 20 best-documented Neandertal burial contexts (Klein, 1989).

Finally, the placement of supposed grave goods in burials, including stone tools, animal bones (such as cave bear), and even arrangements of flowers, together with stone slabs on top of the burials, have all been postulated as further evidence of Neandertal symbolic behavior. However, in many instances, again due to poor excavation documentation, these assertions are questionable. Placement of stone tools, for example, is occasionally seen, but apparently was not done consistently. In those 33 Neandertal burials for which adequate data exist, only 14 show definite association of stone tools and/or animal bones with the deceased (Klein, 1989). It is not until the next cultural period, the Upper Paleolithic, that we see a major behavioral shift, as demonstrated in more elaborate burials and development of art.

Genetic Evidence

As a result of the revolutionary advances in molecular biology (discussed in Chapter 3), fascinating new avenues of research have become possible in the study of earlier hominids. The extraction, amplification, and sequencing of ancient DNA from contexts spanning the last 10,000 years or so are now becoming fairly commonplace (e.g., the analysis of DNA from the 5,000-year-old "Iceman" found in the Italian Alps).

Finding usable DNA in yet more ancient remains is much more difficult because the material has become more mineralized, obliterating organic components, including (usually) the DNA. Nevertheless, in the past few years, very exciting results have been announced relating to DNA found in three different Neandertal fossils. The first of these comes from the original Neander Valley specimen, and analysis was completed in 1997 (Krings et al., 1997); the other two come from Mezmaiskaya Cave, Russia (Ovchinnikov et al., 2000) and from Vindija in Croatia (Krings, et al., 2000). In all cases, the individuals are by far the oldest hominid remains from which DNA has been recovered. The Neander Valley fossil is estimated at 70,000 years old, the Vindija remains are 42,000 y.a., and the Mezmaiskaya material is dated at 29,000 y.a. (*Note:* This places the latter among the most recent of all Neandertal discoveries.)

The technique used in the study of Neandertal fossils involved the extraction of mitochondrial DNA (mtDNA), amplification by PCR (see p. 63), and nucleotide sequencing of portions of the molecule. Results from the three specimens show that they are genetically more different from contemporary *Homo sapiens* populations than these latter populations are from each other (about three times as much). Extrapolating from these comparative data, Krings and colleagues (1997) have

See Virtual Lab 10, section I, for a discussion of the implications of DNA analysis of Neandertals.

hypothesized that the Neandertal lineage separated from that of modern *H. sapiens* ancestors between 690,000 and 550,000 y.a.

The intriguing hypothesis, however, has not been fully confirmed and is most certainly not accepted by all paleoanthropologists. It is still not clear how rapidly mtDNA evolves, nor is it obvious how genetically different we should *expect* ancient hominids to be compared to us. (In other words, at present, we cannot rule out evolutionary relationships on the basis of available genetic evidence.) Nevertheless, such data probably offer the best hope of ultimately untangling the place of Neandertals in human evolution—and perhaps even of understanding something of their fate.

Evolutionary Trends in the Genus *Homo*

To understand the evolution of the various forms of *Homo sapiens* discussed in this chapter, it is useful to briefly review general trends of evolution in the genus *Homo* over the last 2 million years. In doing so, we see that at least three major *transitions* have taken place. Paleoanthropologists are keenly interested in interpreting the nature of these transitions, as they inform us directly regarding human origins. In addition, such investigations contribute to a broader understanding of the mechanics of the evolutionary process—at both the micro- and macroevolutionary levels.

The first transition of note was from early *Homo* to *Homo erectus*. This transition was apparently geographically restricted to Africa and appears to have been quite rapid (lasting 200,000 years at most, perhaps considerably less). It is important to recall that such a transition by no means implies that all early *Homo* groups actually evolved into *H. erectus*. In fact, many paleoanthropologists (part of a growing consensus) suggest that there was more than one species of early *Homo*. Clearly, only one could be ancestral to *H. erectus*. Even more to the point, only *some* populations of this one species would have been part of the genetic transformation (speciation) that produced *Homo erectus*.

The second transition is more complex and is the main topic of this chapter. It is the gradual change in populations of *H. erectus* grading into early *H. sapiens* forms—what we have termed archaic *H. sapiens*. This transition was not geographically restricted, as there is evidence of archaic *H. sapiens* widespread in the Old World (in East and South Africa, in China, India, and Java, and in Europe). Moreover, the transition appears not to have been rapid, but rather quite slow and uneven in pace from area to area. The complexity of this evolutionary transition creates ambiguities for our interpretations and resulting classifications.

For example, in Chapter 11, we included the Ngandong (Solo) material from Java within *Homo erectus*. However, there are several derived features in many of these specimens that suggest, alternatively, that they could be assigned to *Homo sapiens*. The dating (just recently indicating a date of only 29,000 y.a.) would argue that if this is a *H. erectus* group, it is a *very* late remnant, probably isolated *H. erectus* population surviving in southern Asia long after archaic *H. sapiens* populations were expanding elsewhere. Whatever the interpretation of Ngandong—either as a late *H. erectus* or as a quite primitive (i.e., not particularly derived) archaic *H. sapiens*—the conclusion is actually quite arbitrary (after all, the evolutionary process is continuous). We, by the nature of our classifications, have to draw the line *somewhere*.

Another important ramification of such considerations relates to understanding the nature of the *erectus/sapiens* transition itself. In Java, the transition (with late-persisting *H. erectus* genetic components) appears to have been slower than, for example, in southern Africa or in Europe. Nowhere, however, does this transition appear to have been as rapid as that which originally produced *H. erectus*. Why should this be so? To answer this question, we must consider basic evolutionary mechanisms (discussed in Chapters 4 and 14). First, the environments certainly differed from one region of the Old World to another during the time period

350,000–100,000 y.a. And recall that by the beginning of this time period, *H. erectus* populations had been long established in eastern and southern Asia, in North and East Africa, and in Europe. Clearly, we would not expect the same environmental conditions in northeast China as we would in Indonesia. Accordingly, natural selection could well have played a *differential* role, influencing the frequencies of alternative alleles in different populations in a pattern similar (but more intensive) to that seen in environmental adaptations of contemporary populations (see Chapter 15).

Second, many of these populations (in Java, southernmost Africa, and glacial Europe) could have been isolated and thus probably quite small. Genetic drift, therefore, also would have played a role in influencing the pace of evolutionary change. Third, advance or retreat of barriers, such as water boundaries or glacial ice sheets, would dramatically have affected migration routes.

Thus, it should hardly come as a surprise that some populations of *H. erectus* evolved at different rates and in slightly different directions from others. Some limited migration almost certainly occurred among the various populations. With sufficient gene flow, the spread of those few genetic modifications that distinguish the earliest *H. sapiens* eventually did become incorporated into widely separated populations. This, however, was a long, slow, inherently uneven process.

What, then, of the third transition within the genus *Homo*? This is the transition from archaic *H. sapiens* to anatomically modern *H. sapiens*—and it was considerably *faster* than the transition we have just discussed. How quickly anatomically modern forms evolved and exactly *where* this happened is a subject of much contemporary debate—and is the main topic of the next chapter.

Taxonomic Issues

As we discussed in Chapter 11, (and briefly at the beginning of this chapter), there is considerable debate regarding how to classify much of the *Homo* fossil material prior to 35,000 years ago. Our view, followed throughout the discussions in Chapters 10 through 12, proposes a minimum number of species and thus interprets the evolutionary processes influencing the genus *Homo* in a fairly straightforward manner.

However, this interpretation might well be *too* simplistic, and certainly, many paleoanthropologists now suggest much more diversity and complexity in the evolution of our genus. Accordingly, several new species of *Homo* have been proposed. In this text, we have classified the *Homo* fossil materials into three recognized species: *H. habilis*, *H. erectus*, and *H. sapiens*. We further noted that *H. habilis* might well be only one of two species of what we collectively called "early *Homo*." Moreover, in this chapter we made a clear distinction between archaic forms of *H. sapiens* and anatomically modern forms (*H. sapiens sapiens*). A diagrammatic phylogeny representing this interpretation is shown in Figure 12–16a.

Remember, however, that this is a conservative interpretation, implying a minimum amount of species diversity. This scheme is just about as simple as most paleoanthropologists are willing to consider seriously. Yet, there is another view, proposed by Milford Wolpoff of the University of Michigan, which is even more simple (Fig. 12–16b). Wolpoff argues that subsequent to early *Homo*, only one species (*H. sapiens*) should be recognized. In other words, Professor Wolpoff sinks *H. erectus* into *H. sapiens*. Given the significant anatomical (and probably behavioral) differences between *H. erectus* and *H. sapiens*, Wolpoff's suggestion has not received much support from other paleoanthropologists (see particularly the discussion in Rightmire, 1998).

At the other end of the spectrum are views expressed by a number of researchers who subdivide the *Homo* material into a variety of species. In fact, at every major stage of the evolution of *Homo* over the last 2 million years, some professional opinion has argued seriously for more than one species. First, as noted in Chapter 10 (p. 277), early *Homo* is now frequently subdivided into two different species (usually named *H. habilis* and *H. rudolfensis*). Second, as briefly discussed in Chapter 11, what is usually called

 See the Glossary for Virtual Lab 10 for alternative phylogenies of the genus *Homo*.

(a)   (b)

H. erectus is also partitioned into two species (*H. erectus* and *H. ergaster*, the latter referring primarily to African specimens but also including the material from Dmanisi). And third (and most relevant to the present discussion), various forms of archaic *H. sapiens* have been assigned by other paleoanthropologists to two or three additional species of *Homo* (some researchers think even more species might be represented).

The major issues relating to these interpretations (and consequent classifications) of what we have termed "archaic *Homo sapiens*" are as follows:

FIGURE 12–16

(a) Phylogeny showing evolution of genus *Homo*, as discussed in the text. Only very modest species diversity is implied. (Contrast with Figure 12–17.) (b) Highly simplified view of evolution of genus *Homo* with minimal species diversity. (After Wolpoff, 1999.)

1. The classification of individual fossils into "archaic *Homo sapiens*" is viewed by many as imprecise, since this is an ill-defined evolutionary group (and one quite geographically widespread). At minimum, many researchers have urged a more precise anatomical definition of exactly what "archaic *Homo sapiens*" means.
2. Several early archaic specimens are interpreted by paleoanthropologists as showing derived features different from *Homo sapiens*. These fossils come from Africa and Europe (e.g., Kabwe, Mauer) and are now often classified as *Homo heidelbergensis*.
3. Neandertals are also viewed by numerous researchers as representing a distinct species, what is called *Homo neanderthalensis*. In prior discussions, we have interpreted the variation as representing intraspecific differences; this alternative view argues for a greater degree of interspecific variability (with the inference that fertile interbreeding between Neandertals and *H. sapiens* would not have been possible).

FIGURE 12–17

Phylogeny showing multiple species of genus *Homo* with considerable species diversity represented.

Figure 12–17 shows a phylogeny incorporating these more complex, multiple-species interpretations and suggesting possible evolutionary relationships. For an introductory course, it is less important to memorize all the species names than to recognize what such interpretations imply about the evolutionary process—and what these differing views suggest about our origins.

SUMMARY

During the Middle Pleistocene, significant changes occurred in *H. erectus* morphology. The changes, especially in cranial traits, led scientists to assign a new species designation to these forms (*Homo sapiens*). Because they exhibited a mosaic of *H. erectus* and *H. sapiens* characteristics, the name archaic *H. sapiens* is used to indicate that they were forms transitional between *H. erectus* and anatomically modern humans. Some archaic *H. sapiens* populations possessed more derived modern traits than others, and these populations are sometimes referred to as later archaic *H. sapiens* or early *H. sapiens sapiens*. It has been suggested that some later European archaic forms were directly ancestral to Neandertals.

In addition to morphological changes among archaic forms, there were cultural developments as well. Archaic *H. sapiens* invented new kinds of tools and tool-making techniques, exploited new foods, built more complex shelters, probably controlled fire, and may have used some form of speech.

In western Europe, archaic *H. sapiens* developed into a unique form—classic Neandertals—who apparently migrated from Europe to the Near East and then even further into Asia. Neandertals were physically robust and muscular, different from both early archaic forms and modern *H. sapiens*. Their culture was more complex than earlier archaic cultures, and it appears that in Europe and the Near East, they lived in areas also inhabited by modern *H. sapiens*. Whether modern forms in these areas evolved directly from Neandertals or migrated from Africa (or the Near East) and ultimately replaced Neandertals is one of the important issues currently being debated by paleoanthropologists.

Finally, we would emphasize that Neandertals and all humans on earth today belong to the same species, *H. sapiens*. There are physical differences between these forms, of course, and for that reason Neandertals are assigned to the subspecies *H. sapiens neanderthalensis* and anatomically modern forms to the subspecies *H. sapiens sapiens*.

We should point out that this assignment of a *separate* subspecies for the Neandertals emphasizes some notable degrees of variation; that is, Neandertals are viewed as more different from *any* modern group of *H. sapiens* than these groups differ from one another. Some scholars would even more dramatically emphasize this variation and thus assign Neandertals to a separate species from *Homo sapiens*. In this view, Neandertals would be placed in the separate species *Homo neanderthalensis*. Likewise, many paleoanthropologists would also subdivide what we call "early archaic *H. sapiens*" into another species. The behavioral differences between Neandertals and anatomically modern *H. sapiens*, as interpreted from the archaeological record, are also discussed. These differences are emphasized by those scholars who view Neandertals as an evolutionary dead end.

QUESTIONS FOR REVIEW

1. In what respect does *H. sapiens* (broadly defined) contrast with *H. erectus*?
2. What is meant by "archaic" *H. sapiens*?
3. How does archaic *H. sapiens* contrast with anatomically modern *H. sapiens*?
4. In what areas of the world have archaic *H. sapiens* specimens been discovered? Compare and contrast the finds from two separate areas.
5. What do we mean when we say that archaic *H. sapiens* specimens are transitional?
6. Why have Neandertals been depicted (by the popular press and others) as being primitive? Do you agree with this interpretation? Why or why not?

moderns migrate from Africa?
moderns evolve from Neands

7. In what general areas of the world have Neandertal fossil remains been discovered?

8. What evidence suggests that Neandertals deliberately buried their dead? What interpretations do such treatment of the dead suggest to you?

9. What physical characteristics distinguish the Neandertals from anatomically modern *Homo sapiens*?

10. What behavioral characteristics distinguish Neandertal culture from that of the Upper Paleolithic?

11. What two major transitions within the genus *Homo* have been discussed in this chapter and in Chapter 11? Compare these transitions for geographical distribution as well as for aspects of evolutionary pace.

12. Discuss why some paleoanthropologists subdivide the archaic *H. sapiens* material into more than one species. What does this interpretation imply biologically?

SUGGESTED FURTHER READING

Mellars, Paul. 1995. *The Neanderthal Legacy. An Archaeological Perspective from Western Europe.* Princeton, NJ: Princeton University Press.

Shreeve, James. 1995. *The Neandertal Enigma.* New York: Morrow.

Stiner, Mary C. 1995. *Honor Among Thieves. A Zooarchaeological Study of Neandertal Ecology.* Princeton, NJ: Princeton University Press.

Stringer, Christopher, and Clive Gamble. 1993. *In Search of the Neanderthals.* New York: Thames and Hudson.

Trinkaus, Erik, and Pat Shipman. 1993. *The Neandertals: Changing the Image of Mankind.* New York: Knopf.

RESOURCES ON THE INTERNET

 ### Wadsworth Anthropology Resource Center
http://anthropology.wadsworth.com

The companion website for this text includes a range of enrichment material focused on the chapter's topic. While online you can enhance your understanding of the chapter by exploring one of the several additional Internet exercises, by researching topics, and by accessing full articles on InfoTrac College Edition. You can also reinforce the concepts by taking online practice exams.

Internet Exercises

Use your search engine to find articles pertaining to the Neandertals. Specifically, look for information regarding the evidence that Neandertals continued to exist later than previously believed. If you have difficulties finding such information, try **www.archaeology.org**, but we encourage you to look for other websites as well.

 ### InfoTrac College Edition
http://www.infotrac-college.com/wadsworth

Use PowerTrac to search for the subject *Neanderthal.* (InfoTrac College Edition spells "Neanderthal" with the *h*, the older spelling; using the newer spelling will pull up fewer references.) How many articles or abstracts did you find? Read at least one article and discuss how it relates to material in Chapter 12.

CHAPTER

13

CONTENTS

Homo sapiens sapiens

Trail of hominid footprints fossilized in volcanic ash at Laetoli, Tanzania (approximate age, 3.7 million years)

Introduction

In this chapter, we discuss anatomically modern humans, taxonomically known as *Homo sapiens sapiens*. As we discussed in Chapter 12, in some areas evolutionary developments produced early archaic *H. sapiens* populations exhibiting a mosaic of *H. erectus* and *H. sapiens* traits. In some regions, the trend emphasizing *H. sapiens* characteristics continued, and possibly as early as 200,000 y.a., transitional forms (between early archaic and anatomically modern forms) appeared in Africa. Given the nature of the evidence and ongoing ambiguities in dating, it is not possible to say exactly when anatomically modern *H. sapiens* first appeared. However, the transition and certainly the wide dispersal of *H. sapiens sapiens* in the Old World appear to have been relatively rapid evolutionary events. Thus, we can ask several basic questions:

1. *When* (approximately) did *H. sapiens sapiens* first appear?
2. *Where* did the transition take place? Did it occur in just one region or in several?
3. *What* was the pace of evolutionary change? How quickly did the transition occur?
4. *How* did the dispersal of *H. sapiens sapiens* to other areas of the Old World (outside that of origin) take place?

These questions concerning the origins and early dispersal of *Homo sapiens sapiens* continue to fuel much controversy among paleoanthropologists. And it is no wonder, for members of early *Homo sapiens sapiens* are our *direct* kin and are thus closely related to all contemporary humans. They were much like us skeletally, genetically, and (most likely) behaviorally as well. In fact, it is the various hypotheses relating to the behavioral capacities of our most immediate predecessors that have most fired the imagination of scientists and laypeople alike. In every major respect, these are the first hominids that we can confidently refer to as "fully human."

In this chapter, we will also discuss archaeological evidence from the Upper Paleolithic (see p. 326). This evidence will allow us to better understand technological and social developments during the period when modern humans arose and quickly came to dominate the planet.

The evolutionary story of *Homo sapiens sapiens* is really a biological autobiography of us all. It is a story that still has many unanswered questions; but several theories have been proposed that seek to organize the diverse information that is presently available.

See the following sections of the CD-ROM for topics covered in this chapter: Virtual Lab 11, section IV and Virtual Lab 12, sections I and II.

The Origin and Dispersal of *Homo sapiens sapiens* (Anatomically Modern Human Beings)

There are two major theories that attempt to organize and explain modern human origins: the complete replacement model and the regional continuity model. These two views are quite distinct and in some ways diametrically opposed to each other. Moreover, the popular press has further contributed to a wide and incorrect perception of irreconcilable argument on these points by "opposing" scientists. Indeed, there is a third theory, which we call the partial replacement model, that is a compromise hypothesis incorporating some aspects of the two major theories. Because so much of our contemporary view of modern human origins is driven by the debates linked to these differing theories, let us begin by briefly reviewing each. We will then turn to the fossil evidence itself to see what it can contribute to resolving the questions we have posed.

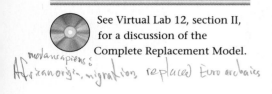

See Virtual Lab 12, section II, for a discussion of the Complete Replacement Model.

[handwritten margin notes:]

modern sapiens:
African origin, migration replaced Euro archaics

✱ for the most part ✱
a new species that cannot breed with Euro archaics

mtDNA

① can make an African tree oldest

or an Asian one

The Complete Replacement Model (Recent African Evolution)

The complete replacement model, developed by British paleoanthropologists Christopher Stringer and Peter Andrews (1988), is based on the origin of modern humans in Africa and later replacement of populations in Europe and Asia (Fig. 13–1). In brief, this theory proposes that anatomically modern populations arose in Africa within the last 200,000 years, then migrated from Africa, completely *replacing* populations in Europe and Asia. This model does not take into account any transition from archaic *H. sapiens* to modern *H. sapiens* anywhere in the world except Africa. A critical deduction of the Stringer and Andrews theory is that it considers the appearance of anatomically modern humans as a biological speciation event. Thus, in this view there could be no admixture of migrating African modern *H. sapiens* with local populations because the African modern humans were a *biologically* different species. In a taxonomic context, all of the archaic *H. sapiens* populations outside Africa would, in this view, be classified as belonging to different species of *Homo* (e.g., the Neandertals would be classified as *H. neanderthalensis*; see p. 339 for further discussion). While this speciation explanation fits nicely with, and in fact helps explain, *complete* replacement, Stringer has more recently stated that he is not dogmatic regarding this issue. Thus, he suggests that there may have been potential for interbreeding, but he argues that very little apparently took place.

A crucial source of supporting evidence for the African origin hypothesis (and complete replacement elsewhere) has come from genetic data obtained from living peoples. Underlying this approach is the assumption that genetic patterning seen in contemporary populations will provide clues to relationships and origins of ancient *Homo sapiens*. However, as with numerous prior attempts to evaluate such patterning from more traditional data on human polymorphisms (e.g., ABO, HLA—see Chapter 14), the obstacles are enormous.

A recent innovation uses genetic sequencing data derived directly from DNA. The most promising application has come not from the DNA within the nucleus, but from DNA found in the cytoplasm—that is, mitochondrial DNA (mtDNA; see Chapter 3). You may recall that mitochondria are organelles found in the cell, but outside the nucleus. They contain a set of DNA, dissimilar from nuclear DNA, inherited only through the mother. Thus, mtDNA does not undergo the genetic recombination that occurs in nuclear DNA during meiosis.

Using mtDNA gathered from a number of different populations, scientists at the University of California, Berkeley, constructed "trees" (something like a family tree) that, they claimed, demonstrated that the entire population of the world today descended from a single African lineage. However, the methodology of these molecular biologists has been faulted. Using the same mtDNA material, other scientists constructed many trees that differed from those of the Berkeley group, and some of them are *without African roots* (i.e., the same data can be used statistically to show that *H. sapiens* arose in Asia, *not* in Africa).

This question of the applicability of the mtDNA evidence continues to generate considerable disagreement. Paleoanthropologist Robert Corruccini of Southern Illinois University has been unimpressed with the entire approach, stating that "critical shortcomings of molecular population genetic assumptions and of analysis . . . render any mtDNA conclusions virtually useless to ruminations about human evolution" (Corruccini, 1994, p. 698). Likewise, Glenn Conroy (1997) has critiqued many of the oversimplifications inherent in the genetic data and consequent interpretations. However, molecular anthropologist Mark Stoneking of the Max Planck Institute (and one of the founders of this approach) remains much more confident in the general reliability of the mtDNA results, especially as they show a much greater diversity among contemporary African groups as compared to other world populations. Stoneking thus concludes: "Because non-African populations that predate the

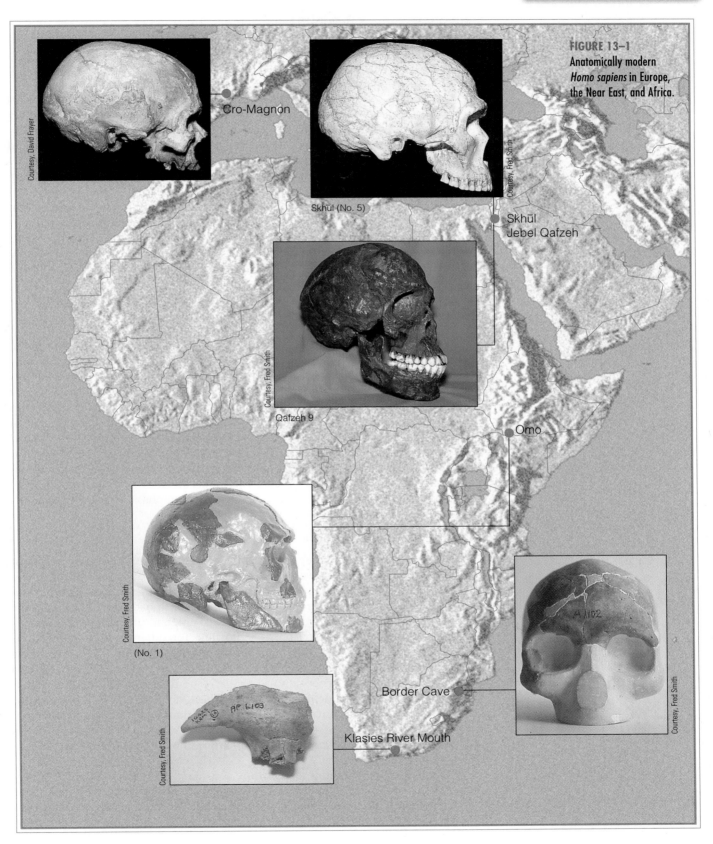

FIGURE 13–1
Anatomically modern *Homo sapiens* in Europe, the Near East, and Africa.

Cro-Magnon

Skhūl (No. 5)

Skhūl
Jebel Qafzeh

Qafzeh 9

Omo

(No. 1)

Border Cave

Klasies River Mouth

mtDNA ancestor apparently did not contribute mtDNAs to contemporary human populations, it follows that the spread of modern populations was accomplished with little or no admixture with resident non-African populations. If it were otherwise, there should be evidence of much more divergent mtDNA types in contemporary human populations" (Stoneking, 1993, pp. 66–67).

Recently, some further genetic data have helped bolster some of the main tenets of the complete replacement model. A team of Yale, Harvard, and University of Chicago researchers (Dorit et al., 1995) has investigated variation in the Y chromosome, finding *much* less variation in humans than in other primates. And another group of Yale researchers (Tishkoff et al., 1996), looking at DNA sequences on chromosome 12, again found much more variation among contemporary Africans than is seen in all the remainder of the world combined. Finally, the recent reports of the distinctive nature of Neandertal mtDNA (see p. 336) also argue that substantial replacement took place. Nevertheless, some geneticists find the results unconvincing (e.g., Ayala, 1995; Templeton, 1996), and many paleoanthropologists (agreeing with the views expressed by Corruccini and Conroy) are extremely skeptical of the main conclusions derived from the genetic data (see Box 13–1 on p. 348–349 for further discussion).

The Partial Replacement Model

The partial replacement model also begins with African early archaic *H. sapiens*. Later, also in Africa, some of these archaic populations evolved into the first anatomically modern *H. sapiens*. This theory, proposed by Günter Bräuer of the University of Hamburg, postulates the earliest dates for African modern *Homo sapiens* at over 100,000 y.a. Bräuer sees the initial dispersal of *H. sapiens sapiens* out of South Africa as significantly influenced by shifting environmental conditions and thus as a gradual process. Moving into Eurasia, modern humans hybridized, probably to a limited degree, with resident archaic groups and eventually replaced them. The disappearance of archaic humans was therefore due to both hybridization and replacement and was a gradual and complex process. This model includes components of regional continuity, hybridization, and replacement, with the emphasis on replacement.

The Regional Continuity Model (Multiregional Evolution)

 See Virtual Lab 12, section II, for an animation of the Regional Continuity Model.

The regional continuity model is most closely associated with paleoanthropologist Milford Wolpoff of the University of Michigan and his associates (Thorne and Wolpoff, 1992; Wolpoff et al., 1994). These researchers suggest that local populations (not all, of course) in Europe, Asia, and Africa continued their indigenous evolutionary development from archaic *H. sapiens* to anatomically modern humans. A question immediately arises: How is it possible for different local populations around the globe to evolve with such similar morphology? In other words, how could anatomically modern humans arise separately in different continents and end up physically (and genetically) so similar? The multiregional model explains this phenomenon by (1) denying that the earliest modern *H. sapiens* populations originated *exclusively* in Africa and challenging the notion of complete replacement and (2) asserting that some gene flow (migration) between archaic populations was extremely likely, in which case modern humans cannot be considered a species separate from archaic forms.

Through gene flow and local selection, according to the multiregional hypothesis, local populations would *not* have evolved totally independently from one another, and such mixing would have "prevented speciation between the regional lineages and thus maintained human beings as a *single*, although obviously *polytypic* (see p. 395), species throughout the Pleistocene" (Smith et al., 1989).

The Earliest *Homo sapiens sapiens* Discoveries

Current evidence strongly indicates that the earliest modern *H. sapiens* fossils come from Africa, but not everyone agrees on the dates or precisely which specimens are the modern and which are the archaic forms. With this cautionary note, we continue our discussion, but there undoubtedly will be corrections as more evidence is gathered.

Africa

In Africa, several early fossil finds have been interpreted as fully anatomically modern forms (see Fig. 13–1). These specimens come from the Klasies River Mouth on the south coast (which could be the earliest find), Border Cave slightly to the north, and Omo Kibish 1 in southern Ethiopia. With the use of relatively new techniques, all three sites have been dated to about 120,000–80,000 y.a. The original geological context at Border Cave is uncertain, and the fossils may be younger than at the other two sites (see Table 13–1 and Fig. 13–5). Some paleoanthropologists consider these fossils to be the earliest known anatomically modern humans. Problems with dating, context, and differing interpretations of the evidence have led other paleoanthropologists to question whether the *earliest* modern forms (Fig. 13–2) really did evolve in Africa. Other modern *H. sapiens* individuals, possibly older than these Africans, have been found in the Near East.

The Near East

In Israel, early modern *H. sapiens* fossils (the remains of at least 10 individuals) were found in the Skhūl Cave at Mt. Carmel (Figs. 13–3 and 13–4a), very near the Neandertal site of Tabun. Also from Israel, the Qafzeh Cave has yielded the remains

TABLE 13–1 Additional Techniques for Dating Middle and Upper Pleistocene Sites

Technique	Physical Basis	Examples of Use
Uranium series dating	Radioactive decay of short-lived uranium isotopes	To date limestone formations (e.g., stalagmites) and ancient ostrich eggshells; to estimate age of Jinniushan site in China and Ngandong site in Java, both corroborated by ESR dates
Thermoluminescence (TL) dating	Accumulation of trapped electrons within certain crystals released during heating	To date ancient flint tools (either deliberately or accidentally heated); to provide key dates for the Qafzeh site
Electron spin resonance (ESR) dating	Measurement (counting) of accumulated trapped electrons	To date dental enamel; to corroborate dating of Qafzeh, Skhūl, and Tabun sites in Israel, Ngandong site in Java, Klasies River Mouth and Border Cave in South Africa, and the Lake Mungo site in Australia

Source: Cook et al., 1984; Aiken et al., 1993.

BOX 13–1   A CLOSER LOOK

Complete Replacement and Mitochondrial Eve

Gathering samples of mtDNA from placentas of women whose ancestors lived in Africa, Asia, Europe, Australia, and New Guinea, biologists Allan Wilson, Rebecca Cann, and Mark Stoneking, while they were at the University of California, Berkeley, postulated a distinctive genetic pattern for each area. They then compared the diversity of the various patterns (Cann et al., 1987).

They found the greatest variation among Africans and therefore postulated Africa to have been the home of the oldest human populations (the assumption is that the longer the time, the greater the accumulation of genetic variation). They also found that the African variants contained only African mtDNA, whereas those from other areas all included at least one African component. Therefore, the biologists concluded, there must have been a migration initially from Africa, ultimately to all other inhabited areas of the world. By counting the number of genetic mutations and applying the *rate* of mutation, Rebecca Cann and her associates calculated a date for the origin of anatomically modern humans: between 285,000 and 143,000 y.a.—in other words, an average estimate of about 200,000 y.a. Indeed, a further contention of the mtDNA researchers is that the pattern of variation argues that all modern humans shared in common a single African female lineage that lived sometime during this time range. Thus was born the popularized concept of "mitochondrial Eve."

Not all scientists, by any means, agree with this scenario. The estimated rate of mutations may be incorrect, in which case the proposed date of migration out of Africa would also be in error. Moreover, differing population size in Africa, compared to elsewhere, would complicate interpretations (Relethford and Harpending, 1994). Also, secondary migration, outside

Africa, could disrupt the direct inheritance of the African maternal line. Even more troubling are the inherent biases in the statistical technique used to identify the primary population relationships ("trees"). More recent reanalyses of the data suggest that the situation is not nearly as clear-cut as originally believed.

Scrutiny of the mitochondrial DNA–based model of modern human origins came when the approach was attempted by other laboratories using similar techniques and statistical treatments. In February 1992, three different papers were published by different teams of researchers, all of which severely challenged the main tenets of the hypotheses as proposed by Wilson, Cann, and Stoneking. The most serious error was a failure to recognize how many *equally valid* results could be deduced statistically from the *same set* of original data. In science, as we have remarked before, beyond the data themselves, the methodological treatments (especially statistical models) greatly influence both the nature and *confidence limits* of the results.

The central conclusion that Africa alone was the *sole* source of modern humans could still be correct. Yet, now it had to be admitted that dozens (indeed, thousands) of other equally probable renditions could be derived from the supposedly unambiguous mitochondrial data. Thus, barely a few months after the original researchers had proposed their most systematic statement of their hypotheses, the entire perspective (especially its statistical implications) was shaken to its very foundations—and, in many people's eyes, falsified altogether.

An interesting twist regarding this entire reassessment is that the team from Pennsylvania State University that challenged the initial results was joined in its critique by Mark Stoneking, one of the original formulators of the now-questioned hypothesis. A viable

of at least 20 individuals (Fig. 13–4b). Although their overall configuration is definitely modern, some specimens show certain archaic (i.e., Neandertal) features. Skhūl has been dated to about 115,000 y.a., and Qafzeh has been placed around 100,000 y.a. (Bar-Yosef, 1993, 1994) (Fig. 13–5 on p. 352).

Such early dates for modern specimens pose some problems for those advocating local replacement (the multiregional model). How early do archaic *H. sapiens* populations (Neandertals) appear in the Near East? A recent chronometric calibration for the Tabun Cave suggests a date as early as 120,000 y.a. Neandertals thus may *slightly* precede modern forms in the Near East, but there would appear to be considerable overlap in the timing of occupation by these different *H. sapiens* forms. And scientific perspective, so well illustrated here, is that new approaches (or refined applications) often necessitate reevaluation of prior hypotheses. It takes both objectivity and courage to admit miscalculations. By so doing, an even more permanent and positive legacy helps contain the inherent personal biases that sometimes have so divided the study of human origins.

On the basis of these new studies, many have proclaimed that mitochondrial Eve is dead—and perhaps the complete replacement hypothesis with her. As could be expected, the proponents of the African origin view are not yet ready to bury Eve or significantly alter their confidence in the complete replacement hypothesis.

As the debate continues, new lines of evidence and new techniques are being pursued: more ways to sequence both mitochondrial and nuclear DNA; more complete evidence of human polymorphisms; genetic sequence data for the Y chromosome; and, it is hoped, more reliable statistical techniques to interpret these complex data. The new data for the Y chromosome are particularly interesting. Since the Y chromosome is inherited *paternally* (and thus most loci are *not* recombined), its pattern of genetic diversity makes for an excellent complement to the maternally inherited mtDNA. Biologist Robert Dorit of Yale University, along with his team of researchers, sequenced a portion of the Y chromosome. Surprisingly, they found absolutely *no* variation in this region, but did see much more Y chromosome variation in great apes (chimpanzees, gorillas, orangutans). Dorit suggests that this lack of variation indicates a recent origin for *Homo sapiens*. He notes at the same time that "the lack of variation in the Y chromosome regions we examined also makes it impossible for us to reconstruct the geographic location of the last common ancestor" (Henahan, 1995).

Further evidence along these lines has come from another group of Yale biologists led by Sarah Tishkoff (Tishkoff et al., 1996). Tishkoff and her colleagues have been investigating genetic patterns within nuclear DNA

(their research target is a region on chromosome 12). Assembling a very large sample of data (1,600 individuals from 42 populations), Tishkoff and her team found by far the most variation among contemporary Africans. (Of 24 possible variants, 21 of these were found in Africa; Europe and the Middle East displayed only 3; Asia, the Pacific Islands, and the New World together displayed a mere 2.) Tishkoff draws the same conclusion as that proposed by both the mtDNA and the Y chromosome researchers—that all modern humans are the result of a single recent evolutionary event. (Tishkoff, in fact, places the date at 100,000–70,000 y.a., even more recent than that suggested by the mtDNA evidence.) Moreover, the results from the chromosome 12 DNA polymorphisms, like those relating to mtDNA, suggest that Africa was the geographical source for all modern humans.

What can we then conclude? Results are still tentative, but various studies are now corroborating one another. First, we can conclude that *Homo sapiens* is not a very genetically variable species; indeed, genetically, we are quite a homogeneous lot (a point we emphasize in Chapter 15). By some estimates, comparisons with other primates suggest that human mtDNA is only about 1/40 to 1/50 as variable as the mtDNA of chimpanzees (Cann et al., 1994)! Does human genetic homogeneity imply a *recent origin* for all *H. sapiens sapiens*? Perhaps. At the least, these increasingly consistent genetic data argue that it is unlikely that the present genetic patterning in *H. sapiens* can be traced back to the early dispersal of *H. erectus* out of Africa (circa 1.8 m.y.a.). It would appear that there must have been one or more later dispersals as well. But how much later? The broadest time limits so far indicated by various genetic techniques would suggest a time frame in the range of 850,000–100,000 y.a. (with the greatest probabilities between 450,000 and 100,000 y.a.). If you were inclined to make a wager on the probabilities of the time of the last major dispersal of hominids, somewhere in this latter range looks like a good bet.

recall, the modern site at Mt. Carmel (Skhūl) is very near the Neandertal site (Tabun). Clearly, the dynamics of *Homo sapiens* evolution in the Near East are highly complex, and no simple model may explain later hominid evolution adequately.

Central Europe

Central Europe has been a source of many fossil finds, including numerous fairly early anatomically modern *H. sapiens*. At several sites, it appears that some fossils display both Neandertal and modern features, which supports the regional continuity hypothesis (from Neandertal to modern). Some genetic continuity from

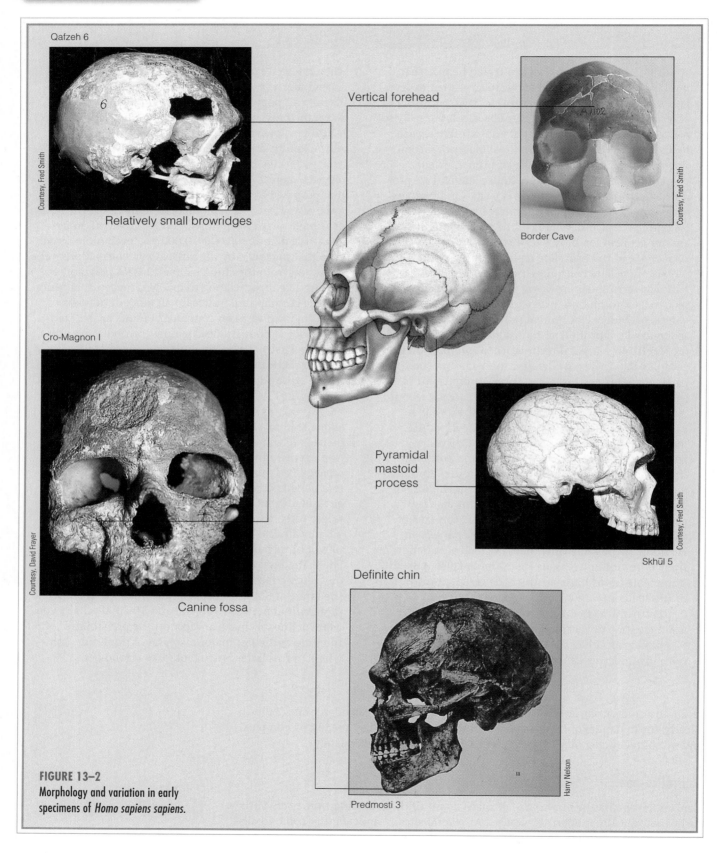

FIGURE 13–2
Morphology and variation in early specimens of *Homo sapiens sapiens*.

(a)

(b)

earlier (Neandertal) to later (modern *Homo sapiens*) populations was perhaps the case at Vindija in Croatia, where typical Neandertals were found in earlier contexts (see p. 330).

Smith (1984) offers another example of local continuity from Mladeč, in the Czech Republic. Among the earlier European modern *H. sapiens* fossils, dated to about 33,000 y.a., the Mladeč crania display a great deal of variation, probably in part due to sexual dimorphism. Although each of the crania (except for one of the females) displays a prominent supraorbital torus, it is reduced from the typical Neandertal pattern. Even though there is some suggestion of continuity from Neandertals to modern humans, Smith is certain that, given certain anatomical features, the Mladeč remains are best classified as *H. sapiens sapiens*. Reduced midfacial projection, a higher forehead, and postcranial elements "are clearly modern *H. sapiens* in morphology and not specifically Neandertal-like in a single feature" (Smith, 1984, p. 174).

FIGURE 13–3

(a) Mt. Carmel, studded with caves, was home to *H. sapiens sapiens* at Skhūl (and to Neandertals at Tabun and Kebara). (b) Skhūl Cave.

FIGURE 13–4

(a) Skhūl 5. (b) Qafzeh 6. These specimens from Israel are thought to be representatives of early modern *Homo sapiens*. The vault height, forehead, and lack of prognathism are modern traits.

(a)

(b)

FIGURE 13–5
Time line of *Homo sapiens sapiens* discoveries.
Note that most dates are approximations.
Question marks indicate those estimates that
are most tentative.

Cro-Magnon
(crow man´yon)

Aurignacian
Pertaining to an Upper Paleolithic stone tool
industry in Europe beginning at about
40,000 y.a.

Western Europe

This area of the world and its fossils have received the greatest paleoanthropological attention for several reasons, one of which is probably serendipity. Over the last century and a half, many of the scholars interested in this kind of research happened to live in western Europe, and the southern region of France happened to be a fossil treasure trove. Also, early on, discovering and learning about human ancestors caught the curiosity and pride of the local population.

Because of this scholarly interest beginning back in the nineteenth century, a great deal of data accumulated, with little reliable comparative information available from elsewhere in the world. Consequently, theories of human evolution were based almost exclusively on the western European material. It has only been in recent years, with growing evidence from other areas of the world and with the application of new dating techniques, that recent human evolutionary dynamics have been seriously considered on a worldwide basis.

There are many anatomically modern human fossils from western Europe going back 40,000 years or more, but by far the best-known sample of western European *H. sapiens* is from the **Cro-Magnon** site. A total of eight individuals were discovered in 1868 in a rock shelter in the village of Les Eyzies, in the Dordogne region of southern France (Gambier, 1989).

Associated with an **Aurignacian** tool assemblage, an Upper Paleolithic industry, the Cro-Magnon materials, dated at 30,000 y.a., represent the earliest of France's anatomically modern humans. The so-called "Old Man" (Cro-Magnon I) became the archetype for what was once termed the Cro-Magnon, or Upper Paleolithic,

(a)

(b)

"race" of Europe (Fig.13–6). Actually, of course, there is no such race, and Cro-Magnon I is not typical of Upper Paleolithic western Europeans and not even all that similar to the other two male skulls that were found at the site.

Considered together, the male crania reflect a mixture of modern and archaic traits. Cro-Magnon I is the most gracile of the three; the supraorbital tori of the other two males, for example, are more robust. The most modern-looking is the female cranium, the appearance of which may be a function of sexual dimorphism.

The question of whether continuous local evolution produced anatomically modern groups directly from Neandertals in some regions of Eurasia is far from settled. From central Europe, variation seen in the Mladeč and Vindija fossils indicate a combination of both Neandertal and modern characteristics and may suggest gene flow between the two different *H. sapiens* groups. However, tracing such relatively minor genetic changes—considering the ever-present problems of dating, lack of fossils, and fragmented fossil finds—has proved extremely difficult.

However, a newly discovered child's skeleton from Portugal has provided some of the best evidence yet of possible hybridization between Neandertals and anatomically modern *H. sapiens*. This important new hominid discovery from the Abrigo do Lagar Velho site in central western Portugal was excavated in late 1998 and is dated to 24,500 y.a. (i.e., at least 5,000 years *later* than the last clearly Neandertal find). Associated with an Upper Paleolithic industry (see p. 355) and interred with red ocher and pierced shell is a fairly complete skeleton of a four-year-old child (Duarte et al., 1999). Cidália Duarte, Erik Trinkaus, and colleagues, who have studied the remains, found a highly mixed set of anatomical features. Many characteristics (of the teeth, lower jaw, and pelvis) were like those seen in anatomically modern humans. Yet, several other features (lack of chin, limb proportions, muscle insertions) were more similar to Neandertals. The authors thus conclude, "The presence of such admixture suggests the hypothesis of variable admixture between early modern humans dispersing into Europe and local Neandertal populations" (Duarte et al., 1999, p. 7608). These researchers thus argue that this new evidence provides strong support for the partial replacement model while seriously weakening the complete replacement model. However, the evidence from one child's skeleton—while intriguing—is certainly not going to convince everyone!

FIGURE 13–6
Cro-Magnon I (France). In this specimen, modern traits are quite clear. (a) Lateral view. (b) Frontal view. (Courtesy of David Frayer.)

See Virtual Lab 12, section I, for a discussion of the transformation in physical characteristics that accompanied the evolution of modern *Homo sapiens*.

Asia

There are six early anatomically modern human localities in China, the most significant of which are Upper Cave at Zhoukoudian and Ordos. The fossils from these sites are all fully modern, and most are considered to be of quite late Upper Pleistocene age. Upper Cave at Zhoukoudian has been dated to between 18,000 and 10,000 y.a. The Ordos find was discovered at Dagouwan, Inner Mongolia, and may be the oldest anatomically modern material from China, perhaps dating to 50,000 y.a. or more (Etler, personal communication) (see Fig. 13–5).

In addition, the Jinniushan skeleton discussed in Chapter 12 (see p. 314) has been suggested by some researchers (Tiemel et al., 1994) as hinting at modern features in China as early as 200,000 y.a. If this date (as early as that proposed for direct antecedents of modern *H. sapiens* in Africa) should prove accurate, it would cast doubt on the complete replacement model. Indeed, quite opposed to the complete replacement model and more in support of regional continuity, many Chinese paleoanthropologists see a continuous evolution from Chinese *H. erectus* to archaic *H. sapiens* to anatomically modern humans. This view is supported by Wolpoff, who mentions that materials from Upper Cave at Zhoukoudian "have a number of features that are characteristically regional" and that these features are definitely not African (1989, p. 83).*

In addition to the well-known finds from China, anatomically modern remains have also been discovered in southern Asia. At Batadomba Iena, in southern Sri Lanka, modern *Homo sapiens* finds have been dated to 25,500 y.a. (Kennedy and Deraniyagala, 1989).

Australia

During glacial times, the Indonesian islands were joined to the Asian mainland, but Australia was not. It is likely that by 50,000 y.a., Sahul—the area including New Guinea and Australia—was inhabited by modern humans. Bamboo rafts may have been the means of crossing the sea between islands, which would not have been a simple exercise. Just where the future Australians came from is unknown, but Borneo, Java, and New Guinea have all been suggested.

Human occupation of Australia appears to have occurred quite early, with some archaeological locales dating to 55,000 y.a. Dating of the earliest Australian human remains (which are all modern *H. sapiens*), however, is controversial. The earliest finds thus far discovered have come from Lake Mungo in southeastern Australia. In agreement with archaeological context and radiocarbon dates, the hominids from this site have been dated at approximately 30,000–25,000 y.a. Newly determined age estimates, using ESR and uranium series dating (see Table 3–1) have dramatically extended the suggested time depth to about 60,000 y.a. (Thorne et al., 1999). The lack of correlation of these more ancient age estimates with other data, however, has provoked serious concerns among some researchers (Gillespie and Roberts, 2000).

Equally intriguing as these proposed early dates for the first Australians are recent reports of mitochondrial DNA sequences derived from the fossil remains from Lake Mungo (Adcock et al., 2001). While the primary researchers are confident that these samples are authentically ancient, the possibility of contamination cannot be entirely ruled out. Indeed, other researchers remain unconvinced that the mtDNA from Lake Mungo is ancient at all (Cooper et al., 2001). Obviously, given the controversies, we will need further corroboration for both the dating and DNA findings before passing judgment.

---

*Wolpoff's statement supports his regional continuity hypothesis. His reference to Africa is a criticism of the complete replacement hypothesis.

Unlike the more gracile early Australian forms from Lake Mungo are the Kow Swamp people, who are thought to have lived between about 14,000 and 9,000 years ago (Figs. 13–7 and 13–9 on p. 354). The presence of certain archaic traits, such as receding foreheads, heavy supraorbital tori, and thick bones, are difficult to explain, since these features contrast with the postcranial anatomy, which matches that of recent native Australians.

Technology and Art in the Upper Paleolithic

Europe

The cultural period known as the Upper Paleolithic began in western Europe approximately 40,000 years ago (Fig. 13–8). Upper Paleolithic cultures are usually divided into five different industries based on stone tool technologies: (1) Chatelperronian, (2) Aurignacian, (3) Gravettian, (4) Solutrean, and (5) Magdalenian. Major environmental shifts were also apparent during this period. During the last glacial period, at about 30,000 y.a., a warming trend lasting several thousand years partially melted the glacial ice. The result was that much of Eurasia was covered by tundra and steppe, a vast area of treeless country dotted with lakes and marshes. In many areas in the north, permafrost prevented the growth of trees but permitted the growth, in the short summers, of flowering plants, mosses, and other kinds of vegetation. This vegetation served as an enormous pasture for herbivorous animals, large and small, and carnivorous animals fed off the herbivores. It was a hunter's paradise, with millions of animals dispersed across expanses of tundra and grassland, from Spain through Europe and into the Russian steppes.

Large herds of reindeer roamed the tundra and steppes along with mammoths, bison, horses, and a host of smaller animals that served as a bountiful source of food. In addition, humans exploited fish and fowl systematically for the first time, especially along the southern tier of Europe. It was a time of relative affluence, and ultimately Upper Paleolithic people spread out over Europe, living in caves and open-air camps and building large shelters. Large dwellings with storage pits have been excavated in the former Soviet Union, with archaeological evidence of social status distinctions (Soffer, 1985). During this period, either western Europe or perhaps portions of Africa achieved the highest population density in human history up to that time.

In Eurasia, cultural innovations allowed humans for the first time to occupy easternmost Europe and northern Asia. In these areas, even during glacial warming stages, winters would have been long and harsh. Human groups were able to tolerate these environments probably because of better constructed structures as well as warmer, better fitting *sewn* clothing. The evidence for wide use of such tailored clothing comes from many sites and includes pointed stone tools such as awls and (by at least 19,000 y.a.) bone needles as well. Especially noteworthy is the clear evidence of the residues of clothing (including what has been interpreted as a cap, a shirt, a jacket, trousers, and moccasins) in graves at the 22,000-year-old Sungir site, located not far from Moscow (Klein, 1989).

Humans and other animals in the midlatitudes of Eurasia had to cope with shifts in climatic conditions, some of which were quite rapid. For example, at 20,000 y.a. another climatic "pulse" caused the weather to become noticeably colder in Europe and Asia as the continental glaciations reached their maximum extent for this entire glacial period (called the Würm in Eurasia). Meanwhile, the southern continents, too, experienced widespread climatic effects. Notably, in Africa around 20,000 y.a. it became significantly wetter, thus permitting reoccupation of areas in the north and south that had previously been abandoned.

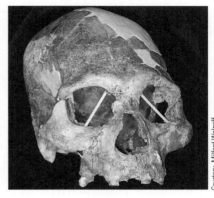

Courtesy, Milford Wolpoff

FIGURE 13–7
Kow Swamp (Australia). Note the considerable robusticity in this relatively late Australian *Homo sapiens sapiens* cranium.

FIGURE 13–8
Cultural periods of the European Upper Paleolithic and their approximate beginning dates.

GLACIAL	UPPER PALEOLITHIC (beginnings)	CULTURAL PERIODS
W Ü R M	17,000 –	Magdalenian
	21,000 –	Solutrean
	27,000 –	Gravettian
	40,000 –	Aurignacian Chatelperronian
Middle Paleolithic		Mousterian

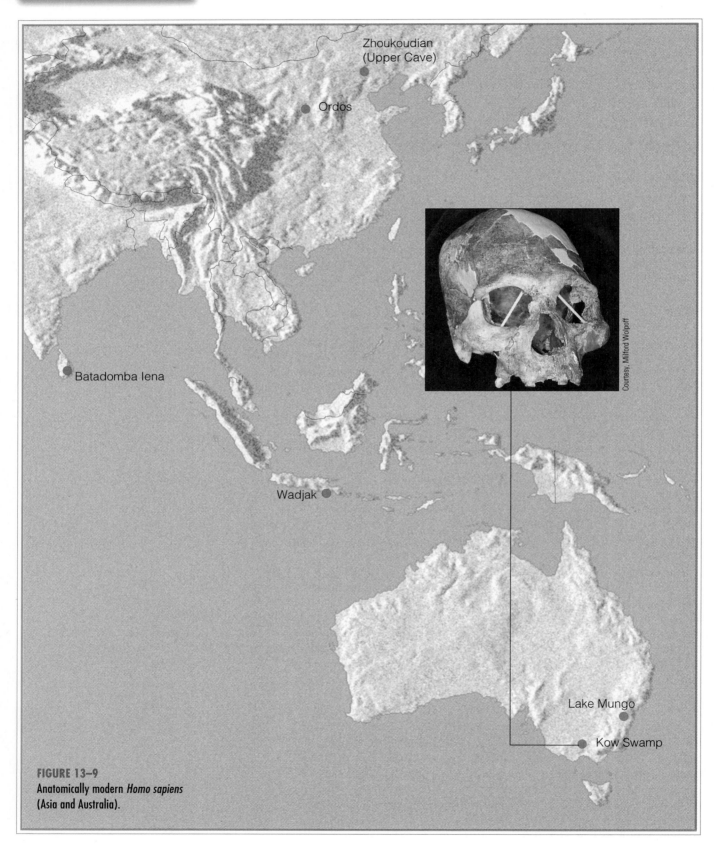

Zhoukoudian
(Upper Cave)

Ordos

Batadomba lena

Wadjak

Lake Mungo

Kow Swamp

Courtesy, Milford Wolpoff

FIGURE 13–9
Anatomically modern *Homo sapiens*
(Asia and Australia).

As a variety of organisms attempted to adapt to these changing conditions, *Homo sapiens* had a major advantage: the elaboration of an increasingly sophisticated technology (and probably other components of culture as well). Indeed, probably one of the greatest challenges facing numerous late Pleistocene mammals was the ever more dangerously equipped humans—a trend that has continued to modern times.

The Upper Paleolithic was an age of technological innovation and can be compared to the past few hundred years in our recent history of amazing technological change after centuries of relative inertia. Anatomically modern humans of the Upper Paleolithic not only invented new and specialized tools (Fig. 13–10), but, as we have seen, also greatly increased the use of (and probably experimented with) new materials, such as bone, ivory, and antler.

Solutrean tools are good examples of Upper Paleolithic skill and perhaps aesthetic appreciation as well (Fig. 13–10b). In this lithic (stone) tradition, stoneknapping developed to the finest degree ever known. Using a pressure-flaking technique (see p. 230), the artist/technicians made beautiful parallel-flaked lance heads, expertly flaked on both surfaces, with such delicate points that they can be considered works of art that quite possibly never served, or were intended to serve, a utilitarian purpose.

The last stage of the Upper Paleolithic, known as the **Magdalenian**, saw even more advances in technology. The spear-thrower (Fig. 13–11), a wooden or bone hooked rod (called an *atlatl*), acted to extend the hunter's arm, thus enhancing the force and distance of a spear throw. For catching salmon and other fish, the barbed harpoon is a clever example of the craftsperson's skill. There is also evidence that the bow and arrow may have been used for the first time during this period. The introduction of the punch technique (Fig. 13–12) provided an abundance of standardized stone blades that could be fashioned into **burins** (see Fig. 13–10a) for working wood, bone, and antler; borers for drilling holes in skins, bones, and shells; and knives with serrated or notched edges for scraping wooden shafts into a variety of tools.

The elaboration of many more specialized tools by Upper Paleolithic peoples probably made more resources available to them and may also have had an impact on the biology of these populations. C. Loring Brace of the University of Michigan has suggested that with more efficient tools used for food processing, anatomically modern *H. sapiens* would not have required the large front teeth (incisors) seen in earlier populations. With relaxed selection pressures (no longer favoring large anterior teeth), incorporation of random mutations would through time lead to reduction of dental size and accompanying facial features. In particular, the lower face became less prognathic (as compared to archaic specimens) and thus produced the concavity of the cheekbones called a *canine fossa* (see Fig. 13–2). Moreover, as the dental-bearing portion of the lower jaw regressed, the buttressing below would have become modified into a *chin*, that distinctive feature seen in anatomically modern *H. sapiens*.

In addition to their reputation as hunters, western Europeans of the Upper Paleolithic are even better known for their symbolic representation, what has commonly been called "art." Certainly, in the famous caves of France and Spain (discussed below), we easily relate to an aesthetic property of the images—one that *may* have been intended by the people who created them. But here we cannot be certain. Our own cultural perspectives create labels (and categories) such as "art," which in itself *assumes* aesthetic intent. While such a cultural orientation is obviously a recognizable part of Western culture, many

FIGURE 13–10
(a) Burin. A very common Upper Paleolithic tool. (b) Solutrean blade. This is the best-known work of the Solutrean tradition. Solutrean stonework is considered the most highly developed of any Upper Paleolithic industry.

Magdalenian
Pertaining to the final phase of the Upper Paleolithic stone tool industry in Europe.

Burins
Small, chisel-like tools (with a pointed end) thought to have been used to engrave bone, antler, ivory, or wood.

FIGURE 13–11
Spear-thrower (atlatl). Note the carving.

(a) A large core is selected and the top portion is removed by use of a hammerstone.

Striking platform

(b) The objective is to create a flat surface called a striking platform.

(c) Next, the core is struck by use of a hammer and punch (made of bone or antler) to remove the long narrow flakes (called blades).

(d) Or the blades can be removed by pressure flaking.

(e) The result is the production of highly consistent sharp blades, which can be used, as is, as knives; or they can be further modified (retouched) to make a variety of other tools (such as burins, scrapers, and awls).

FIGURE 13–12
The punch blade technique.

See Virtual Lab 11, section IV, for a discussion of blade manufacture.

FIGURE 13–13
Magdalenian bone artifact. Note the realistic animal engraving on this object, the precise function of which is unknown.

other contemporary peoples would not relate to this concept within their own cultural context. Furthermore, prehistoric peoples during the Upper Paleolithic did not necessarily create their symbols as true artistic representations. Rather, these representations may have served a variety of quite utilitarian and/or social functions—as do contemporary highway signs or logos on a company's letterhead. Would we call these symbols art?

Given these uncertainties, archaeologist Margaret Conkey of the University of California, Berkeley, refers to Upper Paleolithic cave paintings, sculptures, engravings, and so forth, as "visual and material imagery" (Conkey, 1987, p. 423). We will continue to use the term *art* to describe many of these prehistoric representations, but you should recognize that we do so mainly as a cultural convention—and perhaps a limiting one.

Moreover, the time depth for these prehistoric forms of symbolic imagery is quite long, encompassing the entire Upper Paleolithic (from at least 35,000 to 10,000 y.a.). Over this time span there is considerable variability in style, medium, content, and no doubt meaning as well. In addition, there is an extremely wide geographical distribution of symbolic images, best known from many parts of Europe, but now also well documented from Siberia, North Africa, South Africa, and Australia. Given the 25,000-year time depth of what we call "Paleolithic art" and its nearly worldwide distribution, there is indeed marked variability in expression.

In addition to cave art, there are numerous examples of small sculptures excavated from sites in western, central, and eastern Europe. Beyond these quite well-known figurines, there are numerous other examples of what is frequently termed "portable art," including elaborate engravings on tools and tool handles (Fig. 13–13). Such symbolism can be found in many parts of

(a)

(b)

Harry Nelson

Harry Nelson

FIGURE 13–14
Venus of Brassempouy. Upper Paleolithic artists were capable of portraying human realism (shown here) as well as symbolism (depicted in Fig. 13–15). (a) Frontal view. (b) Lateral view.

Europe and was already well established early in the Aurignacian (by 33,000 y.a.). Innovations in symbolic representations also benefited from, and probably further stimulated, technological advances. New methods of mixing pigments and applying them were important in rendering painted or drawn images. Bone and ivory carving and engraving were made easier with the use of special stone tools (see Fig. 13–10). At two sites in the Czech Republic, Dolni Vestonice and Predmosti (both dated at 27,000 y.a.), small animal figures were fashioned from fired clay—the first documented use of ceramic technology anywhere (and preceding later pottery invention by more than 15,000 years!).

Female figurines, popularly known as "Venuses," were sculpted not only in western Europe, but in central and eastern Europe and Siberia as well. Some of these figures were realistically carved, and the faces appear to be modeled after actual women (Fig. 13–14). Other figurines may seem grotesque, with sexual characteristics exaggerated, perhaps for fertility or other ritual purposes (Fig. 13–15).

It is, however, during the final phases of the Upper Paleolithic, particularly during the Magdalenian, that European prehistoric art reached its climax. Cave art is now known from more than 150 separate sites, the vast majority from southwestern France and northern Spain. Apparently, in other areas the rendering of such images did not take place in deep caves. Peoples in central Europe, China, Africa, and elsewhere certainly may have painted or carved representations on rockfaces in the open, but these images long since would have eroded. Thus, it is fortuitous that the people of at least one of the many sophisticated cultures of the Upper Paleolithic chose to journey belowground to create their artwork, preserving it not just for their immediate descendants, but for us as well.

In Lascaux Cave of southern France, immense wild bulls dominate what is called the Great Hall of Bulls, and horses, deer, and other animals adorn the walls in black, red, and yellow, drawn with remarkable skill. In addition to the famous cave of Lascaux, there is equally exemplary art from Altamira Cave in Spain. Indeed, discovered in 1879, Altamira was the first example of advanced cave art recorded in Europe. Filling the walls and ceiling of the cave are superb portrayals of bison in red and black, the "artist" taking advantage of bulges to give a sense of relief to the paintings. The cave is a treasure of beautiful art whose meaning has never been

Jim Cartier/Photo Researchers

FIGURE 13–15
Venus of Willendorf, Austria. (*Note:* This figure is among the most exaggerated and should be compared with Fig. 13–14.)

Homo sapiens sapiens

satisfactorily explained. It could have been religious or magical, a form of visual communication, or art for the sake of beauty.

Yet another spectacular example of cave art from western Europe was discovered in late 1994. On December 24, a team of three French cave explorers chanced upon a fabulous discovery in the valley of the Ardèche at Combe d'Arc. Inside the cave, called the Grotte Chauvet after one of its discoverers, preserved unseen for perhaps 30,000 years are many hundreds of images, including stylized dots, stenciled human handprints, and, most dramatically, hundreds of animal representations. Included are depictions of such typical Paleolithic subjects as bison, horse, ibex, auroch, deer, and mammoth (Fig. 13–16). But quite surprisingly, there are also numerous images of animals rarely portrayed elsewhere—such as rhino, lion, and bear. Three animals seen at Grotte Chauvet—a panther, a hyena, and an owl—have never before been documented at cave sites (Fig. 13–17). The artwork, at least after provisional study, seems to consistently repeat several stylistic conventions, causing French researchers to suggest that the images all may have been produced by the same artist. Provisional dating has placed the paintings during the Aurignacian (perhaps more than 30,000 y.a.), and thus Grotte Chauvet may be considerably earlier than the Magdalenian sites of Lascaux and Altamira. The cave was found as Paleolithic peoples had left it, and the initial discoverers, as well as archaeologists, have been careful not to disturb the remains. Among the archaeological traces already noted are dozens of footprints on the cave floor, produced by bears as well as by humans. We do not know yet how far the cave extends or what crucial artifactual remains lie along the floor.

A familiar motif seen at Grotte Chauvet and elsewhere is the representation of human hands, usually in the form of outlines. Apparently, the technique used was to liquefy the pigment and blow it onto a hand held flat against the cave wall. At one site in France, at least 159 such hand outlines were found (Leroi-Gourhan, 1986). Another stylistic innovation was the partial sculpting of a rock face—in what is called bas-relief (a technique used much later, for example, by the ancient Greeks at the Parthenon). Attaining depths up to 6 inches, some of the Paleolithic sculptures were quite dramatic and were attempted on a fairly grand scale. In one rock shelter in southwest France, several animals (including mountain goats, bison, reindeer, and horses) and one human figure were depicted in bas-relief. Interestingly, these representations were carved in an area also used as a living site—quite distinct from the special-purpose contexts in the deep cave locations. These bas-reliefs were executed throughout the Magdalenian, always in areas immediately adjacent to those of human habitation.

Strikingly, subject matter seems to differ by location and type of art motif. In portable art, common themes are horses and reindeer as well as stylized human figures; rarely are bison represented. However, in cave contexts, bison and horses are frequently seen, but almost never do we see reindeer (although in Europe, reindeer were probably the most common meat source). Cave artists were thought heretofore to have depicted carnivores only rarely, but the new finds at Grotte Chauvet give us a further perspective on the richness *and* diversity of Paleolithic art.

Ever since ancient art was discovered, attempts have been made to interpret the sculptures, paintings, and other graphic material found in caves or on rocks and tools at open-air archaeological sites. One of the early explanations of Upper Paleolithic art emphasized the relationship of paintings to hunting. Hunting rituals were viewed as a kind of imitative magic that would increase prey animal populations or help hunters successfully find and kill their quarry. As new hypotheses were published, their applicability and deficiencies were discussed. When many of these

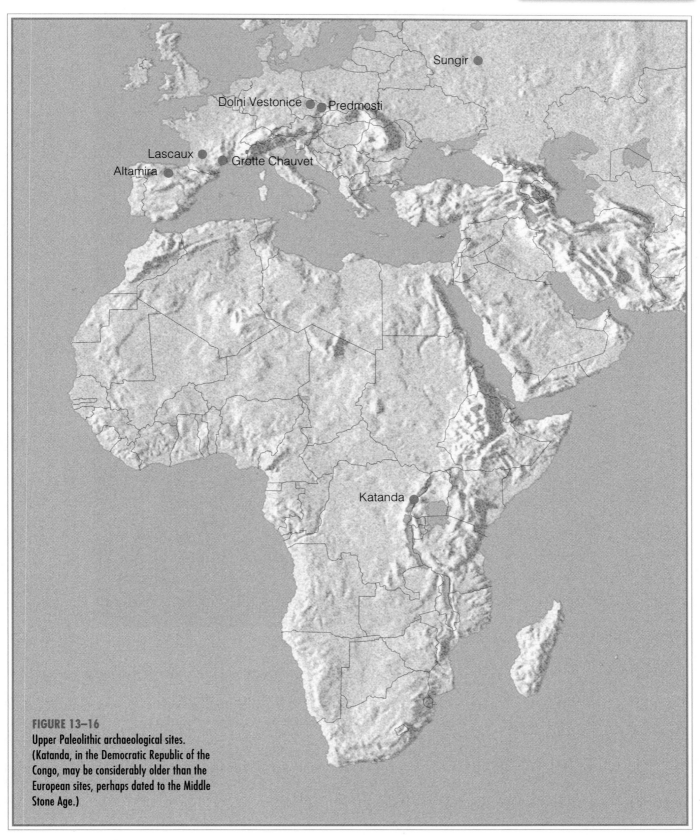

FIGURE 13–16
Upper Paleolithic archaeological sites.
(Katanda, in the Democratic Republic of the
Congo, may be considerably older than the
European sites, perhaps dated to the Middle
Stone Age.)

Homo sapiens sapiens

FIGURE 13–17
Cave art from Grotte Chauvet, France.
(a) Bear. (b) Aurochs and rhinoceros.

(a)

(b)

new hypotheses faded, others were expounded, and the cycle of new hypotheses followed by critiques continued.

Among these hypotheses, the association of religious ritual and magic is still considered viable because of the importance of hunting in the Upper Paleolithic. Nevertheless, other ideas about these graphics have been widely discussed, including the viewing of Upper Paleolithic art from a male/female perspective and the consideration of a prevalent dots-and-lines motif as a notational system associated with language, writing, or a calendar (Marshack, 1972). Other perspectives and ongoing questions include why certain areas of caves were used for painting, but not other, similar areas; why certain animals were painted, but not others; why males were painted singly or in groups, but women only in groups; why males were painted near animals, but women never were; and why groups of animals were painted in the most acoustically resonant areas. (Were rituals perhaps performed in areas of the cave with the best acoustic properties?) It should be noted that given the time depth, different contexts, and variable styles of symbolic representations, no *single* explanation regarding their meaning is likely to prove adequate. As one expert has concluded, "It is clear that there can no longer be a single 'meaning' to account for the thousands of images, media, contexts, and uses of what we lump under the term 'paleolithic art'" (Conkey, 1987, p. 414).

A recent explanation for the florescence of cave art in certain areas has been suggested by archaeologists Clive Gamble (1991) and Lawrence Straus (1993), who point to the severe climatic conditions during the maximum (coldest interval) of the last glacial, around 20,000–18,000 y.a. It was during this period in southwestern France and northern Spain that most of the cave art was created. Straus notes that wherever there are clusters of living sites, there are cave art sanctuaries and residential sites with abundant mobile art objects. The caves could have been meeting places for local bands of people and locations for group activities. Bands could share hunting techniques and knowledge, and paintings and engravings served as "encoded information" that could be passed on across generations. Such information, Straus argues, would have been crucial for dealing with the severe conditions of the last glacial period.

Africa

Early accomplishments in rock art, perhaps as early as in Europe, are seen in southern Africa (Namibia), where a site containing such art is dated between 28,000 and 19,000 y.a. In addition, evidence of portable personal adornment is seen as early as 38,000 y.a. in the form of beads fashioned from ostrich eggshells.

In terms of stone tool technology, microliths (thumbnail-sized stone flakes hafted to make knives, saws, etc.) and blades characterize Late Stone Age* African industries. There was also considerable use of bone and antler in central Africa, perhaps some of it quite early. Recent excavations in the Katanda area of the eastern portion of the Democratic Republic of the Congo have shown remarkable development of bone craftwork. In fact, preliminary reports by Alison Brooks of George Washington University and John Yellen of the National Science Foundation have demonstrated that these technological achievements rival those of the more renowned European Upper Paleolithic (Yellen et al., 1995).

The most important artifacts discovered at Katanda are a dozen intricately made bone tools excavated from three sites along the Semiliki River (not far from Lake Rutanzige—formerly, Lake Edward) (see Fig. 13–16). These tools, made from the ribs or long bone splinters of large mammals, apparently were first ground to flatten and sharpen them, and then some were apparently precisely pressure-flaked to produce a row of barbs. In form these tools are similar to what have been called "harpoons" from the later Upper Paleolithic of Europe (Magdalenian, circa 15,000 y.a.). Their function in Africa, as well, is thought to have been for spearing fish, which archaeological remains indicate were quite large (catfish weighing up to 150 pounds!). In addition, a few carved bone rings with no barbs were also discovered, but their intended function (if indeed they were meant to have a utilitarian function at all) remains elusive.

---

*The Late Stone Age in Africa is equivalent to the Upper Paleolithic in Eurasia.

The dating of the Katanda sites is crucial for drawing useful comparisons with the European Upper Paleolithic. However, the bone used for the tools retained no measurable nitrogen and thus proved unsuitable for radiocarbon dating (perhaps it was too old and beyond the range of this technique). As a result, the other techniques now used for this time range—thermoluminescence, electron spin resonance, and uranium series dating (see Table 13–1)—were all applied. The results proved consistent, indicating dates between 180,000 and 75,000 y.a.*

However, there remain some difficulties in establishing the clear association of the bone implements with the materials that have supplied the chronometric age estimates. Indeed, Richard Klein, a coauthor of one of the initial reports (Brooks et al., 1995), does not accept the suggested great antiquity for these finds and believes they may be much younger. Nevertheless, if the early age estimates should hold up, we once again will look *first* to Africa as the crucial source area for human origins—not just for biological aspects, but for cultural aspects as well.

Summary of Upper Paleolithic Culture

As we look back at the Upper Paleolithic, we can see it as the culmination of 2 million years of cultural development. Change proceeded incredibly slowly for most of the Pleistocene, but as cultural traditions and materials accumulated and the brain (and, we assume, intelligence) expanded and reorganized, the rate of change quickened.

Cultural evolution continued with the appearance of early archaic *H. sapiens* and moved a bit faster with later archaic *H. sapiens*. Neandertals in Eurasia and their contemporaries elsewhere added deliberate burials, technological innovations, and much more.

Building on existing cultures, late Pleistocene populations attained sophisticated cultural and material heights in a seemingly short (by previous standards) burst of exciting activity. In Europe and central Africa particularly, there seem to have been dramatic cultural innovations that saw big game hunting, potent new weapons (including harpoons, spear-throwers, and possibly the bow and arrow), body ornaments, needles, "tailored" clothing, and burials with elaborate grave goods (the latter might indicate some sort of status hierarchy).

This dynamic age was doomed, or so it appears, by the climatic changes of about 10,000 y.a. As the temperature slowly rose and the glaciers retreated, animal and plant species were seriously impacted, and humans were thus affected as well. As traditional prey animals were depleted or disappeared altogether, other means of obtaining food were sought.

Grinding hard seeds or roots became important, and as familiarity with plant propagation increased, domestication of plants and animals developed. Dependence on domestication became critical, and with it came permanent settlements, new technology, and more complex social organization. The continuing story of human evolution and the ways we study contemporary population diversity will be the topics of the remainder of this text.

---

*If these dates prove accurate, Katanda would actually be earlier than Late Stone Age (and thus be referrable to the Middle Stone Age).

SUMMARY

The date and location of the origin of anatomically modern human beings have been the subjects of a fierce debate for the past decade, and the end is not in sight. One hypothesis (complete replacement) claims that anatomically modern forms first evolved in Africa more than 100,000 y.a. and then, migrating out of Africa, completely replaced archaic *H. sapiens* in the rest of the world. Another school (regional continuity) takes a diametrically different view and maintains that in various geographical regions of the world, local groups of archaic *H. sapiens* evolved directly to anatomically modern humans. A third hypothesis (partial replacement) takes a somewhat middle position, suggesting an African origin but also accepting some later hybridization outside of Africa.

The Upper Paleolithic was an age of extraordinary innovation and achievement in technology and art. Many new and complex tools were introduced, and their production indicates fine skill in working wood, bone, and antler. Cave art in France and Spain displays the masterful ability of Upper Paleolithic painters, and beautiful sculptures have been found at many European sites. Sophisticated symbolic representations have also been found in Africa and elsewhere. Upper Paleolithic *Homo sapiens* displayed amazing development in a relatively short period of time. The culture produced during this period led the way to still newer and more complex cultural techniques and methods.

QUESTIONS FOR REVIEW

1. What characteristics define anatomically modern *H. sapiens*?

2. How do the characteristics of modern *H. sapiens* compare with those of archaic *H. sapiens*?

3. What are the three major theories that seek to explain the origin and dispersal of *Homo sapiens sapiens*? Compare and critically discuss these three views.

4. How have data from mitochondrial DNA been used to support an African origin of *H. sapiens sapiens*? What other genetic data have recently been analyzed, and how do they accord with the mtDNA results?

5. Discuss (and compare) the early evidence of anatomically modern humans from two different regions.

6. It is said that the Upper Paleolithic was a time of technological innovation. Support this statement with specific evidence, and compare the Upper Paleolithic with cultural data from earlier in the Pleistocene.

7. From which regions has cave art, dating to the Upper Pleistocene, been discovered? Particularly for the cave art of Europe, what explanations of its meaning have been proposed?

SUGGESTED FURTHER READING

Aitken, M. J., C. B. Stringer, and P. A. Mellars (eds.). 1993. *The Origin of Modern Humans and the Impact of Chronometric Dating*. Princeton, NJ: Princeton University Press.

Klein, Richard. 1999. *The Human Career: Human Biological and Cultural Origins*. 2nd ed. Chicago: University of Chicago Press.

Nitecki, Matthew H., and Doris V. Nitecki (eds.). 1994. *Origins of Anatomically Modern Humans*. New York: Plenum.

Smith, Fred, and Frank Spencer (eds.). 1984. *The Origin of Modern Humans*. New York: Liss.

Wolpoff, Milford. 1999. *Paleoanthropology*. 2nd ed. New York: McGraw-Hill.

RESOURCES ON THE INTERNET

 ### Wadsworth Anthropology Resource Center
http://anthropology.wadsworth.com

The companion website for this text includes a range of enrichment material focused on the chapter's topic. While online you can enhance your understanding of the chapter by exploring one of the several additional Internet exercises, by researching topics, and by accessing full articles on InfoTrac College Edition. You can also reinforce the concepts by taking online practice exams.

Internet Exercises

Some of the most recently discovered cave paintings are those at Grotte Chauvet in France. These paintings were completed between 32,000 and 30,000 years ago. Visit the site on the Web at **http://www.france.diplomatie.fr/label_france/ENGLISH/ SCIENCES/CHAUVET/cha.html**, or use your search engine to find sites for either *Grotte Chauvet* or *Lascaux Cave*. Another suggestion is *Prehistoric France*. Examine the photographs of the cave paintings and read the text. What is portrayed in the pictures? What do you think might have motivated the people to make the images? What do you think they were trying to communicate?

 ### InfoTrac College Edition
http://www.infotrac-college.com/wadsworth

Use PowerTrac to search for *Upper Paleolithic*. This should pull up several references from which you should choose at least two that deal with topics not covered in detail in Chapter 13. After reading these articles, make a list of facts you found particularly interesting. Did these articles change your views of how humans lived during the Upper Paleolithic? If so, how?

The Evolution of Language

One of the most distinctive behavioral attributes of all modern humans is our advanced ability to use highly sophisticated symbolic language. Indeed, it would be impossible to imagine human social relationships or human culture without language.

When did language evolve? First, we should define what we mean by *full* human language. As we discussed in Chapter 7 (see pp. 164–169), nonhuman primates have shown some elements of language. For example, some chimpanzees, gorillas, and bonobos display abilities to manipulate symbols and a rudimentary understanding of grammar. Nevertheless, the full complement of skills displayed by humans includes the extensive use of arbitrary symbols, sophisticated grammar, and a complex *open* system of communication (see p. 166).

Most scholars are comfortable attributing such equivalent skills to early members of *H. sapiens sapiens*, as early as 200,000–100,000 years ago. In fact, several researchers hypothesize that the elaborate technology and artistic achievements, as well as the rapid dispersal of anatomically modern humans, were directly a result of behavioral advantages—particularly full language capabilities. This rapid expansion of presumably culturally sophisticated modern *H. sapiens* (and the consequent disappearance of other hominids) has sometimes been termed "the human revolution."

Of course, this hypothesis does not deny that earlier hominids had some form of complex communication; almost everyone agrees that even the earliest hominids did (at least as complex as that seen in living apes). What is not generally agreed upon is just when the full complement of human language capacity *first* emerged. Indeed, the controversy relating to this process will continue to ferment, since there is no clear answer to the question. The available evidence is not sufficient to establish clearly the language capabilities of any fossil hominid. We have discussed in Chapter 7 that there are neurological foundations for language and that these features relate more to brain reorganization than to simple increase in brain size. Moreover, as far as *spoken* language is concerned, during hominid evolution there were also physiological alterations of the vocal tract (in particular, a lower position of the larynx as compared to other primates).

Yet, we have no complete record of fossil hominid brains or their vocal tracts. We do have *endocasts* (see p. 263), which preserve a few external features of the brain. For example, there are several preserved endocasts of australopithecines from South Africa. However, the information is incomplete and thus subject to varying interpretations. (For example, did these hominids possess language? If not, what form of communication did they display?) Evidence from the vocal tract is even more elusive.

In such an atmosphere of fragmentary data, a variety of conflicting hypotheses have been proposed. Some paleoanthropologists argue that early australopithecines (3 m.y.a.) had language. Others think that such capabilities were first displayed by early *Homo* (perhaps 2 m.y.a.). Still others suggest that language did not emerge fully until the time of *Homo erectus* (2–1 m.y.a.), or perhaps it was archaic forms of *H. sapiens* (such as the Neandertals) who first displayed such skills. And finally, a number of researchers assert that language first developed *only* with the appearance of *H. sapiens sapiens*.

Because the question of language evolution is so fundamental to understanding human evolution (indeed, what it *means* to be human), a variety of creative techniques have been applied to assess the (limited) evidence that is available. We have already mentioned the analysis of endocasts. Other researchers have suggested that the size of the vertebral canal in the thoracic region of the spine might be related to precise muscle control of breathing and thus an indicator of certain language skills. This conclusion was drawn from features of the *H. erectus* skeleton from Nariokotome (see p. 301). Lastly, and perhaps most informative of all, other paleoanthropologists have recently presented provisional data on the size of the hypoglossal canal at the base of the cranium (the size of the canal is thought to reflect the degree of neurological control of the tongue). As we noted earlier (see p. 334), investigators have so far suggested that australopithecines and early *Homo* (with small canals) did not have full articulate language, but that archaic *H. sapiens* (Neandertals) and early *H. sapiens sapiens* probably did (these latter showing canals as large as those of contemporary people).

Subsequent to the initial suggestion that size of the hypoglossal canal might reflect speech capabilities (Kay et al., 1998), the hypothesis has been further tested using a much wider sample of nonhuman primates, fossil hominids, and modern humans (DeGusta et al., 1999). These new data do *not* confirm the hypothesis and in fact seriously question it. For example, many nonhuman primates have hypoglossal canals as large as humans; similarly, some early hominids (members of *Australopithecus*) also have canals as large as contemporary humans. Perhaps even more revealing, the size of the canal, as shown in dissections of human cadavers, does not appear correlated with the size of the (hypoglossal) nerve running through it. Further studies might help resolve some of these issues, but, for the moment, the initial hypothesis concerning the utility of hypoglossal canal size for estimating speech abilities has been seriously weakened.

A final line of inquiry has also focused on language (i.e., speech) by reconstructing in various fossil hominids the presumed position of the larynx within the vocal tract. As first proposed by Lieberman and Crelin (Lieberman and Crelin, 1971; Lieberman, 1992) and more recently by Laitman (Laitman et al., 1993), it is argued that Neandertals and other members of archaic *H. sapiens* could not articulate full speech, since the larynx would have been positioned higher in the throat than is seen in *H. sapiens sapiens*. This inference is based on indirect reconstruction of the vocal tract from the contours of the cranial base. Again, the evidence is far from unambiguous, and interpreta-

tions are often varied (and contentious; see, for example, Falk, 1975; Frayer, 1993). Given these uncertainties, most paleoanthropologists have been reluctant to conclude exactly what *speech* capabilities Neandertals had. The most *direct* evidence was discovered in 1983 and includes an adult Neandertal *hyoid bone* (from Kebara Cave in Israel; see p. 331). This important structure, which supports the larynx, is identical in this Neandertal to that seen in modern humans. Given this information, it would be most imprudent to argue that Neandertals could not articulate full human speech. Nevertheless, simply because Neandertals *could* speak in a fully articulate manner does not necessarily argue that they communicated with the entire array of contemporary human symbolic language. We have noted in Chapter 12 several probable behavioral contrasts of Neandertals with Upper Paleolithic *H. sapiens sapiens*. Was language ability among these contrasts and perhaps the most important difference? Do more advanced language capabilities help explain the rapid success of modern humans in displacing other hominids? Does language, then, mostly account for the human revolution? Surely, these are fascinating and important questions. Perhaps someday we will be able to answer them in a comprehensive, scientifically rigorous manner.

Critical Thinking Questions

1. What is meant by human language? How does it differ from communication seen in great apes?

2. What direct evidence (fossil and archaeological) is used to suggest that early hominids had language capabilities? How sufficient is this evidence?

3. What kind of evidence would convince you that an earlier hominid (Neandertals, for example) did or did not possess language?

Sources

DeGusta, D., W. H. Gilbert, and S. P. Turner. 1999. "Hypoglossal Canal Size and Hominid Speech." *Proceedings of the National Academy of Sciences* 96: 1800–1804.

Falk, Dean. 1975. "Comparative Anatomy of the Larynx in Man and the Chimpanzee: Implications for Language in Neandertal." *American Journal of Physical Anthropology* 43: 123–132.

Frayer, D. W. 1993. "On Neanderthal Crania and Speech: Response to Lieberman." *Current Anthropology* 34: 721.

Kay, R. F., M. Cartmill, and M. Balow. 1998. "The Hypoglossal Canal and the Origins of Human Vocal Behavior" (abstract). *American Journal of Physical Anthropology, Supplement* 26: 137.

Laitman, J. T., J. S. Reidenberg, D. R. Friedland, et al. 1993. "Neandertal Upper Respiratory Specializations and Their Effect upon Respiration and Speech" (abstract). *American Journal of Physical Anthropology* 16: 129.

Lieberman, Phillip. 1992. "On Neanderthal Speech and Neanderthal Extinction." *Current Anthropology* 33: 409–410.

Lieberman, P., and E. S. Crelin. 1971. "On the Speech of Neanderthal Man." *Linguistic Inquiries* 2: 203–222.

MacLarnon, Ann. 1993. "The Vertebral Canal of KNM-WT 15000 and the Evolution of the Spinal Cord and Other Canal Contents." In A. Walker and R. E. Leakey (eds.), *The Nariokotome* Homo erectus *Skeleton*. Cambridge: Harvard University Press, pp. 359–390.

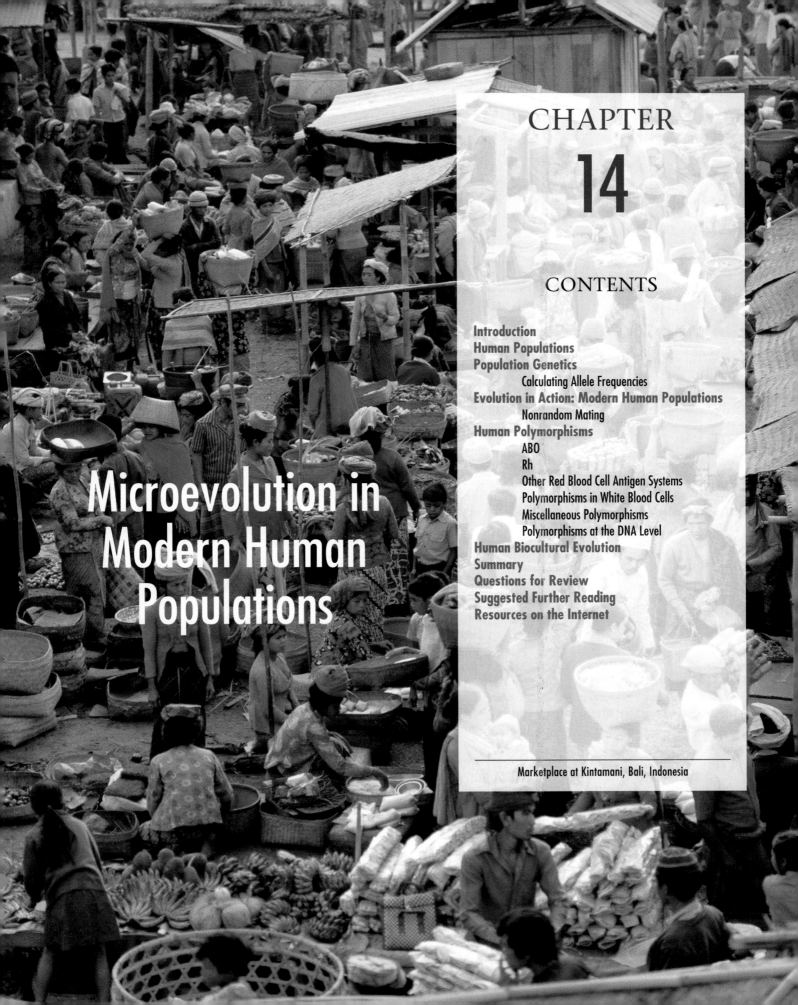

Microevolution in Modern Human Populations

CHAPTER
14

CONTENTS

Marketplace at Kintamani, Bali, Indonesia

Introduction

In the last chapter, we completed our overview of hominid evolution. The dispersal of *Homo sapiens sapiens* was the last major event in our lineage relating to what we have termed *macroevolution*. However, the evolution of our species did not conclude at this point, but has in fact continued over the last several thousand years. This ongoing process of evolutionary change is part of what is referred to as *microevolution.*

How is microevolution evaluated and measured in contemporary species? In earlier chapters, we discussed the mechanisms of inheritance and the manner in which heritable characteristics influence evolutionary change. In this chapter, we will demonstrate how these genetic principles lie at the very foundation of the evolutionary process. Moreover, we will show how these factors interact to produce evolutionary change in contemporary human populations. As with all other organisms, the variation exhibited by *Homo sapiens* can be understood within this contemporary evolutionary framework. Evolutionary change not only characterizes the human past, but also continues as a major factor shaping human beings today. In this explicit evolutionary context, physical anthropologists are able to assess larger patterns of human population diversity.

Human Populations

As we defined it in Chapter 4, a *population* is a group of interbreeding individuals. More precisely, a population is the group within which one is most likely to find a mate. As such, a population is marked by a degree of genetic relatedness and shares a common **gene pool.**

In theory, this is a straightforward concept. In every generation, the genes (alleles) are mixed by recombination and rejoined through mating. What emerges in the next generation is a direct product of the genes going into the pool, which in turn is a product of who is mating with whom.

In practice, however, defining and describing human populations is difficult. The largest population of *Homo sapiens* that could be described is the entire species. All members of a species are *potentially* capable of interbreeding, but are incapable of fertile breeding with members of other species. Our species is thus a *genetically closed system*. The problem arises not in describing who potentially can interbreed, but in isolating exactly the pattern of those individuals who are doing so.

Factors that determine mate choice are geographical, ecological, and social. If individuals are isolated on a remote island in the middle of the Pacific, there is not much chance of their finding a mate outside the immediate vicinity. Such **breeding isolates** are fairly easily defined and are a favorite target of microevolutionary studies. Geography plays a dominant role in producing these isolates by rather strictly determining the range of available mates. But even within these limits, cultural rules can easily play a deciding role by prescribing who is most appropriate among those who are potentially available.

Human population segments within the species are defined as groups with relative degrees of **endogamy** (marrying/mating within the group). These are, however, not totally closed systems. Gene flow often occurs between groups, and individuals may choose mates from distant localities. With the modern advent of rapid transportation, greatly accelerated rates of **exogamy** (marrying/mating outside the group) have emerged.

Most humans today are not so clearly defined as members of particular populations as they would be if they belonged to a breeding isolate. Inhabitants of large cities may appear to be members of a single population, but within the city, social, ethnic, and religious boundaries crosscut in a complex fashion to form smaller popu-

See the following sections of the CD-ROM for topics covered in this chapter: Virtual Lab 2, sections I, II, and III.

Gene pool
The total complement of genes shared by reproductive members of a population.

Breeding isolates
Populations that are clearly isolated geographically and/or socially from other breeding groups.

Endogamy
Mating with individuals from the same group.

Exogamy
Mating pattern whereby individuals obtain mates from groups other than their own.

lation segments. In addition to being members of these highly open local population groupings, we are simultaneously members of overlapping gradations of larger populations—the immediate geographical region (a metropolitan area or perhaps an entire state), a section of the country, the whole nation, and, ultimately, the whole species.

Population Genetics

Once specific human populations have been identified, the next step is to ascertain what evolutionary forces, if any, are operating on this group. To determine whether evolution is taking place at a given locus, we measure allele frequencies for specific traits and compare these observed frequencies with a set predicted by a mathematical model: the **Hardy-Weinberg theory of genetic equilibrium.** This model provides us with a baseline set of evolutionary expectations under *known* conditions.

The Hardy-Weinberg theory of genetic equilibrium postulates a set of conditions in a population where *no* evolution occurs. In other words, none of the forces of evolution are acting, and all genes have an equal chance of recombining in each generation (i.e., there is random mating of individuals). More precisely, the hypothetical conditions that such a population would be *assumed* to meet are as follows:

1. The population is infinitely large. This condition eliminates the possibility of random genetic drift or changes in allele frequencies due to chance.
2. There is no mutation. Thus, no new alleles are being added by molecular changes in gametes.
3. There is no gene flow. There is no exchange of genes with other populations that can alter allele frequencies.
4. Natural selection is not operating. Specific alleles confer no advantage over others that might influence reproductive success.
5. Mating is random. There are no factors that influence who mates with whom. Thus, any female is assumed to have an equal chance of mating with any male.

If all these conditions are satisfied, allele frequencies will not change from one generation to the next (i.e., no evolution will take place), and a permanent equilibrium will be maintained as long as these conditions prevail. An evolutionary "barometer" is thus provided that may be used as a standard against which actual circumstances are compared. Similar to the way a typical barometer is standardized under known temperature and altitude conditions, the Hardy-Weinberg equilibrium is standardized under known evolutionary conditions.

Note that the idealized conditions that define the Hardy-Weinberg equilibrium are just that: an idealized, *hypothetical* state. In the real world, no actual population would fully meet any of these conditions. But do not be confused by this distinction. By explicitly defining the genetic distribution that would be *expected* if *no* evolutionary change were occurring (i.e., in equilibrium), we can compare the *observed* genetic distribution obtained from actual human populations. The evolutionary barometer is thus evaluated through comparison of these observed allele and genotype frequencies with those expected in the predefined equilibrium situation.

If the observed frequencies differ from those of the expected model, then we can say that evolution is taking place at the locus in question. The alternative, of course, is that the observed and expected frequencies do not differ sufficiently to state unambiguously that evolution is occurring at a locus in a population. Indeed, frequently this is the result that is obtained, and in such cases, population geneticists are unable to delineate evolutionary changes at the particular locus under study. Put another way, geneticists are unable to reject what statisticians call the *null hypothesis* (where *null* means "nothing," a statistical condition of randomness).

Hardy-Weinberg theory of genetic equilibrium
The mathematical relationship expressing—under ideal conditions—the predicted distribution of alleles in populations; the central theorem of population genetics.

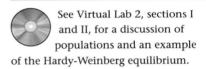

See Virtual Lab 2, sections I and II, for a discussion of populations and an example of the Hardy-Weinberg equilibrium.

The simplest situation applicable to a microevolutionary study is a genetic trait that follows a simple Mendelian pattern and has only two alleles (*A, a*). As you recall from earlier discussions, there are then only three possible genotypes: *AA, Aa, aa*. Proportions of these genotypes (*AA:Aa:aa*) are a function of the *allele frequencies* themselves (percentage of *A* and percentage of *a*). To provide uniformity for all genetic loci, a standard notation is employed to refer to these frequencies:

Frequency of dominant allele *(A)* = *p*
Frequency of recessive allele *(a)* = *q*

Since in this case there are only two alleles, their combined total frequency must represent all possibilities. In other words, the sum of their separate frequencies must be 1:

$$p + q = 1 \text{ (100\% of alleles at the locus in question)}$$
(Frequency of *A* alleles) (Frequency of *a* alleles)

To ascertain the expected proportions of genotypes, we compute the chances of the alleles combining with one another into all possible combinations. Remember, they all have an equal chance of combining, and no new alleles are being added.

These probabilities are a direct function of the frequency of the two alleles. The chances of all possible combinations occurring randomly can be simply shown as

$$
\begin{array}{r}
p + q \\
\times \quad p + q \\
\hline
pq + q^2 \\
p^2 + pq \quad\quad \\
\hline
p^2 + 2pq + q^2
\end{array}
$$

Mathematically, this is known as a binomial expansion and can also be shown as

$(p + q)(p + q) = p^2 + 2pq + q^2$

What we have just calculated is simply:

Allele Combination	Genotype Produced	Expected Proportion in Population
Chances of *A* combining with *A*	*AA*	$p \times p = p^2$
Chances of *A* combining with *a*;	*Aa*	$p \times q$
a combining with *A*	*aA*	$p \times q$ = 2pq
Chances of *a* combining with *a*	*aa*	$q \times q = q^2$

Thus, p^2 is the frequency of the *AA* genotype, *2pq* is the frequency of the *Aa* genotype, and q^2 is the frequency of the *aa* genotype, where *p* is the frequency of the dominant allele and *q* is the frequency of the recessive allele in a population.

Calculating Allele Frequencies

How geneticists use the Hardy-Weinberg formula is best demonstrated through an example. Let us assume that a population contains 200 individuals, and we will use the MN blood group locus as the gene to be measured. This gene produces a blood group antigen—similar to ABO—located on red blood cells. Because the *M* and *N* alleles are codominant, we can ascertain everyone's phenotype by taking blood samples and observing reactions with specially prepared antisera. From the phenotypes, we can then directly calculate the *observed* allele frequencies. So let us proceed.

All 200 individuals are tested, and the observed data for the three phenotypes are as follows:

Genotype	Number of individuals*	Percent	Number of Alleles M	N			
MM	80	40	160	0			
MN	80	40	80	80			
NN	40	20	0	80			
Totals	200	100	240	+	160	=	400
		Proportion	.6	+	.4	=	1

*Each individual has two alleles. Thus, a person who is *MM* contributes two *M* alleles to the total gene pool. A person who is *MN* contributes one *M* and one *N*. Two hundred individuals, then, have 400 alleles for the MN locus.

From these observed results, we can count the number of *M* and *N* alleles and thus calculate the observed allele frequencies:

p = frequency of M = .6
q = frequency of N = .4

The total frequency of the two alleles combined should always equal 1. As you can see, they do.

Next, we need to calculate the expected genotypic proportions. This calculation comes directly from the Hardy-Weinberg equilibrium formula: $p^2 + 2pq + q^2$.

p^2	=	(.6)(.6)	=	.36
$2pq$	=	2(.6)(.4) = 2(.24)	=	.48
q^2	=	(.4)(.4)	=	.16
Total				1.00

There are only three possible genotypes: *MM, MN, NN*. The total of the relative proportions should equal 1. Again, as you can see, they do.

Finally, we need to compare the two sets of data—that is, the observed frequencies (what we actually found in the population) with the expected frequencies (those predicted by Hardy-Weinberg under conditions of genetic equilibrium). How do these two sets of data compare?

	Expected Frequency	Expected Number of Individuals	Observed Frequency	Actual Number of Individuals with Each Genotype
MM	.36	72	.40	80
MN	.48	96	.40	80
NN	.16	32	.20	40

We can see that although the match between observed and expected frequencies is not perfect, it is close enough statistically to satisfy equilibrium conditions. Since our population is not a large one, sampling may easily account for the small observed deviations. Our population is therefore probably in equilibrium (i.e., at this locus, it is not evolving). At the minimum, what we can say scientifically is that we cannot reject the null hypothesis.

BOX 14–1 A CLOSER LOOK

Calculating Allele Frequencies:
PTC Tasting in a Hypothetical Population

For the PTC tasting trait, it is assumed that there are two alleles, *T* and *t*. Moreover, while dominance is displayed, it is incomplete. Thus, it is theoretically possible to ascertain the phenotypes of heterozygotes. To simplify calculations for this example, we assume that *all* heterozygotes can be ascertained.

In our population of 500 individuals, the following observed phenotypic frequencies are found:

Genotype	Number of Individuals	Percent	Number of Alleles T	t
TT	125	25	250	0
Tt	325	65	325	325
tt	50	10	0	100
Totals	500	100	575	425

Thus, the observed allele frequencies are

$T(p) = .575$
$t(q) = .425$

The expected genotypic proportions are

p^2	=	(.575)(.575)	=	.33
$2pq$	=	2(.575)(.425)	=	.49
q^2	=	(.425)(.425)	=	.18

Now we compare the observed and expected genotypic frequencies:

	Expected Frequency	Expected Number of Individuals	Observed Frequency	Actual Number of Individuals with Each Genotype
TT	.33	165	.25	125
Tt	.49	245	.65	325
tt	.18	90	.10	.50

These results show considerable departures of the observed genotypic proportions from those predicted under equilibrium conditions. Both types of homozygotes (*TT* and *tt*) are *less* commonly observed than expected, while the heterozygote (*Tt*) is *more* common than expected.

A statistical test (called a chi-square) can be performed to test the *statistical significance* of this difference. The results of this test are shown in Appendix B.

Of course, sometimes the observed allele frequencies do vary sufficiently from equilibrium predictions to warrant rejection of the null hypothesis. For example, consider the locus influencing the tasting of PTC, an artificial chemical (see p. 383 for further discussion). What makes PTC tasting such a useful characteristic is its ease of ascertainment. Unlike blood antigens like ABO or MN, PTC tasting can be tested by simply having test subjects place a thin paper strip between their lips. This paper contains concentrated PTC, and individuals simply taste or do not taste its presence. Thus, testing is quick and inexpensive and does not expose anyone to the blood of others (a major concern, owing to the risks of HIV or hepatitis infection).

With such an efficient means of screening subjects, we now consider a sample population of 500 individuals. The results from observation of the phenotypes and calculations of expected genotypic proportions are shown in Box 14–1. Further examples of population genetics calculations can be found in Appendix B.

Evolution in Action: Modern Human Populations

Once a population has been defined, a population geneticist will ascertain whether allele frequencies are stable (i.e., in genetic equilibrium) or whether they are changing. As we have seen, the Hardy-Weinberg formula provides the tool to establish whether allele frequencies are indeed changing. What factors initiate changes in allele frequencies? There are a number of factors, including those that

1. Produce new variation (i.e., *mutation*)
2. Redistribute variation through *gene flow* or *genetic drift*
3. Select "advantageous" allele combinations that promote reproductive success—that is, *natural selection*

Note that factors 1 and 2 constitute the first stage of the evolutionary process, as first emphasized by the Modern Synthesis, while factor 3 is the second stage (see p. 88). There is yet another factor, as implied by the condition of genetic equilibrium that under idealized conditions all matings are random. Thus, the evolutionary alteration (i.e., deviation from equilibrium) is called **nonrandom mating.**

Nonrandom Mating

Although sexual recombination does not itself alter *allele frequencies,* any consistent bias in mating patterns can alter the *genotypic proportions.* By affecting the frequencies of genotypes, nonrandom mating causes deviations from Hardy-Weinberg expectations of the proportions p^2, $2pq$, and q^2. It therefore sets the stage for the action of other evolutionary factors, particularly natural selection.

A variety of nonrandom mating, called assortative mating, occurs when individuals of either similar phenotypes (positive assortative mating) or dissimilar phenotypes (negative assortative mating) mate more often than expected by Hardy-Weinberg predictions. However, in the vast majority of human populations, neither factor appears to have much influence.

Inbreeding is a second type of nonrandom mating, and it can have both important medical and evolutionary consequences. Inbreeding occurs when relatives mate more often than expected, and such unions are sometimes referred to as consanguinity. Such matings will increase the amount of homozygosity, since relatives who share close ancestors will more than likely also share more alleles than would two nonrelated individuals.

All living societies have some sort of incest taboo banning matings between very close relatives, such as between parent and child or brother and sister. Therefore, such matings usually occur less frequently than predicted under random mating conditions (which postulates that these matings, like all others, have a certain probability of occurring).

Whether incest is strictly prohibited by social proscriptions or whether biological factors also interact to condition against such behavior has long been a topic of heated debate among anthropologists. For numerous social, economic, and ecological reasons, exogamy is an advantageous strategy for hunting and gathering bands. Moreover, selective pressures may also play a part, since highly inbred offspring have a greater chance of expressing a genetic disorder and thereby lowering their reproductive fitness. In addition, inbreeding reduces variability among offspring, potentially reducing reproductive success (Murray, 1980). In this regard, an interesting note is that incest avoidance is widespread among vertebrates (Parker, 1976). Moreover, detailed studies of free-ranging chimpanzees indicate that they avoid

Nonrandom mating
Patterns of mating in a population in which individuals choose mates preferentially.

Inbreeding
A type of nonrandom mating in which relatives mate more often than predicted under random mating conditions.

375

incestuous matings within their family group (Goodall, 1968); in fact, adults of at least one sex in most primate species consistently establish themselves and then mate within groups other than the one in which they were reared (see p. 147). Apparently, both biological factors (in common with other primates) and uniquely human cultural factors have interacted during hominid evolution to produce this universal behavior pattern among contemporary societies.

Inbreeding has important medical consequences in addition to its influence on genetic equilibrium. When relatives mate, their offspring have an increased probability of inheriting two copies of potentially harmful recessive alleles from a relative that they share in common, such as a grandparent. Many potentially deleterious genes normally "masked" in heterozygous carriers may be expressed in offspring of consanguineous matings and thereby "exposed" to the action of natural selection. Among offspring of first-cousin matings in the United States, the risk of congenital disorders is 2.3 times greater than it is for the overall population. Matings between especially close relatives—incest—often lead to multiple genetic defects.

Human Polymorphisms

The ABO and MN blood groups, as well as the traits discussed earlier in Chapter 4, are *Mendelian* traits. That is, the phenotype of each of these traits can unambiguously be linked to the action of a single locus. These simple genetic mechanisms are much more straightforward than the polygenic traits usually associated with studies of human **racial** variation (discussed in Chapter 15). In fact, the difficulty in tracing the genetic influence on such characteristics as skin color or face shape has led some human biologists to avoid investigations of such polygenic traits. Although physical anthropologists, by tradition, have been keenly interested in explaining such variation, we have seen a trend, beginning in the second half of the twentieth century, toward greater concentration on traits with a clearly demonstrated genetic mechanism (i.e., Mendelian characteristics). In the twenty-first century, this approach will be greatly enhanced through use of genetic variants ascertained directly at the DNA level.

Of greatest use in contemporary studies of human variation are traits that can be used to document genetic differences among various populations. Such a genetic trait is called a **polymorphism.** A genetic trait is a polymorphism if the locus that governs it has two or more variants (i.e., two or more alleles). Recent advances in molecular biology have revealed that such genetic variation can occur in coding regions of DNA (those portions that are translated; see Chapter 3) as well as noncoding areas (those segments of DNA not directly responsible for gene products such as proteins). These noncoding DNA regions occur interspersed within functional loci (where they are called *introns;* see p. 48) or between loci (in what is sometimes referred to as "junk DNA"). Indeed, as we have seen (see p. 50), most of the DNA in humans as well as in other organisms is made up of these noncoding areas. While such regions (making up most of our nuclear DNA) may not be translated into any phenotypic product, this DNA is still passed on to offspring following Mendelian principles. Moreover, this DNA is remarkably variable from person to person as well as from group to group. In other words, these DNA segments (loci) are extremely polymorphic, making them highly useful for numerous types of genetic and forensic analyses (see p. 384 for further discussion).

Clearly, the understanding of human genetic polymorphisms demands evolutionary explanations. As students of human evolution, physical anthropologists use these polymorphisms as a principal tool to understand the dynamics of evolution in modern populations. Moreover, by utilizing these polymorphisms and compar-

Racial
In biology, pertaining to populations of a species that differ from other populations of the same species with regard to some aspects of outwardly expressed phenotype. Such phenotypic variation within a species is usually associated with differences in geographical location.

Polymorphism
A genetic trait governed by a locus with more than one allele.

ing allele frequencies in different populations, we can begin to reconstruct the evolutionary events that link human populations with one another. Hundreds of polymorphisms are now well known in humans, including several determined from analysis of blood.

ABO

With the first use of transfusions as a medical practice at the beginning of the twentieth century, serious problems were immediately recognized. Some patients had severe reactions, such as agglutination (clumping) of their blood cells, kidney failure, and even death. In the year 1901, Karl Landsteiner showed that the underlying cause of these incompatibilities was a genetic trait. As you know, this trait, called the ABO blood system, is expressed phenotypically in individuals as antigens located on the surface of their red blood cells (see p. 76). The blood group (i.e., what antigens a person has) is directly determined by his or her genotype for the ABO locus. The complications sometimes resulting from transfusions are due to *antigen-antibody* reactions. In a highly specific fashion, the body can recognize foreign antigens and combat their invasion by producing specific antibodies that deactivate the foreign substances. Such an *immune response* is normally beneficial, for it is the basis of fighting infections caused by bacteria or viruses.

Usually, antibodies are produced when foreign antigens are introduced. However, in the case of ABO, naturally occurring antibodies are already present in the blood serum at birth. Actually, no antibodies are probably "natural," although they may be (as in ABO) stimulated early in fetal life.

The ABO system is most interesting from an anthropological perspective because the frequencies of the three alleles (*A, B, O*) vary tremendously among human populations. As the distribution maps indicate (Fig. 14–1), it is rare for either *A* or *B* to approach a frequency of 50 percent; frequencies for these two alleles are usually considerably below this figure. Most human groups, however, are polymorphic for all three alleles. Occasionally, as in native South American Indians, frequencies of *O* reach 100 percent, and this allele is said to be "fixed" in this population. Indeed, in most native New World populations, *O* has a frequency of at least 80 percent and usually considerably higher. Unusually high frequencies of *O* are also found in northern Australia, and some islands off the coast show frequencies of 90 percent and higher. Since these frequencies are considerably greater than for presumably closely related mainland populations, founder effect is probably the evolutionary agent responsible.

In general, the lowest frequencies of *O* are in eastern Europe and central Asia. As you might expect, frequencies for *A* and *B* can be relatively higher only where *O* tends to be lower. Generally, *B* is the rarest of the three alleles, and except among the Inuit, it appears to have been completely absent in the pre-Columbian New World. Moreover, the allele has apparently been introduced into Australia only in recent times.

The *B* allele reaches its highest peak in Eurasia, where its distribution is the inverse of *O*. Values up to 20 percent and occasionally slightly higher are found in a broad area in central Asia, western Siberia, and central Mongolia. The highest reported frequencies for *B* are found in the Himalaya area, reaching a peak of 25 to 30 percent. Generally, the frequency of *B* declines gradually in populations the farther westward they are in Eurasia. This pattern of gradual shift in allele frequency over space is called a **cline** (see p. 397 for further discussion).

The *A* allele has two interesting peaks, one among Blackfoot Indians and surrounding groups in North America and the other distributed over almost the

See Virtual Lab 2, section III, for an interactive exercise covering the ABO blood group.

Cline
Gradual change in the frequency of genotypes and phenotypes over geographical space.

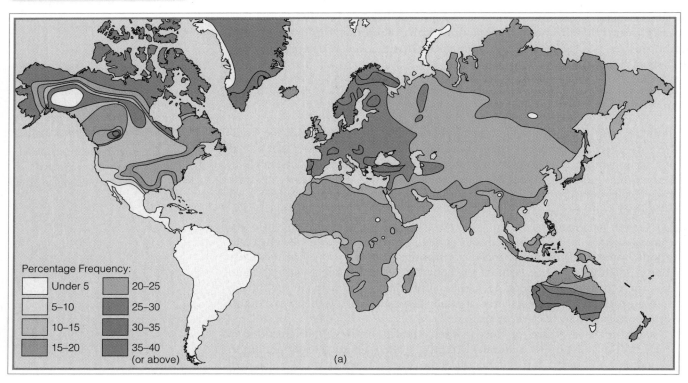

Percentage Frequency:

Under 5	20–25
5–10	25–30
10–15	30–35
15–20	35–40 (or above)

(a)

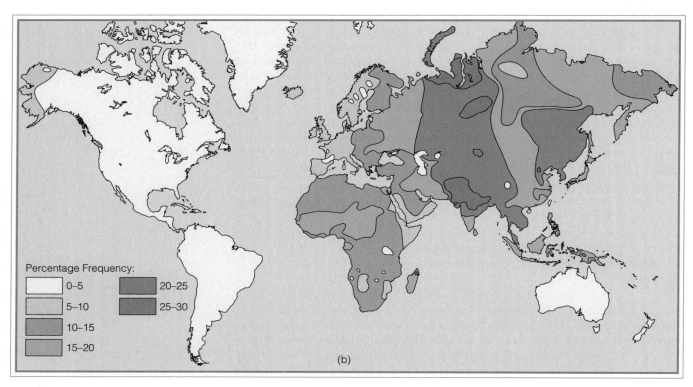

Percentage Frequency:

0–5	20–25
5–10	25–30
10–15	
15–20	

(b)

FIGURE 14–1

ABO blood group system. (a) Distribution of the *A* allele in the indigenous populations of the world.
(b) Distribution of the *B* allele in the indigenous populations of the world. (After Mourant et al., 1976.)

entire Australian continent. With frequencies greater than 50 percent, the Blackfoot display the highest frequencies of *A* anywhere in the world. Certainly, they are divergent from other North American groups, who all have very high frequencies of *O* (and therefore low frequencies of *A*). How did *A* increase so much among this one tribe and its close neighbors, compared to surrounding populations? Possibly drift (founder effect) is the answer, possibly some unknown selective factor. No one knows.

In Australia, except for the northern part, frequencies of *A* are generally high—particularly in central Australia, where they are 40 percent or higher. One tribe has especially high frequencies of *A* (53 percent), significantly higher than any surrounding group. Once again, is founder effect responsible? Over the rest of Australia, frequencies of *A* are fairly even in distribution and gradually decrease as populations become further removed from the center of the continent.

We must point out that distributions of alleles for a single genetic trait like ABO do not conclusively demonstrate genetic relationships between populations. For example, the North American Blackfoot and central Australian Mandjiljara have similar frequencies of *A*, but are obviously not closely related. On the other hand, in South Africa, the San have lower *B* frequencies than some of their close neighbors, with whom they share fairly close genetic ties. To understand *patterns* of population relationships, it is absolutely necessary to consider allele frequency distributions for several traits simultaneously (see p. 397).

Why do frequencies of the ABO alleles vary so much in different populations? In some cases, as with the islands off northern Australia and perhaps with the Blackfoot, drift may be the key factor. However, the even distribution of alleles (as *B* in Eurasia, *A* in Australia) indicates that selection may also be playing an important role, for the regularity in the frequency distributions is thought to mirror gradual changes in environments.

If, in fact, selection is operating, what are the specific factors involved? Unfortunately, unlike the sickle-cell trait, there is not as yet any proven association between ABO frequencies and *any* selective agent (such as a particular disease). There are, however, some clues. For example, *A* individuals have significantly more stomach cancer and pernicious anemia, while *O* individuals have more gastric and duodenal ulcers (Vogel, 1970). Such chronic diseases as these are not that common; moreover, they probably do not affect reproductive success very much, since they occur so late in life.

On the other hand, infectious diseases (as already shown for malaria) are potentially selective factors of enormous significance. Some interesting associations between ABO frequencies and incidence of smallpox, tuberculosis, syphilis, bubonic plague, cholera, and leprosy have been suggested. Moreover, it has also been suggested that *O* individuals are more attractive to mosquitoes and are thus bitten more often than *A*, *B*, or *AB* individuals (Wood et al., 1972). Here, too, could be an important contributing factor for infectious diseases, since many—including malaria, yellow fever, and typhus—are transmitted by insects (Brues, 1990). As yet, none of these associations is well substantiated. Consequently, the evolutionary factors influencing the distribution of ABO alleles are still largely a mystery.

Rh

Another group of antigens found on red blood cells is the *Rh system*, named after the rhesus monkeys that initially provided the blood cells with which to make antiserum. Developed in 1940 by Alex Wiener and Karl Landsteiner (a full 40 years after Landsteiner's discovery of ABO), this antiserum was then tested in a large sample of white Americans, in which 85 percent reacted positively.

BOX 14–2   A CLOSER LOOK

Maternal-Fetal Incompatibility

A maternal-fetal incompatibility occurs when the system of the mother is immunized by cells from a fetus and forms antibodies that then raise problems for that fetus or future ones.

For the Rh trait, complications occur only when the mother is Rh⁻ (*dd*) and the father Rh⁺ (*DD* or *Dd*). Actually, the other loci can also cause incompatibilities, but 95 percent of the problems are due to the D locus.

European populations are the most polymorphic for Rh, and around 13 percent of all matings are at risk. Not all those at risk, however, run into problems. Only about 6 percent of those potentially in danger have any complications. With new preventive treatment, this figure can be expected to decline even further.

The problem of incompatibility arises only if the mother is Rh⁻ and her fetus is Rh⁺. Usually, there are no serious effects in the first pregnancy, for the mother's system has not been immunized. Transfer along the placental boundary does not generally include blood cells, except in the case of rupture. Ruptures, however, do occur normally at birth, so that fetal blood enters the mother's system, stimulating the production of antibodies. Such antibodies do not occur naturally, as in the ABO system, but are produced "on the spot" quite quickly. About 70 percent of all Rh⁻ people have the capability of producing significant amounts of these antibodies, and it requires only one drop of blood to stimulate the process!

When the next pregnancy occurs, transfer of the antibodies from the mother's system takes place across the placental boundary into the fetus. Here is the real problem: The anti-Rh⁺ antibodies react with the Rh⁺ fetal blood, causing cell destruction. Consequently, the fetus will be born with a severe malady called *hemolytic disease of the newborn,* which produces severe anemia with accompanying "oxygen starvation." Because of the lack of oxygen, such newborns are sometimes called "blue babies." In recent decades, doctors, prepared in advance for such complications, administered massive transfusions and often saved the infant. However, previous to modern medical treatment, this disease was probably nearly always fatal. Such incompatibilities were thus fairly common in polymorphic populations and should have exerted a powerful selection pressure.

More recently, physicians have sought to prevent incompatibilities by administering serum containing anti-Rh⁺ antibodies to women at risk after their first birth. These antibodies quickly destroy any fetal red blood cells as they enter the mother's circulation, thereby preventing her from forming her own antibodies. Since the serum given the mother is a passive form of immunization (to her), it will shortly leave her bloodstream. Thus, she does not produce any long-acting antibodies, and the quite low risk of first pregnancies should not be increased in future pregnancies.

It should also be mentioned that maternal-fetal incompatibilities result from ABO as well. However, these are considerably rarer than Rh complications, with less than 0.1 percent of newborns affected. It is possible, though, that some ABO incompatibilities go undetected owing to early fetal death.

The situation with ABO appears to be considerably more complex than for Rh. Some women who experi-

---

Individuals showing such an observable reaction are usually called Rh-positive (Rh⁺), and those whose blood does not react with the antiserum are called Rh-negative (Rh⁻). These standardized designations refer to an apparently simple two-allele system, with *DD* and *Dd* resulting in Rh⁺ and the recessive *dd* resulting in Rh⁻.

Clinically, the Rh factor—like ABO—can lead to serious complications. However, the greatest problem is not so much the incompatibilities following transfusions as those between a mother and her developing fetus (see Box 14–2). For most significant medical applications, Rh⁺ and Rh⁻ phenotypes are accounted for by the three genotypes already noted (*DD, Dd, dd*). However, the actual genet-

FIRST PREGNANCY

SUBSEQUENT PREGNANCIES

FIGURE 1
Rh incompatibility and hemolytic disease of the newborn: the series of events during first and later pregnancies. (After Novitski, 1977.)

ence repeated miscarriages (clinically termed, "recurrent spontaneous abortions") appear to have problems with ABO incompatibilities—where a female's mate and fetus are blood type A and she has anti-A antibodies (i.e., she is either blood type B or O) (Bottini et al., 2001). However, no such problems arise when there is B incompatibility; indeed, there appear to be even fewer difficulties here than seen when there is no incompatibility at all (e.g., when both mates are the same ABO blood type). Thus, some researchers have suggested that there may be some type of protective effect acting in women who have anti-B antibodies.

ics of the Rh system are a good deal more complex than explained by just two alleles at one locus. The famous English population geneticist Sir R. A. Fisher suggested that the Rh system is actually three closely linked loci with at least two alleles each.

The distribution of the various allele combinations within the Rh system (which may be pictured as large genes) varies considerably among human populations. Generally, Rh⁻ (*d*) is quite high in European groups, averaging around 40 percent. African populations also have a fair amount of polymorphism at the D locus, with frequencies of Rh⁻ centering around 25 percent. Native Americans and Australians, on the other hand, are almost 100 percent Rh⁺.

TABLE 14–1 Other Blood Group Systems Used in Human Microevolutionary Studies

Major Systems	Number of Known Antigens
P	3
Lutheran	2
Kell-Cellano	5
Lewis	2
Duffy	2
Kidd	2
Diego	1
Auberger	1
Xg (sex-linked)	1
Dombrock	1
Stolzfus	1

Source: Lerner and Libby, 1976, p. 354.

Other Red Blood Cell Antigen Systems

MN The pattern of inheritance of the MN blood group is very straightforward and is thus a favorite tool in population genetics research. There are three genotypes—*MM, MN, NN*—all clearly ascertainable at the phenotypic level using antisera obtained from rabbits. Clinically, no observable complications arise as a result of transfusions or maternal-fetal incompatibilities; the MN system is anthropologically important because of its variable distribution among human populations.

Almost all human populations are polymorphic (i.e., having both *M* and *N* in "appreciable" frequencies), but the relative frequency of the two alleles varies tremendously. In some areas of Australia, *M* is as low as 2 percent, contrasted with many areas of the New World, where frequencies exceed 90 percent and even reach 100 percent in some areas. The allele *M* is also found in quite high frequency in Arabia, Siberia, and portions of Southeast Asia.

In addition to ABO, Rh, and MN, there are several other polymorphic red blood cell antigen systems. While not clinically significant like ABO or Rh, many of these are important for anthropological studies of population variation. Table 14–1 lists these major antigen systems of human red blood cells.

Polymorphisms in White Blood Cells

An important polymorphic trait called the HLA (human lymphocyte antigen) system has been discovered on some white blood cells (lymphocytes). Of great medical importance, HLA loci affect histocompatibility, or recognition and rejection of foreign tissues—the reason skin grafts and organ transplants are usually rejected. Genetically, the HLA system is exceedingly complex, and researchers are still discovering further subtleties within it. There are at least seven closely linked loci on chromosome 6 making up the HLA system. Taken together, there are already well over 100 antigens known within the system, with a potential of at least 30 million different genotypes (Williams, 1985; Bodmer, 1995). By far, this is the most polymorphic of any known human genetic system.

The component loci of the HLA system function together as a kind of "supergene." In addition to the components of the HLA loci themselves, many other factors affecting immune response are known to exist in the same region of chromosome 6. Altogether, the whole system is called the *major histocompatibility complex* (MHC).

The geographical distribution of the various MHC alleles is not yet well known. Some interesting patterns, however, are apparent. For example, Lapps, Sardinians, and Basques show deviations from frequencies of HLA alleles in other European populations, paralleling evidence for ABO, Rh, and MN. In addition, many areas in New Guinea and Australia are quite divergent, possibly suggesting the effects of drift. It is imperative, however, that care be taken in postulating genetic relatedness from restricted polymorphic information. Otherwise, such obviously ridiculous links as some proposed from HLA data (e.g., Tibetans and Australians; Inuit with some New Guineans) would obscure the evolutionary process in human populations (Livingstone, 1980). Since HLA is involved in the superfine detection and deactivation of foreign antigens, selection relative to infectious diseases (particularly those caused by viruses) may also play a significant role in the distribution of HLA alleles.

Evidence is still tentative, but some HLA antigens are apparently associated with susceptibility to certain diseases. Most severe forms of diabetes, a disease of the spine called ankylosing spondylitis, as well as multiple sclerosis and some varieties of hay fever, all probably result from individuals developing an autoimmune response to their own HLA antigens.

A final interesting and potentially important physiological (and ultimately evolutionary) effect of possessing certain HLA antigens concerns male infertility. Recent data indicate that some HLA antigens are found in higher frequency in males with severe infertility, suggesting that there may be some influence of two or more HLA loci on sperm production or function (van der Ven et al., 2000).

Miscellaneous Polymorphisms

An interesting genetically controlled variation in human populations was discovered by accident in 1931. When the artificially synthesized chemical phenylthiocarbamide (PTC) was dropped in a laboratory, some researchers were able to smell it, while others could not. It was later established that there is a dichotomy among humans regarding those who can versus those who cannot taste PTC. Although tasters vary considerably in sensitivity, most report a very bitter, unpleasant sensation. The pattern of inheritance follows a Mendelian model, with the inability to taste behaving as a simple recessive. In most populations, a majority of individuals are tasters, but the frequency of nontasters varies dramatically—from as low as 5 percent in Africa to as high as 40 percent in India.

The evolutionary function of this polymorphism is not known, although the fact that it is also seen in some other primates argues that it has a long history. Obviously, evolution has not acted to produce discrimination for an artificial substance recently concocted by humans. The observed variation *may* reflect selection for taste discrimination of other, more significant substances. Indeed, taste discrimination, which may allow the avoidance of many toxic plants (which frequently are bitter), may well be an important evolutionary consideration.

Another puzzling human polymorphism is the variability seen in earwax, or cerumen. Earwax is found in human groups in two basic varieties: (1) yellow and sticky with a good deal of lipids (fats and fatlike substances) and (2) gray and dry with fewer lipids. Cerumen variation appears also to be inherited as a simple Mendelian trait with two alleles (sticky is dominant; dry is recessive). Interestingly, frequencies of the two varieties of earwax vary considerably among human populations. In European populations, about 90 percent of individuals typically have the sticky variety, while in northern China, only about 4 percent are of this type.

How do we explain these differences? Even between very large groups there are consistent differences in cerumen type, arguing that drift is an unlikely causal mechanism. However, it is difficult to imagine what kind of selective pressure would act directly on earwax. Perhaps, like that previously suggested for PTC discrimination, earwax variation is an incidental expression of a gene controlling something more adaptively significant. Suggestions along these lines have pointed to the relation of cerumen to other body secretions, especially those affecting odor. Certainly, other mammals, including nonhuman primates, pay considerable attention to smell stimuli. Although the sense of smell is not as well developed in humans as in other mammals, humans still process and utilize olfactory (smell) stimuli. Thus, it is not impossible that during the course of human evolution, genes affecting bodily secretions (including earwax) came under selective influence.

Microevolution in Modern Human Populations

Polymorphisms at the DNA Level

Geneticists and physical anthropologists over the last 50 years have used somewhat indirect techniques to study human polymorphisms, observing some *phenotypic* products. For example, the ABO antigens are phenotypic products (quite immediate ones) of the DNA locus coding for them. In the last decade, with the revolution in DNA technology, much more *direct* means have become available by which to study human genetic variation.

mtDNA   In addition to the DNA found in the nucleus (nuclear DNA), human (and other eukaryotic) cells contain another kind of DNA. This DNA, found in the cytoplasm, is contained within the organelles called mitochondria—and is thus called *mitochondrial DNA (mtDNA)*. While nuclear DNA is extraordinarily long, containing an estimated 3 billion nucleotides, mtDNA is much shorter, containing only 16,500 nucleotides. Using special enzymes (restriction enzymes, derived from bacteria) that cut the DNA in specific locations, researchers have been able to sequence the entire mtDNA genome. Thus, it has become possible to compare variation among individuals and among populations. Ongoing work is establishing that some mtDNA regions are more variable than others but that for the *total* mtDNA genome, variation within *Homo sapiens* is apparently much less pronounced than in other species (e.g., chimpanzees). The possible evolutionary reasons for this surprising finding might relate to a quite recent origin of all modern *Homo sapiens* from a restricted ancestral population base (thus producing genetic drift/founder effect). The evolutionary ramifications of such a process on the dispersal of modern humans was discussed in Chapter 13 (see p. 348).

Nuclear DNA   As with mtDNA analysis, the use of restriction enzymes has permitted much greater precision in direct study of the DNA contained within human chromosomes, that is, nuclear DNA. This work has been greatly facilitated as part of the continuing intense research of the *Human Genome Project*. Untangling the entire human genetic complement is obviously an enormous undertaking, but to date, considerable insight has been gained regarding human variation *directly at the DNA level*. By cutting the DNA of different individuals and comparing the results, researchers have observed great variation in the number and length of the DNA fragments at numerous DNA sites. Accordingly, these genetic differences (caused by variable DNA sequences) are referred to as **restriction fragment length polymorphisms (RFLPs)**.

In addition, new molecular technologies have uncovered a host of other regions of DNA variability. Scattered throughout the human genome are hundreds of sites where DNA segments have been repeated—in some cases, just a few times, in other cases, many hundreds of times. These areas of nucleotide repetitions are called *microsatellites*, and they are extraordinarily variable from person to person. In fact, everyone is unique for their particular arrangement, and using current analytical approaches, the individual pattern produces a distinctive "DNA fingerprint." When using powerful techniques to amplify tiny amounts of DNA (e.g., from a drop of blood, a hair, or a semen stain), millions of copies of the DNA molecule can be produced and then analyzed. As a result, forensic identification of individual human remains at sites of mass disasters (such as the World Trade Center) or from traces left by suspects at crime scenes can be done with great accuracy.

Finally, researchers are beginning to expand their approach and map patterns of variation at individual nucleotide sites. Of course, it has been recognized for some time that individual base substitutions can occur within functional loci, pro-

Restriction fragment length polymorphisms (RFLPs)

Variation among individuals in the number and length of DNA fragments produced by enzymes that break the DNA at specific sites.

mtDNA genome has been sequenced)

ducing what we call a "point mutation" (see p. 52). The sickle-cell allele at the hemoglobin beta locus is the best-known example of such a mutation in humans.

What has only been recently appreciated, however, is that such single nucleotide alterations also frequently occur in noncoding portions of DNA, and these sites, together with those in coding regions of DNA, are all referred to as *single nucleotide polymorphisms (SNPs)*. Already, more than a million such sites have been recognized dispersed throughout the human genome (96 percent of which are in noncoding DNA), and like RFLPs and microsatellites, these single nucleotide polymorphisms are extraordinarily variable (the International SNP Map Working Group, 2001). Thus, at the beginning of the twenty-first century, geneticists have gained access to a vast biological "library," documenting the population patterning and genetic history of our species.

Population geneticists are just beginning to take advantage of these new opportunities. While traditional polymorphic traits, such as ABO and serum proteins, are still being investigated, more and more attention is being directed at the remarkably variable DNA polymorphisms. For example, mitochondrial and nuclear DNA analyses of RFLPs and microsatellites have provided new insights into genetic patterning in India, both between and within major population groups (Raychoudhury et al., 2001; Reddy et al., 2001). Similarly, recent investigations of mitochondrial RFLPs in Indonesian populations are shedding new light on the microevolution of these complex groups (Handoki et al., 2001). Newly discovered variable DNA sites on the Y chromosome are also assisting population geneticists, helping them assess the likely gene flow between North Africa and Iberia (Spain and Portugal) as well as further corroborating the genetic distinctiveness of the native inhabitants of Sardinia (Scozzari et al., 2001). In the New World, recent work has compared the mitochondrial DNA patterning between prehistoric groups (from which ancient DNA was extracted, amplified, and sequenced) and contemporary Native Americans (O'Roruke et al., 2000).

Another fruitful area of recent research holds great promise for future advances. Our specific genetic knowledge of traits under the influence of several loci (what we call *polygenic* traits; see p. 83) has been woefully inadequate. However, by identifying specific loci at the DNA level (or using these highly variable regions as "markers" to direct molecular biologists to ever-smaller areas of specific chromosomes), popular geneticists will soon be able to isolate particular gene variants contributing to skin color, stature, hypertension, and a host of other previously enigmatic human phenotypic traits.

Lastly, using these new tools, the broader history of *Homo sapiens* is coming under closer genetic scrutiny. As we discussed in Chapter 13, analysis of mitochondrial DNA has provided insight into the origins and dispersal of anatomically modern humans (see p. 348). Further investigations, using both mitochondrial and nuclear DNA, will yield more fine-tuned data to help resolve this still-controversial period of our evolutionary history (Mitchell et al., 1999; Harpending and Rogers, 2001).

Human Biocultural Evolution

We have defined culture as the human strategy of adaptation. Human beings live in cultural environments that are continually modified by human activity; thus, evolutionary processes are understandable only within this *cultural* context. You will recall that natural selection pressures operate within specific environmental settings. For humans and many of our hominid ancestors, this means an environment dominated by culture. For example, the sickle-cell allele has not always been an important genetic factor in human populations. In fact, human cultural modification of environments apparently provided the initial stimulus. Before the development of agriculture, humans rarely, if ever, lived close to mosquito breeding areas. With the development and spread to Africa of **slash-and-burn agriculture**, perhaps in just the last 2,000 years, penetration and clearing of tropical rain forests occurred. As a result of deforestation, open, stagnant pools provided prime mosquito breeding areas in close proximity to human settlements. New DNA analyses have further confirmed such a recent origin and spread of the sickle-cell allele in West Africa. A recent study of RFLP sites in the beta locus (on chromosome 11) among a population from Senegal has estimated the origin of the Hb^S mutation in this group at between 1,250 and 2,100 y.a. (Currat et al., 2002).

Thus, quite recently malaria, for the first time, struck human populations with its full impact, and as a selective force it was powerful indeed. No doubt, humans attempted to adjust culturally to these circumstances, and numerous biological adaptations also probably came into play. The sickle-cell trait is one of these biological adaptations. However, there is a definite cost involved with such an adaptation. Carriers have increased resistance to malaria and presumably higher reproductive success, but some of their offspring may be lost through the genetic disease sickle-cell anemia. So there is a counterbalancing of selective forces with an advantage for carriers *only* in malarial environments. The genetic patterns of recessive traits such as sickle-cell anemia are discussed in Chapter 4 (see p. 80).

Following World War II, extensive DDT spraying by the World Health Organization began systematically to control mosquito breeding areas in the tropics. As would be expected, malaria decreased sharply, and also as would be expected, the frequency of the sickle-cell allele also seemed on the decline. The intertwined story of human cultural practices, mosquitoes, malarial parasites, and the sickle-cell allele is still not finished. Forty years of DDT spraying killed many mosquitoes, but natural selection has been acting on these insect populations. Because of the tremendous amount of genetic diversity among insects, as well as their short generation span, several DDT-resistant strains have arisen and spread in the last few years (Fig. 14–2). Accordingly, malaria is again on the rise, with several hundred thousand new cases reported in India, Africa, and Central America.

A genetic trait (such as sickle-cell trait) that provides a reproductive advantage to the heterozygote in certain environments is a clear example of natural selection in action among human populations. The precise evolutionary mechanism in the sickle-cell example is termed a **balanced polymorphism.** A polymorphism, as we have defined it, is a trait with more than one allele in appreciable frequency at a locus in a population. So when an allele like that for sickle-cell is found in a population in frequencies approaching 10 percent, the trait is clearly polymorphic. The sickle-cell allele has a higher frequency than can be accounted for by mutation *alone* and thus demands a fuller evolutionary explanation. In this case, the additional mechanism is natural selection.

This brings us back to the other part of the term *balanced polymorphism.* By "balanced," we are referring to the interaction of selective pressures operating in a malarial environment. Some individuals (mainly homozygous normals) will be removed by the infectious disease malaria and some (homozygous recessives) will die of the inherited disease sickle-cell anemia. Those with the highest reproductive success are the heterozygous carriers. But what alleles do they carry? Clearly, they are passing *both* the "normal" allele and the sickle-cell allele to offspring, thus maintaining both alleles at fairly high frequencies. Since one allele in this population will not significantly increase in frequency over the other allele, this situation will reach a balance and persist, at least as long as malaria continues to be a selective factor.

when a trait persists

balanced polymorphism → when s/ allele, and
oneond die

Slash-and-burn agriculture
A traditional land-clearing practice whereby trees and vegetation are cut and burned. In many areas, fields are abandoned after a few years and clearing occurs elsewhere.

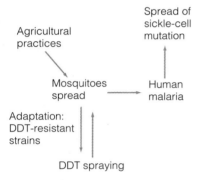

FIGURE 14–2
Evolutionary interactions affecting the frequency of the sickle-cell allele.

Balanced polymorphism
The maintenance of two or more alleles in a population due to the selective advantage of the heterozygote.

See Virtual Lab 2, section I, for a discussion of natural selection and variation.

BOX 14–3   A CLOSER LOOK

Other Genetic Traits Possibly Associated with Malaria

In many parts of the world, malaria has been an extremely important selective factor over the last several thousand years. Sickle-cell is probably only one of several inherited traits that have spread because they provide resistance. It must be noted, however, that none of these other traits have been documented as well as sickle-cell, nor has there been conclusive experimental evidence comparable to the work of A. C. Allison (see p. 94). Concordance between higher incidence of these genetic traits with geographical areas exhibiting high malarial infection provides *indirect* evidence of possible association with the following:

1. Hemoglobin C—produced by an allele at the same locus as that for *Hb^A* and *Hb^S*; distributed in Africa mainly in the west but with a few pockets of high incidence in the south. *Hb^C* is found in many populations where *Hb^S* is also present. Possibly this allele provides resistance to another strain of malaria and *both* alleles occur in populations exposed to multiple varieties of malaria (Weiss and Mann, 1981).

2. Thalassemia—a general term for several inherited disorders. Rather than a defect in the hemoglobin molecule itself, thalassemias involve a block in hemoglobin production (absence of, or deficient production of, the alpha or beta globin molecules). There are probably a variety of genetic mechanisms (mutations) that can lead to thalassemia, including point mutations, deletions, and disruption of gene regulation. For example, one variety of thalassemia (β^+) is caused by inadequate production of mRNA; consequently, protein synthesis of the beta hemoglobin chain is disrupted. The most harmful expression of this disease syndrome is seen in homozygotes, producing severe anemia. In heterozygotes, there are little, if any, harmful effects. Geographical evidence suggests a possible connection between thalassemia and malaria, with the highest frequencies of the disease found among populations around the Mediterranean. The severe form of beta-thalassemia affects as many as 1 percent of newborns in some parts of southern Europe. Tentative experimental evidence suggests that in heterozygotes, thalassemia—like sickle-cell—provides an inadequate environment for malarial infestation and proliferation (Friedman and Trager, 1981).

3. G-6-PD—glucose-6-phosphate dehydrogenase—an enzyme in red blood cells. Individuals with a genetically caused deficiency do not produce this enzyme. The gene for this trait is on the X chromosome (i.e., X-linked), and some populations are up to 60 percent deficient (Bodmer and Cavalli-Sforza, 1976). First discovered by adverse reactions with severe anemia when individuals were given certain antimalarial drugs, anemia can also result from exposure to some foods (fava beans, for example). Distribution is again correlated with malarial areas, but apparently the alleles that cause the deficiency in southern Europe are different from those in sub-Saharan Africa. At the biochemical level, G-6-PD deficiency may act like thalassemia, producing a cellular environment not conducive to malarial infection. When exposed to certain drugs or foods (particularly fava beans), individuals with G-6-PD deficiency may have a severe anemic reaction. It is possible, however, that heterozygous carriers may actually increase malarial resistance by eating such foods—potentially an extremely important biocultural interaction (Friedman and Trager, 1981).

Two other traits that may also be influenced by the selective agent of malaria are G-6-PD deficiency and the thalassemias (results of several different mutations that act to block hemoglobin production). However, in both these cases, evidence of natural selection is not as strong as with the sickle-cell allele. The primary evidence suggesting a link with malaria is the geographical concordance of increased frequency of these traits with areas (especially around the Mediterranean) that historically have had a high incidence of malarial infection (see Box 14–3).

TABLE 14–2 Frequencies of Lactose Intolerance

Population Group	Percent
U.S. whites	2–19
Finnish	18
Swiss	12
Swedish	4
U.S. blacks	70–77
Ibos	99
Bantu	90
Fulani	22
Thais	99
Asian Americans	95–100
Native Australians	85

Source: Lerner and Libby, 1976, p. 327.

Lactose intolerance
The inability to digest fresh milk products, caused by the discontinued production of *lactase*, the enzyme that breaks down lactose, or milk sugar.

Another example of human biocultural evolution concerns the ability to digest milk. In all human populations, infants and young children can digest milk, an obvious necessity for any young mammal. A major ingredient of milk is the sugar *lactose,* which is broken down by humans and other mammals by the enzyme *lactase.* In most mammals, including humans, the gene coding for lactase production "switches off" by adolescence. If too much milk is then ingested, it ferments in the large intestine, leading to diarrhea and severe gastrointestinal upset. Among many African and Asian populations—a majority of humankind today—most adults are intolerant of milk (Table 14–2).

Recent evidence has suggested a simple dominant mode of inheritance for **lactose intolerance.** The environment also plays a role in expression of the trait— that is, whether a person will be lactose-intolerant—since intestinal bacteria can somewhat buffer the adverse effects. Because these bacteria will increase with previous exposure, some tolerance can be acquired, even in individuals who genetically have become lactase-deficient.

Why do we see variation in lactose tolerance among human populations? Throughout most of hominid evolution, no milk was available after weaning. Perhaps, in such circumstances, continued action of an unnecessary enzyme might inhibit digestion of other foods. Therefore, there *may* be a selective advantage for the gene coding for lactase production to switch off. The question can then be asked, Why can some adults (the majority in some populations) tolerate milk? The distribution of lactose-tolerant populations is very interesting, revealing the probable influence of cultural factors on this trait.

European groups, who are generally lactose-tolerant, are partially descended from groups of the Middle East. Often economically dependent on pastoralism, these groups raised cows and/or goats and no doubt drank considerable quantities of milk. In such a cultural environment, strong selection pressures would act to shift allele frequencies in the direction of more lactose tolerance. Modern European descendants of these populations apparently retain this ancient ability.

Even more informative is the distribution of lactose tolerance in Africa. For example, groups such as the Fulani and Tutsi, who have been pastoralists probably for thousands of years, have much higher rates of lactose tolerance than nonpastoralists.

As we have seen, the geographical distribution of lactose tolerance is related to a history of cultural dependence on milk products. There are, however, some populations that rely on dairying but are not characterized by high rates of lactose tolerance. It has been suggested that such populations traditionally have consumed their milk produce as cheese and other derivatives in which the lactose has been broken down by bacterial action (Durham, 1981).

The interaction of human cultural environments and changes in lactose tolerance among human populations is another example of biocultural evolution. In the last few thousand years, cultural factors have initiated specific evolutionary changes in human groups. Such cultural factors have probably influenced the course of human evolution for at least 3 million years, and today they are of paramount importance.

SUMMARY

In this chapter, we have discussed human variation from an evolutionary perspective. We have focused on the contemporary trend to describe simple genetic polymorphisms that can be measured for allele frequencies as well as emphasizing genetic data obtained directly from analysis of mitochondrial and nuclear DNA.

Moreover, we have reviewed the theoretical basis of the *population genetics* approach, the subdiscipline of physical anthropology that seeks to *measure* genetic diversity among humans. Data on polymorphic traits can be used to understand aspects of human microevolution. For humans, of course, culture also plays a crucial evolutionary role, and the sickle-cell trait and lactose intolerance are thus discussed from an explicit biocultural perspective.

QUESTIONS FOR REVIEW

1. How is a population defined? Discuss why, in human groups, defining particular populations can be very difficult.
2. What is meant by genetic equilibrium?
3. What kinds of variation have been discovered at the DNA level? Why is knowledge of such variation important (i.e., what are some of the uses of analysis of such variability)?
4. How has the sickle-cell allele come to be common in some parts of the world? Why is it thought to be a good example of natural selection?
5. What biocultural interactions have occurred that help explain the distribution of lactose intolerance?
6. Discuss how genetic drift may have influenced the geographical distribution of the *A, B,* and *O* alleles.

SUGGESTED FURTHER READING

Cavalli-Sforza, L. L., 2000. *Genes, People, and Languages.* New York: North Point Press.
Cavalli-Sforza, L. L., P. Mendoza, and A. Piazza. 1994. *The History and Geography of Human Genes.* Princeton: Princeton University Press.
Olson, Steve. 2002. *Mapping Human History: Discovering the Past Through Our Genes.* Boston: Houghton Mifflin.
Relethford, John H. 2001. *Genetics and the Search for Modern Human Origins.* New York: Wiley-Liss.

RESOURCES ON THE INTERNET

 Wadsworth Anthropology Resource Center
http://anthropology.wadsworth.com

The companion website for this text includes a range of enrichment material focused on the chapter's topic. While online you can enhance your understanding of the chapter by exploring one of the several additional Internet exercises, by researching topics, and by accessing full articles on InfoTrac College Edition. You can also reinforce the concepts by taking online practice exams.

Internet Exercises

Visit Online Mendelian Inheritance in Man (OMIM—**http://www3.ncbi.nlm.nih. gov/Omim/**) and search for one of the Mendelian traits discussed in Chapter 14, such as sickle-cell anemia, thalassemia, G-6-PD, or lactase deficiency (lactose intolerance). Read part of the discussion and note how complicated the genetic effects of the relevant alleles are. Make a list of facts you learned from this site.

InfoTrac College Edition
http://www.infotrac-college.com/wadsworth

On InfoTrac College Edition, search for *human population genetics*. What does this search find? Choose one article and report on the gene(s) studied and the distribution of that gene in the population investigated. Is an explanation offered for the distribution seen?

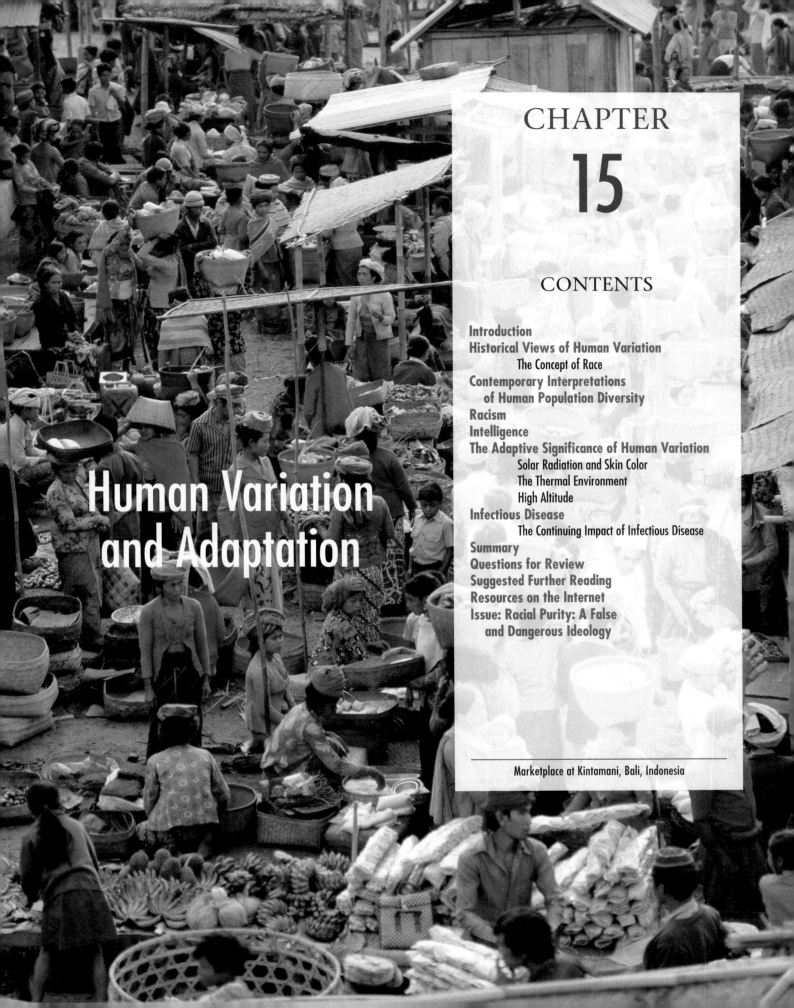

CHAPTER
15

CONTENTS

Human Variation and Adaptation

Marketplace at Kintamani, Bali, Indonesia

See the following sections of the CD-ROM for topics covered in this chapter: Virtual Lab 2, sections III and IV.

Introduction

In Chapter 14, we began our discussion of biological variation in modern human populations, which in turn was based on the genetic principles discussed in Chapters 3 and 4. More specifically, Chapter 14 concerned certain Mendelian characteristics, how they vary among humans, and the underlying genetic factors that influence them, especially at the level of the population.

In this chapter, we continue our discussion of human diversity, beginning with a section on past and current views of human phenotypic variation that primarily deals with the concept of race. The traits that were traditionally used to classify humans into racial groups are polygenic. Hence, our discussion focuses on certain polygenic characteristics and emphasizes their potential adaptive value. We also discuss adaptation to numerous environmental factors, such as temperature, altitude, and infectious disease. Infectious disease has exerted enormous selective pressures on our species and continues to do so today. Thus, we offer a few examples of how infectious disease has altered allele frequencies in some populations. We also consider some of the many cultural and environmental factors that are currently changing the distribution and prevalence of infectious disease. Lastly, there is a discussion of HIV/AIDS that emphasizes evolutionary factors, including recently reported discoveries of genetically determined resistance to HIV.

Historical Views of Human Variation

The first step toward understanding natural phenomena is the ordering of variation into categories that can then be named, discussed, and perhaps studied. Historically, when different groups of people came into contact with one another, they offered explanations for the phenotypic variations they saw, and because skin color was so noticeable, it was one of the more frequently explained traits, and most systems of racial classification came to be based on it.

Egypt as home

As early as 1350 B.C., the ancient Egyptians had classified humans on the basis of skin color: red for Egyptian, yellow for people to the east, white for those to the north, and black for Africans from the south (Gossett, 1963, p. 4). In the sixteenth century, after the discovery of the New World, Europe embarked on a period of intense exploration and colonization in both the New and Old Worlds. Resulting from this contact was an increased awareness of human diversity.

As you learned in Chapter 2, the discovery of the New World was of major importance in altering the views of Europeans, who had perceived the world as static and nonchanging. One of the most influential discoveries of the early European explorers was that the Americas were inhabited by people, some of whom were dark-skinned (compared to most Europeans). Furthermore, these people were not Christian, and they were not considered "civilized" by Europeans. At first, Native Americans were thought to be Asian, and since Columbus believed that he had discovered a new route to India, he called them "Indians."

By the late eighteenth century, Europeans and European Americans were asking questions that challenged traditional Christian beliefs. They wanted to know if other groups belonged to the same species as themselves; that is, were Native Americans and other indigenous peoples indeed human? Were they descendants of Adam and Eve, or had there been later creations of non-Europeans? If the latter were true, then Native Americans had to represent a different species, or else the Genesis account of creation could not be taken literally.

Two schools of thought, known as **monogenism** and **polygenism**, devised responses. In the monogenist view, all humans were descended from a single, orig-

Monogenism
The theory that all human populations are descended from one pair (Adam and Eve), but they differ from one another because they have occupied different habitats. This concept was an attempt to explain phenotypic variation between groups, but did not imply evolutionary change.

Polygenism
A theory, opposed to monogenism, that stated that human races were not all descended from Adam and Eve. Instead, there had been several original human pairs, each giving rise to a different group. Thus, human races were considered to be separate species.

inal pair (Adam and Eve). Insisting on the **plasticity** of human structure, mono-genists contended that local environmental conditions, such as climate and terrain, could modify the original form, resulting in observable phenotypic differences between populations. Monogenist views were initially attractive to many, for they did not conflict with the Genesis version of creation.

The polygenist view, on the other hand, argued that all populations did not descend from a single, original pair, but from a number of pairs. Also, polygenists saw such a wide gap in the physical, mental, and moral attributes between them-selves and other peoples that they were sure that outsiders belonged to different species. Furthermore, polygenists did not accept the monogenist notion of plastic-ity of physical traits, and they rejected the proposition that climate and environ-ment were modifying influences.

Throughout the eighteenth and nineteenth centuries, European and American scientists concentrated primarily on describing and classifying biological diversity as observed in humans as well as in nonhuman species. The first scientific attempt to categorize the newly discovered variation among humans was Linnaeus' taxo-nomic classification, which placed humans into four separate groupings (Linnaeus, 1758). Linnaeus assigned behavioral and intellectual qualities to each group, with the least complimentary descriptions going to African blacks. This ranking was typical of the period and reflected the almost universal European view that Europeans were superior to all other peoples. (To be fair, we should note that the Europeans were not—and are not—the only people guilty of *ethnocentrism*. Most, if not all, human societies participate in the belief that their own culture is superior to others.)

Johann Friedrich Blumenbach (1752–1840), a German anatomist, classified humans into five categories, or races. Although Blumenbach's categories came to be described simply as white, yellow, red, black, and brown, he also used criteria other than skin color. Moreover, Blumenbach emphasized that divisions based on skin color were arbitrary and that many traits, including skin color, were not discrete phenomena. Blumenbach pointed out that to attempt to classify all humans using such a system would be to omit completely all those who did not neatly fall into a specific category. Furthermore, he and other scientists recognized that traits such as skin color showed overlapping expression between groups. At the time, it was thought that racial taxonomies should be based on characteristics unique to partic-ular groups and uniformly expressed within them. Some scientists, taking the poly-genist view, attempted to identify certain physical traits that were thought to be stable or that did not appear to be influenced by external environmental factors. Therefore, these so-called *nonadaptive* traits should exhibit only minimal within-group variation and could thus be used to typify entire populations. Shape of the skull was incorrectly believed to be one such characteristic, and the fallacy of this assumption was not demonstrated until the early twentieth century (Boas, 1912).

In 1842, Anders Retzius, a Swedish anatomist, developed the *cephalic index* as a method of describing the shape of the head. The cephalic index, derived by divid-ing maximum head breadth by maximum length and multiplying by 100, gives the ratio of head breadth to length. (It is important to note that the cephalic index does not measure head size.) Compared to the statistical methods in use today, the cephalic index seems rather simplistic, but in the nineteenth century, it was viewed as a sophisticated scientific tool. Furthermore, because people could be neatly cate-gorized by a single number, it provided an extremely efficient method for describ-ing and ordering phenotypic variation. Individuals with an index of less than 75 had long, narrow heads and were termed **dolichocephalic**. **Brachycephalic** indi-viduals, with broad heads, had an index of over 80. And those whose indices were between 75 and 80 were *mesocephalic*.

Plasticity
The capacity to change; in a physiological context, the ability of systems or organisms to make alter-ations in order to respond to differing conditions.

Dolichocephalic
Having a long, narrow head in which the width measures less than 75 percent of the length.

Brachycephalic
Having a broad head in which the width mea-sures more than 80 percent of the length.

Northern Europeans tended to be dolichocephalic, while southern Europeans were brachycephalic. Not surprisingly, these results led to heated and nationalistic debate over whether one group was superior to the other. Furthermore, when it was shown that northern Europeans shared their tendency to long, narrow heads with several African populations, the cephalic index ceased to be considered such a reliable indicator of race.

By the mid-nineteenth century, monogenists were beginning to reject their somewhat egalitarian concept of race in favor of a more hierarchical view. Populations were ranked essentially on a scale based on skin color (along with size and shape of the head), with Africans at the bottom. Moreover, Europeans themselves were ranked so that northern, light-skinned populations were considered superior to their southern, more olive-skinned neighbors.

The fact that non-Europeans were not Christian and were seen as "uncivilized" implied an inferiority of character and intellect. This view was rooted in a concept now termed **biological determinism**, which in part holds that there is an association between physical characteristics and such attributes as intelligence, morals, values, abilities, and even social and economic differences between groups. In other words, cultural variations are *inherited* in the same manner as biological variations. It follows, then, that there are inherent behavioral and cognitive differences between groups and that some groups are *by nature* superior to others. Following this logic, it is a simple matter to justify the persecution and even enslavement of other peoples simply because their appearance differs from what is familiar.

After 1850, biological determinism was a constant theme underlying common thinking as well as scientific research in Europe and the United States. Deterministic (and what we today would call racist) views were held to some extent by most people, including such notable figures as Thomas Jefferson, Georges Cuvier, Benjamin Franklin, Charles Lyell, Abraham Lincoln, Charles Darwin, and Oliver Wendell Holmes. Commenting on this usually deemphasized characteristic of notable historical figures, Stephen J. Gould (1981, p. 32) emphasizes that "all American culture heroes embraced racial attitudes that would embarrass public-school mythmakers."

Francis Galton (1822–1911), a cousin of Charles Darwin, shared the increasingly common fear among Europeans that "civilized society" was being weakened by the failure of natural selection to eliminate unfit and inferior individuals (Greene, 1981, p. 107). Galton wrote and lectured on the necessity of "race improvement" and suggested government regulation of marriage and family size, an approach he called **eugenics**.

Although eugenics had its share of critics, its popularity flourished in the years following World War I and especially throughout the 1930s. The movement was increasingly popular in Europe and the United States, but nowhere was it more popular than in Germany, where the viewpoint took a disastrous turn. The idea of a "pure race" (see Issue, pp. 416–417) was increasingly extolled as a means of reestablishing a strong and prosperous state. Eugenics was seen as a scientific rationale for purging Germany of its "unfit," and many of Germany's scientists continued to support the policies of racial purity and eugenics during the Nazi period (Proctor, 1988, p. 143), when these policies served as justification for condemning millions of people to death.

But at the same time, many scientists were turning away from racial typologies and classification in favor of a more evolutionary approach. No doubt for some, this shift in direction was motivated by their growing concerns over the goals of the eugenics movement. Probably more important, however, was the synthesis of Mendelian genetics and Darwin's theories of natural selection during the 1930s. This breakthrough influenced all the biological sciences, and many physical anthropologists began to apply evolutionary principles to the study of human variation.

Biological determinism

The concept that phenomena, including various aspects of behavior (e.g., intelligence, values, morals) are governed by biological (genetic) factors; the inaccurate association of various behavioral attributes with certain biological traits, such as skin color.

Eugenics

The philosophy of "race improvement" through the forced sterilization of members of some groups and increased reproduction among others; an overly simplified, often racist view that is now discredited.

The Concept of Race

All contemporary humans are members of the same **polytypic** species, *Homo sapiens*. A polytypic species is one composed of local populations that differ with regard to the expression of one or more traits. Moreover, *within* local populations there is a great deal of phenotypic (and genotypic) variation between individuals.

In discussions of human variation, people have traditionally clumped together various attributes such as skin color, shape of the face, shape of the nose, hair color, hair form (curly, straight), and eye color. People possessing particular combinations of these and other traits have been placed together into categories associated with specific geographical localities. Such categories are called *races*.

We all think we know what we mean by the word *race*, but in truth, the term has had a wide assortment of meanings since it gained common usage in English in the 1500s. It has been used synonymously with *species*, as in "the human race," or to refer to a more limited grouping of individuals all descended from a single individual (e.g., "the race of Abraham").

Since the 1600s, race has also referred to various culturally defined groups, and this meaning still enjoys popular usage. For example, one hears "the English race" or "the Japanese race," where the reference is actually to nationality. Another often-heard phrase is "the Jewish race," when the speaker is really talking about a particular ethnic and religious identity.

Thus, while *race* is usually a term with biological connotations, it is also one with enormous social significance. Moreover, there is still a widespread perception that there is an association between certain physical traits (skin color, in particular) and numerous cultural attributes (such as language, occupational preferences, or even morality). Therefore, in many cultural contexts, a person's social identity is strongly influenced by the manner in which he or she expresses those physical traits traditionally used to define "racial groups." Characteristics such as skin color are highly visible, and they facilitate an immediate and superficial designation of individuals into socially defined categories. However, so-called racial traits are not the only phenotypic expressions that contribute to social identity. Sex and age are also critically important. But aside from these two variables, an individual's biological and/or ethnic background is still inevitably a factor that influences how he or she is initially perceived and judged by others.

References to national origin (e.g., African, Asian) as substitutes for racial labels have become more common in recent years, both within and outside anthropology. Within anthropology, the term *ethnicity* was proposed in the early 1950s as a means of avoiding the more emotionally charged term *race*. Strictly speaking, ethnicity refers to cultural factors, but the fact that the words *ethnicity* and *race* are used interchangeably reflects the social importance of phenotypic expression and demonstrates once again how phenotype is associated with culturally defined variables.

In its most common biological usage, the term *race* refers to geographically patterned phenotypic variation within a species. By the seventeenth century, naturalists had begun to describe races in plants and nonhuman animals, because they recognized that when populations of a species occupied different regions, they sometimes differed from one another in the expression of one or more traits. But even today, there are no established criteria by which races of plants and animals are to be assessed.

Prior to World War II, most studies of human variation focused on visible phenotypic variation between large, geographically defined populations, and these studies were largely descriptive. Since that time, the emphasis has shifted to the examination of differences in allele frequencies within and between populations, as well as the adaptive significance of phenotypic and genotypic variation. This shift in focus occurred partly as a result of the Modern Synthesis in biology (see p. 88), which was based on the recognition of the fundamental importance of the *interaction* of natural

Polytypic
Referring to species composed of populations that differ with regard to the expression of one or more traits.

race ↘ phenotype

selection and other factors, such as gene flow, mutation, and drift, to the processes of adaptation and evolution.

Application of evolutionary principles to the study of modern human variation has replaced the nineteenth-century view of race *based solely on observed phenotype.* Additionally, the genetic emphasis has dispelled previously held misconceptions that races are fixed biological entities that do not change over time and that are composed of individuals who all conform to a particular *type.*

Clearly, there are phenotypic differences between humans, and some of these differences roughly correspond to particular geographical locations. But certain questions must be asked: Is there any adaptive significance attached to observed phenotypic variation? Is genetic drift a factor? What is the degree of underlying genetic variation that influences it? These questions place considerations of human variation within a contemporary evolutionary framework.

Although, in part, physical anthropology has its roots in attempts to explain human diversity, anthropologists have never been in complete agreement on the topic of race. However, no contemporary scholar subscribes to pre-Darwinian and pre–Modern Synthesis concepts of races (human and nonhuman) as fixed biological entities. Among those who accept the validity of the race concept, there are various viewpoints. Many who continue to use broad racial categories do not view them as particularly important, especially from a genetic perspective, because the amount of genetic variation accounted for by differences *between* groups is vastly exceeded by the variation that exists *within* groups. But given these considerations, there are those who see variation in outwardly expressed phenotype, because of its potential to provide information on adaptation, genetic drift mutation, and gene flow, as worthy of investigation and explanation within the framework of evolutionary principles (Brues, 1991).

Forensic anthropologists in particular find the phenotypic criteria associated with race to have practical applications because they are frequently called on by law enforcement agencies to assist in the identification of human skeletal remains. Inasmuch as unidentified human remains are often those of crime victims, and their analysis may lead to courtroom testimony, identification must be as accurate as possible. The most important variables in such identification are the individual's sex, age, stature, and ancestry or "racial" and ethnic background. Using metric and nonmetric criteria, forensic anthropologists employ a number of techniques for establishing broad population affinity, and they are generally able to do so with about 80 percent accuracy.

On the other side of the issue, there are numerous physical anthropologists who argue that race is a meaningless concept when applied to humans. Race is seen as an outdated creation of the human mind that attempts to simplify biological complexity by organizing it into categories. Thus, human races are a product of the human tendency to superimpose order on complex natural phenomena. While classification may have been an acceptable approach some 150 years ago, it is viewed as no longer valid given the current state of genetic and evolutionary science.

Objections to racial taxonomies have also been raised because classification schemes are *typological* in nature, meaning that categories are discrete and based on stereotypes or ideals that comprise a specific set of traits. Thus, in general, typologies are inherently misleading, because there are always many individuals in any grouping who do not conform to all aspects of a particular type.

In any so-called racial group, there will be individuals who fall into the normal range of variation for another group with regard to one or several characteristics. For example, two people of different ancestry might vary with regard to skin color, but they could share any number of other traits, such as height, shape of head, hair color, eye color, or ABO blood type. In fact, they could easily share more similarities with each other than they do with many members of their own populations.

Moreover, as we have stressed, because the characteristics that have traditionally been used to define races are polygenic, they exhibit a continuous range of expression. It thus becomes difficult, if not impossible, to draw discrete boundaries between populations with regard to many traits. This limitation becomes clear if you ask yourself, "At what point is hair color no longer dark brown but medium brown, or no longer light brown but blond?"

The scientific controversy over race will diminish as we increase our understanding of the genetic diversity (and uniformity) of our species. Given the rapid changes in genome studies and the fact that very few genes contribute to outward expressions of phenotype, dividing the human species into racial categories is not a biologically meaningful way to look at human variation. But in spite of all the scientific discussion that has ensued, among the general public, variations on the theme of race will undoubtedly continue (at least for a while) to be the most common view of human biological and cultural variation. Given this fact, it falls to anthropologists and biologists to continue to explore the issue so that, to the best of our abilities, accurate information regarding human variation is available for anyone who seeks informed explanations of complex phenomena.

Contemporary Interpretations of Human Population Diversity

By the 1960s, the study of *clinal distributions* of individual polymorphic traits had become a popular alternative to the racial approach. As discussed in Chapter 14, a cline is a gradual change in the frequency of a single trait, or allele, in populations dispersed over geographical space. In humans, the various expressions of many polymorphic traits exhibit a more or less continuous distribution from one geographical region to another. The distribution of the *A* and *B* alleles in the Old World, discussed in Chapter 14, provides a good example of a clinal distribution (see Fig. 14–1, p. 377). Clinal distributions are generally thought to reflect microevolutionary influences of natural selection and/or gene flow. Thus, interpretations are explicitly framed in evolutionary terms.

Utilizing single traits can be informative regarding potential influences of natural selection or gene flow, but this approach has limitations when we try to sort out population relationships. As noted in our discussion of the HLA polymorphisms, single traits *by themselves* often can yield confusing interpretations regarding likely population relationships. What is needed, then, is a method to analyze a larger, more consistent body of data—that is, to look at several traits simultaneously. Such a *multivariate* approach makes ready use of digital computers.

An excellent example of the contemporary multivariate approach to human diversity was undertaken by Harvard population geneticist R. D. Lewontin (1972). Lewontin calculated population differences in allele frequency for 17 polymorphic traits. In his analysis, Lewontin immediately faced a dilemma: Which groups (populations) should he contrast, and how should they be weighted? That is, should larger population segments, such as Arabs, carry the same weight in the analysis as small populations, such as the one from the island Tristan da Cunha? Lewontin divided his sample into seven geographical areas, and he included several equally weighted population samples within each (Table 15–1). He then calculated how much of the total genetic variability within our species could be accounted for by these population subdivisions.

The results were surprising. Only 6.3 percent of the total genetic variation was explained by differences among major populations (Lewontin's seven geographical units). In other words, close to 94 percent of human genetic diversity occurs *within* these very large groups. The larger population subdivisions within the geographical

TABLE 15–1 Population Groupings Used by Lewontin in Population Genetics Study (1972)

Geographical Group	Examples of Populations Included
Caucasians	Arabs, Armenians, Tristan da Cunhans
Black Africans	Bantu, San, U.S. blacks
Asians	Ainu, Chinese, Turks
South Asians	Andamanese, Tamils
Amerinds	Aleuts, Navaho, Yanomama
Oceanians	Easter Islanders, Micronesians
Australians	All treated as a single group

clusters (e.g., within the category Caucasians: Arabs, Basques, Welsh) account for another 8.3 percent. Thus, geographical and local "races" together account for just 15 percent of all human genetic variation, leaving the remaining 85 percent unaccounted for. The vast majority of genetic differences among human beings is explicable in terms of differences from one village to another, one family to another, and, to a very significant degree, one person to another—even within the same family.

Our superficial visual perceptions tell us that race does exist. But the visible phenotypic traits most frequently used to make racial distinctions (skin color, hair form, nose shape, etc.) may very well produce a highly biased sample, not giving an accurate picture of the actual pattern of *genetic variation*. Simple polymorphic traits provide a more objective basis for accurate biological comparisons of human groups, and they indicate that the traditional concept of race is very limited. Indeed, Lewontin concludes his analysis with a ringing condemnation of traditional studies: "Human racial classification is of no social value and is positively destructive of social and human relations. Since such racial classification is now seen to be of virtually no genetic or taxonomic significance either, no justification can be offered for its continuance" (Lewontin, 1972, p. 397).

Analysis of mitochondrial DNA has produced similar results, especially showing greater genetic diversity among African populations than among other groups (Stoneking, 1993). Because mtDNA is passed solely through the maternal line (and thus does not undergo recombination), it provides certain advantages in reconstructing population relationships. Nevertheless, as a single genetic component, it acts like one large locus; thus, mtDNA results must be supplemented by other genetic data.

Comparative data from nuclear DNA studies (RFLPs or restriction fragment length polymorphisms; see Chapter 14) in conjunction with the studies discussed here are thus potentially illuminating. Initial analysis comparing 80 RFLPs in eight different groups (Mountain et al., 1993) again produced patterns quite similar to those established for the traditional polymorphisms and for mtDNA. And another recent large-scale study (Jia and Chakravarty, 1993) of DNA markers among 59 different groups (and including about 12,000 individuals) found the vast majority of variation (up to 98.5 percent) occurring *within* populations at the *individual* level. These latest data dramatize even further the results obtained by Lewontin, leading one geneticist to conclude, "These results indicate that individual variation in DNA profiles overwhelm any interpopulational differences, no matter how the populations are ethnically or racially classified" (Cummings, 1994, p. 500). And while not quite as overwhelming, *all* the genetically based studies cited here support Lewontin's initial results, strongly indicating that the great majority of human variation does occur within human populations—not between them.

Racism

The most detrimental outcome of biological determinism is racism. Racism is based on the false belief that such factors as intellect and various cultural attributes are inherited along with physical characteristics. Such beliefs also rest on the ethnocentric assumption that one's own group is superior to other groups.

Because we have already alluded to certain aspects of racism, such as the eugenics movement, notions of racial purity, and persecution of people based on racial or ethnic misconceptions, we will not belabor the point here. However, it is important to point out that racism is hardly a thing of the past, nor is it restricted to European and American whites. Racism is a cultural phenomenon, and it is found worldwide.

Ultimately, racism is one of the more dangerous aspects of human behavior because it frequently leads to violence, warfare, terrorism, and genocide. We have seen recent manifestations of racism in many cities in the United States. The rioting that occurred in Los Angeles in 1992 after the acquittal of white police officers accused of beating Rodney King, a black suspect, was a clear example of the tensions among the diverse populations of large urban centers. In the past few years, there has been an increase in racial slurs and hate speech on radio talk shows and, perhaps especially, on the Internet. Sadly, the twentieth century provided numerous examples of ethnic/racial conflict, but it is important to mention that while in some cases there may have been some phenotypic differences between these groups, virtually all these conflicts were due to *ethnic* differences between the participants. The unspeakable genocide of the Holocaust during World War II, in Cambodia in the 1970s, and in Rwanda in 1994; the tragedies of Bosnia, Croatia, and Kosovo; and then the devastating terrorist attacks on the United States on September 11, 2001, all bespeak the senseless outcomes of intolerance of groups we call "others," however we define the term.

What we observe when we see biological variations between populations (and individuals) are the traces of our evolutionary past. Different expressions of traits such as skin color, eye color, and shape of the face are the results of biological adaptations that human ancestors made to local environmental conditions in a process that began perhaps several hundred thousand years ago. Instead of using these differences as a basis for prejudice and persecution, we should recognize them for what they are: a preserved record of how evolutionary forces shaped our species to meet the varied environmental challenges it faced while expanding its geographical range over most of the planet.

We end this brief discussion of racism with an excerpt from an article, "The Study of Race," by Sherwood Washburn, a well-known physical anthropologist at the University of California, Berkeley. Although written almost 40 years ago, the statement is as fresh and applicable today as it was when it was written:

> Races are products of the past. They are relics of times and conditions which have long ceased to exist.
>
> Racism is equally a relic supported by no phase of modern science. We may not know how to interpret the form of the Mongoloid face, or why Rh is of high incidence in Africa, but we do know the benefits of education and of economic progress. We . . . know that the roots of happiness lie in the biology of the whole species and that the potential of the species can only be realized in a culture, in a social system. It is knowledge and the social system which give life or take it away, and in so doing change the gene frequencies and continue the million-year-old interaction of culture and biology. Human biology finds its realization in a culturally determined way of life, and the infinite variety of genetic combinations can only express themselves efficiently in a free and open society. (Washburn, 1963, p. 531)

Intelligence

As we have shown, belief in the relationship between phenotype and specific behavioral attributes is popular even today, but evidence is lacking that personality or any other behavioral trait differs genetically *between* human groups. Most scientists would agree with this last statement, but one question that has produced controversy both inside scientific circles and among laypeople is whether populations vary with regard to intelligence.

Both genetic and environmental factors contribute to intelligence, although it is not yet possible to measure accurately the percentage each contributes. What can be said is that IQ scores and intelligence are not the same thing; IQ scores can change during a person's lifetime, and average IQ scores of different populations overlap. Such differences in IQ scores as do exist between groups are difficult to interpret, given the problems inherent in the design of the IQ tests. Moreover, complex cognitive abilities, however measured, are influenced by multiple loci and are thus strikingly polygenic.

Innate factors set limits and define potentials for behavior and cognitive ability in any species. In humans, the limits are broad and the potentials are not fully known. Individual abilities result from complex interactions between genetic and environmental factors. One product of this interaction is learning, and the ability to learn has genetic or biological components. Undeniably, there are differences between individuals regarding these biological components. However, elucidating what proportion of the variation in test scores is due to biological factors probably is not possible. Moreover, innate differences in abilities reflect individual variation *within* populations, not inherent differences *between* groups. Comparing populations on the basis of IQ test results is a misuse of testing procedures, and there is no convincing evidence *whatsoever* that populations vary with regard to cognitive abilities, regardless of the assertions in some publications.

The Adaptive Significance of Human Variation

Today, physical anthropologists view human variation as the result of such evolutionary factors as genetic drift, founder effect, gene flow, and adaptation (through natural selection) to environmental conditions, both past and present. Although cultural adaptations have certainly played a vital role in the evolution of *Homo sapiens,* in this discussion we are primarily concerned with biological factors.

All organisms must maintain the normal functions of internal organs, tissues, and cells in order to survive, and this task must be accomplished within the context of an ever-changing environment. Even during the course of a single, seemingly uneventful day, there are numerous fluctuations in temperature, wind, solar radiation, humidity, and so on. Physical activity also places **stress** on physiological mechanisms. The body must accommodate all these changes by compensating in some manner to maintain internal constancy, or **homeostasis**, and all life forms have evolved physiological mechanisms that, within limits, achieve this goal.

Physiological response to environmental change is, to some degree, influenced by genetic factors. We have already defined adaptation as a functional response to environmental conditions in populations and individuals. In a narrower sense, adaptation refers to *long-term* evolutionary (i.e., genetic) changes that characterize all individuals within a population or species.

Examples of long-term adaptations in *Homo sapiens* include some physiological responses to heat (sweating) and deeply pigmented skin in tropical regions. Such characteristics are the results of evolutionary change in species or populations, and they do not vary as the result of short-term environmental change. For example, the ability to sweat is not lost in people who spend their lives in predominantly

Stress

In a physiological context, any factor that acts to disrupt homeostasis; more precisely, the body's response to any factor that threatens its ability to maintain homeostasis.

Homeostasis

A condition of balance, or stability, within a biological system, maintained by the interaction of physiological mechanisms that compensate for changes (both external and internal).

cool areas. Likewise, individuals born with deeply pigmented skin will not become pale, even if never exposed to intense sunlight.

Physiological response to a change in environmental conditions is called **acclimatization**. Tanning, which occurs in all people, is a form of short-term acclimatization. Another example is the very rapid increase in hemoglobin production that occurs when lowland natives travel to higher elevations. This increase provides the body with more oxygen in an environment where oxygen is less available. In both these examples, the physiological change is temporary. Tans fade once exposure to sunlight is reduced; and hemoglobin production drops to original levels on return to lower altitudes.

Developmental acclimatization results from exposure to an environmental challenge during a particular period of life, usually during growth. Because this type of acclimatization is incorporated into an individual's physiology, it is not reversible. An example of developmental acclimatization is the physiological responses observed in lifelong residents of high altitude (see p. 407).

In the following discussion, we present some examples of how humans respond to environmental challenges. Some of these examples illustrate adaptations that characterize the entire species. Others illustrate adaptations seen in only some populations. And still others illustrate the process of acclimatization.

Solar Radiation and Skin Color

Skin color is often cited as an example of adaptation and natural selection in human populations. In general, skin color in populations, especially prior to about 1500, follows a particular geographical distribution, especially in the Old World. Figure 15–1 illustrates that populations with the greatest amount of pigmentation are found in the tropics, while lighter skin color is associated with more northern latitudes, particularly the inhabitants of northwestern Europe.

Acclimatization

Physiological response to changes in the environment that occurs during an individual's lifetime. Such responses may be temporary or permanent. The *capacity* for acclimatization may typify an entire population or species. This capacity is under genetic influence and thus is subject to evolutionary factors such as natural selection.

FIGURE 15–1

Geographical distribution of skin color among the indigenous populations of the world. (After Biasutti, 1959.)

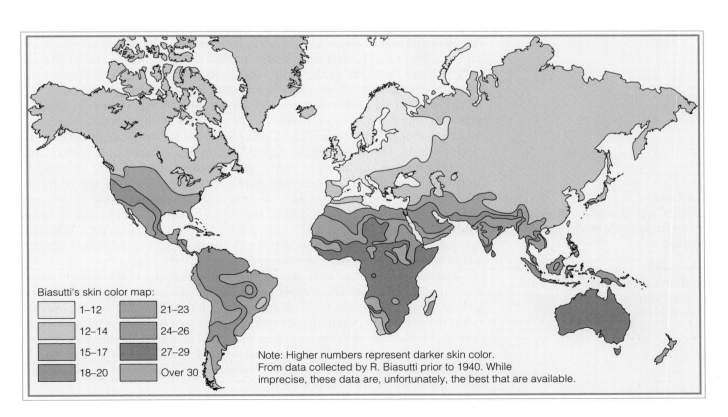

Biasutti's skin color map:

1–12	21–23
12–14	24–26
15–17	27–29
18–20	Over 30

Note: Higher numbers represent darker skin color. From data collected by R. Biasutti prior to 1940. While imprecise, these data are, unfortunately, the best that are available.

Norman Lightfoot/PhotoResearchers

FIGURE 15–2
An African albino. This young man has an
increased likelihood of developing skin cancer.

tan = acclimatization = melanin

See Virtual Lab 2, section IV
for an exercise on the adaptive significance of skin color.

not enough folate?
spina bifida

Neural tube
In early embryonic development, the anatomical
structure that develops to form the brain and
spinal cord.

Spina bifida
A condition in which the arch of one or several
vertebrae fails to fuse and form a protective
barrier around the spinal cord.

Skin color is influenced by three substances: hemoglobin, carotene, and, most important, the pigment *melanin*. Melanin is a granular substance produced by specialized cells in the epidermis called *melanocytes*. All humans appear to have approximately the same number of melanocytes. It is the amount of melanin and the size of melanin granules that vary.

Melanin has the capacity to absorb potentially dangerous ultraviolet (UV) rays that are present (although not visible) in sunlight. Because of this ability, melanin provides protection from overexposure to ultraviolet radiation, which can cause genetic mutations in skin cells. These mutations may ultimately lead to skin cancer, which, if left untreated, can eventually spread to other organs and result in death.

As already mentioned, exposure to sunlight triggers a protective mechanism in the form of temporarily increased melanin production (acclimatization). (The visible manifestation of this increase is a tan.) This protective response occurs in all humans except albinos, who carry a genetic mutation that prevents their melanocytes from producing melanin (Fig. 15–2). Moreover, tanning is limited in many fair-complexioned people of northern European descent who do produce small amounts of melanin, but have a reduced capacity for such temporary increases in melanin production.

Natural selection appears to have favored dark skin in areas nearest to the equator, where the sun's rays are most direct and thus where exposure to UV light is most intense. In considering the cancer causing effects of ultraviolet radiation from an *evolutionary* perspective, three points must be kept in mind: (1) Early hominids lived mostly in the tropics, where solar radiation is more intense than in temperate areas like northwestern Europe; (2) unlike modern city dwellers, most earlier hominids spent the majority of time outdoors; and (3) early hominids did not wear clothing that would have provided some protection from the sun. Given these conditions, ultraviolet radiation could indeed have been a powerful agent selecting for optimum levels of melanin production in early human ancestors.

One objection to this theory is that natural selection acts mainly on traits that affect reproduction. Because cancers tend to occur later in life, after the reproductive years, it should theoretically be difficult for selection to act effectively against any factor that might predispose people to cancer. But in one African study, it was demonstrated that all albino individuals in dark-skinned populations of Nigeria and Tanzania had either precancerous lesions or skin cancer by the age of 20 (Robins, 1991). Clearly, without medical care and protective clothing, the reproductive potential of these individuals is adversely affected by having depigmented skin.

Jablonski (1992; 2001) offers an additional explanation for the distribution of skin color, one that focuses on the role of UV radiation in the degradation of folate. Folate is a B vitamin that is not stored in the body and must be replenished through dietary sources. Folate deficiencies in pregnant women are associated with numerous complications, including maternal death, and in children they can lead to growth retardation and other serious conditions. Folate also plays a crucial role in **neural tube** development very early in embryonic development, and in this context, deficiencies can lead to defects that include various expressions of **spina bifida**. The consequences of severe neural tube defects can include pain, infection, paralysis, and even death. It goes without saying that neural tube defects can dramatically reduce the reproductive success of affected individuals.

A number of studies have shown that UV radiation rapidly depletes folate serum levels both in laboratory experiments and in light-skinned individuals. These findings have implications for pregnant women and children and also for the evolution of dark skin in hominids. Jablonski proposes that the earliest hominids may have had light body skin covered with dark hair, as is seen in chimpanzees and gorillas (who have darker skin on exposed body parts). But as loss of body hair in hominids occurred, dark skin evolved rather quickly as a protective response to the damaging effects of UV radiation on folate.

As hominids migrated out of Africa into Europe and Asia, selective pressures changed. In particular, those populations that eventually occupied northern Europe encountered cold temperatures and cloudy skies sometimes during the summer as well as in winter. Winter also meant fewer hours of daylight, and with the sun well to the south, solar radiation was indirect. Moreover, since physiological adaptations were not sufficient to meet the demands of living in colder climates, these populations had undoubtedly adopted certain cultural practices, such as using fire and wearing animal skins and other types of clothing. As a consequence of reduced exposure to sunlight, the advantages provided by deeply pigmented skin in the tropics were no longer important, and selection for melanin production may have been relaxed (Brace and Montagu, 1977).

However, relaxed selection for dark skin is probably not adequate to explain the very depigmented skin seen especially in some northern Europeans. Perhaps another factor, the need for adequate amounts of vitamin D, was also critical. The theory concerning the possible role of vitamin D, known as the *vitamin D hypothesis,* offers the following explanation.

Vitamin D plays a vital role in the mineralization and normal growth of bone during infancy and childhood and is available in a few foods, including fish oils, egg yolk, butter, cream, and liver. But the body's primary source of vitamin D is its own ability to synthesize it through the interaction of UV light and a cholesterol-like substance found in skin cells. Therefore, if normal bone growth is to occur, adequate exposure to sunlight is essential. Insufficient amounts of vitamin D during childhood result in *rickets,* which leads to bone deformities throughout the skeleton, especially the weight-bearing bones of the lower extremity and pelvis. Thus, people with rickets frequently have bowed legs and pelvic deformities. Pelvic deformities are of particular concern for women, for they can lead to a narrowing of the birth canal, which, in the absence of surgical intervention, frequently results in the death of both mother and fetus during childbirth. This example illustrates the potential for rickets as a significant selective factor favoring less pigmented skin in regions where climate and other factors operate to reduce exposure to UV radiation.

In the past, reduced exposure to sunlight would have been detrimental to darker-skinned individuals in more northern latitudes. In these individuals, higher concentrations of melanin filtered out much of the UV radiation that was available. If, in addition, the diets of groups that came to inhabit northern Europe did not provide adequate amounts of vitamin D, selective pressures would have shifted even further over time to favor less pigmented skin.

There is substantial evidence, both historically and in contemporary populations, to support the vitamin D hypothesis. During the latter decades of the nineteenth century, black inhabitants of northern U.S. cities suffered a higher incidence of rickets than whites. Northern blacks were also more commonly affected than blacks living in the South, where exposure to sunlight is greater. (The supplementation of milk with vitamin D was initiated to alleviate this problem.) Another example is seen in Britain, where darker-skinned East Indians and Pakistanis show a higher incidence of rickets than whites (Molnar, 1983).

Perhaps more social importance has been attached to variation in skin color than to any other single human biological trait. In point of fact, there is no reason this should be so. Aside from its probable adaptive significance relative to UV radiation, skin color is no more important physiologically than many other biological characteristics. But from an evolutionary perspective, skin color provides an outstanding example of how the forces of natural selection have produced geographically patterned variation as the consequence of two conflicting selective forces: the need for protection from overexposure to UV radiation, on the one hand, and the need for adequate UV exposure for vitamin D synthesis on the other.

The Thermal Environment

Mammals and birds have evolved complex mechanisms to maintain a constant internal body temperature. While reptiles must rely on exposure to external heat sources to raise body temperature and energy levels, mammals and birds possess physiological mechanisms that, within certain limits, increase or reduce the loss of body heat. The optimum body temperature for normal cellular functions is species-specific, and for humans it is approximately 98.6°F.

Homo sapiens is found in a wide variety of habitats, with thermal environments ranging from exceedingly hot (in excess of 120°F) to bitter cold (less than −60°F). In such extremes, particularly cold, human life would not be possible without cultural innovations. But even accounting for the artificial environments in which we live, such external conditions place the human body under enormous stress.

Response to Heat   All available evidence suggests that the earliest hominids evolved in the warm-to-hot savannas of East Africa. The fact that humans cope better with heat (especially dry heat) than they do with cold is testimony to the long-term adaptations to heat that evolved in our ancestors.

In humans, as well as certain other species, such as horses, sweat glands are distributed throughout the skin. This wide distribution of sweat glands makes possible the loss of heat at the body surface through evaporative cooling, a mechanism that has evolved to the greatest degree in humans. Indeed, perspiration is the most important factor in heat dissipation in humans.

The capacity to dissipate heat by sweating is seen in all human populations to an almost equal degree, with the average number of sweat glands per individual (approximately 1.6 million) being fairly constant. However, there is variation in that persons not generally exposed to hot conditions do experience a period of acclimatization that initially involves significantly increased perspiration rates (Frisancho, 1993). An additional factor that enhances the cooling effects of sweating is increased exposure of the skin through reduced amounts of body hair. We do not know when in our evolutionary history loss of body hair began, but it represents a species-wide adaptation.

Heat reduction through evaporation can be expensive, and indeed dangerous, in terms of water and sodium loss. Up to 3 liters of water can be lost per hour by an average human engaged in heavy work in high heat. The importance of this fact can be appreciated if you consider that the loss of 1 liter of water is approximately equivalent to losing 1.5 percent of total body weight, and loss of 10 percent of body weight can be life threatening. Therefore, it is essential that water be continuously replaced during exercise in heat.

There are two basic types of heat, arid and humid. Arid environments, such as those of the southwestern United States and parts of East and South Africa, are characterized by high temperatures, wind, and low water vapor. Humid heat is associated with increased water vapor and is found in regions with a great deal of vegetation and precipitation, typical of the eastern and southern United States, parts of Europe, and much of the tropics. Because the increased water vapor in humid climates inhibits the evaporation of sweat on the skin's surface, humans adjust much more readily to dry heat. In fact, people exercising in dry heat may be unaware that they are perspiring because the perspiration evaporates as soon as it reaches the surface of the skin. Although this rapid evaporation increases comfort, it can also lead to dehydration unless these individuals continue to drink water, even if they are not conscious of how much water they are actually losing.

Another mechanism for radiating body heat is **vasodilation**, whereby capillaries near the skin's surface widen to permit increased blood flow to the skin. The visible effect of vasodilation is flushing, or increased redness of the skin, particularly of the face, accompanied by warmth. But the physiological effect is to permit heat, carried

Vasodilation
Expansion of blood vessels, permitting increased blood flow to the skin. Vasodilation permits warming of the skin and also facilitates radiation of warmth as a means of cooling. Vasodilation is an involuntary response to warm temperatures, various drugs, and even emotional states (blushing).

acclimatization—non-sweaters sweat

by the blood from the interior of the body, to be emitted from the skin's surface to the surrounding air. (Some drugs, including alcohol, also produce vasodilation, which accounts for the increased redness and warmth of the face in some people.)

Body size and proportions are also important in regulating body temperature. In fact, there seems to be a general relationship between climate and body size and shape in birds and mammals. In general, within a species, body size (weight) increases as distance from the equator increases. In humans, this relationship holds up fairly well, but there are numerous exceptions.

Two rules that pertain to the relationship between body size, body proportions, and climate are *Bergmann's rule* and *Allen's rule*.

1. *Bergmann's rule (concerning the relationship of body mass or volume to surface area):* Among mammals, body size tends to be greater in populations that live in colder climates. This is because as mass increases, the relative amount of surface area decreases proportionately. Because heat is lost at the surface, it follows that increased mass allows for greater heat retention and reduced heat loss.

2. *Allen's rule (concerning shape of body, especially appendages):* In colder climates, shorter appendages, with increased mass-to-surface ratios, are adaptive because they are more effective at preventing heat loss. Conversely, longer appendages, with increased surface area relative to mass, are more adaptive in warmer climates because they promote heat loss.

According to these rules, the most suitable body shape in hot climates is linear with long arms and legs. In a cold climate, a more suitable body type is stocky with shorter limbs. Considerable data gathered from several human populations generally conform to these principles. In colder climates, body mass tends, on average, to be greater and characterized by a larger trunk relative to arms and legs (Roberts, 1973). People living in the Arctic tend to be short and stocky, while many sub-Saharan Africans, especially the East African pastoralists, are tall and linear (Fig. 15–3). But there is much human variability regarding body proportions, and not all populations conform so obviously to Bergmann's and Allen's rules.

(a)

(b)

FIGURE 15–3
(a) This African woman has the linear proportions characteristic of many inhabitants of sub-Saharan Africa. (b) By comparison, the Inuit woman is short and stocky. These two individuals serve as good examples of Bergmann's and Allen's rules.

Human Variation and Adaptation

Vasoconstriction
Narrowing of blood vessels to reduce blood flow to the skin. Vasoconstriction is an involuntary response to cold and reduces heat loss at the skin's surface.

eating makes heat, higher metab

more cold higher metabolism

Response to Cold   Human physiological responses to cold increase heat production and enhance heat retention. Of the two, heat retention is more efficient because less energy is required. This is an important point because energy is derived from dietary sources. Unless food resources are abundant, and in winter they frequently are not, any factor that conserves energy can have adaptive value.

Short-term responses to cold include increased metabolic rate and shivering, both of which generate body heat, at least for a short time. **Vasoconstriction**, another short-term response, restricts heat loss and conserves energy. In addition, humans possess a subcutaneous (beneath the skin) fat layer that serves as insulation throughout the body. Behavioral modifications include increased activity, increased food consumption, and assuming a curled-up position.

Increases in metabolic rate (the rate at which cells break up nutrients into their components) release energy in the form of heat. Shivering also generates muscle heat, as does voluntary exercise. But these methods of heat production are expensive because they require an increased intake of nutrients to provide needed energy. (Perhaps this explains why we tend to have a heartier appetite during the winter and why we also tend to increase our intake of fats and carbohydrates, the very sources of energy our bodies require.)

In general, people exposed to chronic cold (meaning much or most of the year) maintain higher metabolic rates than those living in warmer climates. The Inuit (Eskimo) people living in the Arctic maintain metabolic rates between 13 and 45 percent higher than observed in non-Inuit control subjects (Frisancho, 1993). Moreover, the highest metabolic rates are seen in inland Inuit, who are exposed to even greater cold stress than coastal populations. Traditionally, the Inuit had the highest animal protein and fat diet of any population in the world. Such a diet, necessitated by the available resource base, served to maintain the high metabolic rates required by exposure to chronic cold.

Vasoconstriction restricts capillary blood flow to the surface of the skin, thus reducing heat loss at the body surface. Because retaining body heat is more economical than creating it, vasoconstriction is very efficient, provided temperatures do not drop below freezing. However, if temperatures do fall below freezing, continued vasoconstriction can allow the skin temperature to decrease to the point of frostbite or worse.

Long-term responses to cold vary among human groups. For example, in the past, desert-dwelling native Australian populations were subjected to wide temperature fluctuations from day to night. As they wore no clothing and did not build shelters, their only protection from nighttime temperatures that hovered only a few degrees above freezing was provided by sleeping fires. They experienced continuous vasoconstriction throughout the night that permitted a degree of skin cooling most people would find extremely uncomfortable. But there was no threat of frostbite, and continued vasoconstriction helped prevent excessive internal heat loss.

By contrast, the Inuit experience intermittent periods of vasoconstriction and vasodilation. This compromise provides periodic warmth to the skin that helps prevent frostbite in below-freezing temperatures. At the same time, because vasodilation is intermittent, energy loss is restricted, with more heat retained at the body's core.

The preceding examples illustrate but two of the many ways in which human populations vary with regard to adaptation to cold. Although all humans respond to cold stress in much the same manner, there is variation in how adaptation and acclimatization are manifested.

High Altitude

Today, perhaps as many as 25 million people live at altitudes above 10,000 feet. In Tibet, permanent settlements exist above 15,000 feet, and in the Andes, they can be found as high as 17,000 feet (Fig. 15–4).

(a)

Courtesy, William Pratt

Courtesy, L.G. Moore

(b)

At such altitudes, multiple factors produce stress on the human body. These include **hypoxia** (reduced available oxygen), more intense solar radiation, cold, low humidity, wind (which amplifies cold stress), a reduced nutritional base, and rough terrain. Of these, hypoxia exerts the greatest amount of stress on human physiological systems, especially the heart, lungs, and brain.

Hypoxia results from reduced barometric pressure. It is not that there is less oxygen in the atmosphere at high altitudes; rather, it is less concentrated. Therefore, to obtain the same amount of oxygen at 9,000 feet as at sea level, people must make certain physiological alterations aimed at increasing the body's ability to transport and utilize efficiently the oxygen that is available.

People who reside at higher elevations, especially recent immigrants, display a number of manifestations of their hypoxic environment. Reproduction, in particular, is affected through increased rates of infant mortality, miscarriage, and prematurity. In Colorado, for example, infant deaths are nearly twice as common above 8,200 feet (2,500 m) as at lower elevations. Low birth weight is also more common and is attributed to decreased fetal growth due to impaired maternal-fetal transport of oxygen (Moore and Regensteiner, 1983).

High-altitude natives and nonnatives exhibit certain differences in acclimatization and adaptation to hypoxia. *Acclimatization* occurs upon exposure to high altitude in people born at low elevation. The responses may be short-term modifications, depending on duration of stay, but they begin within hours of the altitude change. These changes include an increase in respiration rate, heart rate, and production of red blood cells. (Red blood cells contain hemoglobin, the protein responsible for transporting oxygen to organs and tissues.)

Developmental acclimatization occurs in high-altitude natives during growth and development. (Note that this type of acclimatization is present only in people who grow up in high-altitude areas, not in those who moved there as adults.) Compared to populations at lower elevations, lifelong residents of high altitude display slowed growth and maturation. Other differences include larger chest size, associated, in turn, with greater lung volume and larger hearts. In addition to greater lung capacity, people born at high altitudes are more efficient than migrants at diffusing oxygen from blood to body tissues. Hence, they do not rely

FIGURE 15–4
(a) La Paz, Bolivia, at just over 12,000 feet above sea level, is home to more than 1 million people. (b) A household in northern Tibet, situated at an elevation of over 15,000 feet above sea level.

Hypoxia
Lack of oxygen. Hypoxia can refer to reduced amounts of available oxygen in the atmosphere (due to lowered barometric pressure) or to insufficient amounts of oxygen in the body.

407

as heavily on increased red cell formation as do newcomers. Developmental acclimatization to high-altitude hypoxia serves as a good example of physiological plasticity by illustrating how, within the limits set by genetic factors, development can be influenced by environment.

There is evidence that some *populations* have also genetically adapted to high altitudes. Indigenous peoples of Tibet who have inhabited regions higher than 12,000 feet for around 25,000 years may have made genetic (i.e., evolutionary) accommodations to hypoxia. Altitude does not appear to affect reproduction in these people to the degree it does in other populations. Infants have birth weights as high as those of lowland Tibetan groups and higher than those of recent (20 to 30 years) Chinese immigrants. This fact may be the result of alterations in maternal blood flow to the uterus during pregnancy (Moore et al., 1994).

Another line of evidence concerns the utilization of glucose (blood sugar). Glucose is critical because it is the only source of energy used by the brain, and it is also utilized, although not exclusively, by the heart. Both highland Tibetans and the Quechua (inhabitants of high-altitude regions of the Peruvian Andes) burn glucose in a way that permits more efficient use of oxygen. This implies the presence of genetic mutations in the mitochondrial DNA that directs how cells use glucose. It also implies that natural selection has acted to increase the frequency of these advantageous mutations in these groups.

There is no certain evidence that Tibetans and Quechua have made evolutionary changes to accommodate high-altitude hypoxia. Moreover, the genetic mechanisms that underlie these populations' unique abilities have not been identified. The new data are intriguing, however, and strongly suggest that selection has operated to produce evolutionary change in these two groups. If further study supports these findings, we have an excellent example of evolution in action producing long-term adaptation at the population level.

Infectious Disease

Infection, as opposed to other disease categories, such as degenerative or genetic disease, is a category that includes those pathological conditions caused by microorganisms (viruses, bacteria, and fungi). Throughout the course of human evolution, infectious disease has exerted enormous selective pressures on populations and thus has influenced the frequency of certain alleles that affect the immune response. Indeed, it would be difficult to overemphasize the importance of infectious disease as an agent of natural selection in human populations. But as important as infectious disease has been, its role in this regard is not very well documented.

The effects of infectious disease on humans are mediated culturally as well as biologically. Innumerable cultural factors, such as architectural styles, subsistence techniques, exposure to domesticated animals, even religious practices, all affect how infectious disease develops and persists within and between populations.

Until about 10,000 to 12,000 years ago, all humans lived in small nomadic hunting and gathering groups. As these groups rarely remained in one location more than a few days at a time, they had minimal contact with refuse heaps that house disease **vectors.** But with the domestication of plants and animals, people became more sedentary and began living in small villages. Gradually, villages became towns, and towns, in turn, developed into densely crowded, unsanitary cities.

As long as humans lived in small bands, there was little opportunity for infectious disease to have much impact on large numbers of people. Even if an entire local group or band were wiped out, the effect on the overall population in a given area would have been negligible. Moreover, for a disease to become **endemic** in a

See Virtual Lab 2, section III for a discussion of the human adaptive response to malaria.

Vectors
Agents that serve to transmit disease from one carrier to another. Mosquitoes are vectors for malaria, just as fleas are vectors for bubonic plague.

Endemic
Continuously present in a population.

population, sufficient numbers of people must be present. Therefore, small bands of hunter-gatherers were not faced with continuous exposure to endemic disease.

But with the advent of settled living and association with domesticated animals, opportunities for disease increased. As sedentary life permitted larger group size, it became possible for some diseases to become permanently established in some populations. Moreover, exposure to domestic animals, such as cattle, provided an opportune environment for the spread of such maladies as tuberculosis. The crowded, unsanitary conditions that characterized parts of all cities until the late nineteenth century and that persist in much of the world today further added to the disease burden borne by human inhabitants.

sendentism disease

Malaria provides perhaps the best-documented example of how disease can act to change allele frequencies in human populations. In Chapter 4, you saw how malaria has operated in some African and Mediterranean populations to alter allele frequencies at the locus governing hemoglobin formation. In spite of extensive long-term eradication programs, malaria still poses a serious threat to human health. Indeed, the World Health Organization estimates the number of people currently infected with malaria to be between 300 and 500 million worldwide. This number is increasing, also, as drug-resistant strains of the disease-causing microorganism become more common (Olliaro et al., 1995).

Another example of the selective role of infectious disease is indirectly provided by AIDS (acquired immune deficiency syndrome). In the United States, the first cases of AIDS were reported in 1981. Since that time, perhaps as many as 1.5 million people have been infected by HIV (human immunodeficiency virus), the agent that causes AIDS. However, most of the burden of AIDS is borne by developing countries, where 95 percent of all HIV-infected people live. Worldwide, an estimated 40 million people are living with HIV infection, and an estimated 20 million have died. In 2001 alone, there were 5 million new infections worldwide.

HIV is transmitted from person to person through the exchange of bodily fluids, usually blood or semen. It is not spread through casual contact with an infected person. Within six months of infection, most persons test positive for anti-HIV antibodies, meaning that their immune system has recognized the presence of foreign antigens and has responded by producing antibodies. However, serious HIV-related symptoms may not appear for years. HIV is a "slow virus" in that it may persist in a host's body for years before the onset of severe illness. This asymptomatic state is called a "latency period," and the average latency period in the United States is more than 11 years.

Like all viruses, HIV must invade certain types of cells and alter the functions of those cells to produce more virus particles in a process that eventually leads to cell destruction. (The manner in which HIV accomplishes this task is different from that of many other viruses.) HIV can attack various types of cells, but it especially targets so-called T4 helper cells, which are major components of the immune system. As HIV infection spreads and T4 cells are destroyed, the patient's immune system begins to fail. Consequently, he or she begins to exhibit symptoms caused by various **pathogens** that are commonly present but usually kept in check by a normal immune response. When an HIV-infected person's T cell count drops to a level that indicates immune suppression, and when symptoms of "opportunistic" infections appear, the patient is said to have AIDS.

Pathogens
Substances or microorganisms, such as bacteria, fungi, or viruses, that cause disease.

By the early 1990s, scientists were aware of a number of patients who had been HIV positive for 10 to 15 years, but who continued to show few if any symptoms. Awareness of these patients led researchers to suspect that some individuals possess a natural immunity or resistance to HIV infection. This was shown to be true in late 1996 with the publication of two different studies (Dean et al., 1996; Samson et al., 1996) that demonstrated a mechanism for resistance to HIV.

These two reports describe a genetic mutation that concerns a major protein "receptor site" on the surface of certain immune cells, including T4 cells. (Receptor sites are protein molecules that enable HIV and other viruses to invade cells.) In this particular situation, the mutant allele results in a malfunctioning receptor site to which HIV is unable to bind, and current evidence now strongly suggests that individuals who are homozygous for this allele may be completely resistant to many types of HIV infection. In heterozygotes, infection may still occur, but the course of HIV disease is markedly slowed.

Interestingly, and for unknown reasons, the mutant allele occurs mainly in people of European descent, among whom its frequency is about 10 percent. Samson and colleagues (1996) reported that in the Japanese and West African samples they studied, the mutation was absent, but Dean and colleagues (1996) reported an allele frequency of about 2 percent among African Americans. These researchers speculate that the presence of the allele in African Americans may be entirely due to genetic admixture (gene flow) with European Americans. Moreover, they suggest that this polymorphism exists in Europeans as a result of selective pressures favoring an allele that originally occurred as a rare mutation. But, it is critical to note, the original selective agent was *not* HIV. Instead, it was some other, as yet unidentified pathogen that requires the same receptor site as HIV. Researchers may be close to identifying which pathogen, or group of pathogens, it was. In December 1999, a group of scientists reported that the myxoma poxvirus, which is related to the virus that causes smallpox, can use the same receptor site as HIV. These authors (Lalani et al., 1999) suggest that the agent that selected for the altered form of the receptor site may have been smallpox. While this conclusion has not yet been proved, or even really investigated, it offers an exciting avenue of research with the possibility of revealing how a mutation that has been favored by selection because it provides protection against one disease can increase resistance to another malady (AIDS) as well.

Examples such AIDS and the relationship between malaria and sickle-cell anemia are continuously revealing new insights into the complex interactions between disease organisms and their host populations. These insights in turn provide a growing basis for understanding the many variations between individuals and populations that have arisen as adaptive responses to infectious disease.

Smallpox, once a deadly viral disease, may provide a good example of how exposure to infectious agents can produce polymorphisms in host populations. During the eighteenth century, smallpox is estimated to have accounted for 10 to 15 percent of all deaths in parts of Europe. But today, this once devastating killer is the only condition to have been successfully eliminated by modern medical technology. By 1977, through massive vaccination programs, the World Health Organization was able to declare the smallpox virus extinct, except for a few colonies in research labs in the United States and Russia.*

Smallpox had a higher incidence in persons with either blood type A or AB than in type O individuals, a fact that has been explained by the presence of an antigen on the smallpox virus that is similar to the A antigen. It follows that when some type A individuals were exposed to smallpox, their immune systems failed to recognize the virus as foreign and thus did not mount an adequate immune response. Consequently, in regions where smallpox was common in the past, it could have altered allele frequencies at the ABO locus by selecting against the *A* allele.

---

*Concern over the potential use of the smallpox virus by bioterrorists relates to these laboratory colonies. Although the virus is extinct outside these labs, some officials fear the possibility that samples of the virus could be stolen. Also, there are apparently some concerns that unknown colonies of the virus may exist in labs in countries other than Russia and the United States. The use of disease organisms against enemies is not new. In the Middle Ages, the corpses of smallpox and plague victims were catapulted into towns under siege, and during the U.S. colonial period, British soldiers knowingly gave Native Americans blankets from smallpox victims.

The Continuing Impact of Infectious Disease

It is important to realize that humans and pathogens exert selective pressures on each other, creating a dynamic relationship between disease organisms and their human (and nonhuman) hosts. Just as disease exerts selective pressures on host populations to adapt, microorganisms also evolve and adapt to various pressures exerted on them by their hosts.

Evolutionarily speaking, it is to the advantage of any pathogen not to be so virulent as to kill its host too quickly. If the host dies shortly after becoming infected, the viral or bacterial agent may not have time to reproduce and infect other hosts. Thus, selection sometimes acts to produce resistance in host populations and/or to reduce the virulence of disease organisms, to the benefit of both. However, hosts exposed for the first time to a new disease frequently die in huge numbers. Such exposure was a major factor in the decimation of indigenous New World populations after contact with Europeans introduced smallpox into Native American groups. And this has been the case with the current worldwide spread of HIV.

Of the known disease-causing organisms, HIV provides the best-documented example of evolution and adaptation in a pathogen. It is also one of several examples of interspecies transfer of infection. For these reasons, we focus much of this discussion of evolutionary factors and infectious disease on HIV and AIDS.

HIV is the most mutable and genetically variable virus known. The type of HIV responsible for the AIDS epidemic is HIV-1, which in turn is divided into three major subtypes comprising at least 10 different varieties that vary genetically from one population to another (Hu et al., 1996; Gao, 1999). Another far less common type is HIV-2, which is present only in populations of West Africa. HIV-2 also exhibits a wide range of genetic diversity, and while some strains cause AIDS, others are far less virulent.

Since the late 1980s, researchers have been comparing the DNA sequences of HIV and a closely related retrovirus called *simian immunodeficiency virus (SIV)*. SIV is found in chimpanzees and several African monkey species. Like HIV, SIV is genetically variable, and each strain appears to be specific to a given species and even subspecies of primate. SIV produces no symptoms in the African monkeys and chimpanzees that are its traditional hosts, but when injected into Asian monkeys, it eventually causes immune suppression, AIDS-like symptoms, and death. These findings indicate that the various forms of SIV have shared a long evolutionary history (perhaps several hundred thousand years) with a number of African primate species and that the latter are able to accommodate this virus, which is deadly to their Asian relatives. Moreover, these results substantiate long-held hypotheses that SIV and HIV evolved in Africa.

Comparisons of the DNA sequences of HIV-2 and the form of SIV found in one monkey species (the sooty mangabey) revealed that, genetically, these two viruses are almost identical. These findings led to the generally accepted conclusion that HIV-2 evolved from sooty mangabey SIV. Moreover, sooty mangabeys are hunted for food and also kept as pets in West central Africa, and the transmission of SIV to humans probably occurred through bites and the butchering of monkey carcasses.

But although the origin of HIV-2 was established, there was continuing debate over which primate species had been the source of HIV-1. Recently, a group of medical researchers (Gao et al., 1999) compared DNA sequences of HIV-1 and the form of SIV found in chimpanzees indigenous to West central Africa. The results of this research have demonstrated that HIV-1 almost certainly evolved from the strain of chimpanzee SIV that infects the subspecies *Pan troglodytes troglodytes,* which is indigenous to central Africa.

Unfortunately for both species, chimpanzees are routinely hunted by humans for food in parts of West Africa (see Issue, Chapter 5). Consequently, the most probable explanation for the transmission of SIV from chimpanzees to humans was, as with sooty mangabeys, the hunting and butchering of chimpanzees (Gao et al., 1999; Weiss and Wrangham, 1999). The DNA evidence further suggests that there were at least three separate human exposures to chimpanzee SIV, and at some point the virus was altered to the form we call HIV. When chimpanzee SIV was transmitted to humans is unknown. The oldest evidence of human infection is a frozen HIV-positive blood sample taken from a West African patient in 1959. There are also a few documented cases of AIDS infection by the late 1960s and early 1970s. Therefore, although human exposure to SIV/HIV probably occurred many times in the past, the virus did not become firmly established in humans until the latter half of the twentieth century.

From this SIV/HIV example, you can appreciate how, through the adoption of various cultural practices, humans have radically altered patterns of infectious disease. Here, then, is another example of biocultural evolution in our species. The interaction of cultural and biological factors has influenced microevolutionary change in humans (as in the example of sickle-cell anemia) to accommodate altered relationships with disease organisms.

Until the twentieth century, infectious disease was the number one cause of death in all human populations. Even today, in many developing countries, as much as half the mortality is due to infectious disease, compared to about 10 percent in the United States. In the United States and other developed nations, with improved living conditions and sanitation and especially with the widespread use of antibiotics beginning in the late 1940s, infectious disease gave way to heart disease and cancer as the leading causes of death.

Optimistic predictions held that infectious disease would be a thing of the past in developed countries and, with the introduction of antibiotics and improved living standards, in developing nations as well. But by the mid-1980s, such predictions were increasingly seen to be wrong. Between 1980 and 1992, the number of deaths in the United States in which infectious disease was the underlying cause rose from 41 to 65 per 100,000, an increase of 58 percent (Pinner et al., 1996). During that same period, there was a 25 percent increase in infectious disease mortality among people aged 65 and older, from 271 to 338 per 100,000. And deaths due to respiratory tract infections rose from 25 to 30 deaths per 100,000.

Additionally, AIDS contributed substantially to the increase in mortality due to infectious disease in the United States between 1980 and 1992. By 1992, AIDS was the leading cause of death in men aged 25 to 44 years. As of 1998, mortality due to AIDS had decreased significantly, but even when subtracting the effect of AIDS in mortality rates, there was still a 22 percent increase in mortality rates due to infectious disease between 1980 and 1992 (Pinner et al., 1996).

Increase in the prevalence of infectious disease is perhaps partly due to the overuse of antibiotics. It is estimated that half of all antibiotics prescribed in the United States are used to treat viral conditions such as colds and flu. Because antibiotics are completely ineffective against viruses, such therapy not only is useless, but may also have dangerous long-term consequences. There is a growing concern in the biomedical community over the indiscriminate use of antibiotics and pesticides since the 1950s. Antibiotics have exerted selective pressures on bacterial species that have, over time, developed antibiotic-resistant strains (an excellent example of natural selection). Consequently, the past few years have seen the *reemergence* of many bacterial diseases, including influenza, pneumonia, tuberculosis, and cholera, in forms that are less responsive to treatment.

Tuberculosis is now listed as the world's leading killer of adults by the World Health Organization (Colwell, 1996). In fact, the number of tuberculosis cases has risen 28 percent since the mid-1980s worldwide, with an estimated 10 million infected in the United States alone. Although not all infected persons develop active disease, an estimated 30 million are believed to have died from TB in the 1990s worldwide. One very troubling aspect of the increase in tuberculosis infection is that newly developed strains of *Mycobacterium tuberculosis,* the bacterium that causes TB, are resistant to antibiotics and other treatments.

Cholera, a dangerous and often fatal gastrointestinal disease caused by *Vibrio cholerae,* a bacterium found in sewage-contaminated water, has periodically occurred in epidemic proportions throughout history, including outbreaks in the nineteenth century in New York, Philadelphia, and London. Currently, cholera claims about 100,000 lives annually in Asia alone, and an antibiotic-resistant strain, first identified in India in 1992, is spreading throughout Southeast Asia. Recent cholera outbreaks throughout much of South America, India, Bangladesh, China, and parts of Southeast Asia have been partly attributed to rising ocean temperatures, lack of sanitation, and overcrowding.

Various treatments for nonbacterial conditions have also become ineffective. One such example is the appearance of chloroquin-resistant malaria, which has rendered chloroquin (the traditional preventive medication) virtually useless in some parts of Africa. And many insect species have developed resistance to commonly used pesticides.

In addition to threats posed by resistant strains of pathogens, there are other factors that may contribute to the emergence (or reemergence) of infectious disease. Scientists are becoming increasingly concerned over the potential for global warming to expand the geographical range of numerous tropical disease vectors, such as mosquitoes. And the destruction of natural environments not only contributes to global warming; it also has the potential of causing disease vectors formerly restricted to local areas to spread to new habitats.

One other factor associated with the rapid spread of disease and directly related to technological change is the mixing of people at an unprecedented rate. Indeed, an estimated 1 million people per day cross national borders by air (Lederberg, 1996)! In addition, new road construction and wider availability of motor-driven vehicles allow more people (armies, refugees, truck drivers, etc.) to travel farther and faster than ever before.

Fundamental to all these factors is human population size, which, as it continues to soar, causes more environmental disturbance and, through additional human activity, adds further to global warming. Moreover, in developing countries, where as much as 50 percent of mortality is due to infectious disease, overcrowding and unsanitary conditions increasingly contribute to increased rates of communicable illness. One could scarcely conceive of a better set of circumstances for the appearance and spread of communicable disease, and it remains to be seen if scientific innovation and medical technology are able to meet the challenge.

It is still not clear what the long-term consequences of twentieth-century antibiotic therapy, pesticide-based eradication programs, environmental change, and human population growth will be on disease patterns. But there are many scientists who fear that we may not be able to develop new antibiotics and treatments fast enough to keep pace with the appearance of potentially deadly new bacteria and other pathogens. Thus, we have radically altered the course of evolution in some microbial species, just as they have altered our own evolutionary course in the past and clearly continue to do so in the present.

SUMMARY

In this chapter, we have investigated some of the ways in which humans differ from one another, both within and between populations. We explored how this variation has been approached historically in terms of racial typologies and as a function of adaptation to a number of environmental factors, including solar radiation, heat, cold, and high altitude. We have also considered infectious disease, with particular emphasis on AIDS, and the dynamic relationship between pathogens and human hosts.

The topic of human variation is very complicated, and the biological and cultural factors that have contributed to that variation and that continue to influence it are manifold. But from an explicitly evolutionary perspective, it is through the investigation of changes in allele frequencies in response to environmental conditions that we will continue to elucidate the diverse adaptive potential that characterizes our species.

QUESTIONS FOR REVIEW

1. What is a polytypic species?
2. What is a biological definition of race? Why is race socially important?
3. What is biological determinism?
4. What was the eugenics movement, and what were its goals?
5. How did eighteenth- and nineteenth-century European scientists deal with human phenotypic variation?
6. What is homeostasis?
7. Under what conditions might light skin color be adaptive? Under what conditions might dark skin color be adaptive?
8. What physiological adjustments do humans show in coping with cold stress?
9. What physiological adjustments do humans show in coping with heat stress?
10. What do body size and shape have to do with adaptation to climate?
11. What are Bergmann's and Allen's rules?
12. How has infectious disease influenced human evolution?
13. How has susceptibility to HIV been shown to vary between populations? What genetic and biological factors have led to this variation?
14. What is a cline, and how does a clinal approach to human phenotypic variation differ from a racial approach?
15. What components of high-altitude environments are most challenging to humans?
16. What are two effects of exposure to high altitude?
17. Discuss current culturally mediated factors that may contribute to the spread of infectious disease. Provide examples.

SUGGESTED FURTHER READING

Discover. 1994. Special Issue: The Science of Race. 15 (November).

Frisancho, A. Roberto. 1993. *Human Adaptation and Accommodation.* Ann Arbor: University of Michigan Press.

Gould, Stephen Jay. 1981. *The Mismeasure of Man.* New York: Norton.

Jacoby, R., and N. Glauberman (eds). 1995. *The Bell Curve Debate*. New York: Times Books.

Journal of the American Medical Association, 1996. Entire issue, 275 (January 17). (Numerous articles pertaining to climate change and reemergence of infectious diseases.)

Leffell, David J., and Douglas E. Brash. 1996. "Sunlight and Skin Cancer." *Scientific American* 275(1): 52–59.

Nesse, Randolph M., and George C. Williams. 1998. "Evolution and the Origins of Disease." *Scientific American* 279(5): 86–93.

O'Brien, Stephen J., and Michael Dean. 1997. "In Search of AIDS-Resistance Genes." *Scientific American* 277(3): 44–51.

Ramenofsky, Ann F. 1992. "Death by Disease." *Archaeology* 45(2): 47–49.

RESOURCES ON THE INTERNET

Wadsworth Anthropology Resource Center
http://anthropology.wadsworth.com

The companion website for this text includes a range of enrichment material focused on the chapter's topic. While online you can enhance your understanding of the chapter by exploring one of the several additional Internet exercises, by researching topics, and by accessing full articles on InfoTrac College Edition. You can also reinforce the concepts by taking online practice exams.

Internet Exercises

The American Association of Physical Anthropologists (AAPA) have issued policy statements on the subject of race. Go to the AAPA website at **www.physanth.org/** and under *Position Statements,* read the statement entitled, *Biological Aspects of Race.* What aspects of the topic are covered here that are not covered in this chapter?

InfoTrac College Edition
http://www.infotrac-college.com/wadsworth

InfoTrac College Edition provides many articles about eugenics and its effects on public policy. Search for *eugenics* and read at least one article. How has eugenics affected politics and public policy?

Racial Purity: A False and Dangerous Ideology

During the late nineteenth and early twentieth centuries, a growing sense of nationalism was sweeping Europe and the United States. At the same time, an increased emphasis on racial purity had been coupled with the more dangerous aspects of what is termed "biological determinism" (see page 394). The concept of pure races is based, in part, on the notion that in the past, races were composed of individuals who conformed to idealized types and who were similar in appearance and intellect. Over time, some variation had been introduced into these pure races through interbreeding with other groups, and increasingly, this type of "contamination" was seen as a threat to be avoided.

In today's terminology, pure races would be said to be genetically homogenous, or to possess little genetic variation. Everyone would have the same alleles at most of their loci. Actually, we do see this situation in "pure breeds" of domesticated animals and plants, developed *deliberately* by humans through selective breeding. We also see many of the detrimental consequences of such genetic uniformity in various congenital abnormalities, such as hip dysplasia in some breeds of dogs.

With our current understanding of genetic principles, we are able to appreciate the potentially negative outcomes of matings between genetically similar individuals. For example, we know that inbreeding increases the likelihood of offspring who are homozygous for certain deleterious recessive alleles. We also know that decreased genetic variation in a species diminishes the potential for natural selection to act, thus compromising that species' ability to adapt to certain environmental fluctuations. Furthermore, in genetically uniform populations, individual fertility can be seriously reduced, potentially with disastrous consequences for the entire species. Thus, even if pure human races did exist at one time (and they did not), theirs would not have been a desirable condition genetically, and they most certainly would have been at an evolutionary disadvantage.

During the latter half of the nineteenth century, many Americans and Europeans had come to believe that nations could be ranked according to technological achievement. It followed that the industrial societies of the United States and Europe were considered to be the most advanced and to have attained a "higher level of civilization" owing to the "biological superiority" of their northern European forebears. This concept arose in part from the writings of Herbert Spencer, a British philosopher who misapplied the principles of natural selection to societies in a doctrine termed "social Darwinism." Spencer believed that societies evolved, and through competition, "less endowed" cultures and the "unfit" people in them would be weeded out. Indeed, it was Spencer who coined the much abused (and almost always misused) phrase "survival of the fittest," and his philosophy became widely accepted on both sides of the Atlantic, where its principles accorded well with notions of racial purity.

In northern Europe, particularly Germany, and in the United States, "racial superiority" was increasingly embodied in the so-called "Aryan race." *Aryan* is a term that is still widely used, albeit erroneously, with biological connotations. Actually, "Aryan" does not refer to a biological unit or Mendelian population, as the majority of people who use the term intend it. Rather, it is a linguistic term that refers to an ancient language group that was ancestral to the Indo-European family of languages. (Among the many and varied modern Indo-European languages are Hindi, Persian, Greek, Polish, German, and English.)

By the early twentieth century, the "Aryans" had been transformed into a mythical super race of people whose noble traits were embodied in an extremely idealized "nordic type." The true "Aryan" was held to be tall, blond, blue-eyed, strong, industrious, and "pure in spirit." "Nordics" were extolled as the developers of all ancient "high" civilizations and as the founders of modern industrialized nations. In Europe, there was growing emphasis on the superiority of northwestern Europeans as the modern representatives of "true Nordic stock," while southern and eastern Europeans were viewed as inferior.

In the United States, there prevailed the strongly held opinion that America was originally settled by Christian "Nordics." Prior to about 1890, the majority of newcomers to the United States had come from Germany, Scandinavia, and Britain (including Ireland). But by the 1890s, the pattern of immigration had changed. The arrival of increasing numbers of Italians, Turks, Greeks, and Jews among the thousands of newcomers raised fears that society was being contaminated by immigration from southern and eastern Europe.

Moreover, in the United States, there were additional concerns about the large population of former slaves and their descendants. As African Americans left the South in increasing numbers to work in the factories of the North, many unskilled white workers felt economically threatened by new competition. It was no coincidence that the Ku Klux Klan, which had been inactive for a number of years, was revived in 1915 and by the 1920s was preaching vehement opposition to African Americans, Jews, and Catholics in support of the supremacy of the white, Protestant, "Nordic race." These sentiments were widespread in the general population, although they did not always take the extreme form extolled by the Klan. One result of these views was the Immigration Restriction Act of 1924, which was aimed at curtailing the immigration of "non-Nordics," including Italians, Jews, and eastern Europeans, in order to preserve America's "Nordic" heritage.

To avoid the further "decline of the superior race," many states practiced policies of racial segregation until the mid-1950s.

Particularly in the South, segregation laws resulted in an almost total separation of whites and blacks, except where blacks were employed as servants or laborers. Moreover, *antimiscegenation* laws prohibited marriage between whites and blacks in over half the states, and unions between whites and Asians were frequently illegal as well. In several states, marriage between whites and blacks was punishable as either a misdemeanor or a felony, and astonishingly, some of these laws were not repealed until the late 1950s or early 1960s. Likewise, in Germany by 1935, the newly instituted Nuremberg Laws forbade marriage or sexual intercourse between so-called "Aryan" Germans and Jews.

The fact that belief in racial purity and superiority led ultimately to the Nazi death camps in World War II is undisputed (except for continuing efforts by certain white supremacist and neo-Nazi organizations). It is one of the great tragedies of the twentieth century that some of history's most glaring examples of discrimination and viciousness were perpetrated by people who believed that their actions were based in scientific principles. In reality, such beliefs constitute nothing more than myth. There is absolutely no evidence to suggest that pure human races ever existed. Indeed, such an idea flies in the face of everything we know about natural selection, recombination, and gene flow. The degree of genetic uniformity throughout our species (compared to some other species), as evidenced by mounting data from

mitochondrial and nuclear DNA analysis, argues strongly that there has always been gene flow between human populations and that genetically homogenous races are nothing more than fabrication.

The numerous abuses committed in the name of racial purity in the twentieth century were, in part, outgrowths of the rise of nationalism in Europe and the United States during the late nineteenth century. Unfortunately, however, prejudice based on a belief in racial purity and superiority is alive and well. The dogma preached by such white supremacist groups as White Aryan Resistance is no different from that espoused by the Nazi leadership in pre-World War II Germany. The dangers of such thinking have been manifested in incalculable human suffering. As we enter the threshold of the twenty-first century, we can but wonder if the generations who will see it to its conclusion will have learned from the mistakes of their predecessors.

Critical Thinking Questions

1. Given what you know about evolutionary factors, discuss why the notion of "pure races" is inaccurate. Also discuss why you think the concept of racial purity has been (and remains) so prevalent.

2. What is the concept of an "Aryan race," and why is it incorrect? Is this concept dead today?

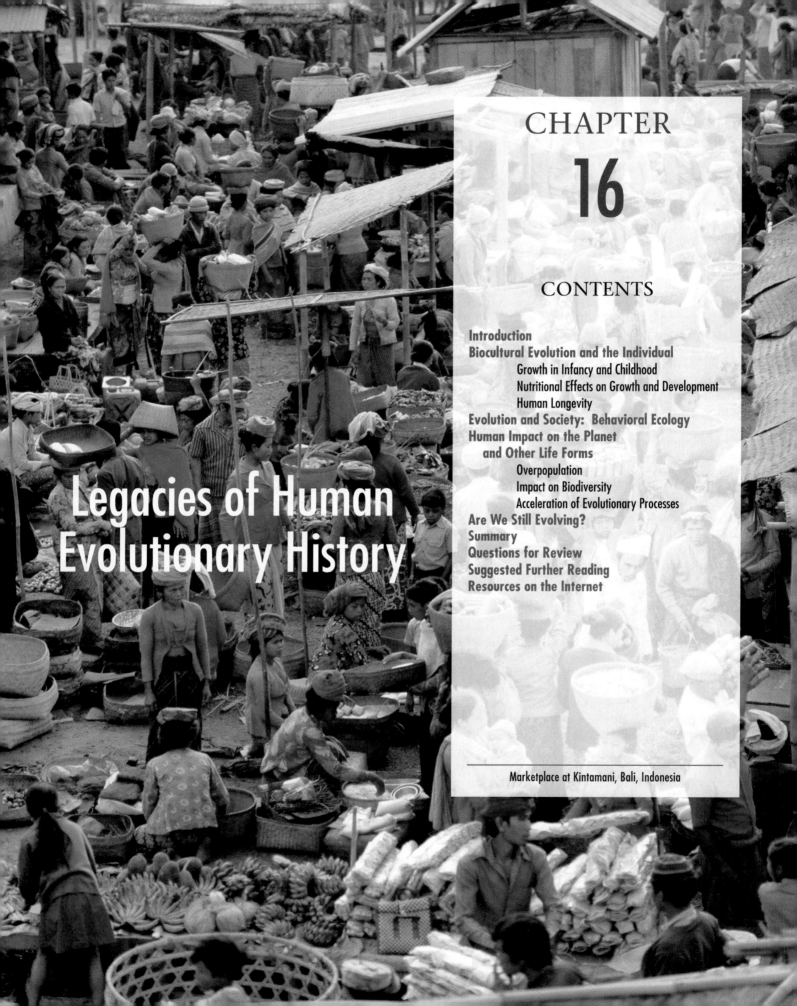

CHAPTER

16

CONTENTS

Marketplace at Kintamani, Bali, Indonesia

Legacies of Human Evolutionary History

Introduction

Because this is a physical anthropology text, we have placed primary emphasis on human biological evolution and adaptation. We have learned that our biology is the result of millions of years of evolutionary history: 225 million years of mammalian evolution, 65 million years of primate evolution, 6 million years of hominid evolution, 2 million years of evolution of the genus *Homo*. But are we just another mammal, just another primate? In most ways, of course, we are like other mammals and other primates. But as emphasized throughout the text, modern human beings are the result of *biocultural evolution*. In other words, human biology and behavior today have been shaped by the biological and cultural forces that operated on our ancestors. In fact, it would be fruitless to attempt an understanding of modern human biology and diversity without considering that humans have evolved in the context of culture. It would be like trying to understand the biology of fish without considering that they live in water.

In the two previous chapters, we have seen that modern human beings are a highly generalized species. This means that we can live in a great variety of climates, eat a wide variety of foods, and respond to most environmental challenges in myriad ways. For example, as human populations moved into cold northern climates, they were able to respond both physiologically and behaviorally to the environmental challenges they faced. As noted in Chapter 15, physiological adaptations to cold include vasoconstriction of the capillaries to conserve heat, increased metabolic rate, and shivering to warm the body. Thinking of these responses from an evolutionary perspective, we can assume that among the members of the earliest populations inhabiting cold regions of the world, those who had genotypes enabling them to respond physiologically had more surviving offspring to pass along these characteristics. Behavioral and cultural adaptations to cold climates probably included fire, house structures, warm clothing, and hunting for foods that provided energy to withstand the cold. In these examples we see evidence of human adaptations to cold that are both biological and cultural and that are rooted in evolution.

In this chapter, we will explore three areas in which the legacies of human evolution have profound impact: the individual, society, and the planet. We begin with a view of the legacies of human evolution that impact each person throughout the life course.

Biocultural Evolution and the Individual

If we consider how a human develops from an embryo into an adult and examine the forces that operate on that process, then we will have a better perspective of how both biology and culture influence our own lives and how our evolutionary history creates opportunities and sets limitations.

There is, of course, much variation in the extent to which cultural factors interact with genetically based biological characteristics; these variable interactions influence how characteristics are expressed in individuals. Some genetically based characteristics will be exhibited no matter what the cultural context of person's life happens to be. If a person inherits two alleles for albinism, for example (see Chapter 4), he or she will be deficient in the production of the pigment melanin, resulting in lightly colored skin, hair, and eyes. This phenotype will emerge regardless of the cultural environment in which the person lives. Likewise, the sex-linked trait for color blindness (also described in Chapter 4) will be exhibited by all males who inherit it, no matter where they live.

Other characteristics, such as intelligence, body shape, and growth reflect the interaction of environment and genes. We know, for example, that each of us is born with a genetic makeup that influences the maximum stature we can achieve in adulthood. But to reach that maximum stature, we must be properly nourished during growth and we must avoid many childhood diseases and other stresses that inhibit growth. What factors determine whether we are well fed and receive good medical care? In the United States, socioeconomic status is probably the primary determinant of nutrition and health. Thus, socioeconomic status is an example of a cultural factor that affects growth. But in another culture, diet and health status might be influenced by whether the individual is male or female. In some cultures, males receive preferential care in childhood and are thus often larger and healthier as adults than are females (Fig. 16–1). And if a culture values slimness in women, young girls may try to restrict their food intake in ways that affect their growth; but if plumpness is valued, the effect on diet in adolescence will likely be different. These are all examples of how cultural values affect growth and development.

As noted in earlier chapters, primatologists and other physical anthropologists view primate and human growth and development from an evolutionary perspective, with an interest in how natural selection has operated on the life cycle from conception to death, a perspective known as *life history theory* (see pp. 161–164). Why, for example, do humans have longer periods of infancy and childhood compared with other primates? What accounts for differences seen in the life cycles of such closely related species as humans and chimpanzees? Life history research seeks to answer such questions.

FIGURE 16–1

This is a mother with her twin children. The one on the left is a boy and is breastfed. The girl, on the right, is bottle-fed. This illustrates both differential treatment of boys and girls in many societies and the potential negative effects of bottle-feeding. (Dr. Mushtaq A. Khan and Dr. Gul N. Rehman, Pakistan Institute of Medical Sciences, Islamabad.)

Dr. Mushtaq A. Khan and Dr. Gul N. Rehman, Pakistan Institute of Medical Sciences, Islamabad

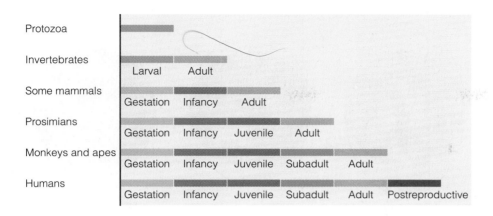

FIGURE 16–2
Life cycle stages for various animal species.

Protozoa					
Invertebrates	Larval	Adult			
Some mammals	Gestation	Infancy	Adult		
Prosimians	Gestation	Infancy	Juvenile	Adult	
Monkeys and apes	Gestation	Infancy	Juvenile	Subadult	Adult
Humans	Gestation	Infancy	Juvenile	Subadult	Adult	Postreproductive

Not all animals have clearly demarcated phases in their lives; moreover, among mammals, humans have more such phases than do other species (Fig. 16–2). Protozoa, among the simplest of animals, have only one phase; many invertebrates have two: larval and adult. Most primates have four phases: gestation, infancy, juvenile (usually called childhood in humans), and adult. Monkeys, apes, and humans add a phase between the juvenile phase and adulthood that is referred to as the subadult period (adolescence, or teenage years, in humans). Finally, for humans there is the addition of a sixth phase in women, the postreproductive years following menopause. One could argue that during the course of primate evolution, more recently evolved forms have longer life spans and more divisions of the life span into phases, or stages.

Most of these life cycle stages are well marked by biological transitions. The prenatal phase begins with conception and ends with birth; infancy is the period of nursing; childhood, or the juvenile phase, is the period from weaning to sexual maturity (puberty in humans); adolescence is the period from puberty to the end of growth; adulthood is marked by the birth of the first child and/or the completion of growth; and menopause is recognized as having occurred one full year after the last menstrual cycle. These biological markers are similar among higher primates, but for humans, there is an added complexity: They occur in cultural contexts that define and characterize them. Puberty, for example, has very different meanings in different cultures. A girl's first menstruation (menarche) is often marked with ritual and celebration, and a change in social status typically occurs with this biological transition. Likewise, menopause is often associated with a rise in status for women in non-Western societies, whereas it is commonly seen as a negative transition for women in many Western societies. As we shall see, collective and individual attitudes toward these life cycle transitions have an effect on growth and development.

Growth in Infancy and Childhood

A characteristic that humans share with most other primates is a relatively large brain compared with body size. In fact, the delivery of a large newborn head through a somewhat small pelvis is a challenge that modern humans share with many other primates, including most monkeys (Fig. 16–3). A further challenge for modern humans, however, is that human brains are somewhat undeveloped at birth, so the babies are more helpless and dependent on their caretakers than are most monkey infants. The continued growth of the brain after birth occurs at a rate far greater than that of any other part of the body, with the exception of the eyeball. At birth, the

FIGURE 16–3
The relationship between the average diameter of the birth canal of adult females and average head length and breadth of newborns of the same species. (After Jolly, 1985.)

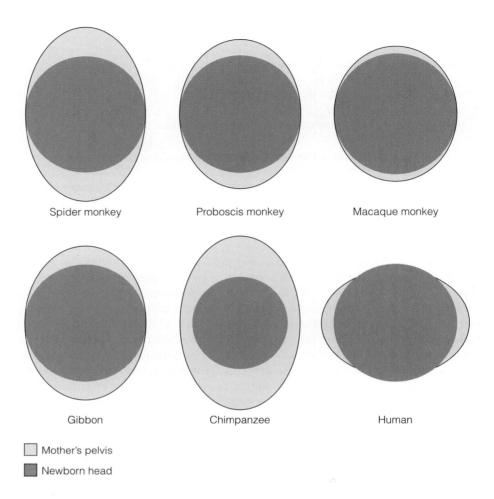

Spider monkey   Proboscis monkey   Macaque monkey

Gibbon   Chimpanzee   Human

☐ Mother's pelvis

■ Newborn head

human brain is about 25 percent of its adult size. By 6 months of age, the brain has doubled in size, reaching 50 percent of adult size. It reaches 75 percent of adult size at age 2½ years, 90 percent at age 5 years, and 95 percent by age 10 years. There is only a very small spurt at adolescence, making the brain an exception to the growth curves characteristic of most other parts of the body. This pattern of brain growth, including the relatively small amount of growth before birth, is unusual among primates and other mammals. By contrast, the typical picture for most mammalian species is that at least 50 percent of adult brain size has been achieved prior to birth. For humans, however, the narrow pelvis necessary for walking bipedally provides limits on the size of the fetal head that can be delivered through it. That limitation, in addition to the value of having most brain growth occur in the more stimulating environment outside the womb, has resulted in human infants being born with far less of their total adult brain size than most other mammals. (As we saw in Chapter 11, this pattern of delayed maturation was probably already established in hominid evolution by 1.5 m.y.a.)

Delayed brain growth may be particularly important for a species dependent on language. The language centers of the brain develop in the first three years of life, when the brain is undergoing its rapid expansion; these three years are considered a critical period for the development of language in the human child.

Infancy is defined as the period during which nursing takes place, typically lasting about four years in humans. When we consider how unusual it is for a mother to nurse her child for even a year in the United States or Canada, this figure may surprise us. But considering that four or five years of nursing is the norm for chimpanzees, gorillas, orangutans, and for women in foraging societies, most anthropologists conclude that four years was the norm for most humans in the evolutionary past (Eaton, Shostak, and Konner, 1988).

Humans have unusually long childhoods and a slowed growth process reflecting the importance of learning for our species. Childhood is the time between weaning and puberty when growth in stature is occurring, the brain is completing its growth, and acquisition of technical and social skills is taking place

Nutritional Effects on Growth and Development

Nutrition has an impact on human growth at every stage of the life cycle. During pregnancy, for example, a woman's diet can have a profound effect on the development of her fetus and the eventual health of the child. Moreover, the effects are transgenerational, because a woman's own supply of eggs is developed while she herself is *in utero*. Thus, if a woman is malnourished during pregnancy, the eggs that develop in her female fetus may be damaged in a way that will impact the health of her future grandchildren.

Nutrients needed for growth, development, and body maintenance include proteins, carbohydrates, lipids (fats), vitamins, and minerals. The specific amount that we need of each of these nutrients coevolved with the types of foods that were available to human ancestors throughout our evolutionary history. For example, the specific pattern of amino acids required in human nutrition (the essential amino acids) reflects an ancestral diet high in animal protein. Unfortunately for modern humans, these coevolved nutritional requirements are often incompatible with the foods that are available and typically consumed today. To understand this mismatch of our nutritional needs and contemporary diets, we need to examine the impact of agriculture on human evolutionary history.

The preagricultural diet, while perhaps high in animal protein, was low in fats, particularly saturated fats. The diet was also high in complex carbohydrates (including fiber), low in salt, and high in calcium. We do not need to be reminded that the contemporary diet that typifies many industrialized societies has the opposite configuration of the one just described. It is high in saturated fats and salt and low in complex carbohydrates, fiber, and calcium (Table 16–1). There is very good evidence that many of today's diseases in industrialized countries are related to the lack of fit between our diet today and the one with which we evolved (Eaton, Shostak, and Konner, 1988).

Many of our biological and behavioral characteristics evolved because in the past they contributed to adaptation; but today these same characteristics may be maladaptive. An example is our ability to store fat. This capability was an advantage in the past, when food availability often alternated between abundance and scarcity. Those who could store fat during the times of abundance could draw on those stores during times of scarcity and remain healthy, resist disease, and, for women, maintain the ability to reproduce. Today, people with adequate economic resources spend much of their lives with a relative abundance of foods. Considering the number of disorders associated with obesity, the formerly positive ability to store extra fat has now turned into a liability. Our "feast or famine" biology is now incompatible with the constant feast many of us indulge in today.

Perhaps no disorder is as clearly linked with dietary and lifestyle behaviors as the form of diabetes mellitus that typically has its onset in later life, referred to variously as Type II diabetes or NIDDM (non–insulin dependent diabetes mellitus).

TABLE 16–1 Preagricultural, Contemporary American, and Recently Recommended Dietary Composition

	Preagricultural Diet	Contemporary Diet	Recent Recommendations
Total dietary energy (%)			
Protein	33	12	12
Carbohydrate	46	46	58
Fat	21	42	30
Alcohol	~0	(7–10)	—
P:S ratio*	1.41	0.44	1
Cholesterol (mg)	520	300–500	300
Fiber (g)	100–150	19.7	30–60
Sodium (mg)	690	2,300–6,900	1,000–3,300
Calcium (mg)	1,500–2,000	740	800–1,500
Ascorbic acid (mg)	440	90	60
*Polyunsaturated: saturated fat ratio.			

Source: From Eaton, Shostak, and Konner, 1988.

In 1900, diabetes ranked twenty-seventh among the leading causes of death in the United States; today it ranks seventh. Moreover, the threat to world health from this disease is growing, with projections of an increase in incidence between 2000 and 2010 of 57 percent in Asia, 50 percent in Africa, 44 percent in South America, and 23 percent in North America (Zimmet, Alberti, and Shaw, 2001). Part of this projected increase will be due to decreases in other causes of death (e.g., infectious diseases), but much of it has to do with lifestyle and dietary changes associated with modernization and globalization, especially the decrease in levels of daily activity and increase in dietary intake of fats and refined carbohydrates.

It is clear that both deficiencies and excesses of nutrients can cause health problems and interfere with childhood growth. Certainly, many people in all parts of the world, both industrialized and developing, suffer from inadequate supplies of food of any quality. We read daily of thousands dying from starvation due to drought, warfare, or political instability. The blame must be placed not only on the narrowed food base that resulted from the emergence of agriculture, but also on the increase in human population that occurred when people began to settle in permanent villages and have more children. Today, the crush of billions of humans almost completely dependent on cereal grains means that millions face undernutrition, malnutrition, and even starvation.

In summary, our nutritional adaptations were shaped in an environment that included times of scarcity alternating with times of abundance. The variety of foods consumed was so great that nutritional deficiency diseases were rare. Small amounts of animal foods were probably an important part of the diet in many parts of the world. In northern latitudes, subsequent to approximately 1 million years ago, meat was an important part of the diet, but because such meat was low in fats, the negative effects of high meat intake that we see today did not occur. Our diet today is often incompatible with the adaptations that evolved in the millions of years preceding the development of agriculture. The consequences of that incompatibility include both starvation and obesity.

Human Longevity

Relative to most other animals, humans have a long life span (Table 16–2). The maximum life span potential, estimated to be about 120 years, has probably not changed in the last several thousand years, although life expectancy at birth (the average length of life) has increased significantly in the last 100 years, probably owing to the decreased influence of infectious diseases, which typically take their toll on the young (Crews and Harper, 1998).

To some extent, aging is something we do throughout our entire lives. But we usually think of aging as **senescence**, the process of physiological decline in all systems of the body that occurs toward the end of the life course. Actually, throughout adulthood, there is a gradual decline in our cells' ability to synthesize proteins, in immune system function, in muscle mass (with a corresponding increase in fat mass) and strength, and in bone mineral density (Lamberts et al., 1997). This decline is associated with an increase in risk for the chronic degenerative diseases that are usually listed as the causes of death in industrialized nations.

As you know, most causes of death that have their effects after the reproductive years will not necessarily be subjected to the forces of natural selection. One explanation for why we age and are affected by chronic degenerative diseases like atherosclerosis, cancers, and hypertension is that genes that enhance reproductive success in earlier years (and thus were favored by natural selection) may have detrimental effects in later years. These are referred to as **pleiotropic genes**, meaning that they have multiple effects at different times in the life span or under different conditions (Williams, 1957). For example, genes that enhance the function of the immune system in the early years may also damage tissue so that cancer susceptibility increases in later life (Nesse and Williams, 1994). Alternatively, cancer-protecting genes may override genes for organ and tissue renewal in later life.

Pleiotropy may help us understand evolutionary reasons for aging, but what are the causes of senescence in the individual? Much attention has been focused recently on free radicals, highly reactive molecules that can damage cells. Protection against these by-products of normal metabolism is provided by antioxidants such as vitamins A, C, and E and by a number of enzymes (Kirkwood, 1997). Ultimately, damage to DNA can occur, which in turn contributes to the senescence of cells, the immune system, and other functional systems of the body. Additionally, there is evidence that programmed cell death is also a part of the normal processes of development that can obviously contribute to senescence.

Another hypothesis for senescence is known as the "telomere hypothesis." In this view, the DNA sequence at the end of each chromosome, known as the telomere, is shortened each time a cell divides. Cells that have divided many times throughout the life course have short telomeres, eventually reaching the point at which they can no longer divide and are unable to maintain healthy tissues and organs. Telomere length changes have also been implicated in cancers. In the laboratory, the enzyme telomerase can lengthen telomeres, making the cell young again. For this reason, the gene for telomerase has been called the "immortalizing gene." Although this research is not likely to lead to a lengthening of the life span, it may contribute to better health throughout an individual's lifetime.

Far more important than genes in the aging process, however, are lifestyle factors, such as smoking, physical activity, diet, and medical care. Life expectancy at birth varies considerably from country to country and among socioeconomic classes within a country. Throughout the world, women have higher life expectancies than men.

A Japanese girl born in 2001, for example, can expect to live to age 84, a boy to age 78. Girls and boys born in that same year in the United States have life

TABLE 16–2   Maximal Life Spans for Selected Species

Organism	Approximate Maximum Life Span (in years)
Bristlecone pine	5,000
Tortoise	170
Rockfish	140
Human	120
Blue whale	80
Indian elephant	70
Gorilla	39
Domestic dog	34
Rabbit	13
Rat	5

Source: Stini, 1991.

Senescence
The process of physiological decline in body function that occurs with aging.

Pleiotropic genes
Genes that have more than one effect; genes that have different effects at different times in the life cycle.

expectancies of 80 and 73, respectively. In contrast to these children in industrialized nations, girls and boys in Mali have life expectancies of only 48 and 46, respectively. Many African nations have seen life expectancy drop below 40 owing to deaths from AIDS. For example, before the AIDS epidemic, Zimbabweans had a life expectancy of 65 years; today life expectancy in Zimbabwe is 39.

Evolution and Society: Behavioral Ecology

Examining human social behavior in an evolutionary framework is known as *behavioral ecology,* which we discussed in Chapter 6 in the context of primate behavior. Of course, humans are primates, and many biological anthropologists are interested in the extent to which evolution can explain contemporary human behaviors. Behavioral ecologists suggest that humans, like other animals, behave in ways that increase their fitness, or reproductive success. This includes behaviors affecting mating and parenting success. Finding mates and taking care of offspring require time and energy, and as we know all too well, both of these commodities exist in finite amounts. Thus, reproductive efforts require trade-offs in time, energy, and resources invested in mating and parenting. When we read about these concepts as they pertain to monkeys and apes, most of us probably do not find much with which to disagree. But to suggest that evolutionary processes have an impact on human behavior today raises a lot of issues, some of which are not so easily resolved.

For example, this view argues that natural selection is not limited to physical and physiological responses, but has had an effect on the way humans think—in other words, on human cognition, perception, and memory. The argument goes something like this: The ability to remember a dangerous event that may have resulted in loss of life would be favorably selected if it prevented a person from being caught in a similar situation. The ability to distinguish a wildebeest (food) from a lion (danger) would be selectively favored. Likewise, economic behaviors involved in the allocation of resources to increase survival and reproductive success would be favored.

The study of how natural selection has influenced how humans and other primates think is often called *evolutionary psychology.* Among the topics explored by evolutionary psychologists are mate attraction, sexuality, aggression, and violence. As you might guess, all of these are hot topics, and there is no end in sight to the controversy that surrounds them.

Many people are uncomfortable with such an explicit evolutionary perspective on contemporary human behavior and thought because it implies that there are constraints on our behavior that we may not be able to overcome. For example, it can be argued that individual males can increase their reproductive success by increasing the number of women with whom they mate. Women, meanwhile, are thought to best increase the health of their offspring (and thus their reproductive success) if they can find faithful mates who will supply resources to them and their children. At first glance, these two recipes for reproductive success seem to conflict. Further examination, however, reveals that the optimal route to reproductive success for males and females represents a compromise between what is argued to be the best strategy for each sex. Males who "love 'em and leave 'em" usually end up with fewer surviving offspring in comparison with males who take on the role of faithful providers.

Aggression and violence, particularly on the part of males, is the subject of a number of books and papers in evolutionary psychology, including the book *Demonic Males: Apes and the Origins of Human Violence,* by Richard Wrangham and Dale Peterson. These authors contrast the behaviors of our two closest living relatives, the chimpanzees and bonobos. Most striking is that chimpanzee society seems to be based on male-male competition and aggression leading occasionally to violence

(a)

(b)

both within and between troops, whereas bonobo society is described as a female-dominated community based on cooperation and peaceful interaction (Fig. 16–4). To Wrangham and Peterson, these two behavior patterns represent the extremes of human societies and also show potentials for both violence and peace that may be rooted in human evolutionary history. On the other hand, they clearly acknowledge the role of culture and society in fostering aggression and violence in males. Mirroring some of the discussions of terrorism today, *Demonic Males* points out that chimpanzee communities with abundant resources have far fewer incidents of violence than communities with limited resources; in general, bonobos live in areas of relative resource abundance. But whatever their roots, it appears to many observers that war, genocide, rape, rioting, and terrorism are unwelcome legacies of human evolutionary history. Unfortunately, because of recent events linked to terrorists, the arguments presented in *Demonic Males* resonate more profoundly and convincingly than they did when the last edition of this textbook was written. Perhaps by the next edition, the pendulum of thinking about world events will have swung toward the idea that peaceful cooperation is more fundamental to human behavior.

To suggest that some of our behaviors reflect our evolutionary history is not to say that there are "genes for" such behaviors. No matter how you cut it, behavior is an extremely complex phenomenon, and its expression depends on a combination of myriad genes, environmental context, and individual experience. There is really no way of predicting how an individual mother or father will allocate resources in the task of child rearing, but behavioral ecologists argue that patterns can be seen when populations (or even the entire species) are examined for allocation of parenting resources.

One aspect of behavioral ecology that may have less emotional baggage than reproductive and parenting strategies is how people make decisions about food acquisition. For example, when a behavioral ecologist examines the hunting strategy on a given day for a band of foragers, the prediction would be that the hunters would pursue a strategy that would maximize return and minimize time and energy invested (Fig. 16–5). In other words, it is predicted that the hunters would pursue an "optimal foraging strategy." But if the analysis considers only the calories in the prey obtained weighed against the calories expended in pursuit of the prey, the theory will always come up short, because other important factors are left out of the model. What dangers were between the hunters and the prey that may have led them to

FIGURE 16–4
(a) These chimpanzees exhibit an aggressive reaction when confronted by others. (b) The bonobos show more relaxed expressions.

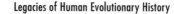
FIGURE 16–5
When these G/wi hunters plan their hunting strategy, they consider many factors in addition to calories expended and acquired.

© Peter Johnson/CORBIS

take an alternate route or avoid that target altogether? Does pursuit of a particular prey take them too far away from home when night falls? Does a smaller prey item provide additional resources such as a pelt that is useful for clothing? And have the people been eating this prey item for several days, and do they desire a bit of variety? All of these factors could explain why a band of hunters might choose to pursue a prey item of less caloric value and thus deviate from the prediction. To return to the idea of an optimal reproductive strategy, would not similar complicating factors apply? Certainly, contemporary humans choose mates based on many more factors than how many offspring they can produce or raise together.

Despite its limitations and challenges, examining human behavior as a product of evolution not only helps explain and understand some aspects of our lives, but also allows predictions that can be examined and tested through field observations, demographic studies, and other methods. We can take an example from the human life cycle to illustrate this. As already noted, the basic argument underlying behavioral ecology is that natural selection will favor individual actions and choices that increase reproductive success. If that is the case, it would make sense for human females to breed as early in their life cycle as possible and for as long as possible and to have children spaced very closely together. Let us examine each of these assumptions more closely.

Menarche
The first menstruation in girls, usually occurring in the early to mid teens.

The onset of **menarche** in girls is affected by several factors, including genetic patterns (girls tend to become mature at about the same age as their mothers), nutrition, stress, and disease. It also appears that a certain amount of body fat is necessary for menarche and the maintenance of ovulation (Frisch, 1988). Both diet and activity levels affect the accumulation of body fat. This may explain the trend toward the lower age of menarche that has been noted in human populations in the last hundred years and the tendency for girls who are very active and thin to mature later than those who are heavier and less active. High activity and low body fat also characterize many ballet dancers and marathon runners, who often cease to menstruate during periods of intense training. Since pregnancy and nursing require an increase in caloric consumption, body fat may serve as a signal to the body that there is enough caloric reserve to support a pregnancy. When the levels of body fat fall too low, ovulation may cease temporarily to prevent initiation of a pregnancy that is likely to fail.

If early maturity results in higher numbers of surviving offspring, then it is predicted that natural selection would favor those members of a population who mature earlier. Until the advent of settled living, it is likely that females became pregnant as soon as they were biologically able to do so. This would be advantageous in view of the fact that individual life expectancy would have been low. Paleodemographic studies indicate a mortality rate of at least 50 percent in subadults in preindustrial populations; and of the half that survived to adulthood, most did not survive to age 50. Given the reality of short life spans combined with the long period of infant dependency, producing offspring as early as possible may have contributed to the reproductive success of females, particularly early hominid females. If we use chimpanzees as a model for this discussion, it is noteworthy that with one exception, no infant chimpanzee orphaned prior to the age of three has survived. Consequently, one could argue that a similar situation applied to early hominids, who, in addition to the numerous risk factors faced by chimpanzees, were subject to greater degrees of predation pressure. Hence, an early hominid female's chances of rearing even one offspring to the point it could survive without her were enhanced by giving birth as soon as she reached sexual maturity.

The high rates of adolescent pregnancy that typify so many cultures today reflect this ancient biological heritage. Today, however, there may be disadvantages to early maturity. If delayed maturity is associated with higher-quality care of the offspring, then offspring survival may improve, resulting in a net increase in fitness for those who mature a few years later. Unfortunately, all too frequently today in many parts of the world, young girls become reproductively mature long before they are socially mature. And if they are also sexually active, they may become pregnant before they have finished school or obtained the skills necessary for economic self-sufficiency. This means that the quality of care that they can provide their offspring will be compromised. It is known that the infant mortality rate in humans rises rapidly as mothers' age at first birth decreases (Stearns, 1992). In contemporary society, it is likely that those who delay reproducing until they are emotionally, socially, and economically mature will have more surviving offspring than those who begin their parenting careers before they themselves have matured. But if the young, maturing parents have sufficient help from their extended families, religious organizations, or government agencies, early childbearing may not compromise their fitness. Clearly, the road to reproductive success is more complicated than most theories of behavioral ecology suggest, although they serve as useful models on which to base predictions about behavior. Scientific models are often simplistic, but this is necessary to test hypotheses about behavior.

What about the number of offspring produced at each birth? Primates such as monkeys, apes, and humans typically give birth to one infant at a time. Twins occur in apes and humans at about the same frequency, but the survival rate of twins (or triplets) is far lower than the survival rate of singletons. Thus, we can argue that humans are physiologically constrained in the number of offspring resulting from each conception. Because we are mammals, we are also physiologically constrained regarding the dependency of our offspring in the first few years of life, as discussed earlier in this chapter (Fig. 16–6). Apes and ancestral humans nurse their infants for three to four years, resulting in an approximate four-year birth interval. That interval can be reduced with earlier weaning or, in the case of humans, by not nursing at all. This means that contemporary humans can easily reduce the birth interval to fewer than two years, potentially doubling the number of offspring produced. But again, in most cases, the quality of parental care is compromised when there are too many dependent offspring. If the number of offspring reaching reproductive maturity is lower in individuals and families with two-year birth intervals than in those with four-year birth intervals, then natural selection will favor the latter.

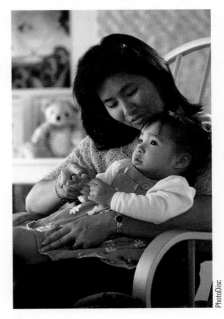

FIGURE 16–6
Human infants require extensive parental care, especially in the first few years of life.

While an evolutionary perspective can help us understand how natural selection has had an impact on offspring quantity, it can also help us understand parenting behaviors that may, at first glance, seem counter to the goal of increasing reproductive success. For example, in Chapter 6 we discussed infanticide in Hanuman langurs, noting that it seems counterproductive to the supposed goal of increasing reproductive success. The evolutionary perspective argues that when infanticide is perpetrated by a male against the offspring of another male, then it can be interpreted as increasing his reproductive success at the expense of the other male. But what about situations in which a mother kills her own offspring? Can this contribute to her reproductive success in any way? Sara Hrdy tackles such challenging questions in her book *Mother Nature: A History of Mothers, Infants, and Natural Selection* (1999). She points out that there are many instances in which maternal behavior defies the claim that there is a natural "instinct" for mother love in mammals. But if the behaviors are placed in an evolutionary context, the discrepancies can often be resolved. For example, consider a mother who abandons her newborn infant when social and economic conditions are so dire that the chances of the child surviving very long are diminished. It may be better (in an evolutionary sense, *not* in a moral sense) to let that child die so that she can bear another as soon as conditions and chances for child survival are improved. This illustrates the concept that for most measures of reproductive success, quality of offspring produced is more important than quantity. This is not to say that all maternal behaviors are adaptive. But a behavior that at first glance seems maladaptive may actually serve to increase reproductive success for the mother.

Can behavioral ecology explain the long period of reproductive sterility in human females following menopause? If increasing reproductive success is what it is all about, then how could natural selection favor cessation of reproductive functioning relatively early in a woman's lifetime?

For women, **menopause**, or the end of menstruation, is a sign of entry into a new phase of the life cycle. Estrogen and progesterone production begin to decline toward the end of the reproductive years until ovulation (and thus menstruation) ceases altogether. This occurs at approximately age 50 in all parts of the world. Throughout human evolution, the majority of females (and males) did not survive to age 50; thus, few women lived much past menopause. But today, this event occurs when women have as much as one-third of their active and healthy lives ahead of them. Such a long period of postreproductive time is not found in other primates. Female chimpanzees and monkeys experience decreased fertility in their later years, but most continue to have reproductive cycles until their death. Occasional reports of menopause in apes and monkeys have been noted, but it is far from a routine and expected event.

Why do human females have such a long period during which they can no longer reproduce? One theory relates to parenting. Since it takes about 12 to 15 years before a child becomes independent, it has been argued that females are biologically "programmed" to live 12 to 15 years beyond the birth of their last child (Mayer, 1982). This suggests that the maximum human life span for preagricultural humans was about 65 years, a figure that corresponds to what is known for contemporary hunter-gatherers and for prehistoric populations. Another theory regarding menopause suggests that it was not itself favored by natural selection; rather it is an artifact of the extension of the human life span. Some have suggested that the maximum life span of the mammalian egg is 50 years (you will recall that all the ova are already present before birth; see p. 423). Thus, although the human life span has increased in the last several hundred years, the reproductive life span has not.

Menopause
The end of menstruation in human women, usually occurring at around age 50.

One final explanation for the long postreproductive period in human females has been proposed by behavioral ecologists and is known as the "grandmother hypothesis." This proposal argues that natural selection may have favored this long period in women's lives because postmenopausal women could provide high-quality care for their grandchildren (Fig. 16–7). In other words, an older woman would be more likely to increase her lifetime fitness by enhancing the survival of her older grandchildren (who share one-quarter of her genes) through provisioning and direct child care than she would by having her own infants. Support of this hypothesis comes from field studies of the Hadza of Tanzania. The Hadza are food foragers who spend hours each day gathering roots, tubers, berries,

FIGURE 16–7
Senior Hadza woman and grandchild.

James F. O'Connell

honey, and other plant foods. Anthropologists Kristin Hawkes, Jim O'Connell, and Nichols Burton-Jones (1997) found that grandmothers with no dependent offspring spent more time per day and were more successful gathering foods than mothers or unmarried girls. The contribution of grandmothers was particularly important when their daughters had recently given birth, resulting in constraints on their own ability to forage for food just when, owing to lactation, their caloric needs were high.

Human Impact on the Planet and Other Life Forms

By most standards, *Homo sapiens* is a successful species. There are currently more than 6 billion human beings living on this planet. Each one of these 6,000,000,000 individuals comprises upwards of 20 trillion cells. Nevertheless, we and all other multicellular organisms contribute but a small fraction of all the cells on the planet—the vast majority of which are bacteria. Thus, if we see life ultimately as a competition among reproducing organisms, bacteria are the winners, hands down.

Bacteria, then, could be viewed as the dominant life form on earth. However, even when only considering multicellular animals, there are additional lessons in evolutionary humility. As mammals, we are members of a group that includes about 4,000 species—a group of animals that has been on the decline over the last several million years. Looking even more specifically, as primates, we see ourselves belonging to a grouping that today numbers not even 200 species (and is also probably declining since its peak several million years ago). Compare these species numbers with those estimated for insects. Over 750,000 insect species have been identified, and estimates are as high as 30 million (Wilson, 1992)! Number of species (as an indicator of biological diversity) is as good a barometer of evolutionary success as any other. By this standard, humans (and our close relatives) could hardly be seen as the most successful of species.

Evolutionary success can also be gauged by species longevity. As we have seen, fossil evidence indicates that *Homo sapiens* has been on the scene for at least 200,000 years and perhaps as long as 400,000 years. Such time spans, seen through the perspective of a human lifetime, may seem enormous. But consider this: Our immediate predecessor, *Homo erectus,* had a species longevity of about 1.5 million years. In other words, we as a species would need to exist another million years simply to match *Homo erectus!* If such considerations as these are not humbling enough, remember that some sharks and turtles have thrived basically unchanged structurally for 400 million years (although many of these species are now seriously threatened).

Overpopulation

No matter what criterion for success is used , there is no question that *Homo sapiens* has had an inordinate impact on the earth and all other forms of life. In the past, humans had to respond primarily to challenges in the natural world; today the greatest challenges for our species (and all others) are environments of our own making.

If we had to point to one single challenge facing humanity, a problem to which virtually all others are tied, it would have to be population growth. We currently are trapped in a destructive cycle of our own making. Population size has skyrocketed in our own species as we have increased our ability to produce food surpluses. As population size increases, more and more land is converted to crops, pasture, and construction, providing more opportunities for yet more humans. Additionally, through the medical advances of the twentieth century, we have reduced mortality at both ends of the life cycle. Thus, fewer people die in childhood, and having survived to adulthood, they live longer than ever before. Although these medical advances are unquestionably beneficial to individuals (who has not benefited from medical technology?), it is also clear that there are significant detrimental consequences to the species and to the planet.

Population size, if left unchecked, increases exponentially, that is, as a function of some percent, like compound interest in a bank account. Currently, human population increases worldwide at an annual rate of about 1.8 percent. Although this figure may not seem too startling at first, it deserves some examination. In addition, it is useful to discuss doubling time, or the amount of time it takes for a population to double in size.

Scientists estimate that around 10,000 years ago, only about 5 million people inhabited the earth (not even half as many as live in Los Angeles County or New York City today). By the year 1650, there were perhaps 500 million, and by 1800, 1 billion. In other words, between 10,000 years ago and 1650 (a period of 9,650 years), population size doubled seven and a half times. On average, then, the doubling time between 10,000 years ago and 1650 was about 1,287 years. But from 1650 to 1800 it doubled again, which means that doubling time had been reduced to 150 years (Ehrlich and Ehrlich, 1990). And in the 37 years between 1950 and 1987, world population doubled from 2 billion to 4 billion.

Dates and associated population estimates up to the present are as follows: mid-1800s, 1 billion; 1930s, 2 billion; mid-1960s, 3 billion; mid-1980s, 4 billion; present, 6 billion (Fig. 16–8). To state this problem in terms we can appreciate, we add 1 billion people to the world's population approximately every 11 years. That comes out to 90 to 95 million every year and roughly a quarter of a million every day!

The rate of growth is not equally distributed among all nations. Although the world's rate of increase has ranged from 1.7 to 2.1 percent since the 1950s (Ehrlich and Ehrlich, 1990), it is the developing countries that share most of the burden (not

FIGURE 16–8
Line graph depicting exponential growth of human population. Note that for almost all of the last 5,000 years, the number of humans increased very slowly. It was not until 1650 that population size was even half a billion (500 million). The rapid increase to 1 billion by about 1850 is, in part, attributable to the industrial revolution. Population increase occurs as a function of some percent (in some developing countries, the annual rate is over 3 percent). With advances in food production and medical technologies, humans are now undergoing a population explosion, as this graph illustrates.

to be interpreted as blame). During the 1980s, the population of Kenya grew at a rate of a little over 4 percent per year, while India added a million per month, and 36,000 babies were born every day in Latin America.

The most recent United Nations International Conference on Population and Development set as its goal the development of a plan to contain the world's population to about 7.3 billion by the year 2015 and to prevent future growth. Otherwise, by the year 2050, human numbers will approach 10 billion. The United Nations plan emphasizes women's education, health, and rights throughout the world, but has met with stiff resistance from religious groups opposed to abortion and contraception.

The United Nations goal is an admirable but ambitious one, and achieving it will be a formidable task. Although the average number of live births per woman declined in developing nations from 5 in 1955 to 3 by the 1990s, it will still be next to impossible to prevent huge population increases in this century. Bear in mind that *approximately half of all people currently living in the developing world are less than 15 years old.* These young people have not yet reproduced, but they will.

You might logically ask, Can we not make technological changes sufficient to feed all these people? Certainly this and similar questions are being asked more frequently today than in the past. There surely are methods that would more efficiently utilize agricultural lands already available. Clearly, there are better ways to distribute the food surpluses already produced (in the United States in particular). But can we continue forever to make technological changes sufficient to feed ever-growing numbers of humans? Is there enough land to support an endless demand for housing, crop cultivation, and grazing? Is there enough water? We probably can develop technologies to meet our species' increasing needs for a while. But can we do so and still meet the requirements of thousands of undomesticated species? The answer for the immediate future is: Probably not. For the long term, without major changes in human population growth, the answer is: Certainly not.

Impact on Biodiversity

Another legacy of the human evolutionary process is expressed in the proposal recently put forth by biologist Stephen Palumbi (2001) that humans are the "world's greatest evolutionary force." What Palumbi means is that we humans, like no other species before us, have profound effects on the evolutionary histories of almost all forms of life, including the ability to alter global ecology and the potential to destroy ourselves and virtually all life on earth. Clearly, such wide and sudden impacts have no precedents in the fossil record. Even massive evolutionary catastrophes and mass extinctions did not wreak the havoc that may result from modern human technology.

The geological record indicates that in the past 570 million years, there have been at least 15 mass extinctions, two of which altered all of the earth's ecosystems (Ward, 1994). The first of these major extinction events took place some 250 million years ago and resulted from climatic change subsequent to the joining of all the earth's landmasses into one supercontinent.

The second event occurred around 65 million years ago and ended 150 million years of evolutionary processes that, among other things, had produced the dinosaurs. This mass extinction is believed by many researchers to have resulted from climatic changes following the impact of an asteroid.

A third major extinction event, perhaps of the same magnitude, is occurring now, and according to some scientists, may have begun in the late Pleistocene or early **Holocene** (Ward, 1994). Unlike all other mass extinctions, the current one has not been caused by continental drift, climate change (so far), or collisions with asteroids. Rather, these recent and ongoing extinctions are due to the activities of a single species—*Homo sapiens.*

Many scientists, in fact, believe that several large mammalian species were pushed toward extinction by overhunting by earlier human populations, particularly near the end of the Pleistocene, some 10,000 years ago. In North America, at least 57 mammalian species became extinct, including the mammoth, mastodon, giant ground sloth, saber-toothed cat, several large rodents, and numerous ungulates (hooved mammals) or grazing animals (Lewin, 1986; Simmons, 1989). Although climate change (warming) was undoubtedly a factor in these Pleistocene extinctions, hunting and other human activities may also have been important. Although there is some dispute as to when humans first entered North America from Asia, it is certain that they were firmly established by at least 12,000 years ago (and probably earlier).

We have no direct evidence that early American big game hunters contributed to extinctions; but we do have evidence of what can happen to indigenous species when new areas are colonized by humans for the first time. Within just a few centuries of human occupation of New Zealand, the moa, a large flightless bird, was exterminated. Madagascar serves as a similar example. In the last one thousand years, after the arrival of permanent human settlement, 14 species of lemurs, in addition to other mammalian and bird species, have become extinct (Jolly, 1985; Napier and Napier, 1985). One such species was *Megaladapis,* a lemur that weighed an estimated 300 pounds (Fleagle, 1999)! Lastly, scientists have debated for years whether the extinction of all large-bodied animals (some 60 species) in Australia during the late Pleistocene was due to human hunting and other activities, or to climate change.

Since the end of the Pleistocene, human activities have continued to take their toll on nonhuman species. Today, however, species are disappearing at an unprecedented rate. Hunting, which occurs for a number of reasons other than acquisition of food, continues to be a major factor (see Issue, pp. 135–136). Competition with

Holocene
The most recent epoch of the Cenozoic. Following the Pleistocene, it is estimated to have begun 10,000 years ago.

FIGURE 16–9
Stumps of recently felled forest trees are still visible in this newly cleared field in Rwanda. The haze is wood smoke from household fires.

Lynn Kilgore

introduced nonnative species, such as pigs, goats, and rats, has also contributed to the problem. But in many cases, the most important single cause of extinction is habitat reduction.

Habitat reduction is a direct result of the burgeoning human population and the resulting need for building materials, grazing and agricultural land, and living areas. We are all aware of the risk to such visible species as the elephant, panda, rhinoceros, tiger, and mountain gorilla, to name a few. These risks are real, and within your lifetime some of these will certainly become extinct, at least in the wild. But the greatest threat to biodiversity is to the countless unknown species that live in the world's rain forests (Fig. 16–9).

It is estimated that over half of all plants and animals on earth live in rain forests. By 1989, these habitats had been reduced to a little less than half their original size—that is, down to about 3 million square miles. The annual net loss between 1980 and 1995 was almost 67,000 square miles. As Harvard biologist E. O. Wilson puts it: "The loss is equal to the area of a football field every second. Put another way, in 1989 the surviving rain forests occupied an area about that of the continuous forty-eight states of the United States, and they were being reduced by an amount equivalent to the size of Florida every year" (Wilson, 1992, p. 275). By the year 2022, half the world's remaining rain forests will be gone if destruction continues at its present rate. This will result in a loss of between 10 and 22 percent of all rain forest species, or 5 to 10 percent of all plant and animal species on earth (Wilson, 1992).

Should we care about the loss of biodiversity? If so, why? In fact, there are many people who do not show much concern. Moreover, reasons as to why we should care are usually stated in terms of the benefits (known and unknown) that humans may derive from rain forest species. An example of such a benefit is the chemical taxol (derived from the Pacific yew tree), which may be an effective treatment for ovarian and breast cancer.

It is undeniable that humans stand to benefit from continued research into potentially useful rain forest products. However, such anthropocentric reasons are not the sole justification for preserving the earth's biodiversity. Each species that is lost is the product of millions of years of evolution, and each fills a specific econiche. Quite simply, the destruction of so much of the planet's biota is within our power. But ethically, we must ask ourselves, Is it within our rights?

Acceleration of Evolutionary Processes

Another of the major impacts that human activities have had is on the acceleration of the evolutionary process for hundreds of life forms. Many of these changes have occurred over one human generation, rather than the millions of years that have been familiar in our discussions of evolution in this text. For example, as noted in Chapter 15, our use of antibiotics has directed the course of evolution of several infectious diseases to the point that many have become resistant to our antibiotics. The analogy often used is that of an arms race: We use slingshots, they come back with spears; we use swords, they come back with guns; we use bigger guns, they come back with bombs; then we come back with weapons of mass destruction. Finally we reach a point where our armaments are matched and no longer work as deterrents to war. Similarly, our antibiotics reach a point where they are no longer effective on strains of infectious diseases that were once relatively mild. Human-invented antibiotics have become the agents of natural selection directing the course of evolution of many bacteria to a more virulent state.

It is even likely that human technology and lifestyles are responsible for the deadly nature of some of the so-called "new" diseases that have arisen in recent decades, such as HIV-AIDS (see p. 409), dengue hemorrhagic fever, Legionnaire's disease, Lyme disease, and resistant strains of tuberculosis, *Staphylococcus,* and *E coli.* As we write this chapter, the fear of anthrax has driven thousands of people to use antibiotics such as ciprofloxacin in the extremely rare event that they will be exposed to the deadly bacterium. Certainly, we understand the desire for preventive action on the part of those at heightened risk. But if more harmful bacteria become resistant as a by-product of this practice, the risk to society from the overuse and improper use of this powerful class of antibiotics is potentially far greater. We could reach a point where we have no antibiotics strong enough to overpower dangerous bacteria that live in our midst.

A similar phenomenon has occurred with the overuse and misuse of insecticides and pesticides on agricultural crops (Palumbi, 2001). Insects evolve resistance to each new generation of toxic agents, eventually reaching a point where they are no longer affected by most of the insecticides used on the fields. Bt toxin (*Bacillus thuringiensis*) has been highly touted as an "organic" and environmentally friendly agent because it is naturally produced (often by the crops it protects), targets specific insect larvae, and is not toxic to humans. Genes for producing Bt toxin have been engineered into millions of acres of plants, but unfortunately, recent evidence suggests that some insects are evolving resistance to it.

Perhaps one of the best-known insecticides to have altered the course of evolution of a species is DDT. When this insecticide was first developed, it was hailed as the best way to reduce malaria, eliminating the mosquitoes that transmit the disease. DDT was highly effective when it was first applied to mosquito-ridden areas, but soon, mosquitoes had evolved resistance to the powerful agent, rendering it almost useless in the fight against malaria. Moreover, the use of DDT proved disastrous to many bird species, including the bald eagle.

From these examples, it is clear that the process of evolution is something that can result in great harm for our species and planet. Certainly, none of the scientists working to develop antibiotics, insecticides, pesticides, and other biological tools intend to cause harm (with the obvious exceptions of those working for bioterrorists), but often those working in these areas lack the understanding of the evolutionary process necessary to foresee long-term consequences of their work. As the great geneticist Theodosius Dobzhansky said, "Nothing in biology makes sense except in the light of evolution." Indeed, we cannot afford even a single generation of scientists who lack knowledge about the process of evolution, which is responsible for the life forms around us, both helpful and harmful. If human actions can cause an organism to evolve from a relatively benign state to a dangerously virulent state, then there is no reason why that process cannot be "turned around." In other words, it is theoretically possible to direct the course of evolution of a dangerous organism like HIV to a more benign, less harmful state (Ewald, 1999). But this requires a very sophisticated understanding of evolution.

Are We Still Evolving?

In many ways, it seems that culture has enabled us to transcend most of the limitations imposed on us by our biology. But that biology was shaped during millions of years of evolution in environments very different from those in which most of us live today. There is, to a great extent, a lack of fit between our biology and our twenty-first-century cultural environment. Our expectations that scientists can easily and quickly discover a "magic bullet" to enable us to resist any disease that arises have been painfully dashed with rising death tolls from AIDS in many parts of the world.

Socioeconomic and political concerns also have powerful effects on our species today. Whether you die of starvation or succumb to disorders associated with overconsumption depends a great deal on where you live, what your socioeconomic status is, and how much power and control you have over your life, factors not likely to be related to biology. These factors also have an effect on whether or not you are killed in a war or spend most of your life in a safe, comfortable community. Whether or not you are exposed to one of the "new" pathogens such as HIV or tuberculosis has a lot to do with your lifestyle and other cultural factors, but whether or not you die from it or fail to reproduce because of it still has a lot to do with your biology. The 4.3 million children dying annually from respiratory infections are primarily those in the developing world, with limited access to adequate medical care, clearly a cultural factor. But in those same areas, lacking that same medical care, are millions of other children who are not getting the infections or are not dying from them. Presumably, among the factors affecting this difference is resistance afforded by genes. By considering this simple example, we can see that human gene frequencies are still changing from one generation to the next in response to selective agents such as disease; thus, our species is still evolving.

Whether we will become a different species or become extinct as a species (remember, that is the fate of almost everything that has ever lived on earth) is not something we can answer. Whether our brains will get larger, our hands will evolve solely to push buttons, or we will change genetically so that we no longer have to eat food is the stuff of science fiction, not anthropology. But as long as new pathogens appear or new environments are introduced by technology, there is little doubt that the human species will continue to evolve or will become extinct, just as every other species on earth has done.

Culture has enabled us to transcend many limits imposed by our biology, and today people who never would have been able to do so in the past are surviving and having children. This in itself means we are evolving. How many of you would be reading this text if you had been born under conditions of 500 years ago?

SUMMARY

In this chapter, we have discussed legacies of human evolutionary history that leave their marks on us today. For the individual, these legacies include patterns of growth and nutritional requirements that result from millions of years of biological evolution and thousands of years of cultural evolution. Our evolutionary history also means that human infants are relatively undeveloped at birth, especially in brain size, and require intense parental investment to reach adulthood and independence. For humans in society, legacies from evolutionary history include thought processes and behaviors that reflect natural selection operating on individuals to increase reproductive success, or fitness. A review of behavioral ecology summarizes the ways in which genes, environment, and culture have interacted to produce complex adaptations to equally complex challenges. Critical review of hypotheses for such human behaviors as aggression, violence, nurturance, and reproduction reveals the complexity of this interrelationship. The final set of legacies reviewed in this chapter concerns the impact of the human species on the planet and other life forms. Through amazing reproductive "success," the human population has reached more than 6 billion from an estimated base of about 5 million people 10,000 years ago. These numbers, coupled with technological developments, have turned humans into what Stephen Palumbi has called "the world's greatest evolutionary force." *Homo sapiens* has become a powerful agent of natural selection, influencing virtually every life form on earth, causing the extinction of many species, and accelerating evolutionary change in others.

Studies of human evolution have much to contribute to our understanding of how we, as a single species, came to exert such control over the destiny of our planet. It is a truly phenomenal story of how a small apelike creature walking on two feet across the African savanna challenged nature by learning to make stone tools. From these humble beginnings came large-brained humans who, instead of stone tools, have telecommunications satellites, computers, and nuclear arsenals at their fingertips. The human story is indeed unique and wonderful. Our two feet have carried us not only across the plains of Africa, but onto the polar caps, the ocean floor, and even across the surface of the moon! Surely, if we can accomplish so much in so short a time, we can act responsibly to preserve our home and the wondrous creatures who share it with us.

QUESTIONS FOR REVIEW

1. What is meant by the analogy, "Water is to fish as culture is to humans"?
2. Briefly describe human brain growth.
3. Give two examples of how culture and biology interact in meeting human nutritional requirements.
4. What were the characteristics of the preagricultural human diet? How does it compare with the diet of modern industrialized nations?
5. What are some of the proposed explanations for why we age?
6. Provide examples for how natural selection might act on human behaviors such as mate selection, parenting, and aggression.
7. Describe circumstances under which adolescent pregnancy might be advantageous, in an evolutionary sense. What are some of the disadvantages of adolescent pregnancy for reproductive success?

8. Under what circumstances might natural selection favor infanticide in humans?

9. What are some of the proposed explanations for menopause in human females?

10. Why do the authors of this text claim that human overpopulation is one of the greatest challenges facing our planet today?

11. Briefly discuss the trends in human population growth from 10,000 years ago to today.

12. How have humans contributed to the decrease of biodiversity on our planet?

13. Provide two examples of how human activities have had an impact on the pace of evolution of other life forms.

14. Are we still evolving? What evidence is there that we are still subject to the forces of evolution?

SUGGESTED FURTHER READING

Bogin, Barry. 1988. *Patterns of Human Growth.* Cambridge: Cambridge University Press.

Cohen, Mark Nathan. 1989. *Health and the Rise of Civilization.* New Haven: Yale University Press.

Diamond, Jared. 1992. *The Third Chimpanzee: The Evolution and Future of the Human Animal.* New York: Harper Collins.

Diamond, J. 1997. *Why Is Sex Fun? The Evolution of Human Sexuality.* New York: Basic Books.

Eaton, S. Boyd, Marjorie Shostak, and Melvin Konner. 1988. *The Paleolithic Prescription.* New York: Harper & Row.

Hrdy, Sarah Blaffer. 1999. *Mother Nature: A History of Mothers, Infants, and Natural Selection.* New York: Pantheon Books.

Palumbi, Stephen R. 2001. *The Evolution Explosion: How Humans Cause Rapid Evolutionary Change.* New York: Norton.

Potts, M., and R. Short. 1999. *Ever Since Adam and Eve: The Evolution of Human Sexuality.* Cambridge, England: Cambridge University Press.

Trevathan, W. R., E. O. Smith, and J. J. McKenna (eds.). 1999. *Evolutionary Medicine.* New York: Oxford University Press.

Ulijaszek, S. J., F. E. Johnston, and M. A. Preece (eds.). 1998. *The Cambridge Encyclopedia of Human Growth and Development.* Cambridge, England: Cambridge University Press.

Ward, Peter. 1994. *The End of Evolution.* New York: Bantam Books.

Wilson, Edward O. 1992. *The Diversity of Life.* Cambridge, MA: Harvard University Press.

Wrangham, Richard and Dale Peterson. 1996. *Demonic Males: Apes and the Origins of Human Violence.* Boston: Houghton Mifflin.

World Resources. 1996–97. *A Guide to the Global Environment.* A joint publication by The World Resources Institute, the United Nations Environment Programme, the United Nations Development Programme, and the World Bank.

RESOURCES ON THE INTERNET

Wadsworth Anthropology Resource Center
http://anthropology.wadsworth.com

The companion website for this text includes a range of enrichment material focused on the chapter's topic. While online you can enhance your understanding of the chapter by exploring one of the several additional Internet exercises, by researching topics, and by accessing full articles on InfoTrac College Edition. You can also reinforce the concepts by taking online practice exams.

Internet Exercises

An evolutionary perspective on human behavior is the focus of study for scholars who are members of the Human Behavior and Evolution Society (HBES). Go to their webpage **http://www.hbes.com/** and read how this group of scholars answers the question *"How can modern evolutionary theory help to advance our understanding of human behavior?"* Explore this website for journal articles that may be of interest to you. You can even go to the section entitled "web-based research" and participate in an ongoing study of human behavior.

InfoTrac College Edition
http://www.infotrac-college.com/wadsworth

1. One of the stages of growth is adolescence. To look at this stage in a little more detail, read "Growth and Normal Puberty" from *Pediatrics,* on InfoTrac College Edition. How does growth during adolescence usually proceed? Think about your own adolescence and puberty. How does your own development correspond to the averages?
2. Read "Why Women Change" by Jared Diamond, from *Discover,* on InfoTrac College Edition. How does Diamond propose that menopause evolved? Does this explanation concur with the theory proposed in the text?
3. How long can people live, and what determines maximum life span? Read "Evolution, mutations, and human longevity: European royal and noble families" by Gavrilova et al., in *Human Biology,* on InfoTrac College Edition. What evidence do these authors propose for the evolution of human longevity?

Appendix A
Atlas of Primate Skeletal Anatomy

Parietal

Temporal

Zygomatic

Occipital

Cervical vertebrae (7)

Lumbar vertebrae (5)

Ilium

Sacrum

Pubis

Ischium

Femur

Patella

Tibia

Fibula

Tarsals (7)
Metatarsals (5)
Phalanges (14)

Frontal

Maxilla

Mandible

Clavicle

Scapula

Sternum

Ribs

Thoracic vertebrae (12)

Humerus

Ulna

Radius

Carpals (8)

Metacarpals (5)

Phalanges (14)

HUMAN SKELETON

FIGURE A–1
Human skeleton
(*Homo sapiens*)—bipedal hominid.

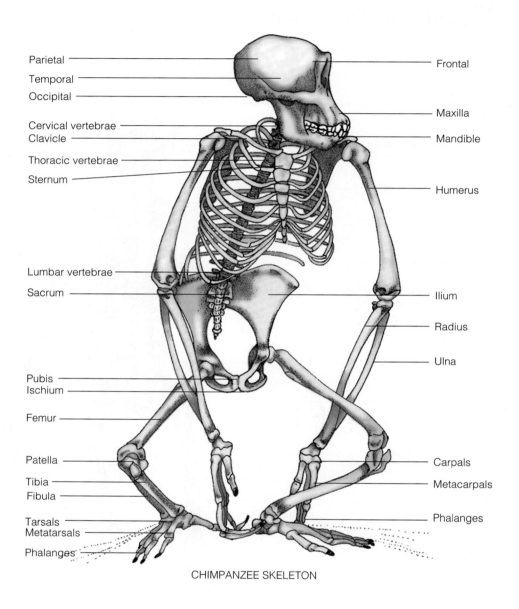

CHIMPANZEE SKELETON

FIGURE A–2
Chimpanzee skeleton (*Pan troglodytes*)—
knuckle-walking pongid.

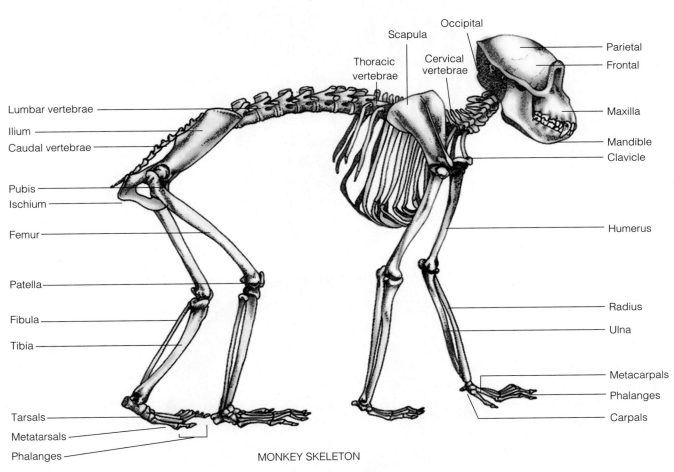

Occipital
Scapula
Thoracic vertebrae
Cervical vertebrae
Parietal
Frontal
Lumbar vertebrae
Ilium
Caudal vertebrae
Maxilla
Mandible
Clavicle
Pubis
Ischium
Femur
Humerus
Patella
Fibula
Tibia
Radius
Ulna
Metacarpals
Phalanges
Tarsals
Carpals
Metatarsals
Phalanges

MONKEY SKELETON

FIGURE A–3
Monkey skeleton (rhesus macaque; *Macaca mulatta*)—a typical quadrupedal primate.

FIGURE A–4
Human cranium.
(continued on next page)

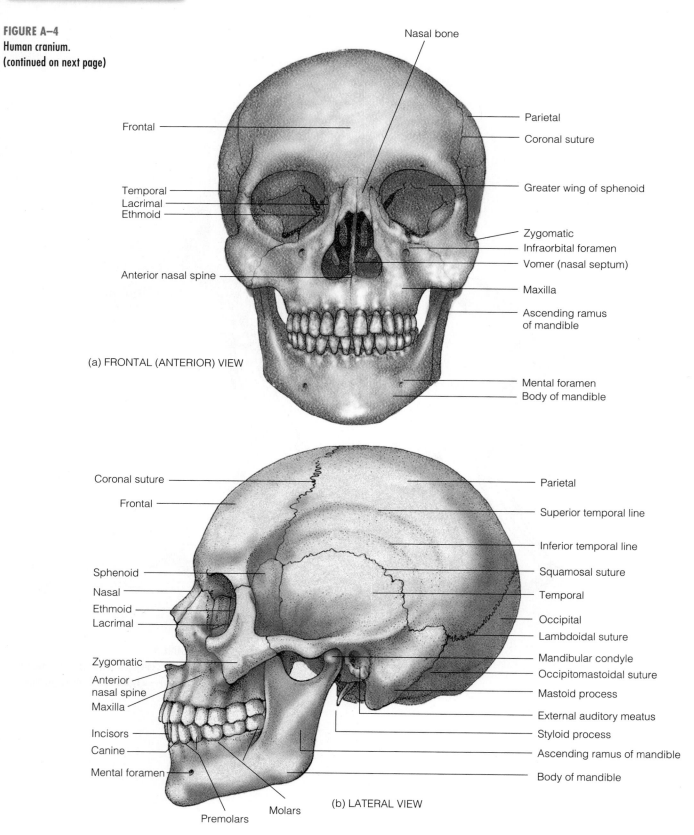

Nasal bone

Frontal

Parietal

Coronal suture

Temporal
Lacrimal
Ethmoid

Greater wing of sphenoid

Zygomatic

Infraorbital foramen

Vomer (nasal septum)

Anterior nasal spine

Maxilla

Ascending ramus
of mandible

(a) FRONTAL (ANTERIOR) VIEW

Mental foramen
Body of mandible

Coronal suture

Frontal

Parietal

Superior temporal line

Inferior temporal line

Sphenoid

Nasal

Ethmoid

Lacrimal

Squamosal suture

Temporal

Occipital

Lambdoidal suture

Zygomatic

Anterior
nasal spine

Maxilla

Incisors

Canine

Mental foramen

Mandibular condyle

Occipitomastoidal suture

Mastoid process

External auditory meatus

Styloid process

Ascending ramus of mandible

Body of mandible

Premolars

Molars

(b) LATERAL VIEW

FIGURE A–4
Human cranium. (continued)

Incisors
Canine
Premolars

Maxilla
Molars
Zygomatic arch
Vomer
Foramen spinosum
Styloid process
External auditory meatus
Jugular foramen
Hypoglossal canal
Mastoid foramen
Inferior nuchal line
Superior nuchal line
External occipital protuberance

Zygomatic bone
Zygomatic process of maxilla
Palatine bone
Zygomatic process of temporal
Sphenoid
Pterygoid process
Mandibular fossa
Carotid canal
Stylomastoid foramen
Foramen magnum
Occipital condyle
Parietal
Occipital

(c) BASILAR VIEW

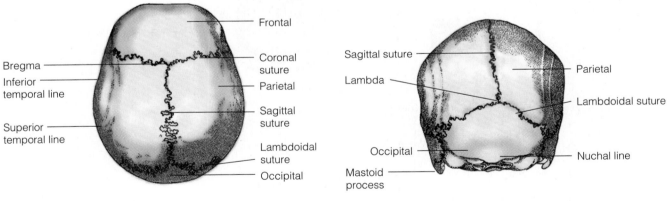

Frontal
Bregma
Inferior temporal line
Superior temporal line

Coronal suture
Parietal
Sagittal suture
Lambdoidal suture
Occipital

(d) SUPERIOR VIEW

Sagittal suture
Lambda
Occipital
Mastoid process

Parietal
Lambdoidal suture
Nuchal line

(e) REAR VIEW

445

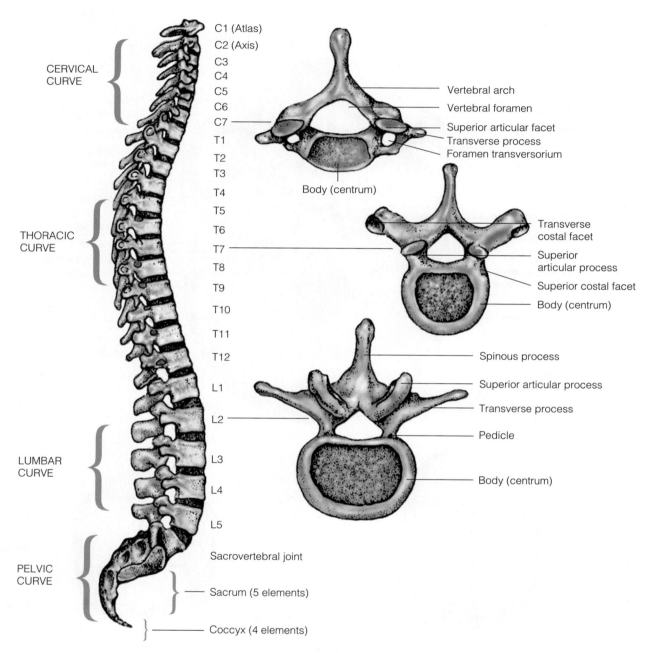

CERVICAL
CURVE

C1 (Atlas)
C2 (Axis)
C3
C4
C5
C6
C7
T1
T2
T3
T4

Vertebral arch
Vertebral foramen
Superior articular facet
Transverse process
Foramen transversorium

Body (centrum)

THORACIC
CURVE

T5
T6
T7
T8
T9
T10
T11
T12

Transverse
costal facet

Superior
articular process

Superior costal facet

Body (centrum)

L1

Spinous process

Superior articular process

Transverse process

Pedicle

Body (centrum)

LUMBAR
CURVE

L2
L3
L4
L5

PELVIC
CURVE

Sacrovertebral joint

Sacrum (5 elements)

Coccyx (4 elements)

FIGURE A–5

Human vertebral column (lateral view) and representative cervical, thoracic, and lumbar vertebrae (superior views).

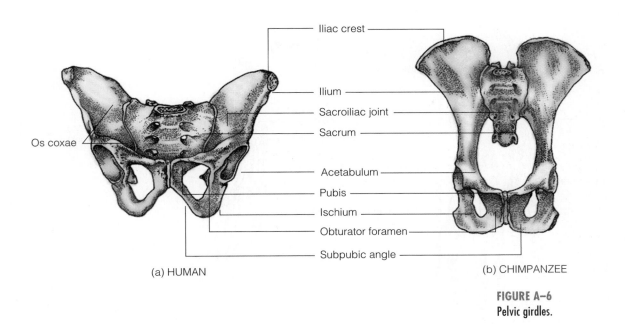

Iliac crest

Ilium

Sacroiliac joint

Sacrum

Os coxae

Acetabulum

Pubis

Ischium

Obturator foramen

Subpubic angle

(a) HUMAN

(b) CHIMPANZEE

FIGURE A–6
Pelvic girdles.

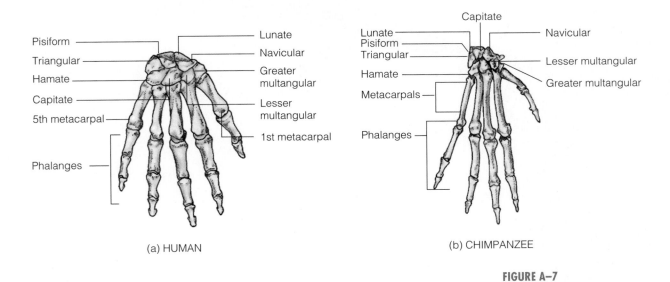

Pisiform

Triangular

Hamate

Capitate

5th metacarpal

Phalanges

Lunate

Navicular

Greater
multangular

Lesser
multangular

1st metacarpal

Capitate

Lunate

Pisiform

Triangular

Hamate

Metacarpals

Phalanges

Navicular

Lesser multangular

Greater multangular

(a) HUMAN

(b) CHIMPANZEE

FIGURE A–7
Hand anatomy.

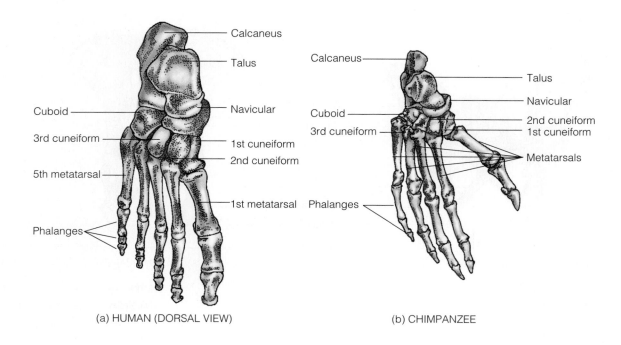

(a) HUMAN (DORSAL VIEW)

Calcaneus

Talus

Navicular

Cuboid

3rd cuneiform

1st cuneiform

2nd cuneiform

5th metatarsal

1st metatarsal

Phalanges

Calcaneus

Talus

Navicular

Cuboid

2nd cuneiform

3rd cuneiform

1st cuneiform

Metatarsals

Phalanges

(b) CHIMPANZEE

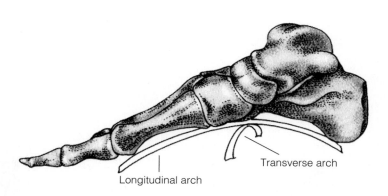

Transverse arch

Longitudinal arch

(c) HUMAN (MEDIAL VIEW)

FIGURE A–8
Foot (pedal) anatomy.

Appendix B
Population Genetics:
The Math of Microevolution

Part A. Further Examples Using the Hardy-Weinberg Equilibrium Formula

Example 1. Hemoglobin Beta Locus in West Africa

As discussed in Chapter 14, there is a high frequency of the Hb^S allele in parts of West Africa. One study (see p. 384) in a Senegalese group found a frequency of the Hb^S allele at 12 percent.

What follows is a hypothetical example for a Senegalese population of 4,000 individuals. Ascertainment is done on all individuals at 6 months of age. Because of incomplete dominance, all three phenotypes (and therefore all three genotypes) can be determined.

Observed frequencies:

	Number of Individuals	Hb^A Alleles	Hb^S Alleles
Hb^AHb^A	3,070	6,140	——
Hb^AHb^S	905	905	905
Hb^SHb^S	25	——	50
Totals	4,000	7,045	955

Allele frequencies:

$Hb^A(p) = 7{,}045/8{,}000 = .881$

$Hb^S(q) = 955/8{,}000 = .119$

Expected genotypic frequencies:

$Hb^AHb^A = p^2 = (.881)(.881) = .776$

$Hb^AHb^S = 2pq = 2(.881)(.119) = .210$

$Hb^SHb^S = q^2 = (.119)(.119) = .014$

Comparison of expected and observed frequencies:

	Expected Frequency	Expected No. Individuals	Observed Frequency	Observed No. Individuals
Hb^AHb^A	.776	3,105	.767	3,070
Hb^AHb^S	.210	839	.227	905
Hb^SHb^S	.014	57	.006	25

As you can see, there is a noticeable difference between the expected and observed frequencies. There are fewer actual (observed) individuals of both homozygotes than expected and more heterozygotes than expected. Indeed, when performing a statistical test (see Part 2 of this appendix), the difference is statistically significant.

We can extend the example further. Let us assume that we again ascertain allele frequencies in this same population 30 years later, at which point there are 3,000 survivors.

Observed phenotypic frequencies:

	Number of Individuals	Hb^A Alleles	Hb^S Alleles
Hb^AHb^A	2,123	4,246	——
Hb^AHb^S	875	875	875
Hb^SHb^S	2	——	4
Totals	3,000	5,121	879

Allele frequencies:

$Hb^A(p) = 5,121/6,000 = .854$

$Hb^S(q) = 879/6,000 = .146$

Expected genotypic frequencies:

$Hb^AHb^A = p^2 = (.854)(.854) = .729$

$Hb^AHb^S = 2pq = 2(.854)(.146) = .249$

$Hb^SHb^S = q^2 = (.146)(.146) = .021$

Comparison of expected and observed frequencies:

	Expected Frequency	Expected No. Individuals	Observed Frequency	Observed No. Individuals
Hb^AHb^A	.729	2,188	.708	2,123
Hb^AHb^S	.249	748	.292	875
Hb^SHb^S	.021	64	.001	2

In this adult sample, the differences between the expected and observed frequencies are even greater than they were for the infant sample (and are even more highly statistically significant; see Part 2). Moreover, these differences are in the same direction as before: There are fewer homozygotes and more heterozygotes than expected under equilibrium conditions. A likely explanation for this pattern of allele frequencies would focus on natural selection. At age 6 months, there are slightly fewer Hb^AHb^A homozygotes than expected and considerably fewer Hb^SHb^S homozygotes than expected. Correspondingly, there are many more heterozygotes (Hb^AHb^S) than expected. These differences could arise from differential mortality of Hb^AHb^A individuals due to malaria (likely in early infancy) and Hb^SHb^S individuals due to sickle-cell anemia occurring both *in utero* and during early infancy.

These same factors would continue throughout childhood and early adulthood, so that by age 30, the effects of differential mortality due to both malaria and sickle-cell anemia are even more dramatic. While hypothetical, these figures represent a good example of how natural selection could operate on this population.

Example 2. Adenosine Deaminase (ADA) in a Sri Lankan Population

ADA is an enzyme present in many types of cells. The locus producing this enzyme has two common codominant alleles, A^1 and A^2. There are also very rare mutant alleles that can cause a fatal form of inherited immune deficiency.

From actual data derived from a polymorphic population in Sri Lanka,* the following observed frequencies were found. (*Note:* Because the alleles are codominant, the three phenotypes correspond directly to the three genotypes.)

	Number of Individuals	A^1 Alleles	A^2 Alleles
A^1A^1	113	216	——
A^1A^2	38	38	38
A^2A^2	3	——	6
Totals	154	264	44

Allele frequencies:

$A^1 = p = 264/308 = .857$

$A^2 = q = 44/308 = .143$

Expected genotypic frequencies:

$A^1A^1 = p^2 = (.857)(.857) = .734$

$A^1A^2 = 2pq = 2(.857)(.143) = .249$

$A^2A^2 = q^2 = (.143)(.143) = .020$

Comparison of expected and observed frequencies:

	Expected Frequency	Expected No. Individuals	Observed Frequency	Observed No. Individuals
A^1A^1	.734	113	.734	113
A^1A^2	.245	38	.247	38
A^2A^2	.020	3	.019	3

As you can clearly see, the expected and observed frequencies are nearly identical (in fact, the raw frequencies are identical). There is thus a probability of 1.0 that the null hypothesis is correct and a 0 percent confidence limit in rejecting the null hypothesis. This population at this locus thus appears to be in equilibrium. Such is often the case in actual population genetics studies, especially when the sample size is small.

---

*Data from Bodmer and Cavalli-Sforza, 1976.

Example 3. Determining the Number of Heterozygous Carriers for PKU in a Hypothetical Population

Another way to apply the Hardy-Weinberg formula is to first *assume* equilibrium and then work the formula in reverse. For example, for many recessive traits where there is complete dominance (or nearly complete dominance), traditionally it has been impossible to ascertain the heterozygotes directly. However, if we make certain assumptions, we can use the formula to estimate the number of heterozygotes (i.e., carriers) in a population.

Let us assume that we are studying PKU in a group of 20,000 students at a university. PKU is an autosomal recessive disorder with an overall frequency in the United States of approximately 1/10,000 (see p. 77). In some subgroups (e.g., individuals of European descent), the frequency of PKU is higher.

In our hypothetical student population, we find two individuals with PKU (which was treated when the individuals were children). Because PKU is an autosomal recessive, the number of PKU homozygotes (2/20,000, or .0001) is equal to q^2.

If q^2 = .0001, then
q = .01   and p = .99

The frequency of the heterozygote is $2pq$:

2(.99)(.01) = .0198

The estimated number of carriers for PKU in the university student sample is

(.0198)(20,000) = 198

An interesting pattern is evident here. In the entire population, there is a total of 200 individuals who possess at least one PKU allele. Of these, the vast majority (99 percent) are carriers.

Example 4. Applying the Hardy-Weinberg Formula to ABO, a More Complex Genetic System

In Chapter 14 and in the three examples given so far in this appendix, we have used examples of loci with only two alleles (and therefore just three possible genotypes). However, many loci are more complex, having three or more alleles. For example, ABO has three alleles and six genotypes (see Table 4–3, p. 78)

How do we utilize the Hardy-Weinberg equilibrium formula for a locus like ABO? First, there are three alleles, so the allele frequencies are designated as:

Frequency of $A = p$
Frequency of B = q
Frequency of $O = r$

Under equilibrium conditions, the genotypic frequencies would be calculated as follows:

$$(p + q + r)^2 = 1$$

This is an expansion of a trinomial (rather than the binomial used in a two-allele system). With a three-allele system like ABO, the genotypic frequency formula is

$$p^2 + 2pq + 2pr + 2qr + q^2 = r^2 = 1$$

There are six terms in this formula, each one representing a different genotype:

Term	Genotype Represented
p^2	AA
$2pq$	AB
$2pr$	AO
$2qr$	BO
q^2	BB
r^2	OO

We will not include actual numbers here. We simply wish to illustrate that population genetics calculations can be considerably more complex than implied by our earlier examples.

Part B. Statistical Evaluation: Testing Hardy-Weinberg Results

Following are the results using statistical tests comparing the expected and observed frequencies for the relevant examples shown in Chapter 14 as well as those discussed in this appendix. The test used is the chi-square (χ^2), which assumes that two variables are independent. In our examples, this independence is tested against a null hypothesis stating that there is equilibrium (in other words, the expected and observed frequencies do not differ any more than would be the case strictly as a result of chance). Further details concerning statistical approaches can be found in any introductory statistics text.

In the data tables that follow, all figures are shown as *raw* frequencies.

MN Data (from Chapter 14, p. 371) Contingency Table:

Observed frequencies	80	80	40
Expected frequencies	72	96	32

$\chi^2 = 2.76$, $p = .251$

This generally accepted confidence limit for rejection of the null hypothesis is less than or equal to .05. Thus, in this case, we cannot confidently reject the null hypothesis.

PTC Tasting Data (from Chapter 14, p. 372) Contingency Table:

Observed frequencies	125	325	50
Expected frequencies	165	245	90

$\chi^2 = 28.17, p < .0000$

This result is highly significant and allows us to reject the null hypothesis with a great deal of confidence. We are able to say there is less than one chance in 10,000 that the null hypothesis applies to these data.

Hemoglobin Beta Locus (Example 1, this appendix) Contingency Tables:

At 6 months:

Observed frequencies	3,070	905	25
Expected frequencies	3,105	839	57

$\chi^2 = 15.18, p = .0005$

This is a highly significant result that allows us to reject the null hypothesis with high confidence.

At Age 30:

Observed frequencies	2,123	875	2
Expected frequencies	2,188	748	64

$\chi^2 = 69.16, p < .0000$

This result is even more highly significant than at age 6 months, as there has been further disruption of equilibrium expectations (i.e., greater evidence of evolutionary shifts in allele frequencies).

Appendix C

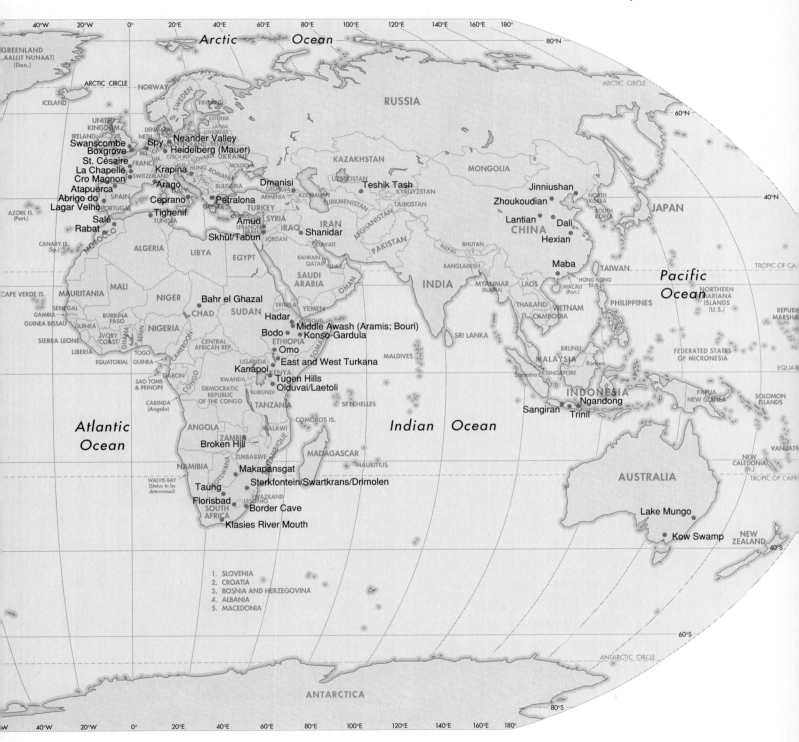

1. SLOVENIA
2. CROATIA
3. BOSNIA AND HERZEGOVINA
4. ALBANIA
5. MACEDONIA

Geographic Distribution of Living Nonhuman Primates

World Political Map

1. SLOVENIA
2. CROATIA
3. BOSNIA AND HERZEGOVINA
4. ALBANIA
5. MACEDONIA

Glossary

Acclimatization Physiological response to changes in the environment that occurs during an individual's lifetime. Such responses may be temporary or permanent. The *capacity* for acclimatization may typify an entire population or species. This capacity is under genetic influence and thus is subject to evolutionary factors such as natural selection.

Acheulian (ash´-oo-lay-en) Pertaining to a stone tool industry of the Lower and Middle Pleistocene characterized by a large proportion of bifacial tools (flaked on both sides). Acheulian tool kits are very common in Africa, Southwest Asia, and western Europe, but are nearly absent elsewhere. (Also spelled "Acheulean.")

Adaptation Functional response of organisms or populations to the environment. Adaptation results from evolutionary change (specifically, as a result of natural selection).

Adaptive niche The entire way of life of an organism: where it lives, what it eats, how it gets food, how it avoids predators, etc.

Adaptive radiation The relatively rapid expansion and diversification of life forms into new ecological niches.

Affiliative Pertaining to amicable associations between individuals. Affiliative behaviors, such as grooming, reinforce social bonds and promote group cohesion.

Allele frequency In a population, the percentage of all the alleles at a locus accounted for by one specific allele.

Alleles Alternate forms of a gene. Alleles occur at the same locus on homologous chromosomes and thus govern the same trait. However, because they are different, their action may result in different expressions of that trait. The term is sometimes used synonymously with *gene*.

Allometry Also called "scaling," the differential proportion among various anatomical structures. For example, the relative size of the brain changes during the development of an individual. Moreover, scaling effects must also be considered when comparing species.

Alloparenting A common behavior in many primate species whereby individuals other than the parent(s) hold, carry, and in general interact with infants.

Allopatric A model of speciation emphasizing complete (or nearly complete) reproductive isolation of divergent populations from their ancestral population.

Altruism Behaving in a manner that benefits another individual but at some potential risk or cost to oneself.

Amino acids Small molecules that are the components of proteins.

Analogies Similarities between organisms based strictly on common function with no assumed common evolutionary descent.

Anatomically modern *Homo sapiens* All modern humans and some fossil forms, perhaps dating as early as 200,000 y.a.; defined by a set of derived characteristics, including cranial architecture and lack of skeletal robusticity; usually classified at the subspecies level as *Homo sapiens sapiens*.

Ancestral (primitive) Referring to characters inherited by a group of organisms from a remote ancestor and thus not diagnostic of groups (lineages) branching subsequent to the time the character first appeared.

Anthropocentric Viewing non-human phenomena in terms of human experience and capabilities; emphasizing the importance of humans over everything else.

Anthropoids Members of a sub-order of Primates, the *Anthropoidea* (pronounced "ann-throw-poid´-ee-uh"). Traditionally, the suborder includes monkeys, apes, and humans.

Anthropology The field of inquiry that studies human culture and evolutionary aspects of human biology; includes cultural anthropology, archaeology, linguistics, and physical anthropology.

Anthropometry Measurement of human body parts. When osteologists measure skeletal elements, the term *osteometry* is often used.

Antigens Large molecules found on the surface of cells. Several different loci governing antigens on red and white blood cells are known. (Foreign antigens provoke an immune response in individuals.)

Arboreal Tree-living: adapted to life in the trees.

Arboreal hypothesis The traditional view that primate characteristics can be explained as a consequence of primate diversification into arboreal habitats.

Archaic *Homo sapiens* Earlier forms of *Homo sapiens* (including Neandertals) from the Old World that differ from *H. erectus* but lack the full set of characteristics diagnostic of modern *H. sapiens*.

Artifacts Objects or materials made or modified for use by hominids. The earliest artifacts tend to be tools made of stone or, occasionally, bone.

Association What an archaeological trace is found with.

Aurignacian Pertaining to an Upper Paleolithic stone tool industry in Europe beginning at about 40,000 y.a.

Australopithecine (os-tra-loh-pith´-e-seen) The colloquial name for members of the genus *Australopithecus*. The term was first used as a subfamily designation, but it is now most commonly used informally.

Australopithecus An early hominid genus, known from the Plio-Pleistocene of Africa, characterized by bipedal locomotion, a relatively small brain, and large back teeth.

Autonomic Pertaining to physiological responses not under voluntary control. An example in chimpanzees would be the erection of body hair during excitement. An example in humans is blushing. Both convey information regarding emotional states, but neither is a deliberate behavior, and communication is not intended.

Autosomes All chromosomes except the sex chromosomes.

Balanced polymorphism The maintenance of two or more alleles in a population due to the selective advantage of the heterozygote.

Behavioral ecology The study of the evolution of behavior, emphasizing the role of ecological factors as agents of natural selection. Behaviors and behavioral patterns have been selected for because they increase reproductive fitness in individuals (i.e., they are adaptive) in specific ecological contexts.

Binocular vision Vision characterized by overlapping visual fields provided by forward-facing eyes; essential to depth perception.

Binomial nomenclature (*binomial*, meaning "two names") In taxonomy, the convention established by Carolus Linnaeus whereby genus and species names are used to refer to species. For example, *Homo sapiens* refers to human beings.

Biocultural evolution The mutual, interactive evolution of human biology and culture; the concept that biology makes culture possible and that developing culture further influences the direction of biological evolution; a basic concept in understanding the unique components of human evolution.

Biological continuum Refers to the fact that organisms are related through common ancestry and that behaviors and traits seen in one species are also seen in others to varying degrees. (When expressions of a phenomenon continuously grade into one another so that there are no discrete categories, they are said to exist on a continuum. Color is such a phenomenon.)

Biological determinism The concept that phenomena, including various aspects of behavior (e.g., intelligence, values, morals) are governed by biological (genetic) factors; the inaccurate association of various behavioral attributes with certain biological traits, such as skin color.

Biological species concept A depiction of species as groups of individuals capable of fertile interbreeding, but reproductively isolated from other such groups.

Biostratigraphy Dating method based on evolutionary changes within an evolving lineage.

Bipedally On two feet. Walking habitually on two legs is the single most distinctive feature of the Hominidae.

Brachiation A form of locomotion in which the body is suspended beneath the hands and support is alternated from one forelimb to the other; arm swinging.

Brachycephalic Having a broad head in which the width measures more than 80 percent of the length.

Breeding isolates Populations that are clearly isolated geographically and/or socially from other breeding groups.

Burins Small, chisel-like tools (with a pointed end) thought to have been used to engrave bone, antler, ivory, or wood.

Catastrophism The view that the earth's geological landscape is the result of violent cataclysmic events. This view was promoted by Cuvier, especially in opposition to Lamarck.

Centromere The constricted portion of a chromosome. After replication, the two strands of a double-stranded chromosome are joined at the centromere.

Cercopithecines (serk-oh-pith´-eh-seens) The subfamily of Old World monkeys that includes baboons, macaques, and guenons.

Chatelperronian Pertaining to an Upper Paleolithic tool industry found in France and Spain, containing blade tools and associated with Neandertals.

Chordata   The phylum of the animal kingdom that includes vertebrates.

Chromatin   The loose, diffuse form of DNA seen during interphase. When condensed, chromatin forms into chromosomes.

Chromosomes   Discrete structures composed of DNA and protein found only in the nuclei of cells. Chromosomes are only visible under magnification during certain phases of cell division.

Chronometric dating   (*chrono,* meaning "time," and *metric,* meaning "measure") A dating technique that gives an estimate in actual numbers of years.

Cladistics   An approach to classification that seeks to make rigorous evolutionary interpretations based solely on analysis of certain types of homologous characters (those considered derived characters).

Cladogram   A chart showing evolutionary relationships as determined by cladistic analysis. It is based solely on interpretation of shared derived characters. No time component is indicated, and ancestor-descendant relationships are *not* implied.

Classification   In biology, the ordering of organisms into categories, such as phyla, orders, and families, to show evolutionary relationships.

Cline   Gradual change in the frequency of genotypes and phenotypes over geographical space.

Clone   An organism that is genetically identical to another organism. The term may also be used to refer to genetically identical DNA segments and molecules.

Codominance   The expression of two alleles in heterozygotes. In this situation, neither allele is dominant or recessive, so that both influence the phenotype.

Codon   A triplet of messenger RNA bases that refers to a specific amino acid during protein synthesis.

Colobines   (kole´-uh-beans) The subfamily of Old World monkeys that includes the African colobus monkeys and Asian langurs.

Communication   Any act that conveys information, in the form of a message, to another individual. Frequently, the result of communication is a change in the behavior of the recipient. Communication may not be deliberate but may be the result of involuntary processes or a secondary consequence of an intentional action.

Complementary   Referring to the fact that DNA bases form base pairs in a precise manner. For example, adenine can bond only to thymine. Thus, these two bases are said to be *complementary* because one requires the other to form a complete DNA base pair.

Conspecifics   Members of the same species.

Context   The environmental setting where an archaeological trace is found. A *primary* context is a setting in which an archaeological trace was originally deposited. A *secondary* context is one to which it has been moved (e.g., by the action of a stream).

Continental drift   The movement of continents on sliding plates of the earth's surface. As a result, the positions of large landmasses have shifted dramatically during the earth's history.

Continuum   A set of relationships in which all components fall along a single integrated spectrum. All life reflects a single *biological* continuum.

Core   Stone reduced by flake removal, and not necessarily a "tool" itself.

Core area   The portion of a home range containing the highest concentration and most reliable supplies of food and water. The core area is frequently the area that will be defended.

Culture   All aspects of human adaptation, including technology, traditions, language, religion, marriage patterns, and social roles. Culture is a set of learned behaviors that is transmitted from one generation to the next by nonbiological means.

Cusps   The elevated portions (bumps) on the chewing surfaces of premolar and molar teeth.

Cytoplasm   The portion of the cell contained within the cell membrane, excluding the nucleus. The cytoplasm consists of a semifluid material and contains numerous structures involved with cell function.

Data   (*sing.,* datum) Facts from which conclusions can be drawn; scientific information.

Deoxyribonucleic acid (DNA)   The double-stranded molecule that contains the genetic code. DNA is a main component of chromosomes.

Derived (modified)   Referring to characters that are modified from the ancestral condition and thus *are* diagnostic of particular evolutionary lineages.

Diploid   Referring to the full complement of chromosomes in a somatic cell—two of each pair.

Direct percussion   Striking a core or flake with a hammerstone.

Displays   Sequences of repetitious behaviors that serve to communicate emotional states. Nonhuman primate displays are most frequently associated with reproductive or agonistic behavior.

Diurnal   Active during the day.

Dolichocephalic   Having a long, narrow head in which the width measures less than 75 percent of the length.

Dominance hierarchies   Systems of social organization wherein individuals within a group are ranked relative to one another. Higher-ranking individuals have greater access to preferred food items and mating partners than lower-ranking individuals. Dominance hierarchies are sometimes referred to as "pecking orders."

Dominant   Describing a trait governed by an allele that can be expressed in the presence of another, different allele (i.e., in heterozygotes). Dominant alleles prevent the expression of recessive alleles in heterozygotes. (This is the definition of *complete* dominance.)

Ecological   Pertaining to the relationship between organisms and all aspects of their environment (temperature, predators, other animals, vegetation, availability of food and water, types of food, etc.)

Ecological niches   The positions of species within their physical and biological environments, together making up the *ecosystem*. A species' ecological niche is defined by such components as diet, terrain, vegetation, type of predators, relationships with other species, and activity patterns, and each niche is unique to a given species.

Ecological species concept   The concept that a species is a group of organisms exploiting a single niche. This view emphasizes the role of natural selection in separating species from one another.

Empirical   Relying on experiment or observation; from the Latin *empiricus,* meaning "experienced."

Encephalization   The proportional size of the brain relative to some other measure, usually some estimate of overall body size. More precisely, the term refers to increases in brain size beyond that which would be expected given the body size of a particular species.

Endemic   Continuously present in a population.

Endocast   A solid impression of the inside of the skull, often preserving details relating to the size and surface features of the brain.

Endogamy   Mating with individuals from the same group.

Endothermic   (*endo*, meaning "within" or "internal") Able to maintain internal body temperature through the production of energy by means of metabolic processes within cells; characteristic of mammals, birds, and perhaps some dinosaurs.

Environmental determinism An interpretation that links simple environmental changes directly to a major evolutionary shift in an organism. Such explanations tend to be extreme oversimplifications of the evolutionary process.

Enzymes   Specialized proteins that initiate and direct chemical reactions in the body.

Epochs   Categories of the geological time scale; subdivisions of periods. In the Cenozoic, epochs include the Paleocene, Eocene, Oligocene, Miocene, Pliocene (from the Tertiary), and the Pleistocene and Holocene (from the Quaternary).

Estrus   (ess´-truss) Period of sexual receptivity in female mammals (except humans), correlated with ovulation. When used as an adjective, the word is spelled "estrous."

Ethnocentric   Viewing other cultures from the inherently biased perspective of one's own culture. Ethnocentrism often results in cultures being seen as inferior to one's own.

Ethnographies   Detailed descriptive studies of human societies. In cultural anthropology, an ethnography is traditionally the study of a non-Western society.

Eugenics   The philosophy of "race improvement" through the forced sterilization of members of some groups and increased reproduction among others; an overly simplified, often racist view that is now discredited.

Evolution   A change in the genetic structure of a population. The term is also frequently used to refer to the appearance of a new species.

Evolutionary pulse theory A view that postulates a correlation of periods of hominid diversification during the Pliocene and early Pleistocene with major shifts in several African mammalian species. These changes in mammalian evolution, in turn, are thought to be related to periodic episodes of aridity.

Evolutionary systematics   A traditional approach to classification (and evolutionary interpretation) in which presumed ancestors and descendants are traced in time by analysis of homologous characters.

Exogamy   Mating pattern whereby individuals obtain mates from groups other than their own.

Fitness   Pertaining to natural selection, a measure of *relative* reproductive success of individuals. Fitness can be measured by an individual's genetic contribution to the next generation compared to that of other individuals.

Fixity of species   The notion that species, once created, can never change; an idea diametrically opposed to theories of biological evolution.

Flake   Thin-edged fragment removed from a core.

Flexed   The position of the body in a bent orientation, with the arms and legs drawn up to the chest.

Foramen magnum   The opening at the base of the skull through which the spinal cord passes as it enters the body to descend through the vertebral column. In quadrupeds, it is located more to the rear of the skull, while in bipeds, it is located farther beneath the skull.

Forensic anthropology   An applied anthropological approach dealing with legal matters. Physical anthropologists work with coroners and others in the analysis and identification of human remains.

Founder effect   Also called the *Sewall Wright effect,* a type of genetic drift in which allele frequencies are altered in small populations that are taken from, or are remnants of, larger populations.

Free-ranging   Pertaining to non-captive animals living in their natural habitat, largely free from constraints imposed by humans.

Frugivorous   (fru-give´-or-us) Having a diet composed primarily of fruit.

Gametes   Reproductive cells (eggs and sperm in animals) developed from precursor cells in ovaries and testes.

Gene   A sequence of DNA bases that specifies the order of amino acids in an entire protein or, in some cases, a portion of a protein. A gene may be made up of hundreds or thousands of DNA bases.

Gene pool   The total complement of genes shared by reproductive members of a population.

Genetic drift   Evolutionary changes—that is, changes in allele frequencies—produced by random factors. Genetic drift is a result of small population size.

Genetics   The study of gene structure and action and the patterns of inheritance of traits from parent to offspring. Genetic mechanisms are the underlying foundation for evolutionary change.

Genome   The entire genetic makeup of an individual or species. In humans, it is estimated that each individual possesses approximately 3 billion DNA nucleotides.

Genotype   The genetic makeup of an individual. Genotype can refer to an organism's entire genetic makeup or to the alleles at a particular locus.

Genus   A group of closely related species.

Geological time scale   The organization of earth history into eras, periods, and epochs; commonly used by geologists and paleoanthropologists.

Grooming   Picking through fur to remove dirt, parasites, and other materials that may be present. Social grooming is common among primates and reinforces social relationships.

Haploid   Referring to a half set of chromosomes, one member of each pair. Haploid sets are found in gametes.

Hardy-Weinberg theory of genetic equilibrium   The mathematical relationship expressing—under ideal conditions—the predicted distribution of alleles in populations; the central theorem of population genetics.

Hemizygous   (*hemi*, meaning "half") Having only one member of a pair of alleles. Because males have only one X chromosome, all their X-linked alleles are hemizygous. All recessive alleles on a male's X chromosome are expressed in the phenotype.

Hemoglobin   A protein molecule that occurs in red blood cells and binds to oxygen molecules.

Heterodont   Having different kinds of teeth; characteristic of mammals, whose teeth consist of incisors, canines, premolars, and molars.

Heterozygous   Having different alleles at the same locus on members of a chromosome pair.

Holocene   The most recent epoch of the Cenozoic. Following the Pleistocene, it is estimated to have begun 10,000 years ago.

Home range   The area exploited by an animal or social group; usually given for one year—or for the entire lifetime—of an animal.

Homeostasis   A condition of balance, or stability, within a biological system, maintained by the interaction of physiological mechanisms that compensate for changes (both external and internal).

Hominidae   The taxonomic family to which humans belong; also includes other, now extinct, bipedal relatives.

Hominids   Colloquial term for members of the family Hominidae, which includes all bipedal hominoids back to the divergence from African great apes.

Hominoidea   The formal designation for the superfamily of anthropoids that includes apes and humans.

Hominoids   Members of the superfamily Hominoidea. This group includes apes (chimpanzees, bonobos, gorillas, orangutans, gibbons, and siamangs) and humans.

Homo habilis   (hab´-ih-liss) A species of early *Homo*, well known from East Africa but perhaps also found in other regions.

Homologies   Similarities between organisms based on descent from a common ancestor.

Homologous Referring to members of chromosome pairs. Homologous chromosomes carry loci that govern the same traits. During meiosis, homologous chromosomes pair and exchange segments of DNA. They are alike with regard to size, position of centromere, and banding pattern.

Homoplasy (*homo,* meaning "same," and *plasy,* meaning "growth") The separate evolutionary development of similar characteristics in different groups of organisms.

Homozygous Having the same allele at the same locus on both members of a chromosome pair.

Hormones Substances (usually proteins) that are produced by specialized cells and that travel to other parts of the body, where they influence chemical reactions and regulate various cellular functions.

Human Genome Project An international effort aimed at sequencing and mapping the entire human genome.

Hybrids Offspring of individuals that differ with regard to certain traits or certain aspects of genetic makeup; heterozygotes.

Hypothesis (*pl.,* hypotheses) A provisional explanation of a phenomenon. Hypotheses require verification.

Hypoxia Lack of oxygen. Hypoxia can refer to reduced amounts of available oxygen in the atmosphere (due to lowered barometric pressure) or to insufficient amounts of oxygen in the body.

Inbreeding A type of nonrandom mating in which relatives mate more often than predicted under random mating conditions.

Intelligence Mental capacity; the ability to learn, reason, or comprehend and interpret information, facts, relationships, meanings, etc.; the capacity to solve problems, whether through the application of previously acquired knowledge or through insight.

Interphase The portion of a cell's cycle during which metabolic processes and other cellular activities occur. Chromosomes are not visible as discrete structures at this time. DNA replication occurs during interphase.

Interspecific Between species; refers to variation beyond that seen within the same species to include additional aspects seen between two different species.

Intraspecific Within species; refers to variation seen within the same species.

Ischial callosities Patches of tough, hard skin on the buttocks of Old World monkeys and chimpanzees.

K-selected Pertaining to an adaptive strategy whereby individuals produce relatively few offspring, in whom they invest increased parental care. Although only a few infants are born, chances of survival are increased for each individual because of parental investments in time and energy. Examples of nonprimate K-selected species are birds and canids (e.g., wolves, coyotes, and dogs).

Karyotype The chromosomal complement of an individual or that which is typical for a species. Usually displayed in a photomicrograph, the chromosomes are arranged in pairs and according to size and position of the centromere.

Knappers Those who flake stone tools.

Lactose intolerance The inability to digest fresh milk products, caused by the discontinued production of *lactase,* the enzyme that breaks down lactose, or milk sugar.

Large-bodied hominoids Those hominoids including the great apes (orangutans, chimpanzees, gorillas) and hominids, as well as all ancestral forms back to the time of divergence from small-bodied hominoids (i.e., the gibbon lineage).

Life history traits Characteristics or developmental stages that influence reproductive rates of individuals in a species. Examples include age at sexual maturity or longevity.

Linked Describing genetic loci or genes located on the same chromosome.

Lithic (*lith,* meaning "stone") Referring to stone tools.

Locus (*pl.,* loci) (lo´-kus, lo-sigh´) The position on a chromosome where a given gene occurs. The term is sometimes used interchangeably with *gene,* but this usage is technically incorrect.

Macaques (muh-kaks´) Group of Old World monkeys comprising several species, including rhesus monkeys.

Macroevolution Changes produced only after many generations, such as the appearance of a new species.

Magdalenian Pertaining to the final phase of the Upper Paleolithic stone tool industry in Europe.

Mammalia The technical term for the formal grouping (class) of mammals.

Material culture The physical manifestations of human activities; includes tools, art, and structures. As the most durable aspects of culture, material remains make up the majority of archaeological evidence of past societies.

Meiosis Cell division in specialized cells in ovaries and testes. Meiosis involves two divisions and results in four daughter cells, each containing only half the original number of chromosomes. These cells can develop into gametes.

Menarche   The first menstruation in girls, usually occurring in the early to mid teens.

Mendelian traits   Characteristics that are influenced by alleles at only one genetic locus. Examples include many blood types, such as ABO. Many genetic disorders, including sickle-cell anemia and Tay-Sachs disease, are also Mendelian traits.

Menopause   The end of menstruation in human women, usually occurring at around age 50.

Messenger RNA (mRNA)   A form of RNA that is assembled on a sequence of DNA bases. It carries the DNA code to the ribosome during protein synthesis.

Metazoa   Multicellular animals; a major division of the animal kingdom.

Microevolution   Small changes occurring within species, such as a change in allele frequencies.

Microliths   (*micro*, meaning "small," and *lith*, meaning "stone") Small stone tools usually produced from narrow blades punched from a core; found especially in Africa during the latter part of the Pleistocene.

Microwear   Polishes, striations, and other diagnostic microscopic changes on the edges of stone tools.

Midline   An anatomical term referring to a hypothetical line that divides the body into right and left halves.

Mitochondria   (*sing.*, mitochondrion) Structures contained within the cytoplasm of eukaryotic cells that convert energy, derived from nutrients, into a form that is used by the cell.

Mitochondrial DNA (mtDNA)   DNA found in the mitochondria that is inherited only from the mother.

Mitosis   Simple cell division; the process by which somatic cells divide to produce two identical daughter cells.

Molecules   Structures made up of two or more atoms. Molecules can combine with other molecules to form more complex structures.

Monogenism   The theory that all human populations are descended from one pair (Adam and Eve), but they differ from one another because they have occupied different habitats. This concept was an attempt to explain phenotypic variation between groups, but did not imply evolutionary change.

Morphological   Pertaining to the form and structure of organisms.

Morphology   The form (shape, size) of anatomical structures; can also refer to the entire organism.

Mosaic evolution   A pattern of evolution in which the rate of evolution in one functional system varies from that in other systems. For example, in hominid evolution, the dental system, locomotor system, and neurological system (especially the brain) all evolved at markedly different rates.

Motor cortex   That portion of the cortex pertaining to outgoing signals involved in muscle use. (The *cortex* of the brain, the outer layer, is composed of nerve cells, or neurons.)

Mousterian   Pertaining to the stone tool industry associated with Neandertals and some modern *H. sapiens* groups; also called Middle Paleolithic. This industry is characterized by a larger proportion of flake tools than is found in Acheulian tool kits.

Mutation   A change in DNA. Technically, mutation refers to changes in DNA bases (specifically called point mutations); also refers to changes in chromosome number and/or structure.

Natural selection   The mechanism of evolutionary change first articulated by Charles Darwin; refers to genetic change or changes in the frequencies of certain traits in populations due to differential reproductive success between individuals.

Neural tube   In early embryonic development, the anatomical structure that develops to form the brain and spinal cord.

Nocturnal   Active during the night.

Nondisjunction   The failure of homologous chromosomes or chromosome strands to separate during cell division.

Nonrandom mating   Patterns of mating in a population in which individuals choose mates preferentially.

Nuchal torus   (nuke´-ul, pertaining to the neck) A projection of bone in the back of the cranium where neck muscles attach, used to hold up the head. The nuchal torus is a distinctive feature of *H. erectus*.

Nucleotides   Basic units of the DNA molecule, composed of a sugar, a phosphate, and one of four DNA bases.

Nucleus   A structure (organelle) found in all eukaryotic cells. The nucleus contains chromosomes (nuclear DNA).

Omnivorous   Having a diet consisting of many food types (i.e., plant materials, meat, and insects).

Osteodontokeratic   (*osteo*, meaning "bone," *donto*, meaning "tooth," and *keratic*, meaning "horn")

Osteology   The study of skeletal material. Human osteology focuses on the interpretation of the skeletal remains of past groups. Some of the same techniques are used in paleoanthropology to study early hominids.

Paleoanthropology   The interdisciplinary approach to the study of earlier hominids—their chronology, physical structure, archaeological remains, habitats, etc.

Paleoecologists   (*paleo,* meaning "old," and *ecology,* meaning "environmental setting") Scientists who study ancient environments.

Paleomagnetism   Dating method based on the shifting magnetic pole.

Paleospecies   Species defined from fossil evidence, often covering a long time span.

Pathogens   Substances or microorganisms, such as bacteria, fungi, or viruses, that cause disease.

Pedigree chart   A diagram showing family relationships in order to trace the hereditary pattern of particular genetic (usually Mendelian) traits.

Phenotypes   The observable or detectable physical characteristics of an organism; the detectable expressions of genotypes.

Phenotypic ratio   The proportion of one phenotype to other phenotypes in a group of organisms. For example, Mendel observed that there were approximately three tall plants for every short plant in the F_2 generation. This is expressed as a phenotypic ratio of 3:1.

Philopatric   Remaining in one's natal group or home range as an adult. In most species, members of one sex disperse from their natal group as young adults, and members of the philopatric sex remain. In the majority of nonhuman primate species, the philopatric sex is female.

Phylogenetic tree   A chart showing evolutionary relationships as determined by phylogenetic systematics. It contains a time component and implies ancestor-descendant relationships.

Phylogeny   A schematic representation showing ancestor-descendant relationships, usually in a chronological framework.

Phytoliths   (*phyto,* meaning "hidden," and *lith,* meaning "stone") Microscopic silica structures formed in the cells of many plants, particularly grasses.

Plasticity   The capacity to change; in a physiological context, the ability of systems or organisms to make alterations in order to respond to differing conditions.

Pleiotropic genes   Genes that have more than one effect; genes that have different effects at different times in the life cycle.

Pleiotropy   A situation whereby several seemingly unrelated phenotypic effects are influenced by the action of a single gene.

Pleistocene   The epoch of the Cenozoic from 1.8 m.y.a. until 10,000 y.a. Frequently referred to as the Ice Age, this epoch is associated with continental glaciations in northern latitudes.

Plio-Pleistocene   Pertaining to the Pliocene and first half of the Pleistocene, a time range of 5–1 m.y.a. For this time period, the earliest fossil hominids have been found in Africa.

Point mutation   A chemical change in a single base of a DNA sequence.

Polyandry   A mating system wherein a female continuously associates with more than one male (usually two or three) with whom she mates. Among nonhuman primates, this pattern is seen only in marmosets and tamarins.

Polygenic   Referring to traits that are influenced by genes at two or more loci. Examples of such traits are stature, skin color, and eye color.

Many polygenic traits are also influenced by environmental factors.

Polygenism   A theory, opposed to monogenism, that stated that human races were not all descended from Adam and Eve. Instead, there had been several original human pairs, each giving rise to a different group. Thus, human races were considered to be separate species.

Polymerase chain reaction (PCR)   A method of producing thousands of copies of a DNA segment using the enzyme DNA polymerase.

Polymorphism   A genetic trait governed by a locus with more than one allele.

Polypeptide chain   A sequence of amino acids that may act alone or in combination with others as a functional protein.

Polytypic   Referring to species composed of populations that differ with regard to the expression of one or more traits.

Population   Within a species, a community of individuals where mates are usually found.

Prehensility   Grasping, as by the hands and feet of primates.

Pressure flaking   A method of removing flakes from a core by pressing a pointed implement (e.g., bone or antler) against the stone.

Primate   A member of the order of mammals Primates (pronounced "pry-may´-tees"), which includes prosimians, monkeys, apes, and humans.

Primatologists   Scientists who study the evolution, anatomy, and behavior of nonhuman primates. Those who study behavior in non-captive animals are usually trained as physical anthropologists.

Primatology The study of the biology and behavior of nonhuman primates (prosimians, monkeys, and apes).

Primitive Referring to a trait or combination of traits present in an ancestral form.

Principle of independent assortment The distribution of one pair of alleles into gametes does not influence the distribution of another pair. The genes controlling different traits are inherited independently of one another.

Principle of segregation Genes (alleles) occur in pairs (because chromosomes occur in pairs). During gamete production, the members of each gene pair separate, so that each gamete contains one member of each pair. During fertilization, the full number of chromosomes is restored, and members of gene or allele pairs are reunited.

Prosimians Members of a suborder of Primates, the *Prosimii* (pronounced "pro-sim´-ee-eye"). Traditionally, the suborder includes lemurs, lorises, and tarsiers.

Protein synthesis The assembly of chains of amino acids into functional protein molecules. The process is directed by DNA.

Proteins Three-dimensional molecules that serve a wide variety of functions through their ability to bind to other molecules.

Protohominids The earliest members of the hominid lineage, as yet basically unrepresented in the fossil record; thus, their structure and behavior are reconstructed hypothetically.

Punctuated equilibrium The concept that evolutionary change proceeds through long periods of stasis punctuated by rapid periods of change.

Quadrupedal Using all four limbs to support the body during locomotion; the basic mammalian (and primate) form of locomotion.

Quantitatively In a manner involving measurements of quantity and including such properties as size, number, and capacity. When data are quantified, they are expressed numerically and are capable of being tested statistically.

r-selected Pertaining to an adaptive strategy that emphasizes relatively large numbers of offspring and reduced parental care (compared to K-selected species). (*K-selection* and *r-selection* are relative terms; e.g., mice are r-selected compared to primates but K-selected compared to many fish species.)

Racial In biology, pertaining to populations of a species that differ from other populations of the same species with regard to some aspects of outwardly expressed phenotype. Such phenotypic variation within a species is usually associated with differences in geographical location.

Random assortment The chance distribution of chromosomes to daughter cells during meiosis; along with recombination, the source of variation resulting from meiosis.

Recessive Describing a trait that is not expressed in heterozygotes; also refers to the allele that governs the trait. For a recessive allele to be expressed, there must be two copies of the allele (i.e., the individual must be homozygous).

Recognition species concept A depiction of species where the key aspect is the ability of individuals to identify members of their own species for purposes of mating (and to avoid mating with members of other species). In theory, this type of selective mating is a component of a species concept emphasizing mating and is therefore compatible with the biological species concept.

Recombinant DNA technology A process in which genes from the cell of one species are transferred to somatic cells or gametes of another species.

Recombination (crossing over) The exchange of genetic material between homologous chromosomes during meiosis.

Replicate To duplicate. The DNA molecule is able to make copies of itself.

Reproductive strategies The complex of behavioral patterns that contributes to individual reproductive success. The behaviors need not be deliberate, and they often vary considerably between males and females.

Reproductive success The number of offspring an individual produces and rears to reproductive age; an individual's genetic contribution to the next generation, as compared to the contributions of other individuals.

Restriction fragment length polymorphisms (RFLPs) Variation among individuals in the number and length of DNA fragments produced by enzymes that break the DNA at specific sites.

Rhinarium (rine-air´-ee-um) The moist, hairless pad at the end of the nose seen in most mammalian species. The rhinarium enhances an animal's ability to smell.

Ribonucleic acid (RNA) A single-stranded molecule, similar in structure to DNA. The three forms of RNA are essential to protein synthesis.

Ribosomes Structures composed of a specialized form of RNA and protein. Ribosomes are found in the cell's cytoplasm and are essential to the manufacture of proteins.

Ritualized behaviors   Behaviors removed from their original context and sometimes exaggerated to convey information.

Sagittal crest   Raised ridge along the midline of the cranium where the temporal muscle (which closes the jaw) is attached.

Scenarios   General, speculative reconstructions derived from various scientific data. In paleoanthropology, scenarios are usually presented as imaginative reconstructions of early hominid behavior. Such interpretations are broader than typical scientific hypotheses and theories and are not as rigorously amenable to verification.

Science   A body of knowledge gained through observation and experimentation; from the Latin *scientia,* meaning "knowledge."

Scientific method   A research method whereby a problem is identified, a hypothesis (or hypothetical explanation) is stated, and that hypothesis is tested through the collection and analysis of data. If the hypothesis is verified, it becomes a theory.

Scientific testing   The precise repetition of an experiment or expansion of observed data to provide verification; the procedure by which hypotheses and theories are verified, modified, or discarded.

Sectorial   Adapted for cutting or shearing; among primates, refers to the compressed (side-to-side) first lower premolar, which functions as a shearing surface with the upper canine.

Selective pressures   Forces in the environment that influence reproductive success in individuals. In the example of the peppered moth, birds applied the selective pressure.

Senescence   The process of physiological decline in body function that occurs with aging.

Sex chromosomes   In mammals, the X and Y chromosomes.

Sexual dimorphism   Differences in physical characteristics between males and females of the same species. For example, humans are slightly sexually dimorphic for body size, with males being taller, on average, than females of the same population.

Sexual selection   A type of natural selection that operates on only one sex within a species. It is the result of competition for mates, and it can lead to sexual dimorphism with regard to one or more traits.

Sickle-cell anemia   A severe inherited hemoglobin disorder that results from inheriting two copies of a mutant allele. This allele results from a single base substitution at the DNA level.

Slash-and-burn agriculture A traditional land-clearing practice whereby trees and vegetation are cut and burned. In many areas, fields are abandoned after a few years and clearing occurs elsewhere.

Social structure   The composition, size, and sex ratio of a group of animals. Social structures, in part, are the result of natural selection in specific habitats, and they function to guide individual interactions and social relationships.

Sociobiology   The study of the relationship between natural selection and behavior. Unlike the approach of behavioral ecology, sociobiological theory does not strongly emphasize ecological factors.

Somatic cells   Basically, all the cells in the body except those involved with reproduction.

Specialized   Evolved for a particular function; usually refers to a specific trait (e.g., incisor teeth), but may also refer to the entire way of life of an organism.

Speciation   The process where a new species evolves from a prior species. Speciation is the most basic process in macroevolution.

Species   A group of organisms that can interbreed to produce fertile offspring. Members of one species are reproductively isolated from members of all other species (i.e., they cannot mate with them to produce fertile offspring).

Spina bifida   A condition in which the arch of one or several vertebrae fails to fuse and form a protective barrier around the spinal cord.

Stable carbon isotopes   Isotopes of carbon that are produced in plants in differing proportions, depending on environmental conditions. Through analyzing the proportions of the isotopes contained in fossil remains of animals (who ate the plants), it is possible to reconstruct aspects of ancient environments (particularly temperature and aridity).

Stereoscopic vision   The condition whereby visual images are, to varying degrees, superimposed on one another. This provides for depth perception, or the perception of the external environment in three dimensions. Stereoscopic vision is partly a function of structures in the brain.

Stratigraphy   Study of the sequential layering of deposits.

Stress   In a physiological context, any factor that acts to disrupt homeostasis; more precisely, the body's response to any factor that threatens its ability to maintain homeostasis.

Sympatric   Living in the same area; pertaining to two or more species whose habitats partly or largely overlap.

Taphonomy   (*taphos,* meaning "dead") The study of how bones and other materials came to be buried in the earth and preserved as fossils. A taphonomist studies the processes of sedimentation, the action of streams, preservation properties of bone, and carnivore disturbance factors.

Taxonomy The branch of science concerned with the rules of classifying organisms on the basis of evolutionary relationships.

Territories Portions of an individual's or group's home range actively defended against intrusion, particularly by conspecifics.

Theory A broad statement of scientific relationships or underlying principles that has been at least partially verified.

Theropods Small- to medium-sized ground-living dinosaurs, dated to approximately 150 m.y.a. and thought to be related to birds.

Transfer RNA (tRNA) The type of RNA that binds to specific amino acids and transports them to the ribosome during protein synthesis.

Transmutation The change of one species to another. The term *evolution* did not assume its current meaning until the late nineteenth century.

Uniformitarianism The theory that the earth's features are the result of long-term processes that continue to operate in the present as they did in the past. Elaborated on by Lyell, this theory opposed catastrophism and provided for immense geological time.

Upper Paleolithic A cultural period usually associated with early modern humans (but also found with Neandertals) and distinguished by technological innovation in various stone tool industries. Best known from western Europe, similar industries are also known from central and eastern Europe and Africa.

Variation (genetic) Inherited differences between individuals; the basis of all evolutionary change.

Vasoconstriction Narrowing of blood vessels to reduce blood flow to the skin. Vasoconstriction is an involuntary response to cold and reduces heat loss at the skin's surface.

Vasodilation Expansion of blood vessels, permitting increased blood flow to the skin. Vasodilation permits warming of the skin and also facilitates radiation of warmth as a means of cooling. Vasodilation is an involuntary response to warm temperatures, various drugs, and even emotional states (blushing).

Vectors Agents that serve to transmit disease from one carrier to another. Mosquitoes are vectors for malaria, just as fleas are vectors for bubonic plague.

Vertebrates
Animals with bony backbones; includes fishes, amphibians, reptiles, birds, and mammals.

Viviparous Giving birth to live young.

World view General cultural orientation or perspective shared by members of a society.

Zygote A cell formed by the union of an egg and a sperm cell. It contains the full complement of chromosomes (in humans, 46) and has the potential of developing into an entire organism.

Bibliography

Adcock, Gregory J., Elizabeth S. Dennis, Simon Easteal, et al.
1   2001   "Mitochondrial DNA Sequences in Ancient
        Australians: Implications for Modern Human
        Origins." *Proceedings of the National Academy of
        Sciences,* 98:537–542.

Aiello, L. C.
1   1992   "Body Size and Energy Requirements." *In: The
        Cambridge Encyclopedia of Human Evolution,*
        J. Jones, R. Martin, and D. Pilbeam (eds.),
        Cambridge, England: Cambridge University Press,
        pp. 41–45.

Aiello, L. C. and B. A. Wood
1   1994   Cranial Variables as Predictors of Hominine Body
        Mass. *American Journal of Physical Anthropology,*
        95:409–426.

Aitken, M. J., C. B. Stringer, and P. A. Mellars (eds.)
1   1993   *The Origin of Modern Humans and the Impact of
        Chronometric Dating.* Princeton, N.J.: Princeton
        University Press.

Alland Jr., Alexander
1   1971   *Human Diversity.* New York: Anchor Press/
        Doubleday.

Altmann, Jeanne
1   1981   *Baboon Mothers and Infants.* Cambridge: Harvard
        University Press.

Altmann, Stuart A. and Jeanne Altmann
1   1970   *Baboon Ecology.* Chicago: University of Chicago
        Press.

Anderson, J. Gunnar
1   1934   *Children of the Yellow Earth.* New York: Macmillan.

Andrews, Peter
1   1985   "Family Group Systematics and Evolution among
        Catarrhine Primates." *In: Ancestors: The Hard
        Evidence,* E. Delson (ed.), New York: Alan R. Liss,
        pp. 14–22.

———
1   1992   "Evolution and Environment in Miocene
        Hominoids." *Nature,* 360:641–646.

Andrews, Peter and Jens Lorenz Franzen (eds.)
1   1984   *The Early Evolution of Man.* Frankfurt: Cour.
        Forsch.-Inst. Seckenberg.

Andrews, Peter and David Pilbeam
1   1996   "The Nature of the Evidence," News and Views.
        Nature, 379:123–124.

Ardrey, Robert
1   1976   *The Hunting Hypothesis.* New York: Atheneum.

Arensburg, B., L. A. Schepartz, et al.
1   1990   "A Reappraisal of the Anatomical Basis for Speech
        in Middle Paleolithic Hominids." *American Journal
        of Physical Anthropology,* 83(2):137–146.

Arensburg, B., A. M. Tillier, et al.
1   1989   "A Middle Paleolithic Human Hyoid Bone."
        Nature, 338:758–760.

Aronson, J. L., R. C. Walter, and M. Taieb
1   1983   "Correlation of Tulu Bor Tuff at Koobi Fora with
        the Sidi Hakoma Tuff at Hadar." *Nature,*
        306:209–210.

Arsuaga, Juan-Luis et al.
1   1993   "Three New Human Skulls from the Sima de los
        Huesos Middle Pleistocene Site in Sierra de
        Atapuerca, Spain." *Nature,* 362:534–537.

Arsuaga, J. L., I. Martinez, A. Garcia, et al.
1   1997   "Sima de los Huesos (Sierra de Atapuerca, Spain).
        The Site." *Journal of Human Evolution,* 33:109–127.

Ascenzi, A. I. Bidditu, P. F. Cassoli, et al.
1   1996   "A Calvarium of Late *Homo erectus* from Ceprano,
        Italy." *Journal of Human Evolution,* 31:409–423.

Asfaw, Berhane
1   1992   "New Fossil Hominids from the Ethiopian Rift
        Valley and the Afar." Paper presented at the
        Annual Meeting, American Association of
        Physical Anthropologists.

Asfaw, Berhane et al.
1   1992   "The Earliest Acheulian from Konso-Gardula."
        Nature, 360:732–735.

———
1   1995   Three Seasons of Hominid Paleontology at
        Aramis, Ethiopia. Paper presented at
        Paleoanthropology Society meetings, Oakland,
        Ca., March 1995.

Asfaw, Berhane, W. Henry Gilbert, Yonas Beyene, et al.
1   2002   "Remains of *Homo erectus* from Bouri, Middle
        Awash, Ethiopia. *Nature,* 416:317–320.

Asfaw, Berhane, Tim White, Owen Lovejoy, et al.
1999 *"Australopithecus garhi:* A New Species of Early Hominid from Ethiopia." *Science,* 284: 629–635.

Avery, O. T., C. M. MacLeod, and M. McCarty
1944 "Studies on the Chemical Nature of the Substances Inducing Transformation in Pneumoccal Types." *Journal of Experimental Medicine,* 79:137–158.

Ayala, Francisco
1995 "The Myth of Eve: Molecular Biology and Human Origins." *Science,* 270:1930–1936.

Badrian, Alison and Noel Badrian
1984 "Social Organization of *Pan paniscus* in the Lomako Forest, Zaire." *In: The Pygmy Chimpanzee,* Randall L. Susman (ed.), New York: Plenum Press, pp. 325–346.

Badrian, Noel and Richard K. Malenky
1984 "Feeding Ecology of *Pan paniscus* in the Lomako Forest, Zaire." *In: The Pygmy Chimpanzee,* Randall L. Susman (ed.), New York: Plenum Press, pp. 275–299.

Baker, Paul T. and Michael A. Little
1976 "The Environmental Adaptations and Perspectives." *In: Man in the Andes,* P. T. Baker and M. A. Little (eds.), Stroudsburg, Penn.: Dowden, Hutchinson, and Ross, pp. 405–428.

Baltimore, David
2001 "Our Genome Unveiled." *Nature,* 409:814–816.

Barash, David
1982 *Sociobiology and Behavior.* (2nd Ed.) New York: Elsevier.

Bartholomew, C. A. and J. B. Birdsell
1953 "Ecology and the Protohominids." *American Anthropologist,* 55:481–498.

Bartlett, Thad.Q., Robert W. Sussman, James M. Cheverud
1993 "Infant Killing in Primates: A Review of Observed Cases with Specific References to the Sexual Selection Hypothesis." *American Anthropologist,* 95(4):958–990.

Bartstra, Gert-Jan
1982 *"Homo erectus erectus:* The Search for Artifacts." *Current Anthropology,* 23(3):318–320.

Bar-Yosef, Ofer
1993 "The Role of Western Asia in Modern Human Origins." *In:* M. J. Aitken et al. (eds.), q.v., pp. 132–147.

——— 1994 "The Contributions of Southwest Asia to the Study of the Origin of Modern Humans." *In: Origins of Anatomically Modern Humans,* M. H. Nitecki and D. V. Nitecki (eds.), New York: Plenum Press, pp. 23–66.

Barzun, Jacques
1965 *Race: A Study in Superstition.* New York: Harper & Row.

Bass, W. M.
1987 *Human Osteology: A Laboratory and Field Manual* (3rd Ed.). Columbia, Mo.: Missouri Archaeological Society Special Publication No. 2.

Beard, K. Christopher, Yong Shenj Tong, Mary R. Dawson, et al.
1996 "Earliest Complete Dentition of an Anthropoid Primate from the Late Middle Eocene of Shanxi Province, China." *Science,* 272:82–85.

Bearder, Simon K.
1987 "Lorises, Bushbabies and Tarsiers: Diverse Societies in Solitary Foragers." *In:* Smuts et al., q.v., pp. 11–24.

Begun, David R.
1992 "Phyletic Diversity and Locomotion in Primitive European Hominoids." *American Journal of Physical Anthropology,* 87:311–340.

——— 1994 "Relations Among the Great Apes and Humans: New Interpretations Based on the Fossil Great Ape *Dryopithecus." Yearbook of Physical Anthropology,* 37:11–63.

Begun, D. and A. Walker
1993 "The Endocast." *In:* A. Walker and R. E. Leakey (eds.), q.v., pp. 326–358.

Behrensmeyer, Anna K. and Andrew P. Hill
1980 *Fossils in the Making: Vertebrate Taphonomy and Paleoecology.* Chicago: University of Chicago Press.

Behrensmeyer, A. K., D. Western, and D. E. Dechant Boaz
1979 "New Perspectives in Vertebrate Paleoecology from a Recent Bone Assemblage." *Paleobiology,* 5(1):12–21.

Berger, Thomas and Erik Trinkaus
1995 "Patterns of Trauma Among the Neandertals." *Journal of Archaeological Science,* 22:841–852.

Bermudez de Castro, J. M., J. L. Arsuaga, E. Carbonell, et al.
1997 "A Hominid from the Lower Pleistocene of Atapuerca, Spain. Possible Ancestor to Neandertals and Modern Humans." *Science,* 276:1392–1395.

Bernor, R. L.
1983 "Geochronology and Zoogeographic Relationships of Miocene Hominoidea." *In:* R. L. Ciochon and R. S. Corruccini (eds.), q.v., pp. 21–66.

Biasutti, R.
1951 *Rassa e Popoli della Terra.* Torino: Unione Tipografico Editria Torinese.

Binford, Lewis R.
1981 *Bones. Ancient Men and Modern Myths*. New York: Academic Press.

_____ 1983 *In Pursuit of the Past*. New York: Thames and Hudson.

_____ 1985 "Ancestral Lifeways: The Faunal Record." AnthroQuest, 32, Summer 1985.

Binford, Lewis R. and Chuan Kun Ho
1985 "Taphonomy at a Distance: Zhoukoudian, 'The Cave Home of Beijing Man'?" *Current Anthropology*, 26:413–442.

Binford, Lewis R. and Nancy M. Stone
1986a "The Chinese Paleolithic: An Outsider's View." *AnthroQuest*, Fall 1986(1):14–20.

_____ 1986b "Zhoukoudian: A Closer Look." *Current Anthropology*, 27(5):453–475.

Birdsell, Joseph B.
1981 *Human Evolution*. (3rd Ed.). Boston: Houghton Mifflin.

Blangero, John, Jeff T. Williams and Laura Almasy
2000 "Quantitative Trait Locus Mapping Using Human Pedigrees." *Human Biology*, 72:35–62.

Blumenschine, Robert J.
1986 *Early Hominid Scavenging Opportunities*. Oxford: Bar International Series 283.

_____ 1995 "Percussion Marks, Tooth Marks, and Experimental Determinants of the Timing of Hominid and Carnivore Access to Long Bones at FLK *Zinjanthropus*, Olduvai Gorge, Tanzania." *Journal of Human Evolution* 29: 21–51.

Blumenschine, Robert J., and John A. Cavallo
1992 "Scavenging and Human Evolution." *Scientific American* (Oct.): 90–96.

Blumenschine, Robert J., and Charles R. Peters
1998 "Archaeological Predictions for Hominid Land Use in the Paleo-Olduvai Basin, Tanzania, During Lowermost Bed II Times." *Journal of Human Evolution* 34: 565–607.

Boas, F.
1910 "Changes in the Bodily Form of Descendants of Immigrants." *American Anthropologist*, 14:530–562.

Boaz, N. T. and A. K.Behrensmeyer
1976 "Hominid Taphonomy: Transport of Human Skeletal Parts in an Artificial Fluviatile Environment." *American Journal of Physical Anthropology*, 45:56–60.

Boaz, N. T. and Russell L. Ciochon
2001 "The Scavenging of *Homo erectus pekinensis*." *Natural History*, 110(2):46–51.

Boaz, N. T., F. C. Howell, and M. L. McCrossin
1982 "Faunal Age of the Usno, Shungura B and Hadar Formation, Ethiopia." *Nature,* 300:633–635.

Bodmer, W. F.
1995 "Evolution and Function of the HLA Region." *Clinical Surveys,* 22:5–16.

Bodmer, W. F. and L. L. Cavalli-Sforza
1976 *Genetics, Evolution, and Man*. San Francisco: W. H. Freeman and Company.

Boesch, C.
1994 "Hunting Strategies of Gombe and Tai Chimpanzees." *In:* Wrangham, R. W., C. MGrew, Frans B. M. de Waal, and Paul G. Heltne (eds.). *Chimpanzee Cultures*. Cambridge: Harvard University Press, pp. 77–91

Boesch, C. and H. Boesch
1989 "Hunting Behavior of Wild Chimpanzees in the Tai National Park." *American Journal of Physical Anthropology*, 78(4):547–573

_____ 1990 "Tool Use and Tool Making in Wild Chimpanzees." *Folia Primatologica*, 54:86–99.

Boesch, Christophe, Paul Marchesi, Nathalie Marchesi, et al.
1994 "Is Nut Cracking in Wild Chimpanzees a Cultural Behaviour?" *Journal of Human Evolution,* 26:325–338.

Bunn, Henry T.
1981 "Archaeological Evidence for Meat-Eating by Plio-Pleistocene Hominids from Koobi Fora and Olduvai Gorge." *Nature* 291:574–577.

Boggess, Jane
1984 "Infant Killing and Male Reproductive Strategies in Langurs (*Presbytis entellus*)." *In:* G. Hausfater and S. B. Hrdy (eds.), q.v., pp. 280–310.

Bogin, Barry
1988 *Patterns of Human Growth*. Cambridge: Cambridge University Press.

_____ 1998 "Social and Economic Class." *In: The Cambridge Encyclopedia of Human Growth and Development,* S. J. Ulijaszek, F. E. Johnston, and M. A. Preece (eds.). Cambridge, UK: Cambridge University Press, pp. 399–401.

Bongaarts, John
1980 Does Malnutrition Affect Fecundity? A Summary of Evidence. *Science,* 208:564–569.

Bordes, François
1968 *The Old Stone Age*. New York: McGraw-Hill.

Bottini, N., G. F. Meloni, A. Finocchi, et al.
2001 "Maternal-Fetal Interaction in the ABO System: A Comparative Analysis of Healthy Mothers and Couples with Recurrent Spontaneous Abortion Suggests a Protective Effect of B Incompatability." *Human Biology,* 73:167–174.

Bowler, Peter J.
1983, 1989 *Evolution: The History of an Idea.* Berkeley: University of California Press.

_____ 1988 The *Non-Darwinian Evolution: Reinterpreting a Historical Myth.* Baltimore: Johns Hopkins University Press.

Brace, C. L. and Ashley Montagu
1977 *Human Evolution* (2nd Ed.). New York: Macmillan.

Brace, C. Loring, H. Nelson, and N. Korn
1979 *Atlas of Human Evolution* (2nd Ed.). New York: Holt, Rinehart & Winston.

Brain, C. K.
1970 "New Finds at the Swartkrans Australopithecine Site." *Nature,* 225:1112–1119.

_____ 1981 *The Hunters or the Hunted? An Introduction to African Cave Taphonomy.* Chicago: University of Chicago Press.

Bramblett, Claud A.
1994 *Patterns of Primate Behavior* (2nd Ed.). Prospect Heights, Ill.: Waveland Press.

Bräuer, Günter
1984 "A Craniological Approach to the Origin of Anatomically Modern *Homo sapiens* in Africa and Implications for the Appearance of Modern Europeans." *In:* F. H. Smith and F. Spencer (eds.), q.v., pp. 327–410.

_____ 1989 "The Evolution of Modern Humans: A Comparison of the African and Non-African Evidence." *In:* Mellars and Stringer (eds.), q.v.

Brock, A., P. L. McFadden, and T. C. Partridge
1977 "Preliminary Paleomagnetic Results from Makapansgat and Swartkrans." *Nature,* 266:249–250.

Bromage, Timothy G. and Christopher Dean
1985 "Re-evaluation of the Age at Death of Immature Fossil Hominids." *Nature,* 317:525–527.

Brooks, Alison et al.
1995 "Dating and Context of Three Middle Stone Age Sites with Bone Points in the Upper Semliki Valley, Zaire." *Science,* 268:548–553.

Brose, David and Milford H. Wolpoff
1971 "Early Upper Paleolithic Man and Late Middle Paleolithic Tools." *American Anthropologist,* 73:1156–1194.

Brown, B, A. Walker, C. V. Ward, and R. E. Leakey
1993 "New *Australopithecus boisei*: Calvaria from East Lake Turkana, Kenya." *American Journal of Physical Anthropology,* 91:137–159.

Brown, F. H.
1982 "Tulu Bor Tuff at Koobi Fora Correlated with the Sidi Hakoma Tuff at Hadar." *Nature,* 300:631–632.

Brown, T. M. and K. D. Rose
1987 "Patterns of Dental Evolution in Early Eocene Anaptomorphine Primates Comomyidael from the Bighorn Basin, Wyoming." *Journal of Paleontology,* 61:1–62.

Brues, Alice M.
1959 "The Spearman and the Archer." *American Anthropologist,* 61:457–469.

_____ 1990 *People and Races* (2nd Ed.). Prospect Heights, Ill.: Waveland Press.

_____ 1991 "The Objective View of Race." Paper presented at American Anthropological Association 90th Annual Meeting, Chicago, Nov.

Brunet, Michel et al.
1995 "The First Australopithecine 2,500 Kilometers West of the Rift Valley (Chad)." *Nature,* 378:273–274.

Buffon, George Louis Leclerc, Compte de
1860 "*Histoire Naturelle Generale et Particuliere.*" Translated by Wm. Smellie. *In: The Idea of Racism,* Louis L. Snyder, New York: Van Nostrand Reinhold, 1962.

Bunn, Henry T.
1981 "Archaeological Evidence for Meat-eating by Plio-Pleistocene Hominids from Koobi Fora and Olduvai Gorge." *Nature,* 291:574–577.

Burkhardt, Richard W., Jr.
1984 "The Zoological Philosophy of J. B. Lamarck." (Introduction) *In:* Lamarck, q.v.

Butzer, Karl W.
1974 "Paleoecology of South African Australopithecines: Taung Revisited." *Current Anthropology,* 15:367–382.

Cann, R. L., M. Stoneking, and A. C. Wilson
1987 "Mitochondrial DNA and Human Evolution." *Nature,* 325:31–36.

Cann, Rebecca L., Olga Rickards, and J. Koji Lum
1994 "Mitochondrial DNA and Human Evolution: Our One Lucky Mother." *In:* M H. Nitecki and D. V. Nitecki (eds.), q.v., pp. 135–148.

Cantalupo, Claudio and William D. Hopkins
2001 "Asymmetric Broca's Area in Great Apes." *Nature,* 414:505.

Carbonell, E. et al.
1995 Lower Pleistocene Hominids and Artifacts from Atapuerca-TDG (Spain)." *Science,* 269:826–830.

Carrol, Robert L.
1988 *Vertebrate Paleontology and Evolution.* New York: W. H. Freeman and Co.

Cartmill, Matt
1972 "Arboreal Adaptations and the Origin of the Order Primates." *In: The Functional and Evolutionary Biology of Primates,* R. H. Tuttle (ed.), Chicago: Aldine-Atherton, pp. 97–122.

_____
1990 "Human Uniqueness and Theoretical Content in Paleoanthropology." *International Journal of Primatology,* 11(3):173–192.

_____
1992 "New Views on Primate Origins." *Evolutionary Anthropology,* 1:105–111.

Cavalli-Sforza, L. L., A. Piazza, P. Menozzi, and J. Mountain
1988 "Reconstruction of Human Evolution: Bringing Together Genetic, Archaeological, and Linguistic Data." *Proceedings of the National Academy of Sciences,* 85:6002–6006.

Censky, E. J., K. Hodge and J. Dudley
1998 "Over-Water Dispersal of Lizards Due to Hurricanes." *Nature,* 395 (6702):556.

Chagnon, N. A.
1979 "Mate Competition Favoring Close Kin and Village Fissioning among the Yanomamo Indians." *In: Evolutionary Biology and Human Social Behavior: An Anthropological Perspective,* N. Chagnon and W. Irons (eds.), North Scituak, Mass.: Duxbury Press, pp. 86–132.

_____
1988 "Life Histories, Blood Revenge, and Warfare in a Tribal Population." *Science,* 239:985–992.

Charteris, J., J. C. Wali, and J. W. Nottrodt
1981 "Functional Reconstruction of Gait from Pliocene Hominid Footprints at Laetoli, Northern Tanzania." *Nature,* 290:496–498.

Cheney, Dorothy L.
1987 "Interaction and Relationships between Groups." *In:* B. Smuts et al. (eds.), q.v., pp. 267–281.

Cheney, D. L. and R. M. Seyfarth
1990 *How Monkeys See the World.* Chicago: Chicago University Press.

Cheney, D. L., R. M. Seyfarth, S. J. Andelman, and P. C. Lee
1988 "Reproductive Success in Vervet Monkeys." In: Clutton-Brock, T.H. (ed.), *Reproductive Success.* Chicago: University of Chicago Press. pp.384–402.

Ciochon, R. L. and A. B. Chiarelli (eds.)
1980 *Evolutionary Biology of the New World Monkeys and Continental Drift.* New York: Plenum Press.

Ciochon, Russel L. and Robert S. Corruccini (eds.)
1983 *New Interpretations of Ape and Human Ancestry.* New York: Plenum Press.

Clark, W. E. LeGros
1967 *Man-apes or Ape-men?* New York: Holt, Rinehart & Winston.
1971 New York Times Books (3rd Ed.).

Clarke, R. J.
1985 "*Australopithecus* and Early *Homo* in Southern Africa." *In: Ancestors: The Hard Evidence,* E. Delson (ed.), New York: Alan R. Liss, pp. 171–177.

Clarke, Ronald J. and Phillip V. Tobias
1995 "Sterkfontein Member 2 Foot Bones of the Oldest South African Hominid." *Science,* 269:521–524.

Cleveland, J. and C. T. Snowdon
1982 "The Complex Vocal Repertoire of the Adult Cotton-top Tamarin (*Saguinus oedipus oedipus*)." *Zeitschrift Tierpsychologie,* 58:231–270.

Clutton-Brock, T. H. and Paul H. Harvey
1977 "Primate Ecology and Social Organization." *Journal of Zoological Society of London,* 183:1–39.

Colwell, Rita R.
1996 Global Climate and Infectious Disease: The Cholera Paradigm. *Science,* 274 (5295):2025–2031.

Conkey, M.
1987 New Approaches in the Search for Meaning? A Review of the Research in "Paleolithic Art." *Journal of Field Archaeology,* 14:413–430.

Conroy, Glenn C.
1997 *Reconstructing Human Origins. A Modern Synthesis.* New York: Norton.

Conroy, G., C. J. Jolly, D. Cramer, and J. E. Kalb
1978 "Newly Discovered Fossil Hominid Skull from the Afar Depression." *Nature,* 272:67–70.

Conroy, G. C., M. Pickford, B. Senut, J. van Couvering, and P. Mein
1992 "*Otavipithecus namibiensis,* First Miocene Hominoid from Southern Africa." *Nature,* 356:144–148.

Conroy, Glenn C., Jeff W. Lichtman, and Lawrence B. Martin
1995 "Brief Communication: Some Observations on Enamel Thickness and Enamel Prism Packing in Miocene Hominoid *Otavipithecus namibiensis.*" *American Journal of Physical Anthropology,* 98:595–600.

Conroy, Glenn C., G. W. Weber, H. Seidler, et al.
1998 "Endocranial Capacity in an Early Hominid Cranium from Sterkfontein, South Africa." *Science,* 280:1730–1731.

Coon, C. S., S. M. Garn, and J. B. Birdsell
1950 *Races—A Study of the Problems of Race Formation in Man.* Springfield, Ill.: Charles C. Thomas.

Cooper, Alan, Andrew Rambaut, Vincent Macaulay, et al.
2001 "Human Origins and Ancient DNA." Letter to *Science,* 292:1655–1656.

Corruccini, R. S., M. Baba, M. Goodman, et al.
1980 "Non-Linear Macromolecular Evolution and the Moleculer Clock." *Evolution,* 34:1216–1219.

Corruccini, R. S. and H. M. McHenry
1980 "Cladometric Analysis of Pliocene Hominids." *Journal of Human Evolution,* 9:209–221.

Corruccini, Robert S.
1994 "Reaganomics and the Fate of the Progressive Neandertals." *In:* R. S. Corruccini and R. I. Ciochon (eds.), q.v., pp. 697–708.

Crapo, Lawrence
1985 *Hormones: The Messengers of Life.* New York: W. H. Freeman and Company.

Crews, D. E. and G. J. Harper
1998 "Ageing as Part of the Developmental Process." *In: The Cambridge Encyclopedia of Human Growth and Development,* S. J. Ulijaszek, F. E. Johnston, and M. A. Preece (eds.). Cambridge, UK: Cambridge University Press, pp. 425–427.

Cronin, J. E.
1983 "Apes, Humans, and Molecular Clocks. A Reappraisal." *In:* R. L. Ciochon and R. S. Corruccini (eds.), q.v., pp. 115–150.

Crook, J. H.
1970 "Social Organization and Environment: Aspects of Contemporary Social Ethology." *Animal Behavior,* 18:197–209.

Crook, J. H. and J. S. Gartlan
1966 "Evolution of Primate Societies." *Nature,* 210:1200–1203.

Culotta, Elizabeth
1995 "Asian Anthropoids Strike Back." *Science,* 270:918.

Cummings, Michael
2000 *Human Heredity. Principles and Issues* (5th Ed.). Pacific Grove: Brooks/Cole.

———
1997 *Human Heredity. Principles and Issues.* 4th ed. Belmont, CA: West/Wadsworth.

Current, M., G. Trabuchet, D. Rees, et al.
2002 "Molecular Analysis of the Beta-Globin Gene Cluster in the Niokholo Mandenka Population Reveals a Recent Origin of the Beta S Senegal Mutation." *American Journal of Human Genetics,* 70:207–223.

Curtin, R. and P. Dolhinow
1978 "Primate Social Behavior in a Changing World." *American Scientist,* 66:468–475.

Curtis, Garniss
1981 "A Matter of Time: Dating Techniques and Geology of Hominid Sites." Symposium Paper, Davis, Ca., May 10, 1981.

Dalrymple, G. B.
1972 "Geomagnetic Reversals and North American Glaciations." *In: Calibration of Hominoid Evolution,* W. W. Bishop and J. A. Miller (eds.), Edinburgh: Scottish Academic Press, pp. 303–329.

Dart, Raymond
1959 *Adventures with the Missing Link.* New York: Harper & Brothers.

Darwin, Charles
1859 *On the Origin of Species.* A Facsimile of the First Edition, Cambridge, Mass.: Harvard University Press (1964).

Darwin, Charles
1871 *The Descent of Man and Selection in Relation to Sex.* Republished, 1981, Princeton: Princeton University Press.

Darwin, Francis (ed.)
1950 *The Life and Letters of Charles Darwin.* New York: Henry Schuman.

Day, M. H. and E. H. Wickens
1980 "Laetoli Pliocene Hominid Footprints and Bipedalism." *Nature,* 286:385–387.

Day, Michael
1986 *Guide to Fossil Man* (4th Ed.), Chicago: University of Chicago Press.

Deacon, T. W.
1992 "The Human Brain." *In: The Cambridge Encyclopedia of Human Evolution,* S. Jones, R. Martin, and D. Pilbeam (eds.), Cambridge, England: Cambridge University Press, pp. 115–123.

Dean, M., M. Carring, C. Winkler, et al.
1996 "Genetic Restriction of HIV-1 Infection and Progression to AIDS by a Deletion Allele of the CKR5 Structural Gene." *Science,* 273:1856–1862.

de Bonis, Louis and George D. Koufos
1994 "Our Ancestors' Ancestor: *Ouranopithecus* Is a Greek Link in Human Ancestry." *Evolutionary Anthropology,*3:75–83.

Defleur, A., T. White, P. Valensi, et al.
1999 "Neanderthal Cannibalism at Moula-Guercy, Ardèche, France." *Science,* 286:128–131.

DeGusta, D., W. H. Gilbert, and S. P. Turner
1999 "Hypoglossal Canal Size and Hominid Speech." *Proceedings of the National Academy of Sciences,* 96:1800–1804.

de Heinzelin, Jean, J. Desmond Clark, Tim White, et al.
1999 "Environment and Behavior of 2.5-Million-Year-Old Bouri Hominids." *Science,* 284:625–629.

Deino, Alan L., Paul R. Renne, and Carl C. Swisher
1998 "^{40}Ar/^{39}Ar Dating in Paleoanthropology and Archeology." *Evolutionary Anthropology,* 6:63–75.

de Lumley, Henry and M. de Lumley
1973 "Pre-Neanderthal Human Remains from Arago Cave in Southeastern France." *Yearbook of Physical Anthropology,* 16:162–168.

Delson, Eric (ed.)
1985 *Ancestors: The Hard Evidence.* New York: Alan R. Liss.

———
1987 "Evolution and Paleobiology of Robust Australopithecus." *Nature,* 327:654–655.

Dene, H. T., M. Goodman, and W. Prychodko
1976 "Immunodiffusion Evidence on the Phylogeny of the Primates." *In: Molecular Anthropology,* M. Goodman, R. E. Tashian, and J. H. Tashian (eds.), New York: Plenum Press, pp. 171–195.

Desmond, Adrian and James Moore
1991 *Darwin.* New York: Warner Books.

Dettwyler, K. A.
1991 "Can Paleopathology Provide Evidence for Compassion?" *American Journal of Physical Anthropology,* 84:375–384.

DeVore, I. and S. L. Washburn
1963 "Baboon Ecology and Human Evolution." *In: African Ecology and Human Evolution,* F. C. Howell and F. Bourliére (eds.), New York: Viking Fund Publication, No. 36, pp. 335–367.

De Vos, J.
1985 "Faunal Stratigraphy and Correlation of the Indonesian Hominid Sites." *In: Ancestors: The Hard Evidence,* E. Delson (ed.), New York: Alan R. Liss, pp. 215–220.

de Waal, Frans
1982 *Chimpanzee Politics.* London: Jonathan Cape.

———
1987 "Tension Regulation and Nonreproductive Functions of Sex in Captive Bonobos (*Pan paniscus*)." *National Geographic Research,* 3:318–335.

———
1989 *Peacemaking among Primates.* Cambridge: Harvard University Press.

———
1996 *Good Natured. The Origins of Right and Wrong in Humans and Other Animals,* Cambridge, Mass.: Harvard University Press.

———
1999 "Cultural Primatology Comes of Age." *Nature,* 399:635–636.

Dolhinow, P.
1978 "A Behavior Repertoire for the Indian Langur Monkey (*Presbytis entellus*)." *Primates,* 19:449–472.

Doran, Diane M. and Alastair McNeilage
1998 "Gorilla Ecology and Behavior." *Evolutionary Anthropology,* 6(4):120–131.

Dorit, R. L., H. Akashi, and W. Gilbert
1995 Absence of Polymorphism at the Zfy Locus on the Human Y Chromosome. *Science,* 268:1183–1185.

Duarte, C., J. Maurício, P. B. Pettitt, et al.
1999 "The Early Upper Paleolithic Human Skeleton from the Abrigo do Lagar Velho (Portugal) and Modern Human Emergence in Iberia." *Proceedings of the National Academy of Sciences,* 96:7604–7609.

Duchin, Linda E.
1990 "The Evolution of Articulate Speech." *Journal of Human Evolution,* 19:687–697.

Dumont, R. and B. Rosier
1969 *The Hungry Future.* New York: Praeger.

Dunbar, I. M.
1988 *Primate Social Systems.* Ithaca: Cornell University Press.

Durham, William
1981 Paper presented to the Annual Meeting of the American Anthropological Association, Washington, D.C., Dec. 1980. Reported in *Science,* 211:40.

Eaton, S. Boyd, Marjorie Shostak, and Melvin Konner.
1988 *The Paleolithic Prescription.* New York: Harper and Row.

Eaton, S. Boyd and Melvin Konner
1985 Paleolithic Nutrition: A Consideration of Its Nature and Current Implications. *New England Journal of Medicine,* 312:283–289.

Eaton, S. Boyd, Malcolm C. Pike, Roger V. Short, et al.
1994 Women's Reproductive Cancers in Evolutionary Context. *The Quarterly Review of Biology,* 69:353–367.

Ehrlich, Paul R. and Anne H. Ehrlich
1990 *The Population Explosion.* New York: Simon and Schuster.

Eiseley, Loren
1961 *Darwin's Century.* New York: Anchor Books.

Eisenberg, J. F., N. A. Muckenhirn, and R. Rudran
1972 "The Relation Between Ecology and Social Structure in Primates." *Science,* 176:863–874.

Eldredge, Niles and Joel Cracraft
1980 *Phylogenetic Patterns and the Evolutionary Process.* New York: Columbia University Press.

Etler, Denis
1992 Personal communication.

Etler, Dennis A. and Li-Tianyuan
1994   "New Archaic Human Fossil Discoveries in China and Their Bearing on Hominid Species Definition During the Middle Pleistocene." *In:* R. Corruccini and R. Ciochon (eds.), q.v., pp. 639–675.

European Union GIS/Remote Sensing Expert Group
1997   Fires in Indonesia, September 1997, a Report to the European Union. Brussels, European Union.

Ewald, Paul
1999   "Evolutionary Control of HIV and Other Sexually Transmitted Viruses," *In: Evolutionary Medicine*, W. R. Trevathan, E. O. Smith, and J. J. McKenna, (eds.), New York: Oxford University Press.

Falk, Dean
1980   "A Reanalysis of the South African Australopithecine Natural Endocasts." *American Journal of Physical Anthropology,* 53:525–539.

_____
1983   "The Taung Endocast: A Reply to Holloway." *American Journal of Physical Anthropology,* 60:479–489.

_____
1987   "Brain Lateralization in Primates and Its Evolution in Hominids." *Yearbook of Physical Anthropology,* 30:107–125.

_____
1989   "Comments." *Current Anthropology,* 30:141.

Fedigan, Linda M.
1982   *Primate Paradigms.* Montreal: Eden Press.

_____
1983   "Dominance and Reproductive Success in Primates." *Yearbook of Physical Anthropology,* 26:91–129.

_____
1986   "The Changing Role of Women in Models of Human Evolution." *Annual Review of Anthropology,* 15:25–66.

Fisher, R. A.
1930   *The Genetical Theory of Natural Selection.* Oxford: Clarendon.

Fleagle, John
1983   "Locomotor Adaptations of Oligocene and Miocene Hominoids and their Phyletic Implications." *In:* R. L. Ciochon and R. S. Corruccini (eds.), q.v., pp. 301–324.

_____
1988   *Primate Adaptation and Evolution.* New York: Academic Press. 2nd ed., 1999.

Fleagle, J. G. and R. F. Kay
1983   "New Interpretations of the Phyletic Position of Oligocene Hominoids." *In:* R. L. Ciochon and R. S. Corruccini (eds.), q.v., pp. 181–210.

Fleischer, R. F. and H. R. Hart, Jr.
1972   "Fission Track Dating Techniques and Problems." *In: Calibration of Hominid Evolution,* W. W. Bishop and J. A. Miller (eds.). Edinburgh: Scottish Academic Press, pp. 135–170.

Foley, R. A.
1991   "How Many Species of Hominid Should There Be?" *Journal of Human Evolution,* 30:413–427.

Foley, R. A. and M. M. Lahr
1992   "Beyond 'Out of Africa.'" *Journal of Human Evolution,* 22:523–529.

Fossey, Dian
1983   *Gorillas in the Mist.* Boston: Houghton Mifflin.

Fouts, Roger S., D. H. Fouts, and T. T. van Cantfort
1989   "The Infant Loulis Learns Signs from Cross-Fostered Chimpanzees." *In:* R. A. Gardner et al., q.v., pp. 280–292.

Francoeuer, Robert T.
1965   *Perspectives in Evolution.* Baltimore: Helicon.

Frayer, David
1980   "Sexual Dimorphism and Cultural Evolution in the Late Pleistocene and Holocene of Europe." *Journal of Human Evolution,* 9:399–415.

_____
1992   "Evolution at the European Edge: Neanderthal and Upper Paleolithic Relationships." *Préhistoire Européenne,* 2:9–69.

_____
n.d.   "Language Capacity in European Neanderthals."

Friedman, Milton J. and William Trager
1981   "The Biochemistry of Resistance to Malaria." *Scientific American,* 244:154–164.

Frisancho, A. Roberto
1978   "Nutritional Influences on Human Growth and Maturation." *Yearbook of Physical Anthropology,* 21:174–191.

_____
1993   *Human Adaptation and Accommodation.* Ann Arbor: University of Michigan Press.

Frisch, Rose E.
1988   Fatness and Fertility. *Scientific American,* 258:88–95.

Froelich, J. W.
1970   "Migration and Plasticity Physique in the Japanese-Americans of Hawaii." *American Journal of Physical Anthropology,* 32:429.

Gabrunia, Leo, Abesalom Vekua, David Lordkipanidze, et al.
2000   "Earliest Pleistocene Hominid Cranial Remains from Dmanisi, Republic of Georgia: Taxonomy, Geological Setting, and Age." *Science,* 288:1019–1025.

Galdikas, Biruté M.
1979   "Orangutan Adaptation at Tanjung Puting
        Reserve: Mating and Ecology." *In: The Great Apes,*
        D. A. Hamburg and E. R. McCown (eds.), Menlo
        Park, Ca.: Benjamin/Cummings Publishing Co.,
        pp. 195–233.
Gambier, Dominique
1989   "Fossil Hominids from the Early Upper
        Palaeolithic (Aurignacian) of France." *In:* Mellars
        and Stringer (eds.), q.v., pp. 194–211.
Gamble, C.
1991   "The Social Context for European Palaeolithic
        Art." *Proceedings of the Prehistoric Society,* 57:3–15.
Gao, Feng, Elizabeth Bailes, David L. Robertson, et al.
1999   "Origin of HIV-1 in the Chimpanzee *Pan
        troglodytes troglodytes.*" *Nature,* 397:436–441.
Gardner, R. Allen, B. T. Gardner, and T. T. van Cantfort
(eds.)
1989   *Teaching Sign Language to Chimpanzees.* Albany:
        State University of New York Press.
Garn, Stanley M.
1965, 1969   *Human Races.* Springfield, Ill.: Charles C.
        Thomas.
Garner, K. J. and O. A. Ryder
1996   "Mitochondrial DNA diversity in gorillas."*Mol.
        Phylogenet. Evol.,* 6:39–48.
Gates, R. R.
1948   *Human Ancestry.* Cambridge: Harvard University
        Press.
Gavan, James
1977   *Paleoanthropology and Primate Evolution.* Dubuque,
        Ia.: Wm. C. Brown Co.
Gao, Feng, Elizabeth Bailes, David L. Robertson, et al.
1999   "Origin of HIV-1 in the Chimpanzee *Pan
        troglodytes troglodytes.*" *Nature,* 397:436–441
Gebo, Daniel L., Marian Dagosto, K. Christopher Beard,
and Tao Qi
2000   "The Smallest Primates." *Journal of Human
        Evolution,* 38:585–594.
Gee, Henry
1996   "Box of Bones 'Clinches' Identity of Piltdown
        Paleontology Hoaxer." *Nature,* 381:261–262.
Ghiglieri, Michael P.
1984   *The Chimpanzees of Kibale Forest.* New York:
        Columbia University Press.
Ghiselin, Michael T.
1969   *The Triumph of the Darwinian Method.* Chicago:
        University of Chicago Press.
Gibbons, Anne
1992   "Mitochondrial Eve, Wounded but Not Dead
        Yet." *Science,* 257:873–875.

1998   "Ancient Tools Suggest *Homo erectus* was a
        Seafarer." Research News, *Science,* 279:1635–1637.
Gingerich, Phillip D.
1985   "Species in the Fossil Record: Concepts, Trends,
        and Transitions." *Paleobiology,* 11:27–41.
Goldizen, Anne Wilson
1987   "Tamarins and Marmosets: Communal Care of
        Offspring." *In:* Smuts et al. (eds.), q.v., pp. 34–43.
Goldstein, M., P. Tsarong, and C. M. Beall
1983   "High Altitude Hypoxia, Culture, and Human
        Fecundity/Fertility: A Comparative Study."
        American Anthropologist, 85:28–49.
Goodall, A. G.
1977   "Feeding and Ranging Behaviour of a Mountain
        Gorilla Group, *Gorilla gorilla beringei* in the
        Tshibinda-Kahuze Region (Zaire)." *In: Primate
        Ecology.* T. H. Clutton-Brock (ed.). London:
        Academic Press, pp. 450–479.
Goodall, Jane
1968   "The Behavior of Free Living Chimpanzees in
        the Gombe Stream Reserve." *Animal Behavior
        Monographs,* 1:(3).

1986   *The Chimpanzees of Gombe.* Cambridge, Mass.:
        Harvard University Press.

1990   *Through a Window.* Boston: Houghton Mifflin.
Goodman, M., M. L. Baba, and L. L. Darga
1983   "The Bearing of Molecular Data on the
        Cladogenesis and Times of Divergence of
        Hominoid Lineages." *In:* R. L. Ciochon and
        R. S. Corruccini (eds.), q.v., pp. 67–86.
Gossett, Thomas F.
1963   *Race, the History of an Idea in America.* Dallas:
        Southern Methodist University Press.
Gould, Stephen Jay
1977   *Ontogeny and Phylogeny.* Cambridge, Mass.:
        Harvard University Press.

1981   *The Mismeasures of Man.* New York: W. W. Norton.

1985   "Darwin at Sea—and the Virtues of Port."
        In: Stephen Jay Gould, *The Flamingo's Smile.
        Reflections in Natural History.* New York:
        W. W. Norton, pp. 347–359.

1987   *Time's Arrow Time's Cycle.* Cambridge: Harvard
        University Press.
Gould, S. J. and N. Eldedge
1977   "Punctuated Equilibria: The Tempo and Mode of
        Evolution Reconsidered." *Paleobiology,* 3:115–151.

Gould, S. J. and R. Lewontin
1979 "The Spandrels of San Marco and the Panglossian Paradigm: A Critique of the Adaptionist Programme." *Proceedings of the Royal Society of London,* 205:581–598.

Gowlett, John
1984 *Ascent to Civilization.* New York: Alfred A. Knopf.

Grant, P. R.
1986 *Ecology and Evolution of Darwin's Finches.* Princeton: Princeton University Press.

Greenberg, Joel
1977 "Who Loves You?" *Science News,* 112 (August 27): 139–141.

Greene, John C.
1981 *Science, Ideology, and World View.* Berkeley: University of California Press.

Greenfield, L. O.
1979 "On the Adaptive Pattern of *Ramapithecus*." *American Journal of Physical Anthropology,* 50:527–548.

Greenleaf, J. E.
1992 "Problem: Thirst, Drinking Behavior, and Involuntary Dehydration." *Med. Sci. Sports Exercise.* 24:645–656.

Grine, F. E.
1993 "Australopithecine Taxonomy and Phylogeny: Historical Background and Recent Interpretation." *In: The Human Evolution Source Book,* R. L. Ciochon and J. G. Fleagle (eds.), Englewood Cliffs, N.J.: Prentice Hall, pp. 198–210.

Grine, Frederick E. (ed.)
1988a *Evolutionary History of the "Robust" Australopithecines.* New York: Aldine de Gruyter.
1988b "New Craniodental Fossils of *Paranthropus* from the Swartkrans Formation and Their Significance in "Robust" Australopithecine Evolution." *In:* F. E. Grine (ed.), q.v., pp. 223–243.

Groves, Colin P.
2001 *Primate Taxonomy.* Washington DC: Smithsonian Institution Press.

_____
2001b "Why taxonomic stability is a bad idea, or why are there so few species of primates (or are there?)". *Evolutionary Anthropology* 10(6):191–197.

Haile-Selassie, Yohannes
2001 "Late Miocene Hominids from the Middle Awash, Ethiopia." *Nature,* 412:178–181.

Haldane, J.B.S.
1932 *The Causes of Evolution.* London: Longmans, Green (reprinted as paperback, Cornell University Press, 1966).

Hamilton, W. D.
1964 "The Genetical Theory of Social Behavior. I and II." *Journal of Theoretical Biology,* 7:1–52.

Handoko, Helina Y., J. Koji Lum, Gustiani, et al.
2001 "Length Variations in the COII-tRNA^{Lys} Intergenic Region of Mitochondrial DNA in Indonesian Populations." *Human Biology,* 73:205–223.

Hanna, Joel M. and Daniel A. Brown
1979 "Human Heat Tolerance: Biological and Cultural Adaptations." *Yearbook of Physical Anthropology,* 1979, 22:163–186.

Harlow, Harry F.
1959 "Love in Infant Monkeys." *Scientific American,* 200:68–74.

Harlow, Harry F. and Margaret K. Harlow
1961 "A Study of Animal Affection." *Natural History,* 70:48–55.

Harrold, Francis R.
1989 "Mousterian, Chatelperronian and Early Aurignacian in Western Europe: Continuity or Discontinuity." *In: The Human Revolution,* P. Mellars and C. Stringer (eds.), Princeton, N.J.: Princeton University Press, pp. 212–231.

Hartl, Daniel
1983 *Human Genetics.* New York: Harper & Row.

Harvey, Paul H., R. D. Martin, and T. H. Clutton-Brock
1987 "Life Histories in Comparative Perspective." *In:* Smuts et al. (eds.), q.v., pp. 181–196.

Hass, J. D., E. A. Frongillo, Jr., C. D. Stepick, J. L. Beard, and G. Hurtado
1980 Altitude, Ethnic and Sex Difference in Birth Weight and Length in Bolivia. *Human Biology,* 52:459–477.

Hausfater, Glenn
1984 "Infanticide in Langurs: Strategies, Counter Strategies, and Parameter Values." *In:* G. Hausfater and S. B. Hrdy, (eds.), q.v., pp. 257–281.

Hausfater, Glenn and Sarah Blaffer Hrdy (eds.)
1984 *Infanticide. Comparative and Evolutionary Perspectives.* Hawthorne, New York: Aldine de Gruyter.

Hawkes, K., J. F. O'Connell, and N. G. Blurton Jones
1997 Hadza Women's Time Allocation, Offspring Provisioning, and the Evolution of Long Postmenopausal Life Spans. *Current Anthropology,* 38:551–577.

Hayden, Brian
1993 "The Cultural Capacities of Neandertals: A Review and Reevaluation." *Journal of Human Evolution,* 24:113–146.

Henahan, Sean
  1995   Men haven't changed in 270,000 years. Access
         Excellence, Genentech Inc., Worldwide Web
         Source.
Heyer, E.
  1999   "One Founder/One Gene Hypothesis in a New
         Expanding Population: Saguenay (Quebec,
         Canada)." *Human Biology,* 71:99–109.
Hiernaux, Jean
  1968   *La Diversité Humaine en Afrique subsahariénne.*
         Bruxelles: L'Institut de Sociologie, Université
         Libre de Bruxelles.
Hill, A., S. Ward, A. Deino, G. Curtis, and R. Drake
  1992   "Earliest *Homo.*" *Nature,* 355:719–722.
Hill, Andrew and Steven Ward
  1988   "Origin of the Hominidae: The Record of African
         Large Hominoid Evolution Between 14 my and
         4 my." *Yearbook of Physical Anthropology,* 1988,
         31:49–83.
Hinde, Robert A.
  1987   "Can Nonhuman Primates Help Us Understand
         Human Behavior?" *In:* B. Smuts et al. (eds.),
         q.v., pp. 413–420.
Hirsch, V. M., R. A. Olmsted, M. Murphey-Corb,
R. H. Purcell, and P. R. Johnson
  1989   "An African Primate Lentivirus (SIVsm) Closely
         Related to HIV-2." *Nature,* 339: 389–392.
Hoffstetter, R.
  1972   "Relationships, Origins, and History of the
         Ceboid Monkeys and the Caviomorph Rodents:
         A Modern Reinterpretation." *In: Evolutionary
         Biology* (Vol. 6), T. Dobzhansky, T. M. K. Hecht,
         and W. C. Steere (eds.), New York: Appleton-
         Century-Crofts, pp. 323–347.
Holloway, Ralph L.
  1969   "Culture: A Human Domain." *Current
         Anthropology,* 10:395–407.

  1981   "Revisiting the South African Taung Australo-
         pithecine Endocast: The Position of the Lunate
         Sulcus as Determined by the Stereoplotting
         Technique." *American Journal of Physical
         Anthropology,* 56:43–58.

  1983   "Cerebral Brain Endocast Pattern of
         Australopithecus afarensis Hominid." *Nature,*
         303:420–422.

  1985   "The Poor Brain of *Homo sapiens
         neanderthalensis.*" *In: Ancestors, The Hard
         Evidence,* E. Delson (ed.). New York: Alan R. Liss,
         pp. 319–324.

Horr, D. A.
  1975   "The Bornean Orangutan: Population Structure
         and Dynamics in Relationship to Ecology and
         Reproductive Strategy." *In: Primate Behavior:
         Developments in Field and Laboratory Research,*
         vol. 4, L. A. Rosenblum (ed.), New York:
         Academic Press.
Howell, F. Clark
  1978   "Hominidae." *In: Evolution of African Mammals,*
         V. J. Maglio and H.B.S. Cooke (eds.), Cambridge:
         Harvard University Press, pp. 154–248.

  1988   "Foreword." *In:* Grine (ed.), q.v., pp. xi–xv.
Howells, W. W.
  1973   *Evolution of the Genus* Homo. Reading, Mass.:
         Addison-Wesley.

  1980   *"Homo erectus*—Who, When, Where: A Survey.
         Yearbook of Physical Anthropology, 23:1–23.
Hrdy, Sarah Blaffer
  1977   *The Langurs of Abu.* Cambridge, Mass.: Harvard
         University Press.

  1984a "Assumptions and Evidence Regarding the Sexual
         Selection Hypothesis: A Reply to Boggess."
         In: G. Hausfater and S. B. Hrdy (eds.), q.v.,
         pp. 315–319.

  1984b "Female Reproductive Strategies." *In:* M. Small
         (ed.), q.v., pp. 103–109.

  1999   *Mother Nature: A History of Mothers, Infants, and
         Natural Selection.* New York: Pantheon Books.
Hrdy, Sarah Blaffer, Charles Janson, and Carel van Schaik
  1995   Infanticide: Let's not throw out the baby with the
         bath water." *Evolutionary Anthropology,*
         3(5):151–154.
Hu, Dale J., Timothy J. Dondero, Mark A. Rayfield, et al.
  1996   "The Emerging Genetic Diversity of HIV.
         The Importance of Global Surveillance, for
         Diagnostics, Research, and Prevention." *Journal of
         the American Medical Association,* 275(3):210–216.
Hublin, Jean-Jacques, F. Spoor, M. Braun, F. Zonneveld,
and S. Condemi
  1996   A Late Neanderthal Associated with Upper
         Palaeolithic Artifacts. *Nature,* 38:224–226.
Hull, David L.
  1973   *Darwin and His Critics.* Chicago: University of
         Chicago Press.

The Institute of Vertebrate Paleontology and Paleoanthropology, Chinese Academy of Sciences
1980   *Atlas of Primitive Man in China.* Beijing: Science Press (Distributed by Van Nostrand, New York).

The International SNP Map Working Group
2001   "A Map of Human Genome Sequence Variation Containing 1.42 Million Single Nucleotide Polymorphisms." *Nature,* 409:928–933.

Isaac, G. L.
1971   "The Diet of Early Man." *World Archaeology,* 2:278–299.

——
1975   "Stratigraphy and Cultural Patterns in East Africa During the Middle Ranges of Pleistocene Time." *In: After the Australopithecines,* K. W. Butzer and G. L. Isaac (eds.), Chicago: Aldine Publishing Co., pp. 495–542.

——
1976   "Early Hominids in Action: A Commentary on the Contribution of Archeology to Understanding the Fossil Record in East Africa." *Yearbook of Physical Anthropology,* 1975, 19:19–35.

Izawa, K. and A. Mizuno
1977   "Palm-Fruit Cracking Behaviour of Wild Black-Capped Capuchin (*Cebus apella*)." *Primates,* 18:773–793.

Jablonksi, Nina
1992   "Sun, Skin Colour and Spina Bifida: An Exploration of the Relationship between Ultraviolet Light and Neural Tube Defects." *Proceedings of the Australasian Society of Human Biology,* 5:455–462.

Jensen, Arthur
1969   *Environment, Heredity, and Intelligence.* Cambridge, Mass.: Harvard Educational Review.

Jerison, H. J.
1973   *Evolution of the Brain and Behavior.* New York: Academic Press.

Jia, L. and Huang Weiwen
1990   *The Story of Peking Man.* New York: Oxford University Press.

Jia, Lan-po
1975   *The Cave Home of Peking Man.* Peking: Foreign Language Press.

Johanson, D. C. and T. D. White
1979   "A Systematic Assessment of Early African Hominids." *Science,* 203:321–330.

Johanson, Donald and Maitland Edey
1981   *Lucy: The Beginnings of Humankind.* New York: Simon & Schuster.

Johanson, Donald, F. T. Masao, et al.
1987   "New Partial Skeleton of *Homo habilis* from Olduvai Gorge, Tanzania." *Nature,* 327:205–209.

Johanson, Donald C. and Maurice Taieb
1976   "Plio-Pleistocene Hominid Discoveries in Hadar, Ethiopia." *Nature,* 260:293–297.

——
1980   "New Discoveries of Pliocene Hominids and Artifacts in Hadar." International Afar Research Expedition to Ethiopia (Fourth and Fifth Field Seasons, 1975–77). *Journal of Human Evolution,* 9:582.

Jolly, Alison
1984   "The Puzzle of Female Feeding Priority." *In:* M. F. Small (ed.), q.v., pp. 197–215.

——
1985   *The Evolution of Primate Behavior* (2nd Ed.), New York: Macmillan.

Jolly, Clifford J.
1993   "Species, Subspecies, and Baboon Systematics." *In:* W.H. Kimbel and L.B. Martin (eds.), *Species, Species Concepts, and Primate Evolution.* New York: Plenum Press, pp. 67–107.

Jones, Rhys
1990   East of Wallace's Line: Issues and Problems in the Colonization of the Australian Continent." *In: The Human Revolution,* P. Mellars and C. Stringer (eds.), Princeton, N.J.: Princeton University Press, pp. 743–782.

Jungers, W. L.
1982   "Lucy's Limbs: Skeletal Allometry and Locomotion in *Australopithecus afarensis.*" *Nature,* 297:676–678.

——
1988   "New Estimates of Body Size in Australopithecines." *In:* F. E. Grine (ed.), q.v., pp. 115–125.

Kano, T.
1980   The Social Behavior of Wild Pygmy Chimpanzees (*Pan Paniscus*) of Wamba: A Preliminary Report. *Journal of Human Evolution,* 9:243–260.

——
1992   *The Last Ape. Pygmy Chimpanzee Behavior and Ecology.* Stanford: Stanford University Press.

Kappleman, John
1996   The Evolution of Body Mass and Relative Brain Size in Fossil Hominids. *Journal of Human Evolution,* 30:243–276.

Katz, D. and J. M. Suchey
1986   "Age Determination of the Male *Os Pubis.*" *American Journal of Physical Anthropology,* 69:427–435.

Katz, S. H., M. L. Hediger, and L. A. Valleroy
1974   Traditional Maize Processing Techniques in the New World. *Science,* 184:765–773.

Kay, R., M. Cartmill, and M. Balow
1998   "The Hypoglossal Canal and the Origins of Human Vocal Behavior (abstract)." *American Journal of Physical Anthropology, Supplement,* 26:137.

Kay, R. F., J. G. Fleagle, and E. L. Simons
1981   "A Revision of the Oligocene Apes of the Fayum Province, Egypt." *American Journal of Physical Anthropology,* 55:293–322.

Kay, Richard and Frederick E. Grine
1988   "Tooth Morphology, Wear and Diet in *Australopithecus* and *Paranthropus, In:* F. Grine (ed.), q.v., pp. 427–447.

Kelly, Mark and David Pilbeam
1986   "The Dryopithecines: Taxonomy, Comparative Anatomy, and Phylogeny of Miocene Large Hominoids." *In: Comparative Primate Biology.* Vol. 1, *Systematics, Evolution, and Anatomy,* D. R. Swindler and J. Erwin (eds.), New York: Alan R. Liss, pp. 361–411.

Kennedy, G. E.
1983   "A Morphometric and Taxonomic Assessment of a Hominid Femur from the Lower Member, Koobi Fora, Lake Turkana." *American Journal of Physical Anthropology,* 61:429–436.

Kennedy, K. A. R.
1991   "Is the Narmada Hominid an Indian *Homo erectus*?" *American Journal of Physical Anthropology,* 86:475–496.

Kennedy, Kenneth A. R. and S. U. Deraniyagala
1989   "Fossil Remains of 28,000-Year-Old Hominids from Sri Lanka." *Current Anthropology,* 30:397–399.

Keyser, André W.
2000   "New Finds in South Africa." *National Geographic,* (May), pp. 76–83.

Kimbel, William H.
1988   "Identification of a Partial Cranium of *Australopithecus afarensis* from the Koobi Fora Formation, Kenya." *Journal of Human Evolution,* 17:647–656.

Kimbel, William H., Donald C. Johanson, and Yoel Rak
1994   "The First Skull and Other New Discoveries of *Australopithecus afarensis* at Hadar, Ethiopia." *Nature,* 368:449–451.

Kimbel, W. H., R. C. Walter, D. C. Johanson, et al.
1996   Late Pliocene *Homo* and Oldowan Tools from the Hadar Formation (Kada Hadar Member), Ethiopia. *Journal of Human Evolution,* 31:549–561.

Kimbel, William H., Tim D. White, and Donald C. Johanson
1988   "Implications of KNM-WT-17000 for the Evolution of 'Robust' *Australopithecus.*" *In:* F. E. Grine (ed.), q.v., pp. 259–268.

King, Barbara J.
1994   *The Information Continuum.* Santa Fe: School of American Research.

Kiple, Kenneth F.
1993   *The Cambridge World History of Human Disease.* Cambridge: Cambridge University Press.

Kirkwood, T. B. L.
1997   "The Origins of Human Ageing." *Philosophical Transactions of the Royal Society of London B,* 352:1765–1772.

Klein, R. G.
1989   *The Human Career. Human Biological and Cultural Origins.* Chicago: University of Chicago Press.

_____
1992   "The Archeology of Modern Human Origins." *Evolutionary Anthropology,* 1:5–14.

Konner, Melvin and Carol Worthman
1980   Nursing Frequency, Gonadal Function, and Birth Spacing among !Kung Hunter-Gatherers. *Science,* 207:788–791.

Kramer, Andrew
1986   "Hominid-Pongid Distinctiveness in the Miocene-Pliocene Fossil Record: The Lothagam Mandible." *American Journal of Physical Anthropology,* 70:457–473.

_____
1993   "Human Taxonomic Diversity in the Pleistocene: Does *Homo erectus* Represent Multiple Hominid Species?" *American Journal of Physical Anthropology,* 91:161–171.

Krings, Matthias, Cristian Capelli, Frank Tschentscher, et al.
2000   "A View of Neandertal Genetic Diversity." *Nature Genetics* 26:144–146.

Krings, Matthias, Anne Stone, Ralf W. Schmitz, et al.
1997   "Neandertal DNA Sequences and the Origin of Modern Humans." *Cell,* 90:19–30.

Kroeber, A. L.
1928   "Sub-human Cultural Beginning." *Quarterly Review of Biology,* 3:325–342.

Krogman, W. M.
1962   *The Human Skeleton in Forensic Medicine.* Springfield: C. C. Thomas.

Krummer, Hans
1971   *Primate Societies.* Chicago: Aldine-Atherton, Inc.

Kunzig, Robert
1997   "Atapuerca. The Face of an Ancestral Child." *Discover,* 18:88–101.

Lack, David
  1966   *Population Studies of Birds.* Oxford: Clarendon.
Lalani, A. S., J. Masters, W. Zeng, et al.
  1999   "Use of Chemokine Receptors by Poxviruses."
         Science, 286:1968–71.
Lamarck, Jean-Baptiste
  1809, 1984   *Zoological Philosophy.* Chicago: University
         of Chicago Press.
Lamberts, S. W. J., A. W. van den Beld, and A-J van der Lely
  1997   "The Endocrinology of Aging." *Science,*
         278:419–424.
Lancaster, Jane B.
  1975   *Primate Behavior and the Emergence of Human
         Culture.* New York: Holt, Rinehart & Winston.
Lancaster, Jane B. and C. S. Lancaster
  1983   "Parental Investment: The Hominid Adaptation."
         In: Ortner, D. J. (ed.), *How Humans Adapt: A
         Biocultural Odyssey.* Washington, DC: Smithsonian
         Institution Press.
Landau, M.
  1984   "Human Evolution as Narrative." *American
         Scientist,* 72:262–268.
Larick, Roy and Russell L. Ciochon
  1996   "The African Emergence and Early Asian
         Dispersals of the Genus, *Homo.*" *American
         Scientist,* 84:538–551.
Lasker, Gabriel W.
  1969   "Human Biological Adaptability: The Ecological
         Approach in Physical Anthropology." *Science,*
         166:1480–1486.
Latimer, Bruce
  1984   "The Pedal Skeleton of *Australopithecus afarensis.*"
         American Journal of Physical Anthropology, 63:182.
Leakey, L. S. B., J. F. Everden, and G. H. Curtis
  1961   "Age of Bed I, Olduvai Gorge, Tanganyika."
         Nature, 191:478–479.
Leakey, L. S. B., P. V. Tobias, and J. R. Napier
  1964   "A New Species of the Genus *Homo* from Olduvai
         Gorge." *Nature,* 202:7–10.
Leakey, M. D.
  1971   "Remains of *Homo erectus* and Associated Artifacts
         in Bed IV at Olduvai Gorge, Tanzania." *Nature,*
         232:380–383.
Leakey, M. D. and R. L. Hay
  1979   "Pliocene Footprints in Laetoli Beds at Laetoli,
         Northern Tanzania." *Nature,* 278:317–323.
Leakey, Meave G. et al.
  1995   "New Four-Million-Year-Old Hominid Species
         from Kanapoi: and Allia Bay, Kenya." *Nature,*
         376:565–571.

Leakey, R. E. F. and M. D. Leakey
  1986   "A New Miocene Hominoid from Kenya." *Nature,*
         324:143–146.
Lederberg, J.
  1996   "Infection Emergent" (editorial). *Journal of the
         American Medical Association,* 275(3):243–245.
Lerner, I. M. and W. J. Libby
  1976   *Heredity, Evolution, and Society.* San Francisco:
         W. H. Freeman and Company.
Leroi-Gourhan, André
  1986   "The Hands of Gargas." *October* 37:18–34.
Lewontin, R. C.
  1972   "The Apportionment of Human Diversity." *In:
         Evolutionary Biology* (Vol. 6), T. Dobzhansky et al.
         (eds.), New York: Plenum, pp. 381–398.
Li, Wen-Hsiung and Masako Tanimura
  1987   "The Molecular Clock Runs More Slowly in Man
         than in Apes and Monkeys." *Nature,* 326:93–96.
Lieberman, Daniel, David R. Pilbeam, and Bernard A.
Wood
  1988   "A Probalistic Approach to the Problem of Sexual
         Dimorphism in *Homo habilis*: A Comparison of
         KNM-ER-1470 and KNM-ER-1813." *Journal of
         Human Evolution,* 17:503–511.
Linnaeus, C.
  1758   *Systema Naturae.*
Lisowski, F. P.
  1984   "Introduction." *In: The Evolution of the East
         African Environment.* Centre of Asian Studies
         Occasional Papers and Monographs, No. 59, R. O.
         Whyte (ed.), Hong Kong: University of Hong
         Kong, pp. 777–786.
Livingstone, Frank B.
  1964   "On the Nonexistence of Human Races." *In:
         Concept of Race,* A. Montagu (ed.), New York: The
         Free Press, pp. 46–60.

  _____

  1969   "Polygenic Models for the Evolution of Human
         Skin Color Differences." *Human Biology,*
         41:480–493.

  _____

  1980   "Natural Selection and the Origin and
         Maintenance of Standard Genetic Marker
         Systems." *Yearbook of Physical Anthropology,* 1980,
         23:25–42.
Lovejoy, C. O.
  1988   "Evolution of Human Walking." *Scientific
         American,* 259(Nov.):118–125.
Lovejoy, C. O., G. Kingsbury, G. Heiple, and A. H. Burstein
  1973   "The Gait of *Australopithecus.*" *American Journal of
         Physical Anthropology,* 38:757–780.

Lovejoy, Thomas E.
1982 "The Tropical Forest—Greatest Expression of Life on Earth." *In: Primates and the Tropical Forest,* Proceedings, California Institute of Technology and World Wildlife Fund—U.S., pp. 45–48.

Lundelius, Ernest L., Jr., and Russell Graham
1999 "The Weather Changed." *Discovering Archaeology,* 1(5):48–53.

MacKinnon, J. and K. MacKinnon
1980 "The Behavior of Wild Spectral Tarsiers." *International Journal of Primatology,* 1:361–379.

MacLarnon, Ann
1993 "The Vertebral Canal of KNM-WT 1500 and the Evolution of the Spinal Cord and Other Canal Contents." *In:* A. Walker and R. E. Leakey (eds.), q.v., pp. 359–390.

Mai, L. L.
1983 "A Model of Chromosome Evolution and Its Bearing on Cladogenesis in the Hominoidea." *In:* R. Ciochon and R. Corruccini (eds.), q.v., pp. 87–114.

Manson, J. H. and R. Wrangham
1991 "Intergroup Aggression in Chimpanzees and Humans." *Current Anthropology,* 32:369–390.

Marshack, A.
1972 *The Roots of Civilization.* New York: McGraw-Hill Publishing Co.

_____
1989 "Evolution of the Human Capacity: The Symbolic Evidence." *Yearbook of Physical Anthropology,* 1989, 32:1–34.

Masserman, J., S. Wechkin, and W. Terris
1964 "'Altruistic' Behavior in Rhesus Monkeys." *American Journal of Physical Anthropology,* 121:584–585.

Mayer, Peter J.
1982 Evolutionary Advantages of Menopause. *Human Ecology,* 10:477–494.

Mayr, Ernst
1962 "Taxonomic Categories in Fossil Hominids." *In: Ideas on Human Evolution,* W. W. Howells (ed.), New York: Atheneum, pp. 242–256.

_____
1970 *Population, Species, and Evolution.* Cambridge: Harvard University Press.

_____
1991 *One Long Argument.* Cambridge: Harvard University Press.

McConkey, Edwin H. and Ajit Varki
2000 "A primate genome project deserves high priority." Letters. *Science,* 289:1295.

McGrew, W. C.
1992 *Chimpanzee Material Culture. Implications for Human Evolution.* Cambridge: Cambridge University Press.

_____
1998 "Culture in Nonhuman Primates?" *Annual Reviews of Anthropology,.* 27:301–328.

McGrew, W. C. and E. G. Tutin
1978 "Evidence for a Social Custom in Wild Chimpanzees?" *Man,* 13:234–251.

McHenry, Henry
1983 "The Capitate of *Australopithecus afarensis* and *A. africanus.*" *American Journal of Physical Anthropology,* 62:187–198.

_____
1988 "New Estimates of Body Weight in Early Hominids and Their Significance to Encephalization and Megadontia in 'Robust' Australopithecines." *In:* F. E. Grine (ed.), q.v., pp. 133–148.

_____
1992 "Body Size and Proportions in Early Hominids." *American Journal of Physical Anthropology,* 87:407–431.

McKenna, James J.
1982a "Primate Field Studies: The Evolution of Behavior and Its Socioecology." *In: Primate Behavior.* James L. Fobes and James E. King (eds.). New York: Academic Press, pp. 53–83.

_____
1982b "The Evolution of Primate Societies, Reproduction, and Parenting." *In: Primate Behavior.* James L. Fobes and James E. King (eds.). New York: Academic Press, pp. 87–133.

McKern, T. W. and T. D. Stewart
1957 "Age Changes in Young American Males, Technical Report EP-45." Natick, MA: U.S. Army Quartermaster Research and Development Center.

McKusick, Victor
1998 *Mendelian Inheritance in Man.* (12th Ed.) Baltimore: Johns Hopkins Press.

McRae, M. and K. Ammann
1997 "Road kill in Cameroon." *Natural History* 106:36–47.

Mellars, P. and C. Stringer (eds.)
1989 *The Human Revolution.* Princeton, N.J.: Princeton University Press.

Mitchell, R. J., S. Howlett, N. G. White, et al.
1999 "Deletion Polymorphism in the Human COL1AZ Gene: Genetic Evidence of a Non-African Population Whose Descendants Spread to All Continents." *Human Biology,* 71:901–914.

Mittermeir, R. A.
  1982   "The World's Endangered Primates: An
         Introduction and a Case Study—The Monkeys
         of Brazil's Atlantic Forests." *In: Primates and the
         Tropical Rain Forest,* Proceedings, California
         Institute of Technology, and World Wildlife
         Fund—U.S., pp. 11–22.
Mittermeir, R. A. and D. Cheney
  1987   "Conservation of Primates in Their Habitats."
         In: B. B. Smuts et al., q.v., pp. 477–496.
Montagu, A.
  1961   Neonatal and Infant Immaturity in Man. *Journal
         of the American Medical Association,* 178:56–57.
Molnar, Stephen
  1983   *Human Variation. Races, Types, and Ethnic Groups*
         (2nd Ed.). Englewood Cliffs: Prentice Hall.
Moore, Lorna G. et al.
  1994   Genetic Adaptation to High Altitude. *In: Sports
         and Exercise Medicine,* Stephen C. Wood and
         Robert C. Roach (eds.), New York: Marcel Dekker,
         Inc., pp. 225–262.
Moore, Lorna G. and Judith G. Regensteiner
  1983   "Adaptation to High Altitude." *Annual Reviews of
         Anthropology,* 12:285–304.
Morbeck, M. E.
  1975   "*Dryopithecus africanus* Forelimb." *Journal of
         Human Evolution,* 4:39–46.

  1983   "Miocene Hominoid Discoveries from
         Rudabánya. Implications from the Postcranial
         Skeleton." *In:* R. L. Ciochon and R. S. Corruccini
         (eds.), q.v., pp. 369–404.
Morgan, Elaine
  1972   *The Descent of Women.* New York: Stein and Day.
Morin, Phillip A., James J. Moore, Ranajit Chakraborty,
et al.
  1994   "In Selection, Social Structure, Gene Flow, and
         the Evolution of Chimpanzees." *Science,*
         265:1145–1332.
Morris, Desmond
  1967   *The Naked Ape.* New York: McGraw-Hill.
Mountain, Joanna L., Alice A. Lin, Anne M. Bowcock, and
L. L. Cavalli-Sforza
  1993   "Evolution of Modern Humans: Evidence from
         Nuclear DNA Polymorphisms." *In:* M. J. Aitken
         et al. (eds.), q.v., pp. 69–83.
Mourant, A. E., A. C. Kopec, and K. Sobczak
  1976   *The Distribution of the Human Blood Groups.*
         Oxford: Oxford University Press.
Moyá-Solà, Salvador and Meike Köhler
  1996   "A *Dryopithecus* Skeleton and the Origins of
         Great-ape Locomotion. *Nature,* 379:156–159.

Mueller, William H. et al.
  1979   "A Multinational Andean Genetic and Health
         Program. VIII. Lung Function Changes with
         Migration between Altitudes." *American Journal
         of Physical Anthropology,* 51:183–196.
Murray, R. D.
  1980   "The Evolution and Functional Significance of
         Incest Avoidance." *Journal of Human Evolution,*
         9:173–178.
Nabhan, G. P.
  1991   Desert Legumes as a Nutritional Intervention for
         Diabetic Indigenous Dwellers of Arid Lands. *Arid
         Lands Newsletter,* 31:11–13.
Napier, J. R. and P. H. Napier
  1967   *A Handbook of Living Primates.* New York:
         Academic Press.

  1985   *The Natural History of the Primates.* Cambridge,
         Mass.: The MIT Press.
Napier, John
  1967   "The Antiquity of Human Walking." *Scientific
         American,* 216:56–66.
Nature
  1986   "Chernobyl Report." *Nature,* 323:26–30.
Neel, J. V.
  1962   Diabetes Mellitus: A "Thrifty" Genotype Rendered
         Detrimental by "Progress"? *American Journal of
         Human Genetics,* 61:1099–1102.
Nesse, R. M., and G. C. Williams
  1994   "Why We Get Sick." New York: Times Books.
Neu, H. C.
  1992   "The Crisis in Antibiotic Resistance." *Science,*
         257:1064–1073.
Newman, Marshall T.
  1975   "Nutritional Adaptation in Man." *In: Physiological
         Anthropology,* Albert Damon (ed.), New York:
         Oxford University Press, pp. 210–259.
Newman, Russell W.
  1970   "Why Man Is Such a Sweaty and Thirsty Naked
         Animal: A Speculative Review." *Human Biology,*
         42:12–27.
Newman, Russell W. and Ella H. Munro
  1955   "The Relation of Climate and Body Size in U.S.
         Males." *American Journal of Physical Anthropology,*
         13:1–17.
Nishida, T.
  1968   "The Social Group of Wild Chimpanzees in the
         Mahale Mountains." *Primates,* 9:167–224.

_____
1979 "The Social Structure of Chimpanzees of the Mahale Mountains." *In: The Great Apes,* D. A. Hamburg and E. R. McCown (eds.), Menlo Park: Benjamin Cummings, pp. 73–122.

_____
1991 Comments. *In:* J. H. Manson and R. Wrangham, q.v., pp. 381–382.

Nishida, T., M. Hiraiwa-Hasegawa, T. Hasegawa, and Y. Takahata
1985 "Group Extinction and Female Transfer in Wild Chimpanzees in the Mahale National Park, Tanzania." *Zeitschrift Tierpsychologie,* 67:284–301.

Nishida, T., H. Takasaki, and Y. Takahata
1990 "Demography and Reproductive Profiles." *In: The Chimpanzees of the Mahale Mountains,* T. Nishida (ed.), Tokyo: University of Tokyo Press, pp. 63–97.

Nishida, T., R. W. Wrangham, J. Goodall, and S. Uehara
1983 "Local Differences in Plant-feeding Habits of Chimpanzees between the Mahale Mountains and Gombe National Park, Tanzania." *Journal of Human Evolution,* 12:467–480.

Noe, R. and R. Bshary
1997 "The Formation of Red Colobus-Diana Monkey Associations Under Predation Pressure from Chimpanzees. *Proceedings of the Royal Society of London, (B) Biological Science,* 264(1379):253–259.

Novitski, Edward
1977 *Human Genetics.* New York: Macmillan.

Oakley, Kenneth
1963 "Analytical Methods of Dating Bones." *In: Science in Archaeology,* D. Brothwell and E. Higgs (eds.), New York: Basic Books, Inc.

Olliaro, Piero
1996 "Malaria, the Submerged Disease." *Journal of the American Medical Association,* 275(3):230–233.

Oates, J. F., M. Abedi-Lartey, W. S. McGrew, et al.
2000 "Extinction of a West African Red Colobus Monkey." *Conservation Biology,* 14(5):1526–1532.

Olson, John W. and R. Ciochon
1990 "A Review of the Evidence for Postulated Middle Pleistocene Occupation in Viet Nam." *Journal of Human Evolution,* 19:761–788.

O'Rourke, D. H., M. G. Hayes, and S. W. Carlyle
2000 "Spatial and Temporal Stability of mtDNA Haplogroup Frequencies in Native North America." *Human Biology,* 72:15–34.

Ortner, Donald J.
1981 "Biocultural Interaction in Human Adaptation." *In: How Humans Adapt.* Donald J. Ortner (ed.), Washington, D.C.: Smithsonian Institution Press.

Ovinnikov, Igor V., Anders Götherström, Galina P. Romanova, et al.
2000 "Molecular Analysis of Neanderthal DNA from the Northern Caucasus." *Nature,* 404:490–493.

Padian, Kevin and Luis M. Chiappe
1998 "The Origin of Birds and Their Flight." *Scientific American,* 278:38–47.

Palumbi, Stephen R.
2001 *The Evolution Explosion: How Humans Cause Rapid Evolutionary Change.* New York: W. W. Norton

Parés, Josef M. and Alfredo Pérez-González
1995 "Paleomagnetic Age for Hominid Fossils at Atapuerca Archaeological Site, Spain." *Science,* 269:830–832.

Parker, Seymour
1976 "The Precultural Basis of the Incest Taboo: Toward a Biosocial Theory." *American Anthropologist,* 78:285–305.

Pennisi, Elizabeth
2001 "The Human Genome." *Science,* 291:1177–1180.

Peres, C.A.
1990 "Effects of hunting on Western Amazonian primate communities." *Biological Conservation* 54: 47–59.

Phillips, K.A.
1998 "Tool Use in Wild Capuchin Monkeys." *American Journal of Primatology,* 46(3):259–261.

Phillips-Conroy, J. E., C. J. Jolly, P. Nystrom, and H. A. Hemmalin
1992 "Migration of Male Hamadryas Baboons into Annubis Groups in the Awash National Park, Ethiopia." *International Journal of Primatology,* 13:455–476.

Pickford, M.
1983 "Sequence and Environments of the Lower and Middle Miocene Hominoids of Western Kenya." *In:* R. L. Ciochon and R. S. Corruccini (eds.), q.v., pp. 421–439.

Pickford, Martin and Brigitte Senut
2001 "The Geological and Faunal Context of Late Miocene Hominid Remains from Lukeino, Kenya." *C. R. Acad. Sci. Paris, Sciences de la Terre et des Planètes,* 332:145–152.

Pilbeam, David
1972 *The Ascent of Man.* New York: Macmillan.

_____
1977 "Beyond the Apes: Pre-*Homo* Hominids: The Ramapithecines of Africa, Asia, and Europe." Symposium Lecture, March 5, 1977, Davis, Ca.

_____
1982 "New Hominoid Skull Material from the Miocene of Pakistan." *Nature,* 295:232–234.

1986   "Distinguished Lecture: Hominoid Evolution and Hominoid Origins." *American Anthropologist,* 88:295–312.

1988   "Primate Evolution." *In: Human Biology,* G. A. Harrison et al., (eds.), New York: Oxford University Press, pp. 76–103.

Pinner, Robert W., Steven M. Teutsch, Lone Simonson, et al.
1996   "Trends in Infectious Diseases Mortality in the United States." *Journal of the American Medical Association,* 275(3):189–193.

Pope, G. G.
1984   "The Antiquity and Paleoenvironment of the Asian Hominidae." *In: The Evolution of the East Asian Environment.* Center of Asian Studies Occasional Papers and Monographs, No. 59, R. O. Whyte (ed.), Hong Kong: University of Hong Kong, pp. 822–847.

1992   "Craniofacial Evidence for the Origin of Modern Humans in China." *Yearbook of Physical Anthropology,* 1992, 35:243–298.

Popp, Joseph L. and Irven DeVore
1979   "Aggressive Competition and Social Dominance Theory." *In: The Great Apes,* D. A. Hamburg and E. R. McCown (eds.), Menlo Park, Ca.: Benjamin/Cummings Publishing Co., pp. 317–318.

Post, Peter W., Farrington Daniels, Jr., and Robert T. Binford, Jr.
1975   "Cold Injury and the Evolution of 'White' Skin." *Human Biology,* 47:65–80.

Potts, Richard
1984   "Home Bases and Early Hominids." *American Scientist,* 72:338–347.

1991   "Why the Oldowan? Plio-Pleistocene Toolmaking and the Transport of Resources." *Journal of Anthropological Research,* 47:153–176.

1993   "Archeological Interpretations of Early Hominid Behavior and Ecology." *In:* D. T. Rasmussen (ed.), *The Origin and Evolution of Humans and Humanness,* Boston: Jones and Bartlett, pp. 49–74.

Potts, Richard and Pat Shipman
1981   "Cutmarks Made by Stone Tools from Olduvai Gorge, Tanzania." *Nature,* 291:577–580.

Proctor, Robert
1988   "From Anthropologie to Rassenkunde." *In: Bones, Bodies, Behavior. History of Anthropology* (Vol. 5), 6. W. Stocking, Jr. (ed.), Madison: University of Wisconsin Press, pp. 138–179.

Profet, M.
1988   The Evolution of Pregnancy Sickness as a Protection to the Embryo Against Pleistocene Teratogens. *Evolutionary Theory,* 8:177–190.

Pulliam, H. R. and T. Caraco
1984   "Living in groups: Is There an Optimal Size?" *In: Behavioral Ecology: An Evolutionary Approach* (2nd ed.), J. R. Krebs and N. B. Davies (eds.), Sunderland, Mass.: Sinauer Associates.

Pusey, Anne E. and Craig Packer
1987   "Dispersal and Philopatry." *In:* B. B. Smuts et al. (eds.), q.v., pp. 250–266.

Radinsky, Leonard
1973   "*Aegyptopithecus* Endocasts: Oldest Record of a Pongid Brain." *American Journal of Physical Anthropology,* 39:239–248.

Rafferty, Katherine L. et al.
1995   "Postcranial Estimates of Body Weight, with a Note on a Distal Tibia of *P. major* from Napak, Uganda. *American Journal of Physical Anthropology,* 97:391–402.

Rak, Y.
1983   *The Australopithecine Face.* New York: Academic Press.

Reddy, B. M., Guangyun Sun, Javier Rodriguez Luis, et al.
2001   "Genomic Diversity of Thirteen Short Tandem Repeat Loci in a Substructured Caste Population, Golla, of Southern Andhra Pradesh, India." *Human Biology,* 73:175–190.

Reithman, H. C., et al.
2001   "Integration of Telomere Sequences with the Draft Human Genome Sequence." *Nature,* 409:948–951.

Relethford, John H. and Henry C. Harpending
1994   "Craniometric Variation, Genetic Theory, and Modern Human Origins." *American Journal of Physical Anthropology,* 95:249–270.

Richard, A. F.
1985   *Primates in Nature.* New York: W. H. Freeman and Co.

Richard, A. F. and S. R. Schulman
1982   "Sociobiology: Primate Field Studies." *Annual Reviews of Anthropology,* 11:231–255.

Rightmire, G. P.
1981   "Patterns in the Evolution of *Homo erectus.*" *Paleobiology,* 7:241–246.

1990   *The Evolution of* Homo erectus. New York: Cambridge University Press.

—— 1998 "Human Evolution in the Middle Pleistocene: The Role of *Homo heidelbergensis*." *Evolutionary Anthropology*, 6:218–227.

Roberts, Charlotte, with Keith Manchester
1997 *The Archaeology of Disease*. 2nd ed. Ithaca, NY: Cornell University Press.

Roberts, D. F.
1973 *Climate and Human Variability*. An Addison-Wesley Module in Anthropology, No. 34. Reading, Mass.: Addison-Wesley.

Roberts, Richard, Rhys Jones, and M. A. Smith
1990 "Thermoluminescence Dating of a 50,000-Year-Old Human Occupation Site in Northern Australia," *Nature*, 345:153–156.

Robins, A. H.
1991 *Biological Perspectives on Human Pigmentation*. Cambridge: Cambridge University Press.

Robinson, J. T.
1972 *Early Hominid Posture and Locomotion*. Chicago: University of Chicago Press.

Rodman, P. S.
1973 "Population Composition and Adaptive Organisation among Orangutans of the Kutai Reserve." *In: Comparative Ecology and Behaviour of Primates*, R. P. Michael and J. H. Crook (eds.), London: Academic Press, pp. 171–209.

Romer, Alfred S.
1959 *The Vertebrate Story*. Chicago: University of Chicago Press.

Rose, M. D.
1991 "Species Recognition in Eocene Primates." *American Journal of Physical Anthropology*, Supplement 12, p. 153.

Ross, Caroline
1998 "Primate Life Histories." *Evolutionary Anthropology*, 6:54–63.

Rovner, Irwin
1983 "Plant Opal Pytolith Analysis." *Advances in Archaeological Method and Theory*, 6:225–266.

Roychoudhury, S., S. Roy, A. Basu, et al.
2001 Genomic Structures and Population Histories of Linguistically Distinct Tribal Groups of India." *Human Genetics*, 109:339–350.

Ruben, John A., Christiano Dal Sasso, Nicholas Geist, et al.
1999 "Pulmonary Function and Metabolic Physiology of Theropod Dinosaurs." *Science*, 283:514–516.

Rudran, R.
1973 Adult Male Replacement in One-Male Troops of Purple-Faced Langurs (*Presbytis senex senex*) and Its Effect on Population Structure. *Folia Primatologica*, 19:166–192.

Ruff, C. B. and Alan Walker
1993 "The Body Size and Shape of KNM-WT 15000." *In:* A. Walker and R. Leakey (eds.), q.v., pp. 234–265.

Rumbaugh, D. M.
1977 *Language Learning by a Chimpanzee: The Lana Project*. New York: Academic Press.

Ruvolo, M., D. Pan, S. Zehr, T. Goldberg, et al.
1994 "Gene Trees and Hominoid Phylogeny." *Proceedings of the National Academy of Sciences*, 91:8900–8904.

Sachick, Kathy B. and Dong Zhuan
1991 "Early Paleolithic of China and Eastern Asia." *Evolutionary Anthropology*, 2(1):22–35.

Samson, M., F. Libert, B. J. Doranz, et al.
1996 Resistance to HIV-1 Infection in Caucasian Individuals Bearing Mutant Alleles of the CCR-5 Chemokine Receptor Gene. *Nature* 382(22): 722–725.

Sarich, V. M. and A. C. Wilson
1967 "Rules of Albumen Evolution in Primates." *Proceedings, National Academy of Science*, 58:142–148.

Sarich, Vincent
1971 "A Molecular Approach to the Question of Human Origins." *In: Background for Man*, P. Dolhinow and V. Sarich (eds.), Boston: Little, Brown & Co., pp. 60–81.

Savage-Rumbaugh, E. S.
1986 *Ape Language: From Conditioned Responses to Symbols*. New York: Columbia University Press.

Savage-Rumbaugh, S., K. McDonald, R. A. Sevic, W. D. Hopkins, and E. Rupert
1986 "Spontaneous Symbol Acquisition and Communicative Use by Pygmy Chimpanzees (*Pan paniscus*)." *Journal of Experimental Psychology: General*, 115(3):211–235.

Savage-Rumbaugh, S. and R. Lewin
1994 *Kanzi. The Ape at the Brink of the Human Mind*. New York: John Wiley and Sons.

Schaller, George B.
1963 *The Mountain Gorilla*. Chicago: University of Chicago Press.

Scheller, Richard H. and Richard Axel
1984 "How Genes Control Innate Behavior." *Scientific American*, 250:54–63.

Schwartzman, Stephen
1997 "Fires in the Amazon: An Analysis of NOAA-12 Satellite Data, 1996–1997." Washington D.C.: Environmental Defense Fund.

Scott, K.
1980 "Two Hunting Episodes of Middle Paleolithic Age at La Cotte Sainte-Brelade, Jersey (Channel Islands)." *World Archaeology,* 12:137–152.

Scozzari, R., F. Cruciani, A. Pangrazio, et al.
2001 "Human Y-Chromosome Variation in the Western Mediterranean Area: Implications for Peopling of the Area." *Human Immunology,* 62:871–874.

Scriver, Charles R.
2001 "Human Genetics" Lessons from Quebec Populations." *Annual Review of Genomics and Human Genetics,* 2:69–101.

Semaw, S., P. Renne, W. K. Harris, et al.
1997 2.5-million-year-old Stone Tools from Gona, Ethiopia. *Nature,* 385:333–336

Senut, Brigitte, Martin Pickford, Dominique Grommercy, et al.
2001 First Hominid from the Miocene (Lukeino Formation, Kenya). *C.R. Acad. Sci. Paris, Sciences de la Terre er des Planètes,* 332:137–144.

Senut, Brigitte and Christine Tardieu
1985 "Functional Aspects of Plio-Pleistocene Hominid Limb Bones: Implications for Taxonomy and Phylogeny." *In: Ancestors: The Hard Evidence,* E. Delson (ed.), New York: Alan R. Liss, pp. 193–201.

Seyfarth, Robert M.
1987 "Vocal Communication and its Relation to Language." *In:* Smuts et al., *Primate Societies.* Chicago: University of Chicago Press, pp. 440–451.

Seyfarth, Robert M., Dorothy L. Cheney, and Peter Marler
1980a "Monkey Responses to Three Different Alarm Calls." *Science,* 210:801–803.

_____
1980b "Ververt Monkey Alarm Calls." *Animal Behavior,* 28:1070–1094.

Shipman, P. L.
1983 "Early Hominid Lifestyle. Hunting and Gathering or Foraging and Scavenging?" Paper presented at 52nd Annual Meeting, American Association of Physical Anthropologists, Indianapolis, April.

_____
1987 "An Age-Old Question: Why Did the Human Lineage Survive?" *Discover,* 8:60–64.

Shipman, Pat
1983 "Early Hominid Lifestyle. Hunting and Gathering or Foraging and Scavenging?" Paper presented at 52nd Annual Meeting, American Association of Physical Anthropologists, Indianapolis.

Sibley, Charles and Jon E. Ahlquist
1984 "The Phylogeny of the Hominoid Primates as Indicated by DNA-DNA Hybridization." *Journal of Molecular Evolution,* 20:2–15.

Simons, E. L.
1969 "The Origin and Radiation of the Primates." *Annals of the New York Academy of Sciences,* 167:319–331.

_____
1972 *Primate Evolution.* New York: Macmillan.

_____
1985 "African Origin, Characteristics and Context of Earliest Higher Primates." *In: Hominid Evolution: Past, Present, and Future.* P. Tobias (ed.), New York: Alan R. Liss, pp. 101–106.

_____
1995 "Egyptian Oligocene Primates: A Review." *Yearbook of Physical Anthropology,* 38:199–238.

Simons, Elwyn L. and Tab Rasmussen
1994 "A Whole New World of Ancestors: Eocene Anthropoideans from Africa." *Evolutionary Anthropology,* 3:128–139.

Simpson, G. G.
1945 "The Principles of Classification and a Classification of Mammals." *Bulletin of the American Museum of Natural History,* 85:1–350.

Simpson, G. G., C. S. Pittendright, and L H. Tiffany
1957 *Life.* New York: Harcourt, Brace and Co., Inc.

Skelton, R. R., H. M. McHenry, and G. M. Drawhorn
1986 "Phylogenetic Analysis of Early Hominids." *Current Anthropology,* 27:1–43; 361–365.

Skelton, Randall R. and Henry M. McHenry
1992 "Evolutionary Relationships among Early Hominids." *Journal of Human Evolution,* 23:309–349.

Skirboll, Lana, et al.
2001 "Stem Cells: Scientific Progress and Future Research Directions." Report from the National Institutes of Health to the Secretary of Health and Human Services, Tommy G. Thompson. Internet version at: *www.nih.gov/news./stemcell/scireport.htm*

Small, Meredith F. (ed.)
1984 *Female Primates. Studies by Women Primatologists.* Monographs in Primatology, Vol. 4. New York: Alan R. Liss.

Smith, Fred H.
1984 "Fossil Hominids from the Upper Pleistocene of Central Europe and the Origin of Modern Europeans." *In:* F. H. Smith and F. Spencer (eds.), q.v., pp. 187–209.

Smith, Fred H., A. B. Falsetti, and S. M. Donnelly
1989 "Modern Human Origins." *Yearbook of Physical Anthropology,* 32:35–68.

Smith, Fred H. and Frank, Spencer (eds.)
1984 *The Origins of Modern Humans.* New York: Alan R. Liss, Inc.

Smith, Fred H., Erik Trinkaus, Paul B. Pettitt, et al.
1999 "Direct Radiocarbon Dates for Vindija G$_1$ and Velika Pécina Late Pleistocene Hominid Remains." *Proceedings of the National Academy of Sciences,* 96:12281–12286.

Smuts, Barbara
1985 *Sex and Friendship in Baboons.* Hawthorne, N.Y.: Aldine de Gruyter.

Smuts, Barbara B. et al. (eds.)
1987 *Primate Societies.* Chicago: University of Chicago Press.

Snowdon, Charles T.
1990 "Language Capacities of 'Nonhuman Animals.'" *Yearbook of Physical Anthropology,* 33:215–243.

Soffer, Olga
1985 *The Upper Paleolithic of the Central Russian Plain.* New York: Academic Press.

Solecki, Ralph
1971 *Shanidar, The First Flower People.* New York: Alfred A. Knopf.

Sponheimer, Matt and Julia A. Lee-Thorp
1999 "Isotopic Evidence for the Diet of an Early Hominid, *Australopithecus africanus.*" *Science,* 283:368–370.

Stanford, C. B., J. Wallis, H. Matama, and J. Goodall
1994 "Patterns of Predation by Chimpanzees on Red Colobus Monkeys in Gombe National Park." *American Journal of Physical Anthropology,* 94(2):213–228.

Stanyon, Roscoe and Brunetto Chiarelli
1982 "Phylogeny of the Hominoidea: The Chromosome Evidence." *Journal of Human Evolution,* 11:493–504.

Steegman, A. T., Jr.
1970 "Cold Adaptation and the Human Face." *American Journal of Physical Anthropology,* 32:243–250.

_____ 1975 "Human Adaptation to Cold." *In: Physiological Anthropology,* A. Damon (ed.), New York: Oxford University Press, pp. 130–166.

Steklis, Horst D.
1985 "Primate Communication, Comparative Neurology, and the Origin of Language Re-examined." *Journal of Human Evolution,* 14:157–173.

Stern, Curt
1973 *Principles of Human Genetics,* 3rd ed. San Francisco: W. H. Freeman.

Stern, Jack T. and Randall L. Susman
1983 "The Locomotor Anatomy of *Australopithecus afarensis.*" *American Journal of Physical Anthropology,* 60:279–317.

Sterns, S. C.
1992 *The Evolution of Life Histories.* New York: Oxford University Press.

Stewart, T. D.
1979 *Essentials of Forensic Anthropology: Especially as Developed in the United States.* Springfield: C. C. Thomas.

Stiner, Mary C.
1991 "The Faunal Remains from Grotta Guatari." *Current Anthropology,* 32(2)April:103–117.

Stoneking, Mark
1993 "DNA and Recent Human Evolution." *Evolutionary Anthropology,* 2:60–73.

Straus, Lawrence Guy
1993 "Southwestern Europe at the Last Glacial Maximum." *Current Anthropology,* 32:189–199.

_____ 1995 "The Upper Paleolithic of Europe: An Overview." *Evolutionary Anthropology,* 4:4–16.

Strier, Karen B.
1999 *Primate Behavioral Ecology.* Boston: Allyn and Bacon.

Stringer, C. B. (ed.).
1985 "Middle Pleistocene Hominid Variability and the Origin of Late Pleistocene Humans." *In: Ancestors: The Hard Evidence,* E. Delson (ed.), New York: Alan R. Liss, pp. 289–295.

_____ 1993 "Secrets of the Pit of the Bones." *Nature,* 362:501–502.

_____ 1995 "The Evolution and Distribution of Later Pleistocene Human Populations." *In: E. Vrba et al. (eds.), op cit., pp. 524–531.

Stringer, C. B. and P. Andrews
1988 "Genetic and Fossil Evidence for the Origin of Modern Humans." *Science,* 239:1263–1268.

Struhsaker, T. T.
1967 "Auditory Communication among Vervet Monkeys (*Cercopithecus aethiops*)." *In: Social Communication Among Primates,* S. A. Altmann (ed.), Chicago: University of Chicago Press.

_____ 1975 *The Red Colobus Monkey.* Chicago: University of Chicago Press.

Struhsaker, Thomas T. and Lysa Leland
1979 "Socioecology of Five Sympatric Monkey Species in the Kibale Forest, Uganda." *Advances in the Study of Behavior,* Vol. 9, New York: Academic Press, pp. 159–229.

____
1987 "Colobines: Infanticide by Adult Males." *In:* B. B. Smuts et al. (eds.), q.v., pp. 83–97.

Strum, S. C.
1987 *Almost Human. A Journey into the World of Baboons.* New York: W. W. Norton.

Sugiyama, Y.
1965 "Short History of the Ecological and Sociological Studies on Non-Human Primates in Japan." *Primates,* 6:457–460.

Sugiyama, Y. and J. Koman
1979 "Tool-using and -making Behavior in Wild Chimpanzees at Bossou, Guinea." *Primates,* 20:513–524.

Sumner, D. R., M. E. Morbeck, and J. Lobick
1989 "Age-Related Bone Loss in Female Gombe Chimpanzees." *American Journal of Physical Anthropology,* 72:259.

Suomi, Stephen J., Susan Mineka, and Roberta D. DeLizio
1983 "Short- and Long-Term Effects of Repetitive Mother-Infant Separation on Social Development in Rhesus Monkeys." *Developmental Psychology,* 19(5):710–786.

Susman, Randall L. (ed.)
1984 *The Pygmy Chimpanzee: Evolutionary Biology and Behavior.* New York: Plenum Press.

Susman, Randall L.
1988 "New Postcranial Remains from Swartkrans and Their Bearing on the Functional Morphology and Behavior of *Paranthropus robustus.*" *In:* F. E. Grine (ed.), q.v., pp. 149–172.

Susman, Randall L., Jack T. Stern, and William L. Jungers
1985 "Locomotor Adaptations in the Hadar Hominids." *In: Ancestors: The Hard Evidence,* E. Delson (ed.), New York: Alan R. Liss, pp. 184–192.

Sussman, Robert W.
1991 "Primate Origins and the Evolution of Angiosperms." *American Journal of Primatology,* 23:209–223.

Sussman, Robert W., James M. Cheverud and Thad Q. Bartlett
1995 Infant Killing as an Evolutionary Strategy: Reality or Myth? *Evolutionary Anthropology,* 3(5):149–151.

Suzman, I. M.
1982 "A Comparative Study of the Hadar and Sterkfontein Australopithecine Innominates." *American Journal of Physical Anthropology,* 57:235.

Swisher, C. C. III, G. H. Curtis, T. Jacob, et al.
1994 "Age of the Earliest Known Hominids in Java, Indonesia." *Science,* 263:1118–1121.

Swisher, C. C., W. J. Rink, S. C. Anton, et al.
1996 Latest *Homo erectus* of Java: Potential Contemporaneity with *Homo sapiens* in Southwest Java. *Science,* 274:1870–1874.

Szalay, Frederick S. and Eric Delson
1979 *Evolutionary History of the Primates.* New York: Academic Press.

Tattersall, Ian, Eric Delson, and John Van Couvering
1988 *Encyclopedia of Human Evolution and Prehistory.* New York: Garland Publishing.

Teleki, G.
1986 "Chimpanzee Conservation in Sierra Leone— A Case Study of a Continent-wide Problem." Paper presented at Understanding Chimpanzees Symposium, Chicago Academy of Sciences, Chicago, Nov. 7–10, 1987.

Templeton, Alan R.
1996 "Gene Lineages and Human Evolution." *Science,* 272:1363–1364.

Tenaza, R. and R. Tilson
1977 "Evolution of Long-Distance Alarm Calls in Kloss' Gibbon." *Nature,* 268:233–235.

Terwilliger, Joseph D. and Harold H.H. Göring
2000 "Gene Mapping in the 20th and 21st Centuries: Statistical Methods, Data Analysis, and Experimental Design." *Human Biology,* 72:63–132.

Thieme, Hartmut
1997 Lower Paleolithic Hunting Spears from Germany. *Nature,* 385:807–810.

Thorne, A. G. and M. H. Wolpoff
1992 "The Multiregional Evolution of Humans." *Scientific American,* 266:76–83.

Thorsby, Erik
1997 "Invited Anniversary Review: HLA Associated Diseases." *Human Immunology,* 53:1–11.

Tiemel, Chen, Yang Quan, and Wu En
1994 "Antiquity of *Homo sapiens* in China." *Nature,* 368:55–56.

Tishkoft, S. A., E. Dietzsch, W. Speed, et al.
1996 "Global Patterns of Linkage Disequilibrium at the CD4 Locus and Modern Human Origins." *Science,* 271:1380–1387.

Tobias, Phillip
1971 *The Brain in Hominid Evolution.* New York: Columbia University Press.

____
1983 "Recent Advances in the Evolution of the Hominids with Especial Reference to Brain and Speech." Pontifical Academy of Sciences, *Scrita Varia,* 50:85–140.

_____
1991 *Olduvai Gorge, Volume IV. The Skulls, Endocasts and Teeth of* Homo habilis. Cambridge: Cambridge University Press.

Todd, T.W.
1920, "Age Changes in the Pubic Bone." *American*
1921 *Journal of Physical Anthropology*, 3:285–334; 4:1–70.

Trevathan, Wenda R.
1987 *Human Birth: An Evolutionary Perspective.* Hawthorne, NY: Aldine de Gruyter.

Trinkaus, E.
1983 *The Shanidar Neandertals.* New York: Academic Press.

_____
1984 "Western Asia." *In:* F. H. Smith and F. Spencer (eds.), q.v., pp. 251–293.

Trinkaus, E. and W. W. Howells
1979 "The Neandertals." *Scientific American,* 241(6):118–133.

Trinkaus, Erik and Pat Shipman
1992 *The Neandertals.* New York: Alfred A. Knopf.

Trivers, R. L.
1971 "The Evolution of Reciprocal Altruism." *Quarterly Review of Biology,* 46:35–57.

_____
1972 "Parental Investment and Sexual Selection." *In: Sexual Selection and the Descent of Man,* B. Campbell (ed.), Chicago: Aldine, pp. 136–179.

Tuttle, Russell H.
1990 "Apes of the World." *American Scientist,* 78:115–125.

Udvardy, Miklos
1977 *The Audubon Society of North American Birds.* New York: Alfred A/ Knopf

Ulijaszek, S.
1998 "The Genetics of Growth." *In: The Cambridge Encyclopedia of Human Growth and Development,* S. J. Ulijaszek, F. E. Johnston, and M. A. Preece (eds.). Cambridge, UK: Cambridge University Press, pp. 121–123.

van der Ven, K., R. Fimmers, G. Engels, et al.
2000 "Evidence for Major Histocompatability Complex-Mediated Effects on Spermatogenesis in Humans." *Human Reproduction,* 15:189–196.

Van Couvering, A. H. and J. A. Van Covering
1976 "Early Miocene Mammal Fossils From East Africa." *In: Human Origins,* G. Isaac and E. R. McCown (eds.), Menlo Park, CA.: Benjamin/Cummings, pp. 155–207.

Varki, A.
2000 "A chimpanzee genome project is a biomedical imperative." *Genome Research,* 8:1065–1070.

Villa, Paola
1983 *Terra Amata and the Middle Pleistocene Archaeological Record of Southern France.* University of California Publications in Anthropology, Vol. 13. Berkeley: University of California Press.

Visalberghi, E.
1990 "Tool Use in Cebus." *Folia Primatologica,* 54:146–154.

Vogel, F.
1970 "ABO Blood Groups and Disease." *American Journal of Human Genetics,* 22:464–475.

Vogel, F., M. Kopun, and R. Rathenberg
1976 "Mutation and Molecular Evolution." *In: Molecular Anthropology,* M. Goodman et al. (eds.), New York: Plenum Press, pp. 13–33.

Vogel, Gretchen
2001 "Objection #2: Why Sequence the Junk? *Science,* 291:1184.

Von Koenigswald, G. H. R.
1956 *Meeting Prehistoric Man.* New York: Harper & Brothers.

Vrba, E. S.
1985 "Ecological and Adaptive Changes Associated with Early Hominid Evolution." *In: Ancestors: The Hard Evidence,* E. Delson (ed.), New York: Alan R. Liss, pp. 63–71.

_____
1988 "Late Pliocene Climatic Events and Hominid Evolution." *In:* F. Grine (ed.), q.v., pp. 405–426.

_____
1995 "The Fossil Record of African Antelopes (Mammalia, Bovidae) in Relation to Human Evolution and Paleoclimate." *In: Paleoclimate and Evolution with Emphasis on Human Origins,* E. Vrba et al. (eds.). New Haven: Yale University Press, pp. 385–424.

Wagner, Gunter A.
1996 "Fission-Track Dating in Paleoanthropology." *Evolutionary Anthropology,* 5:165–171.

Wakayama, T., A. C. F. Perry, M. Zucotti, K. R. Johnson, and R. Yanagimachi
1998 "Full-term Development of Mice from Enucleated Oocytes Injected with Cumulus Cell Nuclei. *Nature,* 394:369–374.

Walker, A.
1976 "Remains Attributable to *Australopithecus* from East Rudolf." *In: Earliest Man and Environments in the Lake Rudolf Basin,* Y. Coppens et al. (eds.), Chicago: University of Chicago Press, pp. 484–489.

1991 "The Origin of the Genus *Homo*." *In:* S. Osawa and T. Honjo (eds.), *Evolution of Life*. Tokyo: Springer-Verlag, pp. 379–389.

1993 "The Origin of the Genus *Homo*" *In:* D. T. Rasmussen (ed.), *The Origin and Evolution of Humans and Humanness*. Boston: Jones and Bartlett, pp. 29–47.

Walker, A., D. Pilbeam, and M. Cartmill
1981 "Changing Views and Interpretations of Primate Evolution." Paper presented to the Annual Meetings, American Association of Physical Anthropologists. Detroit, Mich.

Walker, Alan and R. E. Leakey (eds.)
1993 *The Nariokotome* Homo erectus *Skeleton*. Cambridge: Harvard University Press.

Walker, Alan and Mark Teaford
1989 "The Hunt for *Proconsul*." *Scientific American,* 260(Jan):76–82.

Walters, Jeffrey and Robert Seyfarth
1987 "Conflict and Cooperation." *In:* B. B. Smuts et al. (eds.), q.v., pp. 306–317.

Wanpo, Huang, Russell Ciochon, et al.
1995 "Early *Homo* and Associated Artifacts from Asia." *Nature,* 378:275–278.

Ward, Peter
1994 *The End of Evolution*. New York: Bantam.

Ward, S. C. and D. R. Pilbeam
1983 Maxillofacial Morphology of Miocene Hominoids from Africa and Indo-Pakistan." *In:* R. L. Ciochon and R. S. Corruccini (eds.), q.v., pp. 211–238.

Ward, Steven and William H. Kimbel
1983 "Subnasal Alveolar Morphology and the Systematic Position of *Sivapithecus*." *American Journal of Physical Anthropology,* 61:157–171.

Waser, Peter M.
1987 "Interactions among Primate Species." *In:* B. B. Smuts et al. (eds.), q.v., pp. 210–226.

Washburn, S. L.
1963 "The Study of Race." *American Anthropologist,* 65:521–531.

1971 "The Study of Human Evolution." *In:* P. Dolhinow and V. Sarich (eds.), *Background for Man: Readings in Physical Anthropology,* Boston: Little, Brown, pp. 82–121.

Watson, J. B. and F. H. C. Crick
1953a "Genetical Implications of the Structure of the Deoxyribonucleic Acid." *Nature,* 171:964–967.

1953b "A Structure for Deoxyribonucleic Acid." *Nature,* 171:737–738.

Weiner, J. S.
1955 *The Piltdown Forgery*. London: Oxford University Press.

Weiner, Steve, Qinqi Xu, Paul Goldberg, Jinyi Liu, and Ofer Bar-Yosef
1998 "Evidence for the Use of Fire at Zhoukoudian, China." *Science,* 281:251–253.

Weiss, K. M., K. K. Kidd, and J. R. Kidd
1992 "A Human Genome Diversity Project." *Evolutionary Anthropology,* 1:80–82.

Weiss, Mark L. and Alan E. Mann
1981 *Human Biology and Behavior*, 3rd ed. Boston: Little Brown.

Weiss, K. M., D. W. Stock, and Z. Zhao
1998 "Homeobox Genes." *In: The Cambridge Encyclopedia of Human Growth and Development,* S. J. Ulijaszek, F. E. Johnston, and M. A. Preece (eds.). Cambridge, UK: Cambridge University Press, pp. 137–139.

Weiss, Robin A. and Richard W. Wrangham
1999 "From *Pan* to Pandemic." *Nature,* 397:385–386.

White, T. D.
1980 "Evolutionary Implications of Pliocene Hominid Footprints." *Science,* 208:175–176.

1983 Comment Made at Institute of Human Origins Conference on the Evolution of Human Locomotion (Berkeley, Ca.).

White, T. D. and J. M. Harris
1977 "Suid Evolution and Correlation of African Hominid Localities." *Science,* 198:13–21.

White, T. D., G. Suwa, and B. Asfaw
1995 Corrigendum (White et al., 1994). *Nature,* 375:88.

White, T. D., D. C. Johanson, and W. H. Kimbel
1981 "*Australopithecus africanus:* Its Phyletic Position Reconsidered." *South African Journal of Science,* 77:445–470.

White, Tim D. and Donald C. Johanson
1989 "The Hominid Composition of Afar Locality 333: Some Preliminary Observations." *Hominidae,* Proceedings of the 2nd International Congress of Human Paleontology, Milan: Editoriale Jaca Book, pp. 97–101.

White, Tim D., Gen Suwa, and Berhane Asfaw
1994 *Australopithecus ramidus,* A New Species of Early Hominid from Aramis, Ethiopia. *Nature,* 371:306–312.

Whiten, A., J. Goodall, W. C. McGrew, et al.
1999 "Cultures in Chimpanzees." *Nature,* 399:682–685.

Whyte, Robert Orr (ed.)
1984 "The Evolution of the East Asian Environment." Centre of Asian Studies Occasional Papers and Monographs, No. 59. Hong Kong: University of Hong Kong.

Williams, George C.
1957 "Pleiotropy, Natural Selection and the Evolution of Senescence." *Evolution,* 11:398–411.

_____ 1966 *Adaptation and Natural Selection: A Critique of Some Current Evolutionary Thought.* Princeton: Princeton University Press.

Williams, George C. and Randolph M. Nesse
1991 The Dawn of Darwinian Medicine. *The Quarterly Review of Biology,* 66:1–22.

Williams, Robert C.
1985 "HLA II: The Emergence of the Molecular Model for the Major Histocompatibility Complex." *Yearbook of Physical Anthropology,* 1985, 28:79–95.

Wilson, E. O.
1975 *Sociobiology. The New Synthesis.* Cambridge: Harvard University Press.

_____ 1992 *The Diversity of Life.* Cambridge, MA: The Belknap Press of Harvard University Press.

Wolf, Katherine and Steven Robert Schulman
1984 "Male Response to 'Stranger' Females as a Function of Female Reproduction Value among Chimpanzees." *The American Naturalist,* 123:163–174.

Wolpoff, Milford H.
1983a "Lucy's Little Legs." *Journal of Human Evolution,* 12:443–453.

_____ 1983b "*Ramapithecus* and Human Origins. An Anthropologist's Perspective of Changing Interpretations." *In:* R. L. Ciochon and R. S. Corruccini (eds.), q.v., pp. 651–676.

_____ 1984 "Evolution in *Homo erectus:* The Question of Stasis." *Paleobiology,* 10:389–406.

_____ 1989 "Multiregional Evolution: The Fossil Alternative to Eden." *In:* P. Mellars and C. Stringer, q.v., pp. 62–108.

_____ 1995 *Human Evolution* 1996 Edition. New York: McGraw-Hill Inc, College Custom Series.

_____ 1999 *Paleoanthropology.* 2nd ed. New York: McGraw-Hill.

Wolpoff, Milford H. et al.
1981 "Upper Pleistocene Human Remains from Vindija Cave, Croatia, Yugoslavia." *American Journal of Physical Anthropology,* 54:499–545.

_____ 1994 "Multiregional Evolutions: A World-Wide Source for Modern Human Population." *In:* M. H. Nitecki and D. V. Nitecki (eds.), q.v., pp. 175–199.

Wolpoff, M., Wu Xin Chi, and Alan G. Thorne
1984 "Modern *Homo sapiens* Origins." *In:* Smith and Spencer (eds.), q.v., pp. 411–483.

Wood, Bernard
1991 *Koobi Fora Research Project IV: Hominid Cranial Remains from Koobi Fora.* Oxford: Clarendon Press.

_____ 1992a "Origin and Evolution of the Genus *Homo.*" *Nature,* 355:783–790.

_____ 1992b "A Remote Sense for Fossils." *Nature,* 355:397–398.

Wood, B. C. Wood, and L. Konigsberg
1994 "*Paranthropus boisei:* An Example of Evolutionary Stasis?" *American Journal of Physical Anthropology,* 95:117–136.

Wood, C. S., G. A. Harrison, C. Dove, and J. S. Weiner
1972 "Selection Feeding of *Anopheles gambiae* According to ABO Blood Group Status." *Nature,* 239:165.

Wrangham, R. W.
1977 "Feeding Behaviour of Chimpanzees in Gombe National Park, Tanzania." *In: Primate Ecology,* T. H. Clutton-Brock (ed.). New York: Academic Press, pp. 503–538.

_____ 1980 "An Ecological Model of Female-Bonded Primate Groups." *Behavior,* 75:262–300.

_____ 1986 "Ecology and Social Relationships in Two Species of Chimpanzees." *In: Ecology and Social Evolution: Birds and Mammals,* D. I. Rubenstein and R. W. Wrangham (eds.), Princeton: Princeton University Press, pp. 352–378.

Wrangham, Richard and Dale Peterson
1996 *Demonic Males: Apes and the Origins of Human Violence.* New York: Houghton Mifflin Co.

Wu, Rukang and S. Lin
1983 "Peking Man." *Scientific American,* 248(6):86–94.

Wu, Rukang and C. E. Oxnard
1983 "Ramapithecines from China: Evidence from Tooth Dimensions." *Nature,* 306:258–260.

Wu, Rukang and John W. Olsen (eds.)

1985   *Palaeoanthropology and Palaeolithic Archaeology in the People's Republic of China.* New York: Academic Press.

Wu, Rukang and Xingren Dong

1985   *"Homo erectus* in China." *In: Palaeoanthropology and Palaeolithic Archaeology in the People's Republic of China,* R. Wu and J. W. Olsen (eds.), New York: Academic Press, pp. 79–89.

Yamei, Hon, Richard Potts, Yaun Baoyin, et al.

2000   "Mid-Pleistocene Acheulean-like Stone Technology of the Bose Basin, South China." *Science,* 287:1622–1626.

Yellen, John E. et al.

1995   "A Middle Stone Age Worked Bone Industry from Katanda, Upper Semliki Valley, Zaire." *Science,* 268:553–556.

Yi, Seonbok and G. A. Clark

1983   "Observations on the Lower Palaeolithic of Northeast Asia." *Current Anthropology,* 24:181–202.

Young, David.

1992   *The Discovery of Evolution.* Cambridge: Natural History Museum Publications, Cambridge University Press.

Yunis, Jorge J. and Om Prakesh

1982   "The Origin of Man: A Chromosomal Pictorial Legacy." *Science,* 215:1525–1530.

Zhou Min Zhen and Wang Yuan Quing

1989   "Paleoenvironmental Contexts of Hominid Evolution in China." *Circum-Pacific Prehistory Conference,* Seattle: University of Washington Press.

Zimmet, P., K. G. M. M. Alberti and Jonathan Shaw

2001   "Global and Societal Implications of the Diabetes Epidemic." *Nature,* 414:782–787.

Photo Credits

This constitutes an extension of the copyright page. We have made every effort to trace the ownership of all copyrighted material and to secure permission from copyright holders. In the event of any question arising as to the use of any material, we will be pleased to make the necessary corrections in future printings. Thanks are due to the following authors, publishers, and agents for permission to use the material indicated.

1, Chapter opener, © K. G. Murti/Visuals Unlimited; **2,** Fig. 1–1, Courtesy, Peter Jones; **3,** Fig. 1–2, © Bettmann/CORBIS; **5,** Fig. 1–3a, Institute of Human Origins; Fig. 1–3b, Lynn Kilgore; Fig. 1–3c, Lynn Kilgore; Fig. 1–3d, Robert Jurmain; **10,** Fig. 1–4, Institute of Human Origins; **11,** Fig. 1–5, Robert Jurmain; Fig. 1–6, Courtesy, Judy Regensteiner; **12,** Fig. 1–7a, Courtesy, Bonnie Pedersen/Arlene Kruse; Fig. 1–7b, Robert Jurmain; **13,** Fig. 1–8a, Lynn Kilgore; Fig. 1–8b, Robert Jurmain; Fig. 1–9, Courtesy, Lorna Pierce/Judy Suchey; **24,** Fig. 2–1, Courtesy, Dept. of Library Services, American Museum of Natural History #318607; **25,** Fig. 2–2, Courtesy, Dept. of Library Services, American Museum of Natural History; Fig. 2–3, Corbis; **26,** Fig. 2–4, Corbis; **27,** Fig. 2–6, Courtesy, Dept. of Library Services, American Museum of Natural History #28000; **28,** Fig. 2–7, Courtesy, Dept. of Library Services, American Museum of Natural History #326671; Fig. 2–8, Courtesy, Dept. of Library Services, American Museum of Natural History #32670; **29,** Fig. 2–9, Courtesy, Dept. of Library Services, American Museum of Natural History #326672; **30,** Fig. 2–12, Lynn Kilgore; **31,** Fig. 2–13, Wolf, John Giustina/FPG International; Dogs surrounding wolf, Lynn Kilgore; **32,** Fig. 2–14, Courtesy, Dept. of Library Services, American Museum of Natural History #326696; **33,** Fig. 2–15a, Michael Tweedie/Photo Researchers; Fig. 2–15b,

Breck P. Kent/Animals Animals; **54,** Fig. 3–7, Biophoto Associates/Science Source/ Photo Researchers; **56,** Fig. 3–9, Ifti Ahmed; **71,** Fig. 4–1, Courtesy, Dept. of Library Services, American Museum of Natural History #238141; **85,** Fig. 4–12a, Corbis; Fig. 4–12b, Lynn Kilgore; Fig. 4–12c, Corbis; Fig. 4–12d; Lynn Kilgore; Fig. 4–12e, Lynn Kilgore; Fig. 4–12f, Lynn Kilgore; **101,** Chapter opener, © T. McHugh, Photo Researchers; **106,** Box 5–1, Fig. 1, Lynn Kilgore; **107,** Box 5–1, Fig. 2, Lynn Kilgore; Fig. 3a, Lynn Kilgore; Fig. 3b, Lynn Kilgore; **110,** Fig. 5–4 (Howler species), Raymond Mendez/Animals Animals; (Spider and woolly monkeys)), Robert L. Lubeck/ Animals Animals; (Marmosets and tamarins), © Zoological Society of San Diego, photo by Ron Garrison; **111,** Fig. 5–4 (Baboon species), Courtesy, Bonnie Pedersen/Arlene Kruse; (Macaque species), Courtesy, Jean De Rousseau; (Gibbons and siamangs), Lynn Kilgore; (Tarsier species), David Haring, Duke University Primate Zoo; (Orangutans), © Tom McHugh/Photo Researchers, Inc. #7U5895; (Colobus species) Robert Jurmain; (Galagos), Courtesy, Bonnie Pedersen/Arlene Kruse; (Chimpanzees and bonobos), Courtesy, Arlene Kruse/Bonnie Pedersen; (Mountain and lowland gorillas), Lynn Kilgore; *Cercopithecus* species), Robert Jurmain; (Loris species), Courtesy, San Francisco Zoo; (Langur species), Joe MacDonald/ Animals Animals; (Lemurs), Courtesy, Fred Jacobs; **112, 113,** Fig. 5–5a–d, Stephen D. Nash; **118,** Fig. 5–11, Courtesy, Fred Jacobs; Fig. 5–12, Courtesy, Fred Jacobs; **119,** Fig. 5–13, Courtesy, San Francisco Zoo; Fig. 5–14, Courtesy, Bonnie Pedersen/Arlene Kruse; Fig. 5–15, David Haring, Duke University Primate Zoo; **120,** Fig. 5–17, © Zoological Society of San Diego, photo by Ron Garrison; Fig. 5–18, Raymond Mendez/Animals Animals; **121,** Fig. 5–20, Robert L. Lubeck/Animals Animals; **122,** Fig. 5–22,

Robert Jurmain; Fig. 5–23a, Courtesy, Bonnie Pedersen/Arlene Kruse; , Fig. 5–23b, Courtesy, Bonnie Pedersen/Arlene Kruse; **123,** Fig. 5–24, Robert Jurmain; **125,** Fig. 5–26, Lynn Kilgore; **125,** Fig. 5–27, Robert Jurmain, photo by Jill Matsumoto/Jim Anderson; **126,** Fig. 5–29a, Lynn Kilgore; Fig. 5–29b, Lynn Kilgore; **127,** Fig. 5–30a, Lynn Kilgore; Fig. 5–30b, Lynn Kilgore; **127,** Fig. 5–31a, Robert Jurmain, photo by Jill Matsumoto/ Jim Anderson; , Fig. 5–31b, Robert Jurmain, photo by Jill Matsumoto/Jim Anderson; **129,** Fig. 5–32, Courtesy, Ellen Ingmanson; **136,** Issue Fig. 1, Courtesy, J. Oates; **140,** Fig. 6–1, Courtesy, John Oates; Fig. 6–2, Courtesy, Jean De Rousseau; **142,** Fig. 6–3, Joe MacDonald/ Animals Animals; **145,** Fig. 6–4, Courtesy, John Oates; **149,** Fig. 6–5, Lynn Kilgore; Fig. 6–6, Lynn Kilgore; **152,** Fig. 6–8a, Robert Jurmain; Fig. 6–8b, Courtesy, Meredith Small; Fig. 6–8c, Lynn Kilgore; Fig. 6–8d, Courtesy, Arlene Kruse/Bonnie Pedersen; **153,** Fig. 6–9, Lynn Kilgore; **156,** Fig. 6–10a, Courtesy, David Haring, Duke University Primate Center; Fig. 6–10b, Courtesy, Arlene Kruse/Bonnie Pedersen; Fig. 6–10c, Robert Jurmain; Fig. 6–10d, © Tom McHugh/Photo Researchers, Inc.; Fig. 6–10e, Robert Jurmain; **157,** Fig. 6–11, Harlow Primate Laboratory, University of Wisconsin; Fig. 6–12, Lynn Kilgore; **165,** Fig. 7–1, Lynn Kilgore; **168,** Fig. 7–2, Courtesy, Rose A. Sevcik, Language Research Center, Georgia State University; photo by Elizabeth Pugh; **171,** Fig. 7–4a, Courtesy, Jane Goodall Institute; Fig. 7–4b, Courtesy, Carol Lofton/Distinctive Images; **178,** Fig. 7–5, Lynn Kilgore; **185,** Chapter opener, © J. Reader, Photo Researchers; **203** Fig. 8–12, Hans and Judy Beste/Animals Animals; Fig. 8–13, J. C. Stevenson/ Animals Animals; **204,** Fig. 8–14, Doug Wechsler/Animals Animals; **208,** Fig. 8–18, Robert Jurmain; **209,** Fig. 8–19, Courtesy, David Pilbeam; **221,** Fig. 9–3,

Index

Entries in **bold** indicate glossary terms. Entries in *italics* indicate illustrations or boxed material.